FROGSPAWN AND FLOOR POLISH

Upstairs and downstairs in a National Trust house

MARY MACKIE

ISIS
LARGE PRINT
Oxford

First published in Great Britain 2003
by Summersdale Publishers Ltd.

Published in Large Print 2003 by ISIS Publishing Ltd,
7 Centremead, Osney Mead, Oxford OX2 0ES
by arrangement with Summersdale Publishers Ltd.

British Library Cataloguing in Publication Data
Mackie, Mary
    Frogspawn and floor polish: upstairs and downstairs
    in a National Trust house. – Large print ed. –
    (Isis reminiscence series)
    1. Mackie, Mary – Homes and haunts – England
    – Norfolk 2. Felbrigg Hall 3. Country life – England
    – Norfolk 4. Mansions – England – Norfolk –
    Maintenance and repair 5. Large type books
    6. Norfolk (England) – Social life and customs
    I. Title
    363.6'9'06042612

ISBN 0–7531–9884–3 (hb)
ISBN 0–7531–9885–1 (pb)

CI 52345225

Printed and bound by Antony Rowe, Chippenham

This book is for Harriet, Peter, Ellie and Benjamin, hoping that some day they may visit Felbrigg Hall and discover why their Granma and Grandad Mackie loved it so much.

Acknowledgements

Most of this book is drawn from personal experience and memories, but for extra details and for sharing stories from their own experience, my thanks go to:

Joan Mapperley, our good friend, catering manager at Felbrigg for eighteen years; David Bryden, Jim Watts and Rebecca Howard, property staff at Felbrigg; room stewards and other Felbrigg friends; staff of other properties in both the public and private sectors; and, not least, my husband Chris, whose diaries, talks and memories I have shamelessly pillaged; and our sons Andy and Kevin, for help in recalling those Felbrigg years.

I am also indebted to published sources, most notably:

Felbrigg, the Story of a House, by R. W. Ketton-Cremer (Rupert Hart Davis, 1962)

Staying at Felbrigg as a guest of Wyndham Ketton-Cremer, by Sir Brinsley Ford, National Trust Yearbook 1977–8

The Search for Gainsborough, by Adrienne Corri (Jonathan Cape, 1984)

Felbrigg Hall Guide Books (1971–2000)

Archives based at the Norfolk and Norwich Record Office

INTRODUCTION

Froggie goes a-courtin'

The voice on the telephone was young, female, and deadly serious: "I want to report a disaster."

"Why, what's happened?"

"Your lake's polluted," said the girl.

"Oh dear . . ."

Seated in his office above the Red Corridor at Felbrigg Hall, my husband Chris enjoyed a view across the park, over the Rose Garden and the daffodil-dancing approach to the house. In the middle distance, cows and their young calves grazed across rolling acres of pasture dotted with oak and chestnut trees on which young leaves were sprouting. Beyond them, out of sight in its hollow, the lake lay tranquil under a bright March sky.

None of the staff, neither the blacksmith who acted as a sort of informal water bailiff, nor the woodsmen, had reported any problems to do with the lake, and the last time we took an evening stroll round that way, following the boarded walk across marshy ground and into the trees, all seemed normal. It was too early in the year for fishermen, but rings on the water told us the fish were stirring; moorhens, coots, ducks and geese swam placidly on the glinting water, and the woods were alive with songbirds and pheasant.

1

Even so, the child sounded concerned and her message had to be treated seriously, so Chris replied, "What makes you think that?"

She explained that she and her friends, living in the nearby village, had elected themselves volunteer conservators for the lake. "We're looking after it for you. We watch out for vandals, and fishing line, and litter and things. We think it's important to take care of the environment."

"Absolutely right!" Chris is always keen to encourage youthful conservationists. You never know where such enthusiasm may lead. The girl might grow up to be a young National Trust volunteer, an expert on Elizabethan knot gardens, a countryside warden, property manager, land agent, historic buildings representative, perhaps in time a regional director or even a future director general.

"So we thought you ought to know," the earnest young voice went on. "We went to your lake today. And there's something wrong with the water. It must be poisoned, or polluted, or something."

Thoroughly intrigued, Chris enquired, "How can you tell?"

"Because all the frogs are leaving."

"What?"

"They're trying to escape. We saw them. Hundreds of them! The big frogs are even helping some of the little ones. They're giving them piggy-backs."

"Ah . . . right. Yes."

Of course. It was that time of year. As the verse says, "The spring is sprung, the grass is riz . . ." The

2

camellias were blooming crimson and waxy white in the Orangery, every twig and branch in the woods was bursting with sap, Felbrigg Hall was about to open its doors for another season and, along with the rest of the natural world, the frogs at the lake were doing their natural thing.

As nature lovers will know, frogs tend to hibernate during the winter on the bottom of ponds and lakes. When the spring wakes them and the females become fecund, the males compete for the opportunity to fertilise a clutch of new-laid frogspawn. Whether they fancy the lady frog for her good looks, her fashionable green outfit, her big dark eyes, melodious voice, or her pheromones, I wouldn't like to say (I'm no David Bellamy), but some magical urge draws them. And often, having found a likely specimen, the smaller male will leap on and cling to the lucky female's sturdy back, to await the moment when she lays her clumps of eggs in the water and he can fertilise them.

But how should a National Trust administrator explain the facts of froggie courtship, over the phone, to a child he's never met? She was engagingly keen on matters green, but evidently hadn't yet done enough biology to know about the birds and the bees. Or the amphibians.

"Have you, um, mentioned it to your mum and dad?" Chris enquired.

"No, not yet. I thought I ought to get straight on to you. It's an emergency."

"Well . . . first of all I want to thank you very much for phoning to tell me," said Chris. "It's good to know

3

you're keeping an eye on the lake for us, and if you see anything else you think should be reported, I hope you'll call me again. But . . . I don't think you need to worry this time. I'll get someone to go and have a look, but I really don't think the water's poisoned."

"Then why are the frogs leaving?"

"Well . . . um . . ." Chris picked out his words with care, as if they were bones in one of the delicious kippers from the smoke-house in nearby Cley. "The frogs are . . . well, they often behave like that in the spring. It's natural. Look . . . why don't you go and tell your mum and dad about it? See what they say. But thanks again for reporting it. We really appreciate your interest."

He put the phone down feeling that he'd had a narrow escape, and came through to our flat to share the joke with me. Frogs giving each other piggy-backs to escape pollution. What a jolly thought!

For a time which, in retrospect, seems all too short, Chris and I were privileged to live and work at Felbrigg Hall, in north Norfolk, he as an employee of the National Trust and I as an often-involved onlooker. When you live "over the shop" in a stately home (and work at home as I do, being a writer), you can't help but be the first person summoned every time an emergency arises or an extra pair of hands is needed.

As you may imagine, when Chris and I start reminiscing, the name Felbrigg does tend to crop up, now and again. And again. The opening gambit, "When we were at Felbrigg . . ." has been known to cause close friends to roll their eyes and mutter, "Oh, please!" So we try — honestly folks, we do try — to ration our references to what, in our social circle, has come to be referred to darkly as "the 'F' word".

Some of the stories of our Felbrigg years were told in my earlier books *Cobwebs and Cream Teas* and *Dry Rot and Daffodils*, but since we remain in touch with our F-word friends and every so often find reasons to return and visit the dear old place, new stories continue to accumulate. Some things may have changed, but in essence, much to our delight, Felbrigg remains the same.

This present book continues the theme, recalling Felbrigg tales which had to be left out of earlier books for reasons of space, and bringing the story up to date with more recent happenings. For the sake of readers who have yet to discover the place, I've included some descriptions of the setting and some background details of the history of the house and its owners; enough for them to be able to picture the scene, I hope. Anyone who wants to know more should read *Felbrigg: the Story of a House*, by the distinguished Norfolk historian R. W. Ketton-Cremer, the last squire, who lived at Felbrigg for most of his adult life. As its title suggests, his book tells the story of the house which has stood for almost four hundred years, of the estate that surrounds it, and of the families who lived there, from the days of William the Conqueror to the middle of the twentieth century. The last squire chose to end his book in 1941 and he says little of himself or what happened in the years before he died, nor of course could he know of events which came later, after he bequeathed the house to the National Trust.

This book, I hope, will help to fill in some of those blanks, though I would not presume to compare my own reminiscences with his erudite and scholarly work. My books are not designed for the same purpose, nor are they intended as any kind of sequel. Even so, in their own way, this present book and the two which preceded it do serve to extend Felbrigg's story another sixty years and bring it to the beginning of the third millennium.

If you know Norfolk, I hope you'll enjoy reading more about its history, its humour — and some of its hauntings! And if this county is still a pleasure to be anticipated, perhaps I can whet your appetite with a glimpse of certain delights that await you in this quiet and lovely corner of England's green and pleasant land.

Mary Mackie
Heacham, West Norfolk
January, 2003

CHAPTER
ONE

Felbrigg 2001

In Britain, the wettest autumn in three hundred years merged into a damp, mostly mild winter. The second millennium ended with floods and the third began (on 1 January 2001 — some people celebrated a year too early!) with snowdrifts in Scotland and the north of England. Further south, rain followed yet more rain, bringing disaster to many poor souls whose houses lie in flood-plain areas, while we who live in Norfolk thanked our lucky stars that we had escaped the worst.

On a Thursday in early February the grassed courtyard behind Felbrigg Hall was slick and sticky with mud through which I stepped gingerly as I followed my husband Chris and our friend Elizabeth towards a door hidden in a corner behind an angle of the building. I had been giving a talk, in the Park Restaurant off the stable yard, to around eighty members of the Windham Club, a society formed by and for Felbrigg enthusiasts, most of them volunteers who help out at the Hall in various part-time capacities. Amongst them were several old friends of ours, including Elizabeth. Whenever we meet, she happily recalls how it was Chris who first took her on when he was administrator here; she is now one of the most experienced room stewards.

Over tea and biscuits following the meeting, Elizabeth told us that David, the present property manager, had sent word that he would be happy to show us the Library, if we had time. The exact reasons for this invitation escaped me — I was distracted by answering questions and chatting with people, letting my adrenalin levels settle while my coffee grew cold — but I'm always happy to take another look at our old home, especially when it means a chance to go "beyond the baize door", as it were.

"Sorry we have to go in the back way," Elizabeth apologised as the big house enfolded us in familiar brick wings, tall windows gleaming in grey light. "The front's all locked up when the house is closed." She had obviously forgotten that we know all about winter arrangements here. For seven years this rear courtyard led the way to our home.

When Elizabeth rang the bell, the metal speaker beside the back door crackled an unintelligible answer.

"It's Elizabeth," she told it. "I've brought the Mackies."

In response came the familiar sound of footsteps hurrying down the steep, creaking stairs from the office.

"Brings it all back," Chris murmured. He sounded a bit choked, making me realise how he was really feeling.

I love going back to Felbrigg and do so at every opportunity, but Chris has been a more reluctant visitor. He says he feels much as a vicar must do when

8

he returns to a former parish whose new incumbent has, inevitably, made changes. For him the memories are, perhaps, sharper because he was fully involved all the time, enjoying the good things and riding out the bad, all day and every day ("24/7" as the new verbal shorthand has it), whereas I saw more of the social side of our life here.

In those days the house was run by two resident house staff — the administrator who had charge of the house, shop, restaurant and office, and the houseman whose main responsibilities lay in the more practical areas of security, conservation, and supervision of cleaning and workmen. In practice the two jobs often merged. Now, Felbrigg employs three people to cover similar areas, though in slightly different ways that better suit the needs of a developing, constantly adapting National Trust. Thus the current property manager has responsibility for the financial viability and everyday organisation of both Felbrigg estate and nearby Sheringham; the house manager's main care is the safety and conservation of the house itself; and he now has an assistant, designated the house steward. But, whatever their job descriptions may say, when necessary any or all of them turn their hands to whatever Felbrigg may demand of them. No change there, then!

In the event, on that February day any apprehensions which Chris may have harboured soon dispersed in the warmth of the welcome we received from property manager David. He reminded us that we had met the previous summer, at the retirement party for Ted, who was head gardener for many years. That party was held, appropriately enough, in the Walled Garden, with refreshments in a marquee on the lawn and everyone in summer clothes under a blazing summer sun. Seven months later, meeting again, we were all bundled in thick scarves and warm coats. But, summer or winter, it was a joy to be back again, gazing around us as David relocked the back door.

When Felbrigg first opened to the public in 1971, this long, stone-floored passageway was designated the Red Shutter Corridor because of its red walls and its long row of tall grey shutters all down the south side, framing windows which look out to the Rose Garden. I spent most of one Good Friday washing down these windows and window boards after a film crew let off a smoke device in the lock-up and the corridor filled with a white mist that left an oily film on every exposed surface. (See *Dry Rot and Daffodils*.) Today, however, the shutters were closed, leaving the place lit by dim electric light, and I was saddened to discover that it's no longer a red corridor, even by name. It's now known prosaically as the South Corridor, and instead of the vibrant and characterful deep cherry red that we knew so well, the walls have been repainted a dirty cream, the colour of foam curdling on a polluted river.

"Some expert thought the red wasn't very authentic," said David, starting off a discussion along the lines of "authentic to what era?" After all, over the centuries that corridor has worn uncounted coats of paint whose colours can only be guessed at. It took several meetings, consulting of books and much close

10

analysis of paint samples scraped from the walls before the experts came up with this latest particularly unlovely metamorphosis, which apparently dates from the early 1800s. The colour made me laugh, though — when working on a comic novel set in a stately home something like Felbrigg, I decorated the equivalent area in the most boring colour I could think of and dubbed it, tongue in cheek, the Beige Corridor. A case of life imitating art?

Funny, forgotten, familiar feelings . . .

Through the winter, from November to March, visitors passing through the park may think Felbrigg looks dormant. In fact, during annual hibernation, behind closed doors and blinded windows, great houses undergo the major renovations and conservations which are vital to their well-being. Corridors and stately rooms become a dust-sheeted jumble, often reverberating to hammer and saw, or cluttered with ladder and scaffolding, clanging pipes and gaping drains. The closed season is certainly no rest-cure for resident staff. That winter had been no exception, as evidenced by the gritty dust that coated the old paving stones under our feet. But, as in every winter, all the tables and chairs which furnish the corridor were protected by dust covers tailor-made by the ladies of the Norwich branch of the National Association of Decorative and Fine Arts Societies. They did some of the larger pieces in Felbrigg's spacious Morning Room and I well remember one lady shaking out a vast, flowing piece of material shaped to fit a four-poster bed, saying, "Well, I couldn't very well handle this in my small sitting room!"

Ah, memories. They come crowding round us every time we return.

Indicating my heavy briefcase and the box of books Chris was carrying, David suggested, "Leave your things here."

Leave my precious belongings in a public corridor? For a moment I was appalled. But, of course, this was Felbrigg Hall in February, with dusk approaching. On our way across the courtyard we had passed a couple of workmen heading home. Jim, the house manager, was having a day off and Rebecca, the house steward, was in her flat. There was no one else around in the main house. Just the four of us. And the gathering shadows.

Since we were heading for the Library, David didn't ask us to take off our coats. He himself was clad in thick sweater, corduroys, bodywarmer and scarf. Felbrigg has the reputation of being the coldest house in Norfolk and, on days when ice gathers on the inside of the windows of Dining Room, Drawing Room or Chinese Bedroom, today's residents wouldn't argue. However, fine furniture and paintings prefer cold, dry, dimly lit conditions, so mere mortals must shiver and shake amid a polar chill alleviated only by the tepid draught from the odd small blow-heater which sits, fan rattling madly, in a corner of whichever room is being plastered, painted, or stripped to the bare walls to get at dry rot, deathwatch beetle, woodworm, or . . .

"This way," David invited, heading through a glazed door into the Bird Corridor.

There, too, most of the shutters were closed, everything draped against dust and light, and thick blinds hid the glassed cases in which stuffed birds posed stiffly amid dried grasses and flowers. The exhibits include some very rare birds, such as a bittern, a honey buzzard and, most unusual of all, a cross between a chicken and a pheasant — is it a cheasant, a pheacken, a chickant or a phicken? (Answers on a post card . . .)

Although I wouldn't go quite as far as the regular visitor who told me "I always go through the Bird Corridor with my hands over my eyes. It's horrible, quite horrible!", I must confess that I prefer to watch live birds rather than have them peer at me with dead glass eyes after the taxidermist has done his thing. Beautiful though it is, the honey buzzard in the Bird Corridor isn't half as thrilling as the one Chris saw one fine spring morning using the front railing as a launch pad while giving an early flying and puddle-bathing lesson to her chick. But in the days before the invention of cameras which reveal wildlife in its natural habitat, mating and marauding in glorious colour and intimate close-up, these stuffed specimens provided the best means of studying natural history. The late squire recalled that his paternal grandfather, who lived at nearby Beeston, was a celebrated marksman "in the days when ornithology meant the shooting of rare birds, and in due course their elaborate mounting in glass-fronted cases by Mr Gunn of Norwich". (See

13

Felbrigg, the Story of a House.) In those unenlightened days, Beeston's squire and his friends amused themselves by shooting rare birds both on his own estate and on the wild marshes which grace the Norfolk coastline.

Happily, at the beginning of the twenty-first century these same marshes, stretching for mile after unspoilt mile, are owned by the National Trust and provide a safe haven for all wildlife. All that threatens them now is the inexorable advance of the North Sea.

The Bird Corridor

Like much of the house, the Bird Corridor at Felbrigg has undergone transformations during its long life. Two hundred years ago it was an open colonnade, then during the improvements of 1831 it was enclosed to allow easier passage for servants hurrying with hot dishes between kitchen and dining room. The stuffed birds were not placed here until after the National Trust took over.

Tall shuttered windows look northward on to a garden area set between the two rear wings of the house, and on the inner wall you can peer through sash windows into the butler's pantry and the china closet with its display of willow-pattern plates and dishes. On one of the panes, an impecunious tutor named Benjamin Stillingfleet used a diamond ring to scratch a mournful poem to a lady who had spurned his romantic overtures: "Could Lammy look within my breast / She'd find her image there exprest . . ." Pause to read it and shed a tear for the poor chap if you will.

Against the inner wall, shrouded that February in her made-to-measure cotton dust cover chemise, a matronly marble figure sits on a marble plinth. This Greek funerary statue, swathed in swirling marble draperies, has been sadly battered and no longer has a head. We used to amuse ourselves by warning family and friends against encountering the headless lady in the Bird Corridor — they assumed the place must be haunted!

In fact, the statue is a very substantial presence, though no one knows exactly how she came to Felbrigg. She is first recorded as being in the Walled Garden in 1847, but when Chris and I first encountered her she was incarcerated in a crate in the stables. It has been hypothesised that she may have come to Felbrigg via a vicar at nearby Aylsham, who had been chaplain to Lord Elgin (of Elgin Marbles fame). The tale has yet to be substantiated but seems as likely an explanation as any.

Still, however the Headless Lady came to stand alone and forsaken in her crate in the stables, soon after we arrived the National Trust decided to bring her in to more comfortable quarters in the Bird Corridor. She is, of course, immensely heavy, being a buxom Brunhilde rather than a Twiggy-type sylph; about four feet tall (even seated, and without her head); and sitting on a solid, fluted plinth, all carved from the same block of grey marble. The logistics of moving her caused regional office experts and local workmen to scratch their heads. It was to be no easy task and, like everything else at Felbrigg, became more lengthy and complicated because of the need to protect and conserve the ancient fabric of the house. For one thing, they needed to test the spot where she was going to stand, in case the stone floor collapsed under her weight and sent her plummeting into the cellars.

While they were carefully checking the few square feet that would form her final resting place, they forgot the several yards of stone-paved floor over which she must travel before reaching her destination. The route would trace a diagonal line from the garden door, across the wide corridor, and end by the inner wall. Might not those flagstones, too, give way if subjected to the lady's unsupported weight? "Good point!" the men agreed when Chris raised the question, and when the day came they laid down substantial timbers to spread the load across the floor. That done, the lady was carted, somewhat indecorously, on a large wheeled barrow with half a dozen men guiding her and pushing her to her new home amid the bird cases. They were immensely helped by the woman from regional office who walked alongside with one hand resting on the statue's shoulder "to steady it"!

Having laughed over this story, we moved on, making towards a small lobby at the end of the corridor from where the back stairs climb, up and up, round and round, all the way to the attics.

"Oh, you've taken up the stair carpet!" Elizabeth remarked, agog with interest as the men led the way up the stairs. For her, too, this visit was an adventure.

Room stewards don't often see the hall in its winter state of undress and dishevelment. A few volunteers may be called in to do specific jobs, such as dusting books, mending tray covers, or clearing up after particularly messy projects; but most of them, like the house martins that swoop around the eaves, leave with the autumn and return with the spring. Seeing only the end result of winter renovations, they may not appreciate the massive effort and upheaval that goes into ensuring the conservation of furnishings, fabric and fittings while workmen do their thing.

As we clumped up bare stairs shaped like wedges of cheese (had they grown steeper, or was it my legs that had grown more used to a bungalow?), Elizabeth and I reminisced about the old days, especially the attics and cellars tours which Chris inaugurated with the idea of allowing people, including our keen band of volunteers, to have a glimpse behind the scenes. "I see David's organising some similar tours," I said. "I'm going to book a place on one. I'd love to see the attics and cellars again. How people loved those tours . . ."

I climbed on, up and round another flight of stairs, until Elizabeth called me back, looking bemused. "We have to go this way, Mary."

"Of course we do. Sorry." Talking too much, and distracted by memories of the fascinating bric-a-brac that fills the attics, I had missed the door at first-floor level. I had been instinctively making for the top of the house, where I assumed David and Chris were heading. In fact, as I now realised, the men's voices were awaking hollow echoes in the staircase hall. Elizabeth

17

and I went after them, through the service door and into the West Corridor, where grey daylight filtered through thick cream blinds at small windows. To our left, a more imposing cased door led into the airy stairwell, where an elegant wrought-iron balustrade with a mahogany rail guards the edge of the gallery. On its far side the two men waited by the door to the Library, near to where the main staircase angled down into twilit gloom.

Voices always tend to echo around the gallery, but the effect was even stronger that day because the upper landing had been stripped of its longcase clock, Chinese Chippendale chairs and large oil paintings. The seven classical busts remained in their recesses above the seven door cases, gazing down on a scene of unexceptional winter chaos. Carpets had been removed and someone had covered the dark stained floorboards with cardboard and other packing materials held together with shiny brown parcel tape, while a section of the mahogany rail on the balustrade, outside the door to the Library, was heavily bandaged in what looked like old sheeting. Evidently some major work was in progress.

The staircase hall at Felbrigg is top-lit by a huge, rectangular, domed skylight way up at roof level. This rather unlovely, functional feature, composed of a metal frame and sheets of glass, was erected between the two World Wars when the original skylight, designed by Humphry Repton and his son, threatened to collapse. From its centre depends a long, long chain supporting, at gallery level, a square glass lantern which is empty now but which once held an oil lamp to light the stairs at night (as proved by a photograph in the archives). The sight of it set Chris reminiscing again.

A few years ago, one of his major headaches was the releading of the roof. Whole areas of tile and old, fragile lead were removed and temporarily replaced by tarpaulins, and the skylight also had to come down for renovation. For months much of the main house was encased in scaffolding, with another erection of tubular steel and "deals" (Norfolk for scaffolding planks) towering up through the full height of the staircase hall. Having completed the releading, the workmen replaced the skylight frame and dismantled the internal scaffolding, planning to reglaze the big skylight from the roof above. Panel by panel, they carefully replaced the panes of glass. Then, just as they were about to putty the final window, Chris came up the stairs and noticed that they had forgotten to rehang the lantern.

That chain is very long and heavy; rehanging it so far above the stairwell, with the skylight complete, would have been a nightmare. Even at that stage, to rehook the chain in the centre of the skylight called for some sweat-making manoeuvres and not a little bad language, as one of the men leaned precariously on the outside of the skylight and stretched a long pole through the narrow gap left for the final pane of glass. Steadied by one of his mates, he eventually succeeded in sliding a link of the chain safely onto the hook.

An unexpected site

Seeing these great houses at their best, from Easter to clocks-back time, with furniture artfully set out behind guiding ropes, blinds drawn just so and everything gleaming and grand, summer visitors may find it difficult to imagine the place in total upheaval, covered in dust and grit and filled with scaffolding, or with plasterers plastering and grimy-handed labourers knocking holes in walls or floors.

As an example, let's visit the Library at Felbrigg in mid-season, when lightly clad visitors climb the broad, shallow stairs under the stern gaze of a succession of family portraits.

At the head of the stairs they move into a large, cool, quiet and gracious room, rather dimly lit because the two tall bay windows have their long off-white blinds drawn down to keep out the damaging daylight. The walls are lined with oak bookpresses (the experts' word for large bookcases) designed in the Gothic style by James Paine when he remodelled the house in the 1750s at the behest of William Windham II. The next squire, scholar and statesman William Windham III, added more books, including some which had belonged to his good friend Dr Samuel Johnson. To accommodate them he ordered the building of yet more shelves, some above the doors, some on the sides of the two south-facing bay windows; he even blocked off the window in the west bay and filled that space with more bookpresses. Calfskin-bound volumes, some very tall, some very thick, and many of them bound by

20

William Windham II himself, fill shelves that stretch from "secret" cupboards at floor level up to the elegant finials that grace the tops of the bookpresses, leaving space only for the two south-facing bay windows, the marble chimneypiece and the carved oak overmantel. More books lie waiting on tables, with comfortable chairs here and there, and at the far end of the room, between two large and valuable antique globes printed with a map of the world and a map of the stars, the massive, ornately carved desk holds an inkwell and pen-stand, a leather-bound blotter, and more books. The late squire wanted the room to look as though its owner had stepped aside from his deskwork for a moment, perhaps to climb the library ladder to take down a book from a high shelf, or to relax in one of the big green leather chairs by the hearth. Some people say that the ghost of Windham III has been seen to do just that. Perhaps he still lingers, unseen behind the dust motes floating in the air. Nor is his the only spectral presence to be detected about the Hall, as we shall discover.

Most of Felbrigg's owners were scholars who enjoyed and appreciated books. They have imbued this room with an atmosphere of erudition and studiousness which encourages voices to drop to a whisper. Even on an August day, when people jostle for space on the drugget, the Library seems hushed, an oasis of calm recalling an earlier, orderly, far more leisured world.

However, on that February day in 2001 you wouldn't have recognised the place. It looked like a builder's yard.

David threw the door open, leading us into a murky cave filled with scaffolding and timber, walled in blue plastic, floored in stained, paint-spattered sheeting and ceilinged just above head height by rough planks. A long ladder led up to a square opening in the planks, above which bright lights blazed. It gave me the impression of being in a jungle, hemmed in by a canopy of vast trees with the sun burning far above. As my eyes adjusted to the gloom I found it hard to believe we were standing in Felbrigg's elegant Library.

"We're having the strap-work on the ceiling redone," David explained. "You remember how the main part of the ceiling was plain, with plaster decoration only in the bays? Well, the main ceiling's being . . . no, not restored — there was nothing there to restore — a better word would probably be . . . reconstructed."

Unlike the ceilings of the main rooms on the ground floor, where flowers and birds blend with leaves and branches, the Library ceiling was originally decorated in a geometric strap-work pattern of squares and octagons, to complement the Jacobean origins of this oldest part of the house. It was designed by the architect James Paine and carried out by his master plasterer George Green, the work being completed in 1753.

Unfortunately, by 1923, when Wyndham Cremer Cremer took over the Hall from his reclusive old uncle, Robert Ketton, the whole estate was in sadly neglected condition. The roof of the Hall was in such disrepair, with perished lead and displaced slates, that rain had soaked through to soften the roof timbers and rot the plaster cornices, which obliged the new squire to replace the original skylight with a more utilitarian version, as we have already seen. In the Library in particular, the main part of the eighteenth-century ceiling was so badly damaged that it had to be taken down and, again because of the prohibitive costs of restoration, replaced with a plain flat ceiling. Only in the bays was the plaster still sound enough to be allowed to stay and those small strap-worked areas gave a tantalising hint of what the whole ceiling must once have looked like.

So it had remained, for nearly eighty years.

In the winter of 2000/2001, the painstaking work of replacing the decorative lattice was being undertaken by master plasterer Tom Smith. It looked good, understated and elegant. But ceilings often go unremarked, don't they? You may not even notice this one unless the room steward points it out. But when you crick your neck and gaze up at that seemingly simple ceiling, consider the months of back-breaking work, and the breathless anxiety of plasterers and house staff, that went into bringing it back to that state.

In order to have the job completed by the start of the 2001 season, work began the previous autumn, obliging early closure of the upstairs show rooms. The first task was to clear the Library of most of its books. Hundreds of them. They had to be stored somewhere, and where else but in the adjacent rooms? Soon most of the huge bookpresses were empty and the Library had been stripped to its essentials. Nearby rooms became a cluttered jumble of chairs, desks, carpets, lamps, and piles and piles of books. Along with the resident furniture of each room, the Library's contents had then to be carefully draped in dust covers or wrapped in acid-free tissue paper.

Meanwhile, back in the naked room itself, two men from the regional estate yard moved in to erect, close to the walls, a free-standing wooden framework. This was designed to support a thick shield of blue polythene which would not only protect the remaining books and the bookpresses which contained them, but allow the creation of a micro-climate within which a free flow of dehumidified air could circulate. The moisture in the atmosphere of vulnerable areas is usually maintained at between 50–65 per cent, but the application and drying out of the fresh plaster on the Library ceiling, causing an inevitable rise in humidity, would create ideal conditions for the growth and spread of mould and fungus, so special precautions had to be taken to counter this excess dampness. As the work progressed, the house staff kept a close check on humidity levels as well as controlling other problems such as spreading dirt and the daily risk of damage.

With the blue polythene "greenhouse" in place and the micro-climate established behind it, workmen arrived in lorries laden with steel scaffolding. Having erected suitable platforms outside the house, they proceeded to post a few more tonnes of wood and steel through the Library windows.

When you work in a stately home you need your wits about you at all times, especially with workmen in the house. This time, an alert observer noticed a fine scattering of talcum-like powder in the Great Hall, directly below the Library. Good grief, now what? Was the Library floor about to collapse under all that extra weight?

Work stopped. Experts arrived to examine the structure. Protracted measurement, calculation and consultation took place. Eventually the structural engineers agreed that it might be wise to place strong timbers on the Library floor, directly above the main supporting beams, and to ensure that the weight of the internal scaffolding was evenly spread on those timbers.

The scaffolding supported a platform for the plasterer to work on, within easy reach of the ceiling. The deals were carefully levelled because the plasterer would be looking up most of the time and had to be sure of his footing, and of course he needed to reach every corner of the big room. In effect, the plastering platform cut the Library in half horizontally, with just a small square left to provide a trapdoor through which the plasterers could come and go.

"Come up and see," said David, nimbly climbing the ladder. Chris followed, with me not far behind and Elizabeth bringing up the rear — only one at a time actually on the ladder, of course, with health and safety in mind.

We emerged into a surreal place — a broad, low-ceilinged area with no more than two feet of headroom, on a floor made of rough planks closely abutted and dotted with a discarded distemper-caked bucket or two. Walls of blue, plaster-splattered polythene enclosed the echoing space, and in all four corners electric lamps faced outwards, their brilliant light reflecting across the working area and throwing the fresh strap-work into sharp relief. As close as we were, we could see how sharp and clean were the edges of the ribs, squared each side of a central rounded strip and describing lozenge-shaped patterns across the ceiling.

David told us that when the master plasterer came to take his first close look, he found that the Library is not exactly symmetrical. Its walls are slightly different in length and their corners do not form perfect right angles. This of course made his work all the more difficult since the geometrically exact pattern, as designed, wouldn't fit the geometrically inexact ceiling. However, he also noticed that the existing pattern on the cornice had been cunningly contrived by earlier craftsmen, working by eye and hand, to fit the unequal lengths and still appear consistent. So he used the cornice as a guide, drew his own freehand pattern on the ceiling, and worked to that.

The formation of the new lattice entailed weeks of painstaking work, building up layer upon layer of plaster, using different compositions in different layers, in order to get the shape right and make it stay right. In the final stages as we saw it, the pattern looked perfect.

The latest coat of distemper was still wet in places. It too had been carefully mixed and coloured, the last brush-load applied only a short time before, when the plasterers knocked off for the day. In its liquid state the distemper was an alarming drab khaki, but it was already drying to a tasteful off-white that would

26

complement the age of the room. Brilliant white would look all wrong at Felbrigg, despite the opinion of the visitor who, on her way through the Dining Room, was heard to comment: "It could do with a coat of Dulux, couldn't it?"

Despite the many times I have been in the Library at Felbrigg, I never imagined that I would one day stand in the exact centre of the room, so close to the ceiling. If I had been transported there by magic I would never have guessed where I was. It was a weird and memorable experience.

Later, house steward Rebecca reported that the worst job of all had been the dismantling of the filthy, plaster-caked polythene and the rest of the protective gubbins. To ensure that as little mess as possible reached the rest of the house, a stalwart team of volunteers turned out and, clad in spaceman-type suits that covered them from head to foot, they washed every inch of steel and plastic before it left the Library. The very final stages were completed on a cold and snowy February weekend, when the only "volunteers" available were Rebecca's parents. My own mum, who once stood in as a room steward and even did a stint of washing up in the old tea room, would be glad to know that Felbrigg life goes on as per usual.

As anticipated when talking to Elizabeth, I later telephoned David's secretary and booked a place on one of the advertised attics and cellars tours, which were due to take place at the end of March. I also booked lunch for two in the restaurant, and very much looked forward to the day.

It was not to be. In mid-February of that late, wet, cold, gloom-laden British spring, foot-and-mouth disease took its grim toll on the countryside. Many properties were forced to adopt precautionary measures and close their gates to all but essential visitors. Felbrigg was among them.

CHAPTER
TWO

Historic Felbrigg

The origins of the manor of Felbrigg are traceable way back to Saxon times, but its recorded history begins with the Domesday Book which mentions it as part of the lands belonging to Roger Bigod, first Norman Earl of Norfolk. Two and a half centuries later, a certain Simon de Felbrigg was lord of the manor. The earliest of the brasses in Felbrigg church shows him in old age, dressed in the simple costume of a landowner. His grandson, Sir Simon Felbrigg, knighted by Richard II in the early 1400s, rebuilt the original village church and made it more or less as we see it today. It stands in the park, about half a mile from the house.

During the early Middle Ages the local peasants and cottars dwelled in houses which clustered cosily close to the church, but at some unrecorded date, and for reasons unknown, the village migrated a mile or so. This may have been a consequence of the plague which raged through the area in 1550, or perhaps because of some enclosure of land. It may even have been because the lord of the manor preferred not to have his view defaced by the humble dwellings of his serfs. All we know for sure is that the modern village lies well out of sight of the Hall. Only the church and its cemetery remain, guarded by flint walls — a sacred island in a grassy ocean grazed by sheep and cattle. In dry weather you can still make out various humps and hollows around it, indicating the location of demolished buildings.

The original manor house stood on the same site as the present Hall, but we know very little about it. A few footings have been found during building work, most of these beneath the Rose Garden, but the only substantial evidence of that first building is the undercroft (a sort of cellar or crypt) which lies under the semicircular gravelled courtyard at the front of the house and which adjoins the present Hall's cellars. Heavy vehicles which need to come into the courtyard are directed to park away from the area of the undercroft. Its barrel ceiling might not take the weight of a modern lorry.

The Norman manor house was pulled down in the 1620s and in its place rose a splendid new Jacobean hall with all mod cons, consisting of a central screens passage with a great hall to the left, pantry and buttery to the right, and kitchens behind. When open fires were the only means of cooking, kitchens were kept separate because of the risk of conflagration. As we have seen, over the next century or two this basic structure underwent two further periods of improvement and modernisation, the work being masterminded by two architects who were both famous in their day. William Samwell added the new west wing in the 1670s, and eighty years later James Paine remodelled the rooms and moved the staircase. Later squires added their own adjustments as tastes and lifestyles changed.

A visit to Felbrigg

The Hall lies about 25 miles north of Norwich and a couple of miles south-west of Cromer, the fishing town famous for its crabs and which has one of the few remaining piers in the country, with at the end of it a lifeboat station and a thriving theatre. If you head for Cromer, Felbrigg Hall is easy to find — just follow the brown tourist signs with their oakleaf logo.

Two narrow gatehouses guard a driveway which forms part of a small crossroads lying in the shade of tall trees. Beyond them you follow a winding, tree-lined drive with rhododendrons crowding the woods to your right and arable fields opening eventually to your left. The trees along the drive are mostly oaks, some tall and long-established, others still small enough to need protective fencing: they were planted to replace the 25 mature trees destroyed by the hurricane of October 1987, during which, across the whole estate, many thousands of trees, from ancient chestnuts to tiny saplings, were lost. A cattle grid guards the pasture where the drive dips down, takes a dog-leg left turn, and you pass a pond behind which Hall Farm lies in a hollow to your right. As you climb the next rise you see ahead of you the tall brick wall that shelters the Walled Garden.

From the area reserved for parking, the Hall presents its easterly face, with castellated ramparts surrounding the stable yard and beyond them the house itself, a mass of red brick and weathered, patchy stucco beneath slated roofs and elegant chimneys. Leave your car in the shade of a tree, or on the hard standing near the inner gateway. You might like to follow the drive or walk on the grass for the couple of hundred yards to where you stand square on to the south front and can gain an idea of how the house looked when it was built, between 1621 and 1624, by Sir John Wyndham, of Orchard in Somerset, and his middle son, Thomas, who respelled the name as Windham when he moved here. The oldest, Jacobean part of the house has three bays, above which at attic level the words GLORIA DEO IN EXCELSIS appear in stone letters. Felbrigg's builders were God-fearing men and the Latin translates as "Glory to God in the Highest". It is not, as one visitor brightly surmised, an inscription dedicated to one of the ladies of the manor — "the lady called Gloria"!

If you walk a little further along the road, you have a good view of the west wing, an addition built in the 1680s. Its façade of tall windows set in red brick gives it an almost Georgian elegance which contrasts intriguingly with the craggy outlines of the earlier part, though only six decades separate them. Behind the lawns that front the west wing you can see the Orangery, added by Ash (often spelt Ashe, his mother's maiden name) Windham in 1705. Each springtime, delicate camellias flower here on huge trees which are now almost a century old.

Despite the interior remodelling of the house in the mid-eighteenth century, the only signs of these alterations from the outside are a few blocked-in windows. The covering of the Library's west-facing window gave more room for bookshelves, while the Cabinet and the Chinese Bedroom above it lost their views of the sunset but gained elegant north-facing bay windows instead.

Returning the way you came along the drive, make for the far corner of the house. This south-eastern service wing was added by Paine when he altered the interior of the main house, but in the 1820s it was refaced in Gothic style to match the new stable courtyard to the east of the main buildings. No sign now remains of the earlier stables, which lay to the south-west on a knoll named Stable Hill, inconveniently far from the main house.

These were the last major alterations to take place. Thankfully, Felbrigg escaped the Victorian "improvements" which disfigured many another historic building in Britain.

Behind the black-painted railings and welcoming open gate of the stable courtyard, sunshaded tables and chairs await you, with the tea room on the right. Those tall windows at the back of the courtyard belong to the more formal Park Restaurant, while to the left is the gift shop. You can bypass the stable yard and make straight for the cool, stone-floored reception area where friendly staff wait to greet you.

The new entrance has been formed from what was originally the "knife room" (where the knives were cleaned and sharpened in the days before stainless steel) in an area which, in our experience, was full of what can only be described as junk. These rooms were known to us as the "lock-up" and, being damp, dusty and full of cobwebs, were used only to store things of little worth. When Joan took delivery of some new freezers one year, an old chest freezer with its lid removed for safety was left in the lock-up until it could be disposed of. One winter's day it became a trap for a rat which had leapt in easily enough but couldn't get out. Chris happened to go into the lock-up, then a place of dank gloom and trailing cobwebs, and was startled by a scrabbling of claws and a glimpse of something moving against the lining of the freezer. It gave him quite a fright, even before he saw what it was. Since rats can carry deadly diseases, he decided not to risk trying to catch the thing himself but went to phone for some qualified help. News of the unwelcome freezer-squatter horrified the ladies who were serving lunch to Christmas shoppers, but administrator Robert, a great animal lover, found pathos in its plight. "Poor little thing," he commented. "Should we give it some food and water while it's waiting?" The arrival of pest control officers prevented him from offering the rat a portion of turkey and Christmas pud as a sort of condemned man's last supper.

When next you visit Felbrigg, you'll find the former lock-up rodent-free, swept and dusted, its whitewashed walls graced with display posters and photographs. Show your National Trust membership card or pay the entry fee, and emerge into the Rose Garden, planted in memory of the late squire. At the right season, masses of glorious purple and white wisteria blossom soften the square lines of the windows of the South Corridor as you make your way along to the semicircular front courtyard, crunch across the gravel and walk into the porch past a massive front door of bleached, studded oak.

We'll make this tour a whirlwind one, simply to let you orientate yourself and see the place as it is now. From the main screens passage you turn right and go across a lobby into the dark-panelled Morning Room, then come back again and straight into the Great Hall, whose early Victorian decor includes surprising "Mr Whippy" cones attached to the ceiling (they're turned wood, not plaster, you may like to know). Beyond lie the Dining Room, the sumptuous Red Drawing Room, and the Cabinet with its marvellous display of paintings collected by William Windham II on his Grand Tour. This room lies at the rear of the house and takes you through a jib door into the Stone Corridor, which in turn leads you back southwards and into the main staircase hall. Climb the stairs and you'll find the Library, and through it the Book Room; then return to the gallery and move into the west wing, through the Grey Dressing Room with its intriguing boot-shaped metal bath, and along through the four bedrooms. In the Chinese Bedroom, where a bay window overlooks the Orangery and the shrubberies and trees of the garden, pause to admire the amazing wallpaper where ducks, silver pheasant and birds of paradise stalk amid peonies and lotus blossoms. This paper dates from 1751 and, after suffering from the damp which affected many of the upper rooms in the early 1900s, it was restored and, in some places, repainted in the mid-1970s. Some years later, when Chris and I were there, certain areas of the paper were painstakingly removed for a second time so that workmen could deal with a growth of dry rot in the west wall where a window had been bricked over. When the problem had been dealt with, the restorer replaced and reglued the precious wallpaper, inch by careful inch. Can you see the joins?

Another jib door takes you back along the West Corridor, past the old bathroom with its lino printed with nursery-rhyme scenes, down via the back stairs to the Bird Corridor, and on to the Old Kitchen (once again set out as a working kitchen now that the tea room has its own place). Move on to the South Corridor, which leads to rooms which, during our stay, comprised the shop and its store, but which now, as in much earlier times, are the housekeeper's room, the servants' hall, the tenants' waiting room and the turnery. From there you will find yourself back in the reception area where you can visit the hand-me-down book shop in what is now termed the "strong room" but which may once have been an overnight jail for local miscreants such as poachers. Pause to browse a while, or go round to the gardens, or rest your legs and enjoy the delights of the table service restaurant, the self-service tea room, and of course the shop.

Jib doors

As described by *The Concise Oxford Dictionary*, a jib door is a "Door flush with wall in which it stands, usu. painted etc. so as to be indistinguishable. [orig. unknown]". Such doors are often wrongly termed "secret" doors. A more accurate word would be "hidden", since their purpose is aesthetic, simply to make the room look more tidy and disguise the presence of a door which often led to back corridors frequented by maids and footmen carrying coal, hot water or slop buckets.

Several such doors exist at Felbrigg, but in the main house the most conspicuous examples are in the Cabinet and the Chinese Bedroom; both are made to blend in with the walls around them, and both are opened during the day to allow visitors through. Two other jib doors are so well hidden that without help you wouldn't even suspect their existence. They are both in the Library, where they look just like part of the bookcases and carry a heavy load of books. One of these jib doors leads into a tiny cupboard; the other stands open, allowing access to the Book Room.

Many of our visitors love to have such details pointed out and explained. Don't ever be afraid to ask a room steward for information — they love to talk about "their" house.

Different strokes

Like all stately homes, Felbrigg attracts visitors for a variety of reasons and, at the end of a busy day, volunteer stewards often swap stories of the different, and often unexpected, aspects which have provoked comment. Some want only a cursory glimpse of the house before they go out to enjoy the gardens, or perhaps their interest lies in the woods and the way they were planted. It's wonderful how the landscapers were able to visualise an effect they themselves would never see — swathes of mature trees with coppery foliage making a statement against mid-greens and silver-green and the dark counterpoint of pines. Other visitors may enjoy the house best, but in a variety of different ways. Some wander through imagining what it was like to live amid such splendour. Some ask about the furniture, or perhaps the wood it's made from: "Is it burr yew or burr walnut? Lovely, isn't it?" Smiling, they let their fingers caress the smoothly polished surface before the steward has a chance to stop them; or perhaps the steward hasn't the heart to say, "Please don't touch." Many of us adore the feel of polished wood, so warm and smooth and sensual. Some visitors delight in the wallpapers or the fabrics, the porcelain or the pictures, the clocks or the carpets; to some the Library and the Book Room provide the main magnet, while their companions linger variously amid the sumptuousness of the Drawing Room, the grandeur of the Cabinet, or the delicate femininity of the bedrooms.

I remember my father would spend hours and hours (so it seemed) in each room, wanting to talk to the guides or examine everything minutely. He had been an armament artificer in the REME during the war, his speciality being making the lenses for viewfinders, and though later he worked as a typewriter mechanic before promotion took him up to the boardroom, he never lost his interest in lenses and old machines. My mother, on the other hand, preferred a quick whisk through the main house to get its overall feel and then she'd spend hours in the garden, wondering which flowers she might cultivate in her own small patch.

One man who introduced himself to Chris as "only a coalman", asked if he could take a closer look at the William and Mary chairs, to confirm his thoughts about their construction and to see if they were marked with Roman numerals, as were most such chairs. Evidently he knew his stuff where chairs were concerned. Another man went through the house taking particular notice of the fireplaces; not so much the magnificence of the surrounds, some in marble and some in carved wood, no, his interest was in the ironwork of the grates: "I used to work in a foundry making these things. I love to see them in their rightful setting." But the visitor who displayed perhaps the most extraordinary field of interest was a glamorous American lady. She buttonholed Chris in the front courtyard and spent half an hour discussing with him the different bonding of the brickwork. She knew far more about the subject than he did.

My own interest lies in people, whether from the past or of the present. I enjoy the stories of family quarrels and neighbourly disputes that exercised the Windhams; their romances and heartaches and triumphs; their relationships with their children. Human nature doesn't change, though centuries pass.

Every day at Felbrigg brings some new story of something a visitor had said, a mutual whinge with a member of staff, a dispute between two opinionated room stewards . . . People are endlessly fascinating and surprising. It all serves to prove my theory that a stately home has something for everyone, whether your taste be for fine embroidery, Greek literature, human nature, or something as basic as plumbing.

Natural delights

One of the most constant and yet always changing pleasures is provided by Nature herself. Woods and gardens change with the seasons, drenched in sunlight or bathed in rain; spiky winter branches assume their May mantle of a dozen different shades of green; purple wisteria and lilac augment apple blossom and creamy chestnut candles as delicate spring flowers give way to a riot of summer colour. Trees change into their August suits of uniform green, then gradually begin to yellow or flame into autumn, and leaves fade and fall as the year wanes. We're so lucky to have changing seasons and unpredictable weather. It's what gives our country its charm, and its inhabitants something to talk about.

At Felbrigg we shared this wondrous bounty with a host of other living creatures. Swallows and martins swooped round the eaves, replaced at dusk by bats; water birds patrolled the lake, while duck and geese of many kinds stitched patterns across winter skies; in the woods the sudden *cock-uck, cock-uck* of an alarmed pheasant caused stoats and weasels to pause in their swift hunting, and let's not forget the farm animals, and the dogs brought for walks, and a few stealthy cats. One of Felbrigg's tenants, a charming clergyman who for many years was Dean of King's College, Cambridge, used to make us smile when we met him walking through the woods and calling out in his dulcet ecclesiastical tones, "Purrr-dy, Purrr-dy! Where are you, wretched and abandoned cat?"

A perfect vantage point for enjoying the park was the room we used as our upper sitting room. It mirrors the far half of the Library on the opposite corner of the main Jacobean front and, to give an idea of its size, one Christmas morning we entertained 60 people comfortably in that room to pre-lunch drinks and nibbles. One huge bay window looks east towards the morning sun and the car park, and when the Christmas shop opened we used to decorate a huge tree and stand it in that window like a welcoming beacon. Many visitors and staff still remember those trees with pleasure. Standing at that window one summer's day, I saw a fox trot in leisurely fashion among the parked cars, unnoticed by all the people wandering around. A second bay window faces south across the park, over the invisible lake in its hollow, and on a clear day, using binoculars, you can pick out the spire of Norwich Cathedral 25 miles away.

A big flock of Canada geese regularly visited the park to roost by the lake. They were timid creatures and usually stayed well away from the house. Towards evening we would see them flying in, circling across the park and over the lake before coming in to settle for the night. On a warm June evening as Chris took his ease by an open window, he saw the geese begin to make their usual landing approach, dipping behind the trees in the park. Suddenly, with a loud cackling of alarm and frantic flapping of wings, the great straggling skein of them gained height again and came heading straight towards him, looping right across the front of the house, so close he swears he felt the draught from their wing tips. If only he'd had a video camera handy.

We deduced that the birds must have been startled by the unexpected presence of fishermen, it being the first day of the coarse fishing season, always an event anticipated with delight by the piscatorial enthusiasts of the area (including our son Kevin). The geese eventually got used to these intruders on their space and roosted in the pasture away from the water. They made excellent watchdogs, sounding the alarm if anyone, human or fox, strayed near them in the night.

The cattle which graze in Felbrigg Park belong to the tenant of Hall Farm. Farmer David Rash used to keep a herd of Lincoln Reds, handsome creatures which he used for breeding, not for their milk; so, instead of being driven home to the milking sheds twice daily, they remained out in the pasture most of the year.

We always knew when market time was near because the calves would be corralled in the stockyard ready to be driven off in a huge cattle truck heading for sale next day, while the cows remained in the pasture. All night long we could hear the plaintive cries of youngsters wanting their mothers, answered by the bellowing of cows mourning after their babies. It was almost enough to turn me into a vegetarian, though Chris remains an unrepentant carnivore. Viewing newborn calves skipping merrily in daisy-starred grass, leaping and bounding in youthful delight at being alive, he often wonders how well one might fit into our deep freeze. Or seeing a field full of sweetly gambolling lambs, he'll shout, "Mint sauce!"

Sadist.

However, on one particular spring day — a closed day, with no visitors in the Hall — Chris was in his office catching up on some paperwork when he was distracted by a peripheral glimpse of some unusual activity in the pasture where one of the cows appeared to be attacking one of the trees. A second look revealed that she was actually throwing her hindquarters against the solid tree-trunk again and again in maddened fashion. Grabbing the binoculars which he always kept handy, he focused on the cow and, as she turned to give him a rear view, he spotted a long thin leg protruding from her hind quarters. She was in trouble, unable to give birth because her calf had presented itself in an awkward position.

Not being a cowman, Chris knew he might be making a fool of himself by interfering, but better that than risk losing a calf. He phoned the farm and explained what he could see. A few minutes later, David Rash came out to the pasture, not in a Land-Rover or tractor but in the clapped-out old banger he used for driving about the farm. Chris watched anxiously as the farmer opened connecting gates and, still in his car, slowly circled the herd to make them bunch up. The distressed cow was somewhere among them as they were gradually encouraged to move out of the field and back towards their stockyard, with the farmer in his car bringing up the rear.

Later, David Rash explained that it would have been dangerous, if not impossible, to try to isolate one cow, especially when she had been driven half mad with discomfort and stress. However, in the confines of the stockyard he had managed to separate her from the others and give her the help she needed. The calf had been born. Mother and baby were doing well.

In order to produce calves, of course, a bull has to be involved. Yes, the old-fashioned ways are still employed, much to the amazement of certain town-bred visitors, such as the chap who couldn't understand why the bull was in the field: "But they use artificial insemination these days, don't they?" And milk comes out of bottles, doesn't it? And beans grow in tins. In the real world, at certain times of year the bull is put into the field to enjoy the favours of his harem.

Along with Kevin and his wife Alison, we strolled out one summer evening to enjoy our beautiful surroundings. The bull was in the pasture, grazing close to the electric fence, an enormous brute with curved, pointed horns and a brass ring through his nose.

"He's an old softy," said Chris, who maintains that the female of the bovine species proves the old saying by being far more deadly than the male, especially when she's looking after a calf. If you walk across a field with cows and calves in it, take care not to get between mother and child; the cow will attack without mercy if she thinks you're threatening her baby. The bull, on the other hand, is generally a pretty placid, contented chap — and what male wouldn't be, with plenty of luscious grass to eat and a hundred willing females eager to placate his libido? To prove this point to his own doubting family, Chris carefully climbed over the electric fence and pulled some long grass. This he fed to the bull, who took it much as a pony would, long tongue wrapping round the stalks. All very fine, but however friendly that vast animal seemed, the rest of us sighed in relief when Don Christoforo the toreador climbed back to join us.

Actually, I was almost as worried about the electric fence as about the bull. I've never forgotten the photographer who came in white as a sheet and said he hadn't realised the fence was electrified. Until he was astride it.

Nasty.

CHAPTER
THREE

Days of elegance

We may imagine that spending time in visiting old country houses and wandering round other people's gardens is a relatively new leisure activity. On the contrary, this pleasant pastime has been in vogue for centuries. As readers of Jane Austen will know, Miss Elizabeth Bennett re-encountered the proud but charismatic Mr D'Arcy, quite by chance, when she and her aunt and uncle took a day trip to see his country home, Pemberley, and asked the housekeeper to show them round.

It was on just such a tour of Norfolk in 1764 that Lady Elizabeth Beauchamp Proctor visited Felbrigg and noted:

'Tis a very grand looking old house with three elegant modern rooms added above and below, hung with crimson and India papers, some good pictures, chiefly landscapes . . . There is not much garden, but a very good greenhouse [the Orangery], out of which the gardener gave each of us a fine nosegay of orange flowers, geraniums, &c . . . The park is walled round, and capable of great improvements; but, the owner being a minor, nothing can yet be done. There is a good view of the sea . . .

The orange blossom and geraniums picked for Lady Elizabeth by the gardener came long before the magnificent camellias which grow in the Orangery now. Another change is that "view of the sea": the chill expanse of the North Sea is now, thankfully, hidden by deep plantations of oak, sweet chestnut and beech, a warm shawl that helps to protects Felbrigg Hall from the bitter north-easterlies.

Most of the trees of the Great Wood and the Deer Park were planted at the behest of the youthful owner mentioned in Lady Elizabeth's holiday jottings. He inherited at the age of 11 in 1761 and went on to be the most illustrious of Felbrigg's squires, the Rt. Hon. William Windham III. He became a Member of Parliament and served in Pit's coalition government, becoming Secretary at War in 1794. Marrying late in life, he fathered no children and so left the estate to his step-nephew, Vice Admiral Lukin, who later assumed the name of Windham. It was Lukin who altered the service wing, built the new red-brick stable block and enclosed the north portico to form what is now the Bird Corridor.

Some squires took better care of the fabric of the house; some gave most attention to the woods; others favoured the farms and the shooting pleasures of their estate; one or two neglected the place rather badly and one particularly profligate young squire actually bankrupted the estate. Whatever their differing characters and temperaments, each one of them helped to make Felbrigg what it is today.

The severe damage to the Library ceiling, for instance, was largely a result of the inattention of one particular squire, a crusty old bachelor remembered in the family as "Uncle Bobby" Ketton.

Robert Ketton

In 1861, during a notorious sanity trial held in the Court of Exchequer in Westminster, General Charles Ashe Windham, famous Norfolk hero, tried to prove that his nephew, William Frederick Windham, youthful squire of Felbrigg, was of unsound mind. The old soldier took this action in the hope of saving Felbrigg from ruination, but he failed. After 34 days of enquiry, the court declared the younger Windham to be of sound mind. A year later, another court declared him bankrupt.

The house and much of the estate were purchased by Norwich merchant John Ketton, a dealer in oilcake and other types of cattle feed. Although he and his family had to contend with some initial suspicion from the snobs among their neighbours, they soon settled into the lifestyle of the county set. Mrs Ketton's diaries tell of dinners and balls, afternoon teas and shooting parties, interspersed with much visiting and card-leaving. Like Jane Austen's Mrs Bennett, Mrs Ketton had five marriageable daughters and, also like Mrs Bennett, she found husbands for her three older girls but the younger two remained unwed. However, unlike the heirless Bennetts, the Kettons had two sons: the older one, John, went into his father's business at an early age; the younger one, Robert, the baby of the family, was a small boy when the family came to Felbrigg.

The relationship between John Ketton, senior and his older son appears to have been stormy. It ended in the son's being ordered, as in all the best melodramas, "never to darken my door again". Shortly afterwards, when the old man died, it was young Robert, still a schoolboy at Eton, who became the new owner of Felbrigg.

"Bobby" Ketton lived at the Hall with his mother and his two unmarried sisters, Marion and Gertrude, and in the early days of his tenure he took good care of his estate. Visitors in those days included the Empress of Austria (who ate figs in the walled garden), and Oscar Wilde and his wife. Unlike his staunchly Tory father, Robert Ketton was an enthusiastic Liberal; he played an active part during elections and encouraged the burgeoning Agricultural Workers' Union, even giving work to its pioneer George Edwards, whom other landowners shunned as a troublemaker. But his political leanings and increasingly solitary nature won the disapproval of some of his neighbours, one of whom wrote, "Young Ketton is an awful Radical, and he does not show any sign of marrying".

He never did marry, and his tendency to crankiness grew worse as first his mother died, then his two sisters, leaving him all alone in his great, cold, echoing house.

Still only in his early forties, Robert Ketton seems to have sunk into what today's doctors would probably diagnose as a deeply depressive state. He gave up his interest in politics and slowly turned into a crusty and eccentric old bachelor, a recluse seldom seen by his neighbours.

In the 1980s, an elderly lady who came to visit Felbrigg told Chris that she had been employed at the Hall as a very young housemaid in Robert Ketton's time. She recalled that he would never speak to servants if he happened to pass them in a corridor, and he was often absent on "visits to a lady friend".

What was worse for Felbrigg, Ketton began to neglect both the house and the estate. The untended roof started to let in rain which eventually rotted many of the timbers and softened the plaster ceilings — especially in the Library, as we have seen. Ditches became choked, drains clogged up, lawns turned into hayfields, shrubberies into jungles. A market gardener took a lease on the Walled Garden but allowed the glasshouses to fall into disrepair, and across the estate farm cottages and other buildings deteriorated through lack of maintenance. Robert Ketton's nephew, the next heir, watched the creeping dilapidation of his inheritance with understandable dismay.

In a nice historical twist, the blood of Felbrigg's earlier squires ran in the veins of Robert Ketton's heir. The original Wyndham line had become divided in the sixteenth century, with one branch at Felbrigg and the other at Orchard, in Somerset. The Felbrigg branch changed the spelling of the name to Windham and so it remained. However, during the seventeenth century a third branch, spelling the name with a "y", settled at Cromer Hall. Two hundred years further on, a daughter of the Cromer Wyndhams married into the Cremer family of Beeston Hall and bore a son, named Thomas Wyndham Cremer. He — Tom Cremer — married Anna Ketton, sister of Robert Ketton; thus the two bloodlines merged and Wyndham blood returned to Felbrigg in the veins of Tom and Anna's son, who was blessed with the name of Wyndham Cremer Cremer.

He was only fourteen years younger than his maternal uncle, Robert Ketton, with whom he shared a warm and friendly relationship, shooting being one mutual interest. But it's always awkward to discuss an inheritance with the person who has to die to make it come about, and the nephew could never quite bring himself to raise the subject of the estate and the insidious erosion that threatened it because of his uncle's lackadaisical squirage.

Soon after the First World War, instead of selling off a small parcel of land to settle a debt, Robert Ketton decided to auction off most of the best china, some of the best furniture and plate, and — most unforgivable of all, says Wyndham Cremer's son — many of the most valuable books in the Library. Nor did Ketton secure the best price for them. One can imagine the desperation with which his nephew watched these irreplaceable family treasures go under the hammer, but there was little he could do to prevent it. He finally came to live at Felbrigg in May 1923, after his uncle decided to spend his last few years elsewhere. By then the estate was in dire distress. All its new owner could do was cobble together piecemeal repairs.

Was it Wyndham Cremer who had the first boiler installed to supply hot water to the house? It seems unlikely that the eccentric old recluse Robert Ketton would have done so. Whoever ordered this innovation, at some point around the 1920s the old nursery off the West Corridor was turned into a bathroom. The huge old tub of enamelled cast iron, standing on ball-and-claw feet, is still there to be seen. It was fed with hot water from a boiler situated far away in a cellar under the Old Kitchen (a place which, in later years, head gardener Ted Bullock found ideal for storing dahlia tubers!). The water ran through well-lagged and boxed-in pipes that ran up through the kitchen, along the suite of rooms above (which in the 1980s became the houseman's flat), through other domestic offices and somehow by a roundabout route all the way to the bathroom on the east side of the west wing, where it heated a towel rail and then, finally, reached the brass tap. This advance in plumbing must have been a relief to the maids who had had the task of carting buckets of hot water for baths, but I wonder how long it took for the hot water to come through? Presumably that was why one asked the maid to run one's bath, so that one didn't have to stand waiting until the hot water arrived. It must have caused much alarming clanking and banging as the pipes expanded, and how hot was the water after its long journey, however well insulated the pipes?

The last squire

Because of a clause in John Ketton's will, on coming into his inheritance Wyndham Cremer added the merchant's name to his own and so the family became Ketton-Cremer. Two sons bore this name, Robert Wyndham Ketton-Cremer and Richard Thomas Wyndham Ketton-Cremer. The older brother, known as Wyndham in the family, "Bunny" to his more intimate friends and later simply as "the squire" to most of the local populace, succeeded to the estate in 1933, when he was 27. His profession was history and writing. He liked best to work in the calm atmosphere of his Library, producing numerous published books which are both respected for their erudition and well read by people eager to know more about Norfolk and its history.

Around the house and estate, the squire continued to work on restoration as far as funds allowed, spending all he could spare on the upkeep of the buildings. In the summer of 1958 he reroofed the Orangery. He even sold one of his prized Van de Velde seascapes to the Maritime Museum to raise more money for the estate (happily, the museum returned it, on permanent loan, though they insisted that it be glazed for its protection, which is why it's the only picture in the house behind glass). Evidence suggests that paintings may have been one of his more minor concerns, however; one portrait badly needed cleaning, but he decided the money would be better spent on making improvements to his tenants' cottages.

The squire's abiding passion was reserved for his woods. It has been estimated that over a period of 40 years he planted some 200,000 trees. He loved trees and was fiercely protective of them, abhorring anything that damaged them, from frost to lightning to nails hammered in. Catching David Rash, the Hall Farm tenant, attaching a fence to one of the trees in the park, the usually gentle squire berated him hotly until the farmer pointed out that he hadn't damaged the tree with nails or staples, he'd simply tied wire round it to anchor the fence. Around plantations of young pines the squire liked to plant a border of cherry trees, simply for the pleasure of seeing their blossom in the springtime, and in among the pines he planted a few rowans, so that their berries might add a bright splash of red in the autumn. He also knew his toadstools, being able to tell at a glance which ones were deadly and which merely caused a passing delirium, and when he walked about his estates he carried with him a walking stick with a wickedly barbed point, which he used to spear and pull out thistle roots. The stick is still there among Felbrigg's memorabilia.

If the woods were his chief joy, his greatest sorrow was the loss of his younger brother Dick, an equipment officer with the Royal Air Force, killed in Crete in 1941. After the war, to commemorate VE Day, the squire planted two broad avenues of trees forming a great V shape, a huge arrow in the woods that has provided a landmark for many postwar aircraft. At the apex of the two rides he placed a seat which he dedicated to Dick. What better memorial could a man who loved trees make for his only brother?

During the Second World War, army bases and RAF stations sprang up all over the eastern counties and many great houses were appropriated — and damaged — by military or civil authorities who used them as hospitals, offices and messes, filled their parks with wooden huts, and set guard posts at their gates. Felbrigg escaped this fate for the simple reason that it had no electricity. The frugal squire managed without this modern advantage until 1954, and then, to preserve his decorated ceilings, he had power brought into the main rooms via sockets in skirting boards and walls. This is why today, on dark October afternoons, you will find those rooms softly lit by table and standard lamps. As for heating, the squire and his small staff continued to rely on open fires and electric heaters. For both economy and convenience, he mostly lived in the suite of smaller rooms in the centre of the house, which were later to become living quarters for house staff such as ourselves. He used the main house only when he had guests, and even then the company didn't spend much time in the grandest rooms, nor did they use the best bedrooms, which were a clutter of furniture, porcelain and brass ornaments, and the inevitable piles of books, kept under dust sheets in the dark, behind shuttered windows.

One of the late squire's friends, Sir Brinsley Ford, who visited the house seven times in the 1950s and 1960s, recorded his impressions in an article titled "Staying at Felbrigg as the Guest of Wyndham

Ketton-Cremer". In this he recalls that in May 1953 the house was so cold that an American guest "went in to Cromer on some trumped-up excuse to buy himself the thickest set of long woollen combinations he could find". The cold prevented them from using the grand suite of rooms in the west wing, so the Great Hall became a communal dining-cum-sitting room. That room at least was heated by "a large and ugly anthracite stove round which we sat on the few chairs that were not piled high with books waiting to be reviewed". I love to imagine them sitting around shivering after dinner, wrapped in mufflers and shawls! They chatted or read books by lamplight, went to bed by the light of candles, and generally "enjoyed the pleasant illusion of living in the past". The writer adds that "the house was run on old-fashioned lines by a staff of three . . . Ward, the butler, who had already been at Felbrigg for thirty years, a maid and a cook . . . The brass can filled with hot water, which Ward produced in the morning and again in the evening when one went up to dress for dinner, was always a welcome sight."

Later, Ward the butler was joined by a new cook-housekeeper delightfully named Mrs Muffin. It was the squire's habit to take his guests, at the end of their visit, to see Mrs Muffin and to admire the array of copper in the kitchen. On these occasions Mr Ketton-Cremer would turn his back and pointedly stare out of the tall window into the grass courtyard, allowing his guests "an opportunity of endorsing their compliments to Mrs Muffin with something more precious than copper".

56

Mr Ward continued in service at the Hall until the squire died, when he retired to a bungalow not far away. But he continued to take an interest in the old place and when he was in his nineties he paid a visit during which he regaled Chris with tales of the late squire. He was intrigued to see our apartment, which he said had once been used by Mr Ketton-Cremer and his mother and brother as their private quarters. One small room, which we kept as a cosy guest bedroom, had apparently been used by Mr Ketton-Cremer as a study. I was particularly beguiled by the image of the squire shutting himself into that small room and ordering Ward not to disturb him as he concentrated on reading through the proof of one of his books, or struggled with a copy-edited manuscript. I know the feeling!

It was 1967 before the squire had central heating installed, and then it came only to what he called his Retreat, the cosy bolt-hole which he was creating from former service offices in a corner off the grass courtyard. He planned to move in there every winter, to a modernised apartment that was far easier to heat, service and keep clean. It had a large lounge, lovely dining room overlooking the garden, big kitchen, elegant parquet-floored hallway, downstairs cloaks, upstairs bathroom, bedrooms ... Brinsley Ford thought this retreat a "Lilliputian abode" akin to a hotel annexe. He notes that one room, which in earlier days had been a game larder, a dairy, and then a laundry, had now become a "small dining room". On the occasions when Chris and I had the pleasure of dining there with our neighbours Gill and Henry it didn't seem small to me. You could seat eight or ten people comfortably around the table and there was still room for sideboards and a couple of what-nots. To me the Retreat is a most beautiful, spacious house. (But then I was born in a terrace not far from the Fosse Dyke in Lincoln, so my ideas of grandeur were probably a little different from those of the squire's friend.)

Mr Ketton-Cremer remained a bachelor, but unlike his great-uncle Robert Ketton he did not turn into a lonely recluse. This gentle, kindly, studious and erudite man, a staunch Christian and an amiable if sometimes vague and distracted host, often had friends and relatives to stay. His house also offered hospitality to many local groups while his park became the venue for fêtes and shows, with children from nearby schools and scout groups gathering for picnics by the lake or to camp in the woods. Many of those children, long since grown to adults, still remember him with affection.

Although he finished writing his book in May 1961, he chose to end the narrative 20 years earlier with the death of his only brother. About himself he says little, though between the lines his book reveals much about his character, his great love for his home and his family, and his abiding grief over the loss of his younger brother. In a brief epilogue, he concludes:

Felbrigg survived the war, shaken now and then by bombs, a few windows broken, a few additional cracks in the ceilings, nothing worse . . . And so it stands, with all its associations and memories,

58

confronting the unpredictable future. It may be the scene of happiness, kindness, hospitality in centuries to come. It may be burned to the ground this very night. The story of its first three and a half centuries has now been told; and who can know what lies ahead?

Brinsley Ford writes that the squire visualised himself in old age "crippled by gout", being dragged up to the viewpoint at the apex of his Victory V avenue in the woods "by a ponycart or its modern equivalent" and sitting on the bench he had placed there in memory of his brother, under the oak he had planted to shade it. (That oak was destroyed by lightning, though the National Trust has since planted a new one in the same spot.) However, the squire was not destined to see his old age. As a boy he had suffered from rheumatic fever which left him in delicate health, and as he approached his sixties perhaps he sensed a waning of his physical resources. Having no direct heir, and aware that death duties would in any case enforce the sale of much of the land and many of the remaining treasures, he decided to leave Felbrigg to the nation. He spent his final years organising his house as he hoped it would remain for future visitors to see.

Robert Wyndham Ketton-Cremer died on 12 December 1969 and was buried five days later at the little church in the meadow. He was 63 years old. His unfinished portrait graces the wall of the Great Hall and I like to think that his gentle, genial spirit lingers on and, hopefully, approves of what has happened since he bequeathed his beloved Felbrigg, with its entire contents and estate, to all of us, in care of the National Trust.

CHAPTER
FOUR

Enter the Trust

During the months following the death of Felbrigg's last squire, National Trust staff — under the stewardship of a managing agent — began the work of turning what had been a private home into a place suitable for visitors. They also held a sale, to dispose of excess items such as accumulate in every household. Some of our friends still proudly show off the treasured mementoes they acquired that day when assorted bric-a-brac, books, crockery, kitchen utensils and ornaments were eagerly snapped up.

Felbrigg's first paying visitors, in the 1971 season, saw only the main rooms on the ground floor; that is the Morning Room, the Great Hall (with the staircase hall seen through a roped-off doorway), the Dining Room, the Drawing Room and the Cabinet. From there they turned back to the Drawing Room to leave via a side door, went across to the Bird Corridor and through to the tea room in the Old Kitchen. The Red Shutter Corridor led them to the shop and out via the Rose Garden.

After the first season, the Morning Room was removed from the tour. Isolated to one side of the main entrance where stood the ticket desk, it created a bottleneck because people trying to move back into the Great Hall had to push through the queue of new visitors waiting in the narrow screens passage. As a result, for the ensuing two decades the Morning Room was open for viewing only by special arrangement, being utilised at other times as a gathering place for room stewards and a venue for evening concerts. However, since the mid-1990s, when the new visitor reception area was created well away from the main door of the house, it has resumed its place in the guide book.

The first administrator, Bill Booth, a retired policeman, was appointed in 1971, his wife Molly being employed as his assistant. They were to spend twelve happy years at Felbrigg, Bill running the hall and office while Molly managed first the shop and later also the small tea room which, in later seasons, satisfied those visitors who hungered and thirsted after cream cakes, home-made scones and hot tea. They enjoyed these refreshments in the Old Kitchen, overlooked by "an impressive battery de cuisine consisting of many copper pots, pans, lids and jelly-moulds", to quote the first small guide booklet. That stunning array of gleaming copperware still decorates the kitchen wall and has featured on many a greeting card in the past thirty years.

The Booths were assisted by four ladies who hoovered, dusted and polished the show rooms every morning, then changed their aprons and metamorphosed into shop assistants and/or tea room helpers. For a servery they used a vast rectangular table whose battered, hacked, uneven surface bore witness to many years of vegetable and meat cutting interspersed with much scrubbing and soaking with lye.

This table was still in use as a servery when Chris and I first visited the Hall, but during our first winter as residents, when a more modern counter with display cases and a still were installed, we hauled the huge table to a central position and surrounded it with chairs. It filled nearly a quarter of the room space and was difficult to get one's knees under, not to mention being a ton weight to move when the floor needed scrubbing, but it was well used and especially popular with coach parties who could congregate around it in one big group.

One summer, during our tenure, the news team from BBC's *Look East* came to film the property and interview Chris for a local news item that lasted all of two minutes on screen. A few days after the broadcast, Chris was on his way back to the main house from our flat. His route lay through the Old Kitchen and even before he opened the door he could hear the noise of merry chatter. Around the big refectory table sat an animated party of ladies, their voices filling the spaces under the high ceiling and reverberating off the copper pans. But the din abated when Chris appeared and as he walked through the tea room he became aware of a growing hush. Twenty pairs of eyes fixed on him, following his progress.

"That's him!" someone whispered. Others grinned broadly, and one lady greeted him with a wave: "Hello, Chris!"

He paused, wondering how they knew him. He didn't remember any of their faces. Were they members of a WI group to whom he'd given a talk? "Good afternoon, ladies . . . I'm sorry, should I know you?"

"No, but we know you!" carolled the lady who had waved. "We saw you on the telly the other evening!"

How nice to be famous!

Under the initial guardianship of Bill and Molly Booth, rooms on the first floor were gradually prepared for display, first the Library, then the Rose, Red and Chinese Bedrooms. Access to the bedrooms was originally via individual doors in the West Corridor. However, by 1980, when the last two rooms of this suite opened to public view, the Trust had opened connecting doorways along the far side of the rooms, allowing visitors to flow through more easily.

As the 1970s progressed into the 1980s, thousands more visitors came to enjoy Felbrigg Hall, its gardens, its woods, its lake and its park, and naturally this growing success increased the workload for Bill and Molly and their helpers. Bill's approaching retirement provided an appropriate moment for the Trust to review staffing arrangements.

Bill was due to retire in the autumn, but Molly agreed to continue to supervise the shop and tea room through the Christmas season, after which she too would retire and a new management team would take over. The Trust decided to appoint both a resident administrator and a resident houseman, both of whom would probably come supplied with a spouse who might be willing to help out in time of need (whether or not this is a conscious consideration, in practice that's how it usually turns out). Regional office appears to have hoped that one of the wives of the new appointees might want to fill the gap left vacant by Molly in the shop and tea room, but they were out of luck! In the end the Trust appointed both a seasonal catering manager, Joan, and a seasonal shop manager, Peter, each with a quota of part-time assistants.

The new administrator, Robert, an old hand well versed in the ways of the Trust, came from another East Anglian property. His selected houseman, however, was a novice in the game — a certain Christopher Mackie.

First impressions

Chris had spent twenty-two years as an accountant in the RAF before becoming internal auditor to a firm of excavator manufacturers in Lincoln. But as our sons reached the end of their schooling, Andy going to university to study chemistry while Kevin discovered a vocation for nursing, their father began to wonder if, while he was still young enough to make a new career, there might be life beyond accountancy. Deciding to investigate the possibilities of moving to Norfolk, we subscribed to the East Anglian papers for a while and came across the National Trust advertisement for a houseman to work at Felbrigg Hall.

Apart from the obvious attractions of the county, Norfolk was also the place where Chris had grown up and where his people still lived. We shared a close and happy relationship with them, which was all the more remarkable because Chris was not related to the family in any way. We refer to them as his foster family because that's a concept people understand. The truth is more difficult: "he went to stay with them as an evacuee during the war" doesn't tell half of it.

On the day we moved out of our bungalow near Lincoln, Chris drove the big Granada estate while I took the Mazda, with eighteen-year-old Kevin along as moral support and spare driver. Both vehicles were jam-packed with items necessary for an overnight camp-in before the main removal van arrived. For me it was extra stressful because 120 miles was the longest journey I had yet driven, but luckily, considering it was November, the weather stayed clear and dry. We all arrived without mishap.

Our unfurnished and uncarpeted new quarters lay in the wing over the Old Kitchen. We camped there the first night, cat-napping on sleeping bags and cushions. Being unsettled, I woke long before dawn and lay in the chilly dark, my nose frozen, imagining the busy day ahead. How would the removal men react to the obstacle course that awaited them? Would our furniture fit into the various rooms of the flat? Restless in the dark, I was comforted by the sweet serenade of the courtyard clock only a few yards from the bedroom window. I heard it working up to strike the hour, giving a charming little trill — *ding, ding, dingly, dingly, ding-ding, dingly, ding-ding-ding* — before striking six. How enchanting! Neither Chris nor Kevin had heard it, but I guessed it was a special chime perhaps meant to waken the groomsmen and maidservants of earlier days. I mentioned it to several people, saying how it had made me feel welcome that first anxious morning. It was months before I heard the clock striking six a.m. again, and then to my disappointment it omitted that merry little trill. When I mentioned it to Tom, the head woodsman who had the job of winding the clock, he assured me it had never done anything other than strike the hour. I must have dreamed that welcoming jingle!

Within a day or two we found ourselves selling Christmas trees which Tom brought from the woods and stacked in the Rose Garden to be purchased by friendly people who came up to the Christmas shop. It was our first introduction to some of Felbrigg's regular visitors.

Gradually we made acquaintance with the other staff — Robert and Eve and their bull terrier, a homely but loveable character named Sam; Molly and her four lady helpers; Ted and his assistant gardeners; Tom and his woodsmen — and the few tenants who inhabited dwellings off the grass courtyard and the stable yard. All of these people were invited to a Christmas party that December, along with a few local VIPs and, not least, Felbrigg's team of room stewards.

We cleared the Morning Room in readiness for the evening, leaving a few chairs and the grand piano, with buffet nibbles laid out on the huge table in the Old Kitchen and glasses of wine and orange juice waiting in the entrance lobby. As guests began to arrive by the main front door, Robert and Eve greeted them while Chris and I, dressed in our evening best, waited on tenterhooks near the huge marble fireplace in the Morning Room. No fire blazed in the hearth, sadly, the chimneys not being properly lined. The room had been warmed to just-above-shivering by a couple of small, rattling fan heaters.

Not being much good at small talk, I found the prospect of meeting so many new people daunting. How would the volunteers receive us? They had all grown fond of Bill and Molly and some of them viewed the change of regime with suspicion. We already knew that one or two of the longer-serving volunteers had decided not to carry on into the next season, but half a dozen stalwarts who had been involved at Felbrigg from its first opening had determined to stay and make sure we upstart incomers did right by the house. They felt proprietorial about it and would brook no changes to the status quo. Robert and Eve had been through it all before, but Chris and I felt very much like the new kids on the block — strangers, under scrutiny, under suspicion and probably doomed to be found wanting. However, as the Morning Room filled up, the atmosphere warmed with both body heat and mutual understanding.

Much later, when we all felt part of the same team, we realised that the volunteers too had approached that evening with apprehension and unease.

In the small hours, weary but mellowed by a glass of wine or two, Robert, Eve, Chris and I had a bonding session over the deep stone sink in the Old Kitchen. That is, the men finished closing up the house and then stood about discussing their strategy and swapping anecdotes with much waving of tea towels, while Eve stood up to her elbows in a huge bowlful of sudsy water, washing a hundred-odd plates, pudding dishes, knives, forks and spoons which I dried, dashing upstairs to fetch some of my own tea towels when the Hall's supply became sodden. To my puzzlement, where I would have done the massed trays of wine glasses first, Eve left them to last. "If you rinse them in really hot water, and dry them straight away," she explained, "they come up sparkling, without streaks." (Keen housekeepers please note!) At the time I was less interested in streak-free glasses than in longing for my bed. It must have been nearly three in the morning before we finally crawled up the steep stairs to the houseman's flat.

Having long experience of the Trust's tendency to rely for help on willing wives, Eve preferred her job with a bookseller in Cambridge; she spent most of her time in absentia, appearing usually only at weekends. But for me, a wide-eyed innocent, living at Felbrigg Hall was a great adventure and, despite dire warnings, I threw myself into the role of houseman's helpmeet. And it was a joy. Well, most of the time. To be honest, it was more like the curate's egg — good in parts. And it does tend to get even better when viewed through the rosy lens of retrospect.

Stricter rules

Some of the people whom we met that first night became, and remain, our very good friends. Some have since passed on and we miss having them in our lives. Two couples especially became very close to us and in later years they declared they had known things would be all right the moment they walked into the Morning Room on that December evening. "It was seeing your lovely smiles! You were so friendly and welcoming." But not all of the volunteers succumbed so readily.

During the years since Felbrigg's opening the room stewards had enjoyed certain freedoms which they assumed would continue. In our first season, Chris noticed, a book would occasionally go missing from the Library, only to reappear a week or two later; or he would walk into a room to find the guide displaying the legend on the bottom of a piece of porcelain, or turning the pages of a huge book of maps for the interest of visitors. The Trust had to revoke these privileges and introduce rules which prevented volunteers from handling any of the objects on display. Only house staff and other qualified people are allowed to touch them, and even they must use gloves and other appropriate precautions. A precious piece of porcelain can so easily be dropped, and when it comes to books even careful handling can cause damage, tearing fragile pages or indelibly marking them with grease and sweat from what may seem to be clean, dry fingers.

Blinds, too, are supposed to be kept at an even height, so as to give a neat appearance from outside; all

70

of them fully down on very bright days and all of them lifted to a standard level when clouds dim the daylight. On one moderately dull day when Chris might have expected to find all the blinds at half mast, he was called out to the Orangery and on his return noticed that the blinds in the bedrooms were all pulled right down, except for one, which exposed the whole window. He went up to check with the room stewards, who told him that a courting couple were disporting themselves in the long grass beyond the ha-ha, clearly visible from every bedroom window. The lady room stewards had all closed their blinds so as not to distress the visitors; the only gentleman steward in those rooms had tossed his blind high. "The show was too good to miss!" he said with a grin.

Over the years, some room stewards had developed the habit of giving vent to lengthy expositions on their room-for-the-day, which created unnecessary hold-ups and served to irritate some visitors; so a decree from head office requested them to resist the urge to lecture. At some properties the managers reacted by ordering stewards not to speak to visitors at all, which seems rather sad. Felbrigg chose a compromise: stewards could answer any questions put to them, so long as they did it quietly and unobtrusively.

Most of them appreciated and approved the reasons for the various changes and became allies in the cause of conservation and harmony. They also came to realise that we, too, had grown to love the house just as they did.

Chris's growing fascination with his work and our new home led him to spend most of his sparse free time studying Felbrigg history and doing private research into some of its enigmas. These included the so-called "servants' library", a set of tiny books in a glass-fronted case; the provenance of certain pictures; the stories behind the various bibles; and especially the forgotten treasures which he found secreted in drawers, cupboards, attics and other remote corners of the huge house which no one had had time to properly explore before. After a few years had passed, he was cheered to overhear one of the most knowledgeable room stewards answer a visitor's question by saying, "I don't know, but I'll ask Mr Mackie. If he doesn't know, nobody does!" Quite an accolade coming from that source.

This is not to say we didn't have the odd misunderstanding, as when Chris described the decorative divided top of a bureau, with technical accuracy, as "a broken pediment". A room steward was later heard telling a visitor that the top of the bureau had, unfortunately, been damaged! But friendliness, dedication or homework assiduously studied was not enough to convert one or two of the more stubborn souls. When Chris was promoted to administrator one of the room stewards was heard to cry in the outraged tones of Hyacinth Bucket (Bouquet!), "But he hasn't even been to public school!" He had, actually, for one term, but that's another story.

Felbrigg on TV

Every country house garners its share of media coverage, either for news about its own activities or as a backdrop for someone else's. A reporter will call for a story, or a TV company will ask to record a short item for the local news slot ("News and weather from your part of the world!"), or perhaps a film company wants to use the place as a setting for scenes in a major movie or TV series. Our sons were thrilled to discover that a *Monty Python* sketch had actually been shot in Felbrigg's stable yard. Andy and Kev were both *Python* anoraks and would quote chunks of the script at the drop of a dead parrot. "Look, those are the very green doors you can see in the sketch!" they cried as we drove up to what was then our garage space.

Over the years, Chris lost count of the number of short news pieces he did, seated on dust-sheeted sofas while wearing wellies, or in the Walled Garden with white doves settling as if on cue on the roof of the dovecote or, less charmingly, RAF jets screaming overhead to interrupt the filming and cause retakes. "That wasn't half as good as what I said the first time!" he would groan when the fourth or fifth version was chosen to go on screen. Brief local news items covered such things as the spring opening of National Trust properties, the upheaval caused by dry rot in the Chinese Bedroom, and the attics and cellars tours, to mention only a few. We also played host for several memorable days to a full TV crew and cast of actors filming segments for D. H. Lawrence's *The Rainbow*, and another year the house provided the backdrop for a series about an eighteenth-century tourist going on his Grand Tour of Europe.

A helicopter flew over, filming for a series on Humphry Repton, who took over the mantle of the country's favourite landscape designer after Capability Brown died; and we enjoyed a visit from BBC2 when they produced some programmes on stately homes in the eastern region. This brief series, titled *A Heritage Tour*, was introduced by Lady Victoria Leatham, of Burghley House in Lincolnshire, familiar from her appearances on the *Antiques Roadshow*. With her at Felbrigg, to talk about the contents and pictures, she had John Bligh (also of *Antiques Roadshow* fame) and art expert John Somerville. Chris acted as their guide to show them round and help them decide where best to do the filming and which pieces of art or furniture they should discuss. Although the finished piece ran to only 12 minutes, the filming went on over two days.

The crew arrived on a Monday morning to choose their settings, plan how the piece would go, and of course to complete their homework on the house and its history. They did a little filming in the afternoon when the house was open, though the bulk was shot the next day, a closed Tuesday.

While chatting with Chris outside the house, in between filming her introduction for the piece, Lady Victoria commented on the excellent appearance of the garden and grounds. "However many gardeners do you have?"

"Just two," said Chris. "Plus some occasional part-time help."

"Only two?" She was astounded. Burghley House employed a small team of gardeners.

Television programmes taking viewers behind the scenes have made us all aware of the techniques involved in filming, but what still amazes me is the time it takes, and how many people are involved behind the camera. Enjoying the end results, one can forget the hundred and one small incidents that go unrecorded, scenes shot over and over again to get them just right, filmed out of sequence and later pieced together by the editor, not to mention the "cock-ups" that don't even get an airing in one of those out-take programmes.

On this occasion at Felbrigg, as recorded in his diary, Chris was required to shut down "photogenically". Preparatory to the filming, he was "wired for sound" with a microphone on his lapel. While the crew set up some other shots, Chris went upstairs through the empty house to secure the bedroom shutters, as requested, and found himself called by nature to the staff loo in the west wing. As he left the WC he caught his hand, not for the first time, on the awkward door handle, which made him swear loudly (probably something like, "Oh, blow it!"). It was only when he returned to the ground floor and saw the sound man with his headphones on that he realised he had all the time been monitored. "Oh no!" he groaned. "Did you hear all that?" The sound man just grinned.

Having closed the shutters in the bedrooms, he performed the same chore on the ground floor, leaving a single leaf open in each room. Filmed by a camera which was stationed in the Cabinet looking back through the other rooms, he then closed the downstairs shutters one by one. But it wasn't quite right. "Can you do it quicker?" they asked. Back he went, opened one shutter in each room, and repeated the exercise. This time, as he went out of the camera's line of sight he broke into a run, and after closing the Dining Room shutter he dashed back, slowing to normal speed as he walked back into shot to do it all again in the Drawing Room. Clever stuff. Later, the crew took the camera outside to the far end of the west lawn, where they filmed as Chris re-closed the final shutter (having first raised the blind so that the camera could see what he was doing!). Next, he had to go and secure the main front door while they filmed him from the courtyard. He says he would have loved to put out a couple of milk bottles at the same time, but didn't dare.

When the programme went out, we were fascinated to see how they stitched the various scenes together, beginning with shots of the outside of the house, with Lady Victoria by the gate to the front courtyard, then cutting to the Morning Room with the room stewards gathering for their afternoon duties. We occasionally watch our video recording and enjoy the sight of old friends emoting for all they're worth and Chris saying, "You've got five minutes to get to your rooms," as he lays on the table the draught board and pieces which they used as a means of choosing their stations for that day. Each volunteer had his or her own favourite spot, so much bartering went on. "That's three times I've swapped today!" cries Owen, while Barney uses his charm: "Can I have the Cabinet? That's my favourite," and Robert steps in to announce, "We're expecting no parties today." Cut to the Great Hall where Lady Victoria says a little about the history (and gets a couple of details wrong, much to our dismay, though not many of the viewers will notice or care); then to the Drawing Room where the two experts talk with her about the pictures, the precious Tompien clock, and the boulle table — a wondrous construction covered in an inlay of brass and tortoiseshell. On to the Cabinet, where she and John Bligh discuss the pictures collected by Windham II on his Grand Tour, and the stunning little games table of inlaid marble and carved giltwood. Closing shots show Chris in the front courtyard taking in the "This Way" sign and bolting the big front door, from where we cut to him coming into the Drawing Room and going to close a shutter, plunging the room into darkness. It was nothing like his usual routine, but it looked good on the final TV version.

To our dismay, though, the programme gave the impression that Felbrigg is a lifeless fossil, a sad and sorry place because it is "no longer lived in". Lady Victoria's voice-over concluded with words that infuriated not only Chris and me but many other Felbrigg enthusiasts: "The closing of the shutters is a melancholy business. When the visitors and the administrators have left, the house just dies. The building and contents are preserved for us all, but what of the spirit of the place? What of that?"

No longer anybody's home? The house dies when it closes? What nonsense! What of the resident staff? What of the tenants who live in homes converted out of former domestic areas? All of them are alive, carrying on their normal day-to-day affairs, with families and private visitors dropping in for an evening or coming to stay. And what of the concerts and other events held in supposedly closed periods, when hundreds of people might crowd into the gardens or the Morning Room?

The grandest rooms may, at times, lie dormant for their own protection, but despite the impression given by some historical novelists and dramatists, back across the centuries those rooms were often kept shuttered and dust-sheeted. Many of the earlier squires treated Felbrigg as a shooting lodge — a holiday home. They were absent for much of the time. Ash Windham, for instance, divided his time between Felbrigg and his London house, in Soho Square, while his mother, who "loved Felbrigg dearly", spent months of every year elsewhere, and the rest of the family "moved out into the world".

When the squires and their families did choose to adjourn to their country estate, smaller rooms were then, as now, more economical, more human-sized, more convenient, more friendly. In the larger, showier rooms, the furniture and fittings, the fabrics and wallpapers were much too costly to risk exposing them to bright sunlight, sticky fingers, wine spills, smoke-grime from candles and open fires, or even ordinary everyday dust, except at times when the owners needed to impress important guests. Think of Robert Ketton's five sisters, assigned to bedrooms in the attics. Or their reclusive brother in his later years, living all alone in his great decaying house, keeping himself to one little room downstairs. Or Brinsley Ford, who mentions the "dingy light" in the Library, where the blinds were always kept drawn to preserve the bindings of the books. It was the smaller rooms of their houses that the squires inhabited day to day, as do today's residents.

The exception at Felbrigg may have been the Great Hall. We've already seen how the last squire and his guests used it as a communal dining and sitting room, and there's a charming early photograph of the Victorian Ketton sisters playing billiards on a full size table there; so perhaps the Great Hall was more often in use. For much of the year, however, and especially in the wintertime, the most expensively furnished suites remained uninhabited, shuttered and covered in dust sheets, not so very different from the way they are used today under the National Trust's protection. The difference is that in winter those rooms still come alive to the laughter of cleaners, the voices of workmen, the drone of vacuums, the brushing of a thousand books, the clanging of scaffolding poles . . . The show rooms are being actively conserved for posterity, not simply shut up and left to moulder.

Some years ago, the inauguration of special autumn tours allowed visitors the chance to see the work that goes on to prepare National Trust houses for the winter. Chris launched his own version of these with his attics and cellars tours which proved so popular. But elsewhere some misguided soul — probably someone who never actually worked at a property — named similar events "putting the house to bed". What a misnomer! "Gearing the house for action" would be more apt.

So . . . sorry, Lady Victoria, but the truth is that, unlike a museum, there are people about at Felbrigg all the time. They keep the "essential spirit" of the house very much alive.

CHAPTER
FIVE

It's a fact!

Room stewards enjoy swapping anecdotes of their days on duty and they are often amused by misconceptions which they hear passed on by one visitor to another. One family group had just been to visit Blickling Hall, only 11 miles away, and came through Felbrigg still discussing that trip: "Yes, that's right, Henry the Eighth built Blickling for Anne Boleyn." Nice story, but wrong! The Boleyn family may have owned Blickling estate for a few decades five hundred years ago, but there is no evidence, beyond local legend, that Anne Boleyn ever visited the place. Anyway, the present Blickling Hall was not completed until 1628, a hundred years after Anne was bisected. By that time her family had long faded into obscurity and Blickling had become the seat of the Hobart family.

Then there's the fondly held fallacy that in "the old days" people were smaller than they are today. That's obvious. I mean, you've only to look at the doorways, and the beds, and the armour . . . In fact, doorways were made low for reasons of defence and comfort. You couldn't charge into a room wielding a sword if you were bent double ducking under the lintel; what's more, low doorways, like small windows, kept the fire's warmth in and the sun's heat out. The beds were mostly the same size as we use today, but they look shorter because they're higher and often wider. As for the armour . . . when it's on display you don't see the gaps that would need to be there to allow the wearer to move; actually fitted on a person, the armour would appear larger. Certainly there have been occasions through history when malnutrition led to certain poor people being smaller and ill-formed, but that is still true today. What is not true is the belief that the human race has gradually got bigger as time progressed. If you want proof of that, come and visit our local archaeological dig at Sedgeford. Skeletons from the Saxon cemetery prove that fifteen hundred years ago people were the same size as we are.

The human race has a lot still to learn about its past. Though we can't hope to answer the bigger questions such as how the universe began or what really destroyed the dinosaurs, in his own small way Chris has been instrumental in solving one or two minor mysteries concerning Felbrigg. In the Library, for instance . . .

Playing detective

Many of the books in the Library are bound with calfskin, some in reverse calf (their bindings are white rather than brown), and some of them were bound by William Windham II, or under his close supervision. Bookbinding was one of his practical interests and he owned a complete set of tools and materials with which he bound his collection of three hundred or so pamphlets, plays and poems. His son, William Windham III, added to the Library some volumes which had belonged to his close friend, the great lexicographer Dr Samuel Johnson. Some were a dying gift from Johnson, others bequeathed in his will and others bought at the later sale of his library. Mr Ketton-Cremer particularly treasured these last and kept them in their original tattered state. Scribblings in these books may be in Johnson's hand, but arguments concerning the truth about these marginalia have yet to be resolved.

An amusing and perhaps apocryphal sidelight was unearthed by our good friend John Baker, one of the room stewards who gave many slide shows and talks about Felbrigg history. In an article, he wrote that Johnson bequeathed a volume of Greek poetry to Windham with the quip, "You borrowed it seven years ago, now it's yours!"

Whichever of the squires may have placed them there, the books in the Library are all arranged with care to appear neat and symmetrical. However, if you look carefully at the bookshelves on the right-hand side of the west-end bay you may see that the volumes there are irregular, not matched in size or condition. This anomaly puzzled Chris when he first noticed it. Over time, as he got to know the house and its contents better, he realised that among the books scattered about the house were volumes which would complete the sets on those unevenly filled shelves. A few questions here and there, allied with much use of the "little grey cells", and finally the visit from Mr Ward, the retired butler, provided the answer.

It seems that when the late squire moved into his modernised apartment off the rear courtyard, he took with him some of his favourite books from the Library, leaving gaps on the bookshelves. In the confusion after the squire died and the Trust took over, the spaces were filled with other volumes found around the house, and later when Trust staff came to sort out the Retreat ready for its letting to tenants, they didn't realise that the books they found there belonged in the Library. So, those books were arranged about the Hall, on one or other of the desks, or on bedside tables. Some of them may now be with the collection in the Book Room. When you're in the Library, have a look for those shelves with irregular sizes of books on them.

Later, as you take a stroll in the woods to the north of the house, see if you can find the ice house. It looks like a hummock, and might be taken for a wartime bunker now covered in grass and brambles, but in fact it was the first type of freezer.

The idea of preserving winter ice for use in summer came to Britain around the middle of the 1600s. A century later most country estates possessed their own ice house. These were often some distance from the big house because of the need for the ice pit to be dug deep into the earth, in a spot where temperatures would remain consistently cool. The pit was supplied with a drainage system, lined with brick, given a brick covering (usually dome-shaped though designs varied enormously), and were frequently covered with a final insulating layer of soil.

It fell to the head gardener to organise the task of cutting ice from the nearest river, pond or lake. This was a tedious, time-consuming, labour-intensive chore. One record reports that a team of thirty men took more than five days to shift forty tons of ice. The blocks of ice were broken up and packed tightly into the pit until it was full, then the surface was thickly covered with straw to keep the ice as cold as possible. The following summer, servants would come and chip away a supply of ice, taking it to the kitchen where cooks used it to preserve meat, fish and dairy foods (much the kind of thing we now store in our refrigerator), to make ice creams and sorbets, to cool wine, or fevered brows, and sometimes to cool down rooms in the height of a summer heatwave. Occasionally meat would be stored in the ice house itself, but it needed to be checked frequently to make sure it hadn't gone off and it made the ice melt faster, so generally the ice house was used only to store ice. It was so efficient that, if you were lucky, your ice could last over two or even three summers.

By 1900, however, most ice houses had fallen into disuse. Wealthy households preserved their food with "Arctic crystal" — pure, translucent ice imported from America and Scandinavia. And as the twentieth century progressed domestic refrigerators came into use among people who could afford them. Less affluent households still clung to the time-honoured process of cooling on marble slabs in larders or in meat safes made of wire mesh to keep the flies out, hung outside on sunless walls. This practice continued into the latter half of the twentieth century, and when Chris and I first met, his foster mother still stored her fresh meat and butter that way, much to my horror!

Felbrigg's ice house too fell out of use and, being deep and dangerous, was deliberately filled in with rubbish during Robert Ketton's squireship around a century ago. His men filled the pit with whatever they could find, locked the iron gate and abandoned the place to flying leaves and other blown debris. It remained that way until the summer of 1979 when a party of young National Trust volunteers cleared it out.

At first they found the work easy, with a tractor dragging out packing which proved to be mainly corrugated iron and wire, but as they went deeper the more difficult it became to shift the impacted earth and junk. By the time they finished they were forced to use ladders to climb down the hole and haul up the detritus, which included a number of bottles, some oil and carriage lamps, a bedwarmer, several gin traps (once used to snare animals), some metal signs advertising cigarettes, three old baths and some bullets. What was not so widely reported was the fact that they also found a pistol.

The small hand-gun proved to be the same one which had been owned by Mrs Ketton, wife of the cattlecake merchant. Guns were common items in country houses in those days; the men kept shotguns and even rifles for hunting, and more than one Victorian lady had a small pistol for her own protection. It was especially wise to be prepared in the restless days when farm labourers were burning barns and wrecking steam ploughs in their struggle for a proper trade union, and when republican clubs across Britain preached anarchy and the overthrow of the sleaze-ridden royal family. (This was the 1870s and their target was Queen Victoria and her "brood of Germans", including the pleasure-loving gambler and womaniser Bertie, Prince of Wales, and his strange, ill-fated oldest son.)

Whether Mrs Ketton ever had cause to use her pistol in fear or anger, and how it came to be buried in among the rubbish in the ice house, are part of Felbrigg's enduring mysteries — as is the exact current location of the pistol. When Chris heard about it he set out to try to recover it, to return it to its place on the inventory of the house, where it belongs. It was said to have been taken away by a member of staff who lived locally and after extensive enquiries Chris believed he had discovered who that person might be. But proving it, and broaching the subject of its return without making accusations, was the problem. He still feels it would be wonderful if the pistol could come home where it belongs, back to its rightful place as part of the history of the Hall.

Felbrigg's history became a passion with Chris. He was always thrilled to make a new discovery of some aspect of which even Mr Ketton-Cremer seems to have remained unaware, such as the stewing stove we uncovered in the Old Kitchen; the Jacobean stairs beneath the floor of the Morning Room; and later a new insight into the structure of the cellar windows, which added to our information about that earlier stage of the house.

The earliest part of Felbrigg, the Jacobean great hall and buttery, was built of flint and brick strengthened at the corners and round the windows by stone quoins. At various periods this façade was painted in red, in white, and then in yellow ochre; then the owners decided — or perhaps it became fashionable — to cover the brick with stucco (rough plaster or Roman cement) tied in level with the quoins, to make it look as if the house was built entirely of stone. Natural stone being a rare commodity in Norfolk, stucco was the easiest way of achieving the desired trendy appearance. In similar houses, but where the stone quoins stand proud of the in-fill, it was easy to apply the stucco in a thick and durable layer. However, Felbrigg's quoins are flush with the brick and flint, so the plaster rendering had to be applied fairly thinly, which of course made it more liable to crack and fall out. Over a couple of centuries the façade has become a motley of broken, weathered stucco blotched with patches of bare brick and flint, and in places you can still see traces of the three colours of paint which adorned the house at different periods. After much discussion of the best way to repair the façade, the Trust decided to stabilise it as it was for the time being.

Above the lightwells where the toads live, and all around the base of the Jacobean house, the stucco had been applied in a wide band, like a skirting to protect the base of the walls. The plaster above the lightwells being badly cracked and damaged, the workmen raked it all out and prepared to apply a fresh new layer of stucco. It was at this stage that Chris noticed what the removal of the old stucco had revealed — above the present cellar window there was a filled-in lancet archway. This indicated that at one time the cellar windows had been basement windows which originally extended some two feet above the ground. The arched window to the east of the front porch once shed light into a basement store, where provisions would have been kept below the original Jacobean buttery.

When the house was extended, with wings added at the back, the buttery became the Morning Room and its basement was demoted to a cellar, with the bottom of the connecting stairs removed and the top few steps filled in with rubble and floored over, as we had discovered when the Morning Room panelling was removed to deal with an outbreak of dry rot. It now became apparent that, at the same time, to tidy up the front of the house, they had altered the shape of the windows, covering up the top arch.

Realising that the workmen were about to plaster over the area, Chris rushed for his camera and took some pictures, recording this new discovery for posterity. And when, recently, he showed these pictures to the present house staff, they snapped them up and made instant copies for their archive.

One of the objects which most intrigues and amuses visitors to the Grey Dressing Room is the slipper bath, popularly known as the tin bath, or the boot bath because of its shape. Its charisma annoys some room stewards who would much prefer to talk about the more esoteric contents of the room, or about the void in the ceiling where, through a specially made door set high in the corner, you can see vestiges of the decorative plasterwork which adorned what was once a corner of the original staircase hall. When the west wing was added in the second half of the seventeenth century, the architect William Samwell placed a grand stairway between the Great Hall and the Drawing Room. An observer thought these early stairs "ostentatious", the flights much too long and too high, stupefying the senses with the fatigue of mounting "three or four stretching flights"! Paine's later alterations removed this "pompous and costly" stair, using the space to make a new dining room with two bedrooms above. He built a complete and elegant new stairway in the central well, where it remains to this day.

The strange metal bath which stands near the narrow bed in the Grey Dressing Room was made in Victorian times, of riveted cast iron and shaped like a giant workman's boot, seven league style, maybe. You can see the narrow channel in the front, topped with a little funnel that looks a bit like a soap dish and may have been used for that purpose but also, when the bath was growing cool, allowed the maid to pour in fresh hot water which came out right down at the boot's toe to warm the bather's feet. It's fun to steward in that room and hear the theories people come up with to explain the bath. Children love to touch it and peer inside, making some visitors surmise that it was the bath's purpose "to amuse the children", or perhaps its shape was "for modesty's sake", or "to keep the draughts off".

It's true that if you were lithe enough to slide into the bath and sit down the sides would probably cover you up to your shoulders, and if your maid draped a towel over the top your modesty would be entirely preserved. However, during research for a novel set in the French Revolution I came across another explanation which helped to solve both this conundrum and another. Back in Paris around 1793, during the Reign of Terror when many "aristos" were being sent to face Madame Guillotine, the revolutionary leader Marat was stabbed to death by a woman named Charlotte Corday. This story is well known and well authenticated, but the curious thing is that Charlotte didn't know Marat personally, yet she managed to stab him while he was in his bath! It had always puzzled me as to how on earth she managed to get close enough to do the deed. I mean, if some strange woman came into your bathroom while you were naked in the bath, wouldn't you wonder what she wanted, even before you saw the knife she was holding? Wouldn't you shout to one of the hangers-on who wouldn't be far away (in the Paris tenements there was precious little privacy and Marat at the time was an important figure among the *sans-culottes* rabble). But then I discovered that Marat suffered very badly with psoriasis, the dreadful complaint which in its worst cases turns the skin into a torment of cracking, bleeding scales (remember Dennis Potter's *Singing Detective*?). In Marat's time, one of the ways of alleviating the pain was to soften the skin by soaking in

91

a bath. Apparently he often resorted to this treatment, but, being a very busy man, he turned his bathroom into an office so that he could continue his work. He sat soaking in his boot-shaped bath with a board across the top forming a desk on which he signed all those execution orders, passes to allow citizens to travel, or permits for this and that. People came to see him there, citizens begging for the lives of loved ones or permission to leave the city. So while he soaked in his bath he was surrounded by people, his henchmen and his petitioners, which may explain how Charlotte Corday got close enough to stab him to death (she was caught, of course, and sent to the guillotine for her trouble). And that may also explain why the boot bath at Felbrigg is shaped that way — because it had a medical function.

Old master?

Another small but enduring mystery revived itself after the publication of *The Search for Gainsborough* by the actress Adrienne Corri, who spent six long years doing painstaking research into a portrait she discovered in a theatre and which she believed to be by Thomas Gainsborough. While pursuing this quest, she cracked the code used by eighteenth-century bankers to protect their clients, and revealed a payment to Gainsborough of fifty pounds by a certain "Ash Wyndham" [sic]. (This is another instance of the contemporary spelling of the forename Ash without the "e", though it also gives his surname Windham as "Wyndham".)

This detail was brought to Chris's attention by Maurice Birkbeck, a retired GP and one of Felbrigg's volunteer room stewards, whose particular interest was the study of the pictures in the Hall. He had long been intrigued by the mystery surrounding one of the portraits in the Dining Room, thought to be of Ash Windham's wife, Elizabeth Dobyns, but attributed by various experts to at least three different artists. Since the marriage of Ash and Elizabeth was a disaster (the real love of his life died young so he settled for an heiress and her fortune), and since the portrait seemed to have been painted after her death, there was some question as to whether Elizabeth was the lady portrayed. However, there she hangs on the wall alongside Ash and, timewise, her portrait does seem to fit with the payment recorded by the bank. If the picture could be proven to be a Gainsborough it would become another great asset for Felbrigg.

Her in-depth researches had made Ms Corri an authority on the subject of Gainsborough, so at Maurice's suggestion Chris wrote to ask if the actress turned author and sleuth would be willing to help solve the mystery of the portrait in the Dining Room. Thus began a lively correspondence in which they compared opinions on artists, painting styles, and the relevance of certain dates; in due course Chris sent photographs of the portrait in question for Ms Corri to examine and discussed the matter with her over the phone. He also unearthed some earlier experts' divergent speculations as to the portrait's maker and sitter, and consulted one or two galleries and museums. It all grew rather technical and abstruse, muddying the waters until nothing was clear.

The investigation did, however, throw up some details that, for me, added a human dimension to the esoteric arguments. The Gallery of English Costume observed that it was difficult to date the portrait on costume grounds because "the sitter wears a dress probably supplied by the artist, most definitely not fashionable wear". Another letter confirms the difficulty in exactly dating a picture when the artist may have been "very minor or inexperienced" and painting in "a very conservative or old-fashioned style"; in the eighteenth century, apparently, sitters and artists preferred fashionable details of dress to be indistinct "so that the portrait did not date"! (Even way back then, women liked to leave some doubt about their age, as those of us who were foolish enough to be photographed wearing miniskirts in the 1960s will understand!)

On looking back through the file to remind myself of the details of this tale, I was amused to discover a typical Chris-ism in one of his letters, where he excuses his delay in sending photographs: "My wife tried to poison me on St Valentine's Day — or the cod roes she bought me were off." Ms Corri's reply mainly concerns the portrait, but ends, "I think you malign your wife, I am sure she will agree! . . . At least she can now be attributed — the picture, not your wife!"

94

The mystery still remains to be solved. No authority could date the portrait with complete accuracy; everyone had a different idea as to who the artist might have been; and no one can say for sure who the sitter really was. The inventory simply calls her "a Windham wife" and so until further evidence turns up she remains anonymous. One thing, disappointingly, does seem certain — the paint was not applied by Gainsborough, so the portrait is not of inordinate value.

Be your own expert

Establishing the truth in such debates is far from a precise science, more a proof of the old adage "the more you learn, the less you know", a saying which applies equally to qualified professionals as to the rest of us. In a note to room steward Maurice, Chris confided that over the years he had become both sceptical and cynical about the pronouncements made by some experts.

Those of us who grew up in times when a place at university was a prize that only those with wealthy parents or a very exceptional brain could aim at, tend to feel awed when confronted by someone bearing letters after their name. Alongside a B.Sc., an MA or a Ph.D., even the best O-level results look puny. When Chris and I came to Felbrigg we both tended to take at face value the opinions and assertions of people who were qualified authorities in art, furniture, architecture, history and the like, with university degrees to prove it. But as time went on we realised that learning doesn't have to be confined to educational institutions. Graduates can be fallible, and the University of Life may provide an even broader spectrum of knowledge than a classroom curriculum.

Our neighbours Gill and Henry were wonderful hosts, and Gill the most amazing cook who, not satisfied with providing wonderful starters and main courses, often tempted us with a selection of two or three luscious desserts. One evening over dinner with them at the Retreat, I found myself in deep conversation with one of the Trust's historical gurus. We amicably discussed the Middle Ages, but when I introduced the French Revolution, and then the ancient Celts (both of which I had researched for historical novels) I suddenly realised he was floundering — we'd gone outside his period of expertise and I'd lost him. After that I felt a lot less overawed in such erudite company and began to relax. Or was it the wine?

During the course of his work, Chris met many more of these adepts than I did, and because he was interested and wanted to learn as much as he could, he listened avidly to their informed opinions. About furniture, about paintings . . . He learned a lot in the process, but it struck him that expert conclusions were not necessarily definitive. One specialist might express a different view from another, and occasionally they even contradicted themselves without knowing it, as in the mysterious case of the boulle commode — a chest of drawers covered with an inlay of brass and tortoiseshell. The word "commode" can also mean a cupboard or chair which conceals a chamber pot and you can see some of those in the bedrooms at Felbrigg, though they're not inlaid with boulle-work.

Boulle (or buhl) furniture looks stunning. The brass and the tortoiseshell are cut to fit each other, forming patterns and pictures. With the metal gleaming and the shell sliced thin and laid over coloured paper, usually red, it creates a richly sumptuous effect that screams its owner's wealth and status. (I wouldn't give it house-room, my dears, it's just too, too OTT. Besides, it would look so flashy next to our tasteful MFI furniture!)

This particular chest of drawers had always intrigued Chris because to his eye its top didn't exactly match its body, though he hesitated to say so in case he revealed his ignorance. Then one day a very knowledgeable and highly respected furniture restorer observed without prompting, "Yes, it's a beautiful piece of furniture, except that the top doesn't quite match the bottom." He went on to explain, in great technical detail, why he could say with such certainty that this was so. Chris listened avidly, pleased to know that his guess had been correct. Perhaps he was starting to cultivate an eye for such anomalies. However, a few months later the same man arrived to take away a water-damaged chest for repolishing and as they checked the rest of the furniture Chris commented, "Oh, yes, this is the piece with a mismatched top, isn't it?" The expert surveyed the commode, rubbing his chin. "No, you're wrong about that. It's definitely all one piece." And he went on to explain, in great technical detail, why this was so.

As for paintings, one of the less exciting pictures at Felbrigg is done on a piece of board. Its proportions look wrong, the characters are all facing out of the picture and the perspective is awry, as if it has been chopped down. It's probably the least appealing picture in the Hall, with the exceptions of the ugly lion and the cock-eyed cockerel. (Happily they're all tucked away in gloomy corridors where they go largely unnoticed.) When an art expert arrived to assess the Hall's pictures, Chris asked his opinion about this unprepossessing painting and after taking a good look at it the man said that it had probably come from a larger, damaged painting, the subject being badly balanced and out of proportion to its size and its frame. But the next time he came, when Chris remarked that this was the picture that had been cut from a larger one, the same expert insisted, "Oh, no. No, it's good. This is how the artist intended it." You pays your money and you takes your choice, apparently. Which tends to make one suspect that "expertise" is often a matter of using an authoritative voice and making sure you contradict anyone who dares to advance an alternative opinion. Blind 'em with science — or double-speak!

In fact, anyone can become an expert if they study a subject closely enough. Adrienne Corri is an example to us all.

CHAPTER
SIX

A head for heights

Have you ever been approached by a salesman trying to persuade you to purchase an aerial photograph of your home and its surroundings? Well, one of those chaps came calling at Felbrigg, delighted with the shot he'd produced of the house and gardens from several hundred feet up. The small version of the photo looked quite good, but, even supposing we had had seventy-five pounds to spare, we would not have purchased the framed enlargement — it revealed with unkind clarity that the house had been taken by surprise on an off-day, wearing an unbecoming overcoat of scaffolding topped with green tarpaulins. It looked something like a hedgehog in a rain-hat. Not an image one would wish to keep for posterity.

The scaffolding had been erected to facilitate the releading of the roof. Though the work affected only the west wing and the south front the whole main block of the house was, for several months, covered in a network of galvanised poles linked by ladders and wooden walkways, while the men removed acres of slate and lead skirting (along with the lantern above the staircase hall, as mentioned earlier). To keep the weather from intruding on the attics, the men worked under a substantial shield of corrugated iron, with tough, weatherproof tarpaulins lashed over it. At night, for security reasons, the workmen removed all ladders from the lower sections of the scaffolding and thoughtfully gave us the added protection of bright security lights which blazed through all the hours of darkness (it was like trying to sleep with the noonday sun glaring in our window).

While the work was in progress, a violent storm battered around us one night, howling gales throwing rain at the windows in pailfuls. We were sleeping fitfully anyway, but in the deep of the night a tremendous noise jolted us both awake. Clatterings and bangings and weird, wild shriekings made it sound as if the house was being torn to pieces by demons. We looked out of the window to see, in the glare of the security lights, sheets of corrugated iron flying through the air like playing cards, planks tossed askew, and one long piece of shredded tarpaulin streaming in the wind from a top corner of the scaffolding, like a banner at a tourney.

Chris pulled on a pair of warm trousers, sweater and anorak, and, accompanied by his trusty torch, climbed the stairs to the roof where the storm was battering loudly among the exposed rafters. This storm was worse than the hurricane, certainly more frightening. The hurricane had struck while the roof was intact, but now its temporary defences were being stripped away, leaving the house vulnerable; Chris was obliged to go out and inspect the damage to see if anything could be done to minimise it.

100

He hung on to the scaffolding poles for grim life, thinking that this was one way a landlubber might experience something of what sailors used to feel on a sailing ship during a tempest at sea. At least the deals under his feet didn't surge up suddenly and then drop away, though at times he feared the wind was trying to tip them up and him over the edge. Rain drenched him, the wind tore at his hair and clothes, the torn tarpaulin flapped like the wing of a terrified pterodactyl and, even as he watched, another piece of corrugated iron lifted from its moorings and went sailing away. It sliced through the air and clanged edge-on against the wall, just below the lighted window of our flat where he could see me gazing out wild-eyed. Since there was nothing anyone could do, no means of controlling the storm or preventing damage, Chris headed back down to where I received him with immense relief and a reviving mug of hot coffee. All we could do was wait and wonder what morning would reveal.

We didn't get much sleep for the rest of the night but before dawn came the storm died down. Daylight revealed that this time Felbrigg had been lucky. Some rain had got in and the tarpaulins and corrugated sheeting would need to be replaced, but otherwise little damage resulted.

Work on the roof provided other heart-stopping moments, such as the time when one of the local builders wanted to get from one part of the roof to another. Chris had gone up to see how the men were getting on with repairing one of the bays on the south front and the workman was explaining how he needed to get to an area above the west wing which was relatively close in actual distance but would entail a long trek down and round by normal, safe means. Before anyone could stop him, he had climbed on the parapet and leapt across. He landed safely, thank heaven. When Chris told me about it later he was still disturbed by the risk the man had taken; if an accident had happened, how could he ever have proved that the man did it of his own volition and without his agreement? Scary.

On the plus side, the scaffolding did afford the chance to get some unusual pictures of Felbrigg, including full-face close-ups of the heraldic beasts which face outward from the parapets, and shots looking down into the courtyard. These provided such an extraordinary view of one tenant's residence that she asked for an enlarged copy and displayed it proudly to all her visitors.

While Chris was houseman he frequently had to go out on the roof to check for damage or to clear the gullies of leaves or, since we had a few very cold winters, deep snow. Thick snow may look glamorous when it coats rooftops with a crisp white blanket, but when the thaw begins, especially when the snow is lying on a large expanse of slated peaks, hollows, flat plains and connecting valleys, as at Felbrigg, drainage channels must be kept clear. Melting snow turns to water, which needs to find its way to the drainpipes. If the gullies are clogged with wet snow and ice, the meltwater can't get past, so it builds up under the snow, forming an icy pool that wells up to the top edge of the leads, seeps over and finds its way under the slates. So, while the snow remains, clearing the gullies means daily journeys aloft; another chore for the houseman. This can be a risky business, so high up on a surface slippery with patches of wet ice.

One of the scariest roof incidents happened, again, at night. There had been a lot of snow, and then a freeze which held the snow in shape for a day or two, but one evening the temperature lifted and the TV weatherman forecast a thaw. The icicles outside our windows started to drip and Chris knew he had to go up and make sure all the gullies were clear, otherwise we might wake in the morning to find water seeping through the ceilings of the Hall in a dozen places. Since we were then in the houseman's flat, this meant an expedition down through the house to the Bird Corridor and up to the attics via the back stairway; then a promenade along the west wing, through the attics above the south front and back down the east wing to the roof door. Since the attics had no electric lighting fitted, at night a large torch was the handiest means of illumination. In such conditions, the journey could be an eerie experience. The attics are crammed with all kinds of aged furniture, trunks, lengths of wood, old carpets, pictures and fabrics. Torchlight wakes looming shapes out of the shadows, picks out the sudden wall of a wardrobe, the grinning face of a bad portrait, or a jumble of chairs, while behind you the darkness closes in again. All manner of monsters might be following to leap on you as you pause to negotiate a low slope of the ceiling or a narrow doorway with a step down. And then a cobweb

103

catches in your hair . . . Good thing Chris doesn't share my wild imagination.

On that cold but thawing evening, he made his way through the pitch-dark attics to the little door that opens on to the roof. He clambered out and, following the glow of his torch, picked his way across the slopes and gulleys to make sure that all the various drainpipes were clear, so that if meltwater started running it had somewhere to run to. Task completed, he turned back. And that was when his torch failed. He shook it, hoping the contacts had momentarily parted. But the torch remained lifeless. It being a cloudy night there was no moonlight, nor any stars to guide him. He was out in the middle of that complicated roof in utter blackness. Slowly, as his pupils widened to compensate, he became aware of the glow of Cromer's streetlights three miles away, faintly reflecting from the underside of the clouds and throwing the outline of the roof around him into craggy profile. A little light came, too, from the windows of our flat.

In places on that roof there's a straight drop over the edge — just the slates, the guttering, and a long fall to earth without a parachute. So in those spots, even in daylight on a fine dry day, Chris was always ultra-careful. Thankfully, he knew he could bypass the most dangerous spots, and if he fell over in a gully he'd probably land cradled safely between two slopes. But he didn't want to risk falling and injuring himself, and having to wait for me to realise he was missing and come searching, eventually to discover the spot where he might be lying with a broken leg and hypothermia.

He decided it might be prudent to do the return journey on hands and knees.

Fortunately Chris knew the roof well enough to find his way back without too many detours, but it did mean crawling round the place where the big lantern was missing over the staircase hall, across a ridge and along a gully or two before he reached the narrow door and the comparative safety of the attics — and then he had to feel and fumble his way along the cleared track leading between suitcases, piles of ancient magazines and chests full of old weapons, all across the south front and down the west wing to the back stairs, in wet clothes and with frozen hands and feet. "You should always take two torches," commented some wiseacres later. Hindsight's such a comfort, isn't it?

One autumn day, a gutter clogged by nothing worse than soggy leaves demanded another foray to the heights at a time when Chris's foster sister Shirley happened to be spending the day with us. Unfortunately, the piece of flat roof where Chris was doing his thing happened to be visible from the window where Shirley happened to be passing. Spying him up there without benefit of parapet, crampons, rope or wings, she let out a desolate wail that brought me running, thinking she had hurt herself.

"What's he doing up there?" she cried. "The fool! If he falls he'll be killed. Look at him!"

"I'd rather not," said I, having grown tired of pleading for him to be careful when he went up there. He always said, "Of course I'm careful! What do you think, I'm going to take deliberate risks?"

"Get him down. Oh, get him down!" Shirley threw her hands to her face, peering fearfully through her fingers. She never could stand seeing people work at a height, which was odd because her menfolk — grandfather, father, brother, husband and one of her sons — had been or were slaters and tilers ("ruffers" as they say in Norfolk). Or perhaps that was why she hated it so, because she had lived with the fear all her life, and on occasion had had to nurse her father and husband after nasty falls. For myself, with no way of stopping him from doing this side of his job, I just tried not to think about it. Even so, it was a relief to both of us when Chris moved out of sight, leaving poor Shirley drained with terror and needing a lie down with a cold compress over a migraine. She was furious with him. When he returned to the flat she raged at him, "Don't you dare do that again!"

Next morning, after she had returned home to Heacham and tossed and turned all night in her anxiety, she phoned to repeat her warnings, making Chris promise never to go up on the roof again. "Promise me! I won't be able to sleep unless you do." So he promised. But of course he lied — going up on the roof was part of his job.

The roof also provided its share of leisurely, away-from-it-all moments, such as warm summer evenings when we took a cold supper up to the leaded balcony and enjoyed a bottle of wine while we surveyed the world below and waved at passing strollers and cars.

106

On certain evenings when the late sun was at the right angle, sending long shadows across the park, the light and shade revealed strange lines running along the pasture. Shallow undulations arranged in regular straight rows stretched out from the Hall, from the railings of the house right up to the rise that hid the lake, bisected by the tarmac line of the driveway. These marks are very subtle and not often visible, but with his archaeological hard-hat on, Chris found them intriguing. Are they evidence of an ancient system of strip cultivation? They certainly appear to be man-made and, as such, are probably the oldest remaining signs of human occupation at Felbrigg.

Uneasy spirits?

On really hot nights, if Chris couldn't sleep he would go up to the roof and let the night breeze cool him. So far above the world, with the moon sailing among drifts of cloud, natural sounds seem magnified. Bats squeak as they flitter by; an owl hoots from the woods; somewhere far off a fox barks and his vixen answers faintly, while occasional traffic on the coast road causes only a subliminal disturbance of the peace.

One night Chris heard a noise which he couldn't immediately identify. It sounded for all the world like the crisp crunch of wheels on gravel — iron shod wheels, at that. But since it couldn't possibly be, it must have some other explanation. The only gravel was in the front courtyard, whose gates are locked at night and which, anyway, he could see was empty, spread there below him like a semicircular apron. Besides which, this sound came from further away, further even than the tarmac drive. The more he listened the more sure he became that it emanated from the middle of the park, which was another absurdity. However, before he could decide what it really was, the noise faded into the distance and died away.

Next day he was still trying to figure out what this odd sound might have been and in the course of our discussions I ventured, "You mean, it sounded like the wheels of a carriage?"

"Well, it might have been, except no one around here would be driving a carriage. Not at two in the morning. Anyway, it was out in the pasture — off beyond the church — and there's only grass fields out there."

"But wasn't there once an old carriage drive that used to run out in that direction?"

Etchings show horse-drawn vehicles and people using that old drive, which led from the front of the Hall round by the eastern side of the lake and then curved off in the direction of distant Norwich. The road itself is no longer there but its route is still visible on old maps, and even more tangible proof of its existence lies in the two gate lodges which may still be seen on the boundary of the estate along the Metton road.

"You're surely not suggesting it was a ghostly carriage, are you?" Chris scoffed. "What, pulled by six devil horses and driven by a headless coachman? Oh, come off it. You know I don't believe in ghosts and all that nonsense. There's always a rational explanation."

So he said. Incidents such as the "hand" on his shoulder in the Library at dead of night (which he proved to have been the acorn on the end of a long cord which got caught on his bodywarmer as he checked the shutter) and the figure with a torch moving the opposite way in a bedroom (a reflection of a reflection in two facing mirrors) had, as far as he was concerned, proved his contention that ghosts are all in the mind. He maintains that all so-called "supernatural" events have a natural cause. And if he can't establish that natural cause he'll say it's self-delusion, imagination, hallucination, exaggeration, or deliberate invention because ghost stories find such a ready and gullible audience. So, with this strange occurrence of wheels on gravel in the park, he concluded that his dodgy ear was to blame. Obviously his tinnitus had misled him and he'd misjudged both the direction of the sound and its derivation. He can always explain such things. At least, he can always explain them away, which to my more open mind isn't quite the same.

This is one reason why I didn't insist on being right the morning when I found the door leading from our flat into the Book Room ajar and yet no alarms were ringing, though the door must have been secure the night before or the system wouldn't have set. Nor did I ever mention the cold area that often made me shiver when I walked down the gloomy corridor leading to our bathroom, or the shadowy shape that one night flitted from the bathroom door, across the corridor, and through the wall on the other side. On the few occasions I was left alone overnight I generally went down to use the other lavatory rather than risk that corridor after dark.

Chris has no patience with any story of that kind, such as the cleaner's account of walking through the woods on her way to work from her home in a nearby village. She saw a woman approaching on the same path some distance away and knew they were bound to meet since there were no side paths, only brambles and thick ferns under the trees either side. But after the path had led Dolly down through Dingley Dell and up again to more level ground she found the path clear and the woods deserted for as far as she could see. Was the vanishing walker another hallucination?

One of our close friends among the room stewards preferred not to be assigned to the Library, which she said had a strange atmosphere. It was there, soon after the late squire died, that the managing agent looked up from his work and saw a figure seated in one of the green leather chairs by the fire. In the way of such things, when he looked again the figure was gone, but from portraits in the house he identified the visitor as William Windham III.

Did our son Andy also see the famous squire? When I was working on this book I happened to ask Kevin whether he'd had any odd experiences at Felbrigg and he said, "No, but Andy saw something in the Library. He told me not to mention it, especially to Dad." Seems both of the boys were staying with us one time and, at the end of a long day, they were helping Chris to close up. Doing his usual routine, Chris was working systematically through the rooms making sure all visitors had departed before he relieved the guides. He had reached the bedrooms, with Kev wandering behind him, when Andy came after them up the main stairs. Through the open door of the Library, Andy saw someone bending near the shelves as if taking or replacing a book. He was surprised because he knew his Dad was clearing the house and could hear him along the west wing; so he went into the Library to check. He found no one there. Somewhat shaken, he hurried on to catch up with his brother and tell him, though warning him not to repeat the story. When I recently asked Andy about it, he confirmed that the incident did happen, but he now says it must have been a trick of the light. Like his father, he's a sceptic who can reason away any such occurrence.

Other people have seen or sensed strange things at Felbrigg. Two of the room stewards met on the gallery one quiet day. He had vigil over the Library and she over the Grey Dressing Room, but with no visitors about they had both wandered out to the staircase gallery, where they became engaged (as was their wont) in a lively exchange of opinion. At some point in this argument the lady guide sensed someone by her side and looked round to see a woman standing beside her wearing clothes which were later identified on a figure in a Victorian photograph at the Hall. Our friend was shocked when, a moment later, the figure had disappeared. Then came the day when I discovered a visitor gazing raptly out of a window in the West Corridor onto a view of nothing but a small grassy north-facing area and the walls of the easterly service

wing. Wondering what was holding her so mesmerised
— was she admiring the ornaments on the houseman's
windowsills, or planning the best route for a break-in?
— I paused to ask, "Are you all right? May I help?"

The woman snapped out of her reverie and looked at
me dazedly. "Sorry, I . . . I was just . . . Was there ever a
fire in that room over there?" She indicated the dining
room of the Retreat.

"Not that I know of."

"I mean . . . a long time ago. There were maids in
aprons and long skirts. Laundry maids. I could see
them. They were running out of that room, screaming.
It was all panic, and smoke billowing behind them . . ."
She shook herself and looked embarrassed. "Sorry.
Forget it. I do occasionally see things. I think I'm
psychic."

"Psychic?" Chris snorted when I recounted this
incident. "Most probably she'd had too much wine
with her lunch. There has never been a fire there that I
know of. If there had been, Mr Ketton-Cremer would
have mentioned it."

Maybe. And maybe not. The late squire didn't
include every tiny detail in his history and the woman
only claimed to have seen maids running from a fire,
not that it was a great conflagration such as might be
recorded in official documents. Curiously, though, at
one stage of the house's history the room the lady
pointed to was used as a laundry.

I recount these stories purely for your interest. They
are, inevitably, subjective and anecdotal. Do ghosts
exist? Are some people psychic? I wish I knew. It's true

that certain people suffer from an excess of imagination and suggestibility — myself included, no doubt. Such persons are apt to find a big old country house a bit scary, especially at night.

Take the case of our future daughter-in-law Alison when she came to stay with us at Felbrigg. As fiancé Kevin earnestly explained, "She's terrified of ghosts. So I'd better stay with her. We'll use separate beds, of course." Of course. Well, it was a nice big room, furnished with beds for four people, two single and one double, and our pair were both adults, engaged to be married, it was the late twentieth century and, anyway, they had both been living in the same nurses' home for some time, so it was all the same to me. We still laugh about it, though. What an original excuse!

We also laugh over our memory of Kev, aged twenty-two, bringing three of his male friends over for a weekend's fishing in the lake. "Tell them they're all very welcome," I said. "I'll make up the beds. You can all sleep in the guest room."

"There's only three beds in there," Kev observed.

To which I replied that there were two single beds and one double. "Room for four."

"What?" Kev was appalled. "You want two of us to use the double bed? To sleep together? Two blokes? Mother, do you mind!"

One of them slept on the floor in a sleeping bag. Aren't children quaint?

Storm front

Britain's famously unpredictable weather can affect a country house in many ways. At Felbrigg on a hot summer day visitor figures usually drop because families prefer to stay on nearby beaches or roam in the dappled shade of the woods or wander by the lake, avoiding the house. Some do, of course, still come to walk round rooms kept cool with the blinds firmly down and perhaps a breeze drifting through an open window that gives a glimpse of sundrenched lawns and gardens. But on a cold, wet day people flock for shelter; the house can be crowded and the tea room and restaurant packed, with queues to the doors.

A curious phenomenon of sea mist appears when the cold sea confronts a bank of warm air and causes condensation to form and hang above the margins of the sea. In the north-east of England they call it a haar; in Norfolk we speak of a sea-fret. Sometimes you can see it from a distance, hanging like a low bank of smoky cloud and clinging only near the coast, where it deters beach-lovers and drives them to find amusements inland. At other times it extends inland and envelops a whole swathe of countryside, providing another deterrent to summer visitors since a thick, clinging cold fog doesn't tempt anyone to go out, especially when it happens in July or August. If ever we woke to find Felbrigg shrouded in swirling greyness on our day off, we would probably decide to go to Norwich and do some shopping rather than "bimble" round the countryside as we generally like to do in our free time.

But a short distance inland we would suddenly emerge from the mist and find ourselves enjoying a vividly hot and sunny day. Many times the sea-fret was still there to greet us when we returned, a wall of condensation towards which the car inexorably headed, to plunge into a different climate where we suddenly needed a sweater.

Changing weather made the wide skyscapes a joy, clear blue dotted with candytuft clouds, or darkening with a storm. We often stood in our big sitting room and watched the dance of lightning slowly approaching while the interval before the thunder grew less until it was right overhead, shaking the chimneys before passing on to recede into the distance. Sunsets, too, can blaze amazingly, turning the whole sky over the park a flaming scarlet and orange, with bands of gold-edged purple cloud. In the days when farmers still burned stubble, the rising moon might hang huge and low over the trees, coloured like blood by the particles in the atmosphere. In winter the northern lights occasionally flared around us; and once as the sun set, the sky turned briefly green — perhaps some meteorologist could explain it, but the sight really unsettled me. It was as though normal parameters had gone awry and anything might happen, as when the sun goes into eclipse. No wonder our ancestors feared the sky gods.

Storms, of course, can cause structural damage. Lightning strikes or gale-force winds may knock down chimneys or dislodge slates, allowing rain to pour in. More than once we found ourselves rushing for jugs and bowls to catch the leaks before they spread further than the attics.

But the worst storm of all was the hurricane of October 1987, when during the early hours of the morning gales shook the house, throwing torrents of rain to force their way through many cracks and crevices, while in the woods and along the drive huge trees toppled and fell. How grieved Mr Ketton-Cremer would have been to see the destruction wrought by that one storm in his beloved woods.

I too love trees. They live so very much longer than do we puny humans. One Felbrigg oak that was struck down by lightning proved to have been growing when the Cavaliers and Roundheads were causing each other strife 400 years ago, and some of the sweet chestnuts are so old that they're twisted like corkscrews, as if determined to join themselves more securely with the land. Walking among the stand of ancient beeches, on a thick carpet of rustling leaves, I often used to stretch out my arms and embrace one of the massive old trees — having first made sure no one else was around to see me. Hugging trees is a slightly weird hobby, I know, much like talking to flowers (which I also recommend), but those beeches know so very much about the world; they have stood there for hundreds of years, shedding their leaves every autumn, lying dormant through winter snows, feeling their sap rise with spring . . . Have you ever noticed how soft young beech leaves are? Or observed their delicate colour when the sun shines through them? Or felt the smoothness of the silvery bark that covers those huge trunks? Or experienced its curious warmth against your cheek, where you can almost hear its heart beating? If you need a brief release from stress and tension, go out and hug a tree, listen to its sap singing, become aware of how everything is connected . . . It's a deeply spiritual experience. Don't scoff until you've tried it. Such moments helped me to comprehend what Mother Julian, the anchoress of Norwich, meant when, emerging from years of solitary contemplation, she had one simple, comforting message: "All shall be well, and all shall be well, and all manner of thing shall be well." Go hug a tree and you too might believe it.

The Great Storm destroyed some of those venerable trees, though happily not too many. Most of the thousands that went down on Felbrigg estate were smaller, younger trees, although at least 25 of them were mature oaks lining the drive.

I've written elsewhere about the storm itself and its immediate aftermath, but it's ironic to recall that exactly a year before the hurricane struck a group of young National Trust members were crawling around the Felbrigg woods collecting acorns, beechnuts and seeds from ash, sweet chestnut, hawthorn and blackthorn, in order to start a tree nursery at Blickling Hall from which, it was hoped, they might eventually provide the Trust with home-grown trees. Some of their saplings would, in due time, replace the storm-damaged trees.

The clearing up took several years and by the summer of 1989 another phase of this work was under way at Felbrigg. In order to properly replant areas which had been badly affected, and to allow enough light for the young trees to flourish, in places the few remaining trees also had to be cut down. Phil Scott, the Trust's forester, said that this meant "big holes appearing in the woods, but we have to do this to get the trees away".

There had been a glut of timber after the storm, so the Trust waited until prices rose again before they sold off their mature oak and other hard woods, much in demand since ecological moves to conserve hard timber mean that such valuable trees are seldom felled without compelling reason. Timber merchants took the longer, larger pieces, but because so many trees had been broken up by the violence of the storm there was a residue of smaller, less saleable chunks, which might have been burned as useless. However, in 1990, the head gardener at Ickworth House, near Bury St Edmonds in Suffolk, came up with the idea for a sale of some small pieces of the more unusual storm-damaged timber such as oak, box, yew, mulberry, holly and walnut. Woodturners and other craftspeople flocked to buy this wood and the sale raised over five thousand pounds for Ickworth's tree fund.

But you can't please everyone. During the intensive clearing up operation, an irate letter to a local newspaper editor castigated the Trust for "the desecration of tracts of woodland" that had taken place recently at Felbrigg, comparing it with "the wanton destruction of the rain forests in South America". The writer demanded to know, "is this for profit or management? . . . under the auspices of this organisation,

118

mature woodlands should be protected and preserved".
Quite so. But it was the hurricane that caused the
damage. The National Trust was only trying to restore
order.

If you visit the woods today you may find it hard to
see where the damage was done. Nature may create
chaos, when she chooses, but she also heals the scars.
All shall be well, and all shall be well . . .

CHAPTER
SEVEN

The comedy of manners

Among the thousands who visit Felbrigg every year, we have welcomed many famous (and a few infamous) faces. Norfolk is a favourite retreat for numerous well-known people who have weekend cottages here and some of them come regularly to visit Felbrigg. Some may arrive on official business (Lord Buxton once brought a special party to see the Morning Room), while others simply stroll through, passing time by viewing the house like any other tourist while enjoying a few quiet days at their Norfolk country cottage. Politicians, lords and ladies, royal equerries, EastEnders, and international stars such as Sir John Gielgud . . . all have somehow managed to slip by unnoticed until some sharp-eyed reader of *Hello!* happened to look twice and set the grapevine humming — "You'll never guess who's in the Yellow Bedroom!"

A well-known actress (was it Shirley MacLaine or Barbra Streisand?) once remarked that any famous person could blend in with the background if they wished — it was all in the way they comported themselves. She had noticed that if she sallied out in full warpaint with sunglasses on the top of her head and a sashay to her walk, she was instantly surrounded by a mob of autograph hunters, but if she went supermarket shopping without make-up, wearing flat shoes and a headscarf, she went unrecognised. QED. In west Norfolk they tell of a certain shop in Dersingham, near Sandringham, where the Queen had a habit of dropping in to buy a newspaper or some cough drops for the corgis. Another customer, doing a double-take, laughed and said, "Just for a minute, I thought you were the Queen! You look just like her." To which Her Majesty is said to have replied sweetly, "How reassuring."

Less retiring individuals, however, want everyone to recognise and kowtow to them. We had a few visitors who made a real nuisance of themselves by demanding special privileges at a moment's notice. When politely rebuffed, they would say, "Do you know who I am? I'm Lord Tycoon's daughter!" or "My uncle is the Minister for Hot Air," or even, "I'm secretary to Sir Panjandrum at Head Office!" as if this should excuse their bad manners. Some less well-connected folk have also been known to let themselves down, like the very loud lady who stalked through Felbrigg denigrating everything she saw — "It's all so tatty! Look at that upholstery, it's threadbare! If that suite was mine, I'd have it re-covered. That picture frame's chipped, it needs mending. And as for this crockery . . ." Crockery? Madam, did you perhaps mean our valuable dessert service in Coalport porcelain? She did not endear herself to the room stewards, to whom any slight against Felbrigg is a personal affront.

An irritant to everybody, staff and visitors, room stewards et al, can be the touring party guide who arrives unannounced and proceeds to lecture his group loudly in every room. The National Trust prefers not to let guided parties intrude on usual opening hours. Room stewards are all knowledgeable enthusiasts about "their" property and are well able to explain most points. Some have been known to "hold forth" a bit too freely, but that tendency is gently discouraged, so that visitors may wander through at their own pace and ask questions if they wish to do so. Even so, occasionally a guided tour party will slip through. They're not easy to spot until their accompanying "expert" starts his lecture.

One such unannounced tour guide proved particularly hard to muffle. He ignored room stewards' requests for him to stop lecturing, or at least turn down the volume — he was employed as a tour guide and a tour guide he intended to be! Soon other visitors were complaining of the intrusion, so the steward doing tea relief relayed an SOS to Chris, who hurried down from the office.

"The man's a menace!" said Owen in the Great Hall. In the connecting doorway between Dining Room and Drawing Room, Pam and Vera were discussing the problem, which by now had reached the Cabinet doorway, creating a bottleneck for people trying to get past the tightly-packed group from the coach.

"He's upsetting everybody," Pam said.

"And he's getting it all wrong!" Vera added in annoyance. (To many room stewards, getting facts wrong is the biggest sin of all.)

Chris excuse-me'd his way through the queue of irritated visitors and in among the jam of coach-party members, where he could hear the tour guide going on at length about Windham's Grand Tour and the way the room had been altered. The man had actually climbed over the red rope and was standing in the middle of the room expostulating. Isolated in a corner, penned in and unable to move, room steward Netta was near steaming. "I've asked him to move on, but he won't take any notice. And what he's saying isn't correct!"

Fortunately Chris has a loud voice when he chooses to use it (he once summoned a wing commander from halfway across an airfield). He too crossed the red silk rope and, standing in front of the guide, asked those people nearest the exit door to move along as they were holding up the flow through the house.

"I hadn't finished what I was saying!" the interloper blustered. "I need to keep my party together so they can hear me."

Having seen the flow of visitors moving again, Chris took the offender aside and explained the rules about guided parties. Special arrangements have to be made in advance, and if a tour company wishes to conduct its own guided tour of Felbrigg someone should write to the property manager, arrange to come outside usual visiting hours, and pay the appropriate fee. Otherwise, the guide book gives all the basic information and if any extra details are required the room stewards can usually supply them or, if not, there's a system for answering any query that may require some research.

The man, though less than pleased, appeared to see the logic of this and moved on to catch up with his party while Chris paused to talk with Netta and try to calm her down. He had never seen her so agitated. A few minutes later he decided to continue his walk through the house to visit all the room stewards, as he tried to do every open afternoon, and what did he find in the Library? Another hold-up, with that same tour guide again spouting duff gen, other visitors muttering (some of them were trapped in the Book Room unable to get back through), and another room steward on the verge of exploding.

Much as he would have liked to throw the man out, Chris didn't want to cause a scene. He contented himself with repeating the Trust's policy on guided parties and then had to follow this one through the house quietly asking the guide to move along every time he caused a hold-up. The man stubbornly refused to be silenced, but he did cut his lectures short.

That evening, as the room stewards returned their badges and the ring-binders which contain extra information about each room, the Morning Room sizzled with indignation as they swapped horror stories. Most of them could have done without the extra strain on their blood pressure, and the incident made Chris seethe for hours. We took a long, calming stroll in the peaceful woods that evening, once he'd finished the paperwork.

Heard it on the grapevine

When it comes to oddball visitors or staff, or aggravations peculiar to stately homes, stories both scurrilous and scary pass from old cynics to new ingénues, whispered in regional offices, exchanged over coffee at Queen Anne's Gate or e-mailed between public and private properties. Some of these tales are exaggerated, some probably apocryphal, and one really shouldn't repeat such idle talk. But gossip can be fun, can't it? Shall we indulge a little?

To begin with, warning tales are told of burglaries and thefts, perpetrated by gangs, by couples, or by lone chancers. At Felbrigg we had a break-in which luckily resulted in nothing worse than a broken window, a bent bronze and some muddy footmarks on a table. But not all thieves arrive by night under cover of darkness, running the gauntlet of sophisticated alarm systems and complicated locks; sometimes they call quite openly in full view and bright daylight. At one property an elderly lady fainted, and while the room stewards were rushing around doing their best to help her, a valuable clock disappeared. Any distraction might be deliberate, causing attention to wander just long enough for an accomplice to pocket some small item. Not that many small items are kept within reach any more, we've learned that lesson the hard way! But even the larger items may not be entirely safe. The library at one house lost two huge books of maps during one open afternoon. How they were smuggled out without being noticed is a mystery yet to be resolved. You could hardly slip a couple of those vast tomes into an inner pocket! Some thieves have been known to do a recce beforehand, to make sure just where they can lay their hands on a particular item. They might even be "shopping" for a collector who doesn't mind working outside the law. This may sound like a thriller plot, but it happens.

Smaller thefts of plants and flowers take place all the time. Every head gardener detests the dear, sweet, usually elderly, usually female, folk who wander around helping themselves to "just a tiny cutting, Mabel, they'll never miss it". Some use their fingernails to snaffle their illicit prize; others actually come armed with scissors! One family calmly climbed up Felbrigg's ha-ha and helped themselves to armfuls of camellias from the Orangery — on a bright March morning when the gardens were officially closed! And there was the wheelchair rider who came sailing through the Hall with the tray under her chair stuffed with rhododendron and azalea blooms, obviously picked by the several sweet-faced youngsters who sailed in her wake like Fagin's youthful crew, some of them waving boughs of stolen blossom. Would these people shoplift in Sainsbury's? They'd probably be insulted by the suggestion, but where's the difference? If ten thousand visitors every season took even "just a tiny cutting" there'd be precious few plants left. Please — don't do it!

Fire is another enemy we all have nightmares about, especially since Uppark went up in flames. They've restored it now, but is it the same house or is it a pastiche? Argument rages. At Felbrigg we were always aware of the risks, and even in the private flats smoke alarms adorned every ceiling. Around the main house Chris and his assistant kept a careful watch for anyone working with naked flames. Forgetful or uninformed workmen would arrive with blow-lamps, which in normal venues they wouldn't think twice about using. They were not pleased when asked to find other means of welding or melting or whatever it is men do with blow-lamps. Then there was the outside caterer who arrived to do the food for a staff party when Joan and her team were guests, having a night off for once. The newcomer turned up with what she called "just a little paraffin stove" on which to flambé her prawns. She got very sniffy when prevented from preparing this delicacy. "It's only a tiny flame!" she argued. "I'll have someone standing by with a fire extinguisher if I absolutely must." We went without our seafood delight that evening.

Imagine, then, our horror when workmen came to take up the floorboards in our flat and spray the void with that horrible-smelling stuff that kills woodworm. Between our floor and the ceiling beneath was a thick layer of old, tinder-dry straw, and across it lay a thickly insulated electric cable. The cable had been nibbled by mice, leaving bare wires peeping through the sheathing. Thank goodness they found it in time!

Another near thing occurred when scaffolding surrounded the house, guarded at night by bright security lights. One of the lights, insecurely placed, toppled over and lay face down on one of the deals where, by the time it was found and set upright, it had charred a black patch that might soon have blazed into fire. Yes, having workmen about is another unexpected hazard of life with the National Trust.

Further warnings circulate about staff from hell whose legends grow darker with every telling, from the over-friendly type cordially hated by women at every property across a whole region for his hands-on approach, to certain old-style curators (long gone by now, one hopes) who thought it their right to assume the mantle of the squire. They donned green wellies, deer-stalkers, tweeds and cavalry twill and strode around "their" property barking at gardeners and visitors alike: "Pick up that sweet paper! Get off that lawn! Control that child! What are you doing in my bloody garden when we're closed?" Some kept horses; many owned large and undisciplined dogs; and some seemed to think they were still in the army. One property manager ordered a new assistant to "report to the door of my flat every morning, 8.30 sharp, and I'll give you your orders for the day". As the houseman re-counted wryly, "He thought he was still in the officers' mess, with me as his batman. But half past eight was the middle of the morning for me. So if he wanted me he was forced to come and find me. He soon got tired of playing 'hunt the houseman'. But he never forgave me for it. Insubordination in the ranks!"

Another chap kept two large Labradors which required frequent walking. Their bladder function coincided spookily with busy periods in the house and, if ever a genuine emergency called all hands to the pumps, house staff could rely on their boss to respond, "I'll be there as soon as I've walked the dogs. The poor lads are up there in my apartment with their little legs firmly crossed." Since the walks took anything up to two hours, by the time he returned the crisis had usually passed.

Some types like to show they're boss by going around with a walkie-talkie and loudly issuing orders over it. You see people like that everywhere, in supermarkets, shops and cafés, believing that the louder and bossier they are the more important it makes them seem. And some are much too highly qualified to demean themselves by physical effort. At a conference in Devon, over breakfast, two managers swapped stories of life at their different properties. One described how long his days could be, particularly when his assistant had his day off and there were workmen about, so that the house needed opening up around seven and at the end of the day the paperwork might keep him at it until eight or beyond. "Good heavens!" exclaimed his opposite number. "You mean you're expected to see to security, deal with shutters and things? I wouldn't dream of doing manual work like that. I'm a historian, not a janitor!" One can only assume that his property employed more people than we had at Felbrigg!

The myth remains strong that working for the National Trust must be a sinecure: you're only busy during the summer season, only during visitor opening hours — what, one o'clock to five o'clock, four or five days a week, maybe? The rest of the time — mornings, evenings, closed days and all of the winter, you're free to do your own thing. You wish!

Whenever a post becomes available, persons with dewy-eyed illusions come merrily along and refuse to listen to the warnings about uncertain hours, very hard work, great demands on time, loyalty, stamina and family relationships. "I plan to do an Open University course during the winter," said one ingenuous prospective houseman, while another, a young woman in her twenties, wanted to know who was going to do the heavy work for her: "You mean, I might have to move carpets and things?" Occasionally one of these deluded souls slips through the net and actually gets the job, like the houseman who, in his previous life, had worked on a production line in a factory. Within weeks of taking up his new post, he wrote a letter complaining that he wasn't used to working more than forty hours a week, or cutting his lunch hour short, or not having every weekend to himself; he kept missing his full time off and not getting any in lieu; he also found it very hard to motivate himself to clean ceilings, working all alone in echoing, draughty rooms; and he hadn't expected to be responsible for clearing blocked drains and toilets — in his opinion the Trust ought to employ a caretaker for all those dirty, menial tasks. It wasn't long before he was writing again, to resign his job and go back to the safe parameters of some less challenging occupation.

Every job has its maddening moments, all part of its inevitable downside; but, let's be honest, working for the National Trust does provide its fair share of "up" moments too: a summer's evening when the visitors have all gone and the setting sun lays long shadows across pasture where calves cavort and swallows swoop . . . or a winter morning when you wake to the strange luminosity which means snow, and open your curtains to see everything wearing a thick white shawl, the only footmarks left by birds, or foxes, or deer — or those darn cats! Or simply the enjoyment of sharing your home with the multifarious visitors who enliven every day.

Such as the lady in the Library who enquired breathlessly, "Do you ever lend the books out?" (The answer, of course, is no, though if you have a very good reason for doing so you may write in and ask permission to come and study the books here, under supervision.) Another day, a voice on the phone demanded to speak to Greta and was told, "Sorry, you have the wrong number."

"Wrong number?" retorted the lady. "If it's not your number, why did you answer the phone?" Which reminds me of my dear Mum, who once absent-mindedly enquired, "Yes, but who did write Handel's *Messiah*?" We all say daft things at times, don't we?

Necessaries

Any venue that welcomes the public, be it theme park, country mansion, theatre or truck stop, has to bear in mind a few basic necessities which help to put people at their ease. Visitors must be fed, watered, amused, and provided with facilities to attend to more personal functions such as . . . well, let's admit it, we're talking toilets. (Squeamish readers please skip to the next section.)

Though in polite society one doesn't mention the plumbing — that is, the bathroom, powder room, rest room, ladies' room, gents', the john, the heads, the lavatory, the WC, the outhouse or the privy (any dictionary of euphemisms will supply a whole lot more) — whatever you prefer to call it, we all have to use one. For much of our time at Felbrigg, the subject provided cause for endless argument and anguish. Apart from one somewhat basic comfort station out back (gardeners for the use of), all the loos were deep inside the house. We couldn't let every casual passer-by make use of them. In order to reach those sacred areas you had to buy a ticket or possess a members' card. The gents' convenience lurked at the far end of the Stone Corridor, right next to the calm elegance of the Cabinet, past whose open door a procession of eager chaps came and went every afternoon. Room stewards stationed in the Cabinet observed that the aesthetics of the ornate plaster ceiling, the rococo decor and the Busiri landscapes were better appreciated without the distraction of banging doors and passing strangers.

The ladies' facility, slightly better placed at the end of the Bird Corridor, seemed to provide a magnet for light-fingered visitors fond of collecting lavatory chains and toilet rolls. It did have three cubicles, which were ample except when coach parties arrived (40 restless queuing ladies did create a bit of a crush), but — as young mothers increasingly complained — there was neither the room for changing nappies nor the ambience for feeding a hungry baby. Two young mothers one day decided to prove their point by breast-feeding their infants while seated on a windowboard in one of the bedrooms, while another created a stir by changing her baby's noisome nappy in the lobby next to the ticket desk. Great fun! Thanks, girls, but we did know we had a problem. A solution was what we desperately longed for.

Resident staff and tenants have their own bathroom facilities, of course, but these too used to come into public demand whenever the house was closed. Tenants reported many a stranger hammering at their doors with plaintive pleas for relief. I particularly remember one Boxing Day when an urgent ringing at our own backdoor bell sent Chris rushing downstairs to find outside a gentleman who demanded to know why we didn't have toilet facilities available for visitors using the park or the woodland walks. He was incensed when Chris suggested that most walkers availed themselves of the cover of a convenient oak tree or rhododendron thicket, of which the woods had ample supply. "You expect my wife to squat in the woods? How dare you, you inexpressible animal!" Perhaps we should have suggested he try the three-seater thunderbox privy which once served the communal needs of the inhabitants of the Hall but now provides a conversation-piece in the gardens attached to tenanted apartments behind the main house.

When the Prince of Wales visited us one foggy, snowbound January day, he was amused to hear how, in the privacy of their bedrooms, those fine ladies and gentlemen in their lace ruffles and hooped skirts used close-stools and commodes, and at other times they employed chamber pots tucked away in discreet locations such as sideboard cupboards or desk drawers. Or behind a huge jib door in the Library. Yes, quite.

One curio in the display cabinet of the Stone Corridor is a small vessel which some visitors guess to be a large family-size gravy boat. It has that kind of shape, though without a pouring lip, but in fact it's a bourdalou, a urinal intended "mainly for the use of ladies while travelling" and occasionally "concealed inside a muff", says one authority. How charming. These indispensable items among an itinerant lady's accoutrements were named after a French preacher of the late seventeenth century, one Louis Bourdalou; apparently his tendency to deliver four-hour sermons caused his congregation to come suitably equipped. Perhaps our word "loo" derives from this same source, or maybe it came from the French word *l'eau* and the garbling of the phrase *garde l'eau* (beware the water) into "Gardyloo!" the merry cry which in Renaissance England presaged the emptying of chamber pots from the upper windows of town houses. What elegant days those were, egad!

All of which goes to prove that the problem is not a new one. It must have been going on since the first caveman squatted on a nettle.

134

Every year, at the end-of-season property meeting, someone would raise the same old question and the same old answer would come: "We're hoping to build an outside toilet block very soon." Hooray! But how soon was "very soon"? In the staff newsletter of August 1987, Chris wrote with his usual subtle humour, "If we don't get our new outside loos by next season, as promised, I'm sure to go clean round the bend." Next season? It was March 1989 before, finally, after the first stage of building towards the new Park Restaurant, the long-promised new toilet block became a reality. Equipped with all mod cons, and sited where it can be opened all year round, it is accessible to the public even when the rest of Felbrigg is closed. Wonderful.

The work revealed some interesting sidelights to add to Felbrigg's history. When workmen cleared out the clutter from the old stable, which the gardeners had for years used as a shed, they found two of the original stalls still intact, one bearing a name-plate reading "Jester". It commemorates one of the last horses who lived here. The wooden partitions between the stalls have curved tops made out of single pieces of wood, so pleasing that you want to run your hands over them to enjoy the shape and warmth of the wood. In order to reproduce the effect for the third stall, a huge piece of timber was selected and carved to shape. When you visit Felbrigg, you may be amused to detect which one is the new one; it used to be obvious, but time is mellowing the newer wood.

The builders revealed yet more historic links — of the plumbing kind — when they demolished the old outhouse containing the gardeners' outside loo and came across the cistern of even older lavatories. Evidently that spot has served a similar purpose for generations of servants, grooms, woodsmen and gardeners. Ponder on that when you go. You're sitting on a spot that reeks with history.

Of course, in every complicated job, be it filling in a tax form or building a skyscraper, the possibilities for error are frightening. Those most involved often get so intent picking over details that they forget the whole picture. In the case of the new toilet block, the architectural team were so busy trying to squeeze in as many cubicles as possible that they forgot to provide space in the ladies' for sanitary bins. When this was pointed out at a planning meeting the men shrugged it off: "Oh, that doesn't matter, we'll put an incinerator, or a big bin, out in the main part of the lavatories. What difference does it make?" A great deal of difference, as all the female element at Felbrigg agreed. But the plans were too far advanced for changes to be made. Instead, as a compromise, Chris was given the job of scouring round all the manufacturers to find one that made bins small enough to fit inside the cubicles.

Optimum use of space is always a consideration, but it left the cubicles quite narrow. Fitted with big round toilet-roll holders on their backs, the doors don't open fully; ladies of more generous proportions may have difficulty squeezing in. To alleviate the problem, the workmen could have made all the doors open outwards, but the experts weren't keen on that idea so the squeeze remains. However, as you will discover, the

136

toilet block is spacious and sparkling clean, with a special room for disabled persons and another for babies and their minders. It's a delight to use, not least because the Trust have had the cubicles built to measure in wood, not prefabricated in some plastic laminate or cold steel.

The first visitors that season commented on the splendour of the new facilities and all was well until one busy day which filled all of the ladies' cubicles at the same time. All of the wooden doors closed in their splendid wooden frames and their shiny new bolts slipped across. A few minutes later, the bolts slid open one by one, and one by one the doors refused to budge. They were tightly jammed into the frames, perhaps because the wood had swelled with the damp air after a period of April showers. Cries for help went up and other ladies came to help, but the doors remained stuck. Someone alerted Joan, who in her turn phoned across to the main Hall and spoke to Chris: "Houston, we have a problem . . ." Oh, dear, what could the matter be? As he says when he regales an audience with this riveting story, "We know a song about that, don't we?" I'm sure you'll be thrilled to know that a bit of brute force, shoulder to door, relieved the pressure on the frame and set all the ladies free. Next day a carpenter came and shaved a fraction off the edge of each door. Sorted!

On a sweeter note, the airy lobby of the new block, through which you can reach the old stable and the restaurant, had space enough for a decorative pot in which grew a bay tree. The shrub provided a fragrant stopping place for a goldcrest (Britain's smallest bird), which was often seen flitting in the branches, apparently quite at home. Chris overheard one group of visitors marvelling at the way the tiny bird had been "trained to stay in the lobby!" "Oh, we go to great lengths to please our visitors," he told them before explaining that in fact the bird came and went through the outer door, which was frequently left open. For the goldcrest's sake, he didn't add that he knew exactly where it had its nest, around elbow-height in a wall just outside.

CHAPTER
EIGHT

Swan alert

Occasionally an unusual wildlife visitor would appear, for instance the pelican which for a few days became an aquatic squatter on the lake. We couldn't get near it, nor could we find out where it belonged — none of the zoos or sanctuaries around had lost a pelican. It departed as abruptly as it had arrived, and we never did solve the mystery. (Maybe it was from another dimension, like all those black panthers prowling the countryside!) But most arrivals are less exotic.

The swan pairs who reside by the lake generally build their nests on the northern shore, well away from the walkers and fishermen who are confined to the south side of the water. They introduce a note of elegance and regality, but occasionally their interests conflict with those of their human neighbours, as when a visitor came to the Hall to report a swan in distress, tangled up with fishing line wound round its neck and beak. Chris phoned the local swan-rescue centre, where the man in charge said he would come as soon as he could.

The swan man was known to be a dedicated, single-minded but rather volatile chap who, whilst caring deeply about the welfare of beautiful but vulnerable birds, hadn't much time for humans. We awaited his arrival with interest.

It was the middle of a busy afternoon, when the house was seething with visitors and we were all at full stretch trying to cope with the rush. I was helping Jose, our ticket seller, answering questions and explaining about the choice of guide books while she sold tickets and took money, when with a screech of brakes and a whoosh of gravel a big estate car drew up right bang in front of the main door, causing consternation among a group of arriving visitors. From what I could see from my post by the desk, the back of the car was cluttered with nets and other gear and the trailer behind it contained a dinghy with an outboard motor attached. Was the driver disabled?

Normally the ticket seller would try to deter able-bodied drivers from using the front courtyard. Jose usually performed this duty with a warm smile and a gentle word about leaving the front uncluttered if we possibly could — "thank you so much, you're very kind" — but she was so busy attending to a crowd of new arrivals that I offered to deal with the intruding estate car. Before I could get far through the crush, however, the driver had leapt out, proving that he definitely was not disabled. With little regard for the people around him, he barged through the queue and loudly demanded to see whoever was in charge. He didn't introduce himself, but his purpose soon became apparent.

"There's a swan in difficulties on your lake! Someone phoned me about it. I've been down there to see and the poor thing's all tangled up with fishing line. Bloody fishermen don't give a damn! I spend my life freeing trapped birds and getting hooks out of their mouths. Do you know how much pain and distress it causes? Don't these people care what they're doing to the wildlife? They ought to know better, and so did you people. The National Trust ought to ban fishing on their lakes. It's not good enough . . ."

The tirade went on. I drew the man into the side lobby so as not to cause too much disruption by the ticket desk, but he refused to be calmed. The swan was in the middle of the lake, frightened out of its wits, and he couldn't reach it with his poles and equipment. "Bloody fishermen . . . conservationists who don't give a damn . . . it's all money, these days . . . nobody cares . . ."

When Chris arrived he took the man outside. Visitors going by, coming into the house or going across to the garden gate, had to skirt round the car and trailer, regarding the irate swan man with all the wariness and curiosity they might have displayed at the sight of a snarling Rottweiler. Though I couldn't hear all that was said, body language revealed that the man was growing ever more furious and irrational, shouting and gesticulating, while Chris tried vainly to calm him down.

As Chris told me later, he was trying to explain that, as administrator, he didn't dictate policy over use of the lake. He couldn't personally stop the fishing; we did have notices up asking fishermen to be careful not to leave hooks and lines lying about and our warden kept

141

a close eye out for such dangerous litter. But Chris could certainly promise to report the problem yet again.

That wasn't enough for the angry swan man. "What's the good of reporting it, you fool? They won't do anything. Another piece of paper in a file, and meanwhile swans are dying by the hundred!"

He continued ranting and swearing, furious on behalf of the damaged swan but oblivious to the fact that by creating a disturbance he was doing his cause no good at all. When he continued to insist that the Trust ought to change its policy, Chris suggested he should take it up with the land agent at regional office in nearby Blickling Hall.

"Oh, don't worry, I shall be doing that," the man blustered. "I'll take the bloody swan and put it on his desk!"

Realising the argument was going nowhere, Chris returned to the subject of the swan's rescue. Could he do anything practical to help? Obviously he couldn't leave the property until the end of the afternoon; he was in sole charge since the houseman, Eddie, was having his day off. But once the visitors had gone he would be happy to do what he could. "I'll swim out and drive the swan towards you, if that'll help."

The man dismissed that idea with more scorn, leaving the impression that his main purpose that afternoon was to cause a stir and draw attention to himself and the plight of "his" swans. "I can't wait for you, that's no use. I shall have to get my bloody boat down there somehow!" Eventually, still seething and shouting, he drove away heading for the lake. Chris resumed his duties and peace once more descended.

Later, after the Hall had closed, before he settled down to do his evening's paperwork, Chris walked down to the lake. I didn't go with him. I was cooking our evening meal and anyway someone had to stay and man the Hall in case of unexpected visitors, phone calls or emergencies. Down by the lake, however, tranquillity reigned. The swan had gone, the man and his equipment too. We assumed he had performed his rescue and, of course, we were happy about that. We sympathised with his passion. We heartily agreed with his basic argument: humankind should take more care of the earth's wildlife, yes, of course we should. But does it need verbal abuse and a total disregard of everyone else's rights to prove the point?

Toad in a hole

But sometimes people worry unnecessarily about wildlife. A frequent misconception concerns toads, which are said to fall down cattle grids or through other types of grille, where they get trapped and die. While this might be true of hedgehogs and certain other small mammals, it doesn't apply to toads. They actually like living in dank holes, and they have surprising powers to climb apparently sheer vertical surfaces. In the cellars at Felbrigg we've seen them crawling across windows, supported by tiny suction pads on their feet.

The cellar windows are set in lightwells sunk below ground level and when you're in the front courtyard you may see, close to the wall of the house, a couple of metal gratings protecting them. Down in those dark, dusty, often wet holes, numerous toads and a few lizards live out their lives in peace and harmony. To them, the lightwells are home, a haven watched over by some warty toad god who looks down from the unfathomable heights above their grille and rewards them with feasts of insects and showers of rain. They can easily climb out and go off hunting and foraging whenever they wish, usually in the cool shades of the night when only bats and owls are about. The only time toads need to be close to water is for breeding. So, if you should happen to see a dead one, or a toady skeleton, chances are it died of old age, not from being entrapped in a dungeon. Toad of Monte Cristo? I think not.

People have been coming to Felbrigg to see the toads for many years. Adults recount how they were brought as children and how they now bring their own children and grandchildren to peer down through the gratings. Even so, some caring souls still believe that the toads have fallen down there and can't escape.

After many worried comments from visitors Chris decided on an experiment. One cool evening when all was quiet, he went out and raised one of the gratings, reached down and lifted out a few of the toads. One by one he released them, setting them some yards away on the courtyard, free to head for the pasture, the woods, the lake . . . Within minutes they were all crawling back for the shelter of their familiar home, with the long-suffering air of peaceable beings pointlessly disturbed by some fool.

One afternoon a man came to the front desk to report yet another sighting of trapped toads. "Can you please come and let them out?" he asked Chris, who happened to be there chatting with the ticket seller. "The children are a bit worried about them." Outside, Chris found a family group of several adults and two children all gathered anxiously by the grating. He told them of his experiment and explained that the toads were quite comfortable and happy where they were. But perhaps the children would like to have a closer look? Raising the grating, he asked the little boy to hold it up while he reached down to pick up one of the toads. The grating slipped out of the poor lad's damp fingers and came down on Chris's hand. "Made my eyes water a bit," he told me later, "but no surgery necessary!" Wounded but willing, he tried again and this time brought out a toad, holding it on his hand, stroking it gently and showing the children that it was perfectly fine, healthy and unbothered by the attention.

"Would you like to hold it?" he asked the boy, who looked doubtful. He did touch the toad, stroking it and studying it very closely, but he was not too keen to hold it.

His little sister, about four years old, was watching in amazement, so Chris asked her if she would like to stroke the toad too. He sensed the tension in the adults standing around as the child put out a tentative hand.

145

When she had discovered for herself that the toad was dry and soft, not at all cold and slimey, Chris asked if she would like to hold it. Her mother took a sharp breath, but the little girl nodded, "Yes, please!" and, following Chris's instructions, held out both hands, palms together and spread flat. When the toad was placed on her hands her small face filled with wonder, though Chris was aware of utter silence among the grown-up spectators.

Later, with the resident safely back in its hole, Chris replaced the grating and got to his feet, facing the adults for the first time. The little girl's mother looked pale — the scene had amazed her. "I wouldn't have believed it if I hadn't seen it. I've never known her do anything like that. She hates creepy-crawlies. She's terrified of frogs and toads, won't go near them. It was incredible to see her." Perhaps Chris helped the child to see she had no need to be afraid. He hopes so. He was happy to take the time to introduce another new friend to the toads of Felbrigg Hall.

The father thanked him for his time and patience, then added, "I hope you won't get into trouble for taking so much time out from your work."

"Trouble from whom?" said Chris.

"Well, from . . . whoever's in charge."

Since he himself was "in charge" at Felbrigg, Chris laughed. "No, that's all right. My boss is an understanding chap."

Around the region

Before he became the administrator at Felbrigg, Chris was appointed Health and Safety Representative (HSR) for mansions in East Anglia, the first time this job had been entrusted to a houseman. It entailed making off-season visits to all of the properties in the region to consider aspects of health and safety for both staff and public inside the great houses; other HSRs covered gardens and parks, shops and restaurants. Chris found this new side of his work especially interesting because it gave him a reason to travel around East Anglia, a huge area with National Trust properties as far flung as St George's Guildhall in King's Lynn; Lavenham Guildhall, near Sudbury in Suffolk; and Wimpole Hall and Home Farm on the far side of Cambridgeshire. Since HSRs make their inspections only during the winter season, and bearing in mind all the winter work going on at their own home properties, to cover every property on an annual basis is a physical impossibility. Even so, Chris enjoyed inspecting the usually unseen parts of the places he did visit. At Oxborough, for instance, where the Elizabethan house with its red brick battlements stands four-square behind a broad moat around which lie knot gardens and river walks, the rambling attics were virtually empty. A great contrast to the crowded lumber rooms at Felbrigg.

Once he became administrator, from time to time Chris attended meetings at other East Anglian properties. He particularly remembers one visit to Wimpole (apart from missing the turn and having to drive for miles down the M11 before there was an exit that allowed him to get back!). During the lunch break, Wimpole's administrator, Graham, invited him out to the south front, which was in the process of renovation with consequent scaffolding, machinery, piles of bricks and an assortment of sections of stone balustrade, huge terracotta urns, statues . . . To facilitate the repair of the roof above the main, oldest part of Wimpole Hall, the workmen had brought in a crane to lift down sections of the pediment — a balustrade decorated with urns and a group statue of two classical figures representing Charity, made by the same sculptor who created the statue of the Prince Consort for the Albert Memorial in London. Normally set high above the main front porch, these statues now stood safely on the ground, available for close inspection for the first time since they were set up there on the roof 150 years ago.

Pointing to an object carved in the stone near the feet of one of the figures, Graham asked, "What do you make of that?"

Chris peered at the object, bending to have a closer look. Beside the sandalled feet of the classically robed figure was something formed in a slightly flattened dome shape, set on a curling-edged base that looked for all the world like . . . "It's a bowler hat!"

"That's what we thought," said Graham dubiously. "But it can't be a bowler hat. It's a classical statue, for heaven's sake. Why on earth would Foley have added a bowler hat?"

"It was probably meant as a joke," Chris replied. "He was having a bit of fun. Well, high up there on the roof

148

no one was ever going to see it, were they? Did I ever tell you about the little animals in the plasterwork in our Cabinet Room . . .?"

Ever since he found those tiny animal faces hidden in the fruit-and-flowers ceiling of the Cabinet at Felbrigg, we have been noting examples of this kind of whimsy. You can find them everywhere, perpetrated by artists and artisans of all trades — sculptors, masons, plasterers, builders and painters (of both the portrait-in-oils type and the slap-on-emulsion kind). Grand paintings have little dogs peeking from shrubbery; furniture-maker "Mouse" Thompson was so-called because he carved a mouse somewhere on all his pieces; Alfred Hitchcock liked to play an extra in his own films; even cathedral builders added many a pagan "green man" to their decorations; and, most famously, in Lincoln's magnificent minster, someone hid away a devilish little Imp. They are quirky touches added by someone with a sense of fun.

Humbler workers may leave less artistic marks; nevertheless they too like to think they will be remembered long after they're gone — like the Roman vandal who scratched the Latin for "Marcus was 'ere" on the side of a pyramid in Egypt. When Felbrigg's roof was releaded, the workmen discovered that their nineteenth-century counterparts had pricked out their initials and the shapes of their hands and feet in an obscure position where the squire wouldn't see them. Our twentieth-century lads cut out these pieces and welded them back on to the new roof, adding a few initials of their own for good measure. In the Dining

Room, while doing some high-level work, Chris saw that the men who had repainted it had written their names above the carvings over one of the windows.

But such pranks can rebound, as in the cautionary tale told by a Felbrigg carpenter. He and his colleagues had been remodelling a kitchen for a difficult lady who gave them so much grief that before fitting the final cupboards they wrote rude things about her on the wall. But they came unstuck because they hit a problem and had to take down the cupboards with the lady watching, so she saw the graffiti. Oops.

House and gardens

Felbrigg's few tenants have their own small areas of garden where they can relax behind screening hedges and dry their laundry in the sun and wind. Resident staff have no private garden, though they are allowed to enjoy the Hall's gardens (when they have time). That privilege is especially appreciated on closed days when you have it all to yourself and there are no worries about mowing lawns or weeding in the herbaceous borders or pruning trees — all that is miraculously accomplished by other hands. Not being an enthusiast for soil-tilling, pricking-out rose thorns or dibbling after corms (or whatever it is gardeners do), that state of affairs suited me fine. The only real problem of having no garden of our own was the lack of facilities for drying washing out of doors.

150

After we moved into the larger administrator's flat we had the old slop-room, where damp laundry could hang for days and not intrude on our lives. But in the houseman's flat there was no spare space, so washing hung on airers near the few available storage heaters, or hung dripping over the bath. This was not so bad in summer but during the winter the flat often resembled a Chinese laundry and the condensation was horrendous, even with the washing only two people produced. Extra linen for visitors provided a challenge.

On a damp weekend one winter, Andy and his then-girlfriend, taking a break from university, paused at Felbrigg for a couple of nights en route to her parents' home near Norwich. They arrived late on a Friday night and Andy presented me with three black dustbin bags stuffed with dirty laundry which turned out to be mostly jeans and heavy sweaters. "Can you get them done by Sunday, please? We want to leave Sunday evening."

"I'll happily wash them," I said, "and they can hang up until you leave, but I can't guarantee that jeans and sweaters will be dry by Sunday evening. You may have to pack them still damp."

To this day I'm not sure he understood the logistics of it. Certainly then-girlfriend didn't. The sneer on her face said quite clearly that she thought I was being awkward. "Then we'll take them home to my mother. She won't mind doing them." (Perhaps her mother had a tumble dryer, who knows?) In case you're wondering — no, then-girlfriend didn't become now-wife.

Probably just as well. I'd have been forever damned as the mother-in-law from hell.

As may be apparent, housework is not my favourite occupation. Ironing, hoovering, washing-up and dusting take second place to scribbling, or reading, or going out for coffee and scribbling, or sitting in the garden and scribbling. The gardens at Felbrigg offered many quiet spots where I could sit under a shady hat or a shady tree with my pen and notebook, oblivious to racing children, chattering adults, feet on gravel, cooing doves, splashing fountains, gardeners with wheelbarrows, motor mowers . . .

Even so, inside our quarters I tried to keep the untide from drowning us and, especially after we moved to the larger flat and did much more entertaining, I did my best to keep the place fit to be seen (if only by a cursory glance from a purblind mole). But that second flat was huge, with long stretches of corridor and six flights of shallow stairs, all with wooden edges and ornate, dark-stained balusters that attracted dust and showed off every speck. So at one stage, when I was acting houseman, I employed one of Felbrigg's lady cleaners to come in for a couple of hours once a week (we couldn't afford any more). It was great having her help. She did a wonderful job. But she failed to establish a bond with our very basic vacuum cleaner; she left all my ornaments arranged with regimental precision, when I prefer them in asymmetric groups; and on first sight of my dusters she went white: "I can only work with clean dusters! If you wouldn't mind . . ." Now, forgive me all you wonderwomen out there, but to my mind having to wash dusters before the home help will use them is taking housepride a bit far. The arrangement didn't last long, though she and I remain friends. I must add that whenever I visit her house it's immaculate, whereas if you call on me without warning you'll find the house knee-deep in books, files, papers and, most likely, unwashed dishes arranged artistically round the sink. Perhaps I should offer my kitchen to the National Gallery as an example of modern art! I've given up worrying about it since I heard Quentin Crisp declare that after four years the dust doesn't get any thicker. A comforting thought.

Whenever possible, then, I would escape to the peace and quiet of the garden, away from phones, importuning husbands ("Darling, could you just possibly give us a hand with . . .") and all the other assorted interruptions that impose on one's home life. One of my favourite hiding places was the Walled Garden.

When the last squire died, the garden was in need of some renovation and replanting. The Trust wanted to keep it as a traditional kitchen garden, although, with only a quarter of the staff that might have worked there a hundred years before, they grew fewer vegetables and used more of the garden for decorative planting. Gravel walks lead the visitor round, via flowerbeds and borders full of flocks and peonies and edged with fragrant box, to greenhouses growing lemons and limes, all within the shelter of high red-brick walls where peaches, plums, nectarines and figs are trained. The southern section is mainly lawned and provides a venue for occasional outside entertainments including plays and operas, and for social events such as Ted's retirement party; the central section boasts a collection of hawthorn and quince trees planted in grass, like an orchard; and the northern section has the herb and vegetable gardens, the soft fruit cages and the lily pond presided over by a stone merman. Against the north wall stands the photogenic dovecote, where doves (or white pigeons) still breed happily.

Dovecotes once provided meat for the residents of country houses, especially in winter when other meat was scarce, and the bird's droppings helped to manure the garden. Felbrigg's pretty octagonal dovecote has niches enough for 2,000 doves. It dates from the middle of the eighteenth century, became derelict under Robert Ketton, and was restored by R. W. Ketton-Cremer in 1937. Today it provides a perfect study for artists and photographers, often captured in a frame formed by the archway in the southern wall, with the merman and his lily pond, fringed with purple lavender, in the foreground.

However busy the Hall may be, the Walled Garden remains an oasis of peace and quiet. It seems to invite you to speak quietly, to walk slowly, to enjoy its sights and scents and let cares fall away. Pause to wonder at the incredibly complex design of a single flower; breathe in the lavender and feel the stress depart; watch the doves fly in graceful squadrons across the blue sky . . . It's quite lovely there, at any season.

Head gardener Ted loved his gardens and worked all hours to tend them. He had a real feeling for the land

154

and plants in his care. He had been known to buy plants for the garden with his own money rather than ask the Trust to expend funds, and if the big west lawn needed a good soaking he would turn out at all hours of the night to switch the sprinklers on or off. He exemplified the difference between a dedicated worker and a clock-watcher to whom a job is just something you do to earn money. Nor did he confine himself to gardening. Whenever extra muscle-power was needed in the house, for shifting heavy furniture or statues or some huge picture, he and his assistant Mark could always be relied on to help. And in the gardens their friendly presence was always an added pleasure.

For me, a particular joy of the Walled Garden is the collection of hawthorn trees, foaming with creamy blossom in the spring, dripping with scarlet haws of all sizes in the autumn. Ted felt the same and was upset when a garden adviser suggested the thorns ought to be grubbed up and replaced with yet more apple trees so that the fruit could be sold for profit. It didn't seem to occur to her that someone would have to pick and pack the apples. Was that to be yet another job for Ted and Mark? They were already so busy that they hadn't time to harvest the strawberries, raspberries, gooseberries, blackcurrants, redcurrants, whitecurrants . . . "Please!" Ted begged us each summer. "Go and help yourselves to the soft fruit; it's just dropping off the branches and going rotten." So we very kindly helped him out and spent balmy evenings getting our hands and faces smeared with red juice as we culled basketfuls of fruit for pies, summer puddings, the freezer, to share with

155

our neighbours and friends, or just simply to melt in our mouths with sugar and cream. What a chore that was!

We were sometimes surprised to find that not everyone cherished the aesthetics of the gardens in quite the same way we did. Of course changes have to be made as circumstances alter and times move on, but Chris and I were not alone in feeling that some plans were ill judged. Chris occasionally found himself in hot water for voicing strong opinions, sometimes on behalf of others who daren't speak their thoughts aloud.

Ted did not enjoy making waves. However, if he felt strongly he would make sure someone knew and his opinion would be taken into account. The plan to do away with the hawthorns, for instance, was heard of no more. But a subsequent scheme for the gardens offered a far worse threat and when Ted heard the rumours he came to the office to talk to Chris.

The approaching retirement of farmer David Rash had given the Trust an opportunity to reorganise the environs of Hall Farm. Ted heard that our bosses were planning to bring all vehicles in by the farm road, directing staff and deliveries round behind the gardens and on to the Hall, while visitors' cars would be hidden away in a car park which was to be made in a field behind the Walled Garden. A new entrance route would lead visitors through the dovecote, across the Walled Garden, and on via the meadow to the Hall. The dovecote would be cleaned out and tidied up, of course. It would make a dinky ticket booth. Poor Ted had spent a sleepless night worrying about this awful

156

prospect, and when Chris heard the story he too felt outraged. Surely it couldn't be true? It would be a desecration of the most beautiful, peaceful part of the garden. To have thousands of visitors tramping through, and delivery lorries roaring past only yards away . . .

At the annual property meeting which took place shortly afterwards, Chris got up and asked whether there was any truth in the rumour about the plans to make the dovecote and Walled Garden the new entrance for Felbrigg. To his horror, the answer confirmed that such a scheme was being considered.

"Is that a problem?" they asked.

"A problem!" Every time Chris remembers that meeting he waxes passionate all over again. "It was a crazy idea! The Walled Garden is a haven of peace and tranquillity, waiting to be discovered. A secret, quiet place. You have to make a bit of an effort, walk a few hundred yards, to find it. You come to the wall, and the narrow gate. You go through . . . and that amazing vista opens all around you. Imagine it with hundreds of visitors tramping through every day. It would lose all its magic. And as for using the dovecote as a ticket booth . . ."

He had no idea who had dreamed up this outrageous scheme, but he had to speak up, for himself, for Ted, and for Felbrigg. Right or wrong, he had evolved strong feelings about the way Felbrigg ought to be presented and in his mind this was probably the greatest threat of all to the character of the place, its integrity and its ambience — its "spirit" as Lady Victoria Leatham had put it. He won the day, too. He expressed his feelings with such passion that the scheme was dropped.

Since that time, the powers-that-be have realised that, along with the proliferation of garden centres and TV gardening shows for people who have more leisure time, an increasing number of National Trust visitors come to enjoy the gardens rather than the houses. Some properties whose walled gardens have been paved and turned into car parks are having second thoughts. Obviously gardens are a growing attraction (in every sense of the word!) for the new millennium. Take the example of Anglesey Abbey, where a few years ago the property manager and the head gardener evolved a plan to "do something different". They planted a winter garden and, among other delights, discovered an amazing number of varieties of snowdrops. Now, visitors arrive in droves to visit the winter garden. Anglesey Abbey's busiest months are February and March, with the restaurant humming all through what is usually the quiet season.

So thank goodness they scrapped those plans for such swingeing changes at Felbrigg. There has, however, been one happy innovation — the field which was earmarked as a car park has been planted as an orchard and supplied with picnic tables, an area where children can run free and enjoy themselves. But the Walled Garden still slumbers in the sunlight, with its doves cooing and the soothing scent of herbs drifting on a warm breeze. You still have to walk a hundred yards or so across the meadow to find that gate in the wall, but behind it lies enchantment, an oasis of tranquillity and delight.

The current head gardener is a young woman named Tina, who works with three official helpers and a team of volunteers, so the gardens are looking better than ever. You'll find some flightless bantams strutting the lawns now, along with the doves, a delightful addition to the pleasures of the Walled Garden. Don't miss it.

CHAPTER
NINE

Accustomed as I am . . .

Wearing my writer's hat I've spoken to so many groups
that I've lost count, and after we moved to Felbrigg
Chris too came into demand for his skills as a
raconteur. I confess I've plagiarised most of his stories,
both for my books and for my own talks since Felbrigg
has been added to my list of topics.

Quirky anecdotes of everyday happenings provide
good material. Concerning pheasant, for example . . .
They roam Norfolk's verdant verges, jay-walk on main
roads as if they've never even heard of the highway
code, scream at you from lonely hedgerows, and batter
through undergrowth frightening you to death when
you're taking a peaceful stroll in the woods. They will
walk if they must, break into a run when startled, and
in extremity even launch into flight, but only as a final
resort, and sometimes too late. At Felbrigg, in days
gone by, pheasants liked to perch in the ancient thuya
trees, using the fuzzy foliage as camouflage. Gamekeep-
ers approved this move; poachers had developed an
uncanny knack for knocking birds off more visible
perches by means of ball-bearings shot from catapults. I
must confess that we, too, bagged the odd pheasant,
though not with a catapult, and entirely by accident.

Honest, m'lud! Driving home at dusk one night, we hit something with a resounding thump and discovered it to be a female pheasant. She was beyond resuscitation; in fact she was half-skinned, practically oven-ready. We hung her up in the garage for a few days and then had her *au vin*. Later, a cock pheasant walking down the centre of a country lane suddenly turned the wrong way as we passed and, when we stopped the car, lay limp and lifeless by the roadside. Since he would only be torn to shreds by scavengers, or mangled to a pulp by other traffic, we popped him in the boot intending to give him a more fitting funeral (done to a turn wrapped in bacon, for instance). But as we drove Felbriggward something stirred behind us; something thudded and battered around inside the boot. It was sickening. Pulling into the next field gateway, Chris got out to put the poor bird out of its misery. It was too badly injured to go free and we doubted that the local vet would want to perform radical surgery. The incident turned my stomach and robbed me of all appetite for pheasant (I haven't touched it since), but Chris, being a country-raised boy, wrung its neck and still enjoyed eating it after suitable hanging time.

Audiences like to hear of the glamorous side of our Felbrigg days. Concert evenings, when the house was lit up and looked so alluring, when people came dressed in their best to listen to wonderful music and dine by candlelight. I helped serve the wine one evening and was having trouble opening a fresh bottle until someone pointed out that I had my hand wrapped round the wings of the corkscrew so it couldn't possibly work as it ought. And there was the time in spring when the concert-goers arrived by daylight and departed after dark. They parked their cars in the front courtyard and one man, returning to his hired vehicle, couldn't find the switch that would turn on his lights. Chris had finished closing down and was about to join Joan and me in the kitchen for his first glass of wine that evening when he heard someone hammering on the big front door. Outside, the stranded visitor looked sheepish. "I don't know how to switch on my car lights. Would you believe it . . . I only hired the car today. I've had no reason to use the lights until now, and it's so dark out here I can't see a thing." Problem solved with the aid of a torch.

In snowy periods Felbrigg estate resembles the fairy-tale realm of the Ice Queen. At such a time, the Prince of Wales dropped in quite informally one Sunday afternoon, giving us another memorable occasion that people like to hear about. (See *Dry Rot and Daffodils* for the full story.) At Christmas, we held the local writers' meeting in our upstairs sitting room, reading ghost stories beside the huge tree whose welcoming lights are still remembered by many Christmas shoppers; and on Christmas Eve we heard singing outside in the front courtyard and looked out to see our neighbours and some friends and children from the village grouped round with lanterns gleaming. It was a magical moment that brought the past vividly to life; just so must local folk have come carolling for the squire and his family. They serenaded us sweetly before inviting us round to the Retreat for hot punch and mince pies. We shall always treasure such memories, and delight in sharing them with anyone who will listen.

Invited to speak to some ladies of the WI in Aylsham, Chris went along not realising that it was to be a group meeting of members from several institutes. Approaching the door at the side of the hall, he caught a glimpse of twenty or thirty ladies and a few empty chairs. Fine, he'd faced that many before. Only when he walked in did he realise that what he had seen were the few rows at the back of what proved to be a large hall seething with well over a hundred women, all chattering like starlings, with a row of others arranged on the stage. And he the only male in sight. He survived intact, cossetted half to death by all the attention.

One of his most memorable speaking occasions was a Christmas dinner held in the historic town hall of King's Lynn, a magnificent medieval building of chequered flint, where we dined in the great hall as guests of the King's Lynn National Trust Centre. Chris had been invited to reply, on behalf of the Trust, to a toast proposed by Henry Head, managing director of Norfolk Lavender. Henry was an old acquaintance of ours and it was good to meet him and his wife again, along with many old friends among the National Trust members. During Henry's talk, Chris realised he needed to make some changes to his own remarks, so he scribbled on his cards and added a few topical jokes and anecdotes, including one about Christmas puddings. (Trust members may recall the year that something went wrong with the National Trust's special Christmas puddings and they had all been recalled because some had gone mouldy through being packed before they were entirely cold.) Nearly everyone in the hall had heard this story, so when Chris told them he had a car-load of Christmas puddings that he was prepared to sell for a song, they all laughed. Except for the dear old lady who came up to him afterwards and eagerly enquired, "May I have one of those puddings you've got for sale?"

Every day at Felbrigg provided an extra anecdote, and whenever we return or meet old Felbrigg friends they have more tales to tell. An electric buggy has been added to the Hall's facilities for the disabled, augmenting the more usual wheelchairs; one family availed themselves of it for their elderly father only to return some time later with son scarlet-faced with exertion and fury. "I've had to push the darn thing, with my father still in it, all the way back from the gardens. Nearly creased myself. If you're going to lend these things out you might at least see that the battery's properly charged." Turned out the battery was fine — the problem was they had the buggy in reverse gear.

When a new garden opened with much drum-beating and arrival of panjandrums, it was red faces all round when the regional director realised his organiser had forgotten to invite the press! And prior to another prestigious occasion one of the bosses suggested that some flags might be appropriate. He had in mind a couple of National Trust standards on flagpoles, but he arrived to find the gracious historic property draped like a village fête in fluttering bunting. "But, sir, you said you wanted flags."

Tea rooms and restaurants inevitably add to the story-fund. A lady at the self-service counter ordered three cups of tea and then proceeded to tip the tea out and down the drain because, "The cups don't match the saucers. I want them matching." (They were all blue and white, just slightly different in pattern.)

Then a gentleman came to enquire if the crab was real. Well, of course it was — local Cromer crab, fresh that day. "But my wife's sandwich has got some sort of brown stuff in it, like potted meat," said he. Evidently he didn't realise that crab has brown flesh as well as pink.

Another chap bought a smoked salmon and cream cheese roulade and, after sampling it, called Joan over to inform her that the salmon wasn't cooked. "It's smoked salmon," she pointed out. "It comes like that."

"It's not properly cooked!" the man insisted. "Look, it's all slimy."

And what can one make of the couple who came into the Park Restaurant, sat down and took their time over consulting the menu. When the waitress returned for their order, they looked at her blankly. "We want to see the food first."

"We cook it to order," said the waitress.

The customers didn't understand this regime. "We always like to see it before we choose." Did they usually eat only in canteen-style self-service places? Heaven knows. People are a source of constant amazement.

Since we left Felbrigg, Chris has stopped giving formal talks, though his talent to amuse has come in useful in his post-retirement involvement with the

Sedgeford Historical and Archaeological Research Project (SHARP). His role as a director and supervisor, with special responsibility for media and visitors, includes acting as a tour guide to people visiting the dig, which is in operation for several weeks every summer.

Highlights from my own speaking diary have included a charity lunch at a sailing club near Wroxham, for which my reward was a day's boating on the Broads; an overnight visit to Birmingham to speak to the Seventieth Anniversary Dinner of the Soroptimist International in the glamorous setting of the city's famous Botanical Gardens; and a most amazing evening at a dinner held by the National Trust Centre in Solihull, to celebrate both the centre's golden jubilee and the National Trust's centenary year. That was a fabulous occasion, and horribly nerve-wracking to be the guest speaker in a vast room full of evening-dressed National Trust notables and members. We sat down to dinner at eight o'clock, with so many people to be served that we at the main table had finished our starters by the time the last of the 300-odd guests had been served. The waiters didn't start to clear until everyone had finished, and since one or two were very, very slow eaters (or great talkers!) each course took an age. When we finally finished eating we had the toasts — half a dozen of them: to the Queen; to the National Trust; to the Solihull Centre ... This being an extra-special, once-in-a-hundred-years occasion, each toast-proposer was introduced formally by a few words from the chairman, and then the toast-proposer him- or herself made another speech. Around the room many wine-heavy eyelids were drooping and heads jerked suddenly as another nodder-off woke with a start. Finally, the waiters brought round coffee and we were allowed a comfort break before the main event of the evening — my talk.

I mingled anonymously with the crowd inside the sumptuous ladies' powder room, and in the privacy of the WC I sneaked a look at my watch. It was already half past eleven, and I had been asked to speak for forty minutes! Just then, a voice outside said clearly, "I hope the speaker's not going to drone on too long, I was hoping to be home by midnight."

Back at the table, I asked my congenial host, the chairman, whether I should cut the talk short, it being so late. "No, not at all!" said he. "You've prepared forty minutes. You give 'em forty minutes."

So I did. As far as I could see, no one actually fell asleep before I finished. Bless you, Solihull, it was a magical, memorable night.

Media moments

In a lobby somewhere high in the honeycomb of corridors and rooms that comprise Broadcasting House, Chris and I sat waiting to be called for our scheduled interview on Radio 5. We were to be on air with DJ Johnny Walker, talking about Felbrigg on the publication of my book *Dry Rot and Daffodils*. I felt a bit nervous, awed by our surroundings. We were guests at BBC Radio! What excitement! People came and went about mysterious errands, and every few minutes a female voice from the tannoy pleaded plaintively, "Is Nina Mischow in the building yet? If anyone sees Nina Mischow, will you please tell her there's a message for her? Ask her to contact reception, will you? Please?"

TV viewers who, way back when, watched the talent show *New Faces* will remember Nina Mischow. Her acerbic tongue made the programme such compulsive viewing that years later she's still remembered as the panellist you either loved or hated. Chris tended to the latter view. Or so he claimed.

At last we were called into the studio, where Johnny Walker soon put us at our ease and we began to record the interview, telling tales of ghostly happenings, hilarious mishaps, and hard work, for fifteen minutes without any retakes. Not bad. Best of all, Johnny mentioned the book more than once and asked me to repeat its title, publisher and price. Available from all good bookshops. Naturally.

"Well, thanks very much." Our host rose from behind his console.

"We understand you're expecting Nina Mischow," said Chris.

"Yes, that's right," Johnny replied. "She should have been here by now, but she's been delayed."

"So we gathered," said Chris. "Oh, that woman! Wasn't she horrible to those poor people on *New Faces*? I'd like to punch her in the nose."

"You're not alone!" Johnny laughed and, opening the studio door, he went out into the lobby ahead of us. To my horror, I heard him cry, "Ah, Nina! You're here at last . . . There's a chap here who'd like to punch you in the nose!"

Utterly unabashed, my errant knight marched straight to where Ms Mischow was staring, wide-eyed with surprise, over the back of a red leather settee. "Just a joke," he cried. "It's wonderful to meet you, Nina. How are you?"

And as she rose bemusedly to her feet he grabbed her. And planted a kiss on her cheek. The creep!

He copes far better than I do in such situations. He has the knack of thinking on his feet, while I come up with exactly the right response about half an hour too late. Some years ago, when the BBC's lunchtime magazine show *Daytime Live* was broadcast from the foyer at the Pebble Mill studios in Birmingham, we were invited to appear and do an interview to remind viewers that National Trust properties would be opening the following weekend. This being the BBC we were asked not to mention that my new book on Felbrigg had just come out, though in fact that must have been their reason for inviting us. Why else did they choose us and not some more illustrious National Trust spokesman? "We know you interview well" didn't really explain it.

Since we had been told to be at the studios by nine a.m., the BBC had booked us into a hotel for dinner, bed and breakfast the night before. Chris asked one of the porters if it was far to the Pebble Mill

169

studios and the porter said, "Oh, yes, sir, it's quite a way. It'll take you a good while to get there." So we rose early, breakfasted, and booked out just before eight thirty, giving ourselves half an hour to find the studios. We'd driven barely half a mile before we came upon Pebble Mill Road, so we arrived in exceptionally good time, especially as we discovered we hadn't been expected until ten o'clock anyway. We apologised and said we'd be happy to wait, but the friendly girl on reception said, "No problem. I'll ring through and let them know you're here."

As we sat waiting, arrays of TV monitors relayed silent text messages. We were startled when our own names appeared: "Chris and Mary Mackie have arrived at the studio". Someone soon came to escort us to the hospitality suite, where we found an ample supply of comfortable sofas, coffee and tea facilities, snacks . . . and yet more TV screens letting everyone know what was happening: "Richard Cendal, Ed Watts and skipping children have arrived . . . Judi is in the building . . ." Someone came and took us to be made beautiful for the cameras. This entailed a light dusting of powder and a combing of hair, not the full pancake and eyelashes (more's the pity; I'd looked forward to seeing how they did "proper" make-up). "Chris and Mary Mackie have gone for make-up . . ." we read on all the monitors.

"I'm terrified to go to the loo in case they announce that, too," Chris muttered.

Back in the hospitality room we found a team of American children wolfing down the food as if they were starving, while their coaches Richard and Ed discussed the pros and cons of demonstrating their innovative methods of skipping and tumbling out in the garden as planned, even though the weather had turned foul. Despite the cold weather they did eventually perform in the garden in the middle of the building. "Barbara Hulaniki has arrived," the monitors silently announced as a thin and elegant woman in black joined us — Ms Hulaniki founded the Biba fashion empire that became so famous in the sixties. She stayed quietly in a corner away from the rest of us, though I gained the impression this was more from shyness than aloofness.

Eventually we were taken to the main foyer to be fitted with tiny clip-on microphones, which were then plugged in via connectors in the sofa so that we could do sound checks and rehearse camera angles. The show was transmitted from the big, airy foyer, with windows in the background looking out towards the road, and soon the audience would be coming to take their places on a raised bank of seating to one side. I was horribly nervous, but the technicalities intrigued Chris: one of the autocues kept going wrong, and half a dozen people poked about trying to correct it. What appeared to be pillars supporting the ceiling proved to be conduits containing cables and electronic wizardry.

Having been unplugged from the sound equipment, we were sent back to "hostility" (as Terry Wogan calls it). Chris felt restless and went off on walkabout, pausing to watch a girl typing words for those ubiquitous screens. Further along the lobby he came across a

171

group of people who proved to be the prospective audience, and as he turned back he met a well-known actor marching up and down in a hyper-charged state of nervous distress.

"Are you all right?" Chris asked.

"I've got to do a live broadcast," fretted the star.

"Does that worry you?"

"Of course it does, man! Don't you understand — it's going out live. LIVE!"

This mystified Chris, who is maddeningly calm when confronted by mikes and cameras. It's only when he has to ACT that he becomes a gibbering wreck.

Shortly before going on air we met Judi Spiers, the presenter who was to interview us, and as we chatted Chris told her about a school party who had come to visit Felbrigg. He had pointed out to them a fine example of a commode, only to discover that they didn't understand what that was; so he took off the lid to let them see the porcelain pot inside, and sat astride it to demonstrate, only to realise later that his zip had been unfastened. Judi found this tale very entertaining, however Chris did ask her not to mention it during the broadcast for fear it might be misconstrued. Of course, mention it was exactly what she did, having got us on the interview sofa, tethered by microphone leads: "I understand there was an embarrassing incident . . ." He wagged his finger at her: "I asked you not to mention that!" We were live on air, so they couldn't edit it out.

I might as well not have been there. Judi hardly even looked at me, but talked across me to Chris, laughing and flirting, and he responded with humorous anecdotes. When the spot ended and I realised my book had not merited even a passing reference I was furious — the chance of a lifetime ruined! I fumed most of the way home, while Chris was on a high.

He gets involved with glamorous women nearly every time we have these important interviews. Nina Mischow, Judi Spiers ... on another occasion at Broadcasting House he met and fell for actress Celia Imrie ("Oh, it's my friend Celia," he now cries whenever she appears on our TV). At the time I was having a preliminary chat in the *Woman's Hour* studio with Jenni Murray, who snapped, "Oh, why are people always so nervous?", which really helped to put me at ease!

Visiting the studios of Sky TV for what turned out to be a very enjoyable half hour interview with Jenny Hanley and Tony Blackburn, we were talking about one of the illustrations in the book, a line drawing showing Chris answering the front door of Felbrigg Hall in a striped shortie bathrobe. "Nice legs!" Jenny commented.

"Yours aren't bad, either," Chris returned, quick as light.

Regarding that line-drawing, illustrator Sue Hellard did spend a couple of days following us round and making sketches. But since, as far as I know, she never actually saw Chris in his bathrobe, I've always wondered how she managed to portray his legs with such uncanny accuracy.

Such moments were exciting, but they were only interludes. Back at Felbrigg, real life waited.

The Book Room

The Book Room, which has in its time been a bedroom, a sitting room and, for the last squire, a study, in the 1970s became part of the administrator's flat. However, after Robert and Eve retired its use altered again when it was turned into a display room for some of Mr Ketton-Cremer's own collection of books and pictures. The squire left books all over the house, in cupboards and drawers as well as on his numerous bookshelves; most of them are now lodged with the University of East Anglia, forming the Ketton-Cremer Collection, but a good many volumes from his personal working library remain at the house. They may not be as old as the books in the adjoining Library, but they are of interest because of their connection with the squire. Some provided him with research material; some were written by friends of his; others show his taste in leisure reading. To show off these books, new glass-fronted bookpresses were commissioned from Dan Windham who, by a pleasant coincidence, has family connections with the Felbrigg Windhams.

During the winter before the Book Room opened, the Trust needed to decide which pictures should adorn the walls. Chris's sorting out of the attics had yielded quite a selection of art works, some of which had personal association with the squire, including some modern ones by local artists whom he had liked to encourage. These pictures were brought down and

174

propped round the room, ready for the selection committee to make their choice.

On the appointed day, Lady Harrod, a member of the Trust's regional committee for East Anglia and a friend of Felbrigg's late squire, came along in company with the regional director and the historic buildings representative. Chris left them in the Book Room to deliberate while he went about his usual work, returning later to offer hot drinks to alleviate Felbrigg's winter chill. As he entered the room he sensed an atmosphere of indecision. "Chris . . . what do you think should be hung in here?"

The question disconcerted him as he had never expected to be asked to add his two-penn'orth to the debate. What had they been arguing about exactly, and which way did they hope his verdict would go? Impossible to tell. However, as always where Felbrigg was concerned, he knew exactly what he believed would be the right approach. "Apart from that unfinished portrait in the Great Hall, Mr Ketton-Cremer isn't particularly commemorated anywhere. I think it would be appropriate, in this room, to have some pictures that are connected with him in a personal way." Some of the paintings might not be of great artistic merit, but they were relevant because of their links with Mr Ketton-Cremer's life and interests. One shows his house at Plymouth; another, painted by John Sell Cotman, is of the squire's mother's house at Metton, not far from Felbrigg. There are photographs too — one shows the squire and his brother, Dick, with other members of the Roman Camp Bowls Club. Since the squire liked to support modern artists Chris thought it might be appropriate also to include a couple of rather good examples from local twentieth-century painters — one of an old Norfolk church, the other an evocative, atmospheric study of Norfolk reeds in which you can almost hear the wind blowing across the Broads. Having stated his case, Chris gathered with some relief that he must have reiterated what Lady Harrod had been saying, and her opinion prevailed.

At first they planned to call this addition to the tour by the rather grandiose title "the Muniment Room", but it became popularly known as the Book Room and, happily, that name has stuck. Central in the room stand glass-topped display cases in which the Trust mounts exhibitions of items such as books with their pages open to show particular pictures or writings, or small valuable objects which could not safely be left on open display. Another bonus is the small solar, directly above the main front porch, which leads off the book room and from where you may glimpse the view across the park. If you stand outside and study the front of the house, you'll see that sandwiched between the porch and the solar are another set of windows, giving light to a room somewhat squatter than the solar but with the same view. That too used to be part of the administrator's flat and was where I had my desk; so when you're in the Book Room and climb the couple of steps to the solar to look at the panorama of the park, you'll see the view I had. Glorious, isn't it? Though it's perhaps just as well that the windows are set quite high, so when seated at my desk I could see only the sky. If

I'd been able to see the park and the visitors coming and going I might have spent so much time gazing that I would never have done any work.

As you leave the solar to return to the Library, have a good look at the jib door through which you pass, and on your way out see if you can see the join where its twin stands next to the main Library door. You may remember I mentioned that this jib door opens into a cupboard. In fact, the swing of the door leaves only room in the corner for the chamber pot which used to be kept there for the convenience of whoever happened to need it.

CHAPTER
TEN

Time to move on

Our last few years at Felbrigg blended both sorrow and joy. Our personal lives were shadowed by the deaths of first Shirley and then my father; we also lost one or two of the close friends we had made in north Norfolk. But happier days occurred too — one in Peterborough, when Kevin married Alison; another in Nottingham when Andy was awarded his Ph.D.; a windy day at RAF Cranwell — a passing-out parade followed by a ball, when we all celebrated Kevin's commissioning as an officer of the Princess Mary's Royal Air Force Nursing Service; and a farewell supper before Andy left to spend an eventful year working in Japan. It brought home to us the fact that Chris and I were becoming the older generation; perhaps it was time we thought about our future and what retirement would bring. Reluctantly, we decided that to secure our future we must leave Felbrigg.

Suffice to say that an opportunity arose and we took it. Despite many misgivings about leaving all the people who had grown so close — over the years the team had become more like an extended family — we moved to west Norfolk. It was a difficult period whose details are not relevant here, but in the end we did not regret the move. The time had come to let other people take the helm at Felbrigg Hall.

However, via our Felbrigg friends, and our own occasional visits, we keep in touch with events over in north Norfolk. "It's not the same," some sigh. "When you were here ... those were the best days." Well, of course they were — we're bound to think so. We were a team of friends and we watched Felbrigg expand and win many more visitors under our care; we had that lovely spacious flat; and, let's face it, we were all a bit younger and fitter in those halcyon days not so very long ago. But nothing stays the same for ever. New managers have new ideas, just as we did, and the National Trust continues to evolve to suit the times. It must do so if it's to survive to do the job for which it was formed.

Human beings come and go, but the place itself remains a constant, and so does the work, and the mad incidents. Not so long ago, one autumn Sunday when few visitors came and the daylight waned early, David cleared the house and secured the doors behind his room wardens, one room at a time. "Everyone gone?" he asked the Library steward. "All clear," came the reply. The steward departed down the main stairs, David locked the Library door and moved on into the west wing to secure the bedrooms. He didn't realise that, through in the Book Room, room steward Brian was still performing his final duties of covering the books and exhibition cabinets and unplugging lamps.

Noticing that everything had gone strangely quiet, Brian went into the Library and found it empty, then discovered the door locked. He banged. He shouted, "Help! Let me out!"

No answer.

He bethought himself of the connecting door between the Book Room and the flat, so returned to the shadowy Book Room and slipped the bolts. The door, of course, was bolted on the other side too, for security reasons. The evening was drawing in and the Library loomed with alarming grey shadows, reminding Brian that the ghost of William Windham III was supposed to haunt here. But from the window he could see people walking in the park. He waved at them frantically: "Up here, look. I'm locked in. Help!" People waved back happily.

Eventually, Brian hit on the idea of waving his keys, a sign which one passer-by understood, running off towards the house. A few minutes later, keys jangled in the Library lock. Saved!

Reprise on the roof

The releading project that Chris and I remember so well dealt with only the central part of the roof. Such work is expensive and has to be done in stages. But after we left, the Trust contracted builders to reroof the west wing, which contains the grandest rooms on the ground floor, the four best bedrooms, and above them a long row of attic rooms divided by wooden partition walls. As usual, the men started on the job in midwinter. They always seem to begin in January or

February, with a bare few weeks before opening. Why they can't start in November when the house first closes so that they have five months to complete the work is one of those impenetrable mysteries, like how you always manage to join the slowest queue in a supermarket?

At the time, new property manager David and his wife Helen had been resident at Felbrigg for less than three months. The roofing project proved to be their baptism of fire.

Before work could begin, the west wing had to be covered by a tin roof that would protect the fabric while the old roof was being replaced. Fine, except that it meant erecting a supporting scaffolding, and since the Trust, having regard for the old house's protection, decreed that the scaffolding must not be fixed to the walls, it had be made free-standing and weighted down by large concrete blocks. Also, because the west wing is so wide, owing to the corridors added by James Paine, the roofing-spans that would support the temporary tin roof would need to be extremely long and heavy. These monstrosities had to be bolted together on the ground and then somehow hoisted one by one to roof level, where they would be linked together to form an archway joining the two scaffolding walls.

This might have been relatively easy if an ordinary crane could have been used. But nothing at Felbrigg is ever straightforward. No large machine can be allowed into the gravelled, D-shaped front courtyard, whose surface is vulnerable because of the medieval undercroft and the water pipes beneath; nor could a crane be brought up to the west lawn because the ha-ha created a four-foot step that no machine could climb. So they had to hire a truly enormous crane that could swing the roofing-spans up while standing out in the pasture.

If you can imagine a vast stick insect twice the height of Felbrigg Hall, based on a great slab of machinery with ten gigantic wheels and four hydraulic legs that can be planted to give the whole thing stability, then you have some idea of what the machine looked like when erect. It was bright yellow, brand new and worth a cool two million pounds. Folded into slightly more manageable shape, this monster and its driver, embarking on their first proper job since leaving the manufacturer, camped overnight in a layby on the Aylsham bypass. From there, early next morning, the crane travelled the final few miles and eased through Felbrigg's Cromer gates with inches to spare, gouging up the verges with its huge wheels as it came. It finally rumbled slowly up to the Hall's ancient façade around seven in the morning.

Seeing this leviathan arrive, David went down to make sure the driver and the chief scaffolder knew exactly where to place the machine. The project team had spent hours agreeing the correct spot, so that the crane might have solid standing from where it could reach the far end of the west wing. Yes, the workmen had a copy of the plan; they knew exactly where to put the crane. Reassured, David went up to his flat for breakfast with Helen and later took a camera up to the attics, climbing out onto the leaded balcony behind the GLORIA DEO IN EXCELSIS balustrade.

"What I saw," he told us, "would have made Chris weep — except he was experienced enough to have expected this sort of disaster."

The crane driver had unilaterally decided that he could make his job easier by getting his mechanical dinosaur closer to the building than the plan indicated. What do project officers know about cranes, after all? So he had driven off the prepared track and was directing a JCB driver to position timber baulks to support the crane's four hydraulic legs. They had already placed two of these timbers, and as David arrived on the roof above, the crane driver was just lowering the third leg to mark the correct position for the third timber. The leg penetrated the turf — and a jet of water shot into the air. Felbrigg's first fountain! David recalled, "I was so shocked I didn't even take a picture — I just ran down the stairs like a hare."

The men had managed to plant the crane's massive foot right on top of the fire-hydrant stopcock, fracturing a six-inch water main which fed the Hall itself, several cottages and nearby Hall Farm.

With the usual run of Murphy's Law in these cases, Jim the well-experienced house manager was away, so it was up to new man David to cope, "And me less than three months in the job!" He tried making phone calls, but it was far too early for people to have started work. No answer from the regional estate yard at Blickling; no home phone number for the regional clerk of works; the buildings manager had moved house . . . Finally tracing the new number of the buildings manager, David spoke to him and was told to contact the water board's emergency number. He did so. The water board man logged into his database and, "Sorry, but you've got a private main. Our responsibility ends outside the estate at the stopcock and meter near Felbrigg woodyard. So it's your water, your pipe, your side of the meter. Your problem."

Asking Helen to report this to the buildings manager and ask what next, David went out to find the machine drivers, the scaffolders and sundry other workmen all standing around watching the gusher turn the pasture to mud. "I could see the crane, hired by the day, being bogged down for weeks, so I grabbed a shovel from the crane's toolkit and told them to dig channels to carry the water away into the ha-ha ditch, while I went to look for a decent spade. Helen came out to say she had Steve, the clerk of works, on the phone. What a relief! Steve pulled the right strings and fifteen minutes later (it does help if one of your neighbours happens to be a senior water board engineer!) the water was turned off. Meanwhile Helen had been round to all the neighbours and rung the farm: 'If you want tea today, fill up the kettle now.'"

Order was eventually restored and, one by one, the huge roof spans swung high into the air and were settled into place. The temporary roof didn't cover the entire wing, though. The far end, over the Chinese Bedroom, had to be protected by a tent of canvas. Which was fine until the weekend when a deluge drenched that part of Norfolk. Soaked through, the canvas sagged and turned into a handy receptacle where a puddle soon collected. As the downpour continued, the puddle deepened to a pool. The canvas stretched under the weight. A small hole opened up, letting the water dribble through . . .

During his routine morning walkabout, David found water dripping. He investigated and, discovering the cause of the flood, went down to the office to phone the contractor's emergency team.

This time house manager Jim was at home, with some friends staying over. When they heard what was happening, they all went up to see what they could do to help (if you stay at Felbrigg you automatically qualify as a volunteer). Obviously the canvas had to be rejigged, raised into a tented shape so that the weather would slide off it. But first they had to dispose of that heavy load of water before the canvas split. If the water spilled over, heaven help the Chinese Bedroom — the precious wallpaper would be ruined (again!). Then practical Jim had a brainwave: "Syphon. Hosepipe . . ." David hastened down to the gardeners' shed and sliced eight feet off the end of a garden hose. "You might have made it a bit longer!" said Jim, but he managed. One end of the hose in the water, suck at the other . . . up came the water and he let it gush harmlessly over the side of the house.

Fortunately the builders had left enough timber lying around for the men to make a frame to support the canvas. They had cleaned themselves up and enjoyed a cup of coffee by the time the contractor's emergency team arrived three hours later.

As if that were not enough, the work on the roof revealed the true state of the bay at the west end of the old Jacobean hall. For years we had known something was wrong. The west end of the Library had developed cracks, and the frame of the attic window above it had gone trapezoid. Now, to their horror, the workmen discovered that the bay, added on by Samwell to improve the proportion of the house when he built the west wing extension, was no longer attached to the main building. Its pinnings had all broken, rotted or corroded, and the bay was simply leaning there from habit, as if it hadn't yet realised it was free to fall. Had it gone down, it would have left a wide open view and plenty of fresh air available through gaping holes at the end of the Library and the Great Hall.

Securing the uppermost parts of the bay, working from above, took the whole winter, mainly because there was space for only one man to work, lying horizontally as he picked out all the bits of old, rotten beam, and threaded in rods of stainless steel.

One day the builder doing this work came knocking on the office door looking rather sheepish. "I'm sorry, but, erm . . . I'm afraid I've made a bit of a hole in the Library ceiling."

David and Jim both went rushing up to take stock of the damage, but to everyone's surprise there was no sign of any hole in the Library ceiling.

"Well, there's certainly a hole up where I'm working," said the builder. "Come out and have a look."

Up on the roof they saw that there was indeed a hole. But what lay below it, if not the Library? They enlarged it a little, just enough to get a couple of fingers in, enough to feel the shape of some decorative plasterwork. Wonderful! What they had stumbled upon was a void, an empty space left behind the bookcases which had been built into the Library bay. Not even the architects had realised how big that void was. Not only did it still have some of its original decorative plaster mouldings but evidence inside it proved that, not so very long ago, someone — perhaps the last squire, or his father — had got rid of the glazed window that had long been blanked off there. The gap left by the removal of the window had been bricked up from inside the void, as was clear from the neat pointing of the mortar on most of the area. The bricklayer had evidently left a hole just large enough for him to climb out before he completed the work from outside. Further inspection revealed that the void contained a strange piece of flat, rough timber. This mystified the experts until they realised that those earlier builders had forgotten to remove a final plank from inside the void. There it had remained, bricked in for eighty years.

The French have a saying which translates as "the more things change, the more they stay the same". At Felbrigg it couldn't be more apt.

Foot-and-mouth disease

Only a few days after our visit in February 2001, when we saw the Library wrapped in blue polythene and filled with scaffolding, news of the first outbreaks of foot-and-mouth disease (FMD) began to circulate across Britain. Farmers set footbaths at strategic points and laid absorbent mats soaked with disinfectant across entryways as whole areas of countryside, including many National Trust sites, were declared out of bounds, under strict quarantine. Although National Trust houses were still closed for the winter, at some, like Felbrigg, where the shop and restaurant open at weekends all year round, the ban imposed a complete shutdown. The attics and cellars tours, planned for March, were cancelled.

Many areas of Britain began to feel the effects as hotels lost business, tourist attractions echoed with emptiness and the takings in rural shops and pubs dropped to alarming levels. Clearly, a compromise was called for. On 23 March, in response to the nationwide drive to ease the impact on tourism, the National Trust began a rolling programme for opening selected properties, their golden rule being that animals and visitors must be kept apart, with no public access anywhere near areas with livestock or deer. Property managers were instructed to create fenced-off buffer zones, to require dog-walkers to keep their pets on short leads, to maintain ministry-approved disinfectant regimes and to make sure that local farmers and other residents understood and were happy with the measures being taken.

Official opening day for properties that year should have been Saturday 31 March. Many houses did manage to open as planned and by Easter weekend (with Good Friday falling on 13 April, a doubly bad date for the superstitious) around 200 National Trust sites were available to visitors around the country, in addition to 100 holiday cottages. Most of them were subject to severe restrictions and many country walks were closed. Although Norfolk remained mercifully free of FMD, properties here maintained rigorous preventative precautions.

In the west of Norfolk, our nearest property, Oxborough Hall, opened as planned on 31 March. Hearing that Joan and her catering team had been seconded from Felbrigg because of some crisis in Oxborough's catering arrangements, Chris and I drove over to have lunch there during the first week. Inevitably, it was Joan's day off — the only free day she had during that hectic six weeks when she and her staff travelled across half the county every day, as she later told us. Typical. However, the trip did give us a chance to see FMD precautions in action. Absorbent mats doused in disinfectant lay waiting to bathe the wheels of cars at the entry to Oxborough's driveway, with more squishy mats for visitors to walk over near the gatehouse. Oxborough has no livestock, but even so only the moated house, its shop, restaurant and surrounding formal garden were open; woodlands, meadows and wilderness remained closed because of the risk to roaming wild deer.

Meanwhile over at Felbrigg, where sheep had been wandering freely across the driveway and cattle grazed within petting reach of visitors, the whole estate remained off limits, with no sign of its reopening. I telephoned David to see what was happening and, since we lived in an FMD-free area, he invited us over, advising us to take the back way from the Cromer road, via Lion's Mouth and Sexton's Lodge. "Then drive straight in," he concluded. "Next Thursday? Fine. See you then."

It was 5 April, the sky cold and overcast, the woods still dormant in that wet, chilly spring. As we travelled from Heacham towards Cromer we saw much evidence of FMD precautions, with warning notices in all the roadside copses, farm driveways barred and straw bales protecting field gates.

From the main road between Sheringham and Cromer a little lane curls and twists down through the Lion's Mouth, tunnelling among tall trees which in summer are a leafy delight. There are many different theories about the reason for the name Lion's Mouth, my own favourite being that the little valley resembles a huge mouth, floored by reddish dried leaves and with tall thin, silvery-barked trees growing through like long sharp teeth. As we drove through on that April day the effect was particularly striking, the only greenery being on scrubby dark-leaved evergreens and in the straggling underbrush and weeds poking through blankets of rusty leaves from last autumn. It was all achingly familiar, except for the rash of notices, printed on red paper and posted on trees and stakes every few yards through the woods: "All public rights of way across agricultural and forestry land are closed during the current foot-and-mouth crisis" said some, while others demanded, "Attention, foot-and-mouth precautions. This property is now closed to visitors until further notice".

On the tall brick pillars beside Sexton's Lodge, notices directed "Deliveries this way", but warned "Authorised visitors only". Well, we were authorised, having the property manager's permission, but evidently David's cheerful instruction to "drive straight through" had not been meant literally. A few yards along the drive, just beyond the lodge, thick stakes had been hammered into the ground with a rope slung between them and strung with warning flags, and beside this barrier stood a round tub holding a few gallons of disinfectant. After much rain everything was thick with mud and, when I climbed out to unhook the rope, dunk my boots and let Chris drive through, I discovered the rope had been left to trail on the ground during comings and going of vehicles and was soaked with mud that coated my hands. Ah well . . . I rehooked it and joined Chris in the car. Just beyond the rope barrier we drove through a thick layer of straw heavily doused with more disinfectant. The smell of it came strongly as we followed the curving drive along its undulating way between fields, past picnic areas in the woods, and over a final rise where the house appeared, the west front with its apron of lawns beyond the ha-ha, the Orangery off to the left among the trees of the garden. Bright yellow daffodils starred the grass, but beyond them most of the Hall's shutters were drawn, making the windows blank and grey like sleeping eyes. But, as we know, that slumbrous air is deceptive and this year was no different — behind the unruffled façade three major projects were in progress.

Seen through a veil of chilly April mist, cattle grazed in the distance towards the lake, and as we passed the Hall we saw sheep in the church pasture. Horrible to think of them all having to be killed if the disease came this way. How empty the pastures would seem without them. A surprising number of cars stood on the hard standing in the car park. They belonged to cleaners and workmen, and to volunteers who were working in the Library; they had parked in the public area because the staff-and-tenants car park was hazardous with renovation work going on in the scaffolding-shrouded stable yard. As we left our own car with the rest, the sheep in the church pasture started moving towards us, curious about new arrivals and evidently unaware of the dangers of contact with humans. David later asked us if our car had a diesel engine, as the sheep had come to understand that the sound of a diesel engine probably meant food!

It had been raining almost non-stop for weeks and the grass courtyard was even stickier with thick mud than it had been in February. Hand-made notices warned that it was very slippery. We rang the bell, announced ourselves, and soon David appeared to usher us inside and up to his office.

The desk is in a different place; it has acquired more technology, and there's a secretary installed in an outer office which in our time was a store room. Otherwise little has changed. Turning to his computer screen, David summoned up the latest bulletin on the National Trust website, which announced that some of the stricter rules guarding properties were to be relaxed, allowing more places to open where livestock was well separated from visitor areas. In East Anglia these included Ickworth and Wimpole (though not Wimpole Rare Breed Farm, for obvious reasons).

"And not Felbrigg, either," I observed.

"No, not yet," said David. "Not with our sheep and cattle so close to public areas. Before we can open to the public we've got to erect a thousand metres of extra fencing. All deliveries are being directed round by the woodyard, where their wheels are sprayed with disinfectant before they come up to the house."

Desperate as the situation was, in Norfolk the enforced delay in opening did reveal a positive side. Rather than sitting idle with Felbrigg closed, Joan and her team had been able to fill the catering gap at Oxborough Hall, while shop manager Heather had stepped in to manage Blickling's shop when an unexpected resignation left the post vacant. At Felbrigg itself, belated opening had given three different teams of workmen a little more breathing space to finish their projects before visitors began to arrive. One of the teams was in the house, another working above the restaurant, the third busy on the drive.

Inside the Hall, men had been busy for weeks configuring three separate fire-proof blocks, so that if fire breaks out in one area it should not spread to other parts of the house. This compartmentalisation entailed, among many other things, strengthening the protection around a void which comes up from the Morning Room to become a deep cupboard in what was once our kitchen, creating another fire hazard point. They had also thickened the wall of what we called our "brown room", which lies next to the office. David showed us the room stripped to basics with new plaster drying on the walls. "They've had that floor up, too, so fire can't spread from the houseman's flat to this front part." To help seal off each area of the house, new doors have been fitted with special protection round their hinges, all have been routed and edged with a special strip designed to expand with heat in the event of a fire, to stop air from getting through, and special fire-resistant paint has been applied. As you may imagine, this complicated job took up much of the winter.

Other contractors were restructuring the "base camp" above the restaurant, turning it into holiday accommodation. For many years these rooms were used as a base for teams of voluntary workers, but restrictions and tightened safety rules have severely limited the scope and duration of Acorn Camps, making the dormitories and central living block redundant for most of the year. Now one dormitory will provide a studio flat for a couple, and the main area will accommodate a family. Both will add to the little clutch of holiday properties scattered about the estate. You might even be able to spend a week in Sexton's Lodge, which has been renovated since Ted's retirement. He had always said it was a bit damp, but being Ted he "hadn't liked to bother the Trust" about it. On inspection, his old home turned out to need £30,000 worth of underpinning; so now it's damp-free and highly desirable. Felbrigg's a lovely spot for a quiet holiday. Do write and enquire.

On the main drive, yet another merry band of men were widening the carriageway, which was why David had warned us to come in via the back gates. A one-way system had been in operation on the narrow drive for many years, with cars arriving via the Cromer gates, driving through to the car park and then on past the house and through the woods to leave by the Sexton's Gate and the Lion's Mouth. But some visitors still decided they didn't want to drive out via the narrow and twisting Lion's Mouth lane, so they ignored the signs and drove out by the in way.

The inevitable encounters with incoming traffic forced at least one of the vehicles involved to drive onto the verge, chewing up the grass. So the Trust decided to create some passing places. Owing to the foul, wet winter and equally inclement spring, the work had been delayed until the end of March and, had the Hall opened on time, it would have impeded the flow of visitors. FMD restrictions called for estate workers to be permanently stationed at the Cromer gates, disinfectant sprays at the ready to douse every contractor's vehicle that came past. However, hopefully by the time the Hall opened the drive would be clear, with the benefit of new passing places and new fences to keep the sheep and cows at a safe distance. So David counted his blessings, few as they were.

CHAPTER
ELEVEN

A never-ending story

During our visit in April 2001, David again took us to the Library and proudly displayed the room returned to its usual glory, complete with latticework ceiling. That job, at least, had been finished well before opening. However, in a house like Felbrigg short breaks between projects are all one can hope for. Every day reveals new jobs to be tackled, sometimes urgently, sometimes simply to add to the list of "things to do when time and money allow".

One long-standing problem has been the damp that keeps appearing on the floor of the Great Hall. Long before Chris and I became residents, the Trust drilled exploratory holes under the Great Hall and found only a void infilled with rubble. Later, during our tenure, the irreplaceable carpet had to be raised for a while to let it dry out. But still that void is giving trouble. In 2001 they had an area of the carpet lifted on boards in an effort to stop the rot, but mould began growing on the back of the boards. Perhaps water is seeping into that rubble-filled void. The stone floor itself is laid on timbers and there's no easy way of telling whether they're rotten (unless they collapse!). In hope of solving this problem once and for all, new investigations have been ordered.

To begin with, two structural engineers were called in — at different times — to study the floor. As it happened, each of them arrived after a period of rain. "One said the place would fall down tomorrow," David said, adding drily, "it didn't, of course. The other was more sensible. The theory is that perhaps a new drain was put in, and that it may have broken through a layer of puddled clay that was serving as a damp course, so the water's seeping in now, which it didn't do before. It will have to be done, though it could turn into a huge job."

"So what else is new?" Chris replied with empathy, and they swapped horror stories of dry rot, woodworm, damp, deathwatch beetle . . . not to mention the extra problems created by human error.

One incident that still gives Chris the horrors came soon after the new restaurant had been completed. The place was superb, spacious and gleaming, with all the most up-to-date machinery and gadgets, steel freezers, chillers and vast ovens, production-line dishwashing facilities and the latest type of seamless, space-age, non-slip flooring, ideal for cleaning and hygiene purposes. Sealed underfloor heating promised a perfect working environment both winter and summer, and to protect the hidden pipes prominent notices cautioned "Do not drill into this floor". So what did a workman do when he came to fix a working unit? You've guessed it — drilled through the floor, straight into one of the sealed-unit heating pipes. "Another fine mess you've gotten us into, Stanley . . ."

David can tell a dozen similar stories of his own.

During the enforced lay-off because of FMD one of David's main concerns was that his volunteers might lose heart and interest and find something else to do with their spare time. "They're all highly loyal and understanding, but nobody wants to sit twiddling their thumbs. If this goes on too long, I fear some of them may not come back, and without volunteers we couldn't operate."

Happily, his fears proved groundless. On 5 May, with FMD still being kept at bay in East Anglia, Felbrigg Hall belatedly opened to the public and the faithful volunteers resumed their posts. For everyone, however, severe restrictions remained in force. All of the walks — in the woods, through the park and around the lake — were out of bounds. Warning tapes confined visitors to prescribed areas; house and gardens only at first.

Another set of restrictions, and more yards of plastic tape, kept people clear of the scaffolding which nested the restaurant, above which builders were still at work on the former base camp. Half of the stable yard was a prohibited area, roped off with red and white tape and scaffold-pole fencing, leaving the entry to the shop clear but cutting off the most obvious route to the restaurant and lavatories. Notices by the gates directed visitors round, via an open passageway, to the toilet block and the adjoining stable through which they could gain access to the restaurant.

There are, however, always a few people who don't notice notices — or perhaps they think such warnings apply only to others. Joan and her staff, serving lunches, were startled when a lady came banging on the windows, highly distressed to find herself trapped in a jungle of scaffolding and plastic hazard tape. In an attempt to follow the usual route to the toilets, she had for some reason climbed over the barriers and become disorientated amid the maze of scaffold poles. Joan had to rush to the rescue, smoothing ruffled nerves and leading the lady round by the well-marked temporary route.

Happily, on 23 June, to everyone's relief, all areas of Felbrigg were opened again, including the woodland walks, the lakeside walk and the way to the church. As always, of course, dogs must be kept on leads in fields with grazing animals; only the most irresponsible dog-owners let their pets off the lead around cows and sheep.

Chris and I returned to Felbrigg again at the end of June. It was a beautiful day, with a slight haze of sea-fret misting the distances. This time we drove in by the main entrance and saw for ourselves the new passing places under the trees. Behind new wire fences that kept them well back from the drive, shaggy sheep awaited the shears, standing hock-deep in rich green grass, while on the rise beyond Parsonage Lawn haymakers turned the slope to paler, yellower green dotted with square bales. Further on, behind yet more long stretches of new silver wire, cows and young calves browsed contentedly. A lovely sight.

At the end of the car park, notices read "No Exit" and we could see two new field gates barring the drive in front of the house. Even so, a car was parked there with a passenger out determinedly opening the first gate. The Trust has not imposed an absolute "no go" rule — not yet — but the gates are proving a deterrent and certainly they stop locals from zooming through using the drive as a short-cut. Eventually, if all goes to plan, all traffic will move in and out by the Cromer gates, leaving the front of the Hall and the woodland areas to the west reserved solely for pedestrians.

You can now enjoy the woods by following a paved footway, especially helpful for visitors in wheelchairs or pushing baby-buggies. It extends up to the top of the Victory V, around to Sexton's Lodge and back along the drive to where you can revel in the most splendid view of the house without having to move aside every few minutes to let cars come past. Less traffic means that the area to the west of the house is alive with squirrels and birds. It will also preserve what David calls the "boskiness" of the Lion's Mouth, a peaceful place meant for wildlife and walkers, not for cars.

Global warming

By the end of the year, the British countryside was once again open to all. Foot-and-mouth disease devastated many areas, threatening livelihoods in both the rural communities and the tourist industry. Thankfully, it did not spread into Norfolk and, as I write, here in East Anglia it has left no signs of its passing.

I only wish I could feel as confident about the changes being effected by global warming. If we do not soon stop depleting the ozone layer that protects the earth, we shall find our whole environment altering, and not for the better. The floods of the past few winters are a warning sign and those who scoff, "If the earth's getting warmer, why has it been so wet and cold this summer?" only show their ignorance. It will not be a simple case of the climate growing a degree or two warmer but otherwise everything staying the same: the changes of temperature will affect the winds, the oceans, the seasons, and every eco-system on the earth in ways we cannot hope to predict except to say that they will not be pleasant to live with. Already the changes have started: the past few years have seen too many freak winds, freak floods, droughts, mudslides, earthquakes and eruptions. It may not have affected Britain too badly as yet. No, not yet. But it's coming. As a grandmother, I fear what my grandchildren, and their children, may have to deal with.

The signs are already there, for those who will heed them. At Felbrigg, for instance . . . After my father died, my mother paid for a commemorative tree to be planted at Felbrigg in his name. The young oak was duly placed in a spot where we could see it from the kitchen window of our flat. It didn't appear to be growing too well and when my sister and I visited it a few years on it was still a sickly-looking sapling. In 2001, seeing that the tree had definitely died, I asked David about it and he kindly looked up his records. These revealed that my dad's tree had been replaced

202

three times but the new trees all refused to thrive. No wonder the droopy sapling never seemed to be growing any bigger!

Enquiries reveal that the same problem has been occurring across the estate, making foresters wonder how on earth the earlier Windhams managed to grow so many trees so successfully, raising great plantations of different types of tree to form their woods and coverts. During the last half of the last century, a puzzling change in the success-rate has occurred: trees planted by the late squire in 1953 to mark the coronation are struggling to thrive; others planted by the National Trust in 1977, to celebrate the Queen's silver jubilee, have hardly grown at all. Yes, the estate is exposed to cold north-easterlies, but the same has been true for centuries, and during much colder eras. So what can be the cause of this recent anomaly? If the difficulties are a result of global warming, then nature has been subtly registering climatic changes for some considerable time, and not only at Felbrigg.

On many great Norfolk estates foresters are trying out different methods of rearing young trees. Behind fenced cages across parks and pastureland, you'll see broad-leaf saplings planted inside a sheltering ring of young pines. But since the nurse trees are absorbing more than their share of water and nutrients, leaving the deciduous saplings both hungry and thirsty, this method may not prove viable. In other places foresters have planted parkland trees in large clumps so that they can shelter each other while they grow; in twenty years or so the clumps will be thinned out, leaving only the strongest and best to grow to maturity. In future the National Trust plans to grow commemorative trees this way — in clumps — to avoid the embarrassment of having individually-dedicated trees wither and die. Foresters may also try bringing acorns from further south, where the trees are acclimatised to drier conditions. This is a long-term problem which has been developing for decades. It will not be solved in a few months.

Other complications affecting the trees at Felbrigg have arisen because Hall Farm's new tenant, Graham, is going organic, which means he must grow his food crops from his own seed and do no chemical spraying on arable or pasture. The process takes seven years to reach completion. And this in turn means that the young trees across the pasture are struggling to grow amid fenced enclosures choked with grass and weeds which can't be sprayed with chemicals; neither is there room for a human being to get inside the cages to clear the ground by hand (assuming someone had the time to do it!).

Ever since man turned from hunting and gathering to farming, he has been changing the landscape around him. Nothing stays the same for ever. To those critics who complain that the Trust shouldn't cut down trees or erect fences or make any other of the numerous alterations which may become necessary — "Leave it as it is! Leave it natural!" — all I can say is, what's natural? Left to nature, Norfolk's clay soil areas bred dense forests, while its chalky ridges, including the area where Felbrigg Hall now stands, cloaked themselves in swathes of scrub and heath dotted with gorse which the ancient farmers set alight every spring so that tender fresh shoots would provide food for their livestock. Global warming may see Norfolk growing ever more lavender on its scrubby uplands, or we may face a future of sub-Arctic conditions if the melting ice-caps divert the Gulf Stream. Who knows?

Only one thing is sure — if we don't do something soon, it may be too late to prevent swingeing changes whose exact nature no one can predict. Ultimately, Earth will endure. Whether mankind will also survive is another question.

As to the more immediate future . . . Following modern business practices, the National Trust under its new director general Fiona Reynolds is streamlining itself, cutting down on bureaucracy at both head office and in the regions, and allowing properties more autonomy.

The eastern region is planning to introduce a fee for car parking at properties which at present make no charge. Under this scheme, National Trust members, who will still park for free, will have their visits registered, so the estate will benefit from member-credits awarded. Few people realise how much it costs to keep up these estates. For instance, Felbrigg employs three full-time foresters, but if they sell a thousand pounds' worth of timber in a year they're doing well. The income from the timber won't cover their salaries, but the men are vital to maintaining good order in the woods and countryside.

Inside the great houses, below-stairs areas are proving to be as great an attraction to modern visitors as the rooms inhabited by the lords of the manor. At Felbrigg the South Corridor already provides a glimpse of some of these below-stairs rooms, but in time it may be possible to open up one or two of the attic bedrooms too.

One problem raised in showing such areas is the difficulty of making them authentic to a particular period. The old squires usually kept detailed inventories of the expensive items in their grander quarters, but they didn't take such trouble over their servants' domain. In a bachelors' dormitory, for instance, the inventory may say simply "five beds", which is not much help when you're trying to reconstruct the past in a realistic manner. Research and common sense may help, but the result will inevitably be a pastiche.

Another complication is that the "upstairs, downstairs" lifestyle, as portrayed in the well-known TV series, did not necessarily represent all households. In great country houses, while some servants did sleep in rooms provided by their employer, others — especially the married ones — would return to their homes in the village each evening. At Felbrigg, we believe some unmarried female servants may have used the rear attics as bedrooms, while the single men probably slept over the servants' hall, where the stairs have long been known as the "bachelors' stair". This is, however, conjecture. Nobody really knows for sure.

But perhaps one day you may be able to see one of the attic rooms set up as it might have been in Victorian times, or admire a display of Felbrigg's many fine costumes (currently being conserved at the textile unit at Blickling). There could be an exhibition room for some of the contents of the attics; Felbrigg has a wealth of fascinating collections — swords, shells, toys and games — that people don't usually see, except in brief glimpses during attics and cellars tours. And it's possible that our old sitting room, currently unused, could hold an exhibition covering the whole estate, with photographs and reproductions that wouldn't be affected by the light, so that the blinds could stay up and visitors could enjoy those wonderful views across the park — peaceful views that kept Chris and me sane through the most fraught and frustrating times. Perhaps some generous Lottery winner may offer Felbrigg a million pounds to make it all come true.

One small and charming addition has already been made to the Bird Corridor. A display corner has been opened up where, behind glass, you can see some of the wonderful old toys which belonged to the last squire and his brother. Among other treasures you'll find the old tin taxi, the railway engine, the wooden ark and a selection of its carved animals, and the Stieff "lion that roars". Volunteers have created this display case and added a step-up so that children can see more easily. Pause and enjoy a nostalgic look at this display before you pass on to peer into the butler's pantry and encounter the headless lady.

Pressures are on to keep shops and restaurants in National Trust properties open 365 days a year. Would that mean shoppers and lunchers mingling with winter workmen, tripping over piles of bricks, threading through scaffolding? "People think you have a break during the winter," David informed us (as if we didn't know!). "You could hit them over the head. They say, 'You've got a cushy number, David!' Well, yes, you've got a nice view, but it's a hard-working job. Regional office and head office do not know the pressures that live-in staff are under. You're there for twenty-four hours, you're carrying a bleeper . . ."

Chris always hated the old walkie-talkies which some administrators carried around. His style was so low-key that he seldom even wore a National Trust tie, but he did eventually succumb to having a bleeper in his back pocket — it saved the rest of us having to chase around the house to find him when he was on walkabout.

Today, house staff at Felbrigg find bleepers an essential, linking them to the burglar alarm and the fire alarm, each of which has its own distinctive sound. "We keep the fire alarm on day setting," David explained. "We're always here, so it doesn't need to go directly through to the fire station. But the burglar alarm goes straight through to the police. Even so, if it goes off in the night you've got to go and find out what's going on."

Before they moved out to live in Cromer, he and Helen evolved a system for middle-of-the-night emergencies. If the bleeper went off, they would both get up and Helen would fetch David's dressing gown while he put on his shoes, found his keys, and off he'd go. "We reacted that way whether Jim was in residence or not. If he was, both of us would go. Or if I was on my own I'd take a two-way radio and leave one with Helen, so we had contact. But — as you two know — you get attuned to all this. This is how you respond. Trouble is, you get so attuned that if some other bleeper goes off — for the cooker, or something — you leap up: 'Oh, God, the alarm . . .'"

Came the day when David had to go to London to give a lecture. He told us, "Helen came along, and since I'm a member of the Oxford and Cambridge Club we stayed there. All relaxed, adrenalin all worn down, had a very good supper, sound asleep . . . And the fire bell went! You've just woken up . . . you're in the dark . . . I'm saying, 'Where's my keys, where's my keys, where's my dressing gown?' Helen's instinctive reaction was to get up, go for my dressing gown hanging on the back of the door . . . so she got up, found this strange door, opened it, went out . . . the door shut, the alarm stopped . . . There she was in her nightie, in a gentlemen's club! And me inside thinking, Oh good, it's stopped now, better go back to sleep . . . Where's Helen? Outside, banging on the door!"

They have fun with the livestock, too, just as we did. Some of the sheep, before their confinement over foot-and-mouth disease, had learned how to negotiate cattle grids — they stood at the end of the grid and jumped across to freedom. As for the cows . . . We gather that Felbrigg farmer Graham dines out on our story of some German base campers illicitly "borrowing" the electric fence's battery when their minibus refused to start. In fact, the cows hardly ever went near the fence. But when Chris found out that the battery was missing, he had the remaining campers stand along the fence to shoo the livestock away until the minibus, and had the battery, returned — which taught him a lesson and gave the rest of us a good laugh. To Graham, it's even funnier now because in his experience there hasn't often been a battery to borrow! But the cows don't know that. One bright young calf, jumping for joy as they do, leapt over the electric fence and thoroughly enjoyed the freedom until she was rounded up and returned to her anxious mother.

Having learnt the knack, the calf continued to practise her high-jump, and one summer's day when the bull was in the field among his harem, she decided that the grass looked greener on the other side of the fence. She jumped over yet again. Other calves also liked the look of the lusher grass in front of the Hall. They didn't know how to jump the fence but they soon discovered it was a pretty harmless bit of wire (no battery, you see); some climbed through, others cow-dozed their way. Before long around a dozen of them were mingling skittishly with the human visitors.

Alerted to this problem, David asked his staff to phone and alert the farm while he sallied forth to play cowboy. He picked up a large stick that some youngster had dropped and proceeded to try to herd the excited calves back into the field. These antics attracted the attention of the rest of the herd, who, as curious cows will, came ambling over to take a closer look. Meanwhile someone had helpfully opened the field gate, so David began to drive his little dogies in that direction, some in the field, some outside the fence,

210

with people trying to drive their cars amid the tide . . .
Then Wendy, the farmer's wife, arrived bringing a bag
of cattle-food nuts. She walked calmly out into the field
and shook the bag hard to empty the food in a
scattering pile. The cows all heard the rustling, saw the
nibbles . . . Stampede! Wendy ran for her life, too. "I've
never seen anybody run so fast in my life!"
laughed David. "She belted out of that field, got behind
the gate, all the cows rushing towards her, making
for the food. When they were all inside the field, she
shut the gate — bang! I said to her, 'That was ever so
brave!' and she said, 'Brave! I was frightened silly. But I
had to do it. Graham's away.' Luckily the old bull was
grazing elsewhere at the time," David added, "but you
can get trampled by a few calves, never mind a whole
stampeding herd . . .'"

Another visitor came in one day complaining bitterly
that she had been savaged by a sheep. She had
inadvertently come between a mother ewe and her
lamb, but hadn't counted on the sheep's protective
instinct. "It butted me! It knocked me over!"

All the sheep wear identifying ear-tags, but David
resisted the temptation of asking "Did you take its
number?"

POSTSCRIPT

In the first year or two following our departure from Felbrigg, a rapid turnover of managers left the team of volunteers bemused; so when David, the third new incumbent, arrived he was greeted with caution. His first meeting with the room stewards en masse was at a Christmas luncheon get-together, where one of the experienced volunteers took him aside and warned him darkly, "Property managers come and go, but volunteers go on for ever."

Individually, of course, even volunteers find *anno domini* creeping up on them. To date, a few of our old friends remain in place, but each time we visit the house more and more unfamiliar faces greet us, eager to tell us all about rooms which have given us so many memories. We were delighted, though, to find Heather back managing the shop as she did after Peter, the first shop manager, retired.

The end of 2001 marked the end of an era as Joan Mapperley retired after serving 18 years as catering manager — the last of the old management team with whom Chris and I worked. And as that trying year wound down to its close, David too decided enough was enough. He departed to pastures a little more peaceful.

But there will always be others willing to take over the burden and keep Felbrigg going, and one or two long-serving volunteers will be there to set newcomers on the right path. Felbrigg is in good hands. It will go on, at least for the foreseeable future.

To our surprise and bemusement, Chris and I seem to have earned a footnote in Felbrigg folklore. We're told that visitors arrive saying that they've read *Cobwebs and Cream Teas* or *Dry Rot and Daffodils* and want to see where the incidents happened. Indeed, when we first met, David told us that when he sent change-of-address cards to inform his friends of his move to this remote place called Felbrigg (about which he'd never heard before he applied for the job), some of them replied that they knew all about it — they'd read the books. "So have I now," David assured us. "In fact, if I'd read them before I came here, I might not have been so eager to take the job!"

Felbrigg life goes on just the same, with all its joys, woes, frustrations and hilarity. "If it's been a really rotten day, with everything in chaos," David told us, "we say we've had a Mary Mackie day. Perhaps I ought to do some Mary Mackie tours, taking people to see places and things you've written about . . ." What a good idea! Count me in.

Meanwhile, with the fraught summer of 2001 finally over and as the days grew shorter, Felbrigg held those delayed attics and cellars tours. Chris and I went along as tourists, expecting to remain quietly in the background, incognito. Unfortunately someone recognised us and as we progressed on the tour Chris found himself recounting, yet again, some of the old stories. Can't escape those memories. Wouldn't want to, really.

We remain involved, however distantly, and we are always interested in news of the old place. By the time this book goes to print, will they have solved the problem of the damp carpet in the Great Hall? Or dealt with the rotting glasshouses in the Walled Garden? Or finished work on restoring the staircase? Oh yes, the staircase . . .

At the belated start of the 2001 season, the main stair had to be closed off — it was quietly separating itself from the wall against which it leaned. Not good. At first, in order to ensure that visitors didn't inadvertently wander into unsafe areas, volunteer staff escorted everyone up and down the narrow, winding back stairs. Poor Elizabeth reported that she did the trip 16 times in one afternoon! Then someone had the bright idea of using two-way radios, with one person stationed in the Bird Corridor, the other on the first floor: "Three visitors coming up, Tom." Clump, clump, clump on wooden treads. "Thanks, Sallie. Three visitors, present and correct." By midsummer, much to the relief of the volunteers, the stairs were back in use, having been temporarily shored up by a sturdy supporting partition which reared up from the chequered floor of the staircase hall to bolster the upper flight of stairs. More permanent repairs would have to wait for the winter.

Winter ... You know, that quiet time between October and March, when Felbrigg lies dormant and house staff put their feet up and relax ...

THE ECONOMIC HISTORY OF LATIN AMERICA

The Economic History of Latin America since Independence remains
unfulfilled. Despite the region's abundance of natural resources and favorable
ratio of land to labor, not a single republic of Latin America has achieved the status
of a developed country after nearly two centuries free of colonial rule. If anything,
the gap between living standards in Latin America and those of developed countries
has steadily widened since the early nineteenth century. Burdened with the legacy
of colonialism and its unequal distribution of resources, Latin America is still a
peripheral region in which external influences remain preeminent.

Beginning with the integration of Latin America into the world trading system
centered on Europe and North America during the century before 1930, this
book explores the successes and failures of export-led growth. Using new data
on exports and a simple model to explore the relationship between exports and
growth, the author pays particular attention to the question that has most concerned
policymakers in Latin America: how to transfer growth in the export sector to the
rest of the economy, raising living standards and real income per head.

After the Depression of 1929, a number of countries – mainly the larger republics – withdrew from the world trading system into a model of inward-looking
development based on import-substituting industrialization. Although the benefits of import substitution first appeared substantial, the costs of the inward-looking
model eventually proved to be excessive. Under the weight of the tariff wall, competition from imports – and with it the pressure to improve quality and design –
vanished. Competition from domestic producers might have rescued the situation,
but oligopoly was much more common, with barriers to entry provided by high
initial capital costs. Professor Bulmer-Thomas argues that a major problem with
import substitution was simple timing: The opportunity cost of the inward-looking
model became increasingly high after the Second World War, as world trade started
to expand rapidly. The advantages to be reaped from international specialization,
following the Ricardian ideology of comparative advantage, were abandoned in
favor of growing protection.

The debt crisis of the 1980s effectively ended the inward-looking phase – no
amount of import compression could release the resources needed to service debts
and expand production. The author examines the routes through which Latin American republics extricated themselves from the debt problem in pursuit of a new
version of export-led growth. Taking its narrative from the end of the colonial epoch
to the present, this book provides a comprehensive balanced portrait of the factors
affecting economic development in Latin America.

Victor Bulmer-Thomas is the Director of the Royal Institute of International Affairs
and Professor Emeritus at the University of London. He is the editor of *Regional
Integration in Latin America and the Caribbean: The Political Economy of Open Regionalism*
(2001) and the co–editor of *The United States and Latin America: The New Agenda*
(1999).

For a list of other books in the
Cambridge Latin American Studies series,
please see page 482.

CAMBRIDGE LATIN AMERICAN STUDIES

GENERAL EDITOR
HERBERT S. KLEIN, COLUMBIA UNIVERSITY

77

THE ECONOMIC HISTORY OF LATIN AMERICA
SINCE INDEPENDENCE
SECOND EDITION

Map 1. Leading resources and products of Central and South America, circa 1930. Adapted from Horn and Bice (1949).

THE ECONOMIC HISTORY
OF LATIN AMERICA
SINCE INDEPENDENCE

SECOND EDITION

VICTOR BULMER-THOMAS

Royal Institute of International Affairs
London

 CAMBRIDGE
UNIVERSITY PRESS

CAMBRIDGE UNIVERSITY PRESS
Cambridge, New York, Melbourne, Madrid, Cape Town, Singapore, São Paulo

Cambridge University Press
40 West 20th Street, New York, NY 10011–4211, USA

www.cambridge.org
Information on this title:www.cambridge.org/9780521825672

First edition published 1995
Second edition first published 2003
Reprinted 2004, 2006

Printed in the United States of America

A catalogue record for this book is available from the British Library.

Library of Congress Cataloguing in Publication Data
Bulmer-Thomas, V.
The economic history of Latin America since independence /
Victor Bulmer-Thomas. — 2nd ed.
p.   cm. — (Cambridge Latin American studies ; 77)
Includes bibliographical references and index.
ISBN 0-521-82567-9 — ISBN 0-521-53274-4 (pb.)
1. Latin America — Economic conditions.   2. Latin America — Economic policy.
I. Title.   II. Series.
HC123 .B85   2003
330.98'003 — dc21   2002041243

ISBN-13   978-0-521-82567-2 hardback
ISBN-10   0-521-82567-9 hardback

ISBN-13   978-0-521-53274-7 paperback
ISBN-10   0-521-53274-4 paperback

For the 30 percent who receive 5 percent – a ray of hope;
for the 5 percent who receive 30 percent – a warning.

Contents

Tables, figures, and maps

Tables

Figures

Maps

Preface to the second edition

Since the first edition of this book was published in 1994, the new paradigm based on market-friendly policies and export-led growth has been consolidated in Latin America. At the time of the first edition, it was too early to evaluate the impact of this New Economic Model on long-run economic performance and difficult to make comparisons with the previous paradigms. It is now clear, however, that the outcome of the new paradigm is unlikely to differ substantially from its predecessors. A few countries have been able to lift their long-run growth rates significantly, but most have not and several have performed much worse than during the inward-looking phase of development. Thus, the prospect of Latin America achieving a high standard of living in the near future is still remote and the gap between income per head in Latin America and that in developed countries, notably the United States, is as wide as ever.

The influence of the international context has always been of great importance for Latin America. However, the new wave of globalization – leading to the integration of product and factor markets around the world – has increased the impact of the external environment on the region despite the reduced importance of primary products. Latin America is still struggling to find a way to maximize the benefits of globalization while minimizing the impact of negative external shocks. This dilemma has been made harder by the decline in importance of an independent Latin American school of economic thinking. Most new ideas on economic policy now emanate outside the region and are adopted with only minor adaptations.

The global interest in the impact of the new paradigm on income distribution and poverty has been reflected in recent research on Latin America. This is one of the main advances since the first edition of this book was published. There has also been a revival of interest in regional integration and this now extends to the whole hemisphere as a result of the change of policy by the United States toward regionalism. Debt problems and capital flows have continued to attract a great deal of attention.

Research on the economic history of Latin America has been made easier in recent years by several publications devoted to long-run time series.

Some of these even go back to the independence period at the start of the nineteenth century, although most confine themselves to the twentieth century. This will increase the professionalism of economic history research on Latin America over the next generation and make possible comparisons with many other regions and countries. In the process, many of the ideas presented in this book will be subject to serious examination. I look forward to reading the results of such research and finding out which ideas have stood the test of time.

Preface

Any author whose work covers the whole of Latin America faces a series of problems. These problems are compounded when the period covers nearly two centuries. It is no surprise, therefore, that relatively few studies purport to survey the economic history of Latin America since independence, despite the rapidly expanding literature on the progress of individual countries and provinces. It is, however, the advance at the subregional level that makes necessary and feasible a new economic history for the whole region. From Chile to Mexico, a new generation of scholars has used advanced techniques to mine the primary sources and advance our knowledge across a broad range of issues.

Any economic history of Latin America involves a multidisciplinary approach, which runs the risk of offending the sensibilities of those scholars who prefer to work within a single disciplinary boundary. As a representative of the last generation to be encouraged to stray across disciplines, I have enjoyed the opportunity to draw on a huge literature covering economics, economic history, history, politics, sociology, anthropology, and international relations. As an editor of the multidisciplinary *Journal of Latin American Studies* since 1986, I have been uniquely privileged to gain access to new research in this area before it becomes widely disseminated.

A book such as this one cannot be written without accumulating many debts. Only a few can be mentioned here. Rosemary Thorp and Laurence Whitehead taught me the limitations of a narrow focus on economics. Leslie Bethell gave me the opportunity to work with historians on the monumental *Cambridge History of Latin America*. The late Carlos Díaz-Alejandro, who almost certainly would have written this book had he not died prematurely, and José Antonio Ocampo demonstrated to me how professional economists could provide insights into the economies of nineteenth-century Latin America. Last but not least, I owe a special debt to all those students who have attended my lectures and classes on the economic history of Latin America. Their reaction was often the litmus test of what was, or was not, an acceptable way of presenting new ideas and of making them comprehensible to those groups that are likely to comprise the majority of readers of this book.

xix

Abbreviations

ADRs	American Depository Receipts
ALPRO	Alliance for Progress
AP	Andean Pact
CACM	Central American Common Market
CARICOM	Caribbean Community
CAT	*Certificado de abono tributario*
CBR	crude birth rate
CDR	crude death rate
CEPAL	Comisión Económica para América Latina (y el Caribe)
CET	common external tariff
DC	developed countries
DFI	direct foreign investment
DUA	domestic-use agriculture
EC	European Community
ECLA	Economic Commission for Latin America
ECLAC	Economic Commission for Latin America and the Caribbean
EEC	European Economic Community
EP	export promotion
EPZ	export-processing zone
ERP	effective rate of protection
ES	export substitution
EU	European Union
EXA	export agriculture
FTA	free-trade agreement
FTAA	Free Trade Area of the Americas
GATT	General Agreement on Tariffs and Trade
GDP	gross domestic product
GNP	gross national product
GSP	generalized system of preferences
ICA	International Coffee Agreement
IDB	Inter-American Development Bank

IFI	international financial institution
IMF	International Monetary Fund
IMR	infant mortality rate
ISA	import-substituting agriculture
ISI	import-substituting industrialization
ISS	import-substituting services
ITT	income terms of trade
LA6	Latin America Six (Argentina, Brazil, Chile, Colombia, Mexico, Uruguay)
LA14	Latin America Fourteen (all republics other than the LA6)
LAFTA	Latin American Free Trade Association
LDC	less developed country
MERCOSUR	Mercado Común del Sur
MFN	most-favored nation
MNC	multinational corporation
NAFTA	North American Free Trade Agreement
NBTT	net barter terms of trade
NIC	newly industrialized country
OECD	Organization for Economic Cooperation and Development
OPEC	Organization of Petroleum Exporting Countries
PEA	population economically active
PED	primary-export development
PPE	purchasing power of exports
PPP	purchasing power parity
PREALC	Programa Regional del Empleo para América Latina y el Caribe
REER	real effective exchange rate
RERD	real effective exchange-rate depreciation
RI	regional integration
SOE	state-owned enterprise
TC	trade creation
TD	trade diversion
UNCTAD	U.N. Conference on Trade and Development
USAID	U.S. Agency for International Development
VAT	value-added tax
VER	voluntary export restraints
WC	Washington Consensus
WTO	World Trade Organisation

1

Latin American economic development: an overview

The expression "Latin America," whose origin is still hotly disputed,[1] at first had little more than geographical significance – it referred to all those independent countries south of the Río Grande in which a language derived from Latin (e.g., Spanish, Portuguese, and French) was predominantly spoken. In this original meaning, the only characteristics common to the countries of Latin America were their location in the Western Hemisphere and the origins of their language. In many respects the differences between the countries were considered to be as important – if not more so – as what they shared.

These differences – whether of size, population, ethnicity, natural resources, climate, or level of development – are still very important, but it has also become clear that the republics are held together by much more than geography and language. The shared colonial experience, as divisions above all of the Spanish or Portuguese empires, was crucial in shaping the economic and political destinies of the new republics after independence. The pattern of development in the nineteenth century, based on the export of natural resources to the industrialized countries, reinforced this sense of a shared past.

Thus there is real meaning to the phrase "Latin America," and the factors in common are stronger than those that bind the countries of Africa, Asia, or Europe. Furthermore, the membership of the Latin American club has been fairly stable since independence, with relatively few additions or subtractions as a result of border changes, secession, or annexation (see Maps 2 and 3); indeed, the boundaries of Latin American states, although often the source of interstate conflict and still not entirely settled,[2] have changed much less in the past 150 years than have frontiers elsewhere.

---

1 According to some, it was the Colombian José María Torres Caicedo who first coined the term "Latin America" in 1856 (see Bushnell and Macaulay, 1988, p. 3). Others attribute it either to the French academic L. M. Tisserand or to the Chilean Francisco Bilbao at approximately the same time.

2 The main border disputes (including maritime boundaries) still outstanding are the following: Guatemala and Belize; Colombia and Venezuela; Venezuela and Guyana; Honduras and Nicaragua.

The countries of Latin America are the ten republics of South America (excluding the three Guianas), the six republics of Central America (including Panama but excluding Belize), Mexico, Cuba, the Dominican Republic, and Haiti – a grand total of twenty. Spanish is the main language in eighteen republics, whereas Portuguese is predominant in Brazil and French-derived *kréyol* in Haiti. Indian languages are still spoken by large pockets of the population in Mexico, Guatemala, Ecuador, Peru, Bolivia, and Paraguay, and English is the first language of numerous minorities throughout the region. Japanese can be heard on the streets of São Paulo, Brazil, where at least one million inhabitants are of Japanese descent, and there are important colonies of Chinese origin in many republics.

Puerto Rico, a Spanish colony until 1898, was annexed by and remains a commonwealth associated with the United States.[3] Although clearly part of Latin America in the nineteenth century, Puerto Rico has usually been excluded from the definition since then – a decision which many find harsh but which has been justified by its very different pattern of development as a result of its special relationship with the United States. Thus throughout this book Puerto Rico will appear in discussions of the nineteenth century, but with less frequency in subsequent analyses. By contrast, Panama was not listed as a Latin American country in the nineteenth century because it was still part of Colombia. Its secession in 1903, aided and abetted by President Theodore Roosevelt, led to independence. It is therefore included in the list of post-nineteenth century Latin American republics.[4]

The majority of Latin American countries won independence from their European rulers in the 1820s.[5] Contemporary accounts by Latin Americans and foreigners were filled with glowing reports of the prospects that could be achieved once Spain and Portugal were deprived of their commercial and other monopolies in the region. Standards of living were low, but not much lower than those of North America, probably on a par with those of much of central Europe, and perhaps higher than those of the newly discovered countries in the antipodes. All that was needed, it was thought, were capital and skilled labor to unlock the natural resources in Latin America's vast unexploited interior and unrestricted access to the wealthy markets of western Europe.

The long-standing territorial dispute between Argentina and the United Kingdom over the Falkland/ Malvinas islands also remains unresolved.

3 On Puerto Rican history and its peculiar constitutional status, see Carr (1984). Its people's preference for commonwealth status was reconfirmed by a referendum in December 1998.

4 For the secession of Panama from Colombia and its creation as an independent republic, see Lafeber (1978).

5 The exceptions are as follows: Haiti won its independence from France in 1804, Uruguay was created in 1828 as a buffer state between Argentina and Brazil, the Dominican Republic secured independence from Haiti in 1844, Cuba won its independence from Spain in 1898, and the special case of Panama has already been mentioned (see note 4).

Map 2. Latin America, circa 1826.

Map 3. Latin America, 2000.

Nearly two centuries later, that dream has not been fulfilled. None of the twenty republics in Latin America can be classified as developed, and some remain extremely poor. Pockets of wealth can be found in all republics, but these cannot conceal the deprivation and hardship suffered by the region's poorest inhabitants. Although Latin America is not among the poorest regions in the world, it has now been overtaken by parts of Asia that almost certainly had much lower standards of living throughout the nineteenth century.[6] Latin America's achievements in the fields of literature, art, music, and popular culture rightly win admiration around the world, but this is only partial compensation for failure to bridge the enormous gap between the levels of economic development in the region and those in the developed countries.

Economic development is usually measured by a series of indicators, of which the most commonly used are gross domestic product (GDP) and gross national product (GNP) per person.[7] Other indicators are life expectancy at birth, carbon dioxide emissions per head, infant mortality, telephones per thousand people, and so on. Almost irrespective of the choice of indicators, Latin America comes out midway between the high-income countries of North America and Western Europe and the poorest countries of sub-Saharan Africa and South Asia (see Table 1.1). The World Bank classifies all the Latin American republics as "middle income," except Haiti and Nicaragua, which are classified as "low income"; but this cannot disguise the fact that GNP per head in the region was only 13 percent of the level found in the high-income countries at the begining in the 21st century.[8]

Lack of economic success has not meant stagnation. On the contrary, change has been rapid in Latin America, and this is nowhere more apparent than in the rate of urbanization. Population expansion has been centered on cities, in part as a result of international migration in the nineteenth century and rural–urban migration in the twentieth century. Thus, as Table 1.2 makes clear, Latin America is now predominantly urban, with 75 percent of its inhabitants living in towns or cities. Because the average rate of urbanization for all middle-income countries is 50 percent, this has led to the charge that Latin America is "prematurely mature." Indeed, the spectacular growth of the informal sector in Latin American cities is evidence of the

---

6 Examples are South Korea, Taiwan, Singapore, and Hong Kong (see World Bank, 2002, Table 1.1).
7 GDP refers to the net output generated by factors of production irrespective of whether they are resident; GNP adjusts the GDP figure for net factor income paid abroad. The difference can be important in a number of Latin American republics as a result, for example, of the presence of foreign-owned companies.
8 International GNP comparisons are very dependent on the choice of the exchange-rate. Other comparisons (based, for example, on purchasing power parities) suggest a smaller gap, though the difference still remains considerable. See World Bank (2002a).

Table 1.1. *Comparative development indicators for Latin America, circa* 2000

	GNP per head[a] (in US$)	Life expectancy (in years)	Infant mortality (per 1000)	Carbon dioxide emissions per head (in tons)
Low & Middle Income	1,230	64	85	5.1
South Asia	460	63	99	0.9
Sub-Saharan Africa	480	47	159	0.8
Latin America & Caribbean	3,680	70	38	2.6
High Income	27,510	78	6	12.6
United Kingdom	24,500	77	6	8.8
United States	34,260	77	8	19.4
Switzerland	38,120	80	5	6.1

[a] Economies in World Bank (2002) are divided among income groups according to 2000 Gross National Income per head, calculated using the World Bank Atlas method. The groups are as follows: low income, $755 or less; lower middle $756–2,995; upper middle income, $2,996–9,265; and high income, $9,266 or more.
Source: World Bank (2002), p. 233.

difficulty many new entrants to the urban labor market have in finding secure, productive jobs.[9]

Latin America includes some of the largest urban areas in the world: Mexico City and São Paulo, both of which have some 20 million inhabitants in their metropolitan areas, have all the problems of pollution associated with large conurbations in industrial countries. What is striking about Latin American urbanization, however, is the problem of primacy; that is, the disproportionately rapid growth of the principal city in each republic. Except in Brazil, Venezuela, and El Salvador, the proportion of the urban population living in the main conurbation is far above the world average. Thus the capital city is usually the leading industrial, commercial, financial, and cultural, as well as the administrative, center.[10]

The rate of population growth, as Table 1.2 makes clear, has been steadily declining. The demographic transition, under which birth rates start to fall in line with the earlier fall in death rates, is well under way, and some countries – notably Argentina, Cuba, and Uruguay – have already achieved very modest rates of population growth. Brazil and Mexico, the two most

9 Numerous definitions of the informal sector exist, but it is easiest to think of it as employing all those workers not absorbed by medium- or large-scale firms in the private and public sectors. By that definition the urban informal sector accounts for more than 50 percent of the labor force in many Latin American cities. See, for example, Thomas (1995).
10 The main exception is in Brazil, where the capital was moved from Rio de Janeiro to the newly created Brasília in the 1950s. The new capital, though an important city in its own right, is still overshadowed by Rio de Janeiro and São Paulo in almost all areas of private enterprise.

Table 1.2. *Demographic indicators*

Country	2000 population (in thousands)	Urbanization[a]	Population growth (% per year) 1961–70	1970–80	1980–90	1990–2000
Argentina	37,032	89.4	1.4	1.7	1.4	1.3
Bolivia	8,329	64.8	2.4	2.6	2.5	2.4
Brazil	170,406	81.3	2.8	2.4	2.1	1.4
Chile	15,211	84.6	2.3	1.6	1.7	1.5
Colombia	42,299	74.9	3.0	2.2	2.0	1.9
Costa Rica	3,811	51.9	3.4	2.8	2.9	2.0
Cuba	11,188	75.3	2.0	1.3	0.9	0.5
Dominican Republic	8,373	65.0	3.2	2.6	2.3	1.9
Ecuador	12,646	62.4	3.2	3.0	2.6	2.1
El Salvador	6,276	46.6	3.4	2.3	1.3	2.1
Guatemala	11,385	40.4	2.8	2.8	2.9	2.6
Haiti	7,959	35.7	2.0	1.7	1.9	2.1
Honduras	6,417	46.9	3.1	3.4	3.4	2.8
Mexico	97,966	74.4	3.3	2.9	2.3	1.6
Nicaragua	5,071	64.7	3.2	3.1	2.8	2.8
Panama	2,856	57.7	3.0	2.8	2.1	1.7
Paraguay	5,496	56.0	2.9	3.0	3.1	2.6
Peru	25,661	72.8	2.9	2.7	2.2	1.7
Uruguay	3,337	91.3	1.0	0.4	0.6	0.7
Venezuela	24,170	87.4	3.5	3.5	2.5	2.1
Latin America	**505,889**	**75.4**	**2.8**	**2.4**	**2.1**	**1.6**

[a] Defined as percentage of population living in urban areas. The population classified as urban follows national definitions.
Sources: The World Bank (2002), p. 232; The World Bank (2002a).

populous countries, had high rates of population growth, however, until the 1990s. Their share of the Latin American total – 53 percent in 2000 – can be expected to stabilize now that birth rates are falling.

In most less-developed countries (LDCs) a rapid rate of urbanization is consistent with an increasing rural population. Rural–urban migration is important, but the small size of the urban areas means that they cannot absorb all the increase in the rural population. The expanding populations must still find new work opportunities in rural areas. In many Latin American countries, however, urbanization has been pushed to the point where rural–urban migration leads to a fall in the rural population – not just in its rate of growth. Uruguay, for example, has seen its rural population decline by nearly 50 percent since 1960, and in the year 2000 only 5 percent of its labor force was classified as agricultural.

Table 1.3. *Exports of primary products as a
percentage of the total*

Country	1980	1990	2000
Argentina	76.9	70.9	67.9
Bolivia	97.1	95.3	72.9
Brazil	62.9	48.1	42.0
Chile	88.7	89.1	84.0
Colombia	80.3	74.9	65.9
Costa Rica	70.2	72.6	34.5
Ecuador	97.0	97.7	89.9
El Salvador	64.6	64.5	51.6
Guatemala	75.6	75.5	68.0
Honduras	87.2	90.5	64.4
Mexico	87.9	56.7	16.5
Nicaragua	81.9	91.8	92.5
Panama	91.1	83.0	84.1
Paraguay	88.2	90.1	80.7
Peru	83.1	81.6	83.1
Uruguay	61.8	61.5	58.5
Venezuela	98.5	89.1	90.9
Latin America[a]	**80.0**	**77.2**	**66.4**

[a] Total excludes Cuba, Dominican Republic, and Haiti,
for which data are not provided in source
Source: ECLAC (2001), pp. 518–21.

By contrast, Latin America's population in the 1820s – not much larger in total than Mexico City's is today – was overwhelmingly rural, with the labor force concentrated in agriculture and mining. The natural resources produced by these sectors provided the link with the rest of the world, and international flows of labor and capital were concerned directly or indirectly with increasing the exportable surplus. Some of the commodities for which Latin America is still famous, such as sugar, were already in place by the time of independence; many others, such as coffee, joined the list in the nineteenth century.

The importance of these primary commodities has been declining, but they still accounted for two-thirds of all exports in 2000 (see Table 1.3). Much of the decline, however, has been due to Mexico – Latin America's leading exporter – where goods for processing (*maquila*) have become very important. Furthermore, many of the nontraditional manufactured exports from Latin America – such as textiles, leather products, and furniture – are based on natural resources. Thus it is fair to say that primary commodities still provide the main link with the rest of the world. This statement is even more accurate if we include illegal drugs, such as cocaine and marijuana, in the export list. In the case of Colombia, where the impact of the drug trade is particularly important, the value of narcotics is estimated at 25 percent of exports and 3 percent of GDP.[11]

The exploitation of natural resources in Latin America, as in so many parts of the world, has been carried out with scant respect for the environment. The forest cover has been depleted, rivers and lakes have been polluted, and dangerous chemicals have entered the food chain. Local awareness of these problems has been slowly increasing, but Latin America faces the additional problem that the Amazon Basin – shared by Brazil, Colombia, Ecuador, Peru, Venezuela, and the Guianas – houses the world's largest and most important reserves of tropical rain forests. Their destruction is widely believed to be a major contributor to global warming and to the greenhouse effect, so Latin America finds itself under pressure from the outside world to adopt environmental standards considered appropriate by richer countries.[12]

The problem of environmental damage, however, is not limited to natural resources. Rapid urbanization in the larger republics has been accompanied by impressive industrial growth. Chemical plants, steel mills, cement factories, and automobile assembly lines have proliferated throughout the region as governments have adopted policies that favor industrialization. This process, which began toward the end of the nineteenth century in the major countries of the region, accelerated after 1930 as the Great Depression and the Second World War provided a stimulus for firms that were able to replace manufactured imports with local products. By 1955 the contribution of manufacturing to real GDP had overtaken agriculture,[13] and in 2000 its contribution had reached 21 percent, compared with 7 percent for agriculture (see Table 1.4).

Industrial growth was rapid for much of the twentieth century, but it was not notably efficient. Shielded by tariffs and other barriers to imports, industrial firms (including multinational companies, or MNCs) exploited the domestic market with high-priced, low-quality goods. Most firms were therefore unable to compete internationally, so foreign loans still had to be serviced with earnings from primary products. The rapid accumulation of external debts in the 1970s, in the wake of the two oil crises, left Latin America dangerously exposed, and primary product exports were unable to provide sufficient earnings to service external debts in the 1980s. As a result awareness of the need to make industry internationally competitive has grown, and firms have come under pressure from all sides to cut costs and improve quality.

11 Estimates of the value of narcotics exports from Latin America differ enormously. For a survey of the industry, see Joyce (1998); for Colombia, Steiner (1998).

12 For a good study of the environmental issues raised by the Amazon Basin, see Barbier (1989), Chapter 6. See also Jenkins (2000).

13 At 1970 prices and net factor cost. See CEPAL (1978), Table 5.

Table 1.4. *Sectoral contribution to GDP in* 2000

Country	Agriculture (value added as % of GDP)	Manufacturing (value added as % of GDP)	Country shares of total manufacturing (%)
Argentina	4.8	17.6	14.2
Bolivia	22.0	12.8	0.3
Brazil	7.4	24.0	33.3
Chile	10.5	15.9	3.2
Colombia	13.8	13.8	3.1
Costa Rica	9.4	24.4	1.1
Cuba	6.7	37.2	N/A
Dominican Republic	11.1	17.0	1.0
Ecuador	10.0	16.9	0.7
El Salvador	10.1	23.4	0.9
Guatemala	22.8	13.2	0.8
Haiti	28.0	7.0	0.1
Honduras	17.7	19.9	0.3
Mexico	4.4	20.7	32.2
Nicaragua	32.0	14.0	0.1
Panama	6.7	7.6	0.2
Paraguay	20.6	14.4	0.3
Peru	7.9	14.3	2.3
Uruguay	6.0	16.9	1.0
Venezuela	5.0	14.4	4.9
Latin America	7.0	21.0	100.0

Source: World Bank (2002a).

The extraction of natural resources in Latin America, and related investments in social infrastructure such as railways, attracted foreign capital. The principal investor in the nineteenth century, Great Britain, had, by 1930, been replaced in most countries by the United States. Subsequently, the state steadily increased its participation in economic activity, taking over public utilities, railways, and natural resources that had previously been controlled by foreigners. However, foreign capital remained important in a number of primary commodities, particularly non-oil minerals, and became attracted by the new opportunities in industry after the Second World War.

State participation in the economy, widely accepted in the 1960s and 1970s, failed to reverse the sharp inequality in income distribution found in most Latin American republics. This inequality, at first a product of the unequal distribution of land inherited from colonial times, has been reinforced by industrial and financial concentration in the twentieth century, giving Latin America one of the worst income distributions in the world. Indeed, as Table 1.5 makes clear, it is not uncommon to find the top 10 percent

Table 1.5. *Income distribution: percentage share of household income and Gini coefficient, circa* 2000

Country	Poorest 40%	Next 30%	20% below richest 10%	Richest 10%	Gini coefficient[a]
Argentina[b]	15.4	21.6	26.1	37.0	0.542
Bolivia	9.2	24.0	29.6	37.2	0.586
Brazil	10.1	17.3	25.5	47.1	0.64
Chile	13.8	20.8	25.1	40.3	0.559
Colombia	12.3	21.6	26.0	40.1	0.572
Costa Rica	15.3	25.7	29.7	29.4	0.473
Dominican	14.5	23.6	26.0	36.0	0.517
Republic	14.1	22.8	26.5	36.6	0.521
Ecuador[c]					
El Salvador	13.8	25.0	29.1	32.1	0.518
Guatemala	12.8	20.9	26.1	40.3	0.582
Honduras	11.8	22.9	28.9	36.5	0.564
Mexico	15.1	22.7	25.6	36.7	0.539
Nicaragua	10.4	22.1	27.1	40.5	0.584
Panama	12.9	22.4	27.7	37.1	0.557
Paraguay	13.1	23.0	27.8	36.2	0.565
Uruguay[c]	21.6	25.5	25.9	27.0	0.44
Venezuela	14.6	25.1	29.0	31.4	0.498

[a] The Gini coefficient measures income inequality and varies from 0 in the case of complete equality to 1 in the case of complete inequality.
[b] Greater Buenos Aires.
[c] Urban Total.
Source: CEPAL (2001), pp. 69 and 71.

of households receiving more than 40 percent of total household income, whereas the bottom 40 percent typically receives less than 15 percent. Similarly, the Gini coefficient (a widely used indicator of income inequality) is uniformly high in Latin America (see Table 1.5).

The differences within countries are mirrored to a lesser extent in the differences between countries. In 2000, GNP per head (see Table 1.6) varied from around $6000 to $7000 in the richest countries to around $500 in the poorest. This implies that the average Mexican, for example, is 12 times richer than the average Nicaraguan, whereas the average U.S. citizen (see Table 1.1) is ten times richer than the average Latin American. Thus an economic history of Latin America must explain not only the failure of Latin America as a whole to achieve the status of a developed region but also the differences in standards of living between individual countries within Latin America.

Most theories of economic development have tended to emphasize one side of the explanation at the expense of the other. Racial theories, for

Table 1.6. *GNP per head (in current US$): 1980, 1990, and 2000*

Country	1980	Rank	1990	Rank	2000	Rank
Argentina	2,739	4	4,346	1	7,695	1
Bolivia	519	19	741	17	994	17
Brazil	1,933	9	3,143	3	3,494	7
Chile	2,474	5	2,315	7	4,638	5
Colombia	1,174	13	1,152	12	1,922	13
Costa Rica	2,115	7	1,874	9	4,159	6
Cuba*a*	2,325	6	2,458	6	2,030	12
Dominican Republic	1,164	14	1,002	14	2,349	2
Ecuador	1,474	10	1,041	13	1,076	16
El Salvador	779	16	940	15	2,105	10
Guatemala	1,155	15	874	16	1,668	14
Haiti	273	20	461	19	509	19
Honduras	719	18	626	18	924	18
Mexico	3,308	3	3,157	2	5,864	3
Nicaragua	734	17	264	20	473	20
Panama	1,954	8	2,216	8	3,463	8
Paraguay	1,470	11	1,248	10	1,369	15
Peru	1,193	12	1,219	11	2,084	11
Uruguay	3,477	2	2,990	4	5,908	2
Venezuela	4,597	1	2,492	5	4,985	4
Latin America	2,168		2,586		3,879	

a The Cuban figure for 1980 is an estimate taken from Brundenius and Zimbalist (1989): the 1990 figure applies the growth rate between 1980 and 1990 in Thorp (1998), p. 353, to the 1980 figure; the 2000 figure applies the growth rate for GDP (adjusted for population increase) in ECLAC (2001), pp. 286–7, to the 1990 figure. The Cuban figures for 1990 and 2000 are not strictly comparable with the figures for other Latin American countries, as they are based on constant prices in pesos rather than current U.S. dollars.
Source: World Bank (2002a).

example,[14] now largely discredited, were used to explain the lowly position in terms of real income per head of Bolivia (with its predominantly Indian population) and Haiti (where the population is mainly of African origin) but could not explain the failure of countries with largely European populations, such as Costa Rica and Uruguay, to achieve developed country (DC) status. Racial theories were also hopelessly inadequate at accounting for the transformation of countries from success stories to failures (e.g., Argentina) or vice versa (e.g., Venezuela).[15]

14 See, for example, Bryce (1912) in Chapter 13.
15 Argentina was overtaken in terms of real GDP per head (1970 prices) by Venezuela in 1956 (see CEPAL, 1978, Table 2). Argentina had been the major success story in Latin America in the half-century before the 1920s; Venezuela had been one of the worst failures.

Some theories of economic development for Latin America have put considerable stress on the institutional and structural features of the region.[16] For example, the land-tenure system, which was inherited from the Iberian Peninsula, was seen as an obstacle to development; and the legal and administrative apparatus, which was inherited from the colonial powers, was seen as a barrier to private entrepreneurship and efficient decision making in the public sector. The superficial attractions of these theories should not be allowed to obscure their many deficiencies, however. The institutional and structural landscape inherited from the colonial period was not homogeneous and has changed significantly over time.

On the other hand, dependency theory, which emphasized the dichotomy between the "center" (the advanced countries) and the "periphery" (Latin America) and the unequal relations of exchange between the two regions, seemed at first to be a plausible explanation of the relative failure of Latin America to achieve the high standard of living found in the developed countries, but it was unable to offer much guidance as to why some Latin American countries performed so much better than others.[17] Furthermore, dependency theory was also unable to account for the transformation of a country such as Argentina from success to failure in a relatively short period of time.

Dependency theory is part of a long tradition of theoretical work that has seen the primary obstacle to Latin American economic development in the unequal relations with foreign powers. An abundance of circumstantial evidence illustrates the arrogant attitude toward Latin America on the part of a number of European powers (notably Great Britain and France) in the nineteenth century and of the United States in the twentieth century. It is impossible, however, to sustain the thesis that a negative relationship exists between the closeness of ties to a foreign power and the rate of economic development. Poor and backward countries (e.g., Bolivia) have never received the amount of attention that relatively rich countries have (e.g., Argentina, which, until as late as the 1940s, was often described as being an informal member of the British Empire).[18]

Orthodox theories have fared no better. Numerous theories of export-led growth have argued that countries with the highest levels of integration into the world economy would achieve the highest rates of economic growth and ultimately achieve DC status.[19] Yet some of the poorest Latin American republics, such as Honduras, have been among the most open economies

---

16 See, for example, Griffin (1969) and Frank (1969).

17 The classic statement of dependency theory in the Latin American context is Cardoso and Faletto (1979).

18 On contrasting views of informal empire and the Argentine situation, see Thompson (1992) and Hopkins (1994).

19 For a survey of the literature, see Giles (2000) and Giles (2000a); see also Gylfason (1999).

in the world, whereas the transformation of Brazil from one of the poorest countries in Latin America in the 1920s to one of the richest by the 1970s was achieved against a background of delinking from the world economy for much of that period.

An extreme version of orthodoxy, neoliberalism, has been much in vogue in recent years. It argues that Latin America was crippled by state intervention, which has distorted relative prices, prevented the emergence of a dynamic private sector, and forced many individuals into informal – often illegal – activities.[20] Critics were quick to point out the ahistorical nature of this argument, for state intervention in Latin America – as in many other regions of the world – had been in large part a response to market failure in an unregulated and "liberal" environment. Indeed, the half-century before 1930, which was dominated in Latin America by a liberal ideology, was marked by the modest role of the state and by the importance of private foreign investment. Even if state intervention was not always the appropriate response to market failure, it did not follow that the absence of state intervention would necessarily lead to a more efficient allocation of resources.

No single theory will explain both the intermediate position occupied by Latin America on the scale of world income per head and the differences that have emerged among Latin American countries over time. Yet a theoretical framework is essential if economic history is to be more than mere description. Throughout this book three basic ideas recur to account for the position of the region as a whole and of individual countries within the region: the commodity lottery, the mechanics of export-led growth, and the economic-policy environment.

Latin America's integration into the world economy took place through exports of primary products. As we have seen, this remains the single most important link with the rest of the world. Primary products are not homogeneous, however, and the phrase "commodity lottery" is intended to draw attention to the differences among commodities. Some products (e.g., cattle), lend themselves naturally to forward linkages through further processing before export, whereas others (e.g., bananas), offer little prospect. Commodities with forward linkages can act as a stimulus to industry and urbanization – the clearest example is meat in Argentina in the nineteenth century – but commodities also differ in terms of their demand for inputs (backward linkages). Commodities that are extracted from the ground using labor only (e.g., guano[21]) provide no stimulus to industries that supply

---

20 One of the most forceful statements of the argument can be found in De Soto (1987). For a good survey, see Stokes (2001). See also Gwynne (2000).

21 Guano, a natural fertilizer formed by bird droppings, was found in abundance off the coast of Peru and began to be exploited commercially in the nineteenth century.

inputs, whereas other commodities (e.g., nitrates) demand a range of inputs, including machinery, before they can be exploited profitably.

Commodities also differ in terms of their demand characteristics. Some, such as meat, have enjoyed and still enjoy relatively high income elasticities of demand, so that a 5 percent increase in real-world income brings an increase in demand for the commodity of more than 5 percent. Others, such as coffee, have seen income elasticities decline over time, as the commodity in question has moved from being a luxury good to being an article of basic consumption. Some commodities (e.g., gold) have no close substitute, whereas others (e.g., cotton) face competition from synthetic products, so that the price elasticity of demand is high. In some products (e.g., cocaine), Latin America has a monopoly of world supply; in others (e.g., sugar), international competition is fierce.

The geographical and geological diversity of Latin America meant that each republic had only a limited choice of commodities to export. Chile, a temperate country, could export wheat but not coffee; it has huge deposits of copper but little oil. The commodity lottery dictated that Chile would be integrated into the world economy on the basis of products that were very different from those of, say, Colombia, where the tropical climate and mountainous terrain make coffee production particularly appropriate. Inevitably, these differences among countries in terms of their commodity specialization carried with them important implications for long-run growth.

Commodity specialization led to rising labor productivity in the export sector, bringing with it the prospect of export-led growth. The mechanics of export-led growth, however, are crucial. A well-oiled machine can transfer productivity gains in the export sector to the rest of the economy, raising living standards and real income per head; a faulty machine will leave productivity gains concentrated in the export sector, often to be exploited by foreign companies rather than by domestic factors of production. The capitalist surplus made possible by export specialization is thus no guarantee of capital accumulation.

Three mechanisms are particularly important in the export-led growth machine: capital (including innovation and the transfer of technology), labor, and the state. Where these mechanisms fail to function efficiently, it is possible to have growth in the export sector and stagnation or even decline in the nonexport economy. The result will be rising exports per head and an increase in the share of real GDP accounted for by exports but no guarantee of rapidly rising living standards. Eventually, of course, as exports increase the rate of growth of real GDP must coincide with the rate of growth of exports, but by then export specialization will have reached the point at which the economy is extremely vulnerable to adverse conditions in world markets, and recession induced by cycles in world trade can be deep and long lasting. By contrast, where the three mechanisms function efficiently, the nonexport economy will expand along with the export sector. Exports per head will rise, but the share of exports in real GDP may actually fall, and living standards will certainly increase. The dynamism of the nonexport economy then shields it from adverse external shocks, so that recession induced by cycles in world trade tends to be short lived.

The first mechanism, capital, involves the transfer of part of the capitalist surplus in the export sector to productive investment in the nonexport economy. This transfer is by no means automatic. It is less likely to occur, for example, where the surplus accrues to foreign investors, where there are few financial intermediaries, and where the domestic market is small. It is more likely to occur where the surplus accrues to local factors of production, where financial intermediation is widespread, and where the domestic market is large and expanding.

The size of the domestic market is a function not only of population but also of purchasing power. Where labor – the second mechanism – in the export sector is paid in kind, the domestic market is artificially restricted. A labor force based on slavery, for example, like that in Brazil or Cuba until the late 1880s, is a poor stimulus for transferring productivity gains in the export sector to the nonexport economy. By contrast, a skilled labor force based on wage labor represents not only an important concentration of purchasing power for sellers in the nonexport economy but also a potential source of future entrepreneurs who are able to take their skills and knowledge to other branches of the economy.

The third mechanism involves the state. The expansion of the export sector permits an expansion of imports, and taxes on foreign trade in the first stages of development are invariably the most important source of government revenue. The size of the revenue and the manner in which it is spent are crucial determinants of the success or failure of export-led growth. Where the resources are small and are used primarily to reinforce the export sector, the nonexport sector may remain undynamic; where the resources are substantial and are used to encourage the nonexport economy, both sectors can expand rapidly. The balance is delicate, however, because an excessive tax burden on the export sector can lead to its stagnation.

The commodity lottery and the mechanics of export-led growth have been important determinants of success or failure in Latin America's economic development since independence, but so has the economic-policy environment. Inconsistent economic policies or policies that are applied inconsistently have done considerable damage to both the export sector and the nonexport sector. Consistent economic policies, based on a broad consensus and backed up by political stability, on the other hand, have created an appropriate environment for transferring productivity gains from the export sector to the nonexport economy. As the Latin American economies have become more complex, the economic-policy environment has become more important – to the point that in some republics it is the principal determinant of success or failure.

For most of the first century after independence, all republics in Latin America followed a policy of export-led growth based on primary-product exports. Where the combination of the commodity lottery, the mechanics of export-led growth, and the economic-policy environment were favorable, the results could be impressive. Argentina, for example, which benefited from the commodity lottery and where the mechanics of export-led growth functioned smoothly, was among the twelve richest countries in the world in the 1920s in terms of real income per head, despite numerous deficiencies in economic policy. Where all three elements were unfavorable, as in Haiti and Bolivia, however, the results were bitterly disappointing.

In the half-century after the 1929 Depression a number of countries – mainly the larger republics – turned away from export-led growth toward inward-looking development based on import-substituting industrialization (ISI). In these countries the export sector ceased to be dynamic and the commodity lottery lost its relevance, although primary-product exports remained the main source of foreign-exchange earnings. The new dynamic sector was ISI, and the problem became how to transfer the productivity gains in the ISI sector to the rest of the economy. The need for factor and product markets to function smoothly, therefore, still applied in this new situation, and the economic-policy environment became more important than ever, with mistakes being more costly.[22]

At the end of the 1960s a number of countries began to turn away from inward-looking development toward a new type of integration into the world economy, one based on nontraditional exports, including manufactures. This process gathered pace in the 1980s and 1990s, and by the beginning of the new century a new era of export-led growth was underway throughout Latin America. Much is expected of this new model, but the lessons of the past need to be remembered. The economic-policy environment remains crucial: The global nature of the world economy now means that domestic factors of production are increasingly aware of opportunities outside the region, so policy errors are punished by capital flight and by the drain of skilled labor from Latin America. The mechanics of export-led growth have become more complicated and the transfer and diffusion of technology much more crucial, but the basic problem of transferring productivity gains in the export sector to the nonexport economy remains. The commodity lottery is no longer so important, but the choice

22 With barriers to international trade driving a wedge between domestic and international prices, domestic economic policy became a key determinant of the allocation of resources and the rate of economic growth.

of nontraditional exports can still have an important bearing on success or failure in economic development.

The lessons from Latin America's economic history suggest that nothing about the region's current lowly status in terms of economic development in general and real income per head in particular is predetermined. The alchemy of success is no easier to achieve today than it was at the time of independence, however. There is no magic wand to wave, and international competition is fiercer than ever. Not all the Latin American republics can expect to make the transition to DC status in the next century, but it would be surprising if a few did not succeed.[23] Even so, the lessons from the past – the failures as well as the successes – must be learned if all the grandchildren of today's Latin Americans are to be assured a decent standard of living.

23 Mexico has been accepted as a member of the Organization for Economic Cooperation and Development (OECD), the club to which all DCs belong, but this has more to do with the politics of North American free trade than with Mexico's true economic standing.

2

The struggle for national identity from independence to midcentury

Independence, which most of Latin America had secured by the early 1820s, came at the end of a long period of economic turmoil and political upheaval during which, it can safely be assumed, living standards fell sharply. From the outbreak of hostilities between Great Britain and Spain during the Napoleonic wars, Latin America's external trade – imports and exports – was severely disrupted. The invasion of the Iberian Peninsula by Napoleon in 1808 and the imposition of his brother Joseph as king of Spain drove the Portuguese royal family to Brazil and created a temporary alliance between Great Britain and anti-Napoleonic forces in Spain. Exports from Latin America were adversely affected and domestic trade was undermined by the flood of imports into Latin America as British merchants searched for an alternative to the blocked continental market.[1]

Napoleon's successful invasion of Spain undermined Spanish authority in Latin America and provided the independence movement – until then weak and inchoate – with the impetus it desperately needed. By the time Napoleon had been finally defeated in 1815, the movement had acquired a dynamic of its own, and the reassertion of Spanish and Portuguese authority over the Iberian Peninsula could not be extended to Latin America. Brazil, a separate kingdom since 1815, refused to recognize the demands of João VI in Lisbon and crowned his son, Dom Pedro, as emperor in 1822.[2] New Spain became Mexico (an empire for nine months under Agustín de Iturbide) and extended briefly to the northern border of Colombia following the annexation of Central America.[3] Spain's South American colonies opted for republican government from the beginning, and by the mid-1820s Spain controlled only Cuba and Puerto Rico.[4] Even Santo Domingo, the eastern

---

1 The declared value of British exports to the Americas, other than the United States, jumped from £7.8 million in 1805 to £18.0 million in 1809. See Platt (1972), p. 28.
2 See Bethell (1985), pp. 179–87.
3 See Anna (1985), pp. 86–93.
4 See F. Knight (1990), Chapter 6.

part of Hispaniola, had been seized from Spain in 1822 by Haiti, which had gained its independence from France in 1804.[5]

Political turmoil did not end with independence. On the contrary, national boundaries inherited from Spain and Portugal were often subject to dispute. Central America had separated from Mexico by 1823, losing the province of Chiapas to its northern neighbor in the process, and it proceeded to function with extreme difficulty as a federation until 1838, when it broke up into its five constituent parts.[6] Texas broke away from Mexico in 1836,[7] and the Yucatán did the same in 1839 (although the Peninsula was reincorporated in 1843).[8] Gran Colombia – the union of Venezuela, Colombia, and Ecuador created by Simón Bolívar – finally broke up in 1830 after the Liberator's death,[9] and the short-lived union between Peru and Bolivia in the 1830s collapsed following a Chilean invasion.[10]

Even Brazil, where independence had been achieved without major upheaval, was not exempt from postindependence boundary disputes. Its attempt to incorporate the Banda Oriental into the empire provoked Argentine fury, and the resulting war led to the creation of Uruguay as a buffer state in 1828.[11] Brazil also had to contend with numerous revolts that were clearly secessionist in character,[12] and governments in Argentina and Chile engaged in wars against their Indian populations in an effort to extend the frontiers of the new republics over lands dominated by indigenous peoples undefeated by Spain.[13] Haitian domination of Santo Domingo was brought to an end with the creation of the Dominican Republic in 1844.[14] Paraguay was able only to postpone frontier disputes with its neighbors by retreating into the isolationist cocoon created by the absolutist José Gaspar Rodríguez de Francia.[15]

---

5 See Moya Pons (1985), pp. 237–55.

6 The five republics are Costa Rica, El Salvador, Guatemala, Honduras, and Nicaragua. Great Britain, however, exercised formal and informal rule over much of the isthmus's Atlantic Coast in the nineteenth century through colonies or protectorates in Belize (British Honduras), Mosquitia, and the Bay Islands. See Williams (1916).

7 Texas joined the United States in 1845, so the independent Lone Star republic lasted less than ten years. See Meyer and Sherman (1979), pp. 335–42.

8 See Reed (1964), pp. 4–32.

9 The collapse of Gran Colombia brought to an end the dream of pan-American union outlined by Bolívar in 1826 at the Panama Congress. On the stresses and strains of this early exercise in regional integration, see Bushnell (1970).

10 See Bonilla (1985), pp. 564–70.

11 See Lynch (1985), p. 688.

12 See Bushnell and Macaulay (1988), pp. 167–75.

13 The final defeat and subjugation of the Indian populations did not occur until the 1880s, however.

14 See Moya Pons (1985), pp. 255–68.

15 War did not break out between Paraguay and its neighbors until 1865, but when it did it was disastrous for the landlocked republic. The war of the Triple Alliance between Argentina, Brazil, and Uruguay on one side and Paraguay on the other led to the loss of half the latter's population and much territory.

Table 2.1. *The population of Latin America before and after
independence (in millions)*

Country	1788	1810	1823
New Spain[a]	5.9	7.0	6.8
Guatemala[b]	1.2	—[c]	1.6
Cuba and Puerto Rico	0.6	—[d]	0.8
Venezuela	0.9	0.95	0.79
New Granada[e]	1.8	2.0	2.0
Peru[f]	1.7	2.05	1.4
Chile	—[g]	—[g]	1.1
Río de la Plata[h]	1.1	2.35	2.3
Subtotal	13.2	14.35	16.79
Brazil[i]	1.9[j]	3.3[k]	4.0
Total	15.1	17.65	20.79

[a] Approximately Mexico before the 1850s.
[b] Approximately modern Central America.
[c] Included in New Spain.
[d] Not given.
[e] Equivalent to modern Panama and Colombia.
[f] Equivalent to modern Bolivia, Ecuador, and Peru.
[g] Included in Peru.
[h] Equivalent to modern Argentina, Paraguay, and Uruguay.
[i] Excludes noncatechized Indians.
[j] Data are for 1776.
[k] Data are for 1800.
Source: Rippy (1945), pp. 106, 107, and 127. More recent scholarship
has revised the total population figures downward. See, for example,
Lockhart and Schwartz (1983), p. 338, which gives a figure for circa
1800 of 12,557,000 (excluding Brazil), as a result of a lower estimate
for Río de la Plata.

The territorial disputes were an inevitable consequence of the decline of
Iberian power. Spain in particular had seen no reason to pay special attention
to boundaries that were little more than administrative conveniences. Furthermore, the small size of the population (see Table 2.1) and the low levels
of population density meant that boundaries often ran through areas which
were so underpopulated that local custom was a poor guide to how frontiers
should be drawn. Foreign powers were not afraid to take advantage of this
weakness in the nascent states of Latin America: The modern boundaries
of Belize and Guyana (both former British colonies) were secured in the
early nineteenth century at the expense of the neighboring republics,[16] and

16 On the Anglo-Guatemalan dispute over Belize (formerly British Honduras), see Humphreys (1961).
   On the boundary dispute between Guyana (formerly British Guiana) and Venezuela, see Lieuwen
   (1965), pp. 166–8.

Mexico lost almost half its territory to the United States in the midcentury war between the two republics.[17]

Political turmoil was not confined to disputes between republics. Civil war was an even greater source of friction in most cases, as the political elites struggled among themselves over the nature of the state, over relations with the Catholic Church, and over the organization of key institutions. These tensions, far graver than those that affected the United States at the end of the eighteenth century (where a consensus on many issues had emerged soon after the Revolutionary War), would not be resolved for many decades. A colonial system that had been erected and evolved over three centuries could not be dismantled overnight, and much of the upheaval can be seen as a dispute over how much of the colonial system should be preserved and how much replaced. It is appropriate, therefore, to turn briefly to the main features of the colonial economy inherited by the Latin American republics.

The colonial legacy

The organization of the colonial economy underwent many changes after the conquistadors arrived, but it was always guided by the principles of mercantilism.[18] Under this doctrine a nation's prosperity was linked to the accumulation of capital – and capital was often identified with precious metals. In the case of Spain and Portugal, where gold and silver were not available locally in significant quantities, the doctrine therefore demanded the accumulation of gold and silver (specie) through external trade.

Mercantilism had a number of special consequences for relations between colonial Latin America and the countries of the Iberian Peninsula. The theory demanded that Latin America purchase all of its commodity imports from Spain and Portugal and that it sell its commodity exports (excluding specie) in the same market. The resulting visible trade deficit would then be financed by the transfer of gold and silver to the Iberian Peninsula. The bigger the trade deficit, the bigger – in theory – the accumulation of specie by Spain and Portugal, with the limit being set by the physical capacity of the gold and silver mines in Latin America.

Because trade with other countries would reduce the trade deficit with the Iberian Peninsula, the doctrine of mercantilism required that it be suppressed. Spain and Portugal therefore imposed a trading monopoly and monopsony on their colonies. Latin American commodity exports were encouraged, however, provided they did not compete with, and were sold to,

17 See Bazant (1985), pp. 441–4. Although Mexico's territorial loss was considerable, only 2 percent of its population was affected.
18 On the theory of mercantilism and its pervasive influence throughout Europe at this time, see Blaug (1976), pp. 10 ff.

Table 2.2. *The colonial economic system*

	Iberian Peninsula		Latin America		
	Credits	Debits	Credits	Debits	
Visible commodity exports	500			500	Visible commodity imports
Visible commodity imports		300	300		Visible commodity exports
Balance of trade	200 (surplus)		200 (deficit)		Balance of trade
Net government transfers	100			100	Net government transfers
Imports of bullion		300	300		Exports of bullion
Overall balance	0			0	Overall balance

the mother country. As a result, Latin American exports of such tropical commodities as tobacco and sugar were welcomed.

The visible trade deficit was not the only mechanism under which Spain and Portugal sought to extract specie from the colonies. The division of the output of the mines among the private producers, the colonial administration, and the Iberian monarchs led to significant transfers to the Iberian Peninsula, so the balance-of-payments deficit increased further. This could be financed only by a flow of specie. In addition to taxes on the mines, the proceeds of a number of other local taxes were expected to be transferred to the Iberian Peninsula.

The impact of mercantilism on Iberian–Latin American relations is summarized in Table 2.2, where it is assumed that there is no trade with the rest of the world. The Iberian Peninsula's commodity exports (500 units) therefore equal Latin America's commodity imports, and Latin America's commodity exports (300 units) equal the Iberian Peninsula's commodity imports. The result is a visible trade imbalance (200 units) in favor of the Iberian Peninsula. Net official transfers (100 units) – consisting of such things as the royal tax on mines – leave a current account balance of 300 units. This is then financed by the export of bullion (specie) from Latin America to Spain and Portugal.

Because the shipment of specie was limited by the capacity of the mining industry, it is no surprise that those parts of the empire with the most important deposits of gold and silver – New Spain, Upper Peru, Chile, and New Granada[19] – received the most attention. Other areas, such as the Audiencia of Guatemala,[20] were for the most part neglected and had to fall back on their own (limited) resources. In the case of Portugal, the discovery of gold in central Brazil (Minas Gerais) in the eighteenth century transformed the attention given to the region and was the main reason for moving the capital from Bahia to Rio de Janeiro.[21]

The theory of mercantilism may have guided economic organization in colonial Latin America, but reality was often affected by events over which Spain and Portugal had little control. Thus neither imperial power was ever able to supply all the goods required by the colonies. Efforts to reexport to Latin America goods that had been purchased from the rest of Europe not only increased the cost to Latin America but also led to a flow of specie out of Portugal and Spain to its imperial rivals. Furthermore, in many parts of Latin America the high cost of goods bought from the imperial power led to a lively contraband trade with British, French, and Dutch traders.

Under the Bourbon reforms that started in 1759, Spain made serious efforts to overhaul the external and internal trading systems in Spanish America.[22] Although Spain never formally abandoned its monopoly of external trade, the business of exporting and importing was made easier. Commodity exports from Latin America increased in importance and became more diversified. Agricultural exports, in particular (see Table 2.3), expanded and linked Spanish America not just to Spain but also – through reexport or contraband – to other parts of Europe. A similar process was observed in Brazil, where the Pombaline reforms (named after the Portuguese Marquis de Pombal) eased trading restrictions and provided for an increase in commodity exports that coincided with the decline in gold production in Minas Gerais.[23]

Internal (intraregional) trade (see Table 2.3) also increased. Petty restrictions on intraregional commerce were removed, and a lively trade developed among many parts of the Iberian empires, stimulated by what was in effect a customs union. Agricultural trade, both extraregional and intraregional, led to gains in efficiency, which affected not just the plantation (typically dedicated to a single product for sale to the world market) but also the

---

19 The mining industry of New Spain was located in what is now Mexico, that of Upper Peru in Bolivia, and that of New Granada in Colombia. Maps showing the correlation between colonial and independent Latin America can be found in Humphreys (1946).
20 The Audiencia de Guatemala corresponds to modern Central America, plus Chiapas (annexed by Mexico at the time of independence). Small amounts of specie were produced in Honduras and Nicaragua, but not enough to excite much interest by the crown.
21 See Lockhart and Schwartz (1983), pp. 370–87.
22 The literature on the Bourbon reforms and their economic impact is huge. See, for example, Fisher (1985), Chapter 1.
23 On the Pombaline reforms, see Lockhart and Schwartz (1983), pp. 383–97.

Table 2.3. *Latin America: extraregional and intraregional trade at the end of the colonial era*

Area	Region	Products	Market Extraregional	Market Intraregional
Mexico	Central	Sugar, textiles		✓
	Oaxaca	Grain	✓	✓
	Yucatán	Indigo	✓	✓
	North	Cattle, textiles		✓
	North	Silver	✓	
Central America and the Caribbean	El Salvador	Indigo	✓	✓
	Honduras	Silver	✓	
	Costa Rica	Tobacco		✓
	Antilles	Sugar	✓	
Venezuela	Coast	Cacao	✓	✓
	Plains	Hides	✓	✓
Colombia	Eastern highlands	Gold, silver	✓	
Ecuador	Highlands	Textiles		✓
	Coast	Cacao	✓	✓
Peru and Bolivia	Highlands	Silver	✓	
	Highlands	Mercury		✓
	North coast	Sugar		✓
	South coast	Cotton		✓
Chile	North	Silver	✓	
	Central	Wheat	✓	✓
Argentina, Paraguay, and Uruguay	North and Central	Artisan products		✓
	Cuyo	Wine		✓
	Northeast	Yerba maté, cattle		✓
	Northeast	Sugar	✓	
	Río de la Plata	Tallow, hides	✓	
Brazil	Central	Gold, diamonds	✓	
	South	Cattle		✓
	Amazonia	Forestry	✓	

Source: Cardoso and Brignoli (1979a), pp. 218–20.

hacienda (the large estate on which many different products were produced for its own consumption, for sale in the local market, and for export).

The nonexport economy, neglected to a large extent under the Hapsburgs in the sixteenth and seventeenth centuries, also received attention from the Bourbon and Pombaline reforms. The nonexport economy was dominated by agriculture, but it also contained a large artisan sector, which was housed, for the most part, in the small imperial cities. Despite the presence of an important subsistence economy in most parts of Latin America, particularly in regions with a significant Indian population that still owned land communally, demand for a marketed agricultural surplus existed. This came from the small nuclei in the cities, from nonagricultural workers in the rural areas (especially the mining centers), and from plantation workers (often slaves). As the output of these three activities expanded under the eighteenth-century reforms, so did the need for agricultural goods for internal consumption – to the benefit, in the main, of the *hacienda*.

The artisan sector, shrouded by regulation and an almost feudal network of guilds, had grown up in response to the needs of the colonial administration and to the modest purchasing power of the region's inhabitants. Protected by legislation from non-Iberian imports, it was less able to defend itself from contraband as a result of its high cost and backward technology. Nevertheless, some artisan activities – notably textiles in New Spain[24] – did prosper, and a few commodities entered into intraregional trade (see Table 2.3).

With the exception of a handful of royal monopolies (e.g., tobacco and salt), most productive activities were in private hands. Sources of finance for private investment were limited, and many enterprises depended on reinvestment of profits or on the capital that new arrivals from the Iberian Peninsula brought with them. The other main sources of finance were the Catholic Church and the small merchant class. Means of payment (principally specie) were often in short supply as a result of the drain of bullion to the mother country.

The labor market evolved continuously after the arrival of the Spanish and Portuguese, but in general it was still marked by coercion and the absence of free wage labor, even at the time of independence. On the plantation slave labor remained common and, indeed, was finally abolished in Cuba and Brazil only in the late 1880s; on the *hacienda* the supply of labor often depended on debt peonage – a labor contract that made it virtually impossible for many workers to seek employment elsewhere – and antivagrancy laws added to the labor supply by compelling rural workers to show proof of employment. Some mines relied on wage labor, but others continued to depend on the *mita* – a particularly crude form of forced labor that was designed to guarantee mineowners an adequate supply of (usually) Indian labor.[25]

---

24 A number of good studies on the textile industry in New Spain exist. See, for example, Thomson (1989), part I.
25 The organization of labor in the colonial mining industry has been well researched. For a good survey, see Bakewell (1984), pp. 123–31.

The fiscal system was designed to maximize the flow of resources to the mother country, subject to the constraint imposed by the minimum requirements of administering the colonies. In practice this constraint often overwhelmed the ability of the colonies to remit funds to Spain or Portugal. Revenue came from taxes on external trade (mainly import duties), taxes on mining (the *quinto*), the ubiquitous *alcabala* (in effect, a sales tax), royal monopolies, a share of ecclesiastical tithes, Indian tribute (a poll tax), and the sale of public offices to *peninsulares* (the new arrivals from Spain and Portugal, for whom all the more important public posts were in theory reserved).[26] Expenditures consisted of administrative costs, military spending, and debt-service payments, but in the poorer regions of Spanish America these three items of expenditure exceeded revenue and forced the Spanish crown to implement a system of intraregional transfers from more prosperous regions (such as New Spain). Thus there was often little or no surplus left, even in the wealthier regions, to transfer to Spain, although Brazil was always able to remit some funds to Portugal.

The colonial economy went through a series of cycles, which under the Hapsburgs were determined mainly by the fortunes of the mining industry. The Bourbon reforms, however, produced a secular upswing in the second half of the eighteenth century, based on mining, agricultural exports, and intraregional trade. By 1800, according to one source,[27] Latin America was already the richest part of the Third World, with a real gross national product (GNP) per head (in 1960 prices) of $245 – similar to that in North America ($239). Although the figure for Latin America is almost certainly biased upward (see Coatsworth 1998), Latin America's relatively privileged status within what is now called the Third World at the end of the eighteenth century is difficult to dispute.[28]

This privileged position was undermined by the upheavals associated with the struggle for independence. The economic difficulties encountered in the first two decades of the nineteenth century can safely be assumed to have reduced real income per head in Latin America considerably.[29] External trade declined, there was a drain of capital out of the region through both capital flight and the return of many *peninsulares*, and the fiscal system virtually collapsed. Even worse, the productivity of the mines – the jewel

---

26 The contrast between the local-born *criollos* and foreign-born *peninsulares* and the often-complex relationship between the two have been the focus of numerous studies. For an overview, see Lockhart and Schwartz (1983), Chapter 9.

27 See Bairoch and Lévy-Leboyer (1981), Tables 1.6 and 1.7.

28 Compared to the United States, however, the growth of real per capita GDP in Latin America was disappointing in the eighteenth century. See Coatsworth (1993), Table 3, p. 14.

29 On the dismal economic performance in Mexico at the time of independence, see Coatsworth (1978) and Salvucci (1997). Randall (1977), p. 224, also gives a rough estimate of GDP for Mexico, which confirms the impression of a decline in the first half of the nineteenth century.

in the imperial crown – was seriously affected by flooding and subsidence, in addition to the damage that the disruption of external trade had caused.

The economic consequences of independence

Political independence gave the new republics the right to change many aspects of the colonial economy. The prime candidate was the external trade monopoly, which had proved so irksome throughout the colonial period and which had deprived Latin America of the chance to sell in the best-paying market and buy in the least expensive. The prospect of free trade excited the interest of the non-Iberian powers during the Latin American struggle for independence and provided a powerful incentive for Great Britain in particular, with its exportable surplus of manufactured goods, to recognize the fledgling republics.[30]

The end of the external trade monopoly represented a significant improvement, but the combined effects of the Bourbon and Pombaline reforms and the subsequent decline in Spanish and Portuguese authority had already given Latin America many of the advantages of free trade even before independence was attained. British merchants, for example, had rushed to fill the vacuum left by the Napoleonic invasion of the Iberian Peninsula and had settled in significant numbers in Rio de Janeiro, Buenos Aires, Valparaíso, and Lima.

Independence also gave Latin America the chance to raise capital on the international market. In practice this meant that the London stock exchange and British investors were quick to respond to the bond issues offered by the new republics. Access to the international capital market turned out to be a poisoned chalice, however. A combination of fraud, poor management, and unproductive investment of the proceeds meant that almost all issuing governments were in default by the end of the 1820s.[31]

Moreover, the advantages of free trade and access to the international capital market had to be set against certain disadvantages associated with the collapse of colonial rule. First, the creation of numerous independent republics and one empire (Brazil) brought to an end the de facto customs union that had operated in Latin America. Tariffs now applied on all imports – not just extraregional imports – and the inevitable consequence was trade

---

30 British recognition of Spanish American independence was relatively straightforward, and the story is elegantly told in the contemporary accounts collected in Webster (1938). In Brazil the position was complicated by Great Britain's long and close association with Portugal. The commercial prospects took precedence, however, and Great Britain recognized the independence of Brazil in 1825. See Manchester (1933), pp. 186–219. Recognition of Latin American independence by other countries was also heavily influenced by trade prospects. In the case of the United States, see Gleijeses (1992).

31 This story, laced with intrigue and larger-than-life characters, has been well described by Dawson (1990). Comparisons between this and later debt crises can be found in Marichal (1989).

diversion; that is, the replacement of cheaper imports from a partner with more expensive domestic products.

Second, capital flight was a serious blow to the pressing task of capital accumulation. The problem was not only the drain of finance capital from the region but also the decapitalization of existing enterprises as a result of civil war and political upheaval. The physical capital of the mines was not maintained or repaired, and many *haciendas* became very run down; this in turn led to problems of debt repayment – mainly to the Church – which crippled the domestic capital market in the first years after independence.[32]

Third, the collapse of the fiscal system was not due just to the wars of independence. Republican governments could hardly be expected to maintain royal taxes, the sale of public offices was now frowned on, and there was strong pressure in many countries to remove poll taxes. Early fiscal concessions proved disastrous for the health of the fiscal system, and some "colonial" taxes, such as Indian tributes, had to be reimposed. New administrations lacked the authority, in some cases, to collect traditional revenues and were reluctant to compound their political problems by imposing new taxes.

Fourth, the problem of fiscal balance was aggravated by the additional expenditures that the newly independent republics had to make. National armies had to be maintained, veterans of the wars of independence had to be pensioned off, and boundaries had to be protected. Claims for war damage were considerable and were aggravated by the series of regional disputes that proliferated after independence.

Thus independence offered two great advantages – free trade and access to international capital markets – that in the long run created opportunities for economic advance, but it also brought a series of disadvantages that in the short run swamped the benefits in most republics. Where the costs could be minimized as a result of relatively secure borders, stable government, and healthy tax revenues (as in Chile), the first decades of independence were by no means unsuccessful; where the costs were exacerbated by territorial conflict, political instability, and fiscal crisis (as in Mexico), the economic decline in the first two decades of the century could not be reversed.

Important elements of continuity with the colonial economy also continued to exist after independence. The land-tenure system, revolving as it did around the plantation, the *hacienda*, the small farm,[33] and communal Indian lands, was barely affected. Furthermore, where land grants were made by the newly independent countries on a massive scale (as in Argentina under General Juan Manuel de Rosas), they tended to follow

32 The relationship among the Catholic Church, finance, and capital accumulation has been studied most thoroughly in Mexico. See, for example, Chowning (1990).

33 The small farm, typically family owned and operated, has been relatively neglected in Latin America's economic history. For an exception, see Brading (1978).

the colonial pattern. Some war veterans received small parcels of land as a reward for military services, but these were insufficient to pose a threat to the traditional land-tenure system.

Access to the international capital market, following the disastrous experience of the 1820s, did not constitute a major challenge to the domestic capital market inherited from colonial times. The Church slowly recovered its position, despite the efforts by liberals to reduce its temporal wealth and power, and merchants – their ranks swelled by the numerous foreigners now established in commerce – continued to play a dominant role in financial intermediation. The only major innovation was the creation in Mexico of a state bank, Banco de Avío, to promote import-competing activities – an experiment that, like the first commercial banks in Brazil, did not survive beyond midcentury.[34]

The labor market was more problematic for the political elite in the independent countries. The durability of the land-tenure system and the domestic capital markets implied that no drastic changes could be made in labor relations or in the operation of labor markets. Mass immigration could not be expected, and the traditional labor shortage, from which many colonial activities had suffered, was unlikely to disappear. Yet many members of the political elite, particularly those who were infused with the ideas of the French and U.S. revolutions, were keen to abolish slavery and the numerous forms of coercion that had been applied to Indian labor. Furthermore, those members of the laboring classes who had fought bravely for independence did not welcome a return to coercive labor practices.

As it turned out, the labor market changed only slightly. Slavery was abolished in those republics where it was of little consequence (e.g., Central America) but retained where it played a crucial role in production (e.g., Brazil, Cuba, and Peru).[35] Tribute was abolished at first, but it was often restored when it became clear that the Indian laborer no longer had the same incentive to seek paid work. The *mita* was finally ended, but debt peonage and antivagrancy laws remained in place and were even adopted in those frontier areas, such as the Argentine pampas, where they had not previously been applied. For the Indian majorities in Mexico, Guatemala, Peru, and Bolivia, independence brought no perceptible change, and Black slaves in independent Brazil were in much the same position as their counterparts in the Spanish colonies of Cuba and Puerto Rico.

Continuity with colonialism was found not only in the economic sphere but also in political organization. Some members of the political elite favored major change, but others preferred a system that left the basic power

34 On the Banco de Avío in Mexico, see Potash (1983). On the failure to establish commercial banking in Brazil, see Prado (1991), pp. 135–65.

35 Slavery was abolished in Peru in 1854 – long before its abolition in Brazil and Cuba. A major consideration was the revenue generated by the guano boom, which allowed the Peruvian government to compensate the former slaveowners. See Bushnell and Macaulay (1988), pp. 243–4.

structures unaffected. This was clearest in the case of Brazil, where the colony simply declared itself an independent empire, and it was a major theme in Mexico's postindependence political struggles. These disputes spilled over – as we shall see – into the debates over economic organization and economic policy and in many republics prevented the emergence of that consensus which is indispensable for sound economic management.

The free-trade question

The abolition of the imperial monopoly in international commerce and the transition to free trade did not mean laissez-faire. On the contrary, the issue of which taxes, tariffs, and other restrictions to apply to external trade was an important matter of debate in the first decades after independence. An elite accustomed to innumerable colonial restrictions on the movement of goods and people was ill prepared for full-scale acceptance of Ricardian trade theory and the doctrine of comparative advantage. Furthermore, Great Britain – the most powerful trading nation in the world and the one most committed to free trade – still applied numerous restrictions on its commerce with the rest of the world as well as discriminatory tariffs in favor of its colonies, and Alexander Hamilton's writings in the United States had already established the theoretical case in favor of import taxes on manufactures to promote industrialization.[36]

The free-trade debate was not, therefore, about whether to tax trade but about the degree of taxation and the desired allocation of resources. The "free traders" wanted restrictions on trade to be as low as possible, and their case was most forcibly presented by the foreign merchants who had established themselves throughout the region since the collapse of Iberian power and whose raison d'être was the importation of foreign goods. The foreign traders were generally supported by their governments, although it should be remembered that foreign bondholders (principally British) had an opposite interest because debt-service payments were in many cases supposed to be guaranteed by customs revenues.

Domestic pressure groups favoring low restrictions on foreign trade included producers of exports, merchants engaged in either exporting or importing or both, and the small group of intellectuals who favored an international division of labor based on the exchange of primary products for manufactures. Ranged against these groups were numerous merchants engaged in the distribution of domestically produced commodities, landowners and farmers selling products threatened by imports from other countries (including other parts of Latin America), and the craft guilds concentrated

---

36 Hamilton's influential work was published in 1791 – only fifteen years after the publication of Adam Smith's *Wealth of Nations* had provided the strongest possible case for minimal state intervention and free trade.

in the small urban centers whose artisan production could not be expected to compete with imports without high tariffs.

The battle lines were clearly drawn, therefore, and the final decision rested with government. Since the executive tended to be drawn from precisely those groups lined up on different sides of the free-trade debate, it was not surprising that government positions were often ambivalent, inconsistent, and subject to change. Yet almost all Latin American governments were subject to one overriding constraint – the budget – which tended to be decisive in determining tariff policy.

The transition from colonialism to independence had increased, rather than decreased, dependence on trade taxes. Nontrade taxes were often deeply unpopular, difficult to administer, and easy to evade. Colombia abolished the *alcabala* in 1836 and phased out the tobacco monopoly; by midcentury more than 50 percent of all government revenue came from customs revenues, and the tariff on cloth, shoes, and hats alone accounted for 75 percent of all trade taxes. This example was by no means unique.

Faced with a yawning gap between revenue and expenditure, the governments of the newly independent states – with the exception of isolationist Paraguay – issued bonds through the international capital market in an effort to increase their sources of income. In almost all cases the outcome was unsatisfactory: The loans, reduced by exorbitant commissions and heavy discounts, could not be serviced, and governments were forced to default within a few years.

Foreign loans had therefore ceased to be an option by the end of the 1820s, and trade taxes accounted for a higher proportion of government revenue in the 1830s than they had fifty years earlier. Governments may have been aware of the "protective" function of the tariff, but in a fiscal crisis the revenue purpose had to come first.

Maximizing government revenue from trade taxes did not mean punitive rates of taxation. On the contrary, very high rates of tax would keep out all imports and encourage contraband, leaving the government with no revenue. Thus the trade treaties, which Great Britain in particular desired to sign with the independent states, were generally seen as an acceptable compromise, because they permitted the continuation of tariffs at rates that stood a good chance of maximizing revenue. The one exception, the 1810 trade treaty between Great Britain and Brazil that gave the former preferential access to the latter's market at low tariff rates, provoked an understandable reaction and it was not renewed when it lapsed in 1844. Great Britain lost its preferential status, and Brazilian tariff rates were raised substantially.[37]

---

37 An excellent account of the frictions generated between Brazil and Great Britain by the preferential trade treaty is Manchester (1933), pp. 69–108.

Revenue maximization was an art, not a science. Furthermore, the existence of numerous tariffs set at different rates – typically between 15 percent and 100 percent – on goods competing with domestic production gave ample scope for special pleading. In Peru, for example, the protectionist lobby was able to raise tariffs on a number of goods in the 1830s.[38] In Argentina the 1835 tariff code was almost overtly protectionist. In Mexico the conservative Lucas Alamán was even able to ban the import of British cottons in his efforts to promote the Mexican textile industry.[39]

Thus local interests could exploit the revenue-raising tariff for protectionist purposes in the first years after independence. Yet the element of protection in the tariff – a by-product of revenue maximization – was vulnerable in two ways. First, a failure of local industry to respond with goods in sufficient quality and quantity to compete with imports was bound to cause resentment once living standards started to rise. The tariff was also extremely regressive. An illustrative example was provided for Colombia in 1852 by Salvador Camacho Roldán: Although a peasant might earn 300 pesos a year, he would consume cloth worth 50 pesos and pay 20 pesos in tariffs (7 percent of his income); meanwhile, a wealthy merchant with an income of 6,000 pesos might purchase 50 pesos' worth of imported silks and pay a tariff of only 5 pesos (less than 0.1 percent of his income).[40]

Second, revenue maximization was only a conditional target. If the fiscal crisis should start to abate – as a result, for example, of an expansion of external trade – fiscal targets could be achieved with lower tariff rates. The performance of exports was therefore crucial to the outcome of the free-trade debate. We now turn to that important subject.

The export sector

The Bourbon and Pombaline reforms in the second half of the eighteenth century had paved the way for the emergence of a number of new agricultural exports from Latin America, but for many countries the basis of the export economy was still mining. The mines had suffered badly during the first two decades of the nineteenth century: Foreign markets had been disrupted by the Napoleonic wars, and the struggle for independence had forced many mineowners to abandon production, which led to flooding and subsidence.[41]

---

38 The protectionist lobby and its efforts to influence policy are well illustrated by Gootenberg (1989), Chapter 3.

39 The promotion of the Mexican textile industry after independence became something of a *cause célèbre* among those who did not succumb to the free-trade doctrine. See Salvucci (1987). pp. 166–76.

40 This example is given in Deas (1982) as part of a detailed study of nineteenth-century Colombian public revenue.

41 Prados de la Escosura (1993) provides good case studies for several countries at the time of independence.

Recovery of mining capacity was considered a high priority in those economies that were traditionally dependent on mining exports (Mexico, Colombia, Peru, Bolivia, and Chile). Domestic capital for rehabilitating the mines was scarce, but foreign capitalists – spurred on by (unsubstantiated) stories of the region's fabled mineral wealth – were keen to participate not only in the recovery of mining capacity in traditional areas but also in the search for new deposits. In 1824–5 no fewer than twenty-five British mining associations were formed to operate in Latin America, with a total paid-in capital of £3.5 million. Their activities stretched from Mexico to Chile, with Paraguay the only country excluded.[42]

As with the government bonds issued in the same period, so it was with the mining associations. Virtually all of them failed, the capital was lost, and foreign investors formed a jaundiced view of a region that had promised so much only a few years before. The capital invested had proved insufficient for the task of rehabilitation, and foreigners were perhaps not best placed to cope with the problems of running a successful business in countries that were still subject to major political instability.

It would be wrong, however, to assume that the withdrawal of foreign interest spelled disaster for the mining industry. In most of the mining areas production and export had begun to recover by the 1840s, and in some cases recovery came much sooner. Peruvian silver production doubled in the 1830s; Mexican silver output hit bottom in the 1820s and then began to recover slowly. Colombian gold exports continued to stagnate throughout this period, but Mexican gold production doubled between the 1820s and the 1840s – by which time it was almost back to late-eighteenth-century levels.

In Chile mining output not only recovered, it far surpassed colonial levels of production. This was due above all to the discovery of spectacular veins of silver at Chañarcillo and of new, relatively accessible deposits of copper in several locations, which helped to raise production from an annual average of 1.5 million kg before independence to 12.3 million kg by 1850.[43] The ease of access to the new deposits kept capital costs down and therefore avoided the problem in, for example, Mexico, where the need for heavy capital investments delayed the recovery of production.

The world demand for copper was linked to the Industrial Revolution underway in Europe and North America. In terms of the commodity lottery (see Chapter 1), Chile was clearly fortunate to have gained access to the world market on the basis of a product for which world demand was expanding rapidly, market share could be increased, and costs of production were low. The dominant mineral export for Latin America, however, remained

---

42 The failure of these foreign mining enterprises is described in Rippy (1959), pp. 23–5.
43 On the expansion of Chilean copper and silver production after independence, see Pederson (1966).

silver, for which demand was determined primarily by its use as a means of payment. With the gold standard already established in Great Britain and later adopted by other countries, silver was an industry in long-run structural decline and therefore ill equipped to play the role of leading sector in an export-led growth model.

The restrictions imposed on the nonmining economy until the eighteenth-century Bourbon reforms meant that only a handful of agricultural exports could be described as "traditional." Some of these, such as indigo from Mexico and cochineal from Central America, would soon face competition from synthetic dyes. Another product, sugar, suffered from discrimination by the imperial powers in favor of their colonies and by measures to promote the sugar beet industry in Europe.

It was not surprising, therefore, that many traditional agricultural exports suffered relative and – in some cases – absolute decline in the years after independence. In one instance, however, there was a spectacular boom. This was Cuban sugar, which benefited from the collapse of the sugar industry in the neighboring island of Hispaniola (ruled from Port-au-Prince until the permanent division of the island in 1844) and from the settlement in Cuba of many planters from other parts of Latin America following the collapse of the Spanish and French empires. Indeed, Cuba was the first country in Latin America to construct a railway – a direct response to the growth of the sugar industry – the first lines of which were opened in 1838.[44]

In general, however, the performance of traditional exports was disappointing. The expansion of agricultural exports therefore depended on nontraditional exports – either those that had been established in the latter half of the eighteenth century or new products that had not previously been exported. In Brazil coffee continued its advance, rising to nearly 50 percent of total exports by midcentury; in Colombia it began to take permanent root;[45] and in Costa Rica it was exported for the first time in the 1830s and had established a strong presence by the 1840s. Cacao, almost a traditional export, responded to the growing European demand for chocolate, and exports from both Venezuela and Ecuador rose significantly.[46]

The export of cattle and its by-products (e.g., hides, jerked beef, and tallow) had acquired an important foothold in Argentina even before independence. After a period of virtual stagnation in the 1820s, the industry began to expand, and the rate of growth accelerated in the 1840s. Although cattle exports were also growing in other parts of Latin America (notably

44 The growth of the Cuban sugar industry in this period has been the subject of many studies. See, for example, Thomas (1971), pp. 109–27.

45 Ocampo (1984a), pp. 301–46, provides a superb account of the rise of coffee exports in nineteenth-century Colombia. Although coffee exports became established in the first half of the century, the major expansion was after 1850.

46 On the cacao industry, both in Latin America and elsewhere, see Clarence-Smith (2000).

Venezuela), what is noteworthy about its growth in Argentina is the early evidence of forward linkages. By midcentury many *saladeros* – some with several hundred employees – had been established in Buenos Aires to prepare jerked beef for foreign markets, including Brazil, where it was a staple for many plantation slaves.[47]

The most spectacular nontraditional export was guano from Peru. From a zero base in 1840, guano had reached 350,000 tons annually by the 1850s – nearly 60 percent of all Peruvian exports in that decade. Although Peru's guano age had only just begun by 1850, the main weaknesses were already apparent: Guano, which required very little capital and used cheap, unskilled, imported labor, was a rent-creating activity in which the surplus was divided between the state and the (mainly foreign) merchants. Because neither group was particularly disposed to use its share of the economic rent to promote productive investment in other branches of the economy, the struggle over rental shares made little difference to the long-run growth of the Peruvian economy.[48]

The aggregate export performance of Latin America by midcentury was therefore affected by three broad trends. First, the region was restoring exports lost during the first two or even three decades of the nineteenth century; second, export performance was affected by the presence of certain traditional activities in long-run secular decline; third, exports were affected by the growth or introduction of nontraditional products. Not surprisingly, export performance by midcentury – if compared with the end of the eighteenth century – was not impressive in countries like Mexico and Bolivia, where the negative impact of the first two trends was so strong. Where the initial export decline had been modest (as in Argentina) or where nontraditional exports had jumped in importance (as in Brazil and Peru), exports did manage to grow in the first three decades after independence at a rate that exceeded population expansion. The best performances were recorded by Chile and Cuba, where favorable supply-side conditions allowed both countries to win market share in copper and sugar, respectively.

Export statistics in this period of Latin American economic history are deficient and incomplete, but we can use the evidence available to calculate a rough measure of exports per person by midcentury (see Table 2.4).[49] Some of the results are unsurprising. Cuba, where the sugar industry was forging ahead, achieved a level of exports per head higher than Australia's ($16.5)

---

47 Many excellent monographs deal with this period of Argentine economic history. See, for example, Brown (1979).

48 The classic statement on the weak backward and forward linkages associated with guano can be found in Levin (1960). For a more positive assessment, see Hunt (1985).

49 Bairoch and Etemard (1985), Table 1.5, provide an estimate of exports per head for Latin America in 1829–31 of $5.1. Though based on incomplete figures, this is very similar to the figure of $5.2 in 1850 found in Table 2.4 – confirming the stagnation of exports per head in the first decades after independence.

Table 2.4. *Exports, population, and exports per head, circa 1850*

Country	Exports (in thousands of US$)	Population (in thousands)	Exports per head (in US$)
Argentina	11,310	1,100	10.3
Bolivia	7,500	1,374	5.5
Brazil	35,850	7,230	5.0
Chile	11,308	1,443	7.8
Colombia	4,133	2,200	1.9
Costa Rica	1,150	101	11.4
Cuba	26,333	1,186	22.2
Dominican Republic	500	146	3.4
Ecuador	1,594	816	2.0
El Salvador	1,185	366	3.2
Guatemala	1,404	847	1.7
Haiti	4,499	938	4.8
Honduras	1,125	230	4.9
Mexico	24,313	7,662	3.2
Nicaragua	1,010	274	3.7
Paraguay	451	350	1.3
Peru	7,500	2,001	3.7
Puerto Rico	6,204[a]	495	13.7[a]
Uruguay	7,250	132	54.9
Venezuela	4,865	1,490	3.3
Latin America	159,484	30,381	5.2

Note: A three-year average has been used wherever possible.
[a] The exports and exports per head figures are for 1844.
Source: See Appendix I.

and as high as New Zealand's ($21.4). Uruguay, with its tiny population and high level of trade boosted by reexports from parts of Argentina and Brazil, scored the highest figure. By midcentury Costa Rica had reaped a good harvest from its early specialization in coffee. In general, however, the figures suggest that the efforts to promote external trade had met with only modest success. A handful of countries, notably Paraguay, had eschewed export-led growth after independence,[50] which accounts for the low ratio of exports to population. Yet other countries that were ostensibly committed to the expansion of external trade, such as Colombia and Mexico, appeared to have made virtually no progress.

Export growth after independence was therefore far from spectacular, but at least it appears to have been accompanied by a secular improvement in

50 The isolation of Paraguay in this period is not disputed. See, for example, Pastore (1994). Burns (1980) argues that Guatemala under Rafael Carrera (1838–65) followed a similar path. This would help to explain the extraordinarily low figure for Guatemalan exports per head in Table 2.4.

the net barter terms of trade (NBTT). Although the price of some Latin American primary-product exports (e.g., hides, indigo, and vanilla) did fall, the price of imports (particularly textiles and clothing) fell even further. Leff, for example, finds clear evidence of a substantial improvement in the NBTT for Brazil up to the 1850s; this is confirmed for many other Latin American countries in a study of their trade with France.[51]

The improvement in Latin America's NBTT is not at all surprising for this period. The growth of modern industry in Europe and North America brought a downward shift in industrial supply curves, together with a fall in the price of many manufactures, and competition ensured that this was then passed on to consumers throughout the world. Production of most primary products, however, was not yet subject to the same technological revolution, so prices were determined much more by shifts in the world demand curve. With world demand for primary products growing, this implied price increases for many commodities and an improvement in the NBTT of primary producers. Indeed, classical economists who wrote in the midnineteenth century never questioned the prevailing assumption that the NBTT of primary producers would improve in the long run.

The improvement in the NBTT meant that, despite the problems of the export sector, the capacity to import started to increase. Customs revenue rose, and the fiscal crisis became less acute. The disputes over the tariff did not disappear, but several governments shifted toward a less protectionist stance, and at least one – that of Peru – had become aggressively liberal by the early 1850s.[52] Even Paraguay, following Francia's death in 1840, had slowly begun to dismantle its self-imposed isolation in favor of a more export-oriented development strategy.[53]

The nonexport economy

Not surprisingly, Latin America's postindependence adoption of an outward-looking strategy has led to a great deal of research on the export sector. Much less is known about the nonexport economy, particularly in the first fifty years after independence – which is understandable in view of the paucity of statistics compared with those on foreign trade. The neglect of the nonexport economy in theoretical and empirical work on Latin America's economic history is most unfortunate, for several reasons.

51 For Brazil's NBTT in this period, see Leff (1982a), p. 82. For the terms of trade between France and Latin America, see Schneider (1981).
52 The final triumph of the free traders over their protectionist rivals is well described in Gootenberg (1991).
53 See Lynch (1985b), pp. 668–70. For a spirited defense of the isolationism favored by Francia, see Burns (1980).

First, Latin America inherited a nonexport economy after independence that may have suffered from extremely low levels of productivity and high levels of inefficiency but which was far larger than the export sector. The Bourbon and Pombaline reforms in the eighteenth century could not disguise the fact that levels of international trade and international trade per head were very modest, so the export sector accounted for a very small proportion of real gross domestic product (GDP). In Brazil the ratio of exports to GDP in the early 1820s was probably little more than 5 percent.[54] Such a small ratio kept imports per head to low levels and forced Brazil to meet the bulk of its consumption requirements through domestic production of goods and services. The flood of imports – mainly British – entering Latin America at the time of independence may have temporarily distorted the relationship between consumption and domestic production, but by the end of the 1820s the traditional ratios had been restored.

The small size of the export sector meant that a policy of export-led growth would not produce dividends unless and until the productivity of the nonexport sector improved as a result of the growth of exports. Such a transformation was more likely to occur if a large part of the nonexport sector was complementary to exports. In the first decades after independence, however, this was by no means self-evident. The backward and forward linkages of the export sector to the rest of the economy were generally weak, and the derived demand for goods and services from the payment of factor incomes was just as likely to stimulate imports as local production.

The nonexport economy was extremely heterogeneous and consisted of those activities that in theory competed with imports (tradables) and those that did not (nontradables). The most important tradables were agriculture for domestic use, handicrafts, and artisan production, although some services – notably coastal shipping – also faced foreign competition. Commerce, both wholesale and retail, was penetrated by foreign merchants, but it must still be classified as nontradable because the activity itself could not be satisfied by imports. Other important nontradables were construction, transport, and personal services – above all, domestic servants. Financial services and public administration (very important nontradables today), by contrast, were very undeveloped.

Domestic agriculture centered on the *hacienda*, the small farm (known in Mexico as a *rancho*), and – in some countries – Indian communal lands. Economic growth in the late eighteenth century had led to an increase in the marketed surplus from the *hacienda*, while the small farm had expanded in those areas – such as Minas Gerais in Brazil – in which mining production

54 Brazil's exports per head in the early 1820s were approximately $2 at 1880 prices. See Leff (1982), p. 80. The subsistence level of GDP per head at 1880 prices – that is, the lowest realistic figure – is about $40. Assuming Brazil was close to this level in the 1820s, this implies a ratio of exports to GDP (at 1880 prices) of 5 percent.

had gone into decline. The disruptions faced by domestic agriculture in the first two decades of the nineteenth century were less than those faced by mining, although the collapse of the colonial customs union was a severe blow to farmers, such as those in central Chile, who were accustomed to supplying other parts of the empire.[55]

The move toward free trade by independent Latin America did not pose much of a threat to domestic agriculture. Restrictions on imports of many foodstuffs continued, and the high cost of transportation was an additional barrier against international competition. Land was plentiful, and working capital was available – at least for the *hacienda* – through the traditional conduits of the Church and the merchant class once the disruptions associated with independence had subsided.

The growth of the export sector was not a threat to domestic agriculture either, except in a few isolated cases in which competition for scarce labor drove up wage rates. More serious were the limited spread effects imposed by the inadequate internal transport system in most countries. The growth of henequen exports from the Yucatán, for example, could not do much to call forth a larger marketed surplus from the Mexican Bajío[56] as long as transport links were inadequate. Countries with a littoral population, such as Brazil, were better placed to exploit the opportunities as a result of coastal shipping. Chile, with the same geographical features, went even further at first and restricted coastal shipping to local firms although foreigners (as individuals) were prominent in the trade.[57]

The most problematic part of the tradables sector was artisan or handicrafts production. This sector had developed in response to the consumption needs of a population that was largely deprived of, or unable to pay for, imports. Although in some cases the quality of workmanship was excellent, unit costs were high and the technology used was extremely backward. Furthermore, the absence of appropriate raw materials meant that the goods produced – however ingenious – were often only an imperfect substitute for what was required.[58]

The only way the sector could effectively protect itself against imports was to transform itself into modern manufacturing through the transfer of

55 Chile was able to export wheat and flour to Australia and California during the midcentury gold rush. See García (1989), pp. 84–6.
56 Haber (1992) has drawn attention to the transport bottlenecks that impeded the growth of Mexican industry in the first half-century after independence.
57 The Chilean merchant navy was promoted by an 1835 law which reserved all domestic coastal trade for Chilean ships. By 1850, however, this discrimination against foreign ships had been ended. See García (1989), pp. 112–18.
58 A good example is the widespread use of leather windows in the cattle-producing regions of Latin America, where glass was either unavailable or prohibitively expensive.

imported technology. This process, known as protoindustrialization, had occurred in parts of Europe and was taking place in the United States in response to the Industrial Revolution in Great Britain. Studies of protoindustrialization in Latin America are still in their infancy, but it appears not to have been of any importance.[59] On the contrary, the growth of modern manufacturing in Latin America was an independent process that threatened the handicraft sector as much as imports did.

The textile industry provides the clearest example of these tensions. Consumption, apart from the finest cloths, had traditionally been met by the output of *obrajes*, or workshops, which operated with a simple labor-intensive technology.[60] Following independence, imports expanded and came to represent the single largest item in the import bill. The penetration of these imports, products of modern manufacturing, above all in Great Britain, the United States, and France, encouraged several republics – notably Mexico – to promote modern manufacturing techniques that competed with the production from the *obrajes* as much as with imports.

The failure of the handicraft sector to adapt to the spread of new technology was not immediately apparent. The low level of exports and their slow growth in the first few decades after independence restricted the penetration of imports, and inadequate transport provided artisan production in the interior with high levels of protection. In some cases – for example, traditional Indian dress in Guatemala – imports could never be more than an imperfect substitute, given the complexity and variety of domestic designs.

The handicraft sector was also protected by the very modest growth of modern manufacturing in the first decades after independence. The reasons for this failure are not self-evident. The transition to free trade, as stressed above, did not mean laissez-faire, and both tariff and nontariff barriers provided a significant degree of protection for many industrial goods. Markets were small, but the population was growing and some parts of Latin America had demographic profiles that were not so different from European countries in which the Industrial Revolution was beginning to take root.[61]

The establishment of a modern textile industry in Mexico showed what could be achieved. The state-supported Banco de Avío, financed by tariffs

59 Berry (1987) provides a careful assessment of the obstacles to protoindustrialization in the Colombian case.
60 See Salvucci (1987) and Thomson (1989). For the textile industry in Peru, see Gootenberg (1989), pp. 46–8.
61 At the time of independence the population of Brazil, for example, was roughly comparable to those of Portugal, Romania, and Sweden and was much larger than those of Denmark, Finland, Greece, Norway, and Serbia. See Berend (1982), p. 46.

on imports, channeled finance toward the new activities, while trade policy even prohibited certain classes of competing imports. The transfer of technology was carried out through the importation of machines and, where necessary, skilled labor.[62]

Elsewhere, no such consensus in favor of modern manufacturing existed, and policy was not consistent. Peru, for example, vacillated between liberal import policies and outright prohibition until the 1850s, when the republic finally settled for an open trading regime. Brazil adopted a more protectionist stance, following the end of the preferential trade treaty with Great Britain in 1844, but it failed to adopt other measures in support of modern manufacturing.[63] Even Mexico could not sustain the consensus in favor of modern manufacturing: the Banco de Avío closed in the 1840s, leaving a serious gap in the industrial capital market.

The reluctance to promote modern manufacturing was understandable. Textile manufacturing in Mexico, for example, may have been successful in production terms, but unit costs remained high, and the industry could not compete in export markets. Meanwhile, the price of manufactured imports – including textiles – continued to fall as technological innovations shifted supply curves downward. The case for basing comparative advantage on primary-product exports was strong.

The consequence was a nonexport sector in which many branches were ill equipped to take advantage of the growth of exports. With weak linkages, fast economic growth required exceptional export performance. Yet, as we have seen, export growth in the first few decades after independence was far from spectacular. Thus the transition to free trade put pressure on the import-competing branches of the nonexport sector, while the rest of the nonexport sector received only a modest stimulus from any growth in exports. For many republics it was the worst of both worlds.

Regional differences

By midcentury a consensus had emerged throughout the countries of Latin America in favor of export-led growth. The adoption of this consensus had not been straightforward, however, and in a number of countries (e.g., Mexico and Brazil) the policies designed to support export-led growth were inconsistent. Furthermore, a few republics were still in such a chronic state of political instability (e.g., Central America, Ecuador, and Bolivia) that governments lacked the means of implementing policies in favor of export-led growth, even when a consensus had emerged to support it.

62 On Mexican policies to promote industry in general, see Thomson (1985), pp. 113–42.
63 See Prado (1991), pp. 118–65.

Countries that adopted consistent policies in support of export-led growth tended to be those favored by the commodity lottery. Chile, under the stern influence of the conservative Diego Portales, put in place a series of reforms that reinforced the expansion of external trade facilitated by copper and silver exports. Peru, following its success with guano, adopted a full-fledged export-led model, and in Cuba the colonial administration swept away the remaining obstacles in the path of sugar exports.

The main beneficiaries of the commodity lottery were those countries that were best placed to satisfy the ever-growing demand for foodstuffs and raw materials by the expanding economies of Europe and the United States. Due to high international transport costs, this generally meant countries with well-developed Atlantic ports, such as Argentina and Cuba, but for a country that enjoyed a dominant position in the world market – as in the case of Peruvian guano – a Pacific Coast location was not a serious problem. Furthermore, in the case of minerals – such as Chilean copper – the high ratio of export value to transport costs also meant that location was not so important.

The advantages of the commodity lottery for certain products could easily be swamped by the decline of traditional exports, however. This was clearly the case in Colombia, where expanding exports of quinine, tobacco, and (to a lesser extent) coffee could only partially compensate for the decline in gold exports. It was also true of Brazil, where the decline of cotton and sugar in the Northeast dampened the expansionary impact of the coffee boom, and of Argentina, where the export growth associated with the cattle industry had to compensate for the fall in reexports of silver from the mines of Potosí.[64]

In a few cases the decline or stagnation of traditional exports was not matched by the growth of nontraditional exports, and aggregate export performance was extremely unsatisfactory. In both Haiti and the Dominican Republic the demise of the sugar industry as a result of the struggle for independence left a gaping hole in the economy. Central America, with the exception of coffee in Costa Rica, struggled unsuccessfully to find new products with which to insert itself into the world market, and Bolivia was unable to compensate for the decline of its traditional silver industry.

Paraguay, in self-imposed isolation until the 1840s, was the last country to adopt export-led growth, and by midcentury the results were still barely visible. Forced by its geographical location to export its products mainly through the River Plate, Paraguay was at the mercy of its more powerful Atlantic neighbors. Yet Paraguay had little choice: The years of isolation under Francia had brought little material prosperity, and the absence of

---

64 Under colonial administration, following the Bourbon reforms, silver from Upper Peru (Bolivia) had begun to be exported through Buenos Aires. This profitable trade declined after independence.

imports to buy capital goods was a severe constraint on the emergence of almost all new activities.[65]

Export performance was an important determinant of export-led growth. It was not the only determinant, however, for the links between the export sector and the rest of the economy must also be considered. Although research in this area is still in its infancy, it seems clear that these links varied from moderate to very weak. In Peru fast growth of exports occurred at the same time as a sharp contraction in the number of manufacturing and service businesses in the Lima economy,[66] and only commerce experienced a significant expansion. In Brazil and Cuba the use of slave labor in the expanding exports of coffee and sugar, respectively, reduced the derived demand for consumer goods to a minimum.

The links between the export and nonexport sectors were determined by many considerations. The "ideal" product generated forward linkages through a significant degree of processing, backward linkages through domestically produced inputs, high fiscal revenues through tax receipts, and demand for domestically produced consumer goods through payment of factor incomes. Clearly no products matched all these requirements, but some fared better than others. Thus Chilean copper generated some forward linkages through a simple refining process, earned substantial revenue for the state, and provided a derived demand for consumer goods through payment of high wage incomes. Peruvian guano, on the other hand, had no backward or forward linkages and generated only a modest demand for consumer goods, although it did contribute handsomely to government revenue.[67]

Thus only Chile appeared to enjoy both rapid growth of exports and moderate links between the export and nonexport sectors of the economy. Chile is probably the only country to have come close to the 1.5 percent growth of real income per head recorded by the United States in this period.[68] Elsewhere, given the expansion of the population,[69] growth of real income per head was probably modest indeed, or even negative.

---

65 This is the generally held view of the Francia regime, although it is challenged by Burns (1980). In this and subsequent work – see, for example, Burns (1991) for a study of nineteenth-century Nicaragua – Burns argues that the equality of income distribution and material prosperity for "the folk" varied inversely with the extent of external trade.

66 See Gootenberg (1989), Table 2.1, p. 165.

67 It is the fiscal contribution, allowing an increase in government expenditure, that leads Hunt (1985) to argue that the contribution of guano was much more positive than has usually been claimed.

68 The most detailed study on U.S. growth rates per head after 1774 is that by Gallman (2000). Díaz, Lüders, and Wagner (1998, AE18) estimate the rate of growth of Chilean GDP per head to have been 1.4 percent between 1820 and 1850. By contrast, Maddison (1995, p. 202) estimates a negative rate of growth for Mexico and a mere 0.2 percent for Brazil.

69 By 1850 (see Table 2.4) the population of Latin America had reached 30 million. Assuming the figure given for 1823 in Table 2.1 is accurate, this implies an annual rate of growth of population of 1.4 percent.

Among the many thousands of people who crossed the Atlantic from Europe at this time, few voluntarily chose Latin America as their final destination. Moreover, the trade in African slaves to Brazil, Cuba, and Puerto Rico continued unabated, despite the long diplomatic offensive by Great Britain. Many of the foreign merchants who had arrived with such enthusiasm around the time of independence had returned home, and few skilled workers were attracted as yet by the mining and other export activities. The great expectations formed at the time of independence had not been fulfilled, and Bolívar's vision of Latin American unity had collapsed. For most Latin Americans the major consolation was that things could only improve.

3

The export sector and the world economy, circa 1850–1914

By the middle of the nineteenth century the growth of the world economy and the secular expansion of international trade provided the background for all discussion in Latin America on economic policy and economic development. Throughout the subcontinent a broad measure of agreement had been reached that Latin America's best hope for rapid economic advancement rested on closer integration into the world economy through commodity exports and capital imports, with some countries also favoring European immigration. Alternative theories, which emphasized either protection of domestic import-competing activities or (less realistically) the promotion of manufactured exports, commanded little support among the political elite.

As the early postindependence period had shown, the growth of commodity exports in the presence of a favorable external stimulus could not be taken for granted. The obstacles on the supply side were still considerable, and the political weakness of many of the emerging states was a major handicap. Even an apparently strong state, such as Argentina under General Juan Manuel de Rosas (1829–52), lacked the necessary political consensus to implement successfully a set of consistent economic policies.

The problem was not made any easier by the attentions of foreign powers, whose respect for Latin American independence was sometimes ambivalent. Spain, for example, made an unsuccessful attempt to reestablish its authority over both the Dominican Republic and the Pacific islands off the coast of Peru in the 1860s,[1] but it did succeed in putting down a ten-year struggle for independence in Cuba (1868–78).[2] France intervened in

---

1 The most serious of these episodes was the annexation of Santo Domingo (the Dominican Republic) by Spain in 1861. It took four years to restore the country's independence. See Moya Pons (1985), pp. 272–5.

2 This unsuccessful ten-year struggle for independence launched José Martí as a leader of the Cuban nationalist movement. See Foner (1963), Chapters 15–21. Martí was the leader of the nationalist movement at the start of the war (1895–8) that finally ended Spanish rule in Cuba although he himself was killed in 1895.

Mexico (1861–7) to impose and then support the Hapsburg Maximilian as emperor in an imperialist gesture that the United States, despite the Monroe Doctrine, was at first powerless to resist because of its Civil War.[3]

Great Britain, France, and The Netherlands, which had colonies to protect in the Americas, were all involved in occasional territorial disputes with independent Latin American states, but these were relatively minor.[4] More serious were the frictions with European powers caused by commerce in general and by investments in particular. Brazil broke off diplomatic relations with Great Britain following the latter's vigorous efforts to suppress the slave trade.[5] French intervention in Mexico began as a tripartite effort with Great Britain and Spain in 1861 to enforce bond repayments.[6] In 1902 irritation at nonpayment of bond interest drove Great Britain, Germany, and Italy to blockade Venezuela.[7]

The appearance of European warships off the coast of Venezuela was a challenge not just to the government in Caracas but also to the United States. Flushed by its success in helping to drive Spain out of Cuba, Puerto Rico, and the Philippines,[8] the United States launched itself in the Caribbean in a fashion that was colonialist in all but name.[9] Panama was prized away from Colombia in 1903, and work immediately began on the interoceanic canal.[10]

---

3 The Monroe Doctrine, proclaimed in the 1820s, gave warning of U.S. resistance to all attempts to establish new European possessions in the Americas. The French intervention in Mexico is described in Haslip (1971).

4 In the nineteenth century Denmark and Sweden also had small colonies in the Caribbean. Only Great Britain (British Honduras, British Guiana), France (French Guiana), and The Netherlands (Dutch Guiana) had mainland possessions; all three European powers controlled islands in the Caribbean and – in the British case – in the South Atlantic (the Falkland Islands and dependencies). British protectorates in the Bay Islands (off Honduras) and on the Mosquito Coast of Central America (Honduras and Nicaragua) were abandoned after 1860.

5 The Atlantic slave trade was seen by Brazil as essential to maintaining the supply of slave labor. On the friction between Brazil and Great Britain created by the trade, see Bethell (1970).

6 The liberal reforms launched by President Benito Juárez after the adoption of the 1857 constitution provoked a strong conservative reaction that led to civil war. The Mexican state could not meet its debt obligations, so Europe intervened in 1861. See Marichal (1989), pp. 65–7.

7 This blockade, discussed in detail in Hood (1975), provoked two very different reactions. Latin American states promoted the Drago Doctrine, designed to ensure that nonpayment of debt never became a reason for foreign military intervention. The United States, on the other hand, would shortly proclaim the Roosevelt Corollary to the Monroe Doctrine, the purpose of which was to reduce the justification for European intervention through greater U.S. involvement in the internal affairs of countries "at risk."

8 This projection of U.S. strength, a reflection of its emergence as an economic power of the first rank in the last quarter of the nineteenth century, is discussed in Smith (1986).

9 An excellent "insider" account of this period of U.S. expansion appears in Munro (1964). Dana Munro was a State Department official who worked on Caribbean and Central American affairs for many years.

10 The literature on the part played by the United States in the independence of Panama is huge. See, for example, Schoonover (1991), Chapter 6.

Nicaragua was occupied for the first time in 1912,[11] and a few years later U.S. marines entered Haiti and the Dominican Republic.[12] Puerto Rico traded Spanish rule for U.S. suzerainty, and Cuba narrowly escaped the same fate.[13] Following a tradition established by European powers, the United States took control of the customs house in a number of republics in order to ensure prompt payment of external debts and to reduce the chance of further European interventions.[14]

These episodes in imperial history were both the cause and the effect of political weakness and instability in Latin America. Political stability was also threatened by a number of territorial disputes between Latin American states, which in a few cases even put a country's survival at risk. The most tragic instance was the War of the Triple Alliance (1865–70), which dragged Paraguay, under Francisco Solano López, into a suicidal conflict with Argentina, Brazil, and Uruguay. In the end the defeated Paraguay was allowed to survive as an independent country, but only after it had been deprived of some of its territory and after most of its adult male population had been killed.[15]

Bolivia also suffered dearly for its military weakness. During the War of the Pacific (1879–83) it joined forces with Peru against Chile, but defeat led to the loss of its Pacific coastline and – along with Peru – of a slice of desert rich in nitrates.[16] Some twenty years later, Bolivia lost Acre to Brazil in an episode remarkably similar to Mexico's loss of Texas, and Ecuador lost territory throughout the nineteenth century to Colombia, Peru, and Brazil. In this zero-sum game of territorial transfers, Brazil gained the most. It used a mixture of force and diplomacy to extend its boundaries even beyond those it inherited from Portugal.

The ever-present threat of territorial dispute in the nineteenth century forced governments to keep armed forces, which not only acted as a drain

11 The first phase of U.S. intervention in Nicaragua is described through the eyes of a journalist in Denny (1929). On the whole period of military intervention, which finally ended in 1933, see Bulmer-Thomas (1990b).

12 These U.S. interventions in Hispaniola (the name given by Columbus to the island shared by Haitians and Dominicans) are well described in Langley (1983), Chapters 10–12.

13 Puerto Rico's transition from Spanish colony to U.S. possession is described in Carr (1984). Cuba's independence was formally recognized by the United States, but only after the new republic had agreed to incorporate the Platt Amendment into its constitution. This placed numerous restrictions on Cuban sovereignty and gave the United States the right to intervene under certain circumstances. It also gave the United States control in perpetuity over Guantanamo Bay. On the Platt Amendment, which was finally abrogated in 1934, see Langley (1968).

14 This exercise was part of what has become known as "dollar diplomacy." See Munro (1964).

15 Estimates of the population of Paraguay in the nineteenth century are subject to a large margin of error. The most reliable estimates suggest that the population fell from 350,000 in 1850 to 221,000 in 1870 and that the 1850 figure was not reached again until 1890. See Appendix 1.

16 Bolivia's loss of its Pacific coastline and the implications of the loss for the nation's development are discussed in Bonilla (1985).

on scarce fiscal resources but also impeded the efforts to establish strong civilian-controlled political institutions. By the outbreak of the First World War only a handful of countries (Argentina, Colombia, Costa Rica, Chile, and Uruguay) had come close to establishing a representative political system, and even in these republics such institutions were very far from perfect. Small elites, usually with landed interests, continued to exercise a dominant political and economic influence throughout the region.

In the century leading up to the First World War, for most of Latin America the choice was between anarchy, oligarchic rule, or dictatorship. The latter could bring stability for a time – as it did in Venezuela under Antonio Guzmán Blanco (1870–88)[17] – and even economic progress – as it did in Mexico under Porfirio Díaz (1876–1911)[18] – but it was never based on a broad consensus and therefore reflected only a narrow range of interests.

Throughout the period from midcentury to the First World War, the key issues of public debate were not so much economic as political: liberalism versus conservatism; centralism versus federalism; the relations between church and state, positivism, and social organization; racial questions; the nature of the constitution; and so on.[19] Economic issues, which figured so prominently in public debate in the second half of the twentieth century, were relatively noncontroversial after the midnineteenth century. The free-trade issue had been settled, a certain degree of protection for domestic activity was considered acceptable, and foreign investment and foreign immigration were generally encouraged.

This lack of controversy should not blind us to the problems of implementing a consistent set of economic policies. Governments knew, or thought they knew, what to do to promote the export of primary products – modest export taxes, public investment in social infrastructure, and promotion of foreign investment were considered the key ingredients. There was little consideration of how the growth of the export sector would transform the rest of the economy, however, although the latter – even by the beginning of the First World War – was still far more important than the former.

Thus economic policy was concerned primarily with the needs of the export sector, and its impact on the rest of the economy remained uncertain. The prevailing view emphasized the need to expand the export sector on the assumption that, in some ill-defined fashion, export growth would enhance

17 Antonio Guzmán Blanco was the dominant figure in Venezuelan politics for nearly two decades, during which the republic had its first real taste of political stability since independence and a liberal modernization program like those in other parts of Latin America was adopted. There was nothing "liberal," however, about Guzmán Blanco's system of political control. See Deas (1985).

18 The economic achievements of this period, known as the Porfiriato, are discussed in Rosenzweig Hernández (1989), Chapters 4–6. The politics of the period and the background to the Mexican Revolution are superbly outlined in Knight (1986a), Chapters 1–3.

19 On all these issues of public debate, see Hale (1986).

productivity growth and structural change throughout the economy. Export growth, it was assumed, was virtually the same as export-led growth.

Bearing this in mind, it is not difficult to reconcile the optimism of contemporary reports – particularly in the last decade before the First World War – with what we shall see to have been a generally unsatisfactory economic performance. Contemporaries – both foreign and Latin American – were concerned above all with the export sector and activities (such as railways) complementary to exports: A strong export performance, it was argued, was the key to success. Provided the export sector expanded, the rest of the economy would take care of itself. Such optimism may have been well founded in the case of Argentina, where the benefits of export-sector growth were indeed leading to the transformation of domestic agriculture, manufacturing, and services, but it was clearly misplaced in the case of countries like Bolivia or Ecuador, where the low productivity of the nonexport economy was largely unaffected, even during periods of rapid export expansion.

The policy context is examined in much more detail in the next two chapters, but first it is necessary to consider the logic of the export-led growth model and the expansion of the world economy, which provided the stimulus for development. We must also examine how and why the response of the export sector to this stimulus was not the same across Latin America. These are the principal themes of this chapter.

World demand and the export-led growth model

In the nineteenth century, U.S. real gross national product (GNP) per head increased at an annual rate of nearly 1.5 percent.[20] We can think of this as the target rate of growth for the countries of Latin America after 1850 – the rate that was needed if they were to emulate the extraordinary success of the U.S. economy. This target implied a doubling of living standards in just under fifty years – a modest-enough goal by the more demanding standards of the twentieth century.

In the same period the population of Latin America grew at roughly the same rate (1.5 percent), although there was substantial variation between countries. Thus the target rate of growth for real gross domestic product (GDP) over this period can be thought of as 3 percent per year for the region as a whole, even though for individual countries this figure clearly needs to be adjusted upward or downward, depending on whether population growth exceeded or fell below the regional rate of demographic expansion.

In order to explore the logic of export-led growth, we can think of the real economy as consisting of two parts: an export sector and a nonexport

20 Derived from Gellman (2000), Table 1.6, p. 22, using figures for 1800 and 1909 at constant prices.

sector. The export sector consists of all value added in export activities; the nonexport sector consists of value added in everything else. We can then write the target rate of growth, $g(y)$, as follows:

$$g(y) = w \cdot g(x) + (1 - w) \cdot g(nx) \qquad (3.1)$$

where w is the share of the export sector in real GDP, $g(x)$ is the growth rate of the export sector, and $g(nx)$ is the growth rate of the nonexport economy (with all growth rates expressed as annual averages). It follows that the rate of growth of the export sector consistent with the target rate of growth of real GDP can be written as follows:

$$g(x) = [g(y)/w] - [(1 - w)/w]g(nx) \qquad (3.2)$$

Thus equation (3.2) can be used to solve for the required rate of growth of the export sector, given a target rate of growth of GDP, $g(y)$, while making various assumptions about the share, w, of the export sector in GDP and the growth of the nonexport sector, $g(nx)$.

By midcentury the share of the export sector in real GDP was still modest, although it can safely be assumed to have risen during the period up to the First World War as growth in export activities outstripped the growth of the nonexport economy. If we also assume that the share of the export sector (measured by net output) in GDP and the share of exports (as measured by final expenditure) in GDP are similar, then w can be estimated at between 10 percent to 40 percent for all countries throughout the period (see Appendix 2). The lowest share can be expected to occur in large countries with low levels of exports per head (e.g., Brazil), and the highest share can be expected in small countries with high levels of exports per head (e.g., Cuba).

The growth of the nonexport sector is more complex. We can consider four possibilities. First, labor productivity in the nonexport economy does not change, so value added simply rises in line with labor supply. However, the relative size of the nonexport sector – $(1 - w)$; that is, an estimated 60 percent to 90 percent of GDP – is such that its labor supply can be assumed to grow at roughly the same rate as the population as a whole. Thus in this first case value added in the nonexport sector simply rises at the same rate as population. Second, labor productivity rises modestly, at 0.5 percent per year, as a result of technological progress, so value added in the nonexport sector rises at 0.5 percent plus the annual population growth. Third, labor productivity rises at 1 percent a year, so value added in the nonexport sector increases at 1 percent plus the annual population growth. The fourth possibility is that labor productivity in the nonexport sector grows at the target rate of growth for the economy as a whole – 1.5 percent – so

g(nx) / w	1.5	2.0	2.5	3.0
0.1	16.5	12.0	7.5	3.0
0.2	9.0	7.0	5.0	3.0
0.25	7.5	6.0	4.5	3.0
0.3	6.5	5.3	4.2	3.0
0.4	5.3	4.5	3.8	3.0

Figure 3.1. Required export growth rate to achieve target rate of growth of 1.5 percent real GDP per head: g(nx) = annual rate of growth (%) of nonexport sector; w = share of export sector in GDP; population growth rate = 1.5 percent per annum.

value added in the nonexport sector increases at 1.5 percent plus the annual population growth. This is less likely, however, because it implies that the export sector and the nonexport sector are growing at the same rate, with no increase in the share of exports in GDP. Although this might be a highly desirable outcome at the end of a long period of export-led growth, it could not normally be expected at the beginning.

Using equation (3.2),we can now work out the rate of growth of the export sector in Latin America consistent with a target rate of growth of 3 percent for real GDP (1.5 percent real GDP per head plus 1.5 percent population growth), while making different assumptions about the share of the export sector in real GDP, w, and the rate of growth of the nonexport economy. The result is a matrix (Figure 3.1.) in which the columns record the different assumptions about the annual growth of the nonexport sector and the rows show the different assumptions about the share of the export sector in GDP. The numbers in the matrix indicate the rate of growth of the export sector that is required to achieve a target annual rate of growth of 1.5 percent for real GDP per head under the different assumptions.

The "required" annual rate of growth of exports in Figure 3.1. for Latin America as a whole is between 3.0 percent and 16.5 percent, depending on the assumptions made about the share of exports in GDP, w, and the rate of growth of the nonexport sector, g(nx). This is a very wide range, but it is possible to narrow it considerably by making some additional (and realistic) assumptions. First, the share of w for Latin America as a whole is likely to have varied only between 0.1 and 0.25 in the period under consideration (see Appendix 2). Second, it is safe to assume both that there was some growth of labor productivity in the nonexport sector and that it was less than 1.5 percent per year. This eliminates the first and last columns in Figure 3.1. With these additional assumptions, the relevant range for annual export growth between 1850 and the First World War is 4.5 percent to 12.0 percent per year. Thus the minimum requirement for increasing real GDP per head at 1.5 percent per year was an annual rate of growth of exports of 4.5 percent.

This was the challenge facing the export-led growth model. To see if it was feasible, we must now turn to the growth of world demand. By the second half of the nineteenth century the Industrial Revolution had created four world economic powers (Great Britain, France, Germany, and the United States), whose estimated real GDP growth is recorded in Table 3.1. These rates of growth in turn generated a demand for imports (also recorded in Table 3.1) which generally – the main exception being the United States – rose faster than real GDP.

The specific weight of these four countries in the world economy was enormous. By the last quarter of the nineteenth century they accounted for around 60 percent of world exports and imports,[21] and they played a predominant role in the foreign trade of Latin America. Yet, as Table 3.1 makes clear, the rate of growth of their imports was generally below the rate of growth required by Latin American exports to achieve the target rate of growth of real GDP. Only in exceptional periods, such as 1899–1912 in the United States, did import growth exceed 5 percent a year.

It did not follow that the export-led growth model was flawed. There were, in fact, four main reasons why Latin American exports could grow faster than world imports in the period under consideration. First, the composition of advanced-country imports was changing, and the demand for certain raw materials and foodstuffs (primary products) was growing disproportionately rapidly. The rise of industry had unleashed an unprecedented demand for crude raw materials – in many cases not available in the advanced countries – and the increase in real income was stimulating a demand for foodstuffs, some of which were luxury goods and therefore enjoyed high income elasticities.

Second, industrialization in the advanced countries was producing a shift in resources from agriculture to manufacturing, as well as rapid rural–urban migration. This brought about a reconsideration of protection for agriculture (notably in Great Britain) and tariff and nontariff barriers were progressively lowered. This led, in turn, to an increase in the proportion of consumption that was met by imports. Although agricultural protectionism began to increase toward the end of the century in the less-industrialized parts of Europe,[22] this was not at first a serious threat to Latin America, for only a small fraction of its exports were sold in the European periphery.

Third, the shift toward free trade in the nineteenth century led to a reduction in the preferences received by European colonies. The discrimination

21 The importance of these four countries in the world economy is demonstrated in Lewis (1978). See also Latham (1978) and Solomou (1990).
22 Industrialization in the European periphery is discussed in Berend (1982).

Table 3.1. *Annual growth of world output and imports, circa 1850–1913*

	Growth of real GDP[a] (%)	Growth of imports (%)	Notes
	United States		
1873–1892	4.6	1.2	
1892–1906	4.1	3.9	
1884–1899	4.3	1.9	
1899–1912	3.8	7.9	
1850–1912	4.1	3.7	
	United Kingdom		
1845–1913	2.0	3.2	Imports at constant prices in
1856–1913	1.9	2.7	the nineteenth century
1856–1873	2.1	4.6	doubled every 19 years.
1873–1899	2.1	1.0	This implies an annual
1899–1913	1.3	3.4	growth in volume terms of 3.7%.[b]
	Germany		
1857–1874	2.5	n/a	
1874–1884	1.3	n/a	
1884–1900	3.2	3.7	
1900–1913	2.9	4.9	
1884–1913	3.1	4.2	
	France		
1852–1912	1.5	3.6	Imports from the 1830s to
1852–1869	1.8	7.1	1913 doubled every 22
1875–1892	0.7	1.0	years. This implies an
1892–1912	1.9	3.4	annual growth of 3.2%.[b]
	World		
1882–1890	2.6	3.0	Import growth estimated in
1890–1899	2.8	n/a	volume terms. The
1899–1907	3.1	3.8	periods are slightly
1907–1913	2.6	4.5	different from those used
1881–1913	n/a	3.5	for GDP growth.

[a] For Germany, NDP, net domestic product, is used.

[b] Staley (1944), p. 127.

Sources: United States: GDP growth rates from Solomou (1990), p. 49, except for 1850–1912, which have been derived from Mitchell (1983); import growth rates derived from Mitchell (1983). *United Kingdom:* GDP growth rates from Solomou (1990), p. 28; import growth rates derived from Mitchell (1988). *Germany:* NDP growth rates from Solomou (1990), p. 37; import growth rates derived from Mitchell (1980). *France:* GDP growth rates from Solomou (1990), p. 43; import growth rates derived from Mitchell (1980). *World:* GDP growth rates from Solomou (1990), p. 58; import growth rates taken from Staley (1944), p. 126.

suffered by Latin America in European markets began to erode, and a process of trade creation took place, allowing Latin America to increase market share at the expense of other countries. Great Britain provided the clearest example of this process: By the end of the nineteenth century the advantages enjoyed by its colonies in international trade had almost completely dissipated.[23]

Fourth, the data in Table 3.1 in general refer to the *value* of imports. What was relevant for Latin America's real GDP, however, was the *volume* of exports. If prices were falling, the volume of developed-country imports would be growing faster than their value. This would permit, ceteris paribus, a higher growth of exports by volume from Latin America.

The growth of world trade reported in Table 3.1 was therefore not necessarily inconsistent with the rates of growth of Latin American exports implied by Figure 3.1.. In theory it was possible for Latin American countries to increase exports at a rate consistent with a rise of living standards similar to that in the United States. Nevertheless, a clear dilemma existed. If export-led growth was pursued without much consideration for increasing productivity in the nonexport sector, it required rates of growth of exports (see, for example, the first column of Figure 3.1.) that were possible only under very special circumstances. If, on the other hand, exports could only be expected to grow in line with imports in the industrialized countries, economic policy needed to address the obstacles that prevented a more rapid rise of productivity in the nonexport sector.

Furthermore, international trade was subject to a number of forces that made the task of long-run export growth at fast rates much more difficult. The first problem was the cyclical pattern of international trade that resulted from the long swings to which capitalist economies were prone. Although research casts doubt on the existence of Kondratieff waves (subject to a fifty-year cycle[24]), evidence in all the major capitalist countries clearly reveals both a Juglar business cycle (nine to ten years) and Kuznets swings (approximately twenty years[25]). Unlike the depression at the end of the 1920s, these cycles did not necessarily affect all countries at the same time – international economic integration was not as advanced then as it would be in the interwar period – so not all markets were simultaneously depressed. Nevertheless, a depression in even one major market was a serious blow to a country seeking to sustain long-run export growth at very fast rates.

---

23 The key decision was the repeal of the Corn Laws in 1846, which ended protection for British cereal farmers. The ending of colonial preference took longer to complete, but its effects on Latin America were significant. The region's share of Third World fruit and vegetable exports, for example, rose from zero in 1829–31 to 29 percent in 1911–13. See Bairoch and Etemard (1985), p. 79.

24 See Solomou (1990), Chapter 1.

25 See Lewis (1978), Chapter 2.

Second, international trade was frequently affected by exogenous shocks that had no obvious pattern. The U.S. Civil War, for example, depressed the U.S. market for imports for a number of years in the 1860s;[26] the Franco–Prussian war in 1870 disrupted French imports in the first half of the 1870s; Great Britain's financial crisis in 1890 negatively affected imports from its most important Latin American trade partners for a number of years.[27] In each case trade recovered quickly after the crisis had passed, but the long-run rate of growth of exports was still adversely affected.

Third, in many cases Latin American countries acquired dominant positions in the markets for particular commodities before the First World War. On the eve of the war Brazil contributed more than 70 percent of world coffee production, Bolivia more than 20 percent of world tin production, and Ecuador more than 15 percent of world cacao exports. A dominant position was a tribute to rapid export growth in the past, but it made it much more difficult to sustain the rate of growth of exports on the basis of increased market share. In such a market, exports tended to grow – at best – in line with world imports. This was unlikely to be fast enough to sustain the growth of total exports at a rate consistent with a rapid rise in living standards. Thus the logic of export-led growth pointed to the need for commodity diversification in order to avoid a situation where export earnings depended on one or two commodities in which the country had already acquired a dominant position.

The spread of industrialization into the European periphery and Japan toward the end of the nineteenth century created new demands for raw materials for their expanding manufacturing sectors. Between 1880 and 1913 Japanese import demand doubled every ten years, Russia's every thirteen years, and Sweden's every seventeen years. This was much faster than world imports, which doubled every twenty years over the same period.[28]

The implication was clear: Technological progress and structural change in the established industrial countries were leading to a lower income elasticity for imported raw materials.[29] New industrial activities in the most advanced countries were less dependent on raw materials, and the trade-creating effects of lower protection for agriculture were beginning to play themselves out.[30] Thus the logic of the export-led model required a

---

26 U.S. imports, valued at $336 million in 1860, had fallen to $192 million in 1862. See Mitchell (1993). On U.S. foreign trade before World War I, see Lipsey (2000).

27 See Platt (1972), Appendix 2.

28 See Staley (1944), Chapter 8.

29 Between 1850 and 1913 British imports rose by 600 percent in constant (1913) prices. Raw-material imports, however, rose by only 400 percent. The fastest-growing category of imports was finished manufactured goods, where Latin America could not compete. See Mitchell (1988).

30 Once the trade-creating effects of reduced tariffs on European agricultural imports were complete, the market would grow in line with the income elasticity of demand for foodstuffs. British imports of foodstuffs and livestock, for example, increased their share of imports between 1850 and 1890,

diversification of markets (as well as commodities) in favor of the newly industrializing countries of Europe and Japan.

The export-led model, therefore, needed to be extremely dynamic. New products had to be introduced; new markets had to be found. Under these circumstances it was possible to achieve a significant rise in living standards, provided that the dynamism of the export sector was also reflected in some increase in labor productivity in the nonexport sector. Where productivity in the nonexport sector remained unchanged or even – as has been argued in the case of Mexico – declined, the nature of the world economy made it difficult to believe that exports could achieve the rates of growth needed to sustain long-run growth of real income per head even with geographical and commodity diversification.

The worst situation was clearly one in which exports were concentrated in a single product and single market and in which the productivity of the nonexport sector was unaffected by export growth. Under such circumstances export-led growth was almost certain to be a failure. As is shown, such cases were found all too often in Latin America, even during the so-called golden age of export-led growth.

Export performance

The period from the middle of the nineteenth century to the First World War witnessed the rise of new export products throughout Latin America in response to the demands created by the Industrial Revolution.[31] As a consequence the colonial pattern of exports based primarily on precious metals was finally eclipsed. In Mexico and Peru silver exports remained important – Mexico in 1913 produced more than 30 percent of the world's output – and gold was still an important contributor to export earnings in Colombia. Yet in no case did precious metals account for more than 50 percent of export earnings by 1913. Even in Mexico, where they remained more important than anywhere else in Latin America, their contribution had fallen from nearly 80 percent at the beginning of Porfirio Díaz's rule (the Porfiriato) to around 45 percent on the eve of the First World War. This decline, already underway before the end of the nineteenth century, was accelerated by the discovery of significant oil deposits in the Gulf of Mexico in the early 1900s.[32]

when trade creation was important. The share decreased, however, between 1890 and 1913 – a reflection in part of the relatively low income elasticity of demand for food.

31 For a good overview of this period in Latin America's economic history, see Cárdenas, Ocampo, and Thorp (2000).

32 The buccaneering nature of the Mexican oil industry in its early years is captured in Spender (1930), which tells the story of Weetman Pearson – a British entrepreneur who built a fortune in Mexico during the Porfiriato and became the first Lord Cowdray. See also Young (1966).

Table 3.2. *Export commodity concentration ratios, circa 1913*

Country	First product	Percentage	Second product	Percentage	Total
Argentina	Maize	22.5	Wheat	20.7	43.2
Bolivia	Tin	72.3	Silver	4.3	76.6
Brazil	Coffee	62.3	Rubber	15.9	78.2
Chile	Nitrates	71.3	Copper	7.0	78.3
Colombia	Coffee	37.2	Gold	20.4	57.6
Costa Rica	Bananas	50.9	Coffee	35.2	86.1
Cuba	Sugar	72.0	Tobacco	19.5	91.5
Dominican Republic	Cacao	39.2	Sugar	34.8	74.0
Ecuador	Cacao	64.1	Coffee	5.4	69.5
El Salvador	Coffee	79.6	Precious metals	15.9	95.5
Guatemala	Coffee	84.8	Bananas	5.7	90.5
Haiti	Coffee	64.0	Cacao	6.8	70.8
Honduras	Bananas	50.1	Precious metals	25.9	76.0
Mexico	Silver	30.3	Copper	10.3	40.6
Nicaragua	Coffee	64.9	Precious metals	13.8	78.7
Panama	Bananas	65.0	Coconuts	7.0	72.0
Paraguay	Yerba maté	32.1	Tobacco	15.8	47.9
Peru	Copper	22.0	Sugar	15.4	37.4
Puerto Rico	Sugar	47.0	Coffee	19.0	66.0
Uruguay	Wool	42.0	Meat	24.0	66.0
Venezuela	Coffee	52.0	Cacao	21.4	73.4

Sources: The figures have been derived from Mitchell (1993) wherever possible. The exceptions are Bolivia (Walle, 1914), Colombia (Eder, 1912), El Salvador and Guatemala (Young, 1925), Haiti (Benoit, 1954), Mexico (Enock, 1919), Panama (Bureau de Publicidad de la América Latina, 1916–17), Paraguay (Koebel, 1919), Puerto Rico (Dietz, 1986), Uruguay (Finch, 1981), and Venezuela (Dalton, 1916).

The eclipse of the traditional pattern of colonial exports did not mean the decline of mining. New mineral products emerged in the nineteenth century and rapidly came to prominence in the export structure of certain republics. In Peru copper rose in importance after 1890 and represented more than 20 percent of exports by 1913 (see Table 3.2). In Bolivia the decline of silver exports after 1890 was matched by the rise of tin. As early as 1905 tin represented more than 60 percent of Bolivian exports. By the First World War this figure had increased to more than 70 percent, and silver – 60 percent in 1891 – had fallen to around 4 percent. In Chile the nitrate boom, which had begun after Chile captured nitrate deposits in the northern desert during the War of the Pacific, squeezed out both copper and silver exports, and by 1913 nitrates accounted for no less than 70 percent of total exports.

In the rest of Latin America the new exports that came to dominate export earnings were of agricultural origin. Some, such as rubber (e.g., Brazil and Peru) and wool (e.g., Argentina and Uruguay), were required by the industrial factories of Europe and the United States. Others, such as henequen from Mexico,[33] expanded in response to the new technologies that were being adopted on the North American prairies. Many, such as cereals and meat, represented products to satisfy the food-consumption requirements of the Industrial Revolution. Rising incomes in Europe and North America also created a demand for such tropical "luxuries" as coffee, cacao, and bananas; demand was also strong for tropical forest products like quinine, quebracho extract,[34] and Peruvian balsam,[35] which were needed for medicinal purposes or as industrial raw materials.

In some cases the leading exports represented products that had first been introduced during the Bourbon reforms. Cuban sugar continued its spectacular growth, and the industry survived the final abolition of slavery in 1886 and the wars of independence that ended in U.S. occupation (1898–1902). By 1913 Cuban sugar production represented 25 percent of world sugar-cane output and a much higher proportion of sugar-cane exports. A minor challenge to Cuban success came with the reintroduction of sugar exports in Santo Domingo (the Dominician Republic) after independence in 1844, although it remained a taboo crop in the rest of Hispaniola for many more years because of its association with slavery. In Haiti the leading exports up to the First World War were coffee and cacao (see Table 3.2).

The introduction of new products did not necessarily lead to export diversification. On the contrary, the rise of new exports was often matched by the eclipse of traditional products, so export concentration remained extremely high. In a majority of countries (see Table 3.2), one commodity accounted for more than 50 percent of exports in 1913; in only two countries (Argentina and Peru) did the leading export account for less than 25 percent. The two most important commodities accounted for more than 50 percent

33 The center of the Mexican henequen industry was the Yucatán. The raw material proved ideal for the twine required by mechanized cereal farming in North America. In the United States the gigantic International Harvester Corporation played a dominant role as the major purchaser of henequen from Mexico. See Joseph (1982).

34 Quinine, valued for medicinal purposes, was obtained from the cinchona tree in many of the Andean republics. The quebracho tree, found in abundance in Paraguay and the extreme northern provinces of Argentina, produced a tannin extract once valued as a dye.

35 Despite its name, Peruvian balsam – an extract from a hardwood tree with highly prized medicinal properties – came not from Peru but from El Salvador. See Browning (1971), pp. 61–2. Its description as "Peruvian" almost certainly was due to the idiosyncrasies of colonial trade. In much the same manner, straw hats from Colombia and Ecuador became known as "Panamas" in the nineteenth century because they were transported across the isthmus before being sold in Europe or North America.

of the total in eighteen republics, more than 70 percent in thirteen republics, and more than 90 percent in three republics.

These concentration ratios were high by any standard. No country exporting primary products could expect to escape the impact of a world depression, but high concentration ratios made countries very vulnerable to cycles in single-commodity markets. Coffee, for example, was the leading export in seven republics by 1913, and in all but one (Colombia) it accounted for more than 50 percent of exports (see Table 3.2). It was the second most important export in three other countries (Costa Rica, Ecuador, and Puerto Rico), and it played a dominant role in total Latin American export earnings.[36]

Examples of successful commodity export diversification were few and far between. Peru, after the collapse of the guano boom in the 1880s, managed to spread its export earnings across a wide range of products, including sugar, cotton, coffee, silver, copper, rubber, and wool from sheep and alpaca.[37] Paraguay, its export-led model delayed first by the self-imposed isolation of Francia (1810–40) and then by the disastrous War of the Triple Alliance (1865–70), gradually inserted itself into the world and regional economies on the basis of yerba maté, tobacco, timber, hides, meat, and quebracho extract.

The most successful case of export diversification, however, was in Argentina. The introduction of new products did not eclipse the old, and Argentina simply expanded the range of its exports. By 1913 foreign-exchange earnings came from an impressive array of cereals and livestock products. The former included wheat, linseed, rye, barley, and maize; the latter chilled and frozen beef, lamb, wool, and hides. No other republic came close to matching the range and quality of Argentine exports before the First World War. Indeed, these were so extensive that by 1913 they represented nearly 30 percent of Latin America's export earnings, despite the fact that Argentina had only 9.5 percent of the region's population.

The growth of exports was crucial for the success (or failure) of the export-led model. As the previous section made clear, a *regional* long-run annual rate of export growth of at least 4.5 percent was required even when making fairly optimistic assumptions about the growth of labor productivity in the nonexport sector and about the relative importance of exports. The *national* required rate of growth of exports, however, depended on the rate of demographic expansion in each country. In Figure 3.2. the required export growth rates have been calculated on the same assumptions as in Figure 3.1., but this time with allowances for the different national rates of population growth. Each country has therefore been allocated to a matrix in Figure 3.2.

36 Coffee accounted for 18.6 percent of total Latin American exports in 1911–13. The figure rises to 26.5 percent if Argentina is excluded. See Bairoch and Etemard (1985), p. 77.
37 See Thorp and Bertram (1978), Tables A.1.1 and A.1.2.

(A) PGR = 0.5% pa

w \ g(nx)	0.5	1.0	1.5	2.0
0.1	15.5	11.0	6.8	2.0
0.2	8.0	6.0	4.0	2.0
0.3	5.5	4.3	3.2	2.0
0.4	4.3	3.5	2.8	2.0

(B) PGR = 1.0% pa

w \ g(nx)	1.0	1.5	2.0	2.5
0.1	16.0	11.5	7.0	2.5
0.2	8.6	6.5	4.5	2.5
0.3	6.0	4.8	3.7	2.5
0.4	4.8	4.0	3.3	2.5

(C) PGR = 1.5% pa

w \ g(nx)	1.5	2.0	2.5	3.0
0.1	16.5	12.0	7.5	3.0
0.2	9.0	7.0	5.0	3.0
0.3	6.5	5.3	4.2	3.0
0.4	5.3	4.5	3.8	3.0

(D) PGR = 2.0% pa

w \ g(nx)	2.0	2.5	3.0	3.5
0.1	17.0	12.5	8.0	3.5
0.2	9.5	7.5	5.5	3.5
0.3	7.0	5.8	4.7	3.5
0.4	5.8	5.0	4.3	3.5

(E) PGR = 2.5% pa

w \ g(nx)	2.5	3.0	3.5	4.0
0.1	17.5	13.0	8.5	4.0
0.2	10.0	8.0	6.0	4.0
0.3	7.5	6.3	5.2	4.0
0.4	6.3	5.5	4.8	4.0

(F) PGR = 3.0% pa

w \ g(nx)	3.0	3.5	4.0	4.5
0.1	18.0	13.5	9.0	4.5
0.2	10.5	8.5	6.5	4.5
0.3	8.0	6.8	5.7	4.5
0.4	6.8	6.0	5.3	4.5

Figure 3.2. Required export growth rate to achieve target rate of growth of 1.5 percent real GDP per head in various countries: (A) Bolivia; (B) Cuba, Ecuador, Guatemala, Haiti, Mexico, Nicaragua, Paraguay, and Venezuela; (C) Chile, Colombia, Honduras, Peru, and Puerto Rico; (D) Brazil, Costa Rica, and El Salvador; (E) Dominican Republic; (F) Argentina and Uruguay; $g(nx)$ = annual rate of growth (%) of nonexport sector; w = share of export sector in GDP; population growth rate (PGR); percentages are per annum (% pa).

on the basis of its estimated population growth rate (see Appendix 1), and the required rate of growth of exports has then been calculated according to equation (3.2).

The matrixes in Figure 3.2. provide a very broad range for the required rate of growth of exports. As was the case with Latin America as a whole, however, it is possible to narrow the range through some simplifying assumptions. First, as before, we can assume that labor-productivity growth in the nonexport sector was modest (0.5 to 1.0 percent per year) rather than zero or rapid. This eliminates the first and last columns in each matrix in

Table 3.3. *Annual rate of growth of exports, circa 1850 to circa 1912 (in US$)*

Country	Population Growth (%)[a]	Class[b]	w[c]	Target range[d]	Export growth (%)[e]	In/Out[f]
Argentina	3.1	F	.2–.3	5.7–8.5	6.1	In
Bolivia	0.5	A	.1–.3	3.2–11.0	2.5	Out
Brazil	2.0	D	.1–.3	4.7–12.5	3.7	Out
Chile	1.4	C	.1–.3	4.2–12.0	4.3	In
Colombia (including Panama)	1.4	C	.1–.2	5.0–12.0	3.5	Out
Costa Rica	2.0	D	.2–.4	4.3–7.5	3.5	Out
Cuba	1.1	B	.3–.4	3.3–4.8	2.9	Out
Dominican Republic	2.6	E	.1–.2	6.0–13.0	5.2	Out
Ecuador	1.2	B	.1–.2	4.5–11.5	3.5	Out
El Salvador	1.8	D	.1–.2	5.5–12.5	3.4	Out
Guatemala	1.2	B	.1–.2	4.5–11.5	3.6	Out
Haiti	1.1	B	.1–.2	4.5–11.5	1.5	Out
Honduras	1.5	C	.1–.2	5.0–12.0	1.4	Out
Mexico	1.0	B	.1–.2	4.5–11.5	3.0	Out
Nicaragua	1.2	B	.1–.2	4.5–11.5	2.9	Out
Paraguay	0.8	B	.1–.2	4.5–11.5	3.9	Out
Peru	1.3	C	.1–.3	4.2–12.0	2.9	Out
Puerto Rico	1.4	C	.2–.3	4.2–7.0	3.0	Out
Uruguay	3.5	F	.3–.4	5.3–6.8	3.4	Out
Venezuela	0.8	B	.1–.2	4.5–11.5	2.7	Out
Latin America	1.5	C	.1–.25	4.5–12.0	3.9	Out

[a] See Appendix 1 for sources used to derive this column.
[b] Each letter refers to a matrix in Figure 3.2..
[c] The first number refers to the author's estimate of the export sector share in GDP circa 1850; the second, to the share circa 1912. See Appendix 2.
[d] This range is derived from Figures 3.1. and 3.2..
[e] See Appendix 1 for sources used to derive this column.
[f] "In" means that export growth is inside the target range required to achieve a rate of growth of GDP per head of 1.5 percent per year. "Out" means that it is below the range.

Figure 3.2.[38] Second, it is possible to narrow the export share, *w*, range for individual countries (see Appendix 2). Thus the target range for the growth of exports is a subset of the range implied by each matrix in Figure 3.2.; the best "guesstimates" are given in Table 3.3. Argentina, for example, is assigned a target range of 5.7 percent to 8.5 percent on the basis of a

38 The first column in each matrix in Figure 3.2. implies zero labor productivity increase, which is a very severe assumption. The final column implies an increase in labor productivity (1.5 percent) equal to the target rate of growth for real GDP per head. Such an outcome, however desirable, is improbable in the early stages of export-led growth, for it implies that the export and nonexport sectors are growing at the same rate.

population growth rate of 3.1 percent (matrix F in Figure 3.2.), labor-productivity growth in the nonexport sector between 0.5 percent and 1.0 percent annually, and an export sector share, w, varying between 0.2 and 0.3.

As Table 3.3 makes clear, only two republics, Argentina and Chile, were able to achieve a rate of growth of exports within the target range over the long period from 1850 to the First World War. The Argentine rate of growth (6.1 percent) was impressive and was the result of a steady expansion of the export quantum with only minor interruptions. It was a striking demonstration of the possibilities of export-led growth in the context of world economic expansion in the second half of the nineteenth century. The Chilean export growth rate (4.3 percent) was less impressive, but Chile's much lower rate of growth of population (1.4 percent) meant that the republic's export performance still fell within the target range.

In many countries the rate of growth of exports fell far below the minimum of the target range. Brazil, which faced a minimum target of 4.7 percent, could manage only a long-run rate of growth of exports of 3.7 percent. This put the goal of doubling living standards approximately every fifty years (as happened in the United States) far beyond Brazil's reach. Even in Cuba, despite the apparent success of the sugar industry, the long-run rate of growth of exports (2.9 percent) was below the minimum (3.3 percent) of the target range.

If labor productivity in the nonexport sector had grown more rapidly than assumed, the target range minimum would need to be lowered. In most Latin American republics such an assumption is not justified. Uruguay, however, may be an exception. Its urban centers (particularly Montevideo) proved attractive for European immigrants, and the nonexport sector expanded rapidly in the years before the First World War. Although the long-run rate of growth of exports (3.4 percent) was unimpressive (marginally below population growth), Uruguay may still have been able to raise living standards at a fast rate as a result of above-average performance by its nonexport sector.[39]

No country was able to match Argentina and Chile in the steady expansion of exports, but some republics did achieve rapid growth over at least one subperiod (see Table 3.4). In the two decades between circa 1850 and circa 1870, which bracket the U.S. Civil War, eight countries (Chile, Colombia, Costa Rica, Cuba, Ecuador, El Salvador, Peru, and Venezuela) managed to expand exports at a rate faster than the minimum of the target range in Table 3.3. In Peru the growth rate was due entirely to the guano

---

39 Even if labor productivity in the nonexport sector increased at 1.5 percent per year, it would still not have been sufficient to raise real GDP per head by the target rate of growth in Uruguay. Labor productivity would have to rise by 2 percent a year before export performance in Uruguay could be made consistent with the target (assuming an export share of 0.3 to 0.4).

Table 3.4. *Annual average export growth and export purchasing power growth,*
1850–1870, 1870–1890, and 1890–1912 (in percentages)

Country	1850–1870		1870–1890		1890–1912	
	Export growth	Export purchasing power growth	Export growth	Export purchasing power growth	Export growth	Export purchasing power growth
Argentina	4.9	4.1	6.7	8.2	6.7	5.4
Bolivia	2.8	2.0	2.3	3.8	2.5	1.2
Brazil	4.3	3.5	2.5	4.0	4.3	3.0
Chile	4.6	3.8	3.3	4.8	5.0	3.7
Colombia	7.8	7.0	0.5	2.0	2.4	1.1
Costa Rica	4.7	3.9	5.6	7.1	0.5	−0.8
Cuba	3.5	2.7	2.3	3.8	2.4	1.1
Dominican Republic	4.5	3.7	5.1	6.6	5.9	4.6
Ecuador	4.9	4.1	1.7	3.2	3.9	2.6
El Salvador	5.7	4.9	2.0	3.5	2.6	1.3
Guatemala	3.2	2.4	6.9	8.4	1.1	−0.2
Haiti	2.5	1.7	3.3	4.8	−1.0	−2.3
Honduras	−0.5	−1.3	14.8	16.3	−0.3	−1.6
Mexico	−0.7	−1.5	4.4	5.9	5.2	3.9
Nicaragua	0.8	0	6.1	7.6	2.3	1.0
Paraguay	4.4	3.6	6.0	7.5	2.2	0.9
Peru	6.4	5.6	−4.9	−3.4	6.9	5.6
Puerto Rico	0.1	−0.7	1.8	3.3	7.6	6.3
Uruguay	3.1	2.3	3.7	5.2	3.4	2.1
Venezuela	4.6	3.8	2.4	3.9	1.2	−0.1
Latin America	4.5	3.7	2.7	4.2	4.5	3.2

Note: The data on the purchasing power of exports have been obtained by dividing the
value of exports by an index of import unit values. See Appendix 1 for export data sources
and Appendix 2 for import unit values.

boom that had begun in the 1840s; in Cuba it was due to the rapid expansion of sugar. Thus both countries were vulnerable to changes in the market
conditions for these two products. Peru, in particular, suffered from the loss
of some of the guano deposits to Chile in the War of the Pacific and from
the exhaustion of those that remained in Peruvian territory.[40]

In the next subperiod, circa 1870 to circa 1890, six countries (Argentina,
Costa Rica, Guatemala, Honduras, Nicaragua, and Paraguay) increased exports at a rate faster than the target range minimum, and Mexico came
close. In Guatemala and Nicaragua, as had happened in the previous

40 On cycles in the guano trade, see Hunt (1985).

period in Colombia, Costa Rica, and El Salvador, the rapid growth of exports was due primarily to the expansion of coffee.[41] Mexico, its political stability underwritten by the dictatorship of Porfirio Díaz, was finally able to overcome the dismal export performance in the first half-century after independence through the expansion of nontraditional mineral exports (such as copper), the intensification of silver exports, and the continuation of the henequen boom in the Yucatán.[42] Honduras and Paraguay had the advantage of starting from such a low base that even modest achievements managed to produce a fast rate of export growth.

In the final subperiod, circa 1890 to circa 1912, five countries (Argentina, Chile, Mexico, Peru, and Puerto Rico) recorded export growth rates in excess of the target-range minimum. Peru returned to the high rate of growth it had enjoyed in the 1850–70 period, diversifying away from guano into a broad range of products. Indeed, if Peru had been able to avoid the collapse of exports in the 1870–90 period, when its rate of growth was negative, the long-run rate of growth of exports would have matched that of Argentina. The Mexican rate of export growth accelerated as the Porfiriato entered the twentieth century; Puerto Rico, its sugar industry revitalized by U.S. investments after 1898, experienced a massive export boom.

The basic problems of Latin America's export sector are revealed very clearly by Table 3.4. First, although a large minority of countries were able to sustain satisfactory export growth rates for one or even two subperiods, only two republics, Argentina and Chile, were able to sustain the required rate over the entire period. Second, the least satisfactory subperiod is the last (circa 1890 to circa 1912), when supposedly the world economy was booming and the opportunities for Latin American exports were greatest. The Latin American export growth model was reaching maturity in this period, however, so winning world market share was becoming more difficult. Several of the smaller republics (e.g., Costa Rica, Guatemala, and Nicaragua), whose performance had been satisfactory in the previous subperiod, began to encounter problems in expanding their main export (coffee) as a result – among other things – of the price falls induced by Brazilian overexpansion, and the export performance of others (e.g., Honduras and Paraguay) could not be sustained once their export base had been enlarged.

The export growth rates in Table 3.3 are calculated from the dollar value of exports. Because export prices were falling in some cases, the volume of exports may have risen faster than the value. A more charitable interpretation of Latin America's export performance would therefore make an adjustment to allow for higher volume growth as a result of price declines. If

---

41 In Guatemala, the coffee industry benefited from the strong support provided by President Justo Rufino Barrios under the liberal reforms. See McCreery (1983).

42 The crucial role of railways in this export expansion is now widely accepted. See Coatsworth (1981).

this adjustment is set at 0.5 percent per year, implying that export prices fell by 27 percent between 1850 and the First World War,[43] the target range minimum for each country in Table 3.3 can be lowered by 0.5 percent. Yet even this adjustment makes little difference. Only Cuba now qualifies, along with Argentina and Chile, as having achieved a rate of growth of exports consistent with an increase in real income per head of 1.5 percent per year.

In fact, little evidence supports the idea that export prices declined so sharply over the long run (see Appendix 2). On the contrary, both export and import prices tended to rise in the first subperiod (circa 1850 to circa 1870), fall in the second (circa 1870 to circa 1890), and rise in the third (circa 1890 to circa 1912), leaving them virtually unchanged over the whole period. Sugar prices did fall, however, so it is not unreasonable to include Cuba, whose export performance depended heavily on sugar, in the list of "successful" countries. Indeed, the volume of Cuban sugar exports over the whole period – 1850 to the First World War – did rise faster than the value.

If we use the available information on import prices (see Appendix 2) to calculate the purchasing power of exports (see Table 3.4), the results are different in each subperiod without being any more favorable to Latin America as a whole. In the first subperiod, when import prices were assumed to be rising, only two countries, Colombia and Peru, register a satisfactory export performance. In the second subperiod, with the purchasing power of exports rising faster than the value of exports as a result of the assumed fall in import prices, the number of successful cases jumps from seven to twelve; and in the third subperiod the successful cases fall from five to two (Peru and Puerto Rico). Significantly, taking the whole period from 1850 to the First World War and using the purchasing power of exports as the yardstick, only Argentina now achieves an export growth rate inside the target range. Even in Chile export performance now falls marginally below the target-range minimum.

The test used for successful export growth assumes that the target rate of growth of real GDP per head is 1.5 percent. If we lower the target to a more modest 1 percent, which implies a doubling of living standards every seventy years, the test for the rate of growth of exports is less demanding. Yet, perhaps surprisingly, this less-demanding target makes little difference. The export performance of only three countries (Argentina, Chile, and Cuba) can be considered satisfactory; that is, consistent with a target rate of growth of real GDP per head of at least 1 percent per year. If we add Uruguay to this list, on the grounds that labor productivity in the nonexport sector was growing faster than elsewhere, we are still left with sixteen countries

---

43 This result is obtained by applying the formula for compound interest, $A = P [(0.995)]^{62}$ where P is the initial value (e.g., 100) and A is the final value after 62 years (1850 to 1912).

(seventeen if we include Panama) whose export performance was below the minimum required even for doubling living standards every seventy years. Thus export performance during the golden age of export-led growth left much to be desired.

In fact, the majority of countries recorded a long-run rate of growth of exports that was disappointing. No fewer than seven republics failed to expand exports by more than 3 percent a year between 1850 and the First World War. Even if we concentrate on the period between circa 1890 and circa 1912, when the stimulus from the world economy was supposed to be particularly favorable and when sufficient time had passed for all Latin American countries to overcome supply-side problems in the export sector, as many as eleven republics recorded a growth rate of exports of less than 3 percent a year (see Table 3.4). Only if we concentrate on the last ten years before the First World War do we find a generally satisfactory export performance.[44]

It would be highly misleading to judge the success of the export-led model by the performance of exports in one decade. The truth is that the evolution of the world economy offered a window of opportunity for primary-product exporters after 1850 (if not before) that needed to be seized at an early stage. The window would not remain open forever; indeed, it was never fully opened again after the First World War. Success in one subperiod (e.g., Peru in the guano age) was no guarantee of long-run export performance: The growth of exports needed to be sustained over a much longer period for the export-led growth model to have a real chance of success.

On the eve of the First World War fourteen republics still had exports per head valued at less than $20, and eight countries had not been able to push exports beyond $10 per head, compared with $51.9 in Canada, $87 in Australia, and $98.8 in New Zealand (see Table 3.5). True, the U.S. export per head figure, $24.4, was not much higher than the Latin American average, but the United States had ceased to pursue export-led growth in the usual sense by the middle of the nineteenth century, concentrating instead on its vast domestic market with rapid growth of labor productivity in the nonexport sector. Costa Rica had pushed exports per head above $20 and Chile and Puerto Rico above $40, whereas Uruguay (virtually unchanged since 1850) registered a level of $50. Argentina recorded exports per head in excess of $60 by 1913, although the highest figure in Latin America, $64.7, was enjoyed by Cuba. It must be remembered, however, that Cuba had a much slower rate of population growth than Argentina and began the nineteenth century with a higher value of exports per head as a result of its colonial prominence.

---

44 During this (exceptional) period, Latin America's exports are estimated to have grown at 6.8 percent per year. See Bairoch and Etemard (1985), p. 25.

Table 3.5. *Exports per head in U.S. dollars: three-year averages*

Country	Circa 1850	Circa 1870	Circa 1890	Circa 1912
Argentina	10.3	16.5	32.4	62.0
Bolivia	5.5	8.6	12.4	18.6
Brazil	5.0	8.6	9.6	14.2
Chile	7.8	14.2	20.3	44.7
Colombia[a]	1.9	6.6	5.7	6.4
Costa Rica	11.4	21.2	37.9	27.1
Cuba	22.2	44.3[b]	55.7	64.7
Dominican Republic	3.4	5.0	8.1	15.5
Ecuador	2.0	4.1	4.6	7.9
El Salvador	3.2	7.3	6.8	8.3
Guatemala	1.7	2.5	7.5	7.2
Haiti	4.8	6.5	10.1	6.1
Honduras	4.9	3.6[c]	8.1	4.7
Mexico	3.2	2.3	4.4	10.7
Nicaragua	3.7	3.5	10.1	10.8
Paraguay	1.3	5.8[d]	8.5	8.6
Peru	3.7	10.1	3.3	9.4
Puerto Rico	13.7[e]	9.6	11.0	40.1
Uruguay	54.9	46.6	44.6	50.3
Venezuela	3.3	6.8	8.3	10.5
Latin America	**5.2**	**8.9**	**11.7**	**20.4**
Australia	16.5	63.3	52.8	87.0
Canada[f]	6.4	20.4	21.7	51.9
New Zealand	21.4	97.1	77.3	98.8
United States	7.0	10.0	13.7	24.4

[a] Includes Panama.
[b] Datum is for 1877.
[c] Datum is for 1882.
[d] Datum is for 1879.
[e] Datum is for 1844.
[f] Includes Newfoundland.
Source: See Appendix 1.

The four countries in Latin America with exports above or close to $45 per head before the First World War (Argentina, Chile, Cuba, and Uruguay) were also the four countries that had passed the least stringent tests for export-led growth. These tests, it should be remembered, assumed that the target for real income per head growth was only 1 percent per year. Mexico had failed to record either fast long-run growth of exports or a significant level of exports per head, but at least export performance during the Porfiriato had been impressive. Elsewhere the record of export growth was disappointing.

Export cycles

Only in a relatively few cases were exports stagnant throughout the period from 1850 to the First World War. Virtually all republics[45] experienced boom periods that were then partially or wholly canceled out by slumps. This vulnerability to economic cycles is at the root of the poor export performance of the majority of countries in Latin America in the "golden age" of export-led growth.

The extreme case of an export slump following a boom is provided by Peru. The Peruvian slump in the 1870–90 period (see Table 3.4) was due to the collapse of guano exports as a result of the depletion of an (almost) nonrenewable resource and to the loss of nitrate deposits to Chile. Thus the depression could not be blamed on trade cycles in the world economy. The Peruvian collapse was due above all to the republic's defeat and to its loss of territory in the War of the Pacific. Other examples of export slumps are Mexico (1850–70), when civil war and political unrest undermined export performance, Honduras (1850–70 and 1890–1912), and Haiti (1890–1912). In each case the rate of growth of exports was negative, virtually ruling out any prospect of achieving a long-run rate of growth within the target-range minimum.[46]

Most countries avoided an absolute decline in the value of exports in each subperiod, but this did not necessarily mean that the value of exports per head was rising. As Table 3.5 makes clear, Colombia (1870–90), Costa Rica (1890–1912), El Salvador (1870–90), Guatemala (1890–1912), Nicaragua (1850–70), Puerto Rico (1844–70), and Uruguay (1850–90) all suffered from a decline in the dollar value of exports per head. Such a decline was not necessarily disastrous. The three dominions listed in Table 3.5 (Australia, Canada, and New Zealand) all suffered a decline in exports per head between 1870 and 1890 – a consequence of their dependence on the slow-growing British market[47] – and yet were still able to sustain a

---

45　The worst long-run performances were recorded by Haiti and Honduras, but in both cases there were shorter periods of positive and negative growth rather than long-run stagnation.

46　The Mexican case can be used by way of illustration. Although the republic's export performance was close to the target range minimum after 1870 and well above it after 1890, the long-run export performance was undermined by the absolute decline in the value of exports between 1850 and 1870. Mexican exports needed to reach $372 million in 1912 (more than twice their actual level) to be consistent with the target long-run of growth of real GDP per head.

47　Conventional views on the long British "depression" after 1873 have been recently revised. It is now seen as a period of falling prices rather than declining or stagnant real income. This is confirmed by Table 3.1, in which the rate of growth of British real GDP between 1873 and 1899 (2.1 percent) is wholly consistent with performance in the rest of the century. The value of imports, however, rose by only 1 percent per year as a result of price falls. This import price decline was reflected in the value of exports of those countries (e.g., Australia) that were heavily dependent on the British market.

satisfactory long-run rate of growth of exports.[48] Nevertheless, a temporary decline in exports per head meant that exports had to perform exceptionally well in other subperiods (as happened in the dominions) to sustain the required long-run rate of growth.

It would be quite wrong, despite what has been said about Peru and Mexico, to attribute the generally poor performance of exports to military or political conditions. Brazil, for example, recorded a very modest rate of growth of exports in the (relatively stable) two decades before the end of the empire;[49] during this period (1870–90) export performance was dictated by coffee, with Brazil accounting for more than 50 percent of world exports and coffee representing more than 60 percent of Brazilian foreign-exchange earnings. No country could expect to expand exports indefinitely at a fast rate under such circumstances, and Brazil paid the price for its overexposure to cycles in the world coffee market.[50]

Furthermore, in the period between 1890 and 1913, when political stability was the rule rather than the exception in Latin America, many republics recorded an unsatisfactory export performance. In one case, Bolivia, the explanation was simple: The growth of Bolivian tin exports was certainly dramatic, but overall export performance was dragged down by the relative and absolute decline of silver. In many cases the ores being worked were the same; the only difference was that the mining entrepreneurs now concentrated on extracting the tin rather than the silver content, although some new deposits of tin were also discovered.

In a few cases, where climate and soil were particularly important, the poor performance could partly be blamed on the exhaustion of suitable lands for export crops after many decades of expansion. Costa Rica, El Salvador, Guatemala, Haiti, and Venezuela had begun to face this problem by the end of the nineteenth century in coffee; the Dominican Republic, Ecuador, and Venezuela faced the same problem with cacao. Yet production per hectare in many of these countries for the crops in question was extremely low, and the problem of a shortage of suitable lands could have been overcome through an improvement in yields.

Costa Rica was able to compensate to some extent for the problems of coffee exports through the rapid expansion of bananas. Beginning in the

48 If we assume export shares, w, of between 0.2 and 0.4, the export target range (as in Table 3.3) and long-run exports (circa 1850–circa 1912) for the three dominions are as follows: For Australia the export target range is between 5.3 and 8.5 and export growth is 5.7; for Canada the export target range is between 4.3 and 7.5 and export growth is 5.3; and for New Zealand the export target range is between 8.3 and 11.5, while export growth is 8.8. Thus, the long-run export performance of all three countries exceeded the target range minima and was consistent with an annual increase in real GDP per head of 1.5 percent.

49 The transition from empire to republic in 1889, one year after the final abolition of slavery, was achieved with relatively little social or political upheaval. See Viotti da Costa (1986).

50 See Catão (1991), Chapter 4.

1870s banana exports had replaced coffee as the most important contributor to exports before the First World War.[51] Yet, as happened in the other banana-exporting countries of the region, production was affected by the spread of plant diseases for which no antidote was known. Export earnings in the main banana-exporting countries (Costa Rica, Guatemala, Honduras, and Panama) remained vulnerable to disease and natural disasters even after the First World War.[52]

World trade cycles also played their part in depressing export earnings, although none of the prewar trade depressions appears to have affected all industrialized countries at the same time. Thus countries with geographically diversified exports (see pp. 73–8) were able to compensate for a depression in one market through an expansion of exports to other markets. This, however, was little compensation for countries that sold the bulk of their exports in one market.

The worst case of a trade depression was the stagnation in the value of British imports in the fifteen years after 1873, which was mirrored in the imports of Austria-Hungary, Belgium, Denmark, and Italy. This was a clear threat to all those republics that had come to depend heavily on these markets (of which the British was by far the most important). Colombia, which had been sending more than one-third of its exports to Great Britain at the start of the 1870s, increased its exports to the United States, but the overall performance of exports in this period was still unsatisfactory – at least in value terms. Argentina, in contrast, despite its dependence on the British market, managed an impressive 6.7 percent annual rate of growth of exports between 1870 and 1890 as a result of successful geographic (and commodity) diversification.

External shocks could disrupt foreign-trade expansion for many years in even the most successful countries, as the Baring crisis of 1890 illustrates. The Baring merchant bank had developed such a close and profitable association with the private and public sector in many Latin American republics, particularly Argentina, that the company's credibility depended heavily on the successful operation of its South American portfolio. When the government of President Miguel Juárez Celman in Argentina, following excess borrowing in the international capital market, was unable to meet its payments to the House of Baring, a financial crisis ensued that had serious implications not only for Argentina but also for other Latin American

---

51 Banana exports had begun as a by-product of railways. The heavy expense of constructing the railroad from the Atlantic coast to the capital, San José, made it necessary to find a commodity which could be produced quickly on the fertile lands next to the track in order to generate a source of revenue as the railway advanced from the coast. See Stewart (1964) for a biography of Minor Cooper Keith, the key figure in both railway construction and the banana industry in Costa Rica.

52 The origins of the banana industry and the myriad problems associated with its expansion are discussed in Adams (1914).

countries, particularly Uruguay, and for the whole British financial system. A rescue operation was mounted through the Bank of England, but loans to Argentina (and Uruguay) were severely curtailed, and the two republics had to cut imports sharply. Exports were less affected, but even so the sterling value of Argentine exports did not surpass the 1889 peak until 1898 and imports not until 1904.[53]

The cyclical nature of export performance after 1850 in so many Latin American countries had a variety of causes, both internal and external. The international economy in the sixty years before the First World War provided opportunities for the expansion of primary exports that would never be repeated; the cycles in Latin American export performance were only partly due to external shocks emanating from the international economy. The cycles, as we have seen, had many causes. Some, such as external shocks, gave little or no room for maneuvering. Others, such as commodity concentration and low yields, suggested that much of the remedy for poor export performance lay firmly in national hands.

The pattern of external trade

Industrialization in Europe and the United States was the driving force behind the growth of primary-product exports in the long period between the middle of the nineteenth century and the beginning of the First World War. At the same time, industrialization brought with it a surplus of manufactured goods for which new markets had to be found. Latin America, with its weak industrial base and open trading system, was an obvious market, and competition between the main industrial countries for market share became intense toward the end of the period.

The general pattern of trade was therefore clear, although there were a few exceptions. Some Latin American countries (e.g., Ecuador and Mexico) were major importers of foodstuffs – a trade which tended to benefit the United States rather than Europe. A few republics channeled a large part of their trade through other Latin American countries rather than through the "center." Paraguay, whose main export was yerba maté – a product consumed only in South America – depended mainly on the Argentine market and, indeed, eventually pegged its currency to the Argentine peso. Bolivia purchased many of its imports from neighboring countries, although for much of this "intraregional" trade the countries of origin were almost certainly outside Latin America.

The Bolivian example is indicative of a general problem in interpreting trade statistics before the First World War. The destination of exports was

53 The trade statistics can be found in Ferns (1960), pp. 492–3. On the Baring crisis itself, see Ferns (1992).

assumed to be the port at which the goods were landed, whereas the origin of imports was assumed to be the last port of shipment. Thus British goods shipped to Bolivia through Buenos Aires would appear in Bolivian trade statistics as Argentine. Similarly, Guatemalan exports of coffee shipped to France through Germany would appear in the Guatemalan trade statistics as exports to Germany. The trade figures must therefore be interpreted with caution.[54]

In the midnineteenth century the main export market for all but a handful of Latin American countries was still Great Britain. By 1913 Great Britain was still an importer from Latin America of the first rank, but it was the main market (see Table 3.6) in only four cases (Argentina, Bolivia, Chile, and Peru). France appears as the main market for three republics (Ecuador, Haiti, and Venezuela), but this is almost certainly a statistical illusion (except for Haiti), because the products concerned (meat, wool, coffee, cacao) were destined for final consumption not just in France but in other parts of Europe as well. Germany also appears as the main market for three countries (Guatemala, Paraguay, and Uruguay); this is plausible for Guatemala in view of the presence of a strong German colony (in particular, coffee-growers in Alta Verapaz).

The main export market for most Latin American republics by 1913 was in fact the United States (see Table 3.6). No fewer than eleven of the twenty-one countries reported the United States as their leading market even before the First World War, and these figures are unlikely to be heavily distorted by the way in which exports were recorded.[55] Most of these countries, not surprisingly, were in the Northern Hemisphere; for many, the U.S. market was overwhelmingly the most important. Honduras, Panama, and Puerto Rico sold more than 80 percent of their exports to the United States by 1913; Cuba and Mexico more than 70 percent. The United States was also the main market for Brazil and Colombia, primarily as a result of the strong U.S. demand for coffee.[56]

Exports to the United States remained unimportant in a few countries. U.S. protective tariffs on wool and hides had damaged its trade with Argentina and Uruguay,[57] and Haiti sent almost all its exports of coffee and cacao to Europe. Argentina was by far the most important Latin American exporter by 1913, however, and the high level of its trade with Europe

---

54 A full account of the problems of interpreting nineteenth-century trade statistics can be found in Platt (1971).

55 The most important distortion in the U.S. statistics relates to tobacco imports from Cuba, some of which were destined for reexport. See Stubbs (1985), Chapter 1.

56 The British preference for tea, imported from Asia, has continued to depress per capita coffee consumption in the United Kingdom to this day, although the gap between Great Britain and other consumer countries was more marked in the nineteenth century.

57 See Bureau of the American Republics (1892g), p. 132.

Table 3.6. *Exports by main markets, 1913*

Country	Exports by value (in millions of US$)	United States (%)	United Kingdom (%)	Germany (%)	France (%)	Total (%)
Argentina	510.3	4.7	24.9	12.0	7.8	49.4
Bolivia	36.5	0.6	80.8	8.5	4.9	94.8
Brazil	315.7	32.2	13.1	14.0	12.2	71.5
Chile	142.8	21.3	38.9	21.5	6.2	87.9
Colombia	33.2	44.5	13.5	7.1	2.0	67.1
Costa Rica	10.5	49.1	41.3	4.8	0.9	96.1
Cuba	164.6	79.7	11.2	2.8	1.0	94.7
Dominican Republic	10.5	53.5	2.3	19.8	8.5	84.1
Ecuador	15.8	24.3	10.3	16.6	34.1	85.3
El Salvador	9.3	29.7	7.4	17.9	21.4	76.4
Guatemala	14.5	27.1	11.1	53.0	0.1	91.3
Haiti	11.3	8.8	7.1	37.2	44.2	97.3
Honduras[a]	3.2	86.9	1.8	5.3	0.2	94.2
Mexico[b]	148.0	75.2	13.5	3.5	2.8	95.0
Nicaragua	7.7	35.3	12.9	24.5	22.9	95.6
Panama	5.1	94.1	1.3	4.3	0.3	99.9
Paraguay	5.5	—	na	22.0	0.6	28.1
Peru	43.6	33.2	37.2	6.7	3.5	80.6
Puerto Rico[c]	46.2	84.6	n/a	n/a	n/a	84.6
Uruguay	71.8	4.0	11.2	19.5	17.4	52.1
Venezuela	28.3	29.4	7.6	19.3	34.7	91.0
Latin America[d]	1,588.2	29.7	20.7	12.4	8.0	70.8

[a] Fiscal year 1912–13.
[b] Fiscal year 1911–12.
[c] Data are for 1910.
[d] Excludes Puerto Rico.
Sources: Pan-American Union (1952); Dietz (1986).

was the single most important factor in preventing the United States from acquiring an even more dominant position as a market for Latin American exports. Even so, the United States accounted for 29.7 percent of all exports, compared with 20.7 percent for Great Britain (see Table 3.6), and the U.S. market was fractionally more important than the British even for the exports of the South American republics (all republics south of Panama). In Mexico, Central America, and the Caribbean republics the U.S. market was dominant, accounting for 70 percent of exports on the eve of the First World War.

Geographical concentration cannot be measured as accurately as can commodity concentration, but the statistics certainly indicate a high dependence in the case of exports on the four main industrialized countries (the United States, Great Britain, Germany, and France). By 1913 these four markets accounted for more than 90 percent of exports in ten countries and for more than 70 percent in eighteen (see Table 3.6). Only Argentina, Paraguay, and Uruguay had avoided a high degree of dependence on the four main markets – although in the case of Paraguay this did not mean geographical diversification, because it depended so heavily on the Argentine market.

Once again, therefore, we must note the extraordinarily favorable position of Argentina. With the fastest long-run rate of growth of exports, the highest proportion of total Latin American exports, and diversified commodity exports, Argentina also spread its products across a wide range of markets. Although Great Britain accounted for about a quarter of Argentine exports in 1913, another seven countries each accounted for more than 3 percent.[58] The other republics that had avoided commodity concentration (Mexico, Peru, Paraguay) had not been nearly so successful in avoiding geographical concentration, whereas those countries that enjoyed a satisfactory long-run rate of export growth (Chile and, on some criteria, Cuba) suffered on the eve of the First World War from both commodity concentration and a lack of geographical diversification.[59]

At first glance the pattern of imports (see Table 3.7) appears to tell the same story. In fact, the position was much healthier than the figures imply. First, with a few exceptions, the geographical pattern of imports was more diversified than it had been in the midnineteenth century, when Great Britain was the main supplier for virtually all countries. Second, although the four major countries dominated the import trade into Latin America by 1913, competition between them was often intense, and the use (and abuse) of monopoly power was still relatively rare. Third, as we have already suggested, the structure of imports was probably more diversified than the statistics suggest, as a result of reexports by the European powers.

The shift away from Great Britain was an inevitable consequence of the spread of the Industrial Revolution. Other countries – above all France, Germany, and the United States – acquired a surplus of manufactured goods for sale abroad, and it was natural that their export effort should focus on countries that – in the absence of colonial ties – were free to buy from the cheapest source.

58 See Mills (n.d.), p. 159.
59 Uruguay, however, in common with Argentina, had geographically diversified exports. See Finch (1981), p. 131.

Table 3.7. *Imports by main markets, 1913*

Country	United States (%)	United Kingdom (%)	Germany (%)	France (%)	Total (%)
Argentina	14.7	31.0	16.9	9.0	71.6
Bolivia	7.4	20.3	36.7	3.8	68.2
Brazil	15.7	24.5	17.5	9.8	67.5
Chile	16.7	30.0	24.6	5.5	76.8
Colombia	26.7	20.5	14.1	15.5	76.8
Costa Rica	50.7	14.6	15.2	4.4	84.9
Cuba	53.7	12.3	6.9	5.2	78.1
Dominican Republic	62.2	7.9	18.1	3.0	91.2
Ecuador	31.9	29.6	17.8	4.9	84.2
El Salvador	39.5	27.2	10.8	6.6	84.1
Guatemala	50.2	16.4	20.3	4.0	90.9
Haiti	73.0	7.3	6.6	10.1	97.0
Honduras[a]	67.5	14.7	11.5	2.9	96.6
Mexico[b]	53.9	11.8	13.1	8.6	87.4
Nicaragua	56.2	19.9	10.7	6.9	93.7
Panama	55.5	22.1	9.9	3.1	90.6
Paraguay	6.0	28.6	27.6	6.6	74.8
Peru	28.8	26.3	17.3	4.6	77.0
Puerto Rico[c]	88.5	n/a	n/a	n/a	88.5
Uruguay	12.7	24.5	15.5	8.1	60.8
Venezuela	32.8	25.5	16.5	9.1	83.9
Latin America[d]	**25.5**	**24.8**	**16.5**	**8.3**	**75.1**

[a] Fiscal year 1912–13.
[b] Fiscal year 1911–12.
[c] Data are for 1910.
[d] Excludes Puerto Rico.
Sources: Pan-American Union (1952); Dietz (1986).

The shift in the structure of imports away from Great Britain was also a reflection of a shift in the commodity composition of imports. Throughout the period up to the First World War, British exports to Latin America remained concentrated in textiles and clothing. Rival industrial powers were unable to mount a serious challenge to Great Britain in this field, but they did succeed in outperforming Great Britain in other areas. Thus by the end of the century U.S. agricultural and mining machinery was much in demand, German "fancy" goods were highly prized, and France was considered the best source for luxury consumer goods. As the importance of textiles and clothing imports declined – in Colombia in the 1850s, for example, they still represented more than 60 percent of all imports[60] – the British share of imports tended to fall.

60 See Ocampo (1984), p. 157.

Consider the case of Venezuela on the eve of the First World War. Total textile imports were valued at £876,016, with the British share by far the largest of any country. Imports of foodstuffs and machinery, however, were dominated by the United States. France and Germany had a strong showing in the "general merchandise" category. Because of the decline in the relative importance of textiles, Great Britain had lost first place in the Venezuelan import trade to the United States by the end of the nineteenth century, though it still placed ahead of Germany and France.[61]

By 1913 Great Britain was the main supplier to seven republics, including Argentina, Brazil, Chile, and Uruguay. Almost half of the British exports went to Argentina.[62] As a result of British dominance in the Argentine market – the main market for imports in Latin America – Great Britain was able to match U.S. exports to all Latin America. The two countries each accounted for about one-quarter of total imports in 1913 (see Table 3.7). Needless to say, the British share was much higher in the southern republics than in the northern ones, where the United States had increased its proportion of imports to 54.1 percent by the First World War and where Great Britain's proportion had been reduced to a modest 12.3 percent (still in second place).

In a few of the northern republics the dominance of the United States was a serious problem. With nearly 70 percent of the Honduran market for imports, U.S. suppliers – generally working through the banana companies – faced little competition. The same was true in Costa Rica, Nicaragua, Panama, Cuba, Haiti, and the Dominican Republic. The United States also had a massive share of Mexican imports (more than 50 percent), but the size of the market produced greater competition among suppliers.[63]

The adoption of the gold standard and full currency convertibility among the industrialized nations meant that Latin American countries – even with inconvertible paper currencies – had no reason to balance their trade bilaterally. The Brazilian trade surplus with the United States could be used to pay for the trade deficit with Great Britain and Germany. It was a genuinely multilateral system, with some remarkable examples of bilateral imbalances. In 1913 Haiti shipped less than 10 percent of its exports to the United States but purchased more than 70 percent of its imports from the country that would soon occupy it militarily. Colombia sent nearly half its exports to the United States before the First World War but bought only one-quarter of its imports from that source. Not surprisingly, the collapse

61 See Dalton (1916), pp. 276–7.
62 See Platt (1972), Appendix 1.
63 Although the United States implicitly accepted British trade preeminence in the Southern Cone (Argentina, Chile, and Uruguay) and Great Britain did the same for the United States in the Caribbean and Central America, Anglo–U.S. rivalry in the Mexican market before the First World War was often intense. See Katz (1981).

of currency convertibility in 1914 caused major disruptions in many parts of Latin America as a result of these large bilateral imbalances.

The terms of trade and international transport costs

The external trade of Latin America was dominated by the exchange of primary products for manufactured goods. There were only a few exceptions: Some exports (e.g., straw hats from Ecuador and Colombia,[64] wheat flour from Argentina and Chile) could be classified as manufactures; some imports (e.g., wheat purchased by Mexico) were clearly primary products. Yet these commodities could not alter the general picture: Latin America's place in the world economy depended on the export of primary products and the import of manufactured goods.

The prices of neither primary-product exports nor manufactured imports were stable in the long period that led up to the First World War, so the net barter terms of trade (NBTT) were constantly fluctuating.[65] These fluctuations were part of the natural order of capitalist economic development and would scarcely be worthy of comment were it not for the fact that some authors have claimed to see in the statistics a secular deterioration in the NBTT for Latin America beginning in the nineteenth century.[66]

In the period from independence in the 1820s to midcentury Latin American imports were dominated by textiles. The price of textiles was falling dramatically, however, as the Industrial Revolution drove down the unit cost of production in the exporting countries. Primary-product prices fluctuated considerably, but most Latin American countries experienced an improvement in the NBTT over this period. In the case of Brazil the NBTT are estimated to have doubled between 1826–30 and 1851–5.[67]

Primary-product prices continued to fluctuate from the 1850s to 1913. Cycles in coffee, cacao, and sugar prices were already well established, so countries with exports concentrated in these products were bound to experience significant variation in the export unit values used to calculate the NBTT. Import prices also fluctuated, falling after 1870 and rising after 1890, with no significant long-run trend by most estimates.[68]

For those countries for which we have information, the NBTT were subject to marked swings throughout the period. A trend is difficult, if not

---

64 On the eve of the First World War, these "Panama" hats represented 4 percent of Colombian exports. See Ocampo (1984), p. 100.

65 NBTT are defined as the price of exports, $p(x)$, divided by the price of imports, $p(m)$. Thus an increase (decrease) in the NBTT means a relative increase (decrease) in the price of exports.

66 This hypothesis is discussed in more detail in Chapter 9.

67 See IBGE (1987), Table 11.11.

68 British export prices, for example, which many have used as a proxy for Latin America's import prices, were 100.8 in 1850 (1880 = 100) and 96.9 in 1913. See Imlah (1958), pp. 94–8.

impossible, to discern. Brazil experienced a modest secular improvement in the NBTT between 1850 and 1913, but this conceals enormous fluctuations, including an improvement of 55 percent in the 1850s and an equally dramatic collapse in the 1860s.[69] Colombia suffered a serious deterioration in the NBTT after 1880,[70] but Mexico appears to have experienced an equally dramatic improvement despite the fall in the gold price of silver.[71] Chile, according to one source, experienced a deterioration in its NBTT in the 1890s as import prices started to rise,[72] whereas Peru experienced an improvement in its NBTT during the guano age and a serious decline afterwards.[73]

The interpretation of these figures is further complicated by the methods used to calculate import prices. In view of the widespread use before the First World War of official or declared values of imports in the trade statistics of Latin American countries – neither of which is a reliable guide to actual import prices[74] – it has become common practice to use the export prices of a major exporter of manufactured goods (usually Great Britain) as a proxy for Latin American import prices.

This procedure is subject to a variety of objections. The pattern of British exports (dominated by textiles) did not reflect the changing pattern of Latin American imports. With price falls for textiles concentrated in the first half of the nineteenth century, it is possible that the decline in import prices after 1850 was faster than implied by the use of British export prices. This suspicion is confirmed by Mexican statistics, which show that between 1891 and 1895, for example, British export prices fell by 15 percent and Mexican import prices by 35 percent.[75]

An even more weighty objection comes from the revolution in international transport in the second half of the nineteenth century. The NBTT of any Latin American country should reflect the prices for imports at the port of entry (CIF prices). British export prices, however, are estimated at the port of embarkation (FOB prices). This difference would not matter if international transport costs were stable, but the introduction of steamships on the trade routes to Latin America lowered freight rates and the gap between the CIF and FOB prices of imports.[76] Where FOB import prices were in decline between 1850 and 1913, we can thus be confident that the CIF price was falling even more rapidly. Even if the FOB price was rising,

69 See Leff (1982a), p. 82.
70 See Ocampo (1984), p. 93.
71 See Rosenzweig (1989), pp. 181–2. For the period after 1880, however, there was a decline due to the sharp fall in the price of silver. See Beatty (2000).
72 See Palma (1979), Appendixes 18 and 32.
73 See Hunt (1985), Table 2.
74 See Platt (1971).
75 See Rosenzweig (1989), p. 162.
76 See Oribe Stemmer (1989).

however, it is still possible that the CIF price was moving in the opposite direction.

We must therefore regard any suggestion of a secular decline in the NBTT for Latin America before 1913 with extreme caution. There were certainly long periods when the NBTT for a given country could deteriorate. The crisis of excess supply in the coffee market in the 1890s, for example, caused a serious deterioration in the NBTT of all those countries with exports concentrated in coffee. Sugar prices went through long periods of decline, causing problems for the NBTT of such countries as Cuba and Puerto Rico. Yet it was not difficult to find counterexamples. The boom in nitrate prices caused a sharp improvement in the Chilean NBTT after 1898. The guano age in Peru was also marked by an improvement in the country's NBTT. And the economic expansion in Bolivia in the decade before the First World War was in part a reflection of much higher prices for tin.

The alleged long-run secular decline in the NBTT of Latin America before 1913 was therefore almost certainly a chimera. If anything, the long-run trend was working against the industrialized countries in this period. The causes of changes in the NBTT in the two regions were different, however. A decline in British export prices was in part a reflection of improved productivity in the export sector. The fall in the NBTT was therefore also a reflection of increased productivity and did not necessarily lead to a fall in purchasing power. A decline in a Latin American country's export prices, on the other hand, was often a reflection of changes in the balance between world supply and demand over which the country had no control. A fall in the NBTT could therefore lead to a sharp reduction in purchasing power.[77]

For that reason it is often preferable to work with alternative measures of the terms of trade. One example is the income terms of trade (ITT), which multiplies the NBTT by the volume of exports and therefore measures the capacity to import.[78] ITT have been calculated for a small number of countries before 1913;[79] given the increase in the volume of exports, the ITT generally show a secular improvement. However, it is possible to find periods when the ITT are stationary or even falling. An example is Brazil in the 1890s, when the deterioration in the NBTT was so sharp that the ITT was virtually unchanged despite the growth of export volumes.

---

77 Some price falls, however, were due to productivity increases. This seems to be true of Cuban sugar prices for much of the nineteenth century, with mechanization leading to a rise in labor productivity and a decline in unit costs. See Moreno Fraginals (1986).

78 ITT can be written as $ITT = NBTT \cdot q(x) = [p(x)/p(m)] \cdot q(x) = e(x)/p(m)$, where $q(x)$ is the volume of exports and $e(x)$ is the value of exports. Thus the ITT can be derived from the value of exports through division by the price of imports. It therefore measures the volume of imports that can be purchased for a given value of exports.

79 The most complete series are for Brazil (IBGE, 1987), Chile (Palma, 1979), and Peru (Hunt, 1973). See also Beatty (2000) for Mexico after 1880.

Brazil's experience of coffee-price fluctuations and deteriorating NBTT was influential in the decision of São Paulo and other coffee-producing states to launch a radical and pioneering commodity price stabilization scheme. Known as the Taubaté coffee valorization, the scheme (first adopted in 1906) took advantage of Brazil's quasi-monopoly position in the world market to stabilize prices. By increasing or reducing coffee inventories, Brazil was able to regulate the amount of coffee reaching the world market and thereby to adjust world supply to the level of demand consistent with a target price. However, the higher the target price the more costly the scheme and the greater the risk that coffee exporters in other countries would expand sales and win market share at Brazil's expense. Because coffee trees must mature for five years before their beans can begin to be harvested, the risks associated with coffee valorization were initially discounted. The first coffee-valorization scheme was widely judged to have been a success, even though it collapsed at the outbreak of the First World War.[80]

Coffee was not the only commodity for which market conditions on the eve of the First World War fell far short of the perfect competition described in textbooks. Sugar remained a highly "political" crop,[81] and the production and marketing of bananas were controlled by an oligopoly of foreign-owned companies. Tariff, and even nontariff, barriers were becoming more common for temperate products that competed with agricultural production in Europe and North America. Great Britain had so far resisted all attempts to end its free-trade policies, but the British market was declining in relative importance for Latin America. Joseph Chamberlain's campaign at the turn of the century in favor of imperial preference was a warning of changes to come.[82]

---

80 On the first Brazilian coffee-valorization scheme, see Fritsch (1988), pp. 13–8.

81 Sir Arthur Lewis has often drawn attention to the political nature of some commodity markets, which makes optimizing behavior by economic agents extremely difficult. For a concise summary of sugar diplomacy before 1914, see Chalmin (1984).

82 Joseph Chamberlain, a renegade from the Liberal Party, argued that Great Britain's free-trade policy was leading to a loss of competitiveness. His populist appeal was considerable, and, although he lost the argument, British faith in free trade was undoubtedly undermined by his campaign. See Bulmer-Thomas (1965), vol. 1, pp. 162–3.

4

Export-led growth: the supply side

The growth of exports was a necessary but not sufficient condition for successful export-led growth. Yet, as we saw in Chapter 3, only a small number of countries can be said to have met even this basic condition. The problem was not, in general, a shortage of demand; far more important were the constraints on the expansion of export supply. Countries with fast growth of exports had usually overcome the obstacles to export expansion on the supply side, whereas those with slow growth were unable to break down the often formidable problems that confronted the export sector throughout the nineteenth century.

Export expansion, whether fast or slow, could produce one of three export-led models: additive, destructive, or transformative. In the additive model the export sector was grafted onto the existing structure of production with very little change in the nonexport economy. Resources were attracted into the export sector without reducing output elsewhere, and factor productivity in the nonexport economy was unaffected by the growth of the export sector. An example of additive growth is provided by the expansion of banana exports from Honduras at the start of the twentieth century. The land – previously unutilized – had a zero opportunity cost, the capital was foreign, and the labor was provided in large part by migrant workers from the British West Indies and El Salvador. The impact on the rest of the economy was minor.[1]

In the destructive model the expansion of new exports was achieved by attracting resources from existing activities in the rest of the economy – either from within the export sector itself or from the nonexport economy. A good example of the former is the expansion of tin mining in Bolivia, where the land, labor, and capital all came in large part from resources previously devoted to silver exports.[2] An example of the latter is coffee exports from Puerto Rico after the final abolition of slavery in 1873, which

---

[1] Several good studies have been written on the early days of the banana industry. See, for example, Kepner and Soothill (1935), Chapters 1–2.

[2] On the switch from silver to tin, see Klein (1982), Chapter 6.

were achieved by bidding away resources previously devoted to agricultural production for the home market.[3] The destructive model implied a shift of resources toward higher factor returns (principally for capital and land), although most of the nonexport economy was still unaffected.

In the transformative model the export sector expanded in such a way that the productivity (labor and capital) of the nonexport economy was significantly affected. The resources attracted to the export sector in this model were more likely to come with a nonzero opportunity cost (as in the destructive model), but this time the impact on factor and product markets throughout the economy was considerable. Markets worked in an efficient way, resources were attracted to activities in which they could command the highest rate of return, and the benefits of technological change and productivity gains were transmitted to all branches of the economy. Argentine meat and cereal expansion is the best example of a transformative model of export-led growth in the period before the First World War.

In most countries export-led growth featured elements from all three models. Even in Argentina the growth of some minor exports – such as sugar from Tucumán – was destructive rather than transformative.[4] From the point of view of Latin American economic development the transformative model was far superior to the other two and unambiguously positive. The additive model was (by definition) positive, but its overall impact was often slight. The destructive model could also be positive, because it implied a shift toward activities with higher factor productivity, but the aggregate level of labor productivity depended on whether all the workers released found full employment in the new activities. The underemployment on Caribbean sugar plantations – where workers were idle for up to eight months a year – showed that this assumption could not always be made.[5]

Whether the model of export-led growth was additive, destructive, or transformative depended to some extent on the commodity lottery. The meat-export industry, for example, involved so many separate processes (e.g., pasture, fencing, fattening, slaughtering, and packing) that it could not be mounted successfully without transforming many branches of the nonexport economy. By contrast, banana exports were possible from enclaves both physically and economically separate from the rest of the economy. However, the model also reflected the efficiency with which factor markets functioned. The operation of these markets was an important determinant of whether export growth itself was fast or slow. It is appropriate, therefore, to begin with an examination of the markets for labor, land, and capital in Latin America before the First World War.

---

3 See Bergad (1983), Chapters 3–4.
4 See Rock (1986), pp. 406–7.
5 Moreno Fraginals (1986), pp. 217–29, is a good account of this aspect of the sugar industry.

The labor market

Export-led growth took place against a background of demographic expansion. The natural growth of population – the difference between births and deaths per thousand people – varied between 1 percent and 2 percent per year in the period leading up to the First World War unless exceptional conditions, such as war, prevailed. The crude birth rate (CBR) was remarkably stable – as reflected in the low coefficient of variation – both across countries (see Table 4.1) and over time, at just over 40 per thousand. Only Uruguay, its population more urban and middle-class than any other in Latin America, had experienced a significant reduction in the CBR by 1913.

The crude death rate (CDR) averaged around 26 per thousand, but this concealed significant variations. At first the variations were random – affected above all by epidemics, such as cholera and yellow fever, or by the destructions of war – but gradually the CDR yielded to improvements in sanitation, water supply, and the spread of modern medicine. The extremely high infant mortality rates (IMRs) in the midnineteenth century – in Mexico more than 300 out of every 1,000 children born died before their first birthday – had been reduced by the end of the century; in consequence life expectancy, though still very low by modern standards, had started to climb.[6] Even so the IMR was above 100 throughout Latin America before 1914, compared with 72 in Australia and 57 in New Zealand (see Table 4.1).

The natural rate of population increase was high by international standards throughout the period under consideration (circa 1850 to circa 1914) – a tribute perhaps to the extremely favorable land–man ratios found in most of Latin America – but complaints of labor shortages by employers in the export sector were universal. This was true whether we consider fast-growing export sectors, such as coffee from the state of São Paulo in Brazil, or slow-growing activities, such as nineteenth-century sugar in the Dominican Republic. The annual increase in labor supply implied by past population growth was never enough, it would seem, to satisfy the needs of the export sector for additional workers, and complaints of labor shortages were frequently heard from other branches of the economy as well. The export sector therefore had to attract its labor supply either through internal or international migration.

Let us consider first the case of internal migration. Throughout nineteenth-century Latin America the population was overwhelmingly rural.

6 In Brazil, for example, male life expectancy at birth was 27.1 years in 1879 – typical of much of
   Latin America at the time. By 1920 this had risen to 31.4 years. See Arriaga (1968), pp. 29 and 34.
   Only Argentina, where life expectancy in 1914 reached 48 years, came close to the level in advanced
   countries. See Sánchez-Albórnoz (1986), p. 142.

Table 4.1. *Sociodemographic profiles, circa 1910–1914*

Country	CBR[a]	CDR[b]	IMR[c]	Urbanization[d] (No. of cities)	Newspapers[e]
Argentina	40.3	17.7	121	31.2 (9)	87
Bolivia				4.3 (1)	6
Brazil	47.3[f]			10.7 (14)	9
Chile	44.4	31.5	261	14.5 (2)	44
Colombia	44.1	26.0	177	7.1 (8)	3
Costa Rica	43.0	23.7	191	9.0 (1)	31
Cuba	44.7	21.4	140	15.1 (2)	9
Dominican Republic				3.0 (1)	9
Ecuador	46.5[g]	30.2[g]	188[g]	9.1 (2)	15
El Salvador	44.7	31.1	169	6.3 (1)	13
Guatemala	46.6	33.0	142	5.1 (1)	
Haiti				5.6 (1)	3
Honduras	43.7	24.5	126	3.9 (1)	5
Mexico	43.2	46.6	228	7.6 (11)	12
Nicaragua				7.0 (1)	28
Panama	42.0	19.0	122	11.1 (1)	53
Paraguay				14.2 (1)	20
Peru				5.0 (4)	20
Puerto Rico	35.9	21.8	153	4.3 (1)	
Uruguay	31.5	13.2	103[b]	28.7 (1)	80
Venezuela	44.5	28.3	154	3.6 (1)	16
Mean (unweighted)	42.8	26.3	163		
Coefficient of variation[i]	.098	.313	.27		
Australia	27.8	10.7	72	37.6 (7)	
Canada	31.1	13.0	170	19.4 (11)	
New Zealand	26.2	8.5	57	26.6 (3)	

[a] Crude birth rate (live births per thousand population).
[b] Crude death rate (deaths per thousand population).
[c] Infant mortality rate (infants under one year per thousand live births).
[d] Defined as the proportion of population living in major cities. The number of such cities is given in parentheses.
[e] Daily newspaper circulation per thousand population.
[f] Taken from Sánchez-Albórnoz (1986), p. 144.
[g] Average of 1915–19.
[b] Average of 1921–4.
[i] Defined as the ratio of the standard deviation to the mean.
Sources: CBR, CDR, and IMR from Mitchell (1993). Urbanization figures derived from Mitchell (1993). Newspaper circulation derived from Wilcox and Rines (1917).

This remained the case up to the First World War in all countries except Argentina and Uruguay (see Table 4.1). Thus the export sector faced the task of bidding away labor from rural – mainly agricultural – activities. Because the export sector typically enjoyed above-average growth with above-average labor productivity, it would have been natural for the export sector to offer increased real wages (nominal wages adjusted for the cost of living) on the grounds that the labor-supply curve was upward sloping.

This situation certainly did occur in some parts of Latin America. Migrants who moved from the Central Valley in Chile to the nitrate and other mines in the north were certainly attracted by higher wage rates than they could hope to obtain in their existing employment.[7] Workers who moved to northern Mexico from the center and south to work in the cattle and (after 1900) oil industries were also motivated by higher expected real wages. Some migrants from the Brazilian Northeast, where cotton and sugar were in decline, were attracted by the prospects of higher wages as a result of the coffee boom in São Paulo.

Yet this normal operation of the labor market was thwarted in numerous ways. Real wages in the export sector were often unchanged over long periods of time, and in some cases they even declined. Employers were extremely reluctant to tempt workers with the offer of higher wages. Even when they did pay higher nominal wages they were often able to reduce the real cost through the operation of company stores at which workers had to redeem their wages on goods sold at inflated prices.

Thus coercion – such a marked feature of the labor market in colonial times – was still found in many parts of Latin America on the eve of the First World War. The methods used in Guatemala and El Salvador by coffee producers to secure labor at a fixed or declining real cost were often brutal,[8] and the same could be said for many of those employed in the rubber booms in Brazil and Peru.[9] The labor supply used to produce yerba maté in Paraguay was free only in name,[10] and the situation was not much better for the workers across the border in Argentina producing sugar in Tucumán.[11]

The liberal reforms that swept across many parts of the subcontinent in the second half of the nineteenth century were designed, among other things, to ease the labor shortage faced by employers. The alienation of communal lands belonging to Indian villages introduced private property into the subsistence sector of the economy, and antivagrancy laws were adopted

---

7 See Sunkel (1982), pp. 82–6.

8 For Guatemala, see Jones (1940), Chapter 12. For El Salvador, see Menjívar (1980), pp. 87–112.

9 The rubber boom in Brazil is the subject of a fine monograph by Dean (1987). For Peru, where the treatment of rubber workers became an international scandal, see Vivian (1914), pp. 151–4.

10 Bureau of the American Republics (1892b), pp. 96–104, is an illuminating contemporary account of the yerba maté industry by a U.S. consul.

11 See Bauer (1986), p. 182.

(and adapted) to try to force those without property to offer their labor services to the capitalist sector of the economy. In the absence of higher real wages, however, only coercion could ensure that employers received an adequate supply.[12]

The reluctance of employers to use higher wages to clear the labor market had many explanations. Most of Latin America's exports of primary products competed in the world market with supplies from other parts of the world (including other parts of Latin America); with many exports labor-intensive, labor costs were overwhelmingly the largest single item of expenditure, and higher wages were seen as a zero-sum game in which workers' gains would mean lower rents and profits. Some employers were also pessimistic about the slope of the supply curve and assumed that only a huge increase in wages could voluntarily secure the extra labor required; others shared the prevailing contempt for the lower classes found among most sections of the elite and assumed that only international migration from Europe could solve the problem of labor shortages.

International migration into Latin America before the First World War was, in fact, of two kinds – selective and mass. Selective international migration did not mean a free market in labor; workers were imported for specific tasks. Chinese coolies, for example, were widely employed in the sugar and cotton industries in Peru,[13] on the sugar plantations in Cuba,[14] and in railway construction in Costa Rica.[15] In Mexico they were joined in the henequen industry by indentured laborers from Korea.[16] Workers from the British West Indies were widely employed in the banana industry in the Caribbean Basin, in railway building, and in the construction of the Panama Canal after 1903.[17] The Cuban sugar industry used workers from Puerto Rico, and the sugar industry in the Dominican Republic had begun its traditional dependence on Haitian workers even before the First World War.[18] Many Latin American governments also encouraged the establishment of agricultural colonies made up of European immigrants. Most of these failed, but some in the Southern Cone – notably the south of Chile, southern Brazil, and southern Argentina – were quite successful.[19]

---

12 These issues are the subject of many fine essays in Duncan et al. (1977).

13 See Gonzales (1989).

14 See Thomas (1971), p. 186.

15 The death rate among these workers was high, however, and they were replaced with British West Indians. See Echeverri Gent (1992).

16 See Bauer (1986), p. 184.

17 On British West Indians in Panama, see Conniff (1985), Chapters 1–3.

18 See Hoetink (1986), p. 293.

19 Many nationalities were involved in these agricultural colonies and for very different reasons. For the Welsh, who settled in Patagonia, one of the motivations was preservation of their language. See Williams (1991), Chapter 8. Marshall (1991) contains a good bibliography on European immigration in general.

The most extreme case of selective migration was the international trade in slaves. This trade, finally suppressed in Brazil in the 1850s and in Cuba in the 1860s, was designed to increase the supply of slaves sufficiently to offset the low rate of growth of the slave population and to prevent slave costs from rising. With the suppression of the slave trade Brazil and Cuba were forced to turn to other types of selective migration to hold down wage costs. Only when slavery was finally abolished and – in the case of Cuba – after the Spanish – American War had ended, did the two countries adopt a policy of mass international migration.[20]

Mass immigration was not popular with all governments. Whereas selective migration was a tap that could be turned on and off to suit local labor-market conditions, mass migration – the unrestricted entry of foreigners – carried the risk that the migrants would not work in the areas of labor shortage, that they would bring "dangerous" social or religious ideas, and that they would not leave in times of depression. Furthermore, even if a government favored mass migration, there was no certainty that it could be achieved, because the incentives offered had to compete with the attractions of migration to the United States, Canada, and other countries of "recent settlement."

In fact, mass migration in Latin America was limited to a handful of countries. The outstanding case is Argentina: International migration began in the 1860s, accelerated in the 1870s following the War of the Triple Alliance, and was sustained – with only a brief interlude in the early 1890s – until the First World War. By that time the foreign-born represented 30 percent of the population – a figure far higher than that for the United States. Migrants accounted for half of the increase in population since 1870 and for more than half of the increase in the labor force. Although a high proportion of the migrants chose to stay in Buenos Aires, swelling Argentina's urban population and giving Latin America its first city with more than a million inhabitants,[21] the labor market worked with a fair degree of efficiency. Labor shortages never seriously interfered with the expansion of exports, and there is some evidence of rising real wages even in rural areas before 1914.[22]

Uruguay also favored a policy of mass immigration. As in Argentina, the largest single group of migrants was of Italian origin, but the migrants showed an even greater preference for urban life – in this case Montevideo – than did their Argentine counterparts. The unsettled political conditions until the beginning of the twentieth century restricted the flow of migrants, so the foreign born represented "only" 17 percent of the population in the 1908 census.[23] Brazil also adopted a policy of mass immigration after the

20 On the economics of European migration to Brazil, see Leff (1982), Chapter 4.
21 It had reached more than 1.5 million by 1910. Its only serious rival was Rio de Janeiro, with 870,000. See Mitchell (1993).
22 See Cortés Conde (1986), p. 340.
23 See Finch (1981), p. 25.

abolition of slavery in 1888 and was able to attract large numbers of Italians and Portuguese to the state of São Paulo. After 1907 São Paulo became a major source of attraction for Japanese immigrants. The foreign born never numbered more than 10 percent of the population, however.

Following the defeat of Spain, Cuba opted for mass immigration in a conscious effort to rebuild its war-devastated population and to cure the structural problem of labor shortage in the sugar industry. Racial bias, however, restricted the entry of West Indians until the 1920s, when labor shortages were particularly acute, so the main beneficiaries of Cuban immigration policy were Spaniards (including Fidel Castro's father, who first arrived in Cuba as a member of the Spanish army). Elsewhere, with the partial exception of Chile, policies in favor of mass migration either were never adopted or were unsuccessful. In Mexico, by the time of the revolution, only 1 in 200 was foreign-born, and in Venezuela only 10 percent of those who arrived actually stayed.[24]

The combination of natural growth of population, internal migration, selective immigration, and mass migration relieved the labor shortage but did not usually cure it. Complaints of labor shortages persisted in many parts of Latin America up to the First World War, and the inefficient way in which the labor market operated was certainly one explanation for the low rate of capital formation in some republics. Investors, foreign or national, were naturally reluctant to invest in activities whose profitability could be undermined by labor shortages.

Only in a few countries was the rate of growth of exports not held back by labor shortages. The scale of migration to Argentina, for example, coupled with a relatively efficient labor market that allowed real wages to rise or fall in line with the gap between supply and demand, was such as to eliminate labor shortages over the long run.[25] Not all mass-migration countries, however, were so favored. Brazil after abolition of slavery in 1888 and Cuba after 1898 found that even international migration did not always clear the labor market, and the reason was the same in both countries: manipulation of the labor market by employers in an effort to prevent an increase in real wages.[26]

Countries that depended on minerals for their foreign-exchange earnings (such as Bolivia, Chile, and Mexico) also generally avoided labor shortages

24 See Sánchez-Albórnoz (1986), p. 129.
25 Williamson (1999) has calculated urban unskilled real wages for six Latin American countries before 1914 and compared them with real wages in the United Kingdom. In the case of Argentina, the data show a substantial increase from 1873–83 to 1899–1903. The data can be found in Williamson (1998).
26 International (mass) migration was a clumsy instrument for resolving labor shortages in the export sector. First, not all migrants stayed in the country; second, many chose not to work in the export sector. It has been estimated in the case of São Paulo state in Brazil that 79 percent of those who arrived between 1892 and 1895 stayed permanently, whereas only 9 percent of those who arrived between 1906 and 1910 did so. See Holloway (1980), p. 179.

in the export sector.[27] The mining sector was less labor-intensive than agricultural exports, and employers were more willing to tolerate higher wages as a means of attracting workers. The element of coercion in bringing workers to the mines could still be strong, however, and labor unrest was often met with force.[28]

A final group of countries was those, such as Haiti and El Salvador, where the growth of exports was so modest that the natural rate of population growth even permitted the emigration of labor to neighboring countries. The Northeast of Brazil – a region, not a country – was in a similar position. In these cases the failure of the export sector to grow faster could not be blamed on the operation of the labor market.

Elsewhere, labor shortages persisted and contributed to the slow growth of exports. The root of the problem was the unwillingness of employers to use wages to clear the market. The real wage of Cuban cane cutters, Brazilian coffee growers, and Ecuadorean cacao workers, for example, remained unchanged for long periods despite evidence of labor shortages.[29] Government efforts to increase the labor supply through restricting access to land could alleviate this basic problem but could not resolve it. The authorities were even willing to subsidize international-migration costs (as in Brazil) or to give free parcels of land to foreigners (as in El Salvador) rather than see real wages rise.

In an effort to secure an adequate labor force, without the need to raise real wages, many large landowners expanded the practice (in existence since colonial times) of providing workers with access to land in exchange for their labor. These workers, known as *inquilinos* in Chile; *huasipungueros, colonos, concertados,* or *yanaconas* in the Andes; and *peones acasillados* in Mexico, were often virtually outside the money economy, for their payment was in kind rather than cash. Even day laborers, hired throughout the year for specific tasks, were often marginal to the money economy: This happened when credit was advanced to the worker, often under dubious circumstances, in return for future duties. The advance was not necessarily canceled with the death of the debtor; instead, it could pass to his children, so the system has often been described as debt bondage.[30]

---

27 Even so, there is little evidence of rising real wages. For a careful study of Mexico, see Gómez-Galvarriato (1998).

28 The most infamous example is the suppression of a strike in the nitrate port of Iquique in northern Chile in 1907, with the loss of hundreds of lives. See Blakemore (1986), p. 529.

29 It has been argued for Brazil, for example, that "these conditions seem to have led to an expansion pattern in which the economy's advanced sector could grow for almost a century without rising real wages." See Leff (1982), p. 69. See also Williamson (1998) and (1999).

30 Debt bondage, or debt peonage, has been recently subject to a revisionist interpretation in which labor scarcity is seen as favoring the debtor, not the creditor. See, for example, Miller (1990). Although it can readily be agreed that labor scarcity ought to have favored the debtor, it is by no means certain that it did.

The unwillingness of employers to see real wages rise had macroeconomic as well as microeconomic implications. It concentrated income, in the export sector in particular, in the hands of the owners of land and capital. It also undermined the search for labor-saving technological innovations in response to rising real wages. The contrast with Australia, New Zealand, and Canada — all countries of mass migration with free labor markets (by 1914) and rising real wages — could not be stronger.[31] Only Argentina came close to this model, with technical improvements in agriculture and rising real wages a noteworthy feature of the export sector in the period leading up to the First World War.

Land

The expansion of agricultural exports after the middle of the nineteenth century — and in a few cases even before — required access to new lands. In fifty years, assuming no change in yields, a 5 percent annual increase in agricultural exports implies a tenfold increase in land used. Even allowing for improvements in yield and the more modest rates of growth found in most countries, export-led growth — at least when based on agriculture — still implied very substantial increases in inputs of land.

No Latin American country — not even densely populated El Salvador and Haiti — suffered from a physical shortage of land, either at the beginning of the independence period or on the eve of the First World War. The region was famous throughout the world for its favorable land–man ratios. Some of the largest countries (e.g., Argentina and Brazil) had fewer than 3 inhabitants per square kilometer in 1913; even in El Salvador and Haiti the ratio was below 70.

Access to land was another matter, however. Latin America suffered from two serious problems. First, inadequate transportation meant that vast tracts of land were virtually inaccessible until the coming of the railways; and even then parts of many republics were still physically isolated and were not finally incorporated into the national territory until an extensive road network was established in the twentieth century. Second, Latin America had perpetuated the system of land tenure, inherited from Spain and Portugal, that left the ownership of land highly concentrated.

By all accounts the concentration of landownership had changed very little in the century after independence. Yet it would be wrong to blame this exclusively — as has so often been done — on the land-tenure system inherited from the Iberian Peninsula. The fact is that the area in private

---

31 Australia, despite its inauspicious beginnings as a convict colony, saw a rise of 120 percent in wages between 1841–5 and 1886–90, compared with a rise in prices of 10 percent. See Tregarthen (1897), p. 421.

ownership in the 1820s was only a fraction of the area in private ownership in 1914. The increase over nearly a century was enormous and would have provided many opportunities to alter the concentration ratio if the new lands in private ownership had been allocated more equally. The failure to do so owed more to the balance of political power and to economic exigencies than to inherited colonial patterns. The most striking proof of this was the reproduction in countries long ignored by Spain, such as Argentina, El Salvador, and Uruguay, of the high concentration ratios found in favored colonial areas, such as Mexico and Peru.

The increase in the land area in private hands came from a variety of sources. In some countries it was in part the result of conquest; Indian wars in Argentina, Chile, and Mexico as late as the last quarter of the nineteenth century added substantially to the national patrimony and provided an opportunity for the state to reward its followers. In a few cases the new lands were used to encourage agricultural colonies composed of European immigrants, but they were usually divided up as huge estates. In one case, following the defeat of the Yaqui Indians in northern Mexico during the Porfiriato, a single company was granted 547,000 hectares – equivalent to one-quarter of the area of El Salvador.[32]

The more usual method of increasing the area in private hands was through the sale or grant of former crown lands. Each republic inherited a vast area of such land, which could be disposed of as needs and circumstances changed. The disposal of these public lands provided the state with a powerful instrument to meet numerous different targets, including – if the state had so wished – a less-concentrated pattern of landownership. Smallholdings were occasionally encouraged, but the general pattern of land disposals reproduced – or even aggravated – the inherited concentration.

The same was true of the alienation of *ejidos*, or communal lands. The introduction of private property into villages where land had been held communally for centuries could have created a system of smallholdings and yeoman farming like that in many parts of Europe. Some Indian villages did survive the transition, but all too frequently the main beneficiary was the large landowner with access to credit and political influence. Many of the huge estates in El Salvador and Guatemala, for example, owe their origin to the alienation of communal lands after 1870, when the liberal state was determined to promote the spread of coffee cultivation.

The expropriation of church lands in the second half of the nineteenth century provided a further opportunity to diminish the concentration of landownership. In Mexico the liberal reforms introduced by Benito Juárez after 1857 were specifically intended to encourage smallholding agriculture

---

32 The grant was made to the Richardson Construction Company of Los Angeles. See Knight (1986a), p. 111.

through the disposal of church lands to farmers of modest means. The aims of La Reforma were almost entirely thwarted by large landowners, however, and Mexico entered the twentieth century with one of the most concentrated systems of landownership ever known.[33] Elsewhere, as in Colombia and Ecuador, the disposal of church lands had much the same effect.[34]

The ability of the large landowning class to undermine the stated intention of the Mexican Reforma is a tribute to the political power linked to landownership in nineteenth-century Latin America. In the fifty years before the First World War, there were few occasions when political hegemony was not exercised by landowners who – not surprisingly – used the power of the state wherever possible to reinforce their privileged status. Indeed, in some countries, such as Paraguay after 1870, the overlap between the state and the landowning class was so great as to render meaningless any attempt to distinguish between them analytically.[35]

It would be incorrect, however, to assume that the survival of land concentration was simply a reflection of the political power of the landed elite. The persistence of labor shortages throughout the nineteenth century provided the state with a further justification for restricting access to agriculture landownership by a majority of its citizens. However artificial the labor shortages may have been (after all, they reflected the imperfections and inefficiency of the labor market as much as anything else), the fact remains that a scarcity of labor was perceived by the political elite as a major obstacle to economic development in general and to export promotion in particular. Thus the idea of converting communal lands into family-sized holdings in private hands was seen as counterproductive, because the farm-labor force would have little incentive to seek outside employment.

Some export crops did lend themselves to large-scale farming techniques. The need to process sugar cane within twenty-four hours of cutting required a sophisticated division of labor that would have been difficult to achieve in small-scale agriculture. Much the same could be said of banana exports: In Central America early efforts, controlled by small-scale farmers, to expand sales were thwarted by heavy losses due to deterioration of the crop in the absence of adequate transportation facilities.[36]

Economies of scale in export agriculture were comparatively rare. Crops such as coffee, tobacco, cacao, and wheat were subject to constant returns to

---

33 The census of 1910 – on the eve of the revolution – showed 11,000 landowners (0.1 percent of the population) in control of 57 percent of the land. See Singer (1969), p. 49.

34 In Ecuador church lands expropriated by the state at the end of the nineteenth century were not divided up, and only those with considerable resources were able to gain access. See Deas (1986), pp. 666–7.

35 On this period of Paraguayan economic history, see Abente (1989).

36 On the economics of sugar, see Moreno Fraginals (1986); on economies of scale in the banana industry, see Karnes (1978), Chapter 2.

scale and could therefore be raised just as efficiently on small farms. Indeed, coffee production in Costa Rica and in parts of Colombia provide the best examples of smallholding export agriculture in nineteenth-century Latin America, and independent family farms – often producing cereals, fruits, and vegetables for the home market – prospered in some areas of Chile, Ecuador, Mexico, and Peru. The few successful examples of agricultural colonies, mainly in the Southern Hemisphere, provided evidence of the profitability of medium-sized farms, and tenant farms of modest proportions flourished in parts of the Argentine pampas.[37]

No single explanation accounts for these relatively isolated examples of successful smallholdings. Some of these pockets of yeoman farming developed in parts of Latin America where the shortage of labor was so acute that no amount of manipulation of the labor market could be expected to yield an adequate wage-labor force. Such was the case in Costa Rica throughout the nineteenth century: Many families were obliged to cultivate only an area consistent with the supply of family labor. Others, as in the Mexican Bajío, were the result of the subdivision of estates into family-sized farms in the wake of financial problems faced by large landowners.[38]

Broadly speaking, however, agriculture in general and export agriculture in particular remained dominated by large-scale estates. The incorporation of new lands on the frontier, the sale of public lands within the frontier, and the disposal of communal lands close to villages all reinforced the traditional pattern of landownership inherited from colonial times. Even the sale of large estates in an increasingly transparent and active land market failed to dent the concentration of land in a few hands, for estates were usually sold as one unit without subdivision.

The means available to increase the amount of land in private hands were sufficient to ensure that its supply was rarely an obstacle to the expansion of exports. Only where climatic conditions were highly specific, as in the case of cacao, coffee, or tobacco, could it be claimed that the export quantum was constrained by an absence of suitable lands. Furthermore, within large estates it was often common to leave a high proportion of land uncultivated, providing considerable flexibility to increase production as market circumstances demanded. We must concede that, as an institution capable of responding quickly and flexibly to changing world market conditions, the large estate had certain advantages over the small or even medium-sized farm.

Yet the large estate could not, and should not, be viewed in isolation from the rest of the economy. The labor shortage to which it had responded was often more apparent than real – particularly by the early twentieth century.

37 See Gallo (1986), p. 367. See also Taylor (1948), pp. 190–204.
38 See Brading (1978), Chapter 6. See also Knight (1986a), p. 12.

The political patronage that had promoted the large estate also influenced the fiscal system and encouraged governments to substitute (regressive) import taxes for (potentially progressive) land taxes. The exercise of political hegemony by the landowning class led to the manipulation of factor markets and to a rental share in national income, which marginalized much of the labor force in both economic and political terms and which could only be justified if it led to a high rate of capital accumulation. As we shall now discover, this was very often not the case.

Capital markets

The growth of the export sector under an export-led model required additional inputs of land and labor. It also required capital. This was true whether the primary-product exports were mineral or agricultural, although the capital required per unit of output was generally higher in mining than in agriculture. Furthermore, the growth of labor productivity in the export sector was made possible through the adoption of technical innovations that tended to be embodied in new capital equipment. Thus to a large extent the success of the export-led model hinged on the supply of capital to the export sector.

The profitability of the export sector often depended on complementary investments in related activities, such as transport, public utilities, ports, communications, and housing. Thus the overall capital requirements associated with the export-led model were considerable. A successful mobilization of the resources needed for a high rate of capital accumulation could not guarantee a successful export-led growth model, but it was fairly certain that failure to carry out the necessary investments would undermine the model. Only in exceptional cases, such as guano in Peru, could it be said that export-led growth was not constrained by the supply of capital.[39]

The physical capital required directly and indirectly for the expansion of the export sector consisted of machines, tools, spare parts, construction works, land improvements (including irrigation), livestock, trees, and shrubs. It also included investments in human capital: In the first half of the nineteenth century the most important form of investment in human capital in several Latin American countries was in slaves, but by the end of the century it referred more generally to the costs of training, public education, and subsidized importation of skilled manpower.

For many entrepreneurs in the export sector the supply of working capital was also important. A coffee *fazenda* in Brazil at the beginning of the twentieth century had to spend money on wages, tools, transport, and storage

---

39 Guano could be extracted using unskilled labor and only the most primitive tools (e.g., shovels). See Levin (1960).

many months before payment could be expected from sale of the crop. Fail-ure to obtain access to working capital in sufficient quantities could force a farmer or a mineowner to sell to an export house at a substantial discount to the market price, lowering profitability and discouraging expansion.

The three kinds of capital – physical, human, and working – all required finance, so the first test of the efficiency of the capital market was the channeling of resources from potential lenders to potential borrowers. An export sector that relied exclusively on reinvested profits would not be able to grow sufficiently fast to underpin a successful export-led growth model, but the export sector was not the only potential borrower. Governments – at the national, provincial, and municipal levels – were expected to undertake investments in social infrastructure that could not normally be financed out of current revenue, and new private-sector firms could not invest in activ-ities – such as railways – that were vital to the health of the export sector without access to finance.

The identity of potential borrowers was therefore clear, but no borrow-ing could take place without an institutional framework to put borrowers in touch with lenders. In the first half of the nineteenth century the main lenders had been the church, the merchant class, and foreign sources, but the capital market had not worked well. The economic power of the church was resented by liberal politicians who considered church lending an inefficient way of promoting export-led growth.[40] The merchant class provided loans to hard-pressed governments on numerous occasions, but the finance rarely promoted capital accumulation, and the rent-seeking merchants, not sur-prisingly, demanded various privileges in return. Finally, the funds obtained from abroad through the issue of bonds in the 1820s could not be serviced in virtually all cases, and in general the mining investments promoted by foreigners were failures.[41]

In an attempt to improve the efficiency of the capital market, a small number of governments (notably in Argentina and Brazil) had promoted modern banking facilities. These rapidly deteriorated into institutions for funding government deficits, giving paper currency a bad name in many parts of the subcontinent.[42] The position began to change, however, after the middle of the century. The Banco y Casa de Moneda in Argentina, founded in 1854, functioned like a commercial bank from its origin. It changed its name to Banco de la Provincia de Buenos Aires in 1863 and became one of the foremost financial institutions in that country. In Brazil Baron Maua began to build a financial empire in the 1850s to complement his

---

40 On church lending in Mexico, see Chowning (1990).
41 On mining failures, see Rippy (1959), Chapter 1. A rare exception was the British-owned St. John D'el Rey Mining Company in Brazil. See Eakin (1989); on early bond defaults, see Chapter 2.
42 In the case of Argentina, see Irigoin (2000).

investments in agriculture and mining, and commercial banking became established in many other countries in the 1860s and 1870s.[43]

The spread of commercial banking in Latin America was aided by a change in the rules on limited liability in Great Britain that extended the privilege to financial institutions. British banks were quick to seize the opportunity, and by 1870 three such institutions with branches in many different countries were established in Latin America. French, German, and Italian banks followed suit, but U.S. banks were not allowed to invest in Latin America until just before the First World War.[44] The European banks were foreign, but they raised deposits locally, channeled the resources to Latin American borrowers, and competed with local financial institutions. By the outbreak of the First World War foreign commercial banks were established in most countries in Latin America (see Table 4.2), and some were extremely profitable.[45] Indeed, the yield on British investments in Latin American commercial banks in 1913 has been estimated at 13.4 percent[46] – far higher than the yield on other British investments in the region and well in excess of the average yield on investments in Great Britain itself.[47]

Commercial banking was an important contribution toward mobilizing the resources for capital accumulation in Latin America, but it suffered from two main weaknesses. First, the volume of deposits attracted into commercial banks in most countries by 1914 was still modest. Only in Argentina could it be said that the banking habit had been widely adopted, and even there deposits per head were half the level in Australia and Canada (see Table 4.2). Elsewhere, as Table 4.2 makes clear, the quantitative impact of commercial banking was still small. Ecuador had deposits per head of $1.6 in 1913, and Venezuela – not yet an oil exporter – recorded a mere $1.2 in the same year.

The second weakness was the limited impact of commercial banking on resource allocation in general and on export diversification in particular. Because the deposits taken were short term in nature (as in Europe), orthodox banking precepts demanded that lending be short term as well. Thus many banks concentrated their lending on existing activities in the export sector that required trade finance. This was good news for established export

43 Jones (1977a) contains an excellent account of the spread of commercial banking. For a good study of Mexico's capital market in the nineteenth century, see Marichal (1997).

44 National City Bank (now Citibank) was the first to take advantage of the change in U.S. law, opening a branch in Buenos Aires in November 1914. See Stallings (1987), pp. 64–6.

45 The total assets of the four major Anglo-Latin American banks, for example, rose from £8.9 million in 1870, to £32.6 million in 1890, to £66.3 million in 1910. See Jones (1977a), p. 21.

46 See Rippy (1959), p. 74.

47 The average level of return on productive investments by foreign (British) capital was 6–7 percent. This was some 3–4 percent higher (i.e., approximately double) than the yield on British home and colonial government securities. See Platt (1977), p. 12.

Table 4.2. *Banking in Latin America, circa 1913*

Country	Number of banks	Number of branches of international banks[a]	Note circulatio per head (in US$)	Bank deposits per head (in US$)
Argentina	13	76	45.6	75.7
Bolivia	4	2	3.5	3.3
Brazil	17	48	11.6	9.4
Chile	11	23	11.8	26.0
Colombia	6	2		
Costa Rica	5	0		
Cuba	9	25		
Dominican Republic	3	2		
Ecuador	5	1	2.5	1.6
El Salvador	4	2		2.3
Guatemala	5	0		0.9
Haiti	1	0		
Honduras	3	0		
Mexico	32	14	6.7[b]	
Nicaragua	5	1		
Panama	6	1		
Paraguay	4	0		
Peru	8	20		0.9
Puerto Rico	4	3	7.5[c]	5.6[d]
Uruguay	7	9	16.4	29.5
Venezuela	3	1		1.2
Australia			10.6	150.3
Canada			15.7	142.9
New Zealand			16.4	108.5

[a] The following international banks have been included: Anglo–South American Bank Ltd., Banque Française et Italienne pour l'Amérique du Sud, Commercial Bank of Spanish America, British Bank of South America, Deutsch-Südamerikanische Bank Aktien-Gesellschaft, Deutsche Ueberseeische Bank, London and River Plate Bank Ltd., London and Brazilian Bank Ltd., Banque Italo-Belge, National City Bank of New York, and Royal Bank of Canada.

[b] Derived from Catão (1991), pp. 241–5.

[c] Derived from Carroll (1975), p. 450, and refers to 1898.

[d] Derived from Clark et al. (1975), p. 376, and refers to 1908.

Sources: Data on banks and branches of international banks from Wilcox and Rines (1917). Data on note circulation and bank deposits per head derived from League of Nations (1927) unless otherwise stated.

activities (and contributed to the profitability of the banks themselves), but it did little to help bring into existence new activities and a more diversified export structure.

Some banks experimented with unorthodox lending strategies, tying up loans in projects with long gestations. Such innovations were generally unsuccessful, however, because in the periodic bouts of financial panic – a regular feature of nineteenth-century capitalism throughout the world – depositors rushed to withdraw their funds, and only orthodox banks were equipped to handle the demand. Because foreign-owned banks (particularly British ones) were the keenest on orthodox financial discipline, they tended to survive the crises better than the locally owned financial institutions, and their share of total deposits rose accordingly.

In an effort to overcome these weaknesses of commercial banking, some countries experimented with alternative types of financial institutions. Mortgage banks, for example, issued long-term mortgage bonds and could then lend the money for long-term investments in agriculture, with land offered as collateral. Such banks worked best in countries where title to land was clearly defined and with sufficient credit rating to offer mortgage bonds in foreign markets. Inevitably, Argentina, Chile, and Uruguay were the republics in which such banks prospered best; elsewhere their impact was more limited.[48] The larger countries (e.g., Argentina, Chile, Mexico, and Peru) had also established stock markets by 1914, but they remained little more than an arena for trading government paper.[49]

The inadequate institutional framework for channeling funds from lenders to borrowers meant that many new activities could only be undertaken using more informal channels. Many of the most successful Latin American businesses relied on family networks that allowed the profits of established companies to be channeled toward new ventures. Such was the case of the Di Tella family in Argentina,[50] the Prado family in Brazil,[51] the Edwards family in Chile,[52] and the Gómez family in Mexico.[53] The recurrence of these names in the twentieth-century history of each republic is a tribute to the efficacy of the financial networks established among family members.

---

48 Of fifty-eight financial, land, and investment companies in Latin America, no fewer than nineteen were conducting business in Argentina. See Wilcox and Rines (1917), pp. 840–4.

49 For a case study of Brazil, see Hanley (1998).

50 Lewis (1990), Chapter 4, has a good account of Di Tella and other successful Argentine capitalists.

51 Antonio Prado (1840–1929) was a pioneer in shifting the base of the family fortune away from land toward industry and finance. See Levi (1987).

52 Agustín Edwards had established interests in industry, finance, commerce, and agriculture before the end of the nineteenth century. See Kirsch (1977), p. 102.

53 By the generation before the First World War, the Gómez family were well entrenched in industry and the liberal professions. See Lomnitz and Pérez-Lizaur (1987), p. 106.

Another popular way for promoting capital accumulation, which did not depend on access to financial institutions, was through investment by immigrants. Outside the mass-immigration countries (see pp. 88–89) the trickle of migrants often brought with them small amounts of capital for investment in new activities; the growth of manufacturing before the First World War (see Chapter 5) owed much to this kind of financial transfer.

These devices were useful, but they could not be regarded as a wholly satisfactory solution, and they could not disguise the inefficient nature of the capital market in most Latin American countries. The formal institutional framework tended to reinforce the tendency of the export-led model to concentrate on a limited number of exports and discouraged diversification both inside and outside the export sector. The informal arrangements, on the other hand, put lenders in touch with a limited number of borrowers (among immigrants they were one and the same) and were in any case too weak to have much impact on the overall allocation of resources.

The institutional framework for investment in human capital was even more deficient in most countries. The supply of skilled – or even semi-skilled – labor was constrained by a primary-school system that gave a rudimentary training to a small proportion of children. Adult illiteracy rates of more than 80 percent were not uncommon before the First World War. Argentina under Domingo Faustino Sarmiento, inspired by the example of the United States, had moved toward mass primary education as early as the 1860s;[54] Chile, never far behind, followed suit soon after;[55] Costa Rica had made the same commitment by the 1890s;[56] and Uruguay did so in the following decade.[57] Yet these were the exceptions: In the two largest republics (Brazil and Mexico) the primary-education system remained woefully inadequate, forcing employers to rely on a work force with virtually none of the attributes required for technical progress and innovation.

Some effort went into the creation of professional institutions for training labor in the new skills required by the export-led growth model. Schools for engineers were established, along with institutions specializing in plant breeding, agronomy, and livestock raising.[58] At the university level,

---

54 As early as 1883 some 130,000 children – nearly one-quarter of those of school age – were attending primary school in Argentina. The expenditure per pupil was roughly the same as in the United Kingdom and higher than in the United States. See Mulhall and Mulhall (1885), p. 67.

55 By 1914 Chile had pushed school enrollment up to 380,000, contributing to an increase in literacy from less than 30 percent of the population in 1885 to more than 50 percent in 1910. See Blakemore (1986), p. 527.

56 Fischel (1991) contains a fine study of the Costa Rican educational system and its early commitment to primary schooling.

57 The Uruguayan commitment to education is associated with the rise to power of José Batlle y Ordóñez after the 1903 elections. See Oddone (1986), p. 466.

58 See Wilcox and Rines (1917), pp. 31–9.

however, the situation was far from adequate, for neither the curriculum nor the course structure had changed much since colonial times.[59]

Foreign investment

Given the difficulties encountered in mobilizing domestic resources for capital accumulation, it is not surprising that governments in every republic turned to foreigners as a source of additional finance. At the time of independence the only country with a surplus of capital for export was Great Britain, but by the end of the nineteenth century the list had swelled to include France, Germany, and the United States. Although small amounts of capital might be obtained from other developed countries,[60] the long-run supply of foreign capital depended crucially on attracting funds from these four countries.

Foreign investment could be either portfolio or direct, and the conditions governing the two flows were very different. Portfolio investment consisted mainly of bonds floated on the stock markets of advanced countries. The first bonds had been floated in the 1820s on the London stock market, and the proceeds had been used by governments to try to bridge the gap between revenue and expenditure. The experiment had generally been a failure, but little by little governments had renegotiated the debt in default, so that after 1850 bonds could again be issued.[61] The bonds were issued with heavy discounts to reflect the risk premium, and all too often this proved to be justified.[62] By 1880, for example, most of the £123 million purchased by British bondholders were in default, and regular payment of debt service by governments was not common until the first decade of the twentieth century.[63]

A few governments – notably Argentina, Brazil, Chile, Mexico, and Uruguay – were able to issue foreign bonds regularly (at least after 1870) as a means of funding government expenditures. Bond issues by these countries were generally well received by foreigners: More than 90 percent of British capital invested in Latin American government bonds in 1913 had gone to these five countries (see Table 4.3), and Britons were by far the most important purchasers of such bonds. Even in these favored countries,

---

59 Frustration with the antiquated curriculum and rigid discipline led to a massive protest during 1918 in Córdoba (Argentina), which paved the way for reform in higher education throughout Latin America. See Hale (1986), pp. 424–5.

60 Other developed countries with investments in Latin America included Belgium, Italy, and Spain.

61 The story of how Latin American countries returned to the international capital market after 1850 is well told in Marichal (1989).

62 In 1870, ten years after settling its 1824 debt, the Province of Buenos Aires still had to accept a discount of 12 percent on a flotation of £1,034,000 in the London market. See Rippy (1959), p. 30.

63 Even in 1913, however, the last normal year before the First World War, Guatemala and Honduras were in default. See Rippy (1959), p. 72.

Table 4.3. *Direct and portfolio investment in Latin America, circa 1914*

Country	Public external debt			Direct foreign investment		
	Millions of U.S. dollars	United Kingdom (%)	United States (%)	Millions of U.S. dollars	United Kingdom (%)	United States (%)
Argentina	784	50.8	2.4	3,217	46.7	1.2
Bolivia	15	0	20.0	44	38.6	4.5
Brazil	717	83.4	0.7	1,196	50.9	4.2
Chile	174	73.6	0.6	494	43.1	45.5
Colombia	23	69.6	21.7	54	57.4	38.9
Costa Rica	17	47.1	0	44	6.8	93.2
Cuba	85	58.8	41.2	386	44.0	56.0
Dominican Republic	5	0	100	11	0	100
Ecuador	1	100	0	40	72.5	22.5
El Salvador	4	100	0	15	40.0	46.7
Guatemala	7	100	0	92	47.8	39.1
Haiti	1	0	100	10	0	100
Honduras	26	0	61.5	16	6.2	93.8
Mexico	152	92.1	7.9	1,177	54.0	46.0
Nicaragua	6	50.0	0	6	33.0	67.0
Panama	5	0	100	23	0	100
Paraguay	4	100	0	23	78.3	21.7
Peru	17	47.1	11.8	180	67.2	32.2
Puerto Rico	44					
Uruguay	120	75.0	0	355	43.4	0
Venezuela	21	47.6	0	145	20.7	26.2
Latin America	2,229	67.8	13.8	7,569	47.4	18.4
Agriculture				255	4.7	93.7
Mining				530	19.1	78.3
Oil				140	2.9	97.1
Railways				2,342	71.2	13.0
Public utilities				914	59.7	13.9
Manufacturing				562	14.8	3.0
Trade				485	0.4	7.0
Other and undistributed by sector				2,341	50.0	5.2

Sources: ECLA (1965), pp. 16–17; for Puerto Rico, Clark et al. (1975), p. 586, with data referring to 1928.

however, it was common to fund a proportion of excess expenditure through internal finance, so that foreign bonds were never the only means available to a government to fund a deficit.[64] Yet foreign bonds certainly had their

---

64 In the five years before 1914, for example, some 70 percent of all public-debt-service payments in Brazil could be attributed to foreign loans. See Fritsch (1988), Tables A.11 and A.14. The remaining 30 percent represented payment on internal debt.

attractions for the issuing government: The conditions attached to new bond finance were often loose, and governments could use the funds simply to pay for current expenditure, thereby avoiding the need for unpopular tax increases, even if this did little to contribute to capital accumulation.

In the less-favored countries government bond finance was typically a story of refinancing rather than new investment. Frustration at the continuation of debt defaults in many countries led bondholders to press governments to earmark taxes (usually customs duties) for payment of debt service.[65] In one extreme case (Peru), the British bondholders set up the Peruvian Corporation, which canceled the outstanding bonds in exchange for various state-owned enterprises.[66] Concern in the United States that bond defaults might be used by European powers to intervene in Latin America (in defiance of the Monroe Doctrine) led to several attempts to replace bonds owed to Europeans with loans owed to U.S. investors ("dollar diplomacy"). Where the United States itself intervened – in Cuba, the Dominican Republic, Haiti, and Nicaragua – a high priority was always control of customs revenue to ensure prompt repayment of the debt.[67] These measures ensured that debt default was much more rare in the years just before the First World War than it had been fifty years earlier, but the governments of these countries could still not expect to use foreign finance to cover more than a small part of their total expenditures.

In some cases bonds were issued not by governments but by private sector companies. These bonds were issued to support the operations of firms engaged in railways, public utilities, and financial institutions, and other productive activities. Many such firms had been formed through direct foreign investment, with the capital owned and controlled by nonresidents. The first such firms had been the British mining associations of the 1820s, but only a handful of these had survived, and it was not until the second half of the nineteenth century that direct foreign investment (DFI) recovered.

DFI was attracted to those areas where technological barriers and access to capital restricted the entry of local firms. The bulk of the investment therefore flowed toward railways, public utilities, mining, banking, and shipping (see Table 4.3), although the first two activities were by far the most important. By the First World War the United States had also acquired

---

65 This happened in the Dominican Republic, for example, even before the U.S. occupation. See Hoetink (1986), p. 300.

66 The Grace Contract, named after the immigrant founder of the Grace Company, went into force in 1890. The entire external debt was canceled in exchange for the transfer to the bondholders (henceforth designated as the Peruvian Corporation of London) of the nation's railways for sixty-six years, free navigation of Lake Titicaca, and up to three million tons of guano. See Klarén (1986), pp. 598–9.

67 U.S. control over external-trade taxes in these countries is described in Langley (1983).

important interests in sugar mills in the Caribbean[68] and bananas in Central America,[69] whereas British capital was invested in meatpacking plants in Argentina and Uruguay.[70]

Foreign-owned enterprises in these areas were important – in some cases dominant – and cases of unfair competition or abuse of power can easily be documented.[71] In many areas, however – above all, agricultural production for the home market – DFI played only a minor role in most countries. Furthermore, in the emerging manufacturing sector DFI was still of little importance. In construction a number of foreign-owned firms had been set up to specialize in large-scale public-sector projects – by Weetman Pearson, for example, in Mexico[72] – but the majority of investments in such activities as urban residential housing were carried out by nationals.

By the outbreak of the First World War DFI was subject to relatively few controls. The liberal ideology prevailing in government circles convinced policymakers that DFI was an indispensable adjunct of efforts to promote economic development. Foreign investment in social infrastructure in particular was seen as crucial for creating the conditions under which the export-led growth model could prosper. The growth of the railway network after 1870, though not totally controlled by foreign companies, undoubtedly made a major contribution to the expansion of exports.[73] In relative terms, however, expressed per thousand of the population, the length of track was still modest. Only Argentina came close to the record of Australia, Canada, and New Zealand (see Table 4.4). The spread of public utilities also contributed much to the quality of urban life and increased the productivity of many urban enterprises.[74]

The concentration of DFI in a relatively small number of sectors, most of which did not enter into international trade, created a number of problems. Many of the companies were natural monopolies (e.g., water supply); others enjoyed a quasi-monopoly (e.g., railways). In some cases (e.g., insurance and shipping), foreign companies operated price-fixing cartels, which did not

68 See Moreno Fraginals (1986). The growth of the sugar industry as a result of U.S. investments was spectacular in Puerto Rico after the Spanish had been driven out. See Ramos Mattei (1984).

69 The growth of the banana industry under U.S. control was particularly rapid after the formation in 1899 of the United Fruit Company from a number of smaller companies. See Kepner (1936), Chapter 2.

70 On British investments in the Argentine meat industry, see Hanson (1938), Chapter 5. For Uruguay, see Finch (1981), Chapter 5.

71 A good example is the beef trust created by exporters from the River Plate countries to restrict competition through the allocation of quotas. See Smith (1969), Chapter 3.

72 Pearson finally resolved the engineering problem associated with bringing water to Mexico City from the surrounding area by canal. See Spender (1930).

73 This is demonstrated in the case of Brazil by Summerhill (1998), where the social savings on railroad freight (i.e. the savings on transport costs made possible by railways compared with alternative methods of transport) are estimated at 10% of GDP in 1887.

74 On British public-utility companies in Latin America, see Greenhill (1977). For an excellent case study of a Canadian public-utility company in Brazil, see McDowall (1988).

Table 4.4. *Railways in Latin America, circa 1913*

Country	Number of companies	Length (in kilometers)	Track per 1,000 population (in kilometers)
Argentina	18	31,859	4.3
Bolivia	2	1,284	0.7
Brazil	15	24,737	1.0
Chile	10	8,069	2.4
Colombia	11	1,061	0.2
Costa Rica	1	878	2.5
Cuba	6	3,752	1.6
Dominican Republic	2	644	0.9
Ecuador	2	1,049	0.6
El Salvador	1	320	0.3
Guatemala	1	987	0.6
Haiti		180	0.1
Honduras	6[a]	241	0.4
Mexico	13	25,600[b]	1.8
Nicaragua	1	322	0.6
Panama	4[a]	479	1.4
Paraguay	1	410	0.7
Peru	9[a]	2,970	0.7
Puerto Rico	3[c]	408[c]	0.4
Uruguay	10	2,576	2.3
Venezuela	4	1,020	0.4
Latin America		**83,246**	**1.4**
Australia		31,327	6.9
Canada		49,549	6.5
New Zealand		4,587	4.3

[a] Taken from *South American Handbook 1924*.
[b] Taken from Wilcox and Rines (1917).
[c] Taken from Clark et al. (1975), p. 371.
Sources: Numbers of companies taken from Wilcox and Rines (1917); lengths taken from League of Nations (1927).

endear them to the local population.[75] Many of the railway lines tended to reinforce the pattern of export specialization rather than to encourage diversification, and in some cases price discrimination by the railway companies themselves made the situation even worse.[76] In the smaller republics the resources at the disposal of foreign companies created an unequal relationship

75 See Jones (1977b), pp. 58–63. These price-fixing arrangements were no doubt in part responsible for the wave of hostile legislation that many Latin American countries adopted after 1890, obliging foreign insurance companies to purchase government securities and make local deposits.

76 The most glaring example was provided by International Railways of Central America, a subsidiary of the United Fruit Company (UFCO) in Guatemala, which used price discrimination to shift external trade toward Puerto Barrios – a port controlled by UFCO – on the Atlantic coast. See Bauer Paíz (1956).

with the governments of the countries themselves, and many contracts were signed that – with the benefit of hindsight – look excessively generous to the foreign companies.[77] This was also true in some of the larger countries, such as Peru, where the weak fiscal position gave the government little room to maneuver.[78]

Despite these problems the contribution of DFI to economic development was positive – even if not as spectacular as is often claimed. What is not so clear is the contribution of DFI to the overall financing of capital accumulation. The figures on the stock of foreign-owned capital (see Table 4.3) look impressive, with Great Britain occupying a hegemonic position in South America and the United States playing a similar role in many countries north of Colombia. Nevertheless, part of the finance was obtained through reinvestment of profits and funds raised locally. Furthermore, in a few cases – notably copper mining in Chile and Peru – foreign control was obtained through the purchase of existing – locally owned – enterprises. This process of denationalization undermined the claim that DFI was needed to finance new enterprises.

It is probable, therefore, that the contribution of foreign investment (including bond issues) to the finance of capital accumulation was not as crucial as is often supposed. This suspicion is confirmed by an examination of the trade statistics for the larger republics (Argentina, Brazil, and Mexico), which attracted the bulk of foreign investment.[79] In all three cases a trade surplus – not a deficit – was the normal state of affairs in the years leading up to the First World War. This surplus was needed to finance the outflow of interest and profit on foreign capital, an outflow which lowered the net transfer of resources associated with a given gross inflow of foreign investment.

The fact that the contribution of foreign investment to the finance of capital accumulation may not have been as great as is often supposed does not mean that it did not play a positive role. As a vehicle for transferring technology, encouraging innovation, and promoting new management techniques, DFI could be very important. It did mean, however, that foreign investment could not be regarded as a panacea for resolving the inadequacies of the capital market. The long-run low rate of growth of exports in most of

---

77 This unequal relationship was not confined to the smallest countries. The huge grants of land and tax-free concessions to foreign oil companies in Venezuela by Juan Vicente Gómez after he came to power in 1908 is surely a case in point. See McBeth (1983), Chapter 1.

78 Fiscal weakness, which undermined the capacity to service the debt, was a major factor behind the infamous Grace Contract. See note 66.

79 In Brazil, where unusually comprehensive balance-of-payments statistics have been compiled, there was a trade surplus (exports less imports) in every year except one in the period between 1889 and 1914. This surplus was reduced by interest payments on the foreign external debt, but the current account was still in surplus in all but two years. In eleven of these years, amortization of the public external debt exceeded new capital inflows. See Fritsch (1988). Table A.11.

Latin America was a reflection in part of the low rate of capital accumulation, and the latter reflected the difficulty of mobilizing domestic finance. Foreign investment could be a useful adjunct, but it could not, and did not, resolve the basic institutional weaknesses of the capital market in many Latin American republics.

The policy context

The expansion of the export sector was not just a function of the supply of primary inputs; it was also heavily affected by variations in the profitability of exports, which in turn was influenced by the interaction of fiscal, monetary, and exchange-rate policies (as well as international prices). The policy context was also of great importance in determining the rate of growth of the nonexport sector (see Chapter 5).

Fiscal policy had both a direct and an indirect bearing on the profitability of the export sector. The direct impact came from the incidence of export duties and import tariffs and – to a much smaller extent – from property taxes. The indirect impact resulted, among other things, from the impact of budget deficits on the money supply and on the exchange-rate.

Although all countries collected some public revenue from export duties, few governments relied on such taxes to generate a high proportion of income. International competition meant that most export taxes could not be passed on to consumers without risking market share; indeed, some governments felt constrained to lower export taxes when international prices fell, and exporters were often able to resist a compensating increase when prices rose again.[80] Some regions within countries (e.g., the state of São Paulo in Brazil) relied heavily on export taxes to generate public revenue, but the tax itself represented only a small proportion of the value of the export.[81]

The main exceptions to the unimportance of export duties were provided by minerals. Often facing downward-sloping (rather than horizontal) demand curves and unable to relocate easily, firms that exported minerals offered governments an excellent opportunity to increase public revenue at low cost. The tax on gold, silver, and copper exports was an important element in public finance at the beginning of the Porfiriato in Mexico, although it had declined in importance by the revolution.[82] The most spectacular example of export duties was provided by Chilean nitrates, which

---

80 In Peru, for example, export taxes had been phased out during the guano boom and were not subsequently reimposed, despite the shortage of government revenue, as a result of the political power of exporters. See Thorp and Bertram (1978), p. 30.

81 Before the First World War the coffee-export tax represented around 70 percent of the total tax revenue of the state of São Paulo. See Holloway (1980), p. 46.

82 Export taxes represented 6 percent of all revenue in 1876–7, but this had declined to 0.5 percent by 1910–11. See Catão (1991), p. 132, Table IV.3.7.

provided nearly 50 percent of all public revenue between 1890 and 1914 and in which the tax alone represented 10 percent of the value of exports during the same years.[83]

Given the virtual world monopoly enjoyed by Chile, the nitrate companies were able to pass the tax on to consumers relatively easily, and the nitrate business remained one of the most profitable in Latin America.[84] Indeed, it is difficult to find solid evidence of exports being rendered unprofitable by export duties before the First World War anywhere in Latin America and all too easy to find examples of tax exemption – often on foreign companies – which was probably unnecessary.[85]

Governments throughout the region relied heavily on import tariffs to generate public revenue, and the duties on certain commodities – even in the age of "free trade" – could rise as high as 100 percent. Yet import tariffs on goods of concern to the export sector (machines, equipment, etc.) were usually quite low, and on numerous occasions governments offered duty-free concessions to foreign companies under fixed-term contracts. As in the case of export duties, it is difficult to find important cases in which the growth of the export sector was severely restrained by high tariffs and easy to find cases in which exemptions were generous.[86]

The indirect effects of fiscal policy on the export sector operated mainly through the budget deficit. A tendency toward a deficit in public finance was a marked feature of many Latin American countries in the first few decades after independence, and it remained a problem even in the second half of the nineteenth century, despite the rise in external trade. Tax reform brought about the elimination of many taxes inherited from colonial times and a concentration on external trade taxes; by the time of the First World War no country received less than 50 percent of public revenue from customs duties, and in many cases the share was more than 70 percent.[87]

The emphasis on customs duties resulted in several problems. First, public revenue moved in line with external trade, and in far too many countries –

---

83 See Sunkel and Cariola (1985), Tables 20–22.

84 In 1913 the rate of return on capital on eleven British nitrate companies was more than 15 percent in every case, and in one case (the Liverpool Company) it reached a staggering 150 percent. See Rippy (1959), p. 73. The British engineer John Thomas North, known as the "Nitrate King," had founded many of these companies before his death in 1896. See Blakemore (1974).

85 The Peruvian Corporation, for example, was not subject to taxes on guano exports under the terms of the Grace Contract. See note 66.

86 The banana contracts signed by the fruit companies in Central America and the Caribbean almost invariably provided for duty-free entry on all kinds of imports, including consumer goods sold in company stores.

87 The tax base for customs duties (external trade) tended to vary inversely in proportion to the size of the country. Yet even in Brazil, where external trade in relative terms was less important than in most countries, import duties alone still represented 56 percent of total federal government revenue in 1913. See Fritsch (1988), Table A.14.

as we have seen – the long-run rate of growth of trade was modest. Second, trade was cyclical: The fall in public revenue associated with a trade depression could not easily be met by a cut in expenditure, and deficits were often the consequence, whereas in boom years it was all too easy to spend the surplus.[88] Third, customs duties were usually specific:[89] They did not move in line with domestic (pretax) prices for foreign goods, so the revenue from customs duties was inelastic. This was a serious matter when – as happened frequently – domestic prices were rising.[90]

For all these reasons, revenue per head (see Figure 4.1) was still pathetically low by 1913. The few exceptions were all countries in which either the long-run rate of growth of exports had been respectable (Argentina and Chile) or the tax base – external trade – was relatively large (Uruguay). Yet even a broad tax base (as measured by exports per head) was no guarantee. Cuba and Costa Rica both suffered from excessive use of exonerations for taxes on foreign trade, and the Dominican Republic, Nicaragua, and Panama – their customs houses firmly controlled by U.S. administrators who were intent on maximizing tax collections[91] – had a higher level of public revenue per head than did many other, richer countries.

Expectations about state intervention and the optimal size of the public sector were different before the First World War from what they are today. The private sector was expected to undertake many activities that today are left to the public sector, and in one case (Peru) even the collection of taxes was contracted out to private firms.[92] However, the state had certain basic – and inescapable – functions to perform, and service payments on the public debt were an additional commitment that often forced governments either to default or to go further into deficit. Indeed, public-debt service was the

---

88 When coffee prices rose sharply between 1909 and 1912, Brazilian federal government revenue rose by nearly 40 percent; yet government expenditure rose even faster, leading to a widening of the deficit. See Fritsch (1988), Table A.12. In Peru the Gibbs Contract (1849–61) and the Dreyfus Contract (1869–78) gave the government such a high share of profits that many taxes were phased out or reduced, so the income from sources other than guano was less in the mid-1870s than it had been in the mid-1840s. See Hunt (1985), Tables 3 and 5.

89 Specific duties are levied on the volume of trade (e.g., ten pesos per meter of cloth), while ad valorem duties are levied on the value (e.g., 10 percent on the value of cloth imports). Specific tariffs were favored at a time when it was difficult, if not impossible, to establish whether imports were being correctly valued by the importer. It was also intended to reduce corruption in the customs houses. This explains the use in nineteenth-century trade statistics of "declared" and "official" exports and imports, whose "price" often did not vary for many years.

90 Between 1890 and 1898, for example, the Brazilian cost-of-living index rose by 200 percent. The sterling value of imports (the tax base) was virtually unchanged, whereas the revenue from import duties rose by 120 percent. Thus some attempt was made to raise specific duties in line with domestic inflation, but receipts still declined substantially in real terms.

91 The U.S. controller of customs, once installed, was difficult to remove. U.S. control of Nicaragua's customs houses, for example, began in 1911 and did not finally end for another forty years.

92 See Thorp and Bertram (1978), p. 359, n. 59.

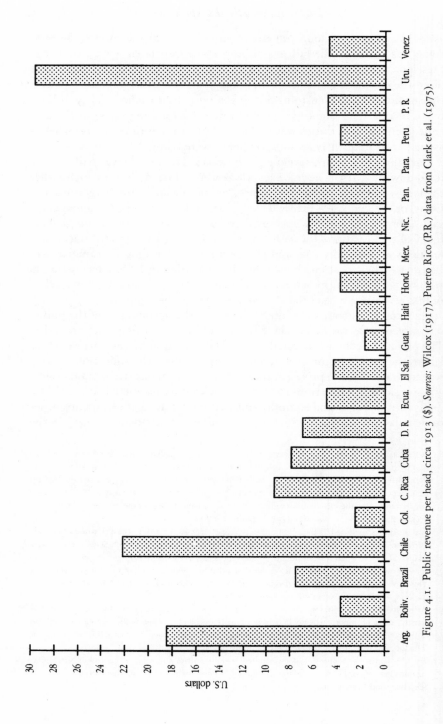

Figure 4.1. Public revenue per head, circa 1913 ($). *Source:* Wilcox (1917). Puerto Rico (P.R.) data from Clark et al. (1975).

single most important item of public expenditure in most Latin American republics before the First World War.[93]

Deficits could be financed either internally or externally. The poor record of external-debt service, however, meant that only a handful of countries could regularly expect to finance a deficit through new bond issues. As late as 1913 the only countries with strong external credit were Argentina, Brazil, Chile, and Uruguay – Mexico's standing having been disrupted by the revolution[94] – and even these countries had to rely on internal debt for at least part of their financing needs.

Internal debt, therefore, was a regular feature of public finance. In a few countries, notably Argentina, capital markets were sufficiently mature to permit the placement of domestic bonds without inflationary consequences, but all too often internal debt involved the issue of inconvertible paper leading to currency devaluation. The Brazilian milreis depreciated steadily against the pound sterling throughout most of the nineteenth century and almost collapsed in an orgy of paper issues in the 1890s.[95] After years of iron fiscal discipline under conservative regimes the Chilean currency began to succumb to the seductive charms of inconvertible paper issues in the late 1870s, and even Argentina had great difficulty for most of the nineteenth century in preventing paper issues from leading to sharp currency depreciations.

The problems of deficit financing were often very serious indeed. At the end of the nineteenth century, during the War of 1,000 Days, Colombia experienced a dramatic collapse of the currency as a result of note issues (including many counterfeits) without any reserve backing.[96] The Guatemalan peso collapsed after 1895 as successive tyrants succumbed to the temptations of paper money.[97] The same was true in Nicaragua, under José Santos Zelaya, until the United States intervened in 1909.[98] The Dominican

---

93 Between 1890 and 1913 public-debt service absorbed 24.7 percent of all government expenditure in Brazil (a fairly typical case) and an even higher proportion of total revenue. See Fritsch (1988), Table A.14. This was much more important than fixed-capital formation and in one year (1898) was more important than all noninterest current expenditure.

94 The revolution began in 1910 and became progressively more violent, until a certain stability was restored with the presidency of Venustiano Carranza in 1917. The intervening years were marked by social, political, and financial upheaval, including a period (1913–16) of hyperinflation.

95 Known as *o encilhamento*, this was the period following the overthrow of the monarchy when the *papelistas* in Brazil threw aside all financial caution. In two years (1889–91), the money supply grew by 200 percent.

96 The civil war began in 1899 and ended in 1902. During this period both liberals and conservatives issued paper currency at such a rapid rate that the value of the currency fell from 30 cents gold to 10 cents in 1900, 2 cents in 1901, and 0.4 cents in 1902. See Eder (1912), p. 75. See also Bergquist (1978), pp. 200–1.

97 Although the process began with President José María Reyna Barrios (1895–8), the real culprit was Manuel Estrada Cabrera (1898–1920), who found inconvertible paper and currency devaluation an indispensable tool for gaining the political allegiance of the powerful coffee class. See Young (1925).

98 In the case of President Zelaya (1893–1909), whose regime faced numerous revolts, deficit financing was often a consequence of increased military expenditure. See Young (1925).

Republic, Haiti, and Paraguay all experienced currency collapse at various times in the nineteenth century as a result of deficit financing.

Currency depreciation could not be avoided even in those countries that followed a responsible policy on note issues. The reason was the fall in the gold price of silver that started in the 1870s after the United States and Germany went on to the gold standard, leaving countries on the silver standard with currencies that were depreciating against major trading partners.[99]

Latin America had inherited from the mother countries a monetary system in which all manner of gold and silver coins circulated freely.[100] After independence the authorities regularly posted tables reporting the rates at which coins could be exchanged for one another (the mint or monetary ratio), and the problem was not too serious as long as the market price of silver in terms of gold did not move too far out of line with the monetary ratio. As the gold price of silver declined after the 1870s, however, gold coins began to be withdrawn from circulation, and many Latin American countries found themselves on a de facto silver standard. Indeed, in a few cases (El Salvador and Honduras) the silver standard was adopted formally, obliging financial institutions to exchange paper for silver at a fixed rate, just as paper was exchanged for gold in the gold-standard countries.[101]

The majority of countries were unable to defend a formal silver standard and retreated into regimes of inconvertible paper after the decline in the gold price of silver.[102] Currency depreciation was therefore the normal state of affairs – even in silver-standard countries – and the losers within each country were easy to identify. Merchants who relied on imports faced an increase in local currency requirements to make payments abroad – not to mention the increase in uncertainty and the currency risks associated with buying goods at one rate of exchange and selling them several months later at another. Governments – their external-debt service payments denominated in gold – had to dig deeper into scarce public revenue to meet their foreign obligations.

99 The fall in the gold price of silver began in 1873 and continued until the beginning of the twentieth century, by which time the average price per fine ounce of silver in New York had dropped from $1.32 to 53 cents.

100 The mixture of currencies was often made even more confusing by the shortage of specie, which obliged countries to use imported coins in daily transactions. The Peruvian sol, for example, played an important part in the monetary life of Guatemala in the second half of the nineteenth century and even found its way into the financial system of British Honduras (Belize) at the beginning of the twentieth century. See Banco de Guatemala (1989), pp. 64–75.

101 El Salvador had tried to adopt the gold standard in 1892, but the gold reserve was insufficient. Gold coins were therefore hoarded as soon as they entered into circulation. The country was forced back on the silver standard until inconvertibility was declared after the outbreak of the First World War. See Young (1925).

102 This was the case, for example, in Bolivia and Guatemala. It was also the case in Mexico until the country adopted the gold standard in 1905.

The winners from currency depreciation should have been the exporters. With exports sold for gold and payments made in local currency, the export sector could be expected to enjoy a windfall gain as long as domestic prices did not rise in line with currency depreciation. This seems to have been the case – indicating a high degree of money illusion – and many domestic prices, including wage rates, do seem to have been remarkably rigid in the face of currency decline.[103] Many exporters benefited handsomely from the system, and adverse movements in the net barter terms of trade could be offset by movements in the exchange-rate.

Even the export sector, however, had reservations about the wisdom of currency depreciation. First, the decline in the gold price of silver was not a steady one: Indeed, a sharp fall in the early 1890s was followed by several years of appreciation in the early 1900s.[104] The narrow market in foreign exchange produced a huge spread between buying and selling rates because of the uncertainty associated with currency movements, and many exporters were forced to sell at times of the year when the rate of exchange was low.[105] Most of the windfall gains in fact went to a handful of traders with sufficient working capital to wait for the most opportune moment to buy and sell. Finally, the costs associated with inconvertible paper were heavy in a world that was growing accustomed to convertibility, and the increase in uncertainty was a serious disincentive to most types of investment.

The widespread existence of money illusion, though it dampened inflationary pressures, had an additional destabilizing effect on public finance. The tax base for nontrade taxes – approximated by the value of domestic sales – did not rise in line with currency depreciation, so nontrade taxes were far from buoyant, and income could only be sustained by regular revision of tax rates. Tax yields from alcohol, tobacco, salt, and other commodities subject to government monopolies tended to lag behind currency depreciation and created additional pressure on public revenue.[106]

---

103 The extent of money illusion is not really surprising. Few countries produced a cost-of-living index, and in societies in which the majority of adults were illiterate even publication of an index was unlikely to make much of an impact. Labor contracts often involved payment in kind as well as in cash. Inflation may have been implied by currency depreciation, but this connection was clearly understood far better by the urban elite than by the rural masses.

104 The average price per fine ounce of silver rose from 53 cents in 1902 to 67 cents in 1906 before declining again to 53 cents in 1908.

105 Guatemalan exporters occasionally faced a huge spread between the highest and lowest exchange-rate in the same year. In 1899 the spread was from 3.00 to 8.50 pesos per U.S. dollar; in 1903 the spread was from 12.15 to 21.00. The difference was quite capable of turning a large profit on a coffee sale into a huge loss.

106 These taxes were often specific, and this was an additional reason why they did not rise in line with currency depreciation. Public external-debt payments, however, rose in proportion to currency depreciation.

Thus there arose throughout Latin America in the last years of the nineteenth century a serious desire for currency stabilization. With the major world economies all on the gold standard, currency stabilization in Latin America implied a movement away from inconvertible paper regimes and the silver standard toward either the gold standard itself or a gold-exchange standard in which the local currency was pegged to a gold currency, such as the U.S. dollar or the pound sterling.

This switch was attempted almost everywhere before the First World War, though it did not always meet with success. The gold standard required a gold reserve sufficiently large to provide a guarantee of full convertibility to holders of paper currency. This was often beyond the resources of the state, and several countries found that newly minted gold coins were being hoarded or exported rather than entering into circulation. El Salvador was forced to abandon its first attempt in the 1890s to leave the silver standard for this reason, and it did not finally succeed until after the First World War.[107]

The ABC countries – Argentina, Brazil, and Chile – adopted a novel solution to the problem of switching to the gold standard. A conversion fund was set up to guarantee the monetary ratio established under the gold standard,[108] and a part of public revenue was earmarked for payment in gold to provide the necessary resources. Taxes were therefore collected partly in gold and partly in paper, and expenditures were similarly divided. The result was, in effect, a two-currency system that was often confusing and sometimes difficult to operate. Indeed, it had collapsed in Chile even before the turn of the century, and the country returned to a regime of inconvertible paper.[109]

A few countries – Costa Rica, Ecuador, Peru, and Uruguay – had made a successful transition to the gold standard by the beginning of the twentieth century and therefore enjoyed a brief period of currency stability before the collapse of convertibility at the start of the First World War. Others – Bolivia, Colombia, Mexico, and Venezuela – made the transition so late that war or revolution (in the Mexican case) undermined the system before it had begun to function properly. Guatemala and Paraguay, still reeling from excessive monetary expansion, had no choice but to stay on inconvertible paper regimes.

Many of the Caribbean Basin countries – their economies heavily dependent on the United States – adopted a gold-exchange standard based on

---

107 El Salvador finally made a successful transition to the gold standard in 1919, when the gold price of silver was high.

108 The conversion fund was established in Chile in 1895, in Argentina in 1899, and in Brazil in 1906. Williams (1920) and Ford (1962) contain classic accounts of the Argentine financial system before and after the adoption of the gold standard, respectively.

109 The Chilean experiment, launched in 1895, collapsed in 1898. See Hirschman (1963), pp. 171–2.

the U.S. dollar. The Dominican Republic and Panama even made the U.S. dollar legal tender,[110] and it circulated freely and widely in Cuba, Haiti, Honduras (on the northern coast), and Nicaragua by the First World War. The gold-exchange standard of these countries brought extreme currency stability, which even survived the First World War and did not require that governments keep costly reserves of gold.

The currency and exchange-rate position of the Latin America republics was therefore varied in the "golden age" of export-led growth before the First World War. Some countries had suffered such long experience of currency depreciation that money illusion had begun to disappear. Such was the case in Brazil, Chile, and Colombia, whose history of inflation dates back to the nineteenth century.[111] Even Argentina – a model economy in so many other respects – had suffered from gross misuse of paper currency in the nineteenth century and had the greatest difficulty in moving toward currency stability and full convertibility. In others, the slide of the currency as a result of the fall in the gold price of silver coupled with money illusion undoubtedly brought major windfall gains to the export sector. The prime example is Mexico under the Porfiriato, but many small countries also reaped the benefit.

By the beginning of the twentieth century the rules of the game for the export sector had begun to change. The gold or dollar standard meant that terms of trade losses could not be compensated through currency depreciation. Greater discipline was needed in the control of costs, and foreign companies, with access to capital at lower rates of interest, sometimes gained the edge over domestic firms as a result. Currency stability, however, eliminated much of the uncertainty associated with exports and encouraged investment for the long term. It is surely no accident that the fastest period of expansion in exports coincided with a decade of relative currency stability just before the First World War.

Given the problems identified in the markets for land, labor, and capital, in the lack of social infrastructure, and in the uncertainty introduced by currency instability (particularly before 1900), it is not surprising that the long-run rate of growth of exports was so unsatisfactory in many countries. Yet solutions to these problems could be found, and the examples of Argentina and Chile show that exports could grow rapidly even when the problems facing the export sector had not all been overcome.

All the republics made some progress toward improving the conditions under which the export sector operated, and the basic framework for export-led growth was in place by 1914. However, timing was all important. The

110 The Dominican Republic adopted the dollar in 1900. Panama has never had any currency other than the U.S. dollar, the local balboa being a useful fiction for purposes of national sovereignty.
111 Chilean inflation before the First World War has been the subject of numerous studies. See, for example, Fetter (1931).

window of opportunity that opened in the nineteenth century for Latin America's primary-product exports began to close with the outbreak of the First World War. Countries like Bolivia or the Dominican Republic, which had waited until the early twentieth century before undertaking a major expansion of exports, would pay a high price for wasting the opportunities provided by the expansion of world trade in the nineteenth century.

5

Export-led growth and the nonexport economy

In the century before the First World War, Latin America followed a model of export-led growth.[1] A successful export-led growth model implies a rapid rise in exports and in exports per head coupled with increases in labor productivity in the export sector. Yet this is only the first, albeit very important, condition for a significant rise in real income per head. The second condition is the transfer of productivity gains in the export sector to the nonexport economy. Thus the export sector needs to become the "engine of growth," stimulating investment outside the export sector itself.

The export sector could provide such a stimulus in many ways. For example, thinking in terms of backward linkages, the growth of the export sector could promote investments in railways, which in turn would generate investments in sawmills (for lumber), capital goods (e.g., locomotives), and workshops for repair and maintenance of the rolling stock. In terms of forward linkages, the export sector could also contribute to a faster rate of investment. For example, cattle raising for export leads not only to investments in beef and beef-extract production but also to investments in the leather industry, the shoe industry, and even the chemical industry.[2]

The growth of some sectors of the nonexport economy was so intimately tied to the fortunes of the export sector that we can think of them as complementary activities. Examples are commerce (wholesale and retail), railway transport, public utilities, construction, and public administration. These service sectors depended directly on the export sector (e.g., railway transport), on the imports and import tariffs made possible by exports (e.g., commerce and public administration, respectively), or on the urbanization associated with the growth of exports (e.g., construction and public utilities).

---

1 The major exception is Paraguay under Francia (see p. 38).
2 The soaps and candles produced as by-products of cattle-raising are early examples of commodities produced by the chemicals industry in Latin America.

However, some activities would not necessarily benefit from the growth of the export sector, because demand could be met by imports rather than by domestic production. A few of these sectors provided services (e.g., coastal shipping) that could be replaced by imports. The Chilean shipping industry, for example, defended by protective barriers until the 1850s,[3] did not benefit from the expansion of exports in the fifty years before the First World War; protection was phased out, and foreign shipping companies increased their share of the coastal trade. Much the same was true of Brazil after the middle of the nineteenth century.[4]

The most important import-competing sectors, however, did provide goods; they are the subject of this chapter. At the dawn of the nineteenth century the majority of the labor force in every Latin American country was employed either in agriculture or in cottage industries producing commodities for the home market. With a very low level of exports per head, this labor force faced little competition from imports, and domestic consumption was satisfied mainly by domestic production. As exports per head increased, imports started to rise, and establishments producing for the home market faced greater foreign competition. A failure to increase the capital stock per worker in the import-competing sector would then leave a large proportion of the total labor force with such low productivity that the growth of the export sector could not lead to a large rise in real income per head except under exceptional circumstances.[5] Thus the response of the import-competing sector to the growth of exports was vital for the success of the export-led growth model.

In terms of the labor force, the most important import-competing sector was domestic-use agriculture (DUA). This branch of agriculture, which employed everyone in the sector not producing exports, included *latifundistas*, *hacendados*, *rancheros*, *colonos*, and *peones*; it included huge estates and tiny plots of land, owner-occupied farms and rented properties, and efficient and inefficient estates. As late as 1913 the labor force in DUA was the largest component of the population economically active (PEA) in virtually all republics and represented a majority of the PEA in many countries. It was a heterogeneous sector, and yet, despite its heterogeneity, it produced an output which in principle could always be replaced by imports.

---

3 Chilean shipping was heavily protected from competition from 1835 to 1849, when the California gold rush created new opportunities for Chilean exporters and led to the phasing out of preferences for domestic ships. See Véliz (1961).

4 The protection given to Brazilian ships in the coastal trade was phased out after 1862, and free competition was finally established in 1873. See Prado (1991), pp. 196–8.

5 These exceptional circumstances arise when nearly all output is exported and almost all consumption is met by imports. In this case the rates of growth of exports and of GDP are approximately the same. No Latin American country ever approached such a high level of export specialization, however. See Appendix 2.

The other main import-competing sector was cottage industry. The establishments were small, the technology was simple, and the main input was labor, so it does no great harm to think of it as the handicrafts or artisan sector. However, because its output consisted of goods competing with manufactured imports, we can also think of it as the manufacturing sector. The establishments in this sector could be (and were) rural or urban, although even at the beginning of the nineteenth century the majority of such workers were employed in urban areas. Slavery was not unknown, but wage labor was more common. The labor force was often organized in craft guilds, which enjoyed certain privileges and a high level of protection at the time of independence.

These two import-competing sectors are the focus of this chapter. They are often ignored in studies of export-led growth, yet their performance could be crucial. Without a positive response by the two sectors to the stimulus from exports, it was unrealistic to expect that even a fast rate of growth of exports would result in significant growth of real income per head. As is shown, the response could be positive, but situations also existed in which countries were robbed of the potential gains from the export-led growth model as a result of the poor performance of the import-competing sectors.

Domestic-use agriculture

The task of transferring productivity gains from the export sector to DUA was often very difficult. This branch of agriculture, representing all its nonexport activities, had traditionally absorbed a majority of the labor force, and a generalized increase in living standards was therefore difficult to imagine without the transformation of DUA. Although the proportion of the labor force absorbed by DUA declined slowly in the nineteenth century, as a result both of the growth of the export sector and of urbanization, it remained enormously important throughout the period up to the First World War.

The exact size of DUA in the period before 1914 is not known. We do, however, have figures for some countries on the proportion of the labor force in all agriculture – including export agriculture (EXA) – and on the share of agriculture in gross domestic product, or GDP (see Table 5.1). It can be seen that the agricultural labor force represented around two-thirds or more of the total PEA everywhere except those republics (Argentina, Chile, Cuba, and Uruguay) in which the high level of exports per head had brought significant structural transformation. After making educated guesses for the proportion of the labor force employed in EXA, it is probable

Table 5.1. *Agriculture and the agricultural labor force, circa 1913*

Country	Year	Agricultural labor force		Agricultural net product (1970 prices)		
		Number, in thousands	Percentage of total	Millions of U.S. dollars	Percentage of GDP	Per worker, in U.S. dollars
Argentina[a]	1914	1,051	34.2	882	26.5	839
Brazil[b]	1920	6,377	66.7	835	22.9	131
Chile[c]	1913	455	37.7	198	15.5	435
Colombia[d]	1913	1,270	70.5	307	54.6	241
Cuba[e]	1919	462	48.9	n/a	n/a	n/a
Dominican Republic[e]	1920	138	67.6	n/a	n/a	n/a
Mexico[f]	1910	3,581	63.7	824	24.0	230
Nicaragua[g]	1920	170	83.7	55	55.8	322
Uruguay[h]	1908	103	28.0	n/a	n/a	n/a
Venezuela[i]	1920	n/a	72.0	n/a	n/a	n/a
Australia[e]	1911	481	24.8	n/a	n/a	n/a
Canada[e]	1911	1,011	37.1	n/a	n/a	n/a
New Zealand[e]	1911	116	26.1	n/a	n/a	n/a

Note: Local currency data have been converted at official exchange rates.

[a] Labor-force data from Díaz-Alejandro (1970), p. 428. Production data from CEPAL (1978).

[b] Labor-force data from IBGE (1987). Production data from CEPAL (1978).

[c] Labor-force data for 1907 from Ballesteros and Davis (1963), adjusted to 1913 assuming no change in the structure of PEA and in the ratio of PEA to population. Production data from CEPAL (1978) for 1940, adjusted to 1913 using the index in Ballesteros and Davis (1963).

[d] Labor-force data from Berry (1983), p. 25, for 1918, adjusted to 1913 assuming a rate of growth equal to the rate of growth of the population between 1913 and 1918. Production data from CEPAL (1978) for 1929, adjusted to 1913 using the index for GDP in Maddison (1991) and assuming no change in the ratio of agriculture to GDP between 1913 and 1929.

[e] Labor-force data from Mitchell (1993).

[f] Labor-force data from Mitchell (1993). Production data from CEPAL (1978) for 1920, adjusted to 1910 using data in Solís (1983).

[g] Labor-force data from Cantarero (1949), p. 61. Production data from Bulmer-Thomas (1987).

[h] Labor-force data from Finch (1981), p. 76.

[i] Labor-force data from Karlsson (1975), p. 34.

that DUA accounted for more than 50 percent of the labor force in many republics at the beginning of the twentieth century.[6]

The high proportion of the labor force employed in agriculture in most countries[7] was a reflection of the low level of labor productivity. The proof of this is the fact that agriculture accounted for a much smaller proportion of GDP than its share of the labor force (see Table 5.1). In the case of Brazil and Mexico the agricultural share of GDP around the time of the First World War was 23 percent and 24 percent, respectively, whereas agriculture's share of the labor force was more than 60 percent in both countries. Considering that labor productivity in EXA was far superior to labor productivity in DUA, one can confidently assume that in these two large republics (and in others with similar structures) labor productivity in DUA was no more than one-fifth the national average at the beginning of this century.[8]

Given the size of DUA, therefore, an export-led growth model that left labor productivity in DUA unchanged was almost certain to fail. Thus it was important to consider the circumstances under which the growth of the export sector would lead to the transformation of DUA – often misleadingly referred to as the "subsistence" sector.[9]

First, in a few countries the export commodities were also the staples of the national diet; in these cases (e.g., wheat in Argentina and beef in Uruguay) it was almost inevitable that the technological changes that brought productivity gains to EXA would do the same for DUA. Improved fencing techniques for livestock, for example, and new breeding methods could not fail to affect the whole output of the livestock sector – irrespective of its end use.

Second, labor productivity in DUA could expect to benefit from some of the changes associated with the growth of the export sector. The most

6 The PEA in DUA is equal to the proportion in the agricultural sector less the proportion in the export sector (E). The latter – $L(E)/PEA$ – can be expressed as

$$(E/GDP) \cdot (GDP/PEA) \cdot [L(E)/E] = (E/GDP) \cdot [APL/APL(E)],$$

where (E/GDP) is the ratio of exports to GDP, APL is the average productivity of labor, and $APL[E]$ is the productivity of labor in the export sector. Before 1914, in many Latin American republics the proportion of the labor force in the agricultural sector was around 70 percent and the ratio of exports to GDP was around 20 percent. Thus, provided that labor productivity in the export sector was higher than the national average – that is, $[APL/APL(E)] < 1$ – the share of DUA in the PEA would exceed 50 percent.

7 The lowest figures are found in Argentina, Chile, and Uruguay, but even in these three cases the share was higher than it was in Australia and New Zealand.

8 In Brazil agriculture accounted for around 25 percent of GDP, whereas exports (and EXA) represented around 15 percent of GDP. Thus 10 percent of GDP was produced by the 50 percent of the labor force that was engaged in DUA. This implies productivity of labor in DUA equal to 20 percent of the national average.

9 A subsistence sector consumes what it produces, so no marketed surplus exists. This was rarely the case in Latin American rural communities, although the marketed surplus was sometimes only a small proportion of total output.

important was the lowering of transport costs as a result of railway construction and other transportation improvements. The circulation of the bulky products in DUA, such as basic grains, was held back by high unit transport costs in the days of mule or oxcart transport, so the effective market was often limited to the area within a few miles of the farm. Large farmers, too, could expect to benefit from the growth of financial institutions linked to the export sector, while rising productivity in the export sector, a more sophisticated division of labor, and population growth expanded the market for DUA.

Under some circumstances, however, the relationship between the growth of EXA and that of DUA could be negative, with adverse consequences for productivity in the latter. Where export specialization was carried to extremes, leading to the exhaustion of the land frontier, the most appropriate lands were monopolized by EXA, leading to a squeeze on DUA and either driving its farmers out of business or onto less productive land. Similarly, the rise in land rents associated with the growth of EXA could render the production of DUA unprofitable and could lead to a rise in imports of foodstuffs.

Such cases were more than theoretical possibilities. In some Central American and Caribbean countries up to 40 percent of the import bill was accounted for by foodstuffs on the eve of the First World War (see Table 5.2). In Puerto Rico the growth of the main export crops in the nineteenth century (coffee, tobacco, sugar) had seen the farm area devoted to DUA fall from 71.1 percent in 1830 to 31.6 percent in 1899.[10] Export specialization had undermined DUA, leading in some cases to an absolute decline and a retreat by many small farmers into defensive strategies based on very low levels of labor productivity.

These special cases are worth noting. In general, however, DUA kept pace with the growth in demand. The share of imports accounted for by foodstuffs in most of South America on the eve of the First World War was not unduly high, and food imports per head (except in Cuba and Puerto Rico) were quite modest (see Table 5.2). Furthermore, the import bill for foodstuffs tended to be concentrated on a handful of essential products. In Colombia wheat, rice, sugar, lard, and maize represented 66.7 percent of the food-import bill around 1870; the proportion had risen to 91.3 percent by 1905.[11] Indeed, wheat alone was responsible for around half the food-import bill for most of the period in Colombia and was also a major item in Brazil and Peru.

Although it would have been physically possible in many cases to replace imported foodstuffs by domestic production, it would not necessarily have made economic sense. The opportunity cost – in terms of the land, labor,

10 See Dietz (1986), Table 1.3, p. 20.
11 See Ocampo (1984), Table 3.11, p. 158.

Table 5.2. *Food imports per head and as share of total imports, circa 1913*
(current prices in US$)

Country	Year	Food imports Thousands of U.S. dollars	Food imports Percentage of total imports	Per head (in US$)
Argentina	1913	60,452	12.4	7.7
Brazil	1913	45,004	13.9	1.9
Chile	1913	11,183	9.3	3.2
Colombia	1913	4,928	17.9	0.9
Costa Rica	1913	2,093[a]	23.8	5.5
Cuba	1913	36,279	25.9	15.0
Ecuador	1913	1,028	11.6	0.7
Guatemala	1913	962	9.6	0.8
Honduras	1911–2	492	15.1	0.9
Mexico	1911–2	9,358	10.3	0.6
Nicaragua	1913	890	15.4	1.6
Panama	1913	3,414[a]	30.1	9.4
Paraguay	1913	1,991[a]	25.3	3.1
Peru	1913	3,648	12.6	0.9
Puerto Rico	1914	14,818	40.7	12.9
Uruguay	1907	6,525	17.4	5.7
Venezuela	1909–10	2,218	19.8	0.9

[a] Includes beverages.
Sources: Pan-American Union (1952), except for Honduras, Koebel (n.d.); for Puerto Rico Clark et al. (1975); for Uruguay Koebel (1911); for Venezuela Dalton (1916).

and capital employed – needed to be lower than the cost of importing. For most republics in the nineteenth century, labor and capital were scarce; land in general was abundant, but land suitable for growing imported foodstuffs (e.g., wheat) was not always available. Thus the pattern of food imports – exclusive of the sugar islands – was not a major cause for concern, and, by implication, DUA had in general expanded in line with the demand for foodstuffs.

A satisfactory rate of production did not guarantee that labor productivity was rising, however. Whether it did depended on how the technique of production responded to the growth of output. If an x percent increase in output was achieved by an x percent increase in all inputs, clearly productivity would be unaffected. If, on the other hand, labor inputs expanded less rapidly than output, average labor productivity would rise.

With labor in general scarce throughout the nineteenth century, it would have been natural for technological progress in DUA to be labor saving; that is, nonlabor inputs would have to grow faster than labor inputs. Even with a proportionate increase in all factor inputs, an increase in labor productivity could still be achieved if output rose more rapidly – a consequence perhaps of the demonstration effect associated with export sector growth or as a result of economies of scale in DUA production.

Such increases in labor productivity in DUA were indeed recorded throughout nineteenth century Latin America, but they tended to be concentrated in the Southern Cone.[12] It is impossible to measure DUA labor productivity with accuracy; if, however, we use figures on net output per worker to measure labor productivity in agriculture (biased upward by the inclusion of EXA), we may note (see Table 5.1) a significant difference between productivity levels in Argentina and those in the rest of Latin America. Indeed, net agricultural output per worker in Argentina was more than six times higher than the level in Brazil and nearly four times higher than that in Mexico.

Although it is not a very reliable guide to labor productivity, the statistics on land productivity (output per hectare) tell a similar story for DUA of dynamism in the Southern Cone and unchanging yields in the rest of Latin America. Furthermore, because land-productivity data refer to individual crops they provide a more detailed picture of DUA than can be obtained from aggregate labor-productivity figures. In Chile yields for all the major crops doubled in the forty years before the First World War, and the maize yield quintupled.[13] Indeed, land productivity (yield per hectare) was higher in Chile than in the United States for the most important components of DUA. By contrast, Mexican yields for many domestic crops (e.g., maize) were among the lowest in all Latin America and far below those recorded in Australia, Canada, New Zealand, and the United States.[14]

It is clear, therefore, that some republics were able to transfer productivity gains quite successfully from the export sector to DUA. In Argentina and Uruguay the transfer was almost effortless, because the products were very often the same (e.g., beef). The Chilean case is more impressive: Despite the success of wheat exports, foreign-exchange earnings were derived mainly from minerals. Yet the productivity of Chilean farming could still benefit from mineral production because the concentration of workers around the nitrate mines in arid northern Chile, where no food could be grown, was a powerful stimulus to the growth of output, technological change, and labor productivity in the fertile central valley.[15]

12 The Southern Cone is the geographical name given to Argentina, Chile, and Uruguay.
13 See Sunkel (1982), Table 43, p. 158.
14 The maize yield in Mexico just before the First World War was 8.5 quintals per hectare, compared with 16.3 in the United States, 17.7 in Australia, 31.2 in New Zealand, and 35.2 in Canada. See League of Nations (1925), Table 51.
15 These backward linkages from nitrate mining in northern Chile to agriculture in the central valley are explored in great detail in Sunkel and Cariola (1985). Under these circumstances it is perhaps puzzling that the share of the Chilean labor force in agriculture was so much higher than the contribution of agriculture to GDP (see Table 5.1). The problem may reflect the quality of the 1907

For many reasons other Latin American republics failed to transfer productivity gains from the export sector to DUA. The most important cause was the long delay in improving transport systems, leaving unit transport costs so high that many farmers could not reap the benefits of access to a wider market. Once the railway network had been consolidated in Brazil, solid evidence suggests a much more dynamic performance on the part of DUA; yet the network was slow in coming, so the Brazilian productivity figures in Table 5.1 are dismal.[16]

The railway age also took a long time to reach Mexico. Only after the Porfiriato had guaranteed political stability did foreign investors register an enthusiasm for railway construction. Even so, the network overwhelmingly favored the carriage of export products, and during the Porfiriato the growth of DUA failed even to keep pace with population growth.[17] That this did not lead to a major explosion in food imports must have been due to the fall in real agricultural wages for much of the period.[18]

The fall in real agricultural wages in Mexico in the Porfiriato seems to have found an echo in many other republics. At a time of apparent labor scarcity the decline may seem perverse; the artificial manipulation of the labor market by the authorities and landowners (see pp. 84–91), coupled with a steady acceleration of population growth, reduced the tightness in the labor market. Only in Argentina and Uruguay can much evidence be found for rising real wages in nonexport agriculture in the half-century before the First World War.

Faced with falling or static real wages, farmers had little incentive to rely on machinery imports to replace labor. Such labor-saving technical progress, capable of producing a huge increase in labor productivity, was not found in DUA outside Argentina and Uruguay – and even there it was not universal. Furthermore, the cost of machinery – burdened by tariffs and high internal-transport costs – was often considerable, and credit could not always be obtained, even by large farmers. Thus DUA remained technologically backward throughout most of Latin America, a fact that was bound to depress productivity levels.

The lack of formal education and high levels of illiteracy in rural areas were further barriers to raising labor productivity in DUA. High illiteracy rates had not prevented productivity from rising in the export sector, but this was due above all to the increase in the capital stock per worker. In the absence of machinery, productivity could still be raised (e.g., through the

census, from which the labor-force data are drawn and which has prompted some to argue that the method of enumeration "may have resulted in an overestimate (relative to subsequent censuses) of the active population in agriculture at the time of the census." See Ballesteros and Davis (1963), p. 159.

16 See Leff (1982), pp. 146–9.
17 See Coatsworth (1981), Chapter 4.
18 See Rosenzweig (1989), Table 16, p. 250.

application of improved agricultural methods), but high levels of illiteracy were a formidable barrier to the spread of information and knowledge.

Nothing could demonstrate the abysmal state of DUA in most of Latin America better than the livestock industry. With an abundance of land, fine natural pastures, and plenty of water, most Latin American republics enjoyed a potential comparative advantage in cattle raising, and many could say the same for sheep raising. Yet, outside the main beef-exporting countries, the quality of the herds was generally considered to be poor, and hides were often riddled with blemishes. Only three republics (Argentina, Paraguay, and Uruguay) could boast a stock of cattle twice as large as their populations by 1914, and the majority had less than one head of cattle per person.[19] Yet improvements in the industry (such as breeding) were not particularly capital intensive, and the biggest barrier of all was ignorance of the best technologies available.

It would be tempting to argue that the poor productivity performance of DUA in most of Latin America was linked in some way to the landtenure system, to the concentration of farmland in a few hands, or to both. In Mexico the already unequal distribution of land became even more acute during the Porfiriato; on the eve of the revolution in 1910 more than half the land was controlled by less than 1 percent of the population, and 97 percent of Mexicans were landless.[20]

In fact, no empirical support exists for either of these claims. In Argentina the proportion of farms classified as owner occupied fell sharply after the 1880s as tenant farming increased; by 1914 nearly 40 percent of all farms were tenanted, and the figure was more than 50 percent in the crucial provinces of Buenos Aires and Santa Fe.[21] Contemporaries lamented the decline of owner occupation and traditional colonization in Argentina, but it does not seem to have had a negative impact either on the rate of growth of DUA or on the rate of growth of agricultural labor productivity. By contrast, Costa Rica – where the vast majority of farms were owner occupied[22] – did not achieve significant increases in labor productivity in DUA in the period before the First World War.

The *latifundio*, villain of so much post-1950 writing on Latin America, does not appear to have been any worse than other farm sizes in contributing to an improved performance by DUA. Microeconomic studies of these large estates suggest that they were not unresponsive to new opportunities in the nineteenth century, and their owners or managers were often best placed

19 Nicaragua, for example, with vast natural pastures stretching from the cordillera to the Atlantic coast, only had 252,000 head of cattle in 1908, when the population exceeded 500,000.

20 See Singer (1969), p. 49.

21 See Taylor (1948), p. 191.

22 The debate over the degree of land concentration in Costa Rica in the nineteenth century is lively, but all scholars agree that the proportion of the agricultural labor force that owned its own land was very high. See Gudmundson (1986), Chapters 1–2.

to absorb the flow of new information regarding markets, prices, and techniques of production.[23] Indeed, the increased output from the large estates helps to explain why the supply of DUA did not lag far behind demand. However, labor hoarding was frequent, production remained labor intensive, and labor productivity growth suffered in consequence.

The emergence of a labor surplus in the twentieth century has meant that any proposals to improve labor productivity in DUA through labor-saving technical progress carry high social costs. Although those who remain in the sector can enjoy higher standards of living, the displaced labor may have no alternative source of employment. For much of the nineteenth century, however, this dilemma did not exist in such sharp form. Labor scarcity meant that workers who were displaced from DUA by productivity-raising-techniques could still find employment elsewhere. Argentines and foreigners alike could lament the passing of the colorful *gaucho*, but the economic gain to the country from fencing the pampas was unambiguous.[24]

In the United States the response to labor scarcity had brought a massive investment in labor-saving farm technology – so much so that many of the global innovations in farm machinery throughout the nineteenth century originated in the United States. In this way the United States was able not only to raise productivity and real wages in its nonexport sector, but also to build up its own technical expertise and capital-goods industry.[25] In much of Latin America the response to labor scarcity in the nineteenth century – as, indeed, in the colonial period – was artificial manipulation of the labor market, coercion of the work force, and restrictions on access to land. The reason for the different responses in the two halves of the Western Hemisphere cannot be discussed here (it can be traced in part to the different postindependence political systems), but we may safely conclude that most of Latin America – particularly those republics north of the Southern Cone – paid a high price in the long run for a refusal to recognize relative scarcities.

Manufacturing and its origins

The expansion of the export sector promoted urbanization, contributed to the growth of a wage-earning working class and a salaried middle class, and widened the market for manufactured goods. As in the case of DUA, this

23 See, for example, the study of the Mexican *hacienda* in Miller (1990).

24 The *gaucho*, whose demise was most eloquently recorded in the poem "Martín Fierro," by José Hernández, declined in economic importance with the introduction of barbed wire on the Argentine pampas, because his primary function had been to herd the cattle that roamed wild over miles of territory.

25 As early as the 1840s the United States was not merely producing farm machinery but also exporting it. Domingo Sarmiento, who later became president of Argentina, was particularly impressed by the application of machinery to agricultural production during his visit to the United States in 1847. See Rockland (1970).

growth in demand could be met either by increased domestic production or by imports. To the extent that it was met by the former, it created opportunities for transferring productivity gains from the export sector to the nonexport economy, thereby contributing to the emergence of modern manufacturing.

In the first decades of the nineteenth century real income per head was low throughout Latin America, and demand for manufactured goods was correspondingly modest. Nevertheless, the depressed level of exports per head (see pp. 34–9) made it impossible to satisfy much of this modest demand through imports. The surge of imports that followed the abolition of colonial restrictions on foreign trade could not be sustained, and the countries of the region returned to a more "normal" state of affairs, in which a high proportion of the low level of demand for manufactured goods was in fact met by local production.

This local production consisted almost entirely of handicrafts rather than modern manufacturing. The artisan sector in both urban and rural areas turned out a variety of simple manufactured goods that could be used to satisfy the basic needs of the mass of the population. The demand for processed foods (bread, biscuits, flour, etc.) was met by cottage industry; the textile industry turned out simple cloth and finished goods in establishments known as *obrajes*.[26] The by-products of the livestock industry were used in the handicraft sector to provide a broad range of simple consumer goods, such as shoes, candles, soap, and riding equipment, and small foundries were capable of making the simpler products involving metals, such as stirrups, cutlery, and hand tools.[27] The demand for more sophisticated products of superior quality was typically met by imports, but their consumption was limited to a small proportion of the population.

The main exceptions to the dominance of cottage industry within manufacturing were found in the export sector. Thus those raw materials that required a degree of processing before export were often handled in large-scale establishments that warranted the label "factory." The sugar mills in the main export countries (e.g., Brazil and Cuba) were of this kind, although the processing of cane sugar in countries without sugar exports was far too crude to be described as modern manufacturing.[28] The meat-processing plants (*saladeros*) in the River Plate Basin, which produced jerked beef for export, had all the characteristics of factory production, and the refining of some minerals (e.g., copper in Chile) had also reached the stage at which the label "manufacturing" was not inappropriate.

---

26 See pp. 41–2.

27 These early examples of industrial production are well described in Lewis (1986).

28 Described by a variety of names (e.g., *trapiches* in Costa Rica), these units for processing sugar were usually horse or mule driven, with little machinery. The sugar was typically sold to households, but the cane juice was often sold to rum factories. See, for example, Samper (1990), p. 63.

However, the fact that virtually all these modern manufacturing establishments fell within the export sector meant that the rise in domestic demand for manufactured goods, associated with the expansion of exports, was felt mainly by the handicraft sector. A similar process had occurred in parts of Europe and had led to protoindustrialization,[29] in which the low-productivity, small-scale units in the handicraft sector were transformed into modern manufacturing establishments that employed a sophisticated division of labor and enjoyed higher labor productivity through the use, above all, of modern machinery. Not surprisingly, whether such a process can be observed in Latin America has sparked considerable interest among scholars.

The answer must be in the negative.[30] In no country can the origin of the modern factories in existence at the end of the nineteenth century be traced directly to the cottage industries in existence at the beginning of that century. On the contrary, the modern factories were often direct competitors and contributed significantly to the reduction in importance of the handicraft sector in the period after 1870. On the eve of the First World War cottage industry still survived and had acquired a niche in a number of specialized markets (e.g., Mexican *rebozos* and Guatemalan *huipiles*),[31] but it was apparently incapable of transforming itself into high-productivity modern manufacturing.

The origins of modern manufacturing in Latin America cannot, therefore, be traced to a process of protoindustrialization. Yet the handicraft sector functioned for many decades after independence, despite the competition provided by the growth of imports. Although the share of domestic consumption of manufactures met by imports almost certainly rose in the first fifty years after independence, that is quite consistent with modest growth in the handicraft sector. The "natural" protection provided by high transport costs was not finally eroded until the railway age in the last quarter of the nineteenth century, and tariffs (see pp. 137–41) always provided an additional barrier to imports.

The survival of handicrafts meant the continuation of a low-productivity sector that employed a significant proportion of the labor force. As late as 1900 employment in cottage industry was more important than employment in modern manufacturing in almost all republics outside the Southern Cone. Indeed, even in the mid-1920s some 80 percent of manufacturing

29 The classic work on European protoindustrialization is Mendels (1972). On industrialization in the United States after independence, see Engerman and Sokoloff (2000).

30 Numerous investigations have been carried out on protoindustrialization in Latin America. See, for example, Berry (1987) on Colombia and Libby (1991) on Minas Gerais, in Brazil. Batou (1990, 1991) are excellent comparisons of early industrialization efforts in Latin America and the Middle East, with many case studies.

31 These female garments were (and are) difficult to produce under factory conditions because they often involve elaborate hand embroidery.

employment in Colombia was in cottage industry.[32] In the absence of pro-toindustrialization in Latin America, therefore, the transfer of the productivity gains in the export sector to the domestic branches of manufacturing could be achieved only through investment in modern factories.

The inability of the handicraft sector to transform itself into high-productivity activities can be traced to a number of causes. First, lack of finance for working and fixed capital costs was a major problem. The absence of barriers to entry in the sector kept profit margins low, so self-financing of expansion was difficult, and the few financial institutions in existence had little interest in lending to the microenterprises that made up the artisan sector. Second, the entrepreneurs in the sector were definitely not part of the social or political elite and lacked the bargaining power to influence public policy in their favor. Third, family labor constituted an important component of labor inputs, and reliance on family labor clearly imposed limits on the size of each establishment.

The inability of cottage industry to transform itself meant that the growth of manufacturing capacity would have to fall disproportionately on new, modern factories if the share of consumption met by imports were not to keep on rising. However, modern manufacturing itself faced a number of obstacles that needed to be overcome before production in large-scale units could begin.

The first problem was the supply of energy. The Industrial Revolution in Europe and North America had relied on coal and water. Only a few countries in Latin America (Brazil, Chile, Colombia, and Mexico) had coal deposits, but most of these were of poor quality, and imported coal was expensive. All Latin America had a plentiful supply of water, but water power in its natural state was often unreliable, because it was excessive in the rainy season and insufficient in the dry season. The problem of energy supply became much less serious following the creation of electricity-generating public utilities after 1880 (frequently linked to the introduction of trams in urban areas). Indeed, the construction of hydroelectric plants at the beginning of the twentieth century in some countries provided not only a reliable but also a cheap source of energy.[33]

Second, modern manufacturing needed markets. The tiny cities at the time of independence and a rural labor force, which received only a small portion of its earnings in cash, were not the ideal combination for starting large-scale manufacturing. Gradually, however, export expansion widened the market, because primary-product exports were associated with a process of urbanization and the growth of urban real incomes. By 1900 Argentina – the most successful primary-product exporter – was heavily urbanized, and

---

32 See Berry (1983), Table 2.1, p. 10.
33 In 1910 Brazil produced 374 million kilowatt hours of electricity, of which 315 came from hydro-electricity. See Bairoch and Toutain (1991), p. 106.

Buenos Aires was one of the great cities of the world; less successful exporters (e.g., Bolivia) tended to have a much more modest rate of urbanization.[34]

Third, modern manufacturing needed transport not only to market its products but also to supply its inputs of intermediate and capital goods. The obstacles in the path of modern industry before the railway age were formidable, and even after the railway age unit transport costs were still high enough to create regional monopolies[35] and to favor imports in certain coastal areas far from the main centers of domestic production. Nevertheless, the spread of railways went a long way toward breaking down the barriers faced by large-scale manufacturers.

Fourth, the factory system needed finance. Although financial institutions were unreceptive to the needs of cottage industry, on occasion they were prepared to lend to modern manufacturing establishments. Yet banking rules did not favor the long-term loans that industry needed, and many banks continued to favor the primary exports with whose expansion their own fortunes were often intimately tied. It is surely no accident that immigrants figure disproportionately in the early history of modern manufacturing in Latin America: Immigrants – faced with rising land prices and coming from countries in which the Industrial Revolution was already underway – were more prepared to risk their capital in new manufacturing ventures than were their local counterparts.[36] Indeed, the Italian immigrant community in many countries of Latin America was distinguished by its willingness to create banks designed primarily to service industry.[37]

Finally, modern manufacturing needed a reliable supply of raw materials. This did not need to be of domestic origin, because – as Great Britain had shown in textiles – comparative advantage could be based on imported raw materials. In the case of imports, however, a growing supply of foreign exchange was required in order to pay for their purchase, so the expansion of exports was almost a precondition for the early growth of modern manufacturing.[38]

Overcoming all these obstacles did not guarantee that modern manufacturing would be profitable. Yet for those firms selling to the local market there was always the possibility that the price could be influenced in their

---

34 Bolivia in 1990 was still not as urban as Argentina in 1900. The scattering of so much of the population across small communities in rural areas was bound to have a major impact on the rate of industrialization.

35 In Mexico, for example, even the railway age did not break down many of these regional monopolies. See Haber (1989), pp. 84–6.

36 Good studies on the relationship between immigration and manufacturing are numerous. See, for example, Dean (1969) on São Paulo, Brazil, and Lewis (1990) on Argentina.

37 The Peruvian Banco Italiano, founded in 1889, provided financial support for many manufacturing ventures. See Thorp and Bertram (1978), p. 32.

38 This rather obvious point is usually overlooked in the writings of the dependency school on early manufacturing in Latin America. See pp. 182–4.

favor through the manipulation of policy instruments (e.g., tariffs). Indeed, policy could make production profitable even before the obstacles listed above had been overcome, provided that consumers were willing to pay prices far above those in world markets. These issues are discussed on pp. 137–46.

Our description of obstacles to modern manufacturing during the nineteenth century provides useful insights into both the timing and the location of factory production in Latin America. Before 1870 markets were still too small, the energy supply too unreliable, and transport costs too high to permit more than a handful of large-scale factories to be built to serve the home market. Most of the large-scale factories that were built processed raw materials for export, so the small size of the domestic market was not an obstacle. These factories (e.g., sugar mills in Brazil and Cuba, copper foundries and flour mills in Chile, silver works in Mexico, and *saladeros* in Argentina) all processed a local raw material that was too bulky or perishable to export in unprocessed form. Although the manufacturing part of the operation could no doubt have been handled more efficiently abroad, the industrialized countries lacked the raw material, and it was too expensive for them to import in unprocessed form. Thus the value added by manufacturing had to be accomplished in the country of origin, very often providing Latin American countries with their first taste of modern factory production.

The earliest examples of modern factories serving the local market were usually textile mills. Their appearance – despite the formidable obstacles – was due not so much to the availability of raw materials (cotton or wool) as to the existence of a large and protected market and to economies of scale in production. Everyone had to be clothed, and textile imports throughout the nineteenth century attracted relatively high tariffs, providing a level of protection for local production that was able to sustain cottage industry for many decades and to compensate factory production for its numerous deficiencies. The modern textile industry in Mexico had also received official support since the early 1830s and, despite the failure of the Banco de Avío, growth in the number of spindles and looms had been steady throughout the turbulent half-century leading up to the Porfiriato.[39]

Not until the last quarter of the nineteenth century, however, did factory production geared toward the home market became firmly established. Even then it was confined to a small number of republics in which market size (Brazil and Mexico), rapidly growing exports (Peru), income per head (Chile and Uruguay), or all three (Argentina) was sufficient to overcome the other obstacles faced by modern manufacturing. Some of the larger republics, in

---

39 On the growth of productivity in the Mexican textile industry, see Razo and Haber (1998). For a comparison between the Mexican and Brazilian textile industry, see Haber (1997).

which export expansion had been particularly unsatisfactory (e.g., Colombia and Venezuela), had made only the most modest beginnings in factory production by 1914,[40] and in nearly all the small republics even a satisfactory export performance was unable to compensate for the deficiencies of market size.[41]

The rapid growth of the rail network after 1870, the spread of electricity-generating public utilities after 1880, and the steady rise in the purchasing power of exports all played their part in undermining the obstacles to factory production. The location of the factories, however, was closely linked to proximity to markets. The Brazilian textile industry migrated from the Northeast (where it enjoyed access to cotton) to the south as the growth of coffee exports produced huge urban concentrations in Rio de Janeiro and São Paulo.[42] The city of Buenos Aires, with 20 percent of Argentina's population by 1913, was always a prime location for modern manufacturing, and the attractions of Montevideo and Lima were almost irresistible for would-be industrial entrepreneurs in Uruguay and Peru, respectively. Only Mexico, where both Puebla and Monterrey were important industrial cities at the beginning of the twentieth century,[43] resisted this trend toward concentrating industry in the largest city,[44] although even in Mexico the lion's share of factory production was located in the capital.

Location may have been dictated primarily by proximity to markets, but the level of production was influenced primarily by real income per head. Argentina, with a population far smaller than that of Brazil or Mexico, had the highest level of value added in manufacturing on the eve of the First World War, although its net output of manufacturing per head of population was still far below the comparable figures for other countries of recent settlement. Brazil and Mexico came next in terms of total manufacturing net output, but value added per head of population was very small. Indeed, even in 1920 Brazilian manufacturing net output per head was only $16 (1970 prices), compared with a prewar Argentine figure of $84 (see Table 5.3).

40 Some evidence indicates that Colombia began its economic "takeoff" after 1905. See McGreevey (1985). This was too late, however, to have much of an impact on the main macroeconomic indicators before 1914, and in any case factory production was still very unimportant until long after the First World War. See Berry (1983), Table 2.1, p. 10. See also Ocampo (2000).

41 Most of the Central American republics enjoyed rapid export growth between 1870 and 1890 without any evidence of significant investment in modern manufacturing.

42 The migration of the textile industry from the Northeast to the south is well described in Stein (1957).

43 Puebla, dominated by the textile industry, was in relative decline, whereas Monterrey was growing rapidly in importance as a result of the location of new, dynamic industries in the city.

44 In the postwar period, however, Colombia reversed the trend toward concentration of industry in the capital, with the emergence of Medellín as a major manufacturing center.

Table 5.3. *Indicators of manufacturing output, circa 1913 (1970 prices)*

Country	Year	Value added			
		Millions of U.S. dollars	Percentage of GDP	Per worker employed ($)	Per head of population ($)
Argentina[a]	1913	619	16.6	977	84
Brazil[b]	1920	440	12.1	744	16
Chile[c]	1913	184	14.5	1,061	53
Colombia[d]	1925	58	6.7	142	8
Mexico[e]	1910	371	12.3	713	24

[a] Production data from CEPAL (1978). Labor-force data from Díaz-Alejandro (1970), p. 428.

[b] Production data from CEPAL (1978). Labor-force data from IBGE (1987) include mining and construction workers; these were adjusted assuming that manufacturing employment accounted for 75 percent of the total figure.

[c] Production data from CEPAL (1978) for 1940, adjusted to 1913 using the index in Ballesteros and Davis (1963). Labor-force data for 1907 from Ballesteros and Davis (1963) include construction workers; these were adjusted assuming that manufacturing employment accounted for 80 percent of the total figure and that the labor force grew at the same rate as the population between 1907 and 1913.

[d] Production data from CEPAL (1978). Labor-force data from Berry (1983), p. 10, using the lower employment figure.

[e] Production data from CEPAL (1978) for 1920, adjusted to 1910 using data in Solís (1983). Labor-force data from Mitchell (1993) include construction workers; these were adjusted assuming that manufacturing employment accounted for 80 percent of the total figure.

The low Brazilian figure may come as something of a surprise to those who are accustomed to the idea that Brazil's Industrial Revolution was well under way by 1900. Brazilian manufacturing production had indeed grown rapidly since 1870, its labor productivity was not too far below the level in neighboring Argentina (see Table 5.3), and 75 percent of local consumption was met by domestic production as early as 1919.[45] Nevertheless, the extremely low level of real income per head in Brazil put an upper limit on the level of industrialization geared to the home market. At the beginning of the 1920s only 3 percent of the labor force was employed in modern industrial factories,[46] and much of the agricultural labor force (nearly 70 percent of the total) was too poor to buy more than the most essential items of food and clothing.

45 See Fishlow (1972), p. 323. The measurement of this seemingly simple statistic is in fact fraught with problems, as Fishlow makes clear.

46 Derived from Tables 7.6 and 3.1 in IBGE (1987).

Table 5.4. *The structure of manufacturing output (in percentages)*

Country	Year	Food and beverages	Textiles	Clothing	Subtotal	Metals
Argentina[a]	1914	53.3	1.7	7.9	62.9	6.3
Brazil[b]	1920	40.7	25.2	8.2	74.1	3.3
Chile[c]	1914	53.8	6.0	14.4	74.2	3.6
Colombia[d]	1925–9	67.0	(.......... 5.0 ....)		72.0	1.5
Costa Rica[e]	1929	65.1	(.......... 4.0 ....)		69.1	3.3
Mexico[f]	1930	37.7	23.4	6.1	66.9	7.8
Peru[g]	1918	74.8	(.......... 7.5 ....)		82.3	n/a
Uruguay[b]	1930	51.9	3.8	7.5	63.2	4.5
Venezuela[i]	1913	33.1	4.3	14.1	51.5	0

[a] Taken from ECLA (1959).
[b] Taken from IBGE (1987).
[c] Taken from Palma (1979).
[d] Taken from Ocampo (1991), p. 227.
[e] Based on data on the number of establishments reported in Dirección General de Estadística y Censos (1930), p. 65.
[f] See Dirección General de Estadística (1933), pp. 63–7.
[g] Based on number of establishments; see Thorp and Bertram (1978).
[b] Taken from Finch (1981), p. 165.
[i] Based on data on employment; see Karlsson (1975), Table A1.

The modest advances in Latin American manufacturing were reflected in the structure of industrial production. The dominant position occupied by food processing and beverages (see Table 5.4) reflected Engel's law,[47] although in Argentina and Uruguay the figure is pushed upward by the inclusion of processed food exports. The second most important sector was textiles and clothing, with Brazil reaching the million mark in spindles by 1910 and Mexico not far behind.[48] Argentina's textile industry, however, remained extremely underdeveloped until the 1930s – a victim of the ideological commitment of the Argentine elite in favor of a traditional reading of the law of comparative advantage.[49]

The rapid spread of urbanization in the three decades before the First World War provided outstanding opportunities for firms selling nonmetallic materials to the construction industry (where international transport costs were often prohibitively high and kept out imports). By 1914 cement

47 The nineteenth-century German statistician Engel established an inverse relationship between the level of household income and the proportion of income spent on foodstuffs. This implied that the demand for foodstuffs was income inelastic, so that the share of food production in total industrial production would fall, ceteris paribus, as average income rose.
48 The Mexican figure was 726,000 in 1910. See Clark (1911), Part 4, p. 118.
49 The law of comparative advantage stated that a country should export those products in which it had the greatest relative cost differential. In the Argentine case, this was clearly agroindustrial exports.

industries had been established in Brazil, Chile, Mexico, Peru, Uruguay, and Venezuela, but in Argentina – despite the attractions of the market – early efforts proved unsuccessful.[50] The metals industry was still very backward: Only Mexico had constructed an integrated, modern iron and steel industry by 1910. In view of the unprofitable nature of this firm, however, the delay in establishing the industry in the rest of Latin America may have been justified.[51]

Food processing, textiles, and clothing thus accounted for around 75 percent of manufacturing in most of Latin America on the eve of the First World War – an unsophisticated structure that in general reflected the level of real income per head and consumption patterns in the region. As a consequence of growth in these branches of industry, import patterns began to change, and the share taken by nondurable consumer goods fell rapidly in the countries in which modern manufacturing had begun to take root. By 1913, in the larger republics, imports were dominated by capital and intermediate goods, the consumer-goods share having been reduced to around one-third.[52] Only in the countries in which modern manufacturing had not yet established itself was the share of consumer goods more than 50 percent.

Despite the recent interest in early industrialization efforts in Latin America, it is difficult to escape the conclusion that the results were modest before the First World War. The majority of republics – even some of the larger countries – had not undertaken any significant investments in modern manufacturing. The most developed country, Argentina, had a relatively backward industrial structure for a country of its income and wealth. Indeed, industrial labor productivity was lower than in Chile (see Table 5.3), despite Argentina's superior income per head. Industry in Mexico had advanced rapidly, but by all accounts it was very unprofitable, and it accounted for only 12 percent of GDP on the eve of the revolution. Peruvian industrialization exhibited signs of stagnation even before 1914.[53] Brazilian manufacturing was showing high growth rates, but the small proportion of the labor force employed in modern factories made it difficult for industry to be a vehicle for the transfer of productivity gains from the export sector to the nonexport economy, and real income per head remained extremely low. In the next section we explore the extent to which the policy context was responsible for this disappointing outcome.

---

50 On the origins of the cement industry in Latin America, see Kock-Petersen (1946).
51 Fundidora Monterrey was so unprofitable that it never declared a dividend before the First World War. See Haber (1989), Chapter 7.
52 As early as 1900–4 the consumer-goods share of imports was less than 40 percent in Argentina. See Díaz-Alejandro (1970), p. 15.
53 Thorp and Bertram (1978) argue that the industrial dynamism of the 1890s – based on local firms – had given way to a much less impressive performance in the decade before the First World War.

Industry and relative prices

Although the level of real income per head and population size are the most important determinants of the level of manufacturing output per person,[54] the rate of growth of manufacturing in any given period is nevertheless also affected by the incentives being offered. In Latin America, before the First World War one of the most important incentives was the price of domestic production relative to competing imports.

This relative price embodied five main variables. First, the price of each manufactured good was influenced by the rate of growth of real income and the rate at which domestic prices were changing. The second influence was the foreign-currency price of competing imports and the rate of price change. The third was the rate at which international transport costs were falling, because, ceteris paribus, this made competing imports cheaper. The fourth was the nominal rate of exchange, expressed as the number of units of domestic currency required to purchase one unit of foreign currency. The fifth variable was the structure of protection embodied in the nominal tariff rate.

Some of these variables (e.g., international transport costs) were beyond the control of Latin American policymakers. The tariff, however, was a matter of national policy. Throughout the first century after independence the function of the tariff was primarily to raise revenue. It was the main source of government income in all countries and virtually the only source in a few republics.[55] This was quite different from the situation in the United States or Germany, where tariffs were widespread but were explicitly adopted to provide protection for domestic producers.[56] However, even though a protective tariff can be set so high that it yields no revenue, a revenue tariff will always give some protection. Thus to say that the Latin American tariff was primarily intended to raise revenue does not rule out a secondary protective function. Indeed, the protective element in the Latin American tariff had become quite significant in a number of republics by 1914.

The tariff structure was inherited by independent Latin America from its colonial masters, and no great changes were observed in the first few decades

---

54 This basic relationship was established in Chenery (1960) and has been subject to numerous refinements. See, for example, Syrquin (1988).

55 See pp. 107–109.

56 The protective function of the tariff had been recognized in the United States ever since the publication in 1791 of Alexander Hamilton's famous work on manufactures. Prewar protection reached its peak with the McKinley tariff of 1890, which raised the general level of duties from 38 percent to 49.5 percent. Indeed, U.S. protection was so strong that one economic historian could write, "The key-note of our commercial policy has from the very beginning been the reservation of the home market for the domestic manufacturer, and the exclusion of foreign competition." See Bogart (1908), p. 396.

after independence.[57] The most important exception was Brazil, where the imperial government was obliged to honor the 1810 treaty between Portugal and Great Britain that gave the latter preferential tariff treatment in the Brazilian market.[58] This treaty, the source of much (justifiable) Brazilian resentment, expired after twenty-five years and was replaced by the 1844 tariff law, which raised tariffs significantly and removed preferential treatment for Great Britain. At that time the average level of tariffs in Latin America was around 25 percent to 30 percent, with relatively few items admitted duty free.

The reluctance of independent Latin American countries to change the tariff was not due just to their dependence on the tax for revenue. Handicrafts were very important, and the craft guilds still had some influence. For the artisan sector the tariff had a protective function, and artisans fought hard to retain it. Although the "free traders" might have been expected to press for the reduction of tariffs, their enthusiasm was tempered by the knowledge that government revenue had to be raised somehow, and one obvious alternative to the tariff – a tax on land – was abhorrent to the powerful *latifundistas*.[59]

During the third quarter of the nineteenth century a tendency toward tariff liberalization emerged in a number of countries. The Brazilian law of 1853 and the Chilean ordinance of 1864 lowered tariffs on a range of consumer goods, and in Colombia the average tariff fell to 20 percent in the 1860s.[60] These changes were due not so much to the decline in the influence of the artisan class (never great) as to the growing awareness that a tariff cut could increase revenue if the import price elasticity was greater than one.[61] Furthermore, as the export quantum expanded, the volume of imports (the tax base) started to rise sharply in some republics, making possible a cut in the average rate of protection (the tax rate).[62]

The third quarter of the nineteenth century was the closest Latin America ever came to free trade. Yet the level of protection was far from zero. In the late 1860s the average tariff on textiles was nearly 50 percent in Brazil,[63]

57 In Colombia, for example, tariff rates in the period before 1820 were in the 30–40 percent range. See McGreevey (1971), p. 34. The average tariff has been calculated as 27.9 percent for the early 1840s. See Ocampo and Montenegro (1984), p. 264.

58 See p. 32.

59 "Free" trade in Latin America, therefore, unlike Great Britain, never implied zero tariffs. In fact, "fair" trade would be a more accurate description of nineteenth-century commercial policy.

60 See Ocampo and Montenegro (1984), pp. 265–6. Other sources imply an even lower figure. See, for example, McGreevey (1971), p. 170.

61 The price elasticity of demand is the ratio of the percent change in demand to the percentage change in price. Thus if the elasticity is greater than one, total revenue can be increased by lowering price.

62 This effect was stronger during those periods when the Net Barter Terms of Trade (NBTT) were improving. An increase in the NBTT, ceteris paribus, implied an increase in the purchasing power of exports and in the capacity to import.

63 See Versiani (1979), p. 19.

and in Colombia the tariff on *domésticas* (local textiles) was as high as 88 percent in 1859.[64] In 1877 Argentina adopted a tariff on wheat and flour that was frankly protectionist and turned the country from a net importer (mainly from Chile) to a major exporter in a few years.[65] Even in Peru, where income from guano provided the main source of government revenue, the average tariff in the 1860s was about 20 percent.[66]

The last quarter of the century, when import prices were generally falling, witnessed a rise in protection in the main Latin American republics. This was achieved by leaving specific duties unchanged, thereby raising implicit average tariff rates (e.g., Uruguay), increasing the variance of tariff rates[67] (e.g., Chile, Argentina), or both (Brazil). Thus the tariff system continued to be the main source of government revenue, but it was combined with a protective element in those republics in which the level of income per head or population size made possible the introduction of modern manufacturing. By 1913 the ratio of duties collected to the value of imports in Latin America was at least as great as that found in Australia (16.5 percent), Canada (17.1 percent), or the United States (17.7 percent), and in some countries, such as Brazil (39.7 percent), Uruguay (34.4 percent), or Venezuela (45.8 percent), it was considerably higher.[68]

In the case of Mexico, we are fortunate to have a detailed study of tariff protection from 1892 to 1909 (see Marquez, 1998). This shows a reduction in ad valorem tariffs reinforced by exchange-rate movements. However, this was offset to some extent by a rise in nontariff barriers. The monetary reform of 1905 provided an opportunity to establish an explicit policy of protection through tariff reform.

These figures are only a rough measure of the rate of protection, for numerous reasons. First, Latin American countries used official values for imports, which did not necessarily reflect actual values. These official values, introduced to avoid tax evasion by importers, were revised infrequently, so the published figures for imports did not necessarily take into account rises or falls in import prices. Thus, if the official value was above the true value, the true rate of protection would be higher (and vice versa).[69]

---

64 See McGreevey (1971), p. 80.

65 See Rock (1987), p. 150.

66 See Thorp and Bertram (1978), p. 30. See also Hunt (1985), Table 13, which shows the decline in ad valorem tariff rates for a number of products before the 1860s.

67 A high variance, with the average unaffected, would still imply an increase in protection, because the higher rates almost always applied to products for which some possibility of local production existed.

68 For Argentina, Australia, Canada, and the United States, see Díaz-Alejandro (1970), p. 285. For Brazil, see Leff (1982), p. 175; for Uruguay, see Finch (1981), p. 168; for Venezuela, see Karlsson (1975), p. 64.

69 The differential has been calculated for Argentina for the years 1910 to 1940. See Díaz-Alejandro (1970), p. 282.

Second, not all imports were subject to duty. If a high proportion entered free of tariffs, the rate of protection for those goods subject to duty would be greatly increased. In the United States such a high proportion of imports entered duty free that the implied rate of protection jumps from 17.7 percent to 40.1 percent when duties collected are expressed as a percentage of dutiable imports.[70] In Latin America, by contrast, the increase was much more modest (e.g., from 20.8 percent to 25.8 percent in Argentina, from 25.4 percent to 33 percent in Peru, and from 32.2 percent to 38.1 percent in Paraguay).

Third, what matters to domestic producers is not the nominal rate of production but the effective rate of protection (ERP). Whereas nominal rates refer only to the tariff on competing imports, the ERP also takes into account tariffs on inputs to calculate the percentage increase in value added as a result of the structure of protection. If there are high tariffs on competing imports and low tariffs on raw materials, intermediate inputs, and machinery, the effective rate of protection will exceed the nominal rate.

It is impossible to take into account all these other factors that influence the rate of protection. Nevertheless, a number of observations can be made. In general, sterling and dollar import prices had fallen in the last quarter of the nineteenth century but had risen in the decade before 1913. The net effect, for those countries that had not revised official values for some time, was probably to leave "official" protection slightly below the "true" rate of protection, whereas for those countries (e.g., Argentina) that had revised official values at the start of the century the opposite was true.[71]

Latin American countries did exempt some imports from duties, but the proportion exempted was never much higher than 20 percent – far lower than in the United States – because the primary function of the tariff remained the collection of revenue. The most important items on the free list were those commodities allowed in duty free under special contracts with foreign companies. Following the Mitre law in Argentina in 1907, for example, all railway companies (not just the foreign-owned companies) were free to import most of their material requirements duty free – a concession that is widely assumed to have contributed substantially to the subsequent rapid expansion of the railway network.[72]

Growing sophistication on the part of policymakers in combining the revenue and protective functions of the tariff produced high ERPs for some consumer goods. As early as 1864 the Chilean average tariff had been lowered, but it was lowered much less on consumer goods than on intermediate

---

70 See Díaz-Alejandro (1970), p. 286.

71 In 1913 the average import tariff in Argentina, calculated on the basis of official import values, was 20.8 percent; this falls to 17.7 percent when the market value of imports is used. See Díaz-Alejandro (1970), pp. 280–6.

72 On British railway investments in Argentina, see Lewis (1983); on French investments, see Regalsky (1989).

or capital goods, so the ERP increased for some manufacturers.[73] Brazilian treatment of textiles, clothing, and shoes provides clear evidence of a desire to combine high tariffs on competing imports with low tariffs on inputs, so the ERP for many consumer nondurables is estimated to have exceeded 100 percent.[74] In Argentina raw materials for the furniture, metals, and construction-materials industries were subject to much lower tariffs than were competing imports in the same sectors.[75]

Relative prices, however depended not just on the tariff but also on the other variables we have discussed. The fall in foreign-import prices and the decline in international freight rates in the second half of the nineteenth century had been offset to a certain extent by depreciation of the exchange-rate. The rate of depreciation had been particularly marked in the countries on the silver standard after 1873, but those countries on an inconvertible paper standard (e.g., Chile after 1878) also experienced devaluation of the nominal exchange-rate. Although it would be wrong to argue that the change in the nominal value of the currency represented a conscious pursuit of a stable real exchange-rate, there is not much evidence that those countries which were free to vary the parity suffered a serious erosion in international competitiveness.

The only countries that were not free to alter the exchange-rate were those which adopted the gold standard. Under these circumstances a fall in foreign import prices or international freight costs could have serious consequences for the profitability of domestic production competing with imports. Yet the first Latin American countries to adopt the gold standard only did so at the end of the 1890s, by which time foreign-import prices were about to rise. Of course, domestic prices could still rise faster than foreign prices, and gold-standard countries would then be unable to use exchange-rate devaluation as a mechanism for restoring international competitiveness. This does seem to have been a problem for a few republics in the years before 1914 (e.g., Peru),[76] although it could be offset by further tariff increases (e.g., Brazil).[77]

In general the true rate of industrial protection in the Latin American republics was not far below the rate in many other parts of the world. However, the disadvantages faced by Latin American manufacturing were such that protection was almost certainly less than what was required to achieve an industrial performance consistent with the level of real income per head and population size. Indeed, regression analysis shows that in some

73 See Palma (1979), Chapter 2.

74 It should be noted, however, that Brazil imposed high tariffs on certain raw materials, so industries that depended heavily on these inputs may have had effective rates below nominal rates of protection. See Leff (1982), p. 176.

75 See Díaz-Alejandro (1970), p. 290.

76 See Thorp and Bertram (1978), p. 125.

77 See Versiani (1979), pp. 18–23. On the link between coffee prices and industrial tariffs in Brazil, see Abreu and Bevilaqua (2000).

important cases manufacturing net output per head in Latin America (see Table 5.3) was below the level predicted by international comparisons.[78]

The major disappointment was Argentina. The wealthiest country in Latin America, Argentina had a level of manufacturing per head that compared unfavorably with many European countries with lower real incomes per person and with smaller population sizes.[79] The contrast would be even more striking if the contribution to manufacturing of processed primary exports (e.g., beef, lamb, and flour) were deducted. Although Argentina was the most industrialized of all the Latin American countries, its manufacturing sector was still smaller than what one might have expected from international comparisons.[80]

The outstanding weakness of Argentine industrialization was in the textile and clothing sectors. Although food processing, beverages, tobacco products, construction materials, chemicals, and even metals were quite well advanced (and well protected), the textile and clothing sectors were extremely underdeveloped and far behind the levels in Brazil and Mexico. Indeed, most of the industrial gap between Argentina and comparable countries abroad would have disappeared if Argentina had developed its textile industry as far as Brazil had before 1914.[81]

The weakness of Argentine industry was therefore highly specific and not due to some conspiracy on the part of the nation's landowners. Yet it was true

---

78 Using data on thirteen countries (excluding Latin American republics) in Maizels (1963) for which comparable figures can be found, the following equation was obtained for 1913 (using 1955 prices):

$$lnMAN(pc) = -2.57964 + 1.497379 \; lnGDP(pc) + 0.135668 \; lnPOP \quad R^2 = .72,$$
$$\quad\quad\quad\quad\quad\quad (0.290418) \quad\quad\quad\quad (0.16763)$$

where $lnMAN(pc)$ is the logarithm of manufacturing net output per head of population, $lnGDP(pc)$ is the logarithm of real GDP per head, $lnPOP$ is the logarithm of population, and the figures in parentheses are the standard errors of the coefficients. This equation was then used to predict manufacturing net output for the countries in Table 5.3. After making adjustments for the difference between U.S. dollar 1955 and 1970 prices (assumed to have risen by 50 percent) and for the difference between official and purchasing-power parity exchange rates [see Maizels (1963), Table F.2, p. 546], the ratio between the actual and predicted value of manufacturing net output for the five countries was then as follows: Argentina (0.55), Brazil (1.15), Chile (1.29), Colombia (0.68), and Mexico (1.03). This confirms the view that Argentina, given its level of income per head and population size, was relatively underindustrialized.

79 At 1955 dollar prices (using purchasing-power parity exchange rates), manufacturing net output per person in Argentina in 1913 was $70. Sweden, with a smaller population and a lower income per head, recorded a figure of $145; The Netherlands and Norway, with similar GDPs per head and smaller populations, had figures of $105 and $120, respectively. See Maizels (1970), Tables B.2 and B.4.

80 It is surely relevant that Argentina did not hold its first industrial census until 1908 – twenty years after the first national agricultural census – and that it would not take a second until 1937. See Travis (1990).

81 If Argentina had achieved the same value added in textiles as Brazil (see Tables 5.3 and 5.4), it would have increased manufacturing net output per head by nearly 15 percent.

that industry and industrialists failed to acquire the same status as agroexports. Policies were adopted to promote industry, but they were not always consistent. Differential tariffs, for example, were employed in the textile and clothing sectors to push the ERP above the nominal rate of protection, but the difference was far lower than in Brazil or Mexico, and the ERP was nowhere near as high. The tariff on imported cloth was just over 20 percent, following the 1906 tariff law – clearly not a sufficient incentive for domestic producers who enjoyed tariff rates above 50 percent on many classes of foodstuffs and beverages.[82]

Although the rate of protection in Latin America was sufficient to stimulate some domestic production of manufactures in the larger countries, that did not necessarily mean that tariff policy was optimal. The Latin American tariff was deficient in a number of ways that had adverse consequences for growth, distribution, and the allocation of resources. The use of "official" values for imports made the "true" rate of protection difficult to measure, so that – in the absence of frequent revisions – changes in the rate of protection were almost arbitrary and difficult to anticipate. The "passive" nature of protection may have discouraged industrial investment in those republics in which the state was not prepared to give a strong lead. As official values became out of date, the classification of new imports became more and more difficult – an open invitation to importers and corrupt officials alike to allocate commodities to categories with lower tariffs.

The use of official values also meant that Latin American tariffs were in effect specific even when they were described as ad valorem. If a poor-quality article attracted the same rate of duty as a high-quality commodity in the same import category, it encouraged the higher priced "luxury" import over its lower-priced, mass-produced equivalent. In Colombia this system was taken to extremes: Duties were calculated on the weight of imports, providing a strong incentive to import luxury goods. Specific tariffs, on the other hand, encouraged local production of low-quality goods for mass consumption and discouraged domestic production of luxury goods. With the slow growth in real wages before 1913 in most countries and the concentration of income in the upper deciles, the system of specific tariffs may have encouraged an unnecessarily fast growth of imports.

The Latin American tariff had a protectionist element in the larger republics by 1914, but a tax imposed primarily for revenue reasons would never give the same rate of protection as a tax imposed primarily for protectionist purposes. Thus the rate of tariff protection in the United States may have appeared to be the same as in Argentina, but in practice U.S. protection was much higher because the duties were concentrated on those products deemed to need protection from foreign competition. Furthermore, a rate of protection of 20 percent in the United States was qualitatively

---

82 See Díaz-Alejandro (1970), p. 291. See also Cortés Conde (2000).

different from a similar rate in Latin America, because the disadvantages in domestic production that the tariff was designed to overcome were so much higher in the subcontinent.

The revenue function of the tariff stemmed from the absence of politically acceptable alternative sources of government revenue. On the rare occasions when such alternatives were found, the tariff could be used to strengthen its protective role at the expense of collecting revenue. This seems to have been the case in Chile, following the windfall gain in export taxes associated with the rise of nitrate exports after 1880. On the other hand, there was no guarantee that the tariff would be used in this way: We have already seen the example of Peru after 1850, where guano income made possible tariff liberalization and a fall in the rate of protection.[83]

The shift in tariff policy in the last quarter of the nineteenth century in favor of greater protection was not due to the rise of powerful industrial associations. The new industrialists were overwhelmingly immigrants, merchants, or miners; associations were formed in all the more important countries to defend their interests, but their influence could not compare with that of the landowners and agroexporters.[84] However, we have already seen that for the latter tariff revenue was a relatively painless way of financing central government and servicing foreign debt. Because the tariff affected primarily the price of domestic and imported consumer goods, its cost was mainly borne by urban consumers – a social group with no organized strength and little political power.

Here again we may note an intriguing difference between Argentina and the rest of Latin America. Not only was Argentina an immigrant country par excellence, but this immigration was concentrated in urban areas. Italians, Spaniards, and Britons in Buenos Aires looked first to imports to satisfy their consumption requirements and were presumably particularly reluctant to pay high prices as a result of tariffs, for they would have known the "true" cost of the same articles abroad. The concentration of immigrants in Argentine cities, with knowledge of foreign markets, may therefore have been one reason why the textiles and clothing industry was so underdeveloped by 1914.

The five countries of Latin America that had made progress toward industrialization before the First World War (Argentina, Brazil, Chile, Mexico, and Peru) had all achieved a high level of import substitution in consumer goods. In these five countries the share of apparent consumption met by domestic production of consumer goods was between 50 percent and 80 percent. In some commodities domestic production had virtually eliminated imports. Yet when we examine nontraditional exports of consumer goods

83 See p. 109, n. 88.
84 On the first industrial associations in Latin America, see Lewis (1986), pp. 310–19.

(i.e., excluding such commodities as beef and sugar) we find that they are of negligible importance.

The absence of manufactured exports before 1914 is all the more surprising when we take into account the sharp rise in trade in such goods during the First World War (see Chapter 6). Once the competition from European and North American imports was removed, Latin American industrialists were able to export to neighboring countries with considerable success. The failure to compete with exports from other countries in peacetime conditions must therefore have been due to too-high prices, to too-low quality, or to both.

We have already seen that the tariff system in Latin America favored production of low-quality articles of mass consumption. Such commodities, acceptable to low-income consumers in Latin America, may not have been saleable in the more discerning markets of North America and Europe. Yet the problem of high prices was almost certainly much more serious than the problem of quality. Although domestic tariffs could offset some of the advantages enjoyed by foreign manufactures in raw-material, energy, and transport costs, the loss of tariff protection in foreign markets left Latin American industrialists with the advantage only of lower real wages. However, the difference in real wages was usually not sufficient to compensate for differences in productivity.[85]

The most important nontraditional manufactured exports from Latin America before 1914 were flour and Panama hats. Each used a raw material in which Latin American exporters had an advantage over developed countries, and Panama hats relied on family labor (women and children) at costs that more than compensated for any realistic productivity differential. However, just as Argentina had developed its flour industry through a protective tariff on imports from Chile, so other developed countries would do the same, making flour exports increasingly difficult.

Manufactured exports faced other obstacles as well. One reason why unit costs of production were so high in Latin America was the failure to exploit economies of scale and the low levels of capacity utilization.[86] In part, of course, these well-known problems of industrialization in Latin America stemmed from the low level of effective demand, but they were also caused by internal barriers to trade. Provincial governments in Brazil, Mexico, and Colombia were still applying taxes on interstate traffic. These taxes tended to foster regional monopolies, which in turn undermined the chances of full-capacity utilization and exploitation of economies of scale.

---

85 Haber (1989) provides an outstanding account of the problems faced by Mexican exporters of manufactured goods as a result of high prices.

86 The Mexican steel industry, for example, was running at 4 percent of capacity in 1905. This is an extreme figure, but it never rose above 40 percent during the Porfiriato. See Haber (1989), p. 33.

The fact that Latin American producers of consumer goods were not able to export under normal conditions raises the question of whether in some sense tariffs may have been too high. Tariff protection was clearly needed in Latin America, just as it was in Australia, Germany, and the United States, to provide incentives for industrial investment. With domestic competition and learning-by-doing, unit costs should then fall and industry could move into export markets. This classic infant-industry argument had worked in the case of Argentine flour after 1877 but had not operated with much success elsewhere.

Although it might be argued that tariff rates in Brazil, Uruguay, and Venezuela were excessive, they certainly were not in the other republics. The problem of international competitiveness was due much more to the failure of domestic competition to drive prices below the level permitted by tariff protection. Barriers to entry were quite high, and the market – restricted by internal tariffs, high transport costs, and an unequal distribution of income – was small. It was all too easy for a few firms to dominate local markets in the larger republics – not to mention the smaller ones – and unit costs and prices therefore stayed above the level that would have prevailed in a more competitive environment.

Regional differences on the eve of the First World War

By 1914 Latin America had been following a model of export-led growth based on free (unrestricted) trade for nearly a century. Each republic had become more closely integrated into the world markets for commodities, capital, and even labor (through international migration), but regional variations were sharper than they had been at the beginning of the nineteenth century. These differences under export-led growth could arise for two reasons: Republics could differ in the rate at which long-run exports per head expanded; and differences could arise in the rate of transfer of productivity gains in the export sector to the nonexport economy. The result was a wide differential in living standards: Income per head, for example, was nearly five times higher in Argentina than in Brazil (see Figure 5.1.).

The regional differences that arose from the growth of exports have already been examined (see Chapter 3). By 1914 the most successful countries in terms of exports per head were in the Southern Cone (Argentina, Chile, and Uruguay) and in the Caribbean (Cuba and Puerto Rico). Elsewhere, performance had been patchy, with some countries (e.g., Peru) recording such marked export cycles that the long-run rate of growth was undermined and with others (e.g., Mexico) moving into top gear too late to reverse a dismal earlier performance.

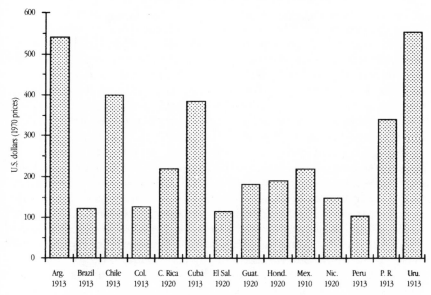

Figure 5.1. GDP per head in 1970 dollars circa 1913. *Source:* See Appendix 3.

The regional differences that arose from the transfer of productivity gains in the export sector to the nonexport economy have been explored in this chapter. Clearly, where the productivity gains in the export sector were negligible, very little existed to transfer to the nonexport economy. The stimulus from the export sector was too weak to promote productivity gains in DUA and manufacturing, and the growth of productivity in other sectors (e.g., commerce) was linked to the fortunes of the export sector itself. On the other hand, a successful export performance did not necessarily guarantee a fast growth of the nonexport economy. The stimulus from exports could simply lead to higher levels of imports, leaving the level of productivity in many branches of the nonexport sector unchanged.

We therefore need to distinguish among three groups of countries. The first contains those republics with high rates of growth of exports (and/or high levels of exports per head) and an increase in productivity in the nonexport sector, the second those with a high rate of growth of exports but little increase in the productivity of the nonexport sector, and the third those in which the growth of exports was modest and in which productivity levels in the nonexport sector remained depressed.

The only countries that can be placed with any certainty in the first group are Argentina and Chile. Not only did they enjoy fast long-run rates of growth of exports (see Chapter 3), they also had some success in transferring the productivity gains in the export sector to the other branches of the economy. If Argentine industrial development and Chilean export diversification left much to be desired, the rise in living standards had been noticeable and was frequently commented on by foreigners. A case can be made for including Uruguay in this group: Despite its modest export growth, the nonexport economy performed well and the estimated real GDP per head (see Figure 5.1.) was as high in Uruguay as it was in Argentina. The three countries of the Southern Cone therefore represent Latin America's success stories before the First World War.

Although the long-run performance of these three republics may have compared favorably with the rest of Latin America, their achievement was only relative. By international standards the performance was not so outstanding. Exports per head in 1913, even in Argentina, were below the levels recorded in Australia, Canada, New Zealand, Sweden, and Norway, and the gap in manufacturing net output per head was even greater. Although it is true that Argentina could claim to have the tenth highest level of real income per head in the world in 1913 (see Maddison, 2001, pp. 185 and 195) this was due more to the depressed level of living standards in many Northern Hemisphere countries that was caused by a huge peasant sector with very low levels of productivity. France, for example, had a real income per head just below Argentina's in 1913 (despite the fact that it was a much more industrialized country) because a very high proportion of its labor force was still occupied in low-productivity peasant activities. When comparisons are made with other countries of "recent settlement" – in which the peasantry was not important either – the Argentine level of real income per head looks less impressive. Indeed, the Argentine figure was well below the level recorded in Australia, Canada, and New Zealand in 1913.[87]

The second group of countries comprises Cuba and Puerto Rico. The growth of exports per head, though quite rapid, did not lead to the transformation of the nonexport economy. Real income per head in Cuba in 1913 was only 70 percent of the level in Argentina, despite the fact that Cuba had the highest level of exports per head in Latin America. Although Cuba's real GDP per person was similar to Chile's (see Figure 5.1.), Cuba had not developed a modern manufacturing sector, DUA had declined in importance, and the economy remained hopelessly dependent on sugar.[88] Puerto Rico had a relatively low level of real income per head despite the fact that its exports per head were among the highest in Latin America. Like

---

87 Using purchasing-power parity exchange rates at 1990 prices, Maddison (2001) estimates GDP per head in Argentina at $3797. The comparable figures for Australia, Canada, and New Zealand are $5715, $4447, and $5152 respectively.

88 The ratio of sugar exports to GDP in 1913 was nearly 40 percent, which made the economy extremely vulnerable to world sugar policy and fluctuations in sugar prices. See Alienes (1950).

Cuba, modern manufacturing had not yet emerged in Puerto Rico, and nonexport agriculture had been undermined by the expansion of coffee and sugar.

The countries in this second group were small economies, so it would be tempting to argue that the weak stimulus from the rapid growth of the export sector was a consequence of economic size. Uruguay was economically small, too, yet it had managed to transfer some of the productivity gains from the export sector to the nonexport economy. The disappointing performance of the second group cannot therefore be attributed entirely to economic size. The strong foreign presence in the export sector of both countries was a more important factor, which led to much of the productivity gain being transferred abroad. The semicolonial character of Cuba and Puerto Rico after 1898 – not forgetting their colonial status before then – inhibited the adoption of fiscal, monetary, and exchange-rate policies conducive to the development of the nonexport economy.[89]

The third group contains all the other republics. The long-run rate of growth of exports per head had been very disappointing, and the level of exports per head in 1913 was low. Not surprisingly, real income per head was depressed (see Figure 5.1.). Some of these countries, however, had improved their performance significantly in the last few decades before the First World War. Mexico (during the Porfiriato) and Peru (after the War of the Pacific) recorded rates of growth of exports per head that raised productivity and stimulated investment and growth in the manufacturing sector. The failure of export-led growth in these two countries was therefore a reflection, above all, of their inability to produce a consistent export performance in the first sixty years after independence. This inability was due in part to the commodity lottery (e.g., the rise and fall of guano in Peru) and in part to the social and political disruptions associated with the formation of nation-states (e.g., Mexico).

Even if we exclude Mexico and Peru from the third group, it is still the largest. Fourteen republics (thirteen if we exclude the special case of Panama) neither managed to record a satisfactory long-run rate of growth of exports per head nor displayed much evidence of dynamism in the last few decades before the First World War. This group includes medium-sized countries (e.g., Colombia and Venezuela) as well as small countries (e.g., El Salvador), mineral exporters (e.g., Bolivia) as well as agricultural exporters (e.g., Guatemala), and semicolonies (e.g., the Dominican Republic) as well as staunchly independent republics (e.g., Paraguay). It also includes Brazil, where – despite the rise of modern manufacturing – both exports and real GDP per head were low in 1913.

---

89 The restrictions in the case of Puerto Rico are well described in Carroll (1975), pp. 385–94.

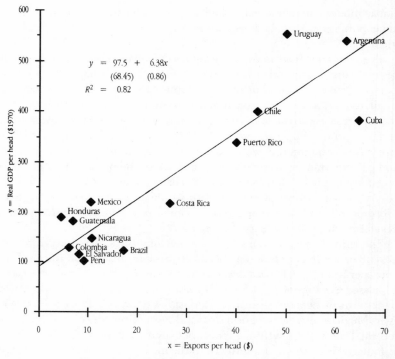

Figure 5.2. Real GDP and exports per head, circa 1913. *Source:* See Tables A.1.1, A.1.2, and A.3.2.

The fact that the countries with low exports per head tended to have low real income per head invites a statistical comparison. The relationship between exports and real income per head almost a century after independence is plotted in Figure 5.2. The line of best fit, using simple regression analysis, is also shown in the figure (with the standard error of the coefficients in brackets). Points above the line refer to countries (e.g., Uruguay) whose real GDP per head is higher than predicted by export performance. Points below the line refer to countries (e.g., Cuba) with below predicted income per head.

The results of the simple regression analysis indicate that variations in exports per head "explain" 82 percent of the variation in real GDP per head. Despite all the known deficiencies of the data (see Appendixes 1 and 3), it is difficult to deny that export performance was an important determinant of the standard of living in Latin America before the First World War. Countries could "underperform" (e.g., Cuba) or "overperform" (e.g., Uruguay) as a result of the many factors not taken into consideration by simple regression analysis, but the significant correlation between the two variables is clear.

The fact that the export-led model had yielded such modest results in many republics has led some scholars to question the wisdom of export-led growth itself. Yet it is difficult to escape the conclusion that any model adopted by the thirteen countries in the third group would have shown a poor rate of return. Political instability, administrative incompetence, poor transport systems, lack of capital, shortages of labor, and the small sizes of internal markets would have overwhelmed any conceivable alternative to export-led growth in the nineteenth century.

Other republics had faced the same problems, but the sustained growth of the export sector had partially resolved them. Indeed, the progress toward solving these problems in the third group of countries tended to be linked to the evolution of the export sector. The railway and banking systems, however rudimentary, were a consequence of the development of the export sector, and only export growth could pay for the imports on which tariffs – the bedrock of government revenue – were collected.

The basic problem among the "failures" was therefore the slow rate of growth of exports per head. Because the world market in primary products was subject to fewer restrictions before the First World War – particularly after 1850 – than at any other time in history, the blame for failure must be put firmly on the supply side (see Chapter 4). The price of failure was high, however. Not only were the inhabitants of the republics in the third group condemned to low levels of real income per head, but the window of opportunity provided for primary products was beginning to close. Already, even before 1914, protection for agriculture had raised its ugly head in continental Europe, and in Great Britain an influential section of the Conservative Party, led by Joseph Chamberlain, had nailed its colors to the mast of imperial preference. In the United States domestic competition was yielding to the formation of trusts and cartels, with a diminution in the bargaining power of producers (including Latin American exporters) selling raw materials. By the 1920s the climate for export-led growth was less favorable, and the odds on success in the commodity lottery were beginning to lengthen.

6

The First World War and its aftermath

When war broke out in Europe on 2 August 1914, it was not just the international balance of power that was shattered; the global trade and payments system, which had slowly evolved since the end of the Napoleonic wars, was also thrown into disarray. With the signing of the armistice in 1919, a brave face was put on attempts to reconstruct the prewar system. The old international economic order had perished, however, and the new one was dangerously unstable. This instability was scarcely perceived at the time, leaving peripheral regions, such as Latin America, extremely vulnerable to the collapse of international trade and capital flows at the end of the 1920s.

The main feature of the old order had been the existence of relatively unrestricted international trade – a reflection of the interests of the dominant economic power (Great Britain) in the nineteenth century; the limited restrictions in force generally took the form of tariffs, which had the advantage for all concerned of being transparent. Both capital and labor were free to move across international boundaries, and passports were the exception rather than the rule. The gold standard, adopted first by Great Britain, had spread to all the main industrial countries by the end of the century and provided a well-established mechanism for balance-of-payments adjustment. Internal equilibrium (full employment and zero inflation) was regarded as less important than external equilibrium, so the burden of adjustment to adverse shocks was usually achieved through price deflation and underemployment.

Latin American countries had slotted into this scheme relatively easily on the basis of primary-product exports, capital inflows, and – in Argentina, Brazil, and Uruguay, in particular – international migration. Balance-of-payments adjustment was never smooth, and capital flows were usually procyclical, falling at just the moment when they were most needed, but these disruptions with rare exceptions (e.g., the Baring crisis) had little impact on the dynamics of world economic growth. Internal adjustment was cushioned by the existence of a large nonexport agricultural sector with low productivity, to which many workers could withdraw in the event of a fall in the demand for labor.

The collapse of the old order

At the apex of the prewar international economic system stood Great Britain. Although its dominant position in manufactured exports and its leadership in science and technology were threatened by the end of the nineteenth century, Great Britain was still the financial powerhouse of the world, a source of capital for the periphery and a major importer of primary products. British financial preeminence underwrote the rules of the international system, and its navy stood ready to block all attempts at restricting the freedom of trade and capital movements.

The first casualties of the Great War were the gold standard and the movement of capital. Currency convertibility was suspended by the belligerent countries, new capital issues were canceled, and old loans were recalled to shore up the balance sheet of financial insitutions in Europe. Latin American republics such as Argentina and Brazil, which depended heavily on the European market for balance-of-payments finance, were particularly badly hit, as European-owned banks called in loans and provoked a domestic financial crisis. New long-term public loans to Brazil, for example, which had reached $19.1 million in 1913, fell to $4.2 million in 1914 and to zero in 1915, and in the last quarter of 1914 the money supply shrank to the level that had been recorded in the third quarter of 1910.[1]

The hostilities in Europe also brought to an end the inflows of direct foreign investment (DFI) from the Old World. The United States, neutral in the Great War until 1917, sharply increased its DFI in Latin America, particularly in the extraction of strategic raw materials, but was not in a position to increase portfolio lending until the 1920s. U.S. banks, however, prevented until 1914 by law from investing in foreign subsidiaries, began to set up branch operations in Latin America. By 1919 National City Bank, the first U.S. multinational bank, had forty-two branches in nine Latin American republics.[2]

The upheavals in the capital market were mirrored in the disruption of commodity markets, but here the short-run impact was different from the long-run effect. Shortages of shipping at the start of war, coupled with the absence of trade credit, disrupted normal supplies, but demand fell even

---

1 See Fritsch (1988), Tables A.11 and A.16.
2 See Stallings (1987), p. 66. For an excellent study of foreign investment in Latin America throughout the twentieth century, see Twomey (2000). On U.S. Direct Foreign Investment, see O'Brien (1996).

faster and drove down prices in many markets. The fall in short-run export earnings, together with the decline in new capital inflows, reduced the demand for imports (the supply of which was in any case also disrupted by shipping shortages). The fall in imports was so sharp that Latin America as a whole was estimated to be running a current-account surplus by 1915,[3] but this rapid short-run adjustment to external disequilibrium brought a big decline in real government income – dependent as it was on import tariffs. In Chile, for example, government revenue fell by nearly two-thirds between 1911 and 1915.[4]

The short-run impact of commodity-market disruption was soon overwhelmed by the shift toward a war economy in the main industrial countries. The demand for strategic raw materials (e.g., copper and petroleum) soared, and shipping space was made available by the allied powers. The export of oil from Venezuela began for the first time with foreign companies leading the search for deposits.[5] The prices of strategic materials rose sharply, and countries that were exporting a high proportion of strategic materials (e.g., Mexico with its oil, Peru with its copper, Bolivia with its tin, and Chile with its nitrates) even enjoyed an improvement in the net barter terms of trade (NBTT) despite the rise in import prices. However, although the capacity to import rose sharply, the volume of imports remained restricted in many cases. The consequent rise in import prices, coupled with trade surpluses[6] and budget deficits, provoked domestic inflation. The impact of this inflation on urban real wages was a contributory factor in the political upheavals in a number of Latin American countries during and immediately after the First World War.[7]

Countries that exported nonstrategic raw materials (e.g., coffee) were not so favored. Prices rose, but the terms of trade deteriorated, and shipping remained a serious constraint on the volume of exports. Brazil, heavily dependent on the export of coffee, was unable to sustain its first coffee-valorization scheme and saw its barter terms of trade fall by 50 percent between 1914 and 1918, even though the quantum of exports was unchanged.[8] Small countries in Central America and the Caribbean were

3 See Stallings (1987), p. 174.

4 See Sunkel (1982), Table 6, p. 125. See also Palma (2000b).

5 The legal framework for extracting minerals in Venezuela had been overhauled by Juan Vicente Gómez at the beginning of his long dictatorship (1908–35), and foreign companies were quick to exploit the new opportunities. See McBeth (1983), Chapter 2.

6 A trade surplus, if it raised international reserves, would normally lead to an increase in the money supply (money of external origin) and would provoke inflationary pressures. This monetization of reserve movements is discussed in more detail in note 58.

7 See Albert (1988), Chapter 6, for an excellent account of these social upheavals in Argentina, Brazil, Chile, and Peru.

8 See Albert (1988), pp. 56–7.

protected to some extent by their proximity to the United States, although banana exports suffered badly from a shortage of shipping until the end of the war.[9]

The outbreak of hostilities in Europe did not lead to the total loss of traditional markets. Great Britain remained heavily dependent on food imports (e.g., meat and sugar), and strenuous efforts were made to maintain supplies of Latin American exports. However, almost equally strenuous efforts were made by the allied powers to prevent German access to Latin American raw materials. Although the major countries in the region (except Brazil) were neutral throughout the war, trade with Germany became increasingly difficult, and both the United States and Great Britain employed a blacklist of firms in Latin America that they believed to be under the control of German nationals. The result was a sharp squeeze on the share of Latin American exports and imports accounted for by Germany.[10]

The principal beneficiary of this squeeze was the United States (see Table 6.1). During the war the United States, already the main supplier for Mexico, Central America, and the Caribbean, became the most important market for most Latin American countries, and its share of imports reached 25 percent in South America and nearly 80 percent in the Caribbean Basin (including Mexico). The fortuitous timing of the opening of the Panama Canal at the beginning of the war, when transatlantic trade was becoming dangerous and difficult, allowed exports from the United States to penetrate markets in South America that had previously been supplied from Europe in general and Germany in particular. The network of U.S. branch banks that followed this trade, coupled with an aggressive diplomatic effort in support of U.S. business,[11] ensured that the outbreak of peace would still leave the United States in a hegemonic position in the northern republics and a strong position elsewhere.

The eclipse of Germany as a trading partner not only contributed to the rise in importance of the United States but also softened the decline in importance of Great Britain. British dominance was retained only in trade with Argentina, but this was still by far the largest market in Latin America, and Argentina remained the region's most important exporter. However, Argentine exports to Great Britain substantially exceeded its imports from the same source, and this trade surplus was roughly matched by a trade deficit with the United States. This triangularity of foreign trade – observed in reverse in the case of Brazil – could only work in a world system of convertible currencies and multilateral payments, so the external trade

9 See Karnes (1978), Chapter 4.
10 For a case study of how Germany was squeezed out by the United States in Central America, see Schoonover (1998), Chapter 9.
11 See Tulchin (1971), Chapter 1.

Table 6.1. *External trade between Latin America and the United States,*
circa 1913, 1918, and 1929 (in percentages of totals)

Country	Exports to the United States			Imports from the United States		
	circa 1913	1918	1929	circa 1913	1918	1929
Latin America	**29.7**	**45.4**	**34.0**	**24.5**	**41.8**	**38.6**
Mexico, Central America, and Panama	67.2	83.5	57.4	53.5	78.1	65.7
Cuba, Dominican Republic, and Haiti	73.9	66.1	68.9	55.2	76.8	59.6
South America	16.7	34.9	25.1	16.9	25.9	31.4
Argentina	4.7	29.3	8.3	14.7	21.6	23.2
Brazil	32.2	34.0	45.5	15.7	22.7	26.7
Chile	21.3	56.8	33.1	16.7	41.5	30.8
Peru	33.2	35.1	28.8	28.8	46.8	41.4
Uruguay	4.0	25.9	10.7	12.7	13.2	30.2
Venezuela	28.3	60.0	26.5	32.8	46.7	57.5

Sources: Pan-American Union (1952); Wilkie (1974); individual country data for circa 1913 taken from Tables 3.6 and 3.7.

of the major Latin American republics became vulnerable in the 1920s to any departure from gold-standard orthodoxy.[12]

The restoration of the gold standard was indeed a priority after the Treaty of Versailles,[13] but it took some years to achieve and – in the case of Great Britain – involved great hardship as a result of the adoption of an over-valued parity for the pound sterling.[14] The slow growth of the British economy in the 1920s[15] was a blow for those Latin American countries that had traditionally looked to Great Britain as a market for exports, and the emergence of the United States as the dominant economic power was little consolation for those republics that were selling goods in competition

12 The triangularity of foreign trade has been studied in a number of articles. See, for example, Fodor and O'Connell (1973).

13 The Treaty of Versailles, signed in 1919, imposed massive war reparations on Germany. Subsequent international conferences were concerned with the reestablishment of a multilateral payments system under the gold standard.

14 The decision by Great Britain in 1925 to return to the gold standard at the prewar parity of £1 equals U.S. $4.86 is now widely recognized to have been a serious error. See Kindleberger (1987), pp. 28–32.

15 See Broadberry (1986), Chapter 2.

with U.S. farmers.[16] Between 1913 and 1929 U.S. trade with Latin America rose far more rapidly that did British trade, but U.S. exports to the region outpaced imports from the region by a considerable margin.[17] Thus Latin America, which had run a substantial trade surplus with the United States before and during the war, was in the reverse position by the end of the 1920s. Exports to the United States in 1929 represented 34 percent of all exports, and U.S. suppliers took nearly 40 percent of all imports (see Table 6.1).

The surplus enjoyed by the United States in its commodity and service trade with Latin America reflected its emergence as a capital exporter. After the war New York replaced London as the leading international financial center, and Latin American republics increasingly turned to the United States for the issue of bonds, public-sector loans, and direct foreign investment. At first supported by U.S. government efforts in favor of dollar diplomacy,[18] the flow of capital soon acquired a momentum of its own: Foreign investment (direct and indirect) poured into Latin America (see Table 6.2), and the proportion of the stock controlled by U.S. investors steadily rose at the expense of European countries. Great Britain and France continued to invest in parts of Latin America, but the new investments were modest and commensurate with the weak balance-of-payments position of the two countries.[19]

The emergence of the United States in the 1920s as a major source of foreign capital was a mixed blessing for Latin America. The appearance of dynamic new capital markets in the Western Hemisphere was clearly of great importance in view of the shrinking capital surplus available from traditional European markets, but the new borrowing was only achieved at a price. In the smaller republics the new lending was intertwined with U.S. foreign-policy objectives, and many countries found themselves obliged to submit to U.S. control of the customs house or even national railways to ensure prompt debt payment.[20] In some of the larger republics the new lending reached such epidemic proportions that it became known as "the

16 The emergence of the United States as a global economic power of the first rank led to no reduction in its protectionist tendencies. Exporters of temperate products from Latin America (e.g., beef) were particularly at risk from new restrictions imposed in the 1920s.

17 Between 1913 and 1929 U.S. imports from Latin America rose by 110.6 percent, while Latin American imports from the United States rose by 161.2 percent. The British figures were 45.5 percent and 34.5 percent, respectively. See Cardoso and Brignoli (1979b), Chapter 5.

18 Dollar diplomacy, coupled with European financial weakness, had vastly increased U.S. financial penetration in many parts of Latin America by the mid-1920s. See Tulchin (1971), Chapter 5.

19 Both France and Great Britain had been forced to disinvest to help pay for the war, and it was some time before normal capital outflows could be restored. German capital outflows were crippled by the need to meet reparation payments. See Kindleberger (1987), Chapter 2.

20 For an excellent survey of many of these U.S. interventions, see Munro (1964).

Table 6.2. *U.S. investments in Latin America, 1914 and 1929*

Region and sector	Direct		Portfolio		Total	
	1914	1929	1914	1929	1914	1929
Latin America (in millions of US$)	1,275.8	3,645.8	365.6	1,723.9	1,641.4	5,369.7
	By region (in percentages)					
Mexico, Central America, and Panama	53.0	26.3	73.8	17.5	57.7	23.5
Cuba, Dominican Republic, and Haiti	21.5	26.5	15.0	7.4	20.0	20.4
South America	25.5	47.2	11.2	75.1	22.3	56.1
	By sector (in percentages)					
Agriculture	18.7	24.1				
Mining and smelting	43.3	22.0				
Oil	10.2	20.1				
Railroads	13.8	6.3				
Public utilities	7.7	15.8				
Manufacturing	2.9	6.3				
Trade	2.6	3.3				
Other	0.8	2.2				

Source: ECLA (1965).

dance of the millions."[21] Little effort was made to ensure that the funds were invested productively in projects that could guarantee repayment in foreign exchange,[22] and the scale of corruption in a few cases reached pharaonic proportions. U.S. officials might occupy the customs house in pursuit of fiscal rectitude, but they had little or no control over U.S. bankers issuing bonds to cover widening public-sector deficits.

The changing international balance of power and the shifts in the international capital market were not the only problems in the 1920s with which Latin America had to grapple. Even more serious were changes in

21 This famous phrase was allegedly coined by two Colombians, Laureano Gómez and Alfonso López Pumarejo, who were highly critical of the loan bonanza. See Banco de la República (1990), p. 219.
22 Although only 4.7 percent of the value of all U.S. loans to Latin America in the 1920s were stated as "purpose unknown," no less than 50.3 percent were for "refinancing" and 12.1 percent for "general purpose." See Stallings (1987), Table 10, p. 131.

commodity markets and the increase in commodity price and earnings instability. The unstable conditions during and after the war led to sudden shifts in demand curves that could play havoc with commodity prices. The world recession in 1920–1 was a case in point. Prices for many commodities (notably sugar) collapsed as stocks held for strategic purposes were unwound.[23] The abolition of wartime price controls, enforced by civil servants with draconian powers in the major countries, led to an initial price surge, a dynamic supply response, and a subsequent price collapse in many markets.[24]

The 1920–1 world depression was short lived, but the problem of commodity oversupply was to last much longer. Although the long-run growth of demand for primary-product exports in the center was slowing down – as a result of demographic change,[25] Engel's law,[26] and the creation of synthetic substitutes[27] – the long-run rate of growth of supply was speeding up as a result of technological progress, new investments in social infrastructure (including transport), and the protection of agriculture in many parts of Europe.

These demand and supply shifts produced changes in long-run equilibrium prices that should have acted as signals for a change in resource allocation in Latin America. For many countries the NBTT deteriorated between 1913 and 1929. A number of factors distorted the information provided by price signals, however, and the uncertainty created by war and its aftermath made it difficult for private entrepreneurs and public-sector officials in Latin America to draw appropriate conclusions. As a result Latin America not only failed to adjust its external sector to the new international conditions in the 1920s but even increased its dependence on primary-product exports quite markedly.

The first problem was the short-run instability of commodity prices, which concealed long-run trends. This had been a problem for Latin

---

23 World coffee stocks – 11.77 million bags at the end of 1917 – had fallen to 5.33 million by the end of 1922. See Fritsch (1988), Table A.6.

24 U.S. wholesale prices (1913 = 100) had reached 188 by 1918. They then jumped to 221 in 1920 before falling to 143 in 1921 and to 130 in 1922. See League of Nations (1928), Table 102. A similar pattern was observed in France and Great Britain, whereas in Germany prices continued to rise after 1920 as hyperinflation was unleashed.

25 By the 1920s the crude birth rate (live births per thousand population) had fallen to around 20 in the main countries of the center and the death rate to between 12 and 17. This implied a considerable reduction in the natural rate of population increase compared with the prewar period.

26 Engel's law stated an inverse relationship between household income and the proportion of income spent on foodstuffs. Although its impact on primary-product exports could be ignored in the short run, its long-term impact was bound to be considerable if real incomes were rising.

27 The world chemical industry made giant strides in the 1920s, with new discoveries making substitutes possible for such natural materials as cotton, rubber, forest dyes, timber, and nitrates.

American primary-product exporters before the war, but it was much greater in the 1920s. In Chile export-price instability was double what it had been before 1914, and export-value instability was nearly five times higher.[28] Even in Argentina, with its much more diversified exports, export instability was greater in the 1920s than at any other time in the republic's history.[29]

The second problem was the continuation of "strategic" demand for minerals for a number of years after the war. The need to control supplies of oil, copper, tin, and so forth led to official encouragement of U.S. firms to invest heavily in Latin America. With European powers doing the same in colonies and dominions, the danger of world oversupply of certain minerals was real. Furthermore, as these new investments came on stream in the second half of the 1920s, strategic demand had in many cases abated, and stocks began to increase. When world interest rates rose in the wake of the stock-market boom in 1928, the costs of holding stock rose sharply and discouraged additional purchases.

The third problem was the manipulation of prices in a number of key markets. The Brazilian coffee-valorization scheme, revived in the 1920s, reduced Brazilian supplies reaching the world market and raised prices. However, other coffee exporters (e.g., Colombia) responded to higher world prices by increasing plantings. This increased production hit the market a few years later, and the coffee market was saturated as early as 1926. Brazil attempted to repeat the experiment with rubber, but its share of the world market was too small to have a significant impact on prices.

The final problem was the weakness of the nonexport sector in so many Latin American countries. The idea that resources would shift smoothly out of primary-product exports in response to falling long-run equilibrium prices assumed not only that the long-run prices were observable but also that the resources could find alternative employment. In those republics in which industrialization had made a promising beginning (see pp. 127–36), this was a legitimate assumption. However, most of the Latin American republics had taken only a modest step toward industrialization by the 1920s, so only a massive drop in the long-run equilibrium price – such as that which occurred in the 1929 Depression – was likely to induce the required shift in resources. Small declines in the long-run equilibrium price – even if they were observable – could always be offset by exchange-rate depreciation, export tax reductions, or more favorable credit terms. Indeed, as shown in Chapter 7, some of the smaller republics were prepared to resort to such policies even in the 1930s rather than promote a wholesale shift of resources from the export sector.

---

28 See Palma (2000a), Table 3.1, p. 47.
29 See O'Connell (2000), p. 213, note 3. See also Cortés Conde (2000).

Trade strategies

The difficulties facing primary-product exports in the period after 1913 were intense even before the collapse of prices at the end of the 1920s. In addition to the upheavals associated with the First World War, Latin American exporters experienced a particularly sharp decline in prices in the 1920–1 depression as the world economy adjusted to peacetime conditions. Prices and volumes recovered in the next few years, but over the whole period from 1913 to 1929 only a few countries enjoyed an increase in their NBTT.[30]

The main problem was the slow growth of world trade. In the sixteen years after 1913, the growth in the dollar value of world exports barely exceeded 3 percent a year.[31] The modest nature of this increase is underlined by the fact that much of it consisted of a rise in prices. Indeed, the increase in the volume of world trade was little more than 1 percent per year.[32] This was an insufficient stimulus under normal conditions for those countries that were following export-led growth. Furthermore, world trade in many commodities was growing more slowly than world production. This discrepancy – a sure sign of import substitution in agriculture in a number of countries – reflected the growth of agricultural protection in Europe and North America and adversely affected world exports of rye, barley, linseed, cotton, and wool.

The slow growth of aggregate world trade did not mean that world demand for all commodities was growing slowly. However, of the twenty-two commodities that dominated the exports of Latin America at the time (see Table 6.3), only three (oil, cacao, and rubber) recorded annual rates of increase in world volume terms above 5 percent a year between 1913 and 1928, and fifteen had rates of increase below 3 percent a year. Indeed, for six commodities of importance to Latin America (silver, gold, rye, barley, cotton, and wool), world production or exports in volume terms did not increase by more than 1 percent a year.

Faced with such difficult world trading conditions, Latin American republics had to choose from a number of different trade strategies. The first

30 The impact of the 1920–1 depression on the NBTT of primary producers is examined in detail in Cuddington and Urzúa (1989) and in Powell (1991). Even when the terms of trade are adjusted for growth in the volume of exports to give their real purchasing power, only five Latin American countries (Colombia, Honduras, Mexico, Peru, and Venezuela) experienced fast growth (more than 5 percent per year). See Thorp (1986), Table 5, p. 68.

31 Sources differ on the dollar value of world trade in 1913. These differences place the range of values for annual growth from 1913 to 1929 at between 3.1 percent and 3.7 percent.

32 At 1913 prices, total exports from the industrial countries have been estimated at $11,101 million in 1913 and $13,916 million in 1929 – an average annual rate of growth of 1.4 percent. See Maizels (1970), Table A.2. A similar rate of growth has been estimated for the volume of world primary-product exports over the same period. See Maizels (1970), Table 4.1, p. 80.

Table 6.3. *Commodity world market shares by region, 1913 and 1928 (in percentages)*

Commodity	World rate of growth[a]	Latin America		Europe[b]		United States and Canada		Asia		Africa		Oceania	
		1913	1928	1913	1928	1913	1928	1913	1928	1913	1928	1913	1928
Minerals[c]													
Petroleum	8.5	7.2	15.9	22.1	9.1	64.5	67.4	6.0	6.8	0	0.1	0	0
Copper	3.7	9.3	21.3	18.6	9.2	60.6	58.0	6.5	4.1	0.8	6.8	4.3	0.7
Tin	1.8	19.9	23.0	4.2	2.0	0	0	65.3	66.9	4.8	6.4	5.8	1.6
Silver	1.0	38.2	54.0	7.3	4.6	43.6	31.0	2.4	5.7	0.5	0.8	8.0	3.9
Gold	-1.6	16.5	6.2	6.1	0.8	20.6	21.9	5.9	6.5	40.5	61.2	10.4	3.4
Lead	2.6	4.8	13.5	46.8	22.7	36.6	48.1	2.0	5.1	0	1.6	9.7	9.0
Nitrates	1.9	97.4	81.2	2.6	18.8	0	0	0	0	0	0	0	0
Others[d]													
Wheat	1.5	14.7	25.6	48.4	4.4	20.3	59.0	8.6	1.4	1.1	2.1	6.8	7.5
Wheat flour	2.6	5.7	5.4	28.4	17.2	51.6	56.1	4.9	7.5	1.1	0.7	6.2	12.0
Rye	-2.1	0.4	12.2	98.5	44.4	0.9	43.1	0.3	0.2	0	0.1	0	0
Barley	-2.8	0.8	7.2	83.4	21.4	4.7	48.1	7.0	7.5	4.1	15.2	0	0.6
Maize	1.9	42.8	70.8	36.8	7.6	16.0	7.3	2.3	4.4	2.1	9.9	0	0.1
Bananas	4.4	49.2	65.5	12.1	7.0	0	0	0.5	4.2	0	0.4	0.3	0.2
Sugar	3.7	29.2	40.0	30.6	14.0	0.6	1.0	23.7	30.1	3.6	3.2	7.3	8.4
Cacao	5.1	41.5	23.0	10.1	2.6	0	0	2.3	0.9	31.3	61.4	0.3	0.5
Coffee	1.2	82.0	83.7	10.5	2.1	1.6	0.3	4.0	9.1	1.0	3.7	0.2	0.2
Linseed	1.0	42.4	86.8	22.7	1.8	11.3	3.2	23.0	7.5	0.6	0.6	0	0
Cotton	0.1	1.2	3.0	10.2	4.0	61.4	57.4	16.9	22.4	10.1	11.6	0	0.1
Rubber	13.5	33.8	2.5	39.3	13.9	0	1.0	12.9	78.5	12.2	0.8	0	0.1
Cattle	1.0	30.4	19.1	36.6	57.7	13.8	3.2	13.1	6.1	5.3	7.4	0.6	0.3
Wool	0	20.3	18.0	33.1	22.6	0.1	0.4	4.7	7.2	7.4	13.5	34.1	38.1
Beef	3.7	64.0	72.8	12.4	9.4	0.2	2.9	2.0	1.3	0.2	1.8	15.3	11.8

[a] Annual volume rate of growth between 1913 and 1928.
[b] Includes the Soviet Union.
[c] Statistics refer to world production.
[d] Statistics refer to world exports.
Sources: League of Nations, *Statistical Yearbook* and *International Yearbook of Agricultural Statistics*.

option was to rely on the commodity lottery. If the country's leading export was one of those facing fast growth of world demand, the value of exports would still rise rapidly provided that market share did not decline. Yet Latin America suffered a severe loss of market share in cacao and rubber, two of the three commodities that enjoyed rapid growth (see Table 6.3). Wild-rubber exports from Brazil and Bolivia collapsed in the face of exports of plantation rubber from the Far East; Brazil, Ecuador, Venezuela, the Dominican Republic, and Haiti all lost market share to numerous European African colonies in which exports of cacao were vigorously promoted. Only in the case of oil did the commodity lottery favor Latin America: The principal beneficiary was Venezuela, where oil had begun to be exported in the First World War, although Colombia, Ecuador, Peru, and Argentina all reaped a modest harvest as well.[33]

The second option was to increase market share in commodities for which world demand was growing modestly. For many decades Latin American governments had been honing the tools at their disposal for promotion of primary-product exports, so this strategy was by no means impossible. Domestic prices and rates of return on capital for products traded in world markets could be altered through changes in exchange rates, export taxes, import tariffs, and so forth, so a deterioration in the external (net barter) terms of trade did not necessarily imply a fall in the internal (rural–urban) terms of trade or in the profitability of exports.[34]

In the period under consideration, among the main products of particular importance to Latin America we can identify sixty-one cases in which commodity exports changed their share of the world total by more than 0.5 percent of the world total between the beginning (1913) and end (1928) of the period. In forty-one of these cases (more than two-thirds), market share increased (see Table 6.4). If cacao is excluded, market share increased in nearly three-quarters of all cases. This trade strategy was therefore a popular option. Indeed, in only four countries (Brazil, Ecuador, Haiti, and Paraguay) did market share fail to increase in at least one case.

The market-share strategy affected all kinds of primary products. Despite the rise in agricultural protection in the Northern Hemisphere, Argentina managed to increase market share in eight cases (see Table 6.4). The British meat market remained open to imports and was sufficiently dynamic to compensate for the restrictions imposed on the meat trade in other markets. European protection did not yet extend to maize, and Argentina increased

---

33 Production and export of Mexican oil, however, declined in the 1920s, with unit costs of production far in excess of those in Venezuela.

34 The internal terms of trade, often measured by the domestic price of agricultural commodities relative to that of manufactured goods, is only a rough guide to intersectoral resource allocation. The rate of return on capital in different sectors is a superior measure, but evidence for Latin America in this period is not available in a systematic form.

Table 6.4. *Changes in commodity world market shares by country, 1913–1928*

Country	Increase in share[a]	Decrease in share[b]
Argentina	Wheat, rye, barley, maize, linseed, beef, oil, cotton	Cattle, wool
Bolivia	Tin, silver	Rubber
Brazil		Coffee, rubber, cacao
Chile	Copper, wool	Nitrates
Colombia	Oil, bananas, coffee	
Costa Rica	Cacao, coffee	Bananas
Cuba	Sugar	Cacao
Dominican Republic	Sugar	Cacao
Ecuador		Cacao
El Salvador	Coffee	
Guatemala	Coffee, bananas	
Haiti		Cacao
Honduras	Bananas	
Mexico	Silver, lead, bananas, coffee, cotton	Oil, cattle
Nicaragua	Bananas, coffee	
Panama	Bananas, cacao	
Paraguay		
Peru	Copper, silver, oil, sugar, cotton	
Puerto Rico	Sugar	Coffee
Uruguay	Linseed, wheat	Cattle, wool
Venezuela	Oil	Gold, cacao, coffee
Totals	41	20

[a] Small increases (less than 0.5 percent) have been ignored.
[b] Small decreases (less than 0.5 percent) have been ignored.
Sources: League of Nations, *Statistical Yearbook* and *International Yearbook of Agricultural Statistics.*

its share of world exports from around 40 percent before the First World War to 70 percent in 1928. Even more remarkable were the gains recorded by Argentina in wheat, rye, barley, and linseed – all commodities receiving protection in a number of Northern Hemisphere countries. In the case of linseed, Argentina had doubled market share to more than 80 percent of world exports by the end of the 1920s.

The market-share strategy also affected minerals. Their strategic nature had led to a feverish search by foreign and domestic companies in Latin America for new deposits of oil, copper, lead, and tin. Venezuela led the way in oil, with British and U.S. investments encouraged by the generous contracts allowed by the dictatorial government of Juan Vicente Gómez; by 1928 Venezuela had captured nearly 10 percent of the world market despite the fact that oil exports were nonexistent as late as 1913. Colombia and Peru, under the stimulus of U.S. investment, also gained market share in oil exports, and a small beginning was made by Ecuador and Argentina. In Argentina, however, nationalism was sufficiently strong to bring about partial state control of the oil industry as early as 1923.

The rise in Venezuela's oil market share was achieved in part at the expense of Mexico, where oil exports had soared in the decade before the First World War. The industry, based in Tampico, suffered much less than other sectors from the upheavals associated with the 1910 revolution, and production and exports continued to expand. The 1917 Constitution raised the specter of nationalization,[35] but the Carranza government went out of its way to reassure U.S. oil companies that their investments were secure. The Bucareli Treaty of 1923 was intended to settle all outstanding disputes with the United States and to pave the way for renewed foreign investment in mining.[36] To some extent it succeeded, with Mexico increasing its market share significantly in silver and lead, but oil exports peaked in 1921 and declined steadily thereafter. No amount of honeyed words from the Mexican government could compensate for the exceptional conditions enjoyed by foreign investors in the Venezuelan oil industry.[37]

Tropical products were at risk from protection because of the preference that could be given to colonies by imperial powers. We have already noted the rise in African production of cacao and in Asian production of rubber, leading in both cases to a sharp fall in Latin America's market share (see Table 6.3). Yet there were two cases of tropical products, both involving U.S. investment, for which the Latin American market share increased sharply.

The first was bananas. The novelty of this tropical fruit, a relative newcomer to the dinner table in both Europe and North America, permitted world exports to grow rapidly. In addition, nearly all the main Latin American exporters managed to increase market share, so earnings from banana exports soared. Exports were dominated by a small number of foreign fruit companies, whose decision to concentrate production in Central America and Colombia was based on low average costs of production and exceptionally favorable tax treatment. The most dynamic case was Honduras, a country that had enjoyed virtually no success in export-led growth in the nineteenth century; the value of its exports, almost entirely based on bananas, grew faster than the exports of any other Latin American country in the sixteen years after 1913.[38]

35 The 1917 Mexican Constitution vested subsoil rights in the nation, so that oil production required government concessions and all land owned by oil companies had to be converted to leasehold. See Knight (1986b), p. 470.
36 On the Bucareli Treaty, see Smith (1972).
37 The generous nature of oil concessions awarded by the Gómez administration in Venezuela is well described in McBeth (1983).
38 Exports increased from $3.2 million in 1913 to $24.6 million in 1929 – an annual rate of increase of 13.6 percent. See Pan-American Union (1952).

The second was sugar. Despite the risks associated with imperial preference and the ever-present threat of protection for beet-sugar growers in temperate countries, many Latin American exporters increased market share. The increase was focused mainly on Cuba and Puerto Rico, whose combined share of total world exports of sugar (including beet) rose to more than one-third by the end of the 1920s. Investments in these Caribbean islands, mainly by U.S. companies, pushed output to record levels and obliged Cuba to experiment with quantity controls from the mid-1920s. Any increase in price simply encouraged increased exports by rival producers, however.[39] Although Cuba enjoyed a preferential tariff in the crucial U.S. market, some of its rivals – notably Puerto Rico and Hawaii – faced no tariff at all, while Cuban exports to Europe were increasingly threatened by the recovery of the European beet-sugar industry in the late 1920s. Prices peaked in January 1927, and their long descent was well underway before 1930.

The problem of restricting volume in order to regulate prices was much easier in the coffee market, in which Brazil controlled 60 percent of world exports by 1913. When Brazilian coffee valorization was renewed in the 1920s, it produced an increase in world coffee prices. However, Brazilian restraints on coffee exports were not matched by other countries in Latin America, whose market share increased at the expense of Brazil. Colombia and the Central American countries were particularly successful at reaping the price harvest Brazil had sown, and their combined share of world exports doubled to 20 percent in the fifteen years to 1928. Their increased market share was not just at the expense of Brazil (which still accounted for 55 percent of world exports at the end of the 1920s): Venezuela also lost market share, its high exchange-rate undermining the profitability of coffee exports and providing an early example of the notorious "Dutch disease."[40]

The strategy of increasing market share in Latin America was therefore widespread, popular, and profitable. It allowed the majority of Latin American countries[41] to increase export earnings faster than the world value of exports in the period under consideration (1913–29), and it reinforced the

---

39 This was exactly the same problem faced by Brazil when its (unilateral) coffee valorization scheme was in force.

40 The phrase "Dutch disease" was coined to describe the impact of natural-gas discoveries in the 1960s on the Dutch balance of payments. The increase in energy exports led to an appreciation of the real exchange-rate, which undermined traditional (manufactured) exports while leaving the balance of payments in equilibrium. It has become clear, with the benefit of hindsight, that many countries have suffered from a form of Dutch disease, although in the Venezuelan case the traditional export activities undermined by the strong exchange-rate were agricultural rather than industrial. For the case of Chile, see Palma (2000b).

41 Among the twenty-one countries (i.e., including Puerto Rico with the twenty republics), fourteen (66 percent) exceeded the world rate of growth exports. The seven "failures" were Bolivia, Brazil, Ecuador, Haiti, Nicaragua, Panama, and Uruguay – all small countries, with the exception of Brazil.

export-led model that had been adopted in the nineteenth century. A decline in the external terms of trade could be offset by manipulating the internal terms of trade in favor of the rural sector, and many countries enjoyed the illusion in the 1920s that the First World War was simply a temporary setback in the long march of export-led growth.

The strategy was fraught with problems, however. Although no one could reasonably have been expected to anticipate the depth of the depression at the end of the 1920s, the risk of agricultural protection in the Northern Hemisphere countries and imperial preference for their colonies was present for all to see. The market-share strategy rendered many Latin American republics extremely vulnerable to changes in world trading conditions, and that vulnerability was simply reinforced by the risk of depression. By 1928 Argentina, Bolivia, Brazil, Chile, Cuba, Honduras, and Mexico all controlled more than 20 percent of world exports in at least one commodity,[42] and Argentina was a leading supplier to the world market in virtually all her exports.

The export boom was also associated with a significant loss of national control of the export sector in many countries. In those countries in which the value of exports grew at more than 5 percent a year between 1913 and 1929 (Colombia, the Dominican Republic, Honduras, Paraguay, Peru, Puerto Rico, and Venezuela), foreign penetration of the export sector was particularly marked. These foreign investments occurred above all in commodities (e.g., oil, copper, bananas, and sugar) for which world demand was in any case rising relatively rapidly. Coupled with an increase in market share for these products, the foreign-owned enclaves at times acquired a dominant position. The extremely generous contract terms open to foreign investors at the time led to low tax yields and to high profit remittances; this reduced the returned value[43] associated with export growth in many countries and undermined the stimulus to the nonexport sector associated with the export-led model.

Detailed studies on returned value are rare, but carefully documented research on the Cerro de Pasco Copper Corporation in Peru is available. This giant mineral company, acquired by purchase from Peruvian capitalists in the first decade of the twentieth century, grossed approximately $20 million a year in the 1920s from its Peruvian operations.[44] Payments within Peru to workers, suppliers, and the government (in taxation) averaged $10 million,

---

42 The commodities and countries were as follows: Argentina (beef, linseed, maize, wheat), Bolivia (tin), Brazil (coffee), Chile (nitrates), Cuba (sugar), Honduras (bananas), and Mexico (silver).

43 The "returned value" of exports refers to the proportion of declared export earnings that remain in the country as a result of expenditure on wages and salaries, tax payments, and local material costs. It is therefore theoretically (and practically) possible for the declared and returned value of exports to move in opposite directions in the short-to-medium term. The concept of returned value was pioneered by Reynolds (1965) in his work on the Chilean copper industry.

44 See Thorp and Bertram (1978), p. 87.

so returned value was 50 percent of recorded earnings. The balance was accounted for by imports and profit remittances. This case was by no means atypical; indeed, in the Venezuelan oil industry, returned value was a much lower proportion of total exports.[45]

The market-share strategy also suffered from the risk of retaliation. With the exception of coffee, for which Latin American gains and losses approximately canceled each other, export intensification by so many countries meant that the region as a whole was winning market share from other continents across a broad range of primary products (see Table 6.3). In the fragile geopolitical environment after 1913 and in view of the rising threat of protection, it was unrealistic not to expect other regions to retaliate, either through discrimination against imports from Latin America or through support for their own primary-product industries.[46]

The market-share strategy was not successful in all cases. Indeed, a few Latin American republics failed even to raise export earnings in line with the growth of world trade in the sixteen years before 1929 – further confirmation of the pitfalls associated with the export-led model in the new international economic order that was constructed after the First World War. The unstable nature of commodity prices, the risk of disease, and competition from synthetic products could all play havoc with export earnings, even in countries in which policy was determined primarily by the needs of the export sector.

The instability of export prices was the major reason for the poor performance of export earnings in Bolivia and was also responsible for the less-than-spectacular Cuban trade performance. In both republics, the *volume* of exports grew rapidly: Bolivia won market share for its leading export, tin, and Cuba did the same for sugar. By the end of the 1920s, however, prices were barely higher than the level recorded on the eve of the First World War,[47] and the *value* of exports had grown only modestly. Although Cuban export earnings rose at a rate close to the world average, its position was very vulnerable at the end of the 1920s, with exports at risk from European protection for beet sugar, imperial preference, and mainland U.S. imports from Puerto Rico and Hawaii. Bolivia, on the other hand, had seen its exports fall under an oligopoly dominated by the tin magnate Simon Patiño, who had shrewdly invested in downstream smelter capacity in the

---

45 See McBeth (1983), pp. 117–18.

46 Some of the largest market-share losses (e.g., barley, rye, and wheat) were recorded by the Soviet Union (aggregated with the rest of Europe in Table 6.3). This would not in itself invite retaliation, because the Soviet Union was deliberately withdrawing from international trade. However, the rest of Europe was also losing market share in many of these commodities (the main exception being barley), so retaliation was a very real possibility.

47 Raw sugar averaged 3.5 cents per pound in 1913. The average price in 1929 was 3.77 cents per pound. See League of Nations (1930), Table 204.

United Kingdom;[48] thus Bolivian capital earned profits on processing as well as producing tin, although the benefit to the Bolivian economy began to shrink as Patiño increasingly moved his business interests toward Europe in the 1920s.[49]

Disease could also play its part in wiping out efforts in support of export-led growth. The Costa Rican banana industry was hit by the spread of Panama disease in the 1920s, and world market share plummeted from 15.6 percent in 1913 to 6 percent in 1928. For the fruit companies the easiest "solution" to the spread of disease was to develop new plantations on virgin land, even if this meant moving production to a different country. Fortunately for Costa Rica, the growth of earnings from coffee was sufficiently rapid to offset the collapse of bananas, and total export earnings grew above the world average. Ecuador was not so lucky: The spread of disease on the cacao plantations reduced the republic to the status of a minor exporter,[50] and other exports (including coffee, gold, and oil) did not expand fast enough to prevent a decline in foreign-exchange earnings.

The country most affected by competition from synthetics was Chile. The nitrate industry, in which British capital played a large part,[51] had enjoyed high prices during the first World War, and nitrate exports continued to account for around 70 percent of total exports. The collapse of demand at the end of the war was instrumental in persuading British investors to sell their interests to other (mainly Chilean) capitalists, under whom the nitrate industry staged a recovery in the 1920s.[52] Technological progress in the German chemical industry made possible the production of synthetic nitrates at competitive prices, however, and the Chilean nitrate industry was finally killed off by the interwar depression. The spectacular growth of the copper industry after 1913 went a long way toward compensating Chile for the loss of dynamism in nitrate exports, but the growth of export earnings in the fifteen years after 1913 still fell short of the world average.

Brazil and Uruguay, where export-earnings growth also fell far below the world average, enjoyed an improvement in their NBTT between 1913 and

---

48 The Bolivian tin industry had fallen under the control of three local capitalists by the 1920s. Simon Patiño, the most important of the three, acquired the world's largest tin smelter in Great Britain in 1916. See Klein (1982), p. 165. See also Contreras (2000).

49 By the end of the 1920s Patiño had in effect become a foreign capitalist, for much of the profit from his Bolivian mining operations was invested in new activities in Europe.

50 The cacao crop was affected by two plagues, the more serious of which was witchbroom. See Linke (1962), p. 135. As a result, Ecuador's share of world cacao exports fell, from 16.4 percent in 1913 to 4.2 percent in 1928.

51 Although John Thomas North, the nitrate "king," had died in 1896, British interests in the nitrate industry had remained strong, with new companies being formed up to the eve of the First World War. See Rippy (1959), pp. 57–65.

52 The volume of exports, which fell sharply at the end of the First World War, had recovered to wartime levels by 1928. See Sunkel (1982), Table 8, p. 127.

1928. Thus the poor performance of export earnings was due unambiguously to the virtual stagnation in the volume of goods sold abroad. These two countries therefore offer a partial exception to the pursuit of export-led growth by Latin America up to the 1930s.

The stagnation of Brazilian exports was due both to the decline of rubber, wiped out by competition from plantations in the Far East, and to coffee valorization. However, the various efforts by the São Paulo government to restrict the volume of coffee exports[53] reaching the world market had a pronounced effect on coffee prices, so real incomes from coffee climbed steadily. Thus the state of São Paulo – where so much Brazilian industry was located – experienced a rise in effective demand from the export sector, and policy encouraged resources to move out of coffee toward the nonexport economy. This powerful combination was an important explanation for Brazilian industrialization during the period.[54]

Despite high prices for Uruguay's exports (principally meat and its extracts, hides, and wool), the volume of exports was virtually unchanged in the fifteen years after 1913. Wartime shipping problems provided part of the explanation, and the volume of exports did expand briefly in the mid-1920s, but the cartelization of the meat industry was an important deterrent to increased production. The *frigoríficos*, dominated by foreign capital, had joined forces with their Argentine counterparts to create a meat pool that allocated cargo space on routes to London (the principal market).[55] The pool gave processing companies the upper hand in price negotiations with farmers, for whom "the 1920s was a decade of disillusion and resentment with the operations of the foreign-owned frigorifico industry."[56]

A further consideration in the Uruguayan case was the ideology of Batllismo. José Batlle y Ordóñez, president of Uruguay on two occasions in the early twentieth century and the dominant public figure until his death in 1929, was a representative of the urban middle classes who was not afraid to tax agriculture in order to finance urban welfare-state services. Although no evidence exists that agricultural exports were crippled by Batllismo, the rate of taxation was significantly higher than in other countries that pursued export-led growth, and the ideology of Batllismo certainly encouraged nonexport urban activities. Coupled with the operations of the meat pool, it is perhaps not so surprising that Battle's Uruguay – despite its small size – was among the first Latin American republics to shift away from traditional export-led growth.[57]

53 During the 1920s responsibility for coffee valorization shifted between the state of São Paulo and the federal government in Rio de Janeiro. This dual responsibility reflected the different functions of coffee: a key source of income for state planters, and a major influence on federal-exchange rates, fiscal, and monetary policies. See Fritsch (1988).

54 See pp. 188–9 for a more detailed discussion of Brazilian industrialization in the 1920s.

55 See Hanson (1938), pp. 62–7.

56 See Finch (1981), p. 140.

57 On the ideology of Batllismo and the creation of a welfare state in Uruguay, see Oddone (1986).

Exchange-rate, financial, and fiscal reform

The export-led model, with its emphasis on growth in the value of exports, was subject to strong cycles that reflected the fortunes of the export sector itself. The fiscal and financial systems, far from operating in a counter-cyclical fashion, reinforced the cycles that emanated from the export sector and contributed to the instability in exchange rates, prices, and nominal incomes.

The fiscal system was typically procyclical. The value of imports tended to move in line with the value of exports. Because such a high proportion of government revenue was derived from customs duties, government revenue and expenditure tended to move in line with external trade. At the same time, any rise (fall) in the value of foreign trade was linked to a rise (fall) in the net output of sectors, such as commerce and transport, that depended on the movement of exports and imports. Thus the real economy also tended to move procyclically with the change in the nominal value of exports.

Changes in the value of exports were also highly correlated with changes in the money supply. As exports increased (decreased), foreign exchange flowed into (out of) the country. Because money of "external origin" tended to be such a high proportion of the total money supply in countries that followed export-led growth, it could not easily be offset by a decrease (increase) in money of "internal origin" through budget deficits or domestic credit creation.[58]

The procyclical nature of monetary policy was particularly acute in Latin American countries that were on the gold standard, for the latter was designed to bring about automatic adjustment to balance-of-payments problems. Industrialized countries that ran balance-of-payments deficits as a result of excess credit creation would experience an outflow of gold and a reduction in the money supply and prices, and they would then be able to increase exports and reduce imports in order to achieve a new balance-of-payments equilibrium. For all the criticism subsequently leveled against it, the prewar gold standard worked tolerably well for industrialized countries,[59] and it seemed only natural that Latin American republics should adopt it as well.

Unfortunately, this argument was based on two misconceptions. First, balance-of-payments problems in Latin America usually arose from instability in the world markets for primary products; they were not in general a

---

58 Because the money supply represents the (monetary) liabilities of the consolidated banking system, it can also be expressed as the sum of banks' net foreign and domestic assets. Thus a change in the money supply can be expressed as a change in either net foreign assets (money of external origin) or net domestic assets (money of internal origin). This useful distinction is now recognized in many textbooks on the monetary system in developing countries and was first explicitly used by Robert Triffin in the 1940s. See Thorp (1994).

59 Numerous good works have been written about the operation of the gold standard in industrialized countries. See, for example, McCloskey and Zecker (1981), pp. 184–208.

consequence of domestic financial disorder. An outflow of gold, for example, would not necessarily lead to an increase in exports through its impact on prices, so that balance-of-payments correction had to be achieved almost entirely by reducing imports, with damaging effects on the level of real economic activity. Second, the gold standard was not designed for countries in which the value of exports was subject to huge swings according to the level of world prices. An inflow of gold, for example, following a (temporary) increase in prices, would simply raise imports to a level that could not be sustained when export prices fell.

Perhaps for these reasons Latin American republics approached the gold standard circumspectly before the First World War. Those countries that did adopt it operated exchange offices which tended to suspend convertibility in periods of gold outflow, thus reducing the deflationary impact of balance-of-payments deficits and passing some of the burden of adjustment to the exchange-rate.[60] Countries were prepared to pursue gold-standard orthodoxy in good times with gold flowing in, but were much more reluctant to restore the balance-of-payments equilibrium in bad times by exclusive reliance on gold outflows. Furthermore, international pressure was not a serious obstacle to this rather asymmetrical interpretation of the rules of the gold-standard game.

The suspension of the gold standard in 1914 ushered in a period of great instability for countries that were following the export-led model. The volume of imports fell as shipping space was reallocated in accordance with the needs of the war effort in Europe, and the price of imports soared. Government revenue declined in line with the volume of imports in most countries, producing a severe fiscal crisis, and budget deficits were common. In the absence of foreign loans the deficits had to be financed domestically, which often generated price increases over and above the inflation brought by higher prices for imports.[61] In Mexico these inflationary pressures reached extreme proportions as revolutionary upheaval from 1913 to 1916 led to an explosion of paper money without a gold or silver backing.[62]

A further source of instability came from currency fluctuations. With the gold standard suspended, only those currencies that were tied to the U.S. dollar (e.g., Cuba) could expect to avoid currency instability; elsewhere, currencies first depreciated against the dollar in line with the problems of the export sector and then rose or fell according to their ability to increase export earnings. Republics with strategic exports (e.g., Chile and Peru) were

---

60 See Triffin (1944), pp. 94–6.

61 In Brazil, for example, retail prices rose by 158 percent between 1913 and 1918 – an annual increase of 20.9 percent. This was far higher than could be justified by reference to the dollar value of imports alone.

62 The inflationary pressures in Mexico were so intense that the exchange-rate collapsed from 2.01 pesos per U.S. dollar in January 1913 to 217.4 in December 1916. See Cárdenas and Manns (1989), p. 68.

Table 6.5. *Exchange rates per U.S. dollar, 1913, 1918, 1923, and 1928*

Country	Unit	1913	1918	1923	1928
Argentina	Paper peso	2.38	2.27	2.86	2.38
Bolivia	Boliviano	2.57	2.44	3.23	2.86
Brazil	Milreis	3.09	4.00	10.00	8.30
Chile	Paper peso	4.50	3.45	8.33	8.33
Colombia	Peso	1.00	0.94	1.05	1.02
Costa Rica	Colón	2.15	4.55	4.55	4.00
Cuba	Peso	1.00	1.00	1.00	1.00
Dominican Republic	Peso	1.00	1.00	1.00	1.00
Ecuador	Sucre	2.05	2.56	4.76	5.00
El Salvador	Colón	2.43[a]	2.43[a]	2.04	2.00
Guatemala	Peso	20.00	35.00	60.00	1.00[b]
Haiti	Gourde	5.00	5.00	5.00	5.00
Honduras	Peso	2.50	2.00	2.00	2.00[c]
Mexico	Peso	2.00[d]	2.00	2.04	2.08
Nicaragua	Córdoba	1.00	1.00	1.00	1.00
Panama	Balboa	1.00	1.00	1.00	1.00
Paraguay	Peso	1.43[e]	1.00	1.27	1.04
Peru	Libra	0.21	0.19	0.24	0.25
Uruguay	Peso	0.96	0.83	1.27	0.97
Venezuela	Bolívar	5.27	4.55	5.26	5.26

[a] Silver peso.
[b] Quetzal (equivalent to 60 old pesos).
[c] Lempira.
[d] Datum is for 1911–12.
[e] Datum is for 1910.
Sources: Mills (n.d.), Young (1925), and Pan-American Union (1952) for 1913; Wilkie (1974) for 1918, 1923, and 1928.

experiencing currency appreciation by the end of the war, while countries with nonessential exports (e.g., Brazil and Costa Rica) suffered from further depreciation (see Table 6.5).

The combination of imported inflation, internally financed budget deficits, and (in some cases) currency depreciation produced an upsurge in the domestic price level. Although this phenomenon also occurred in Europe and North America, it produced greater social tensions in Latin America. Workers, including the urban middle class, were less able to defend the value of their real wages, and appeals for wartime sacrifices had less force. Social unrest was often met with violence, notably in Argentina during the *Semana trágica*,[63] and a climate of political instability pervaded the region by the end of the war.

63 The crushing of labor unrest in Argentina in January 1919, following mass protests, is described in Rock (1986).

Any hopes that the end to hostilities in Europe would eliminate the outstanding economic problems were undermined by the sharp depression in 1920–1. Although mercifully short, this trade-induced depression was a forceful reminder of the procyclical nature of the export-led model. The collapse of primary-product prices in world markets once again induced an outflow of foreign exchange, a fall in the money supply, a reduction in imports, and a decline in government revenue.[64] Most dramatic of all was currency depreciation in almost all the republics without a fixed link to the U.S. dollar (see Table 6.5). Brazil and Ecuador, for example, saw the nominal value of their currencies halved between 1918 and 1923.

The extreme nature of export instability in the years after 1913 led governments in Latin America to look more favorably on financial and fiscal reforms that could eliminate some of the worst excesses of the export-led model. Currency instability was seen as one of the biggest problems, and the return to (or adoption of) fixed exchange rates became a symbol of the new orthodoxy. With the emphasis given to the gold standard by the newly formed League of Nations,[65] Latin American republics came under pressure to join the system and to play by the rules of the game.

Currency stability was not necessarily in everyone's interests, however. It was well known that exporters and domestic debtors benefited from currency depreciation, and this had often been cited as a reason for the failure of a number of republics (e.g., Chile[66] and Guatemala[67]) to join the gold standard before the war. Currency instability could bring appreciation as well as depreciation, however, and the uncertainty associated with currency movements after 1913 reduced the resistance of many to the adoption of fixed exchange rates. Furthermore, the urban middle class – the rising social force in Latin America – unambiguously favored currency stabilization;[68] as governments in the 1920s began to take into consideration the interests

---

64 One of the most extreme examples of this vicious cycle was found in Cuba as a result of the republic's openness to foreign trade. See Wallich (1950).

65 The League of Nations, established at the end of the war, had called a conference as early as 1920 to discuss various problems in international finance, among which a return to the gold standard was considered crucial. See Kindleberger (1987), pp. 46–8.

66 Numerous attempts had been made in the forty years before the First World War to restore currency stability in Chile, but they all failed. In an influential work, Fetter (1931) attributed this failure to the influence of landlords on government policy. It is now recognized that this influence was only one of many which led to currency depreciation. See Hirschman (1963).

67 The survival of Estrada Cabrera as dictator of Guatemala from 1898 to 1920 was undoubtedly made easier by the windfall gains that currency depreciation yielded for the powerful coffee oligarchy.

68 This social group, whose income was derived from wages and salaries, was the first to suffer when currency depreciation raised the domestic-currency cost of imports. Without indexation or powerful trade unions, there was no certainty that remuneration would rise in line with prices.

of this class, a consensus in favor of orthodox exchange-rate management began to emerge.[69]

For a number of the smaller republics in the Caribbean Basin the preference of the United States for fixed exchange rates was the overriding factor leading to the adoption of currency stability. The United States had emerged from the war with its world economic and financial position greatly strengthened. Its influence in Central America and the Caribbean, considerable even before the war, was now undisputed. Even in Mexico and South America, however, there were good reasons for taking note of the U.S. preference for stable exchange rates. The United States was fast becoming the principal supplier of capital to all Latin American republics, both portfolio and direct, and the adoption of reforms leading to exchange-rate stability was seen as a relatively painless way of opening the door to inflows of U.S. capital. With the demand for foreign capital rising and the supply from traditional sources – notably Great Britain, France, and Germany – restricted by postwar economic difficulties, no republic could afford to be wholly indifferent to U.S. preferences for financial and fiscal reform.

In a handful of republics (see Table 6.5) currency stability had survived the war years and continued throughout the 1920s. Without exception, however, these countries (Cuba, the Dominican Republic, Haiti, Nicaragua, and Panama) were all semicolonies of the United States[70] in which the U.S. dollar circulated freely and monetary policy was completely passive. Elsewhere the shift to stable exchange rates was adopted only after the war – and in most cases after the 1920–1 depression. In a few republics (notably Argentina, Bolivia, Brazil, Ecuador, and Peru) currency stability was delayed until 1927–8, but by the beginning of 1929 all Latin American countries had stabilized their exchange rates in relation to the U.S. dollar.[71]

The stabilization of exchange rates was usually associated with the adoption of the gold-exchange standard. This was much less demanding than the gold standard for peripheral countries because it was no longer necessary to guarantee the exchange of local currency for gold. Instead, the gold-exchange standard allowed countries to exchange local currency for a foreign currency, such as the dollar, which was in turn fully convertible into gold.[72] Even so, the gold-exchange standard was not without its

---

69 During and after the First World War a number of governments came to power that could be said to represent this new social force. Good examples are the Radicals in Argentina under Hipólito Yrigoyen (1916–30) and the Liberals in Chile under Arturo Alessandri (1920–5).

70 The close relationship between these countries and the United States produced many detailed monographs on economic conditions and financial policies. See, for example, Cumberland (1928).

71 In some cases the currency was not explicitly linked to the U.S. dollar. The Paraguayan peso, for example, was linked to the Argentine currency; the Bolivian peso, to the pound sterling. However, the operation of the gold standard provided an indirect link to the U.S. dollar for all these currencies.

72 The gold-exchange standard is described in Kindleberger (1987), pp. 46–9.

problems. Countries such as Honduras and Mexico, where silver coins were the preferred medium of exchange for historical reasons, suffered from the depreciation of silver in the 1920s as the gold price of silver started to rise. This led to a withdrawal of gold currency from circulation that could only be offset by increasing the coinage of gold and reducing that of silver.[73]

The prewar gold standard in Latin America had often broken down as a result of the suspension of gold outflows by the exchange office. In order to reduce this risk in the new postwar environment, exchange-rate stability was buttressed by financial reform, with the creation of new banking institutions, financial supervision, and bank regulation. The most striking example of this change was the creation of central banks in the Andean countries,[74] many of which had been the least orthodox in exchange-rate management before 1914.

The creation of these central banks was usually preceded by a visit from E. W. Kemmerer, a U.S. academic and specialist in monetary economics. The Kemmerer missions were independent of the U.S. State and Treasury departments, but both looked with favor on the financial and fiscal reforms invariably proposed by Kemmerer and his team. Indeed, a visit by Kemmerer was often seen as an essential precondition for future U.S. loans – even from the private sector – and Kemmerer on occasion lobbied hard for private-sector loans to countries that adopted his package of reforms.[75]

The success of the Kemmerer missions was due in large part to the fact that his recommendations coincided with changes that were likely to have happened anyway. Countries without Kemmerer missions (e.g., Brazil) carried out similar reforms. Throughout Latin America free banking disappeared,[76] one bank (the central bank if there was one) was given a monopoly of the note issue, and the ability of the government to finance a budget deficit through the printing press was reduced.

Financial reform in the 1920s was extremely orthodox. The main purpose was to provide an institutional framework that would underpin exchange-rate stability and the gold-exchange standard. In practice it did not allow governments to operate countercyclical monetary policies, and techniques for sterilizing the impact of a surge of foreign-exchange inflows on the

---

73 This process in Honduras is well described in Young (1925). For Mexico, see Cárdenas (2000).

74 The Andean countries affected were Bolivia, Chile, Colombia, Ecuador, and Peru.

75 Drake (1989) provides an excellent account of the Kemmerer missions to South America and the efforts by Kemmerer to underpin his proposed reforms through foreign-capital inflows.

76 "Free banking" is the name given to the process under which commercial banks are "free" to issue their own currency, subject to normal prudential banking requirements. It has virtually disappeared throughout the world in favor of granting a monopoly of note issue to a single bank, although a version of it has survived in Scotland.

money supply and on the domestic price level were extremely rudimentary. Although Great Britain and the United States enjoyed almost a decade of price stability after the 1920–1 depression, many Latin American countries suffered from severe price fluctuations even after the currency was stabilized.[77]

The adoption of an exchange-rate target had implications not only for the financial system but also for fiscal policy. Budget deficits, financed by inflationary methods, would undermine currency stability, so pressure to increase revenue was strong. However, the close dependence of revenue on the trade cycle meant that the tax base needed to be broadened in order to increase the stability of government income. Thus fiscal reform was needed to complement financial and currency reform.

All these arguments suggested the need for new taxes that were not directly tied to exports and imports. The obvious candidates were income, property, and sales taxes, but little progress was made in most republics in this direction. The share of trade taxes by the end of the 1920s (see Table 6.6) was still very high throughout the region. Income taxes were generating more than 5 percent of government revenue in only a few cases. Both Uruguay and Venezuela enjoyed high yields from direct taxes – the former relying on the progressive tax rates (mainly on real estate) associated with Batllismo and the latter capturing a small part of the large rent associated with oil exports. Even so, fiscal effort, as measured by revenue per head (see Table 6.6), was still modest, with many countries generating $10 per head or less in government income. Only Argentina, Chile, and Uruguay raised more than $25 per head in the form of public revenue. Argentina, however, after a heated congressional debate in 1915, rejected the introduction of an income tax and initiated export taxes instead.[78] In many other republics the yield from income taxes was undermined by the numerous exemptions permitted.

An additional obstacle in the path toward fiscal reform was provided by external debt-service payments. In the tense international context before, during, and after the war a failure to meet debt-service payments – owed mainly to European powers – could be interpreted as an excuse for European intervention in the Western Hemisphere. This potential challenge to the Monroe Doctrine had persuaded successive U.S. governments since the turn of the century to use their influence to ensure that debt-service payments were made. The most effective way to do this was to insist that Latin American republics pledge their revenue from external trade to service their

---

77 Although U.S. and Argentine wholesale prices, for example, were virtually the same in 1927 as they had been in 1922, the standard deviation in Argentina over this period was much higher, with prices rising or falling by as much as 10 percent in a single year.

78 See Albert (1988), p. 145.

Table 6.6. *Public revenue, circa 1929*

Country	Amount		Structure (in percentages)			
	Total (in millions of US$)	Per head (in US$)	Import duties	Export duties	Direct taxes[a]	Income tax
Argentina	308.3	27.5	45.7	2.4	3.6	0
Bolivia	17.8	5.9	32.3	13.7	9.0	n/a
Brazil[b]	282.1	7.2	43.9	0	4.0	3.1
Chile	148.1	34.0	30.0	24.3	17.7	12.6
Colombia	73.2	9.2	54.0	0.5	4.9	3.6
Costa Rica	8.9	18.0	56.8	7.9	2.8	0
Cuba	79.3	22.1	50.3	4.5	5.7	5.5
Dominican Republic	15.4	15.0	32.5	n/a	n/a	n/a
Ecuador	12.1	6.1	32.9	6.4	6.6	1.8
El Salvador	13.5	7.8	50.7	11.9	5.2	0
Guatemala	15.4	7.2	47.4	13.6	1.3	0
Haiti	8.5	3.4	59.5	23.1	1.9	1.2
Honduras	6.9	9.8	58.6	1.3	0	0
Mexico	146.0	9.7	37.7	3.5	6.7	6.7
Nicaragua	6.6	10.1	58.6	1.2	0	0
Panama	6.5	13.0	48.8	1.6	4.7	0
Paraguay	5.8	6.9	49.3	10.0	6.9	0
Peru	56.2	9.1	27.7	6.5	10.3	6.0
Uruguay	61.3	34.1	(....... 40.8 ....)		19.2	1.2
Venezuela	44.5	14.4	51.1	0	20.1	0

[a] Includes income tax.
[b] Federal government.
Sources: Council of Foreign Bondholders (1931); League of Nations (1938).

external debts; thus, in order to protect against any backsliding, U.S. officials were placed in the customs houses of many Latin American countries. Indeed, by the mid-1920s U.S. officials "had served or were serving in some supervisory capacity" in ten of the twenty republics.[79]

The emphasis on debt-service payments made it more difficult for governments to reduce their dependence on trade taxes because – unlike most other taxes – they could be paid in gold.[80] Although wartime inflation had sharply reduced the share of total revenue derived from import duties, this share recovered quickly in the 1920s. By the end of the decade the

79 See Tulchin (1971), p. 80.
80 External debt obligations were denominated in currencies linked to gold, so there was an understandable preference by finance ministers for tax revenues that could also be collected in gold. Trade taxes were the most obvious candidate.

contribution to total government income from trade taxes was not much lower than it had been in 1913, so revenue was still vulnerable to fluctuations in the value of exports. Fiscal reform had therefore been very timid, and it remained extremely difficult for governments to pursue countercyclical fiscal policies.

One reason for the timidity of fiscal reform was the growing awareness on the part of Latin American governments that foreign loans were available to finance budget deficits in a noninflationary manner. The emergence of the United States as a capital-surplus country led to a substantial transfer of resources to Latin America in the form of loans to national, state, and municipal governments. Other capital-exporting countries could not match the explosion of U.S. lending to Latin America, and by 1929 the United States had become the most important foreign investor in every Latin American republic except Argentina, Brazil, Paraguay, and Uruguay.

At times this inflow of resources, the infamous "dance of the millions," was beyond the absorptive capacity of the recipient country, and stories of graft and corruption were legion. In 1927 Peru received an inflow of portfolio capital equivalent to more than 50 percent of total export receipts.[81] In the period between 1926 and 1928 the United States alone exported more than \$1 billion (net) to Latin America, most in the form of government loans.[82] The temptation to rely on foreign loans to avoid the need for painful fiscal reform was strong. This was true even in those countries, such as Colombia, that did use the inflow to invest in productive assets (e.g., social infrastructure).[83]

The combination of orthodox exchange-rate management, conservative financial reform, and timid fiscal policies was not an appropriate response to the growing instability in the world markets for primary products. Although it encouraged the inflow of foreign capital – particularly U.S. capital – it left the region dangerously vulnerable to external shocks. This had been demonstrated clearly in 1920–1, and the experience was to be repeated even more disastrously after 1929. Furthermore, at a time of deterioration in the external terms of trade, financial and fiscal reform in most countries was too timid to bring about a significant shift in resources from the export sector of the economy to the nonexport sector. Small countries found themselves going into the 1930s depression with a nonexport sector too weak to act as an "engine of growth," while the nonexport sector in the larger countries was still handicapped by lack of finance, poor infrastructure, and a policy climate that favored primary-product exports.

81 See Thorp (2000), p. 72.
82 See Stallings (1987), Table I.A.
83 The contrast in the use of resources between Colombia and Peru is one of the important themes in Thorp (1991), Chapters 1–2.

External shocks, relative prices, and
the manufacturing sector

By the time war broke out in Europe, modern manufacturing had already established itself in Argentina, Brazil, Chile, Mexico, Peru, and Uruguay, and modest beginnings were visible in Colombia and Venezuela. Many factors contributed to the emergence of domestic industry geared to the home market. On the demand side the creation of urban concentrations as a by-product of export-led growth produced expanding markets based on wage labor and a growing middle class. As the market increased, the unit cost of production fell, so local firms could compete more easily with imports across a broad range of tradable goods. Small republics, in which urban concentration was modest, were at a disadvantage, and modern factory production (excluding establishments engaged in processing raw materials for export) was extremely limited before the war. The exception was Uruguay, where the high level of exports per head and economic policies with an urban bias had produced an urbanized society with a sufficiently large market to justify production of many manufactured goods.[84]

The growth of social infrastructure was also important in promoting modern manufacturing. As internal transport links improved, the products of modern factories could begin to compete more easily with the artisan and handicraft production that had traditionally satisfied the needs of the rural population. The appalling transport system in Colombia was a major obstacle to the emergence of modern manufacturing before the war, whereas Mexican industry had benefited substantially from the spread of the railway network during the Porfiriato. The growth of public utilities and financial institutions also played an important part in the rise of modern factories.

The third crucial element in the rise of industry was relative prices. With output destined primarily for the home market, profitability was sensitive to any change in the domestic price of competing imports. When imports became cheaper – through, for example, tariff reductions, exchange-rate appreciation, or falling world prices – domestic production was adversely affected, and resources flowed out of industry. Conversely, when the real domestic price of imports rose, domestic production was encouraged, and industry attracted resources from other branches of the economy.

The First World War shattered the "normal" environment in which modern manufacturing had arisen before 1914. The first big change was the decline in imports as a result of shipping and other difficulties. Cut off from competing imports, local industry no longer had to worry to the same extent about relative prices. In effect, tariffs on imports had been replaced

---

84 At the end of the 1920s Guatemala and Uruguay had roughly the same population (1.7 million). Yet Montevideo, the capital of Uruguay, was home to nearly 500,000 inhabitants with a relatively high average income, whereas Guatemala City was a modest urban center with only 120,000 inhabitants.

by quotas, and domestic prices were free to rise until the market cleared. Import restrictions, however, applied to all products, and firms were frequently denied access to imports of capital goods to expand their capacity; thus in many cases demand had to be met by more intensive use of existing capacity, which was not always possible.

Demand was also affected by the war. In almost all republics the immediate impact of the war was a decline in export values; this fall, aggravated by multiplier effects, produced a decline in the domestic demand for manufactured goods. It is tempting to assume that this produced a fall in manufacturing output, but such was not necessarily the case. We must distinguish between three branches of modern manufacturing. The first processed primary products for export (e.g., *frigoríficos* in Argentina and Uruguay) and was clearly adversely affected by any fall in export values. The second produced nontraded goods (e.g., bread and bricks) or goods that had already replaced imports in the domestic market and were therefore effectively nontraded (e.g., matches and tobacco products). Because the output did not compete with imports, a decline in domestic demand would automatically imply a decline in production. The third produced tradable goods in competition with imports (e.g., textiles and shoes). Provided that imports fell faster than demand, the output of this branch could be expected to increase. Thus the direction of change of manufacturing output could not be easily predicted from the knowledge that export values had fallen. Furthermore, import restrictions did not apply to imports from other Latin American countries, so output was free to expand through exports to neighboring countries.

As the war in Europe intensified, the demand for strategic materials rose. Prices soared, and a number of Latin American countries enjoyed a spectacular improvement in their export earnings and NBTT. Coupled with the continuing restrictions on competing imports, this provided a strong stimulus for those countries with sufficient industrial capacity to expand output without the need for major investments. In the small republics without significant manufacturing capacity, however, domestic output could not expand; the stimulus simply provoked higher prices.

The position was further complicated by proximity to the United States. The restriction on imports was felt most severely by countries that received most of their supplies from Europe. The small republics of Central America and the Caribbean were less affected by import restrictions, because the United States was already their main supplier before the war and was able to replace European imports without too much difficulty. Thus these small countries still had the possibility of buying capital equipment from abroad, but they lost the stimulus to industrial production associated with the fall in competing imports. Although U.S. exports to all republics increased, the increase could not compensate for the decline in imports from Europe for those countries (e.g., Argentina) that had not previously bought much from the United States. Consequently, the stimulus to domestic manufacturing from import restrictions was much more important in the southern republics.

We may now turn to the performance of the manufacturing sector in Latin America during the war, a subject that has excited much attention and acrimonious debate.[85] The first point to note is the almost-universal acknowledgment that countries which went into the war with very little manufacturing capacity made little progress. These small republics in Central America and the Caribbean, together with Bolivia, Ecuador, and Paraguay, continued to follow a traditional export-led growth model in which the fortunes of the economy varied in line with export performance. Colombia and Venezuela experienced some increase in output, based on prewar investments in textiles, shoes, cement, and food processing, but progress in manufacturing was still modest.[86] The performance of industry in Mexico, on the other hand, was overwhelmingly dictated by the impact of revolutionary upheaval rather by than the Great War itself. The output of textiles – by far the most important sector – fell by 38 percent between 1913 and 1918, and by 1921 manufacturing output was still 9 percent below its 1910 level.[87] The decline in demand brought about by civil war, by the collapse of real wages in the hyperinflationary episode from 1913 to 1916, and by the damage to the country's social infrastructure (particularly railways) dwarfed whatever positive stimulus might have been provided by import restrictions.[88]

Countries that faced a combination of rising exports and import restrictions were particularly well placed to improve manufacturing performance. In that case the war provided a positive stimulus not only for import-competing firms, but also for those establishments that were directly linked to exports and those that sold nontradables in the home market. Chile and Peru were in such a position, although both countries faced a brief decline in exports at the start of the war. The statistics on industrial output are not very reliable, but all the indicators suggest that output in Chile rose rapidly after 1914 and that many new firms were established despite the problem of importing capital equipment.[89] The Peruvian data are even more deficient, but the import-competing sector (notably textiles and shoes) did expand, and some evidence indicates that new factories were founded even during

---

85 This particular debate was sparked off by the claim of the dependency school that Latin America's industry stood to gain from external shocks to the economy because manufacturing firms were then subject to reduced international competition. See Frank (1969).

86 For Colombia, see Ocampo and Montenegro (1984), Part 1; for Venezuela, see Karlsson (1975), Chapter 2.

87 See Haber (1989), Chapter 8.

88 The grim social and economic conditions in these years are well described in Knight (1986b), pp. 406–20.

89 See Kirsch (1977), pp. 45–8; see also Palma (1979).

the war years: The number of factories doubled between 1905 and 1918, and it is difficult to believe that all this expansion occurred before 1914.[90]

Argentina and Uruguay provide a less-encouraging picture. Although both countries suffered a sharp drop in imports as a result of restrictions on shipping, a significant part of manufacturing value added (between 10 percent and 20 percent) was directly tied to the performance of exports.[91] Because the volume of exports declined during the war and the terms of trade deteriorated, demand for manufactured goods was adversely affected. Some branches of the import-competing sector (e.g., textiles) expanded rapidly, but others (e.g., metals in Argentina) did not have sufficient capacity to respond to the stimulus of import restrictions, so output actually fell.[92] Some new firms were established (particularly in Uruguay),[93] but overall industrial performance was sluggish. The manufacturing index for Argentina suggests that the 1913 level of output was not surpassed until 1919.[94]

The war did have some beneficial effect on industry in these two countries. Both republics managed to increase manufactured exports to neighboring countries: Argentina, for example, shipped flour to Brazil, and Uruguay sent hats to Argentina. The chemical industry in Argentina received a boost with the production for the first time of sulfate of aluminum, and automobile assembly began in 1916.[95] Nevertheless, the negative impact of the fall in demand was severe for many industries, and the efforts in Argentina to balance the budget at a time of falling real revenue caused a deep recession in the construction-materials industry, which had come to rely on public-works contracts. Finally, import restrictions in Argentina seem to have been more severe for capital and intermediate goods (which could not easily be replaced by domestic industry) than for consumer goods (which could be replaced), because the share of consumer goods in total imports actually rose from less than 40 percent before the war to nearly 50 percent in the period between 1915 and 1919.[96]

The Brazilian experience stands in strong contrast to those of Argentina and Uruguay. Although the volume of exports fell and terms of trade deteriorated, domestic demand did not decline to the same extent because Brazil chose to "accommodate" the budget deficit by following loose fiscal and monetary policies. The resulting inflation accelerated the rate of

90 See Thorp and Bertram (1978), Chapter 6.
91 For Argentina, Díaz-Alejandro (1970) remains a classic source for this period. For Uruguay, see Finch (1981).
92 See Albert (1988), Chapter 3.
93 See Finch (1981), p. 164.
94 As late as 1917, net manufacturing output (1970 prices) was still 16.9 percent below the 1913 level. See CEPAL (1978), Table 12. A more detailed study can be found in CEPAL (1959).
95 See Wythe (1945), p. 83.
96 See Albert (1988), pp. 72–5.

currency depreciation and lowered real wages, but it also increased nominal demand and encouraged firms to expand production at the expense of imports. Brazilian industrial output was also much less directly tied to exports (dominated by coffee), so the import-competing sector was proportionately more important than it was in Argentina or Uruguay.

It is no surprise, therefore, to find that all the available statistics point in the direction of industrial expansion during the war years after an initial sharp drop in 1914.[97] The number of industrial workers almost doubled between 1912 and 1920, and many new firms were set up despite restrictions on imports of capital equipment.[98] Indeed, in contrast with Argentina, the consumer-goods share of total imports fell during the war years in Brazil,[99] with the United States moving into the market for investment goods previously supplied from Europe. Pig-iron output soared, and Brazil even began to find export markets in the rest of Latin America; the chemicals industry received a boost with the beginning of caustic-soda production in 1918.

Brazil's countercyclical fiscal and monetary policies in the war were highly unorthodox and were replaced in the 1920s by more traditional techniques of economic management. The fact that they were successful during the war had much to do with the restrictions on imports and with the presence of spare capacity in many branches of industry as a result of prewar investments. Unorthodox fiscal and monetary policies in other countries (e.g., Guatemala) produced rampant inflation rather than industrial expansion. The Brazilian case could not therefore be generalized to all countries, although it might well have succeeded in Argentina and Uruguay.

Just as the war years had brought a reduction in the import quantum, so too the return to peacetime conditions brought a flood of goods into the main Latin American markets. This increase in competing imports was not simply a reflection of a return to the prewar situation; it was also due to the fact that the relative price of imports had fallen sharply as a result of the erosion of tariff rates. Domestic inflation in Latin America had undermined the protection given by the region's specific tariffs to the point that by 1919 duties collected represented only 7.5 percent of imports in Argentina, 9.6 percent in Peru, and 11.2 percent in Uruguay.[100] Domestic firms could not compete with cheap imports. The textile industry in many countries saw a fall in output, and the situation for the import-competing sector was rescued only by the 1920–1 world depression, which forced Latin American

---

97 See Albert (1988), pp. 183–98. For the cotton textile industry, see Haber (1997).

98 The number of industrial establishments increased between 1912 and 1920 from 9,475 to 13,336. See IBGE (1987), Tables 7.2 and 7.6.

99 The consumer-goods share of imports was 30.1 percent in 1913 and 34 percent in 1914. By 1918 it had fallen to 23.1 percent, See Albert (1988), Table 5.3, p. 189.

100 See Finch (1981), Table 6.8, p. 168.

countries to protect the balance of payments through exchange-rate depreciation. The sharp drop in the price level also improved tariff protection, because the same specific tariffs were now collected on imports whose foreign currency price had fallen.[101]

Latin American export earnings recovered quickly after 1921, with growth propelled not only by the recovery of world demand but also by the increase in market share (see pp. 161–70) Demand for manufactured goods was stimulated through the usual mechanisms that operated under export-led growth, and domestic industry was now free to import capital equipment to expand production. Both Colombia and Venezuela, where export growth was rapid, were able to make substantial progress toward the first stage of industrialization, with textiles, shoes, hats, furniture, and paper products in the vanguard. Argentina enjoyed strong industrial growth in almost every year of the 1920s, and the consumer-goods share of total imports fell back to its prewar level as consumer durables and nondurables (particularly textiles) expanded rapidly at the expense of competing imports. Intermediate industries, such as oil refining, chemicals, and metals, also flourished; only construction materials remained below the prewar levels.

The intense mining activity in Chile, where copper was replacing nitrates as the leading export, contributed to the rise of a small capital-goods industry. By the end of the 1920s the share of demand for intermediate, capital, and durable goods met by local production had reached 30 percent – it had been 16.6 percent in 1914 – and more than 80 percent of the demand for nondurables was met locally.[102] This impressive performance has led to some suggestions that industry had already become the leading sector in Chile even before the Great Depression,[103] its performance no longer dependent on the fortunes of the export sector. Such claims cannot be fully justified, however;[104] the external terms of trade remained an enormously important determinant of Chilean industrial performance, and the small capital-goods sector proved unable to adapt to the growing sophistication in product design demanded by the mining companies, many of which were U.S. owned and imported their capital requirements from abroad.[105]

---

101 Between 1919 and 1922 tariff protection in Argentina, Peru, and Uruguay rose by more than 50 percent in the first two countries and by more than 40 percent in Uruguay. See Finch (1981), Table 6.8, p. 168.

102 See Palma (1979).

103 This claim is made most forcibly by Palma (2000a), pp. 49–53.

104 Regression analysis testing the log–linear relationship from 1914 to 1929 between net manufacturing output and constant price export revenues suggests a weak correlation. See Palma (2000a), p. 50. However, it is not clear that constant-price exports are the correct explanatory variable, in view of the enormous impact of the terms of trade in Chile on purchasing power and effective industrial demand.

105 See Ortega (1990), pp. 22–3.

Although there were some industrial successes in the 1920s, there were also many disappointments. The small republics – even the more prosperous ones – were in general unable to take even the first steps toward industrialization. Tariff increases were adopted in Cuba, Haiti, and the Dominican Republic in the second half of the 1920s, but the main beneficiary was nonexport agriculture, which was able to expand quickly at the expense of food imports.[106] The decline of Mexico's export earnings after 1925, coupled with severe monetary contraction, contributed to the stagnation of industrial output, and textile production fell after 1926.[107] The spectacular growth of Peruvian exports was much more modest when expressed in terms of returned value,[108] and the stimulus to domestic production was further eroded by the failure of tariff rates to return to their prewar level.[109]

Once again Brazil is the enigma whose industrial performance in the 1920s has excited the most attention.[110] Coffee valorization after the 1920–1 depression eventually stabilized export earnings, and the policy of export restrictions (on coffee) encouraged resources to move into other activities. Tariff protection in Brazil remained high, although it never reached prewar levels,[111] and foreign companies were sufficiently attracted by the captive home market (as also in Argentina, Chile, and Mexico) to establish branch plants in such products as automobiles, sewing machines, paper, and tires.[112] Yet a superficial reading of Brazilian industrial statistics can give the impression that industrial performance was very undynamic, with cotton-textile production in particular falling after 1922.

There can be little doubt that industrial output did not rise very rapidly in Brazil after the 1920–1 depression. The orthodox policies pursued in the middle of the decade in preparation for the readoption of the gold standard led to monetary contraction and to some extent counteracted the favorable stimulus from the terms of trade.[113] Nevertheless, it would be wrong to conclude that industry was undynamic. Output expanded rapidly from 1921 to 1923 and again from 1926 to 1928: Excluding cotton textiles, where ferocious international competition took its toll, industrial output

---

106 See Wythe (1945), pp. 324–43.

107 See Haber (1989), Chapter 9.

108 The International Petroleum Company (IPC) in Peru, for example, had total sales (mainly exports) of $305.6 million between 1916 and 1929. Yet only $43.9 million represented returned value (local-currency expenditures). See Thorp and Bertram (1978), Table 5.8, p. 104.

109 As a result of price deflation (see note 101), the rise in implicit tariff protection at the end of the war was still not sufficient to compensate for the erosion of protection caused by wartime inflation. Even in 1928 the average tariff (import revenues as a percentage of the value of imports) was still only 20.4 percent–less than the 25.4 percent estimated for 1910. See Finch (1981), Table 6.8, p. 168.

110 There is an excellent survey of the debate in Versiani (2000).

111 See Leff (1982), Table 8.8, p. 175.

112 See Phelps (1936).

113 See Fritsch (1988), Chapter 6.

Table 6.7. *Net manufacturing output, circa 1928 (in 1970 US$)*

Country	Year	Total[a] (in millions of US$)	Per head (in US$)	Share of GDP (in percentages)
Argentina	1928	1,279	112	19.5
Brazil	1928	660	20	12.5
Chile	1929	280	65	12.6
Colombia	1928	65	9	5.7
Costa Rica	1928	10	20	9.0
Honduras	1928	10	11	4.9
Mexico	1928	469	29	11.8
Nicaragua	1928	7	10	5.0
Peru	1933	107	18	7.7
Uruguay	1930	160	93	15.6
Venezuela	1928	64	21	10.7

[a] Local currency values have been converted to U.S. dollars at the 1970 official exchange-rate. See Table A.3.1.
Sources: The basic source is CEPAL (1978), which has been used for Argentina, Brazil, Colombia, Honduras, and Mexico. However, the starting point in CEPAL (1978) is after 1930 for many countries. Thus an index has been formed for earlier years from other sources (where available) and spliced to the earliest year in CEPAL (1978): for Chile, Ballesteros and Davis (1963); for Costa Rica and Nicaragua, Bulmer-Thomas (1987), with the data adjusted from purchasing-power parity to official exchange rates; for Peru, Boloña (1981), Tables 6.1 and 6.3; for Uruguay, Millot, Silva, and Silva (1973); and for Venezuela, Rangel (1970).

rose by 55 percent between 1920 and 1929 – an annual rate of increase of 5 percent. Many new industries were established in the 1920s, including a number of firms making capital goods, and the iron and steel industry made some progress. Perhaps most important of all, imports of industrial equipment rose sharply in the 1920s, creating new industrial capacity and modernizing existing plants. Indeed, imports of industrial machinery hit a peak in 1929 – the last year before the Great Depression.[114]

By the end of the 1920s, throughout Latin America the industrial sector was still the junior partner in the export-led model. Industrial output depended heavily on the home market – the brief surge in exports during the war had been reversed in the 1920s, as cheaper imports from Europe and North America again became available – and domestic demand was still closely linked to the fortunes of the export sector. Furthermore, industrial maturity was clearly correlated with past rates of growth of exports and with the level of exports per head. Argentina, the richest republic, was still in a class of its own in terms of industrial advance, with manufacturing accounting for nearly 20 percent of gross domestic product (GDP) at the end of the 1920s and with a manufacturing output per head of $112 at

114 See Versiani (2000), Table 7.4, p. 148.

1970 prices (see Table 6.7). The second rank of countries included Chile and Uruguay, with a share of manufacturing in GDP between 12 percent and 16 percent and with production of manufactured goods per head at $65 and $93, respectively. The third rank included Brazil, Mexico, and Peru, where net manufacturing output per person was below $30. Elsewhere, even in Colombia and Venezuela, the modern manufacturing sector was still small.[115]

Argentina, despite its high level of net manufacturing output per head, compared unfavorably with its neighbors in terms of the share of total demand met by domestic manufactures. This ratio was lower than that found in Brazil, Chile, or even Uruguay.[116] This did not mean that Argentina was less industrialized than those countries – though many have made the mistake of assuming this to be so – but it did mean that Argentine industry had not been particularly successful in meeting the enormous demand for manufactured goods derived from its rapid export growth. The textile industry, capital goods, and consumer durables were all less advanced than could legitimately be expected in a country of Argentina's wealth. Although the demand for industrial goods was strong, modest tariff protection, a social infrastructure geared to agroexports, a powerful rural elite, and the close ties with Great Britain – whose exports would have been the first to suffer from an increase in the output of import-competing industries in Argentina – robbed Argentine industrialists of some of the potential benefits that export-led growth might have brought.[117] In addition, industry suffered from a lack of competitiveness (as in the rest of Latin America), with unit costs of production too high to generate manufactured exports under normal conditions. A handful of firms dominated sales in most markets, with little incentive to improve the technique of production or to make innovations in product design and managerial methods. Thus the growth of total factor productivity remained modest, and increases in output were essentially achieved through an increase in all factor inputs. This was not the optimal route to achieve the fall in unit production costs that was required if industry was to become internationally competitive.

---

115 The rate of growth of manufacturing in a number of countries from 1913 to 1929 is estimated in Thorp (1998), Appendix III.

116 This ratio, the share of total industrial demand met by domestic output, is the subject of much confusion. In addition to problems of measurement – see Fishlow (1972) – it is quite impossible to identify a higher ratio with a higher level of industrialization. It is worth remembering that Paraguay in 1840 – hardly an industrialized society – almost certainly had a very high ratio, in view of the low level of manufactured imports.

117 There is a huge literature on the factors behind the apparent failure of industry in Argentina to match the country's growth and prosperity before 1930. For an excellent survey of the issues, see Korol and Sábato (1990). See also Cortés Conde (1997).

7

Policy, performance, and structural change in the 1930s

The first decade after the First World War brought about some resource shifts in the major Latin American economies in the direction of structural change, industrialization, and diversification of the nonexport economy. In addition, financial and monetary systems were overhauled in many republics – prompted in some cases by the missions led by E. W. Kemmerer – as governments returned to exchange-rate orthodoxy and the gold standard in the postwar years.[1] Without exception, however, economic performance remained heavily dependent on the fortunes of the export sector. By the end of the 1920s (see Table 7.1) exports still accounted for a high proportion of the gross domestic product (GDP), and the openness of the economy – measured by the ratio of the sum of exports and imports to GDP – varied from nearly 40 percent in Brazil to more than 100 percent in Costa Rica and Venezuela.[2]

Structural change in the 1920s brought no diversification within the export sector. On the contrary, the composition of exports by the end of the decade was very similar to what it had been on the eve of the First World War, with a high degree of concentration. The three leading export products accounted for at least 50 percent of foreign-exchange earnings in all republics, and one product accounted for more than 50 percent of exports in ten countries (Bolivia, Brazil, Colombia, Cuba, the Dominican Republic, El Salvador, Honduras, Guatemala, Nicaragua, and Venezuela).[3] Virtually all export earnings came from primary products, and nearly 70 percent of

---

1 Financial reform and exchange-rate orthodoxy in the 1920s are discussed on pp. 171–79.
2 Data (of varying quality) on GDP in the 1930s exist for most of the Latin American republics. See Thorp (1998), Appendix IX. Not all countries can be used, however, because of the need for comparable data on real exports and imports, so only 13 countries are included in Table 7.1. At 1929 prices the trade ratios are on average lower – significantly so in the case of Mexico. See Maddison (1985), Table 6.
3 In five of these ten cases (Brazil, Colombia, El Salvador, Guatemala, and Nicaragua) the commodity was coffee; in two cases (Cuba and the Dominican Republic) it was sugar; and the remainder were bananas (Honduras), tin (Bolivia), and oil (Venezuela).

Table 7.1. *The external sector in Latin America: trade ratios in 1928 and 1938 (1970 prices, in percentages)*

	Exports / GDP		(Exports + imports) / GDP	
Country	1928	1938	1928	1938
Argentina	29.8	15.7	59.7	35.7
Brazil	17.0	21.2	38.8	33.3
Chile	35.1[a]	32.7	57.2[a]	44.9
Colombia	24.8	24.1	62.8	43.5
Costa Rica	56.5	47.3	109.6	80.7
El Salvador	48.7	45.9	81.0	62.4
Guatemala	22.7	17.5	51.2	29.5
Honduras	52.1	22.1	69.8	39.5
Mexico	31.4	13.9	47.7	25.5
Nicaragua	25.1	23.9	54.9	42.3
Peru	33.6[a]	28.3	53.2[a]	42.6
Uruguay	18.0[b]	18.2	38.0[b]	37.1
Venezuela	37.7	29.0	120.4	55.7

[a] Data are for 1929.
[b] Data are for 1930.
Sources: Rangel (1970); Millot, Silva, and Silva (1973); CEPAL (1976, 1978); Finch (1981); Palma (2000a); Bulmer-Thomas (1987); Maddison (1991). Data have been converted to a 1970 price basis where necessary, and official exchange rates have been used throughout.

external trade was conducted with only four countries (the United States, Great Britain, France, and Germany).[4]

Thus on the eve of the Great Depression the Latin American economies continued to follow a development model that left them highly vulnerable to adverse conditions in the world markets for primary products. Even Argentina, by far the most advanced Latin American economy in the late 1920s, with a GDP per head that was twice the regional average and four times higher than Brazil's,[5] had been unable to break the link under which a decline in export earnings would undermine imports and government revenue, leading to expenditure cuts and a decline in internal demand.

4 The combined share of these four industrial powers in Latin American trade had remained fairly stable for several decades, although the United States had gained market share at the expense of the others.
5 At purchasing-power parity exchange rates (1970 prices), the real income per head in Argentina in 1929 was $748 and in Brazil, $179. See CEPAL (1978). Thus the proportionate difference between the two countries in the late 1920s was as great as the difference between South Korea and the United States at the end of the twentieth century.

The Depression of 1929

The onset of the Great Depression is usually associated with the stock-market crash on Wall Street in October 1929, but for Latin America some of the warning signals came earlier. Commodity prices in many cases peaked before 1929, as supply (restored after wartime disruption) tended to outstrip demand. The price of Brazilian coffee reached its maximum in March 1929,[6] of Cuban sugar in March 1928, and of Argentine wheat in May 1927. The boom in stock markets before the Wall Street crash led to excess demand for credit and to a rise in world interest rates, raising the cost of holding inventories and reducing demand for many of the primary products exported by Latin America.

The rise in interest rates – the discount on New York commercial paper jumped by 50 percent in the eighteen months prior to the stock market crash – put additional pressure on Latin America through the capital market. Flight capital – attracted by higher rates of interest outside the region – increased, while capital inflows declined as foreign investors took advantage of the more attractive rates of return offered in London, Paris, and New York.[7]

The stock-market crash in October set in motion a chain of events in the main markets supplied by Latin America. The fall in the value of financial assets reduced consumer demand through the so-called wealth effect. Loan defaults led to a squeeze on new credit and to monetary contraction, and the whole financial system came under severe pressure. Interest rates started to fall in the fourth quarter of 1929, but importers were unable or unwilling to rebuild stocks of primary products in the face of credit restrictions and falling demand.

The subsequent fall in primary-product prices was truly dramatic. Every Latin American country was affected. Between 1928 and 1932 (see Table 7.2) the unit value of exports fell by more than 50 percent in ten of the countries for which data are available; the only countries with a modest fall in unit values were those (e.g., Honduras and Venezuela) in which the prices of primary products were administered by foreign companies and were not an accurate reflection of market forces.

Prices of imports also fell, as the decline in world demand and the fall in costs produced a double squeeze on the unit value of goods sold to Latin

---

6 Even a seemingly homogeneous commodity such as coffee, however, was subject to market segmentation. Thus the prices of some Latin American varieties peaked as early as the first quarter of 1927.

7 The Central Bank rate of discount in Chile, for example, was almost twice as high as that of the U.S. Federal Reserve Bank in 1926. In the first half of 1929 it was virtually the same. See League of Nations (1931), p. 252.

Table 7.2. *Price and quantity changes for exports, net barter terms of trade, and export purchasing power, 1932 (1928 = 100)*

Country	Export prices	Export volumes	Net barter terms of trade	Purchasing power of exports
Argentina	37	88	68	60
Bolivia	79[a]	48[a]	n/a	n/a
Brazil	43	86	65	56
Chile	47	31	57	17
Colombia	48	102	63	65
Costa Rica	54	81	78	65
Dominican Republic	55[b]	106[b]	81[b]	87[b]
Ecuador	51	83	74	60
El Salvador	30	75	52	38
Guatemala	37	101	54	55
Haiti	49[b]	104[b]	n/a	n/a
Honduras	91	101	130	133
Mexico	49	58	64	37
Nicaragua	50	78	71	59
Peru	39	76	62	43
Venezuela	81	100	101	100
Latin America	36	78	56	43

[a] 1929 = 100.
[b] 1930 = 100.
Sources: CEPAL (1976); Bulmer-Thomas (1987); Ground (1988) .

America. Import prices did not generally fall as fast or as far as export prices, however, and the net barter terms of trade (NBTT; see Table 7.2) declined sharply for all but two Latin American countries between 1928 and 1932. The exceptions are Venezuela, where the unit value of oil exports fell by "only" 18.5 percent (roughly in line with the fall in import prices), and Honduras, where the export "price" of bananas was set by the fruit companies simply to cover their local-currency costs and was reduced between those years by 9 percent.[8]

All of the republics faced a fall in price for their primary-product exports, but the volume of their export sales differed sharply. Worst affected were those republics – including Bolivia, Chile, and Mexico – with a severe drop in the price and volume of exports (see Table 7.2). Significantly, the exports of all three countries were dominated by minerals, as firms in importing countries reacted to the depression by running down existing inventories

8 Administered export prices were used for bananas for balance-of-payments purposes until 1947. The fruit companies calculated their domestic costs in local currency and set a dollar price for exports that – at the official exchange-rate – would meet their domestic obligations.

rather than by placing new orders.[9] Not surprisingly, these countries experienced the steepest decline in the purchasing power of exports (PPE; the NBTT adjusted for changes in the volume of exports). In Chile (see Table 7.2) the 83 percent fall in the PPE was the largest ever recorded in Latin America in such a short period and was one of the most severe in the world.[10]

Cuba, though not mentioned in Table 7.2 owing to lack of comparable data, should also be included in this first group.[11] Exports, dominated by sugar, fell rapidly after 1929 as the island suffered the consequences of its specialization in sugar and its heavy dependence on the United States. A committee led by Thomas Chadbourne, a New York lawyer with Cuban sugar interests, divided the U.S. market in 1930 in a way that implied a steep reduction in Cuban sugar exports,[12] and the next year an international sugar agreement was signed between the main producers and consumers that imposed further limits on Cuban exports.[13]

A second, more numerous, group of countries experienced a modest decline (less than 25 percent) in the volume of exports. This group – Argentina, Brazil, Ecuador, Peru, and all of Central America – produced a range of foodstuffs and agricultural raw materials the demand for which could not be so easily satisfied from existing stocks.[14] The United Kingdom, for example, held port stocks of imported wheat in August 1929 equivalent to only 2 percent of annual wheat imports.[15] Similarly, the steep fall in price was in some cases sufficient to sustain consumer demand despite the fall in real income in importing countries. The volume of world coffee imports, for example, was still as its 1929 level in 1932.

A third group of countries experienced a small (less than 10 percent) decline in the volume of exports between 1928 and 1932. Colombia,

---

9 The decline of Mexico's oil production meant that copper, lead, and zinc – all commodities with significant inventory levels in importing countries – were among the country's leading exports at the end of the 1920s.

10 Chilean dependence on nitrates and copper proved to be a most disastrous combination: Nitrates were beginning to be challenged by cheaper synthetic substitutes manufactured by the world's chemical industry; copper exports competed with U.S. domestic production, where the protectionist lobby was strong.

11 Trade ratios for Cuba, however, can be constructed at current prices. See Alienes (1950) and Pan-American Union (1952). These show an export ratio in 1929 of 47.7 percent – one of the highest in the region.

12 The committee, although insisting, "in nothing that we suggest here is there an effort made to interfere with the immutable laws of Supply and Demand," limited Cuban exports in 1931 to the 1928 level – the lowest in any year between 1922 and 1930. See Swerling (1949), pp. 42–3.

13 The island's problems were further compounded in 1934 by the Jones–Costigan Act, which established a reduced quota for U.S. sugar imports from Cuba.

14 Peru's main exports were minerals, but the most important was oil, in which stock holding was not so important and the price of which suffered less than other minerals in the Depression.

15 See League of Nations (1933), p. 577.

exploiting the confusion caused by the collapse of Brazil's coffee-valorization scheme,[16] managed a small increase in the volume of coffee exports. Venezuela suffered a decline in the volume of oil exports after 1929, but this merely offset the huge increase between 1928 and 1929. Exports from the Dominican Republic, dominated by sugar, steadily increased during the worst years of the depression, as sugar exporters took advantage of the restraints on Cuba that were imposed first by the Chadbourne Committee and later by the 1931 International Sugar Agreement, which was not signed by the Dominican Republic (or by Brazil).[17]

The combination of falling export prices for all countries and falling export volumes for most countries produced a sharp decline in the PPE over the worst years of the Depression (see Table 7.2). Only Venezuela, protected by oil, and Honduras, helped by a decision of the fruit companies to concentrate global production on their low-cost Honduran plantations, escaped. Elsewhere the impact of the depression on the PPE was severe: It affected mineral producers (e.g., Mexico), temperate-foodstuff producers (e.g., Argentina), and tropical-foodstuff exporters (e.g., El Salvador).

While export and import prices were falling after 1929, one "price" remained the same: the fixed nominal interest rate on public and private foreign debt. As other prices fell, the real interest rate on this debt (mainly government bonds) rose, increasing the fiscal and balance-of-payments burden for those governments that were anxious to preserve their credentials in the international capital market through prompt payment of debt service.

The rise in the real burden of the debt meant that an increasing share of (declining) total exports had to be allocated to debt-service payments. Argentina, for example, devoted 91.2 million pesos to foreign debt-service payments in 1929 against total exports of 2,168 million pesos. By 1932 exports had dropped to 1,288 million pesos while foreign debt-service payments remained at 93.6 million pesos, implying a virtual doubling of the real debt burden.[18]

The combination of unchanged debt-service payments and falling export receipts exerted a strong squeeze on imports. As the volume and value of imports fell, governments had to come to terms with a new problem caused by the heavy dependence of fiscal revenue on external trade taxes. The principal source of government revenue, tariff duties on imports, could not be maintained in the wake of an import collapse. Brazil, for example, collected 42.4 percent of total government revenue from taxes on imports

---

16 The Brazilian coffee *defesa* collapsed in 1929. See Fritsch (1988), pp. 152–3.
17 See Swerling (1949), pp. 40–50.
18 The real burden of debt also rose sharply as a proportion of public expenditure. See Alhadeff (1986),
      p. 101.

in 1928. By 1930 import tax collection had been cut by one-third and government revenue by one-quarter.[19] Those countries that also depended heavily on export taxes (e.g., Chile) experienced a particularly severe cut in government revenue.[20]

The rise in the real burden of debt service affected the fiscal position in much the same way as it affected the balance of payments. The combination of falling government revenue and debt-service payments fixed in nominal terms put intense pressure on government expenditures. Efforts were made at creative accounting (Honduran civil servants, for example, were paid in postage stamps for a time), but this could not conceal the underlying crisis. Most Latin American republics witnessed a change of government during the worst years of the Depression, with the swing of the pendulum favoring the parties or individuals out of government at the time of the Wall Street crash.[21] The most important exceptions were Venezuela, where the autocratic government of Juan Vicente Gómez, in power since 1908, survived until the dictator's death, in 1935,[22] and Mexico, where the recently formed Partido Nacional Revolucionario (later Partido Revolucionario Institucional, or PRI) presided over a country exhausted by revolutionary upheaval and civil war.[23]

In a less crisis-ridden international environment a Latin American government might have hoped to borrow its way out of its difficulties with the help of international loans. However, the flow of new lending to Latin America – already in decline even before the Wall Street crash – had ground to a halt by 1931. In that year repayment of U.S. portfolio capital exceeded new U.S. portfolio investment for the first time since 1920, and the net flow remained negative (with the minor exception of 1938) until 1954.[24] Even Argentina, which by any standards had the highest credit rating in

19 See IBGE (1987), Tables 12.1 and 12.2.
20 In some years during the 1920s export duties had been even more important than import tariffs in Chile. Because the marginal export tax was higher than the average, the yield fell disproportionately rapidly as export prices collapsed.
21 Many governments fell as early as 1930. A military coup brought Getúlio Vargas to power in Brazil, for example, and President Hipólito Yrigoyen was overthrown in Argentina. In Chile political instability became so acute that a socialist republic was even established by an army officer in 1932, although it only lasted for twelve days. See the relevant chapters in Bethell (1991).
22 A coup against Gómez was attempted in 1928, but the dictator faced no major challenge to his authority in the depression years despite a fall in oil prices and production. See Ewell (1991), pp. 728–9.
23 Mexico, which endured a long, drawn-out revolution in the 1910s, enjoyed no respite in the 1920s. The army rebelled twice, the *Cristero* rebellion brought renewed bloodshed, and former president and president-elect Alvaro Obregón was assassinated in July 1928. By the end of the decade, however, the foundations of the modern state had been laid, and institutional rule began to replace personalist rule. With the election of Lázaro Cárdenas as president (1934–40), the Mexican Revolution came of age. See A. Knight (1990), pp. 4–7.
24 See Stallings (1987), Appendix I.

Latin America, was unable to obtain significant new loans during the first years of the Depression.

No Latin American country escaped the Great Depression, but its impact was much worse in some countries than in others. The most disastrous combination was a high degree of openness, a large fall in the price of exports, and a steep decline in the volume of exports. It is no surprise, therefore, that the most seriously affected republics were Chile and Cuba, where the external shock was strongest. Indeed, estimates of Cuban national income during the interwar years show a drop of one-third in real national income per head between 1928 and 1932,[25] and the decline in Chilean real GDP between 1929 and 1932 has been estimated at 35.7 percent.[26]

The impact of external shock could be mitigated under exceptional circumstances, but not avoided. Thus the Dominican Republic – dependent on sugar exports – was able to exploit its position as a nonsignatory of the post-1929 sugar agreements. Venezuela took advantage of its position as the oil producer with the lowest unit costs in all the Americas. Countries with exports dominated by foreign companies (e.g., Peru) saw some of the burden transferred to the outside world through a reduction in profit remittances and an increase in returned value as a proportion of total exports. Generally, however, the external shock was severe, and the introduction of stabilization measures to restore external and internal equilibrium could not be delayed for long.

Short-term stabilization

The external shocks associated with the depression created two disequilibria that policymakers in each republic had to address as a matter of urgency. The first was the external imbalance created by the collapse of earnings from exports and the decline in capital inflows; the second was the internal imbalance caused by the decline in government revenue, which gave rise to budget deficits that could no longer be financed from abroad.

During the 1920s the republics of Latin America had either adopted the gold-exchange standard for the first time (e.g., Bolivia) or had returned to it (e.g., Argentina[27]). Under the gold-exchange standard, adjustment to external disequilibrium was supposed to be automatic – indeed, this was one of its principal attractions. As exports fell, gold or foreign exchange would be drained out of a country, lowering money supply, credit, and demand

25 See Brundenius (1984), Table A.2.1. The primary source is Alienes (1950).

26 See Palma (2000a), Table 3.5, in which the GDP estimate is derived from ECLA (1951). Long-run GDP estimates, as well as the sectoral breakdown, can also be found in Díaz (1998).

27 Argentina may have returned to exchange-rate orthodoxy in the 1920s, but – like Brazil – it still lacked a central bank. Furthermore, gold payments (effected through a *caja de conversión*) were not resumed until August 1927.

for imports; at the same time, monetary contraction would lower the price level, making exports more competitive and imports more expensive. Thus imports would fall both through expenditure reduction and through expenditure switching, and the process would continue until external equilibrium was restored.

The decline in the value of exports was so severe after 1929, however, that it was by no means clear whether external equilibrium could be restored automatically. Furthermore, the decline in capital inflows and the initial determination to service the foreign debt meant that the drop in imports needed to be particularly steep to eliminate a balance-of-payments deficit. Argentina saw the value of its exports drop from $1,537 million in 1929 to $561 million in 1932 – and this was by no means the most severe case. With imports in 1929 valued at $1,388 million, Argentina needed to cut foreign purchases by 70 percent if it wished to maintain debt-service payments in 1932 on the same terms as in 1929.[28]

Those countries that did try to play by the rules of the gold-exchange standard saw their holdings of gold and their foreign-exchange reserves fall rapidly. Colombia struggled on until four days after the British suspension of the gold standard (on 21 September 1931), by which time the republic had seen its international reserves fall by 65 percent.[29] Most countries, however, either abandoned the system formally (e.g., Argentina in December 1929)[30] or limited outflows of gold and foreign exchange through a variety of banking and other restrictions (e.g., Costa Rica).[31] This did not avoid the need for stabilization policies to reduce imports and reestablish external disequilibrium, but it did mean that the process would no longer be automatic.

Three countries (Argentina, Mexico, and Uruguay) suspended the gold standard before the British decision to stop selling gold and foreign exchange on demand, although Peru – alone in Latin America – twice introduced a new gold parity.[32] Most countries, however, adopted exchange

28 Imports did in fact fall by 74 percent – from $1,388 million in 1929 to $364 million in 1932. See CEPAL (1976), p. 27.

29 The newly created central bank in Colombia, Banco de la República, reacted with extreme orthodoxy to the first signs of depression. Thus discount rates were increased above their pre-Depression level and averaged 8–9 percent at a time when prices were falling sharply. See Ocampo (2000), p. 112. The real discount rate therefore rose above 20 percent, though this was not unique to Colombia. See Ground (1988), p. 182, note 16.

30 Thus Argentina returned to the system of inconvertible currency that it had operated before August 1927. This did not at first imply devaluation, however. See O'Connell (2000), p. 179.

31 In Costa Rica the *caja de conversión* set the exchange-rate, and a board of control (established in January 1932) restricted the size of applications. Thus the demand for foreign exchange was rationed by administered prices and quantities. See Bulmer-Thomas (1987), p. 54.

32 A new gold parity was the only way of devaluing within the orthodox rules of international finance before the collapse of the gold standard. Peru also used the occasion of a change in the gold parity in 1930 to replace the libra with the sol (the country's traditional currency unit), at ten soles per paper libra.

control in one form or another and created a rationing system for imports. The only countries that did not make use of exchange controls were the small Caribbean Basin republics that used the U.S. dollar as means of payment, either officially (Panama and the Dominican Republic) or unofficially (Cuba and Honduras[33]).

The desire to stick to the international rules of the game meant that devaluation – currency depreciation – was at first used sparingly. No one expected the depression to be as severe as it turned out to be: The last world depression (1920–1) had passed quickly, without permanently disrupting the international financial system. Furthermore, many Latin American republics had overhauled their financial systems in the 1920s, created central banks, and struggled for monetary discipline. The 1929 depression was seen as the first real test of the institutions, and their reluctance to admit failure through currency depreciation was natural.

By the end of 1930 only five countries (Argentina, Brazil, Paraguay, Peru, and Uruguay) had seen their currencies depreciate by more than 5 percent against the U.S. dollar since the end of the previous year. Peru, however, had changed its gold parity. The Paraguayan peso, officially pegged to the Argentine gold peso, also depreciated against the U.S. dollar as an unintended consequence of exchange-rate policy. The British suspension of the gold standard and the subsequent depreciation of the pound sterling meant that those Latin American currencies with a sterling link – Argentina, Bolivia, Paraguay (via the Argentine peso), and Uruguay – fell sharply against the U.S. dollar after September 1931, until the U.S. suspension of the gold standard in April 1933 produced an equally abrupt appreciation.[34]

The decision by Great Britain and the United States to abandon the gold standard finally forced all the republics to address the problem of exchange-rate management. Six small republics (Cuba, the Dominican Republic, Guatemala, Haiti, Honduras, and Panama) all pegged their currencies to the U.S. dollar throughout the 1930s. Three others (Costa Rica, El Salvador, and Nicaragua) tried to do the same but were eventually forced to devalue.[35] Even in South America, among the larger republics many attempts were

---

33 Cuba introduced exchange control in June 1934 but suppressed it one month later because it was ineffective. Honduras introduced exchange control in March 1934, but it had virtually no impact as a result of the widespread use of the U.S. dollar in the banana zones. See Bratter (1939).

34 U.S. depreciation against gold was rapid. By the fourth quarter of 1933 the value of the dollar had fallen to 60 percent of its 1929 gold parity. Whether this translated into a devaluation against other currencies depended on their movement in relation to their former gold parity. Thus the scene was set for a series of competitive devaluations among the industrial powers that contributed to the instability of the international financial system before the Second World War. See Kindleberger (1987), Chapters 9–11 and Temin (2000).

35 The devaluations in Costa Rica and El Salvador were relatively modest and did not set off an inflationary spiral. In Nicaragua, however, Anastasio Somoza ("elected" president in 1936) found currency depreciation a most convenient way of undermining political opposition from agroexport interests. See Bulmer-Thomas (1990b), p. 335.

made to peg currencies to the pound sterling or the U.S. dollar. Paraguay persisted with its policy of tracking the Argentine peso (albeit with little success); Argentina (with some success) and Bolivia (with none) tried to link their currencies to the pound sterling after January 1934 and January 1935, respectively. Brazil (December 1937), Chile (September 1936), Colombia (March 1935), Ecuador (May 1932), and Mexico (July 1933) all tried to link their currencies to the U.S. dollar.[36]

Examples of genuinely floating currencies were rare. The Venezuelan bolívar was floated and promptly appreciated by 50 percent against the U.S. dollar between the end of 1932 and the end of 1937.[37] Several of the South American countries (Argentina, Bolivia, Brazil, Chile, Ecuador, and Uruguay) adopted a dual exchange-rate system after the suspension of the gold standard by the United States, with the nonofficial rate allowed to fluctuate freely. This free rate was used for a variety of transactions, including capital exports, profit remittances, nontraditional exports, and nonessential imports. This experience – which was in many cases a source of exchange-rate profits for the public sector[38] – was to prove invaluable for exchange-rate management after the Second World War.

In view of the reluctance to adopt genuinely freely floating exchange-rate regimes, the majority of republics were forced to rely on other techniques for achieving external equilibrium. The most popular was exchange control and a nonprice rationing system for imports. This technique was not limited to the larger republics, for several small countries (Bolivia, Costa Rica, Ecuador, Honduras, Nicaragua, Paraguay, and Uruguay) adopted the system aggressively. In most countries tariff rates were raised at a time when the CIF price of imports was falling, which raised the real cost of imports sharply and encouraged a switch in expenditure toward domestic substitutes. Even where tariff rates were not formally raised, the real cost of imports tended to increase as a result of the widespread use of specific tariffs.[39]

36 In Mexico currency stabilization was complicated by the expansionary monetary policies adopted in 1932 by Alberto Pani, the minister of finance who had replaced the orthodox Luis Montes de Oca in December 1931. The first attempt at stabilization therefore had to be abandoned. The second attempt was much more successful, and the peso was unchanged against the U.S. dollar from November 1933 to March 1938. See Cárdenas (2000), pp. 201–4.

37 Foreign-exchange receipts rose, with higher oil production and an increase in returned value from oil exports. Meanwhile, the oil companies cut back on their (import-intensive) investment expenditures, and Venezuela did not have to make any debt-service payments. Under the circumstances, the appreciation of the bolívar is hardly surprising. See McBeth (1983), Chapter 4.

38 Multiple exchange-rate systems can produce losses as well as profits, as Latin American governments discovered in the postwar period. However, in the 1930s the purpose of multiple-rate systems was to make almost all imports more expensive, so exchange-rate profits were the rule rather than the exception.

39 On average, import prices were about one-third lower in 1932 than in 1929. Thus a meter of imported cloth that cost $1.00 in 1929 and attracted a specific tariff of 20 cents might have cost only 70 cents three years later. With an unchanged specific tariff, the implicit tariff rate would have risen from 20 percent to 28.6 percent – an increase of more than 40 percent.

In a few cases external equilibrium was achieved without exchange control and nonprice import rationing through a gold-standard-like mechanism: Current-account deficits were financed through an outflow of international reserves, which reduced the money supply so sharply that nominal demand fell into line with the required reduction in nominal imports. The clearest cases of this automatic adjustment to external equilibrium can be found in Cuba, the Dominican Republic, Haiti, and Panama. Mexico also experienced a sharp decline in its nominal money supply in the first years of the depression as a result of its peculiar monetary system, in which silver and gold coins made up most of the money in circulation.[40]

By the end of 1932 external equilibrium had been restored in virtually all of the republics, at a much lower level of nominal exports and imports and at a slightly lower level of nominal debt-service payments. A balance-of-trade surplus for Latin America in 1929 of $570 million had increased to $609 million by 1932, despite a two-thirds fall in nominal exports, from $4,683 million to $1,663 million.[41] The eight countries that had recorded a balance-of-trade deficit in 1929 were reduced to six by 1930, to five by 1931, and to four by 1932. These four (Cuba, the Dominican Republic, Haiti, and Panama) were the exceptions that proved the rule, however: All were economies in which the dollar circulated freely, without exchange control, so a trade deficit and foreign-exchange outflow was the mechanism by which nominal demand was brought into line with the PPE.

The achievement of external equilibrium, however painful, was inevitable. Most of the republics could not pay for imports in their own currency, so the supply of foreign exchange set a limit on available imports once international reserves were exhausted. Internal equilibrium was different, because a government could always issue its own currency to finance a budget deficit. Only in countries such as Panama, where the dollar circulated freely and where no central bank existed, could one be certain that the achievement of external equilibrium also implied internal equilibrium.[42]

In most republics suspension of the gold standard and the adoption of exchange control drove a wedge between external and internal adjustment. Where budget deficits persisted and were financed domestically, the supply of nominal money would not fall into line with the decrease in nominal imports. This would cause the ratio of domestic credit to imports to rise,

40 See Cárdenas (2000), pp. 197–8.

41 Latin America had traditionally run a trade surplus; that is, commodity exports exceeded commodity imports. See Horn and Bice (1949), p. 103. Nevertheless, the size of the surplus varied considerably, falling in the late 1920s and rising in the 1930s.

42 Although the local Panamanian currency was (and is) called the balboa, this was (and is) a legal fiction because the U.S. dollar is in effect the unit of account. Thus the Panamanian government could not run a budget deficit without access to foreign borrowing – which was virtually impossible in the 1930s.

Table 7.3. *The money supply: commercial bank time and demand deposits,*
1930–1936 (current prices; 1929 = 100)

Country	1930	1931	1932	1933	1934	1935	1936
Argentina	101	90	90	89	88	86	94
Bolivia	84	78	133	144	322	520	547
Brazil	97	101	115	109	125	131	141
Chile	84	68	82	96	110	124	143
Colombia	87	78	90	94	102	110	120
Ecuador	98	59	92	145	187	187	215
El Salvador[a]	74	68	64	57	42	44	37
Mexico[b]	111	67	74	107	108	136	143
Paraguay	100[c]	76	64	72	125	191	170
Peru	69	63	62	78	100	116	137
Uruguay	114	115	126	114	116	124	139
Venezuela	49	68	69	76	85	106	89
United States	101	92	71	63	72	81	92

[a] Includes dollar deposits.
[b] The data were compiled on a different basis in 1932 and 1935, so the series is not consistent.
[c] 1930 = 100.
Source: League of Nations, *Statistical Yearbook.*

creating an excess supply of money that in turn would stimulate domestic expenditure in nominal terms. Whether the increase in nominal expenditure was reflected in price or quantity increases would be crucial in determining how quickly and how successfully a country escaped the depression.

The idea of a monetary overhang finds empirical support in many countries. Whereas the United States experienced a nearly 40 percent drop in nominal commercial bank deposits in the 1929–33 period (see Table 7.3), some Latin American republics (e.g., Bolivia, Brazil, Ecuador, and Uruguay) saw the nominal value of commercial bank deposits rise, and others (e.g., Argentina, Chile, and Colombia) experienced only a modest fall. In real terms (i.e., adjusted for the change in the price level), the performance is even more remarkable: Prices fell between 1929 and 1933 in all of the Latin American republics (except Chile) for which price data exist.[43]

The nominal money supply was relatively buoyant for several reasons. First, the decision to impose exchange control in many republics restricted the outflow of gold and foreign exchange and therefore limited the reduction

43 Chilean prices (wholesale and retail) did fall in 1930 and 1931. However, the subsequent depreciation of the currency was reflected in price rises with only a short lag – a consequence, perhaps, of the inflationary expectations established in Chile as a result of the long experience of exchange-rate devaluation. See Hirschman (1963), Chapter 3.

in the supply of money of external origin. Uruguay, one of the first countries to impose exchange control, suffered only a modest drop in international reserves. Mexico, which had no exchange controls, was drained of the gold and silver specie that constituted such a high proportion of its monetary stock.

Second, budget deficits persisted, despite enormous efforts to raise revenue and cut expenditures. Brazil managed to increase the yield from direct taxes on income by 24 percent between 1929 and 1932 despite the contraction in real GDP, but the overwhelming importance of external trade taxes forced fiscal revenue down in line with the collapse in imports and exports.[44] Furthermore, the initial determination to service the public debt (internal and external) and the difficulties associated with sharp cuts in nominal wages and salaries for public employees made it virtually impossible to cut expenditures by enough to eliminate budget deficits. In the absence of new external loans, the deficits had to be financed through the banking system, which had an expansionary effect on the money supply.

Third, the decline of private domestic credit was by no means as sharp as might have been expected in view of the close links between the banking system and the export sector. The small number of banks – Mexico, for example, had only eleven – and their high public profile created a powerful incentive to avoid bank failure. The close relationship between bankers and exporters (who sometimes were the same individuals) allowed for greater flexibility in debt rescheduling than would have been permitted in a more competitive environment. Banks also tended to operate in the 1920s with cash reserves well above the legal minimum, leaving a certain cushion available for the difficult times after 1929. Foreign banks, unable to remit profits after exchange control, had additional resources to sustain themselves through the Depression years.[45]

Thus monetary policy in the depth of the Depression was relatively slack in many republics, so internal equilibrium – unlike external equilibrium – had not been restored by the end of 1932. Efforts to raise taxes, including tariffs, had proved insufficient, and further increases promised to be self-defeating. Cuts in the public sector wage-and-salary bill were made more difficult by the turbulent political circumstances at the start of the 1930s, so policies for reducing the budget deficit increasingly came to focus on debt-service payments.

Debt default was nothing new in Latin American economic history; indeed, the customs houses of some small republics (e.g., Nicaragua) were

---

44 Brazilian fiscal problems were compounded in 1932 by the insurrection in the state of São Paulo which obliged the federal government to increase expenditure sharply. See Schneider (1991), pp. 118–25.

45 A good example is provided by the British-owned Bank of London and South America, which held cash ratios high at most branches to avoid a loss of confidence. See Joslin (1963), p. 250.

still full of U.S. officials appointed to collect external-trade taxes and to avoid a repetition of past debt defaults. At first all the republics made strenuous efforts to maintain debt-service payments, in the hope that they would preserve access to international capital markets. This created an intriguing dilemma: The main creditor in terms of the stock of international bonds remained Great Britain, where stock-exchange rules made it impossible for countries in default to float new bond issues; meanwhile, the annual flow of new capital to Latin America had become increasingly dependent on the United States, where the penalties for default were less clear. As it became apparent that Latin America could not in general expect additional finance from Great Britain, the temptation to default became almost overwhelming.

Mexico, still caught up in the aftermath of its revolution, had suspended debt-service payments as early as 1928. Generally, however, suspension began in 1931 and gathered pace in the next few years. Default was unilateral, but no country repudiated its external debts, and not all issues were treated equally. Brazil, for example, established seven grades of bonds in 1934, with treatment varying from full service to complete default on interest and principal.[46] Thus the impact on government expenditure varied substantially even among defaulting countries, although the resources committed to debt service tended to decline everywhere as the decade advanced.

Not all countries defaulted on the external debt, and default on the external debt did not necessarily imply default on the internal debt (or vice versa). Venezuela, under Gómez, completed the redemption of its external debt – begun fifteen years earlier – in 1930.[47] Honduras defaulted on its internal debt but serviced its external debt in full[48] (as did the Dominican Republic and Haiti). Of the major countries (apart from Venezuela), only Argentina serviced its internal and external debt in full, for reasons that are still controversial. Its special relationship with Great Britain, the close trading links, and the prospect of continuing loans were some of the factors that persuaded Argentine policymakers to service the debt, the bulk of which was owed to Great Britain. In addition, the financial orthodoxy of the conservative Argentine administrations in the 1930s provided a strong bias in favor of debt repayment.[49]

Debt default eased the pressure on the budget deficit in most countries and (in the case of the external debt) released foreign exchange that

46 See Eichengreen and Portes (1988), pp. 25–31.
47 A small amount of foreign debt remained on the books, because the authorities were unable to trace the owners. However, no interest payments could be made for the same reason.
48 Honduran orthodoxy on the external debt was due to the fact that the country's nineteenth-century obligations, including fraudulent loans made to the state railway company in the 1860s, had finally been settled only in 1926. The settlement terms were generous, involving a cancellation of all arrears of interest and a reduction in principal. See León Gómez (1978), pp. 177–81.
49 The literature on the reasons for Argentine orthodoxy in the 1930s is huge. See, for example, Rock (1991) and Abreu (2000).

could be spent for other purposes. The decline of debt-service payments, however, took some of the pressure off fiscal policy because it avoided the need for further tax increases or expenditure cuts. Budget deficits therefore remained common, and internal equilibrium was still a distant goal in most republics. The tension between external equilibrium and internal disequilibrium produced serious financial and economic instability in some republics (e.g., Bolivia),[50] but it also contributed to economic recovery at a faster pace than was found in countries in which tight fiscal and monetary policies left the nonexport sector with insufficient demand and unable to respond to the new vector of relative prices.

Recovery from the Depression

The policies adopted to stabilize each economy in response to the Depression were intended to restore internal and external equilibrium in the short term. Inevitably, however, they also had longer-term implications in those countries in which they permanently affected relative prices.

The collapse of export prices after 1929, the deterioration in the NBTT, and the rise in nominal tariffs favored the nonexport sector (both nontradables and importables[51]) over the export sector in terms of relative prices. Where real devaluation occurred (i.e., nominal devaluation more rapid than the difference between home and foreign prices), both exportables and importables received a price advantage relative to nontraded goods. Thus the price of the import-competing sector improved relative to both exportables and nontraded goods in every case, whereas the nontraded sector increased its price relative to the export sector unless real devaluation occurred (in which case the result was indeterminate).

Whether these short-term shifts in relative prices persisted depended to a large extent on the movement in export and import prices. For Latin America as a whole, export prices fell steadily until 1934. At that point a new cycle began, which produced a sharp recovery in prices in 1936 and 1937, followed by two years of export price falls. Import prices remained weak, however, so the NBTT improved from 1933 to 1937 and even in 1939 were still 36 percent above the 1933 level and equal to the 1930 level. Thus for the region as a whole a permanent improvement in the relative price of the import-competing sector depended less on movements in the NBTT and more on increases in tariff rates and real devaluation.

---

50 Bolivian fiscal imbalances escalated with the need to increase military expenditure following the outbreak of war with Paraguay in 1932. Defense spending rose eightfold between 1932 and 1933, and revenue only covered 25 percent of total expenditure.

51 Importables are commodities that are produced locally in competition with imports; nontradables are those goods and services that are not exported and that do not face competition from imports. On relative price movements in the 1930s, see Ground (1988).

The import-competing sector consisted of all activities that were capable of substituting for imports. It has conventionally been identified with import-substituting industrialization (ISI) in view of the importance of manufactures in the import bill. However, many countries in the 1920s were importing substantial quantities of agricultural goods that could in principle be produced by domestic activities. Thus, it is also necessary to consider import-substituting agriculture (ISA) as part of the import-competing sector.[52]

The change in relative prices encouraged resource shifts and acted as a mechanism of recovery from the depression. This was only part of the story, however. A fall in the output of the export sector, for example, and a rise in the output of the import-competing sector would not necessarily produce a recovery in real GDP, though it would produce structural change. Recovery was assured only if the import-competing sector expanded without a fall in the export sector or if the import-competing sector grew so rapidly that it could compensate for export decline. The first possibility points to the importance of export-sector performance in the 1930s, a much-neglected topic; the second requires consideration of the growth of nominal demand.

We have shown that stabilization programs were very successful in restoring external equilibrium in almost all republics by 1932, but that many countries had less success in eliminating budget deficits. The persistence of deficits in some republics, even after debt-service payments were reduced through default, provided a stimulus to nominal demand that under certain circumstances could be expected to have real (Keynesian) effects. These conditions included the existence of spare capacity and a price-elastic supply response in the import-competing sector, together with a financial system that was capable of supplying finance for working capital at low real rates of interest. Where these conditions did not exist (e.g., Bolivia), the consequence of fiscal deficits and the growth of nominal demand was simply inflation and a collapse of the nominal exchange-rate;[53] where they did exist (e.g., Brazil), loose fiscal and monetary policies could contribute to recovery. Thus for some republics the consequences of incomplete stabilization measures in pursuit of internal equilibrium after 1929 were by no means unfavorable. By contrast, some "virtuous" republics (e.g., Argentina) faced the paradox that orthodox fiscal and monetary policies in pursuit of balanced budgets may have lowered the rate of economic growth in the 1930s.

---

52 In theory it is also necessary to consider import substitution in services (ISS). In the 1930s, however, international trade in services was very limited, so in practice it can be ignored.

53 Retail prices rose by 300 percent in Bolivia between 1931 and 1937. The powerful mining industry demanded currency depreciation by way of compensation for the rise in local costs, so a vicious cycle soon prevailed. See Whitehead (1991), pp. 520–1.

With only two minor exceptions (Honduras and Nicaragua[54]), recovery from the Depression, in terms of real GDP, began after 1931–2. In the remainder of the 1930s all republics for which data are available[55] achieved positive growth, and all surpassed the predepression peak in real GDP, with the same two exceptions. The speed of recovery varied considerably, however, and so did the recovery mechanisms. In particular, almost no countries relied exclusively on ISI for their recovery, and some simply depended on the return of more favorable conditions in export markets.

Following Chenery,[56] we can explore Latin America's recovery during the 1930s through a growth-accounting equation that breaks down the change in real GDP into its main components: import substitution, export promotion, and the growth of home final demand.[57] It is then possible to identify a number of recovery mechanisms that correspond loosely to the entries in the growth-accounting equation. This is presented in Table 7.4, in which the fourteen republics for which GDP data exist are grouped into three categories of recovery: fast, medium, and slow.

The fast-recovery group comprises the eight republics in which real GDP rose by more than 50 percent between the trough year (1931 or 1932) and 1939. Two countries (Brazil and Mexico) can be considered large, four (Chile, Cuba, Peru, and Venezuela) medium sized, and two (Costa Rica and Guatemala) small. Thus no correlation exists between size and speed of recovery. ISI is an important recovery mechanism in most of the group, but not in Cuba, Guatemala, or Venezuela. Indeed, Cuban recovery was due mainly to better prices for sugar, which contributed to a doubling of the value of exports between 1932 and 1939; Venezuelan recovery was due primarily to the growth of oil production; and Guatemalan recovery depended heavily on ISA.

The medium-recovery group comprises the republics in which real GDP rose by more than 20 percent between the trough year and 1939. Only three republics (Argentina, Colombia, and El Salvador) can be placed with certainty in this group, though some other republics (Bolivia, Ecuador, the Dominican Republic, and Haiti), for which national accounts in this period do not exist, all registered a significant increase in the volume of exports

---

54 Honduras, its economic destiny intimately linked to the fortunes of the banana industry, was crippled by the spread of disease on the banana plantations after 1931. Nicaragua also suffered from a weak export sector and in addition had to contend with the economic problems caused by the final withdrawal of U.S. marines in January 1933.

55 Some estimate of GDP growth in the 1930s exists for fourteen republics. See Table 7.6.

56 See Chenery (1960). See also Syrquin (1988), in which numerous refinements to the original methodology are discussed.

57 The sources-of-growth equation is more usually applied to a particular sector (e.g., industry), with the change in output broken down into the contribution from import substitution, export promotion, intermediate consumption, and home final demand. The data for this equation are not generally available for the 1930s.

Table 7.4. *Qualitative analysis of sources of growth in the 1930s.*

Country	Import-substituting industrialization	Import-substituting agriculture	Export growth
	Fast-recovery countries		
Brazil	*		$
Chile	*		$
Costa Rica	*	#	
Cuba		#	$
Guatemala		#	
Mexico	*	#	
Peru	*		$
Venezuela			$
	Medium-recovery countries		
Argentina	*	#	
Colombia	*		
El Salvador		#	$
	Low-recovery countries		
Honduras		#	
Nicaragua		#	
Uruguay	*		

Note: Fast-recovery countries assumed to increase real GDP from trough year to 1939 by more than 50 percent, medium-recovery countries by more than 20 percent and less than 50 percent, low-recovery countries by less than 20 percent. * = ratio of manufacturing net output to GDP assumed to increase significantly; # = ratio of Domestic Use Agriculture to GDP assumed to increase significantly; $ = ratio of exports to GDP assumed to increase significantly in either nominal or real terms.
Sources: Rangel (1970); Millot, Silva, and Silva (1973); CEPAL (1976, 1978); Finch (1981); Palma (2000a); Bulmer-Thomas (1987); Maddison (1991). Data have been converted to a 1970 price basis where necessary, and official exchange rates have been used throughout.

after 1932 and are likely to have experienced a rise in GDP that would place them in this second category. ISI was important as a recovery mechanism in Argentina and Colombia, but export growth was not significant.

The final group includes the republics with the least successful performance. Only three (Honduras, Nicaragua, and Uruguay) are listed in Table 7.4, but the disastrous export performances of Paraguay and Panama (for which national-accounts data are not available) suggest that they should also be included. All five were small economies with little possibility (with the exception of Uruguay) of offsetting a weak export performance through an increase in import-competing activities. Uruguay did experience a rise in industrial output, and ISI was important, but this was not sufficient to compensate for the stagnation of the crucial livestock industry. In Panama, where service exports are so important, the decline in world trade volumes produced a drop in the number of ships using the canal in the 1930s; this had an adverse impact on overall economic performance.[58] Paraguay, though victorious in the Chaco War with Bolivia (1932–5), suffered terrible losses, and the nominal value of exports continued to fall until 1940.

If we limit ourselves to the 1932–9 period, when the recovery was at its strongest in Latin America, twelve countries[59] provided sufficient national-accounts data to produce a limited version of a growth-accounting equation in which the change in real GDP is broken down into the proportion due to the growth in home final demand (with no change in import coefficients), the proportion due to the change in import coefficients, and the proportion due to export recovery (see Table 7.5). By far the most important contribution in all cases is the recovery of home final demand, followed by export promotion; the contribution due to changes in import coefficients is generally negative, as import coefficients tended to rise rather than fall after 1932.

If a year in the 1920s rather than 1932 is used as the starting point, the picture changes considerably (see Table 7.5), because import coefficients in 1939 were invariably lower than they had been a decade earlier. Nevertheless, export promotion was still a positive source of growth in most cases, and the contribution of home final demand (assuming an unchanged import coefficient) was more important than import substitution in all the major countries except Argentina. These results do not mean that import substitution in industry was not important, because the sources of growth equation applied to the manufacturing sector alone can yield a different outcome. Yet, using a longer period (1929–50), the contribution of import substitution to industrial growth in the larger countries (Argentina, Brazil, Chile, Colombia, and Mexico) has been estimated at a weighted average of 39 percent – implying that the growth of home final demand (the contribution of industrial exports can be ignored) was important for the manufacturing sector as well.[60]

The recovery of home final demand was a reflection of the loose fiscal and monetary policies referred to above. Budget deficits were common and – in the absence of foreign loans – were usually financed through the banking system, with an expansionary effect on the money supply. Financial institutions, strengthened by the creation of central banks in several countries (e.g., Argentina[61] and El Salvador) or underpinned by the monetary reforms

---

58 For economic purposes the Panama Canal Zone was treated as U.S. territory until 1979. The government of Panama received an annuity from the United States, but this covered only a small part of total government expenditure. A new treaty, which gave Panama certain commercial advantages in its dealings with the Canal Zone, was signed with the United States in 1936; in practice, however, these advantages were largely ignored. See Major (1990), p. 657.

59 The twelve countries are all those except Uruguay in Table 7.1.

60 See Grunwald and Musgrove (1970), Table A.4, pp. 16–17.

61 The Argentine Central Bank was created in 1935, with Raúl Prebisch as its general manager. Prebisch, however, remained thoroughly orthodox in his economic thinking during the 1930s. See Love (1994).

Table 7.5. *Quantitative analysis of sources of growth, 1932–1939 and 1929–1939 (in percentages)*

Country	1932–1939			1929–1939		
	(1)	(2)	(3)	(1)	(2)	(3)
Argentina	+102	+6	−8	+51	+84	−36
Brazil	+74	−11	+37	+39	+31	+31
Chile	+71	−24	+53	+67[a]	+28[a]	+5[a]
Colombia	+117	−35	+18	+61	+24	+15
Costa Rica	+96	−21	+25	+36	+64	0
El Salvador	+39	−4	+65	+31[b]	+11[b]	+58[b]
Guatemala	+92	+2	+6	+64	+30	+6
Honduras	—[c]	—[c]	—[c]	+55[b]	+17[b]	+28[b]
Mexico	+108	+1	−9	+113	+61	−74
Nicaragua	+98	−1	+3	+64[d]	+47[d]	−11[d]
Peru	+85	−2	+17	+68	+30	+2
Venezuela	+80	−1	+21	+19	+67	+14

Key: (1) Percentage contribution to increase in real GDP of home final demand, assuming no change in import coefficient;
(2) percentage contribution to increase in real GDP of change in import coefficient; and
(3) percentage contribution to increase in real GDP of export promotion.
[a] Data are for 1925–39.
[b] Data are for 1920–39.
[c] Sources of growth equation cannot be applied, because home final demand fell between 1932 and 1939.
[d] Data are for 1926–39.
Sources: Author's calculations, using data from Rangel (1970); Millot, Silva, and Silva (1973); CEPAL (1976, 1978); Finch (1981); Palma (2000a); Bulmer-Thomas (1987); Maddison (1991). Data have been converted to a 1970 price basis where necessary, and official exchange rates have been used throughout. See also Hofman (2000), Table B.2.

of the 1920s, were able to compensate for losses on loans to the export sector with this new and profitable source of lending. Given the extremes to which capacity utilization had fallen, the growth in the money supply was only mildly inflationary and had real as well as price effects.[62]

Home final demand consists not just of government expenditure, but also of investment and private consumption. Public investment, sharply cut between 1929 and 1932, was stimulated by road-building programs in virtually all republics, as governments seized on a form of investment

---

62 Prices began to rise after 1931–2, but the rate of increase was generally modest. As late as 1939, for example, using 1929 as the base (100), wholesale prices in Argentina stood at 112, in Brazil at 101, in Mexico at 122; and in Peru at 116. The main exceptions (Bolivia and Chile) have already been mentioned. See notes 43 and 53.

expenditure with a low import content.[63] The growth of the road network was truly impressive in some republics[64] and contributed indirectly to the growth of both manufacturing and agriculture for the home market. Even private investment, despite its high import content, was able to recover after 1932, as the balance-of-payments constraint began to be relaxed.[65]

Increases in private consumption – the most important element in home final demand – were a necessary condition for industrial growth in the 1930s. Private consumption was promoted both by the recovery of the export sector and by loose fiscal and monetary policies. As home demand recovered, domestic firms were provided with an excellent opportunity to satisfy a market in which the relative price of imports had increased. Few financial institutions – even the new ones established in the 1930s – were concerned primarily with providing consumer credit, so demand for expensive consumer durables (e.g., motor cars) was still modest; however, nondurable consumption such as beverages and textiles experienced substantial growth.

Some people have speculated that the growth of consumer demand in the 1930s may have been fueled by shifts in the functional distribution of income.[66] The data do not exist to confirm or deny this hypothesis, but it is clear that within certain sectors important changes occurred in the return to labor relative to capital. In the export sector, for example, the impact of the depression fell most heavily on the owners of capital, with real rates of return falling more sharply than real wages. Recovery of the sector after 1932 helped to rebuild profit margins, but it is unlikely that the rate of return on capital was restored to its pre-1929 level. Thus in the export sector it is realistic to talk of a shift in the functional distribution of income in favor of labor.

In the import-competing sector, on the other hand, the opposite is more likely to have occurred. The growth of the sector on the back of depreciated exchange rates and higher nominal tariff rates created a relative price shift from which the owners of capital would have been the primary beneficiaries.

---

63 The priority in the 1930s was simple roads (often unsurfaced), which could be used for transport by the rapidly increasing number of vehicles. Road building was therefore labor intensive and often involved only modest expenditure on tools and equipment. The extreme example was Jorge Ubico's Guatemala, where the *ley vialidad* provided the state with virtually costless labor. See Grieb (1979), Chapter 9.

64 In Argentina the road network expanded particularly rapidly. The incentives for the government were very strong because – in addition to its low import content – the road-building program gave farmers an alternative to the (mainly foreign-owned) railways.

65 Brazilian industrial machinery imports (at constant 1913 prices), for example, were back to their pre-Depression peak by 1938. See IBGE (1987), p. 345.

66 The functional distribution refers to the division of income into wages, rent, and profits. It should not be confused with the size distribution of income, which refers to the share of income received by a particular decile or quintile of the population.

At the same time, nominal wages were slow to respond to the gentle rise in prices in countries with depreciating currencies, and a further shift toward profits may well have taken place. In the nontraded sector both the Depression and the subsequent recovery are likely to have left the functional distribution largely unchanged, so the aggregate change in the functional distribution of income cannot have been very large.[67] Thus it is improbable that the growth of consumer demand in the 1930s can be attributed to sharp changes in income distribution.

The international environment and the export sector

The recovery of the export sector, in terms of both volume and price, contributed to the increase in import capacity after 1932 and to the restoration of positive rates of economic growth. Yet this export recovery was not simply a return to the pre-1929 world trading system. On the contrary, the international economic environment in the 1930s underwent a series of changes that had an important bearing on the fortunes of individual republics.

The main change in the world trading system was the growth of protectionism. The notorious Smoot–Hawley tariff in 1930[68] raised the barriers faced by Latin American exporters in the U.S. market, and a specific tariff imposed on U.S. copper imports in 1932[69] hit Chile particularly hard. Great Britain's retreat behind a system of imperial preference at the Ottawa conference in 1932 left Latin America facing discriminatory tariffs in its second-largest market. The rise of Adolf Hitler in Germany produced the aski-mark, an inconvertible currency paid to exporters that could only be used to buy German imports. Some staples (notably sugar) were subject to an international agreement that set export quotas for the main producers (e.g., Cuba). Bolivian tin was regulated by the International Tin Agreement.[70]

Despite the retreat into protectionism, world trade in dollar terms grew steadily after 1932 – at least until a new U.S. depression drove down U.S. imports and world trade in 1938. The imports of the major industrialized countries reached a turning point between 1932 and 1934 (only in France

---

67 The aggregate change is a weighted average of the change in the three sectors – exportables, importables, and nontradables. Where the import-competing sector was unimportant or confined to (labor-intensive) agriculture, the distribution of income in the 1930s may have improved, with the main burden of adjustment being carried by profits in the export sector.

68 The Smoot–Hawley tariff act became law in June 1930. It had passed the House of Representatives in May 1929, however – even before the stock-market crash – as tariff increases were being applied in numerous countries at the end of the 1920s. Needless to say, Smoot–Hawley provided many governments with the "justification" they needed for further tariff increases in the 1930s. These retaliatory tariff changes exacerbated the trade depression of the decade.

69 See Maddison (1985), p. 28.

70 See Hillman (1988), pp. 83–110.

was recovery delayed until after 1935). In the crucial U.S. market, imports recovered by 137 percent between 1932 and 1937 – stimulated in part by the efforts of Secretary of State Cordell Hull to dilute the impact of Smoot–Hawley through bilateral trade treaties involving reciprocal tariff cuts.[71]

For Latin America as a whole the export performance after 1932 at first glance appears undistinguished. In the seven years before the outbreak of the Second World War exports in value terms were virtually unchanged, while the volume of exports rose by a modest 19.6 percent. This is very misleading, however, because the figures are heavily influenced by Argentina – by far the most important exporter from Latin America, with almost 30 percent of the regional total. Excluding Argentina, the volume of exports rose by 36 percent between 1932 and 1939. If Mexico is also excluded, the volume of exports of the remaining eighteen republics rose by 53 percent over the same period – an annual rate of 6.3 percent.

The poor performance of Mexico is easy to explain, for exports in fact grew rapidly between 1932 and 1937 – only to collapse in the wake of oil nationalization in 1938.[72] Higher prices for gold and silver after the collapse of the gold standard could not compensate for the trade embargo imposed in retaliation against the expropriation of the foreign oil companies and exports fell by 58 percent between 1937 and 1939.

Argentine exports have been the subject of much analysis. In volume terms, the steady decline after 1932 was not reversed until 1952. The trend was obscured, however, by the favorable prices and NBTT that Argentina enjoyed for much of the 1930s. Between 1933 and 1937, for example, the NBTT improved by 71 percent, in response to a series of bad harvests in North America that drove up the prices of grain and meat.

The dependence of Argentina on the British market was a major obstacle to export expansion, however. The Roca–Runciman pact of 1933[73] may have given Argentina a quota in the British market for exports of its main primary

---

71 Cordell Hull deplored the retaliatory tariff increases of the 1930s and had attempted, without success, to reverse the trend at the World Economic Conference in 1933. He had more success with the bilateral trade treaties that were signed between the United States and numerous Latin American countries in the second half of the decade.

72 Oil nationalization arose from a dispute between the foreign-owned companies and their Mexican workers. It was immensely popular, but it also generated serious problems for the Cárdenas administration as the companies orchestrated an international boycott. See A. Knight (1990), pp. 42–7.

73 The Roca–Runciman pact (known officially as the London Treaty) was a logical response to the adoption of imperial preference by Great Britain, for it allowed Argentina continued access to the British market for its beef and grains. However, the protocol to the trade treaty obliged Argentina to lower tariffs on many British imports and allowed British companies to pay remittances by means of a subtraction from Argentina's exports to Great Britain. Thus Great Britain extracted the maximum advantage from its negotiating position, but the long-run cost was extremely high as a result of Argentina's humiliation. See Rock (1991), pp. 21–4. A similar agreement was reached with Uruguay.

products, but the best that could be hoped for under this arrangement was the preservation of import market share. British farmers, on the other hand, now had a price incentive provided by discriminatory tariffs to increase production at the expense of imports. Thus even the preservation of import market share could not prevent a small decline in Argentine exports to Great Britain.

Argentine exports were also undermined by real exchange-rate movements. Traditional exports in many Latin American republics enjoyed long-run real depreciation, but Argentine exporters faced a real exchange-rate that tended to appreciate in the 1930s. For example, with British wholesale prices falling by 20 percent in the decade after 1929 and Argentine wholesale prices rising by 12 percent, the nominal devaluation of the peso against the pound sterling needed to keep Argentine exports to Great Britain competitive was at least 32 percent. This was far more than the actual depreciation of the official exchange-rate over the decade, and the marked year-to-year fluctuations did little to bolster confidence in the export sector. By contrast, over the same period Brazilian exporters enjoyed a 49 percent real devaluation based on the official exchange-rate and an 80 percent real depreciation based on the free-market rate.[74]

In the rest of Latin America export performance after 1932 was surprisingly robust (see Table 7.6). Of the seventeen countries providing data on the volume of exports, only Honduras – in addition to Argentina and Mexico – saw a decline between 1932 and 1939. Furthermore, if 1929 is taken as the base, half of the reporting countries experienced an increase in the volume of exports, despite the exceptionally difficult circumstances that prevailed throughout the 1930s.

Three factors accounted for the relatively strong performance of exports. The first was the commitment of the authorities to the preservation of the traditional export sector – the engine of growth in the export-led model – through a network of policies, from real exchange-rate depreciation to debt moratoria. The second was the movement in the NBTT after 1932. The third was the commodity lottery, which produced a number of winners from the Latin American menu of exports in the 1930s.

In the early 1930s few, if any, republics could afford to ignore the traditional export sector. This was particularly true of the smaller republics, in which the sector remained the major source of employment, capital accumulation, and political power. Even in the larger republics a decline in the export sector threatened to undermine the nonexport sector, as a result of the direct and indirect linkages between the two. Significantly, all but one of the thirteen countries with real GDP and export data for the 1930s recorded an increase in real exports and real GDP at the same time. The

---

74 Author's calculations, based on adjustment of the nominal exchange-rate for the difference between Brazilian and foreign (British and U.S.) wholesale prices.

Table 7.6. *Annual average rates of growth, 1932–1939 (in percentages)*

Country	GDP	Export volume	Import volume	Net barter terms of trade
Argentina	+4.4	−1.4	+4.6	+2.1
Bolivia		+2.4		
Brazil	+4.8	+10.2	+9.4	−5.6
Chile	+6.5	+6.5	+18.4	+18.6
Colombia	+4.8	+3.8	+16.1	+1.6
Costa Rica	+6.4	+3.4	+14.0	−5.4
Cuba	+7.2			
Dominican Republic		+3.0	+4.4	+15.2
Ecuador	+4.4	+9.7	0	
El Salvador	+4.7	+6.7	+4.2	+1.9
Guatemala	+10.9	+3.4	+11.2	+2.0
Haiti		+4.9		
Honduras	−1.2	−9.4	+0.8	−0.3
Mexico	+6.2	−3.1	+7.8	+5.7
Nicaragua	+3.7	+0.1	+5.6	+5.5
Peru	+4.9(a)	+5.4	+5.0	+7.2
Uruguay	+0.1(a)	+3.5	+3.0	+1.4
Venezuela	+5.9(a)	+6.2	+10.4	−3.4

Note: Much of this data is conveniently summarized in Thorp (1998) Statistical Appendix. See also Hofman (2000), Table 3.2

a Data are for 1930–9.

Sources: Rangel (1970); Millot, Silva, and Silva (1973); CEPAL (1976, 1978); Brundenius (1984); Finch (1981); Palma (2000a); Bulmer-Thomas (1987); Maddison (1991). Data have been converted to a 1970 price basis where necessary, and official exchange rates have been used throughout. See note 25.

exception was Argentina, where – as we have already seen – the quantum of exports failed to recover.

Argentina was the exception that proved the rule, however. The richest country by far in Latin America in the early 1930s (its only rival in terms of income per head was Uruguay), Argentina had the most diversified economic structure and the strongest industrial base. The nonexport sector was sufficiently robust to become the new engine of growth in the 1930s, so real GDP and real exports moved in opposite directions. At the same time, it must be remembered that the NBTT improved significantly in Argentina, which gave a boost to home final demand and private consumption after 1932. Thus even Argentina could not entirely escape its inherited dependence on the export sector.

Measures to sustain and promote the export sector in Latin America were varied, complex, and often unorthodox. Only six of the twenty republics (Cuba, the Dominican Republic, Guatemala, Haiti, Honduras, and

Panama) eschewed all forms of exchange-rate management, preferring instead to preserve their pre-1929 peg to the U.S. dollar. Elsewhere, nominal devaluation was frequent and multiple exchange rates were common. As the example of Argentina has shown, nominal devaluation did not necessarily mean real depreciation, but domestic price increases were generally modest, and only Bolivia collapsed into a vicious cycle of high domestic inflation and exchange-rate devaluation – a victim of the chaotic financial conditions created by the Chaco War and its aftermath.

The decline of credit for the export sector after 1929, from both domestic and foreign sources, threatened many firms with foreclosure by banks. Overwhelmingly, governments intervened with debt moratoria to prevent the erosion of the export base.[75] In some cases new financial institutions were set up with state support or government participation to channel additional resources to the export sector. Pressure groups representing the export interests were strengthened or set up for the first time, and export taxes were frequently revised downward.[76]

The improvement in the NBTT after 1932 was a further boost to the export sector. Of fifteen reporting countries (see Table 7.6), only four recorded a deterioration in the 1932–9 period. Two of these (Costa Rica and Honduras) were major banana exporters and suffered from the downward revision in the administered prices for bananas used by the giant fruit companies in their global operations; because these prices were highly artificial, the deterioration in the NBTT was not serious in practice. The same is true of Venezuela, where world oil prices remained weak and caused the fall in the NBTT; however, Venezuela began to squeeze a higher returned value from the foreign oil companies after the fall of Gómez through the revision of contracts and an increase in tax revenue, so the PPE increased steadily.[77]

The only other country to experience a fall in the NBTT was Brazil. The collapse of coffee prices after 1929 hit Brazil hard. A new coffee support scheme, financed in part by a tax on coffee exports and in part by government credits,[78] provided the funds to destroy some of the crop. This reduced the supply that reached the world market and allowed Brazil to sell at higher dollar prices than would otherwise have been possible. At the same time,

---

75 The debt moratoria prevented banks from foreclosing on their clients by selling collateral in exchange for unpaid debts. Bank resistance to such unorthodox practices was undermined by the knowledge that property prices were falling and would fall even faster if banks had to unload unwanted properties to maintain their liquidity.

76 In addition, Argentina created a series of state marketing boards that provided farmers with domestic prices above world prices. The implicit losses of the boards were covered by the profits from management of the multiple exchange-rate system. See Gravil (1970).

77 See McBeth (1983), Chapter 5.

78 The macroeconomic impact of this funding scheme has been the subject of much debate. See, for example, Furtado (1963) and Peláez (1972). Fishlow (1972) contains a good survey of the debate, generally favoring Furtado's interpretation of the scheme as expansionary.

devaluation raised the local currency price of coffee exports, so the fall in coffee income was much less severe than the NBTT deterioration implied. No amount of tinkering with the instruments available could conceal the fact that the coffee sector was in deep crisis, however. With the price of cotton relative to coffee rising in the 1930s, resources were reallocated and Brazilian cotton production and exports soared. From 1932 to 1939 the area planted to cotton increased nearly fourfold and production nearly sixfold, while exports rose so rapidly that exports in volume terms grew faster in Brazil than in any other republic (see Table 7.6). Brazilian dollar earnings from exports may have remained weak, but the growth in volumes and in domestic-currency terms was impressive.[79]

The commodity lottery produced a series of winners and losers in Latin America. The main loser was Argentina, its traditional exports hurt by their dependence on the British market. Cuban tobacco exports, including cigars, also lost, for they suffered severely from the protectionist measures adopted in the U.S. market.[80] The main winners were exporters of gold and silver, because prices rose steeply in the 1930s. This windfall from the lottery benefited Colombia and Nicaragua in the case of gold and Mexico in the case of silver. Bolivia benefited from the price increases for tin achieved by the International Tin Committee after 1931, and a further boost to tin prices came from rearmament in the late 1930s.[81] Chile, too, having suffered the most severe drop in export prices in the worst years of the Depression, saw its NBTT increase by an average of 18.6 percent a year between 1932 and 1939, as rearmament fed its way through to copper prices. The Dominican Republic exploited its position outside the International Sugar Agreement to enjoy higher prices and increased volumes from sugar sales.

The recovery of the traditional export sector was the main reason for the growth of export volumes after 1932. Export diversification (with the exception of cotton in Brazil) was of limited importance, for only a few sporadic efforts were made – such as cotton in El Salvador and Nicaragua and cacao in Costa Rica (on abandoned banana plantations).[82] The rise of

---

79 Peláez (1972), Chapter 3, provides an excellent account of the rise of cotton production in the state of São Paulo during the 1930s and draws attention to the predepression investments in cotton research financed by the state government.

80 Attracted by the opportunity to avoid import duty, the American Tobacco Company transferred its operations from Cuba to New Jersey in 1932. See Stubbs (1985), Chapter 4.

81 The disruptions associated with the end of the Chaco War against Paraguay left Bolivia unable to meet its quota under the international cartel agreement, however. See Hillman (1988), pp. 101–3.

82 The United Fruit Company (UFCO) had begun to shift its banana production from Costa Rica's Atlantic coast to its Pacific coast in the early 1930s. Because the contract between UFCO and the government denied free movement to the many black workers on the Atlantic coast plantations, unemployment was a serious problem in the Puerto Limón area. The planting of cacao on disused UFCO lands was seen by the government as a solution to the dilemma it had helped to create. See Harpelle (1993).

Nazi Germany and its aggressive trade policy based on the aski-mark meant that the geographical composition of foreign trade changed quite sharply, however. By 1938, the last year not affected by war, Germany was taking 10.3 percent of all Latin American exports and supplying 17.1 percent of all imports compared with 7.7 percent and 10.9 percent, respectively, in 1930.[83] The main loser from the increased German share was Great Britain, although the United States also declined as a market for Latin American exports (from 33.4 percent in 1930 to 31.5 percent in 1938).[84]

The rise in importance of the German market owed a great deal to the commerical policy of the Third Reich. The carrot to induce countries to accept the inconvertible aski-mark was the offer of higher prices for their traditional exports. Brazil, Colombia, and Costa Rica, for example, all of which were searching for new markets for coffee, saw a steep rise in the importance of the German market – the loss of which was to cause serious problems following the outbreak of war. Uruguay, facing problems of access to the British market, saw exports to Germany rise to 23.5 percent of the total by 1938. By contrast, the reciprocal trade treaties promoted by Cordell Hull failed to achieve an increase in U.S. market shares, although they did contribute to the increase in the absolute value of trade.[85]

By the end of the decade the export sector still had not fully recovered its earlier importance, but it had contributed in no small part to the recovery of real GDP after 1932. Comparing 1928 with 1938 (see Table 7.1), most reporting countries experienced a drop in the ratio of real exports to real GDP. Only in Mexico, Honduras, and Argentina – the special cases already examined – was there a major decline; and Brazil even experienced an increase.

The recovery of the export volume in most Latin American republics helps to explain the steep increase in the volume of imports after 1932 (see Table 7.6). It is not the whole story, however, for imports recovered in every reporting case – including the three in which the volume of exports fell. The additional explanations for the movement in imports are provided by changes in the NBTT and by reductions in factor payments due to debt default, exchange control, and the fall in profit remittances. Thus even in Argentina – where the external debt was serviced punctually and the volume of exports fell – favorable movements in the NBTT and a reduction in profit

83 The German share is all the more remarkable when it is remembered that in 1920, just after the First World War, Germany accounted for only 1.8 percent of Latin America's exports and 3.4 percent of its imports.

84 See Horn and Bice (1949), Chapter 5.

85 The increase in the value of trade with the United States was disrupted by the U.S. depression after 1937. U.S. imports fell sharply in 1938, and all the main Latin American countries except Venezuela were seriously affected. This U.S. depression was not as deep as the previous one, however, and had a more limited effect on the rest of the world, so the overall impact on Latin America was not so severe.

remittances made possible an annual increase in the volume of imports of 4.6 percent between 1932 and 1939.

The growth in the volume of imports for every republic after 1932 is so striking that it is worth examining the correlation between changes in real imports and real GDP. For the twelve republics for which data are available,[86] there is a strong, positive relationship, with a least-squares correlation coefficient of 0.75 significant at the 1 percent level. Considering the standard view of the 1930s as a period of economic recovery based on ISI and import compression, this result is a salutary reminder of the overwhelming importance of the external sector and foreign trade even after the 1929 Depression.

It is worth exploring this point further, because the standard view is so firmly established. Import substitution in industry was indeed important, as is shown in the next section, and over the decade between 1928 and 1938 the ratio of real imports to real GDP did fall. However, import compression was most severe in the worst years of the Depression (1930–2) and led to an intense squeeze on consumer imports. After 1932 industrial growth was able to satisfy much of the demand for consumer goods that had previously been met by imports, but at the same time real imports rose faster than real GDP in virtually all cases, as the marginal propensity to import remained extremely high. The composition of imports shifted away from consumer goods – particularly nondurable consumer goods – but economic performance was still highly sensitive to and dependent on the growth of imports. Without export recovery, or at least an improvement in the NBTT, it would have been much more difficult for Latin America in the 1930s to carry out successful ISI.

Recovery of the nonexport economy

The recovery of the export sector – in terms of volumes, of prices, or, in many cases, of both – contributed to the growth of the Latin American economies in the 1930s. The resurgence of the export sector, coupled with loose monetary and fiscal policies, brought about an expansion of nominal home final demand. With price increases kept to modest levels in most republics, this corresponded to an increase in real home final demand that permitted the nonexport sector to expand rapidly in some cases. The major beneficiary was manufacturing, although domestic-use agriculture (DUA) also increased and growth in some nontraded activities, such as construction and transport, was significant.

Argentina was the only country in which the recovery of real GDP is not associated with the recovery of the export sector. On the contrary, the

---

86 See note 59. The period chosen was 1932 to 1939.

nominal and real value of exports continued to fall in Argentina for several years after real GDP reached its trough in 1932. Argentina had the largest and most sophisticated industrial structure (with the exception of textiles) of any republic by the end of the 1920s, however, and this industrial maturity allowed manufacturing to lead the Argentine economy out of recession in response to the abrupt change in the relative price of home and foreign goods brought about by the Depression.

The change in relative prices – which affected all importables, not just manufactured goods – came about for three reasons. First, the widespread use of specific tariffs in Latin America meant that tariff rates started to rise as import prices fell. Specific tariffs – a serious disadvantage in times of rising prices – brought increasing protection in times of falling prices, even without state action. However, most republics responded to the Depression by raising tariffs, thus giving a further twist to nominal protection.[87] These increases were often designed primarily to raise government revenue, but – as usual – they also acted as a protective barrier against imports. Venezuela, for example, saw the average tariff rate rise from 25 percent in the late 1920s to more than 40 percent by the late 1930s.[88]

The second reason for the change in relative prices was exchange-rate depreciation. In the early 1930s, when prices were falling almost everywhere, a nominal exchange-rate depreciation was a reasonable guarantee of real devaluation. By the mid-1930s, with modest price increases in some countries, real devaluation was assured only if the nominal depreciation exceeded the difference between domestic and foreign price changes. Many countries, particularly the larger ones, met these conditions, and exchange-rate policy became a powerful tool for shifting relative prices in favor of home goods that competed with imports. In those republics that used multiple exchange rates (most of South America), a further opportunity was provided for raising the domestic currency cost of those consumer-good imports that local firms were best placed to produce.

Exchange control provided the third reason for the change in relative prices. The rationing of foreign exchange for nonessential imports effectively drove up their local currency cost, even without devaluation. Thus some of the republics that pegged their exchange-rate to the U.S. dollar still enjoyed a de facto devaluation as a result of exchange control. The outstanding exception is Venezuela, where the bolívar appreciated sharply against the dollar and wiped out much of the advantage offered by the increase in tariff rates.

---

87 This is disputed by Ground (1988), p. 193, who argues that "tariffs were not used to ease the adjustment to the Great Depression." However, this conclusion can be disputed using the figures on tariffs in his own Table 7 – and even more so using alternative calculations. See, for example, Díaz-Alejandro (1970), p. 282.

88 See Karlsson (1975), p. 220.

The change in relative prices, coupled with exchange control in many cases, provided an excellent opportunity for manufacturers in those countries in which industry had already taken root. Even better placed were those countries in which the manufacturing sector had developed spare capacity before 1929. In such countries production could respond immediately to the recovery of internal demand and to the change in relative prices, without expensive investments dependent on imported capital goods.

A number of Latin American countries did indeed meet these conditions. Argentina has already been mentioned. Brazil, though much poorer than Argentina, had been steadily developing its industrial base and had taken advantage of favorable circumstances in the 1920s to expand its manufacturing capacity. Mexico had seen a wave of industrial investments during the Porfiriato and, following the upheavals of the revolution, had begun to invest again on a modest scale. Among the medium-sized countries, Chile had succeeded in building a relatively sophisticated industrial base even before the First World War, and Peru had enjoyed a boom in industrial investment in the 1890s that was subsequently sustained only during periods of favorable relative prices. Colombia, its industrial progress delayed by the failure to build a strong internal market in the nineteenth century, had finally begun to build an important industrial base in the 1920s. Among the small republics, only Uruguay could be said to have established modern manufacturing, with firms attracted by the concentration of population and high incomes in Montevideo.

These seven republics were best placed to take advantage of the exceptional conditions facing the manufacturing sector after domestic demand began to recover. Indeed, the annual rate of growth of manufacturing net output exceeded 10 percent in a few cases (see Table 7.7). Although spare capacity was used at first to meet the increase in demand, this had begun to be exhausted by the middle of the decade. In Mexico the giant iron and steel works in Monterrey – unprofitable for most of the century – was finally able to pay healthy dividends as utilization reached 80 percent of capacity in 1936.[89] Thereafter demand could only be satisfied through new investment involving the purchase of imported capital goods. Thus industrialization began to change the structure of imports, with a declining share accounted for by consumer goods and an increasing share by intermediate and capital goods.

Argentina remained the most industrialized republic, in terms of both the share of manufacturing in GDP and net manufacturing output per head (see Table 7.7). However, the Brazilian manufacturing sector made considerable progress in the 1930s. Despite the decline in world coffee prices, local currency income derived from coffee fell much more modestly, as a result of the coffee-support program, and cotton exports provided a dynamic new

89 See Haber (1989), p. 177.

Table 7.7. *Industrial sector indicators in the 1930s*

Country	A	B	C	D
Argentina	7.3	22.7	122	12.7
Brazil	7.6	14.5	24	20.2
Chile	7.7	18.0^a	79	25.1
Colombia	11.8	9.1	17	32.1
Mexico	11.9	16.0	39	20.1
Peru	6.4^b	10.0^c	29	n/a
Uruguay	5.3^d	15.9	84	7.0

Key: A = Annual rate of growth of manufacturing net output, 1932–9; B = Ratio of manufacturing to GDP, 1939 (1970 prices, %); C = Net manufacturing output per head of population (in 1970 dollars, converted at official exchange-rate), circa 1939; and D = Number of workers per establishment, circa 1939.
^{a} Datum is for 1940.
^{b} Datum is for 1933–8.
^{c} Datum is for 1938.
^{d} Datum is for 1930–9.
Sources: Author's calculations, using data from Wythe (1945); Rangel (1970); Millot, Silva, and Silva (1973); CEPAL (1976, 1978); Boloña (1981); Finch (1981); Palma (2000a); Maddison (1991). Data have been converted to a 1970 price basis where necessary, and official exchange rates have been used throughout. For data at purchasing power parity exchange rates, see Thorp (1998), Statistical Appendix, which also contains estimates for Cuba and Venezuela derived from Pérez-López (1977) and Baptista (1997) respectively.

source of earnings. At the same time the combination of real depreciation, tariff increases, and exchange controls gave consumers a strong incentive to switch from imported commodities to local products. This stimulus was at work in other countries, but capacity constraints often prevented firms from responding more positively. In Brazil, however, manufacturing capacity had been significantly enlarged by the high level of imported capital equipment made possible during the 1920s. Thus Brazilian firms were poised to meet demand, not only in traditional industries such as textiles, shoes, and hats, but also in new industries producing consumer durables and intermediate goods.

Even the Brazilian capital-goods industry advanced in the 1930s. However, its share of value added was still only 4.9 percent in 1939.[90] Brazilian industrialization therefore remained heavily dependent on imported capital goods, so capacity constraints in several branches began to reassert themselves in the late 1930s. In common with other large Latin American countries, these capacity constraints encouraged labor-intensive operations and the substitution of labor for capital wherever possible. Manufacturing

90 See Fishlow (1972), Table 7. See also Leff (1968).

employment growth in Brazil was rapid, especially in São Paulo, where the annual rate of increase was more than 10 percent after 1932. Indeed, labor inputs "explain" most of the growth in Brazilian industry in the 1930s, so productivity increases were modest. The efficiency of this industrialization and the ability of firms to compete internationally can therefore be questioned.

The industrialization of the 1930s brought about an important shift in the composition of industrial output in the major countries. Although food-processing and textiles remained the most important branches of manufacturing, several new sectors began to acquire importance for the first time. These included consumer durables, chemicals (including pharmaceuticals), metals, and papers. The market for industrial goods also became more diversified. Although the majority of firms continued to sell consumer goods (durable and nondurable) to households, interindustry relations were now more complex, with a number of establishments providing inputs that were previously purchased abroad.

These changes were significant, but they should not be exaggerated. By the end of the 1930s, for example, industry's share of GDP remained modest (see Table 7.7). Only in Argentina did the share exceed 20 percent, and even there agriculture was still more important. Despite its late industrial spurt, the manufacturing sector in Colombia accounted for less than 10 percent of real GDP in 1939. Brazil and Mexico had made important progress toward industrialization, but the net output of manufactures in both countries per head of population was still far below the levels in Argentina, Chile, and Uruguay.

The industrial sector faced other problems in the 1930s. Attracted by the highly protected internal market, it had no incentive to overcome its many inefficiencies and to start to compete in export markets. By the end of the 1930s the sector was still small scale, with the average number of employees per establishment ranging from 7.0 in Uruguay to 32.1 in Colombia (see Table 7.7). The productivity of the labor force was also low, with value added per worker even in Argentina only one-quarter of the U.S. level, and in most republics more than half the work force was employed in food products and textiles.

The problems of low productivity in the industrial sector could be traced to shortages of electric power, lack of skilled labor, restricted access to credit, and use of antiquated machinery. By the end of the 1930s the governments of several republics had accepted the need for indirect state intervention on behalf of the industrial sector and had set up state agencies to promote the formation of new manufacturing activities with economies of scale and modern machinery. A notable example was the Chilean Corporación de Fomento de la Producción (CORFO); similar development corporations were formed in Argentina, Brazil, Mexico, Bolivia, Peru, Colombia, and

Venezuela.[91] Most of these corporations came too late to have much impact on industrial developments in the 1930s – the Chilean one was formed in 1939 – but their influence was felt in the 1940s.

In a few cases state intervention was direct rather than indirect. The nationalization of the oil industry in Mexico in 1938 brought the oil refineries into public ownership.[92] State ownership in social democratic Uruguay was extended into meat packing and cement manufacture. Generally, however, industry was controlled by private domestic interests, with a vital role played by recently arrived immigrants from Spain, Italy, and Germany. Only in Argentina, Brazil, and Mexico were foreign-owned subsidiaries of overseas companies important, and even in those countries their contribution to total industrial output was still modest.[93]

The change in relative prices of home and foreign goods favored ISA as well as ISI. Before 1929 the export-led model had brought specialization to the point that imports of many foodstuffs and raw materials were required to meet home demand. The change in relative prices provided an opportunity to reverse this and encouraged production of DUA.

The expansion of agriculture for the home market was particularly impressive in the Caribbean Basin. These small republics, lacking a significant industrial base, found in ISA an easy way of compensating for the lack of opportunities in ISI. By the end of the 1920s export specialization and the existence of numerous foreign-owned enclaves had created a huge demand for imported foodstuffs to feed the rural proletariat and the growing populations of the urban centers. With surplus land and labor, together with the incentives provided by the change in relative prices, it was a relatively simple matter to expand domestic production at the expense of imports.[94]

Although ISA was most important in the smaller republics of Central America and the Caribbean, it also affected South America. A clear pattern can be discerned for many agricultural staples, with imports falling sharply in the Depression in line with the collapse of purchasing power and then failing to recover their predepression peak as domestic production of food and raw materials expanded. The main exceptions (e.g., cotton and hemp) were all raw materials required by the rapidly expanding industrial sector, so imports remained important.

---

91 See Hughlett (1946), pp. 7–13.
92 The Mexican oil nationalization was not the first. Standard Oil in Bolivia had been expropriated in 1937 following an outbreak of populism in the aftermath of the Chaco War. See Whitehead (1991), p. 522.
93 Foreign investment in manufacturing in the 1930s, however, was considered sufficiently important to attract a fine monograph. See Phelps (1936).
94 For the five Central American republics, where the possibilities of ISI were very limited, see Bulmer-Thomas (1987), pp. 79–82.

The change in the relative prices of home and foreign goods was an important explanation for the expansion of DUA and industry. Nontraded goods and services also advanced, however, in line with the growth of the real economy and with the recovery of home final demand. The shift of resources toward the industrial sector and the related increase in urbanization drove up the demand for energy, for example, and stimulated new investments in electricity supply (including hydroelectric dams), oil exploration, and petroleum refineries. The gap between supply and demand remained a problem through much of the 1930s, but the existence of excess demand was a powerful stimulus for the growth of both public utilities and the construction industry.

The construction industry was also a beneficiary of new investments in the transport system. By the 1930s Latin America's railway boom was over, but the region had barely begun to develop the road system needed to cope with the demand for trucks, buses, and cars. The construction of roads – overwhelmingly financed by the state – had the great merit of using labor and local raw materials rather than being heavily dependent on complementary imports. The road system expanded throughout Latin America in the 1930s, with a particularly impressive increase in Argentina, and this expansion provided an opportunity to absorb unemployed labor in many rural areas.

The expansion of the road system required an increase in government expenditure, which put further pressure on the limited fiscal resources of the state. Some authoritarian governments, notably Jorge Ubico's Guatemala, relied on coercion to obtain the labor inputs needed for expansion of the road system. Once built, however, the network of roads permitted isolated regions to market an agricultural surplus and contributed to the growth of DUA. This has been clearly demonstrated in the case of Brazil.[95]

The air-transport system also expanded rapidly in the 1930s, although it started from such a low base that its ability to carry passengers and freight was still limited at the end of the decade. Nevertheless, in countries where geography made travel by train impossible and by road difficult, the creation of an air-transport system was an important step toward modernization and national integration. In Honduras, for example, where President Tuburcio Carías Andino granted a monopoly to a New Zealand entrepreneur as a reward for his role in converting civilian planes into bombers during the 1932 civil war, the newly formed Transportes Aéreos Centroamericanos (TACA) played an important part in linking the country's isolated eastern provinces to the capital city. Colombian airlines flew more than a million miles in 1939.[96]

---

95 See Leff (1982a), p. 181.
96 See Collier (1986), p. 255.

Although the Depression in Europe and North America cut a swath through the financial system of the developed countries, with runs on deposits and bank collapses a common experience, Latin America came through the worst years of the Depression with only modest damage to its financial system. Furthermore, the 1930s witnessed the creation of new central banks, the expansion of the insurance industry, and the growth of secondary banking (including state-owned development corporations).

The stability of the financial system was all the more remarkable in view of the close relationship between many banks and the export sector. As the value of export earnings collapsed after 1929, many exporters could not meet their financial commitments, and the position was made even worse for the banks when a number of governments declared a moratorium on foreclosures.

Several factors helped to mitigate the situation and contributed to the survival of the banking system. The wholesale financial reforms of the 1920s, spurred on in many cases by Professor Kemmerer, had led to the creation of a much stronger financial system with clearly defined rules by the time of the Depression. The novelty of the system meant that in many countries cash-reserve ratios were far above the legal limits, so it was easier to absorb the inevitable decline in deposits.

A second explanation was provided by exchange control. The close links between banks in Latin America and foreign financial institutions had led to a high degree of dependence on foreign funds. The existence of exchange control rescued a number of banks from having to make payments of interest or principal to foreign creditors that might have bankrupted the institutions.

Perhaps the most important reason for the survival of the banking system was its role in funding budget deficits during the 1930s. Banks contributed handsomely to domestic bond issues by governments and were rewarded with a steady stream of interest payments. Bank funding of the deficit may have contributed to the rise in prices in Latin America after the early 1930s, but inflation remained modest, and for the banks the interest receipts became a useful source of income. Furthermore, as the export sector began to recover, the banks were able to return to a more normal relationship with many of their traditional clients, and some began to exploit the new opportunities opening up outside the export sector.

The recovery of real GDP in the 1930s was rapid (see Table 7.6). By 1932 Colombia, where the Depression was relatively mild, had already surpassed its predepression peak of real GDP. Brazil followed in 1933; Mexico in 1934; and Argentina, El Salvador, and Guatemala in 1935. Chile and Cuba, where the Depression had been particularly severe, had to wait until 1937 before real GDP overtook its pre-Depression peak, and the luckless Honduras – overwhelmingly dependent on the export of bananas –

had to wait until 1945. With the population growing at around 2 percent a year, most republics had recovered the pre-Depression levels of real GDP per head by the late 1930s – the most serious exceptions being Honduras and Nicaragua.

The transition toward inward-looking development

The world depression that began at the end of the 1920s was transmitted to Latin America through the external sector. In almost all cases, the recovery from the Depression was also associated with the recovery of the external sector. The growth of exports, coupled with debt default, with a reduction in profit remittances, and with an improvement in the NBTT, permitted a substantial growth in the volume of imports, with which the growth of real GDP in the 1930s is highly correlated. Loose fiscal and monetary policies, the change in relative prices in favor of domestic production competing with imports, and the availability of complementary imports through the relaxation of the balance-of-payments constraint combined to produce significant structural change in the 1930s, which particularly favored the manufacturing sector in the larger countries and DUA in the smaller republics.

The performance and policy of the Latin American economies in the 1930s should therefore not be seen as marking a turning point, as has so often been claimed.[97] Although it is true that the industrial sector was particularly dynamic, growing faster than real GDP in almost all countries, that was also true in the 1920s. Only in Argentina, where the manufacturing sector led the recovery from depression in the early 1930s, could it be claimed that by the beginning of the decade the economy had reached a sufficiently advanced level for performance not to be seriously affected by the decline in the volume of exports. Elsewhere, there is no evidence that larger countries with a broader industrial base performed better than the small republics with virtually no modern manufacturing. In both cases performance was highly dependent on the recovery of import capacity, and even in Argentina performance was not insensitive to the sharp improvement in the NBTT after 1933.

By the end of the decade, however, it could be argued that industrial growth had produced a qualitative as well as a quantitative change in the structure of the economies of the larger republics. In the 1940s and 1950s (see Chapter 8) these changes matured to the point that industry and real GDP in many republics were capable of moving in the opposite direction

---

97 This claim is made with equal vigor by structuralists in the *Cepalista* tradition, who favor inward-looking development, and by neoconservatives in the laissez-faire tradition, who oppose it.

to primary-product exports, so the export-led growth model had ceased to be an accurate description of their performance. Thus changes in the 1930s can be seen as laying the foundations for a transition toward the pure import-substitution model, which reached its most extreme form in the 1950s and 1960s. This was certainly true of Brazil, Chile, and Mexico, which had joined Argentina by the end of the 1930s as the only countries to have pushed industrialization and structural change to the point that internal demand was no longer determined primarily by the export sector.

The most important change in the 1930s involved the switch from self-regulating economic policies to policy instruments that had to be manipulated by the authorities. By the end of the 1920s attachment to the gold standard had left most Latin American republics without an independent exchange-rate policy. The operation of the gold standard also meant that monetary policy was largely passive, with inflows and outflows of gold underpinning movements in the money supply to bring about automatic adjustment to external and internal equilibrium. Even fiscal policy had lost much of its importance. In the smaller republics dollar diplomacy and high conditionality in many cases had produced foreign control of external trade taxes – the major source of government revenue – and in the larger countries the "dance of the millions" had made it much easier to finance expenditure by foreign borrowing than by fiscal reform.

The collapse of the gold standard forced all of the republics to address the question of exchange-rate policy. A few (smaller) republics preferred to peg to the U.S. dollar, thereby abandoning the exchange-rate as an active instrument. Most republics, including some of the smaller ones, opted for a managed exchange-rate. In highly open economies the exchange-rate has an immediate and powerful effect on the prices of many goods, so it is the single most important determinant of relative prices and of the allocation of resources. An independent exchange-rate policy also encourages the formation of pressure groups to lobby the authorities in support of exchange-rate changes to favor their interests. Not surprisingly, in the 1930s many republics in Latin America opted for a multiple exchange-rate system as a way of resolving these competing pressures. That is one reason why in 1945, after the Bretton Woods Conference, the newly formed International Monetary Fund (IMF) found that thirteen of the fourteen countries in the world that operated multiple exchange-rate systems were in Latin America.[98]

The balance-of-payments constraint in the 1930s, coupled with exchange control, meant that movements in international reserves – money of external origin – ceased to be a major determinant of the money supply. Instead,

---

98 See de Vries (1986), p. 21.

base money was driven more by government budget deficits and by the rediscount policy of the central bank, and the money multiplier was affected by changes in reserve ratios. Thus changes in the money supply were due more to changes in money of internal origin, which implied the adoption of a more active monetary policy in almost all republics. The main exceptions were those countries, such as Cuba and Panama, that lacked a central bank and were therefore unable to influence the money supply through changes in the monetary base.

The recovery of the export sector and import capacity did not necessarily imply an increase in the value of external trade. Thus government revenue from taxes on trade was seriously affected, and the reduction was not fully compensated by the need to spend less on public external-debt service as a result of default. The crisis provoked fiscal reform and a more active fiscal policy in all republics. A prime candidate was upward revision of tariff rates, but a further modest shift toward direct taxes – income and property – can be detected in the 1930s, as can the introduction of a variety of indirect taxes aimed at home consumption. By the end of the decade the correlation between the value of external trade and government revenue had been loosened, thereby undermining a crucial link in the operation of the export-led growth model.

The adoption of more aggressive exchange-rate, monetary, and fiscal policies was so widespread that it is difficult to sustain the thesis that Latin American republics can be divided into larger countries adopting "active" policies and smaller countries following "passive" policies. Although all the larger republics did indeed follow active policies, so did many of the smaller countries, including Bolivia, Costa Rica, Ecuador, El Salvador, Nicaragua, and Uruguay.[99] The most obvious examples of passive countries (Cuba, Haiti, Honduras, and Panama) were all semicolonies of the United States in the 1930s, but not all semicolonies (e.g., Nicaragua) could be described as passive.

These changes in the management of key instruments of economic policy did not amount to an intellectual revolution. On the contrary, the theory of inward-looking development was still inchoate, the export sector was still dominant, and its supporters were still politically powerful. Yet the choices forced on the authorities in the 1930s in the fields of exchange-rate, monetary, and fiscal policy do mark an important stepping stone on the way to the intellectual revolution associated with the U.N. Economic Commission for Latin America (ECLA) and the explicit development of the import-substitution model at the end of the 1940s (see Chapter 8). Policy management in the 1930s showed the sensitivity of resource allocation

---

99 See Díaz-Alejandro (2000), pp. 19–31.

to relative prices, and the response of the manufacturing sector in the larger republics was a salutary reminder of how efficacious economic policy could be.

The management of economic policy in the 1930s was indeed quite successful, and it compared favorably with the postwar experience. What the authorities lacked in experience was compensated in a number of ways. First, the officials in charge of fiscal and monetary policy (e.g., Raúl Prebisch at the Argentine Central Bank) were often competent technocrats who benefited from public ignorance of economic science and were able to make decisions in a relatively apolitical environment. Second, perfect foresight and perfect information – the two conditions required for the rational-expectations conclusion on the impotence of government policy – were clearly absent in the 1930s, so there was much less danger that the intended thrust of a change in economic policy would be thwarted by the omniscience of the private sector. Third, the scourge of economic policy in the postwar period – the acceleration of inflation – was much less of a problem in the 1930s. Money illusion (based in part on the absence of price statistics), falling prices in the world economy, and spare capacity in the domestic economy meant that expansionary economic policies were less likely to collapse in a vicious cycle of budget deficits and inflation.

Loose fiscal and monetary policies in the 1930s underpinned the growth of home final demand. As Table 7.5 shows, this was of enormous importance in pulling the republics out of depression and in providing the stimulus needed for the growth of importables and nontraded goods and services. Associated with this growth was an increase in urbanization, so a number of republics could be described as primarily urban by the end of the 1930s, and all republics saw a big fall in the proportion of the population classified as rural.

Even though economic performance was generally satisfactory in the 1930s – at least after 1932 – there were a number of deviations from the regional pattern. Some republics – the "slow-recovery" countries in Table 7.4 – were marked by stagnation or even decline in economic activity. The basic problem was the export sector, which remained depressed through most of the 1930s for reasons beyond the control of the authorities. In Honduras, banana exports collapsed after 1931 as a result of disease, and the real value of exports did not recover its 1931 peak until 1965. With exports depressed, the best hope for recovery lay in the import-competing sector (ISA and ISI), but the small size of the market made it difficult to compensate for the decline in the export sector.

With the important exceptions of Argentina and Colombia, the "medium-recovery" countries based their recovery from the Depression mainly on the export sector. Economic growth in the 1930s therefore did not imply significant structural change, and the composition of exports changed little. Recovery in Bolivia depended crucially on the formation of the International Tin Cartel in 1931, which brought higher prices for tin exporters and therefore higher revenue for the government from export taxes.

The export sector did expand in Colombia, but its growth was overshadowed by the spectacular rise of the manufacturing sector, in which the increase in textile production was particularly impressive. In Argentina the export sector stagnated in real terms, so the recovery depended crucially on the nonexport sector. The performance of this sector, whether in industry, transport, construction, or finance, was generally satisfactory, so it is difficult to conclude that the long-run decline of the Argentine economy dates from the 1930s.[100]

The "fast-recovery" countries include republics in which the impact of the Depression was relatively minor (e.g., Brazil) as well as severe (e.g., Chile and Cuba). Fast growth in the second group of countries therefore consisted primarily of a "recovery" of real output lost in the worst years of the Depression, although Chile also enjoyed a considerable amount of new ISI. In Brazil, on the other hand, fast growth primarily involved additions to real output. Although export recovery was important in Brazil, the structure of the economy began to shift in favor of industry. Brazil remained desperately poor, however, with a real GDP per head in 1939 only one-quarter of that in Argentina and only 60 percent of the Latin American average. Mexico also enjoyed significant structural change: Land reform under President Lázaro Cárdenas (1934–40) strengthened nonexport agriculture,[101] the state became a major source of investment, and many firms in the industrial and construction sectors began to rely on public-sector contracts.[102]

The 1930s in Latin America may not have represented a sharp break with the past, but the decade did not represent a lost opportunity, either. In the face of a generally hostile external environment, most republics did well to rebuild their export sectors. Where it was feasible, and with only a few exceptions, republics expanded the production of importables and increased the supply of nontraded goods and services. These changes provided the basis for a significant growth in intraregional trade in the early 1940s, when access to imports from the rest of the world was cut off (see

100 The literature on the origins of the long-run Argentine economic decline is vast. See, for example, Korol and Sábato (1990).

101 Land reform had been on the agenda ever since the 1917 Constitution, but not until the time of President Cárdenas was it applied with vigor. Some 18 million hectares were distributed to 800,000 recipients, leading to a huge increase in the importance of the *ejido*. See A. Knight (1990), p. 20.

102 Mexican administrations in the 1930s were also active in the creation of financial institutions to tap new sources of saving and channel resources to new activities. The best-known example is Nacional Financiera, created in 1934. See Brothers and Solís (1966), pp. 12–20.

Chapter 8). Changes in economic policy in the 1930s were also generally rational. A wholesale retreat from the export sector and the construction of a semiclosed economy would have involved a massive increase in inefficiency, a slavish commitment to the export-led model of growth would have locked the region into an allocation of resources that was no longer consistent with long-run dynamic comparative advantage. These changes were also sufficiently wide ranging to permit the 1930s to be described as marking the transition from export-led growth to inward-looking development – even though the majority of countries had not completed the transition by the end of the decade.

8

War and the new international economic order

The Second World War, which began in Europe in September 1939, was the third major external shock to strike Latin America in twenty-five years.[1] Despite many similarities with the impact of the First World War and some with the 1929 Depression, the implications of the Second World War for Latin America were quantitatively and qualitatively different from the earlier shocks.

First, the war was far more devastating for Latin America in terms of disruption to its traditional markets. By 1940 the Axis powers[2] controlled much of the European coastline from northern Norway to the Mediterranean Sea, and the consequent British blockade deprived the Latin American republics, despite their initial neutrality in the war,[3] of access to continental European markets. Furthermore, the British market – so important for Argentina and Uruguay – started to shrink as the United Kingdom retreated into a war economy in which only the most essential imports were permitted.

Second, the war erupted after nearly a decade of growing disillusionment with the traditional export-led model in Latin America. World trade in the 1930s had recovered, but it was increasingly "managed," often bilateral, and heavily distorted by higher tariffs and a plethora of nontariff barriers. The great powers had frequently acted irresponsibly (e.g., the Smoot–Hawley tariff[4]) or selfishly (e.g., the Roca–Runciman pact[5]). The result was a growing sense of nationalism in a number of Latin American

---

1 The others were the First World War (see Chapter 6) and the 1929 Depression (see Chapter 7). In addition, Latin America had been adversely affected by the brief world trade slump in 1920–1, when commodity prices collapsed, and the (mainly U.S.) depression between 1937 and 1939, when world trade volumes declined.

2 In 1940 the Axis powers were Germany and Italy. They were joined by Japan in December 1941, following the Japanese attack on the U.S. Navy at Pearl Harbor, Hawaii.

3 All of the Latin American countries were neutral until Japan attacked the United States in December 1941. At that point all the republics north of the equator either declared war on the Axis powers or broke off diplomatic relations. It was a different story, however, in the countries south of the equator: Argentina and Chile remained neutral until almost the end of the war. See Humphreys (1982).

4 See Chapter 7, note 68.

5 See Chapter 7, note 73.

republics and a greater commitment – albeit poorly articulated – to inward-looking development and industrialization as an alternative model to traditional export-led growth.

These changes in the intellectual and policy climate had begun to manifest themselves in the 1930s. The rise of nationalism was reflected in the expropriation of foreign oil interests in Bolivia (1937)[6] and Mexico (1938) and in the commitment to industry through the creation of new institutions – such as the Corporación de Fomento de la Producción (CORFO) in Chile – to promote investment in manufacturing. The war years, however, accelerated the process. State intervention in support of industry, particularly in the larger republics, now became direct, with important investments in basic commodities as well as in the infrastructure needed to support a more complex industrial system.

This change, encouraged by the United States even before it entered into the war in December 1941, became more marked as the vast majority of the republics joined in the war against the Axis powers.[7] The allocation of resources distorted by shipping shortages and the lack of imports as well as by price controls and nontariff barriers, became increasingly determined by the Allied war effort on the one hand and by state preferences for industrialization on the other. The rise of new industrial establishments was spectacular in some republics, but the efficiency of the manufacturing sector remained suspect. With economies of scale ruled out by the small size of the market and the lack of long-term investment finance, protected from foreign competition by the shortage of imports in wartime and high tariff and nontariff barriers in peacetime, the new industry was a fragile base on which to construct an alternative to export-led growth in the postwar period.

Trade and industry in the Second World War

The recovery of Latin America's external trade in the 1930s was accompanied by a change in its geographical distribution, which increased the importance of the German, Italian, and Japanese markets at the expense of Great Britain and, to a lesser extent, the United States (see Table 8.1). By 1938 Europe

---

6 Nationalism in Bolivia after the Chaco War bore similarities to national socialism in Europe. The Axis sympathies of President Germán Busch were a source of deep concern to the United States and Great Britain. His unexplained suicide in August 1939 paved the way for the entry of Bolivia into the Pan-American fold just as the war began. See Dunkerley (1984), pp. 28–9.

7 A formal declaration of war was not always needed to join in the war effort. Mexico, its differences with the United States over oil nationalization conveniently resolved even before Pearl Harbor, opened its ports and airfields to the U.S. military as early as January 1942. Not until May, after German submarines sank Mexican tankers, did Mexico declare war on the Axis powers. See Humphreys (1981), pp. 118–19.

Table 8.1. *Latin American trade shares, 1938–1948*
(in percentages)

Country	1938	1941	1945	1948
	Exports			
United States	31.5	54.0	49.2	38.2
United Kingdom	15.9	13.1	11.8	13.3
France	4.0	0.1	—	2.9
Germany	10.3	0.3	—	2.1
Japan	1.3	2.7	—	0.9
Latin America	6.1	n/a	16.6	9.3
All others	30.9	n/a	22.4	33.3
	Imports			
United States	35.8	62.4	58.5	52.0
United Kingdom	12.2	7.8	3.6	8.1
France	3.5	0.1	—	1.9
Germany	17.1	0.5	—	0.7
Japan	2.7	2.6	—	0.1
Latin America	9.2	n/a	25.6	10.9
All others	19.5	n/a	12.3	26.3

Note: n/a = not available; — = negligible.
Sources: Horn and Bice (1949), Table 7, p. 112; Pan-American Union (1952).

was purchasing nearly 55 percent of all exports and supplying nearly 45 percent of all imports – a situation that clearly left Latin America extremely vulnerable to the outbreak of hostilities in Europe and to the imposition of the British blockade.

Great Britain tried its best to purchase as much as possible from Latin America in 1940 in a desperate effort both to supply itself and to prevent essential commodities falling into the hands of its enemies.[8] Yet the parlous state of the British economy made it quite impossible for Great Britain to compensate Latin America for the loss of the continental market. Inevitably, the only economy large enough to absorb commodities previously destined for Europe was the United States.

The Roosevelt administration – more sensitive to Latin American needs than its predecessors – was acutely aware of the importance of avoiding economic collapse in the region. With certain political groups vocally

---

8 These efforts, concentrated on such commodities as sugar from the Dominican Republic, oil from Venezuela, and tin from Bolivia, sustained the value of British trade with Latin America in the first months of the war. Indeed, an official trade mission was dispatched to South America in October 1940 at the height of hostilities with Germany. By the time the mission returned, however, British trade priorities had shifted toward the Commonwealth and colonies. See Humphreys (1981), pp. 52–3. See also Miller (1993), Chapter 9.

supporting fascism – and even national socialism – in the 1930s, Latin American solidarity with the United States in the event of a war could not be guaranteed. At the same time, the United States needed to secure supplies of raw materials and strategic commodities in case its traditional sources outside Latin America were disrupted.

The result was the system of inter-American economic cooperation, whose foundations were laid at a Pan-American conference in Panama in September 1939 – only three weeks after the outbreak of war in Europe.[9] An Inter-American Financial and Economic Advisory Committee was created, which established the Inter-American Development Commission (IADC), with subsidiaries in all twenty-one republics (i.e., including the United States), in 1940. The IADC's tasks were to stimulate trade in noncompetitive goods between Latin America and the United States, to promote intra–Latin American trade, and to encourage industrialization. Soon after, Nelson Rockefeller was appointed to head the Office for the Coordination of Commercial and Cultural Relations between the American republics.[10]

The main U.S. priority was securing access to strategic materials. In 1940, therefore, the Roosevelt administration set up the Metals Reserve Company and the Rubber Reserve Company to stockpile essential supplies. Although the commodities could be bought anywhere, Latin America was the main beneficiary because it was the only major raw-material-exporting region not directly affected by hostilities. After the Japanese occupied many parts of Asia, the U.S. search for alternative supplies became frenetic, and the Latin American republics cooperated in a major effort to provide alternative sources of supply for such commodities as abaca, kenaf, cinchona, and rubber.[11] U.S. direct foreign investment in Latin America, much of it in strategic materials, soared during the war to levels not seen since the late 1920s, and official U.S. loans through the Export–Import Bank and Lend–Lease[12] – though not restricted to the extraction of strategic materials – became increasingly important.[13]

9 The Panama conference, though paving the way for wartime cooperation, reflected the improvement in U.S.–Latin American relations in the wake of President Roosevelt's Good Neighbor Policy. The new U.S. policy had been warmly endorsed at the Seventh Pan-American Conference in 1933 in Montevideo. See Mecham (1961), pp. 116–21.

10 See Connell-Smith (1966), p. 119.

11 These "exotic" tropical products acquired a special importance in wartime. Both kenaf and abaca were used in the manufacture of rope, cinchona was an essential ingredient in malaria control, and rubber was needed for footwear and tires.

12 The Export–Import Bank had been established under Roosevelt's New Deal program in 1934, but it had virtually no impact on inter-American trade relations until the outbreak of war. The Lend-Lease Act, adopted by the United States in March 1941, was primarily designed to help Great Britain. By the end of the war, however, nearly all of the Latin American republics (the main exception being Argentina) had received some Lend-Lease aid.

13 U.S. government loans to Latin America, virtually zero until 1938, averaged $15 million in the first years of the war and reached a peak of $178 million in 1943. See Stallings (1987), Table 1.A.

Inter-American cooperation was not confined to strategic materials. In recognition of the crucial role played by coffee exports in a dozen republics, the United States promoted the Inter-American Coffee Convention (IACC), which provided quotas, favorable prices, and a guaranteed market.[14] The IACC, set up in 1941, was a lifeline for the smaller republics and a great boon for the larger republics – many of which had become heavily dependent on the German market in the 1930s. U.S. largesse did not, however, extend to temperate products from the Southern Cone, which remained tied to the British market in particular.

Increased U.S. purchases led to a massive increase in the importance of the U.S. market for Latin American exports, but it could not fully compensate for the loss of Japan, continental Europe, and the shrinking British market (see Table 8.1). Attention therefore turned to intra–Latin American trade as a way of sustaining the volume of exports. This trade, a mere 6.1 percent of the region's exports in 1938, had never been of much importance since independence. Only landlocked Paraguay, which exported timber, yerba maté, and quebracho extract to its neighbors, relied heavily on Latin American markets. Moreover, many republics had better transport links with Europe and the United States than with each other.[15]

All this changed as a result of both war and the system of inter-American economic cooperation. As early as 1940 Argentina's minister of finance, Federico Pinedo, produced a plan that envisaged a customs union for the southern republics,[16] and a conference in Montevideo of the five River Plate countries came close to adopting such a proposal in January 1941.[17] In the end, however, intra-Latin American trade was promoted through a multitude of bilateral agreements that provided tariff and nontariff concessions for pairs of neighboring countries. The result was an increase in the share of exports going to other Latin American republics to 16.6 percent in 1945 (see Table 8.1). This same value of intraregional trade represented no less than 25.6 percent of all imports (a figure that has yet to be surpassed), because total purchases from abroad – affected by wartime shortages and shipping problems – were much less than total exports.

14 See Wickizer (1943), pp. 233–9.
15 The transport system between many countries was so inadequate that the Pan-American Highway, first proposed at the Seventh Pan-American Conference in 1933, was finally given high priority. By the end of the war it was at last possible to reach the Panama Canal from the United States by road. See James (1945), pp. 609–18.
16 The Pinedo Plan is more normally associated with the scheme of the Argentine government, the Concordancia, to promote industry during the early years of the war. Although the plan was rejected by the Congress, it anticipated the creation of a customs union between Argentina and her neighbors to provide an outlet for the manufactured exports that industrial promotion was supposed to achieve. See Cramer (1998), pp. 519–50.
17 The five countries were Argentina, Bolivia, Brazil, Paraguay, and Uruguay. See Chalmers (1944), pp. 212–14.

Table 8.2. *Annual average rates of growth by sector, 1939–1945*
(*in percentages*)

Country	Value of exports[a]	Volume of exports[b]	GDP[c]	Agriculture[d]	Industry[e]
Argentina	8.0	−2.9	2.1	0.2	3.6
Bolivia	15.7	+6.0			
Brazil	13.6	−2.0	2.4	0	5.3
Chile	7.1	+3.4	4.0[f]	0[f]	9.3[f]
Colombia	10.4	+3.4	2.6	2.2	5.1
Costa Rica	5.6	−2.2	−0.1	0	−3.5
Cuba	17.1	+2.0[g]	1.8	n/a	4.3
Dominican Republic	15.4	−1.4			
Ecuador	20.1	+2.5	4.2	2.7	5.2
El Salvador	9.8	−1.1	2.2	1.4	3.9
Guatemala	8.5	+3.7	0.9	−6.3	4.4
Haiti	15.2	+1.5			
Honduras	3.5	+2.1	3.5	2.4	4.7
Mexico	9.4	+1.3	6.2	2.3	9.4
Nicaragua	6.2	−4.9	3.9	−2.6	7.9
Panama	4.7	−9.3			
Paraguay	21.6	+8.0	0.4	−1.7	1.0
Peru	6.6	−1.8	4.8[f]	n/a	4.8
Uruguay	11.7	+1.8	1.7	−1.0	3.5
Venezuela	13.6	+8.9	5.3	0	9.2
Latin America	10.5	+0.5	3.4	0.8	5.7

[a] Based on dollar values at current prices.
[b] Based on constant (1963) prices.
[c] Based on 1970 prices.
[d] Net agricultural output (1970 prices).
[e] Net manufacturing output (1970 prices).
[f] Data are for 1940–5.
[g] Based on volume of sugar exports only.
Sources: Pérez-López (1974); CEPAL (1976, 1978); Boloña (1981); Brundenius (1984); Bulmer-Thomas (1987).

The system of inter-American cooperation – both between the republics and with the United States – was the major factor preventing a collapse of exports after 1939. The volume of exports only surpassed its 1939 level in 1945, however, and a number of the most important republics (notably Argentina and Brazil) had still not reached the prewar level of real exports by the end of the war (see Table 8.2). Inter-American cooperation could not fully compensate Argentina and Uruguay for the shrinking of the British market, and the IACC could not realistically replace all of Brazil's lost coffee sales. Only a handful of countries secured a significant increase in export volumes in the war years: Bolivia benefited from a U.S. decision to purchase all surplus tin not destined for smelting in Great Britain[18] – a decision made possible by prewar investments in a tin smelter in Texas – and Venezuela reaped a rich harvest from British and U.S. determination to secure oil supplies from a reliable source.[19]

The value of exports, unlike the volume, grew rapidly in all the republics (see Table 8.2) as a result of higher dollar prices – a reflection above all of wartime dollar inflation. Import prices and the domestic cost of living also increased sharply, however. Thus most republics experienced little if any stimulus to real consumption from the development of the export sector. In Argentina real household expenditure on manufactured goods in 1946 was still below the 1937 level.[20]

In an earlier epoch the stagnation of the export sector and real consumption would have held out little prospect for industrial growth even in the larger republics. The war years were different, however, and several republics managed to raise industrial output rapidly despite the slow growth – or even decline – in real household disposable income. Three factors explain this apparent paradox.

First, just as in the First World War, the sharp decline in the volume of imports after 1939 allowed domestic manufacturers to expand production even with an unchanged level of real consumption. The recovery of industrial imports in the second half of the 1930s provided a cushion that could be squeezed through import substitution in the war years even in those republics that had been following import-substituting industrialization (ISI) for many years. Although the growth of manufacturing capacity was difficult under such conditions because of the shortage of imports of equipment and machinery, the ISI process benefited from the technical assistance provided by U.S. personnel to the Latin American republics through the network of IADCs.[21] Furthermore, the growing sophistication of industry in Argentina, Brazil, Chile, and Mexico had brought into existence a small capital-goods industry that was able to meet some of the demand for manufacturing investment.[22]

Second, and in complete contrast to the 1930s, the rise of intra-Latin American trade made it possible for manufacturers to sell their output in neighboring countries: Brazilian textile exports soared,[23] and Argentina

---

18 See Hillman (1990), pp. 304–9.
19 See Knape (1987), pp. 279–90.
20 See CEPAL (1959), vol. 1, p. 252.
21 See Hughlett (1946), p. 10; see also Thorp (1994).
22 This should not, however, be exaggerated. Even Brazil, where capital-goods production had made a promising beginning, had difficulty sustaining the sector's growth because capital goods remained import intensive. As late as 1949 the sector still accounted for only 5.2 percent of industrial value added. See Fishlow (1972), Table 9, p. 344. See also Gupta (1989).
23 Brazil's textile exports were so successful that at one point they contributed 20 percent of total export receipts. See Baer (1983), p. 47.

exported nearly 20 percent of all its manufacturing production in 1943. Indeed, Latin America's manufactured exports even penetrated markets outside the region. South Africa, cut off from its traditional British suppliers, bought significant quantities of Latin American manufactured exports in the war, and joint ventures between the United States and Mexico in manufactures led to a flow of nontraditional industrial goods northward across the Rio Grande.[24]

The third factor in the growth of industry among the larger republics was the rise of firms not dependent on consumer demand. These factories, which produced mainly intermediate goods but also some capital goods, looked to productive sectors and the state, rather than to households, for their markets. A spectacular example was the Volta Redonda integrated steel mill in Brazil,[25] financed in part by the United States, which sold its output mainly to construction firms and manufacturing enterprises – its output replacing goods that had previously been imported. Other examples were cement factories, basic chemical plants, oil refineries, plastics, rayons, and machinery. These industries – restricted in the main to Argentina, Brazil, Chile, and Mexico – represented a new (secondary) stage of ISI that transformed the structure of manufacturing, reducing the relative importance of consumer goods in general and nondurables in particular.[26] By 1946 less than half of all industrial output in Argentina was destined for households – down from nearly 75 percent in 1937 – and nearly one-third consisted of intermediate goods sold to productive sectors.[27]

The change in industrial structure and the emergence of new industries was linked to the rise of a more interventionist state in Latin America. Even deeply conservative governments could not avoid an increase in state responsibilities during the war years, because free markets could not handle the problems posed by dollar inflation, import shortages, and unsold agricultural surpluses. Prices could not be used exclusively to clear markets, price control was endemic, and rationing by the state was essential in the allocation of foreign exchange, import licenses, and many essential commodities. The war effort and the system of inter-American cooperation placed additional demands on the state through the need for infrastructure improvements and public works. The Pan-American Highway, intended to run from Alaska to Tierra del Fuego, had been agreed to as early as 1933 at the Pan-American Conference in Montevideo, but only as a result

24 See Wythe (1945), p. 296.
25 Before the war the Getúlio Vargas regime had been on the point of signing an agreement with Krupps, the German arms manufacture, for assistance in construction of a steel mill. A U.S. loan was quickly arranged after the outbreak of hostilities to replace the need for German participation. The mill, begun in 1941, was completed in 1944. See Baer (1969).
26 The fastest-growing industrial sectors in Brazil during the war years (e.g., nonmetallic minerals, metal, and rubber products) all produced intermediate goods. See Baer (1983), Table 10, p. 47.
27 See CEPAL (1959), vol. I, p. 252.

of wartime strategic considerations and generous funding from the United States was real progress made.

The expropriation of properties owned by Axis nationals was an additional factor in the spread of state intervention. German capital, in particular, had spread in the 1930s from its traditional base in agriculture and banking into transport and insurance. Many of the airline companies that had sprung up before the war were German owned and provided a highly visible target – so much so that some had even been taken over before the host republic declared war on Germany. Not all the newly acquired properties remained in state hands, but even their sale to private owners took the state into relatively unfamiliar territory.[28]

In a few cases state intervention went further. Following the 1943 military coup the Argentine government – soon to be dominated by Colonel Juan Perón – finally cast aside the republic's traditional hostility to state interference in economic activity and invested directly in productive assets.[29] Direct state intervention in Brazil was not limited to the steel works at Volta Redonda; it also embraced mining, chemicals, and heavy motors.[30] Everywhere the state became more heavily involved in electricity generation, construction, and transport in an effort to provide the infrastructure that would not only assist the new allocation of resources demanded by wartime exigencies but also remove some of the obstacles faced by the industrial sector.

In view of the stimulus provided by state intervention, it is scarcely surprising that a number of nontraded sectors grew rapidly during the war years. Construction grew at an annual rate of 6.6 percent for the region as a whole between 1939 and 1945, with a rate in excess of 7 percent recorded in Chile, Colombia, Ecuador, Honduras, Mexico, and Venezuela. Transport, public utilities, and public administration also grew rapidly in most republics.

The expansion of the nontraded sectors provided a direct stimulus to manufacturing and helps to explain industry's healthy growth in most countries (see Table 8.2). Chile, Mexico, and Venezuela were the star performers, but all reporting countries except a few small republics (in which internal demand remained almost entirely dependent on real disposable household income) recorded rates of growth well in excess of population increase. By contrast, agriculture performed dismally (see Table 8.2). Its export component was depressed by the problems of expanding volumes under wartime conditions; and agriculture for domestic use was constrained by the slow growth of real consumption – domestic sales being heavily dependent on

---

28 Inevitably, the transfer of Axis properties provided the region's more venal leaders with an opportunity for graft. Anastasio Somoza, for example, was able to secure German properties in Nicaragua at ridiculous prices. See Diederich (1982), p. 22.

29 Most of this direct intervention occurred after 1946, however. See Lewis (1990), Chapter 9.

30 See Trebat (1983), Chapter 3.

household purchases – and the limited opportunities left for replacing imports after a decade of import-substituting agriculture (ISA).

Only a handful of countries managed to expand agricultural output. The most important was Mexico, where the extensive land-reform program under Lázaro Cárdenas in the second half of the 1930s began to bear fruit: Supported by state investment in roads and irrigation, by private investment in transport and by an increase in wheat yields made possible by research and development,[31] agricultural output kept pace with population growth.[32] Ecuador – despite the problems of "witchbroom" disease in the cacao industry – and Colombia also managed modest expansion of their agricultural sectors. Both countries, however, had the advantage of an expanding volume of exports that sustained real disposable incomes and the demand for agricultural goods.[33]

Everywhere (with one minor exception[34]) industrial growth exceeded agricultural growth, so the aggregate performance of the economy depended above all on the weight of these two sectors. In the small Central American republics and Cuba the dominant position of agriculture dragged down the rate of growth of gross domestic product (GDP) despite some advance in manufacturing; in Argentina, Brazil, and Chile industrial growth supported a modest expansion of GDP despite the stagnation of agriculture. GDP growth was most impressive in Mexico, where proximity to the United States yielded significant benefits throughout the war years, and in Venezuela, where the government of Isaias Medina Angarita used its strong wartime bargaining position to achieve a fairer division of the oil rent with foreign-owned companies.[35]

The war marked a further transition from traditional export-led growth toward an inward-looking model based on ISI. This transition, not to be completed even in the larger republics until the 1950s, steadily weakened the link between the external sector and aggregate economic performance as structural change both increased the importance of the nonexport sectors and shifted the composition of industrial output toward intermediate and capital goods.

Many new manufacturing establishments were established in the war years despite the unfavorable external environment. Refugees from Europe brought their skills and capital to Argentina, Brazil, Chile, and Uruguay, and many highly qualified Spaniards fled to Mexico to escape living in

31 See Hewitt de Alcantara (1976), Chapter 3.

32 Mexico's population expanded at 2.3 percent per year between 1939 and 1945 – exactly the same as the rate of growth of net agricultural output.

33 Ecuador, as part of the inter-American wartime cooperation, experienced a huge expansion in rice exports to the United States. This contributed directly to agricultural growth and provided an increase in real incomes – much of which was then spent on foodstuffs. See Linke (1962), pp. 137–8.

34 The exception is Costa Rica, where real GDP fell in the war years, with a more negative impact on industry than agriculture.

35 See Knape (1987), pp. 284–9.

Franco's Spain. Generally, however, these new firms were built on fragile foundations. Responding to the scarcity of capital and finance, the new enterprises were often even smaller in scale than were their predecessors. In Argentina nearly 30 percent of all firms in existence at the end of the war had been established between 1941 and 1946; yet these new firms accounted for only 11.4 percent of the value of production.[36] The inability to exploit economies of scale hardly mattered in years when international competition was ruled out by import shortages, but it was an appropriate basis for launching an industrialization program under peacetime conditions. Far too many of the new firms – including a large number of those established in the 1930s – prospered only because of the artificial conditions made possible by high protection, import restrictions, and indirect state subsidies.

Trade surpluses, fiscal policy, and inflation

As the world shifted to a war economy, the price deflation of the 1930s was replaced by price inflation. In the main industrialized countries huge increases in government expenditure, coupled with a reduction in the supply of consumer goods, created excess purchasing power that even draconian price-control legislation could not keep from spilling over into higher prices. With the end of hostilities in 1945 the supply of consumer goods increased, and fiscal deficits were brought under control. Inflation in the main developed countries fell sharply, although it proved impossible to eliminate entirely.[37]

The war years therefore represented an aberration in price terms for the developed countries. In a number of the more important Latin American countries, however, the price inflation of the war years was to prove a cancer that was never excised, despite repeated attempts, in the postwar period. Thus for these republics – which included Argentina, Brazil, Chile, Colombia, and Uruguay – the price inflation of the war years, far from being an aberration, was the beginning of a long-run trend that kept annual increases far above the average in their main trading partners.

Latin America was no stranger to inflation even before the 1940s, but earlier inflationary episodes had tended to be country-specific and linked to political and monetary disorder. The huge rise in prices in Colombia at the turn of the century and in Mexico during the revolution were both caused by the explosion of paper money in the middle of civil war; as more normal times returned, the money supply was brought under control and

36 See Lewis (1990), p. 40.
37 Although the advent of peace reduced inflationary pressures, the abolition of price control provided firms with an opportunity to raise prices. The main developed countries did not restore price stability until 1947–8. See Scammell (1980), Table 5.8, p. 70.

prices stabilized. Similarly, the rises in the cost of living in Brazil in the early 1890s during the *encilhamento*, in Guatemala during the presidency of Manuel Estrada Cabrera (1898–1920), and in Nicaragua in the first decade of the twentieth century were all linked to the excessive issue of inconvertible paper currency.[38]

The 1930s had also seen a large increase in the cost of living in a few Latin American republics – in contrast to what was happening in the main industrialized countries. Again, however, the explanation for nearly all of these inflationary episodes was straightforward. The Chaco War, between Bolivia and Paraguay, provoked huge increases in government expenditure financed by printing money; in Brazil and Colombia the more modest rise in prices was clearly linked to currency depreciation, tariff increases, and loose monetary policies. Where exchange rates were fixed (e.g., Guatemala) or even appreciating (e.g., Venezuela) price deflation was the normal state of affairs. Only in Chile, where the cost-of-living index had risen steadily since the 1870s and where prices had almost doubled in the 1930s, was inflation endemic – and even there the price level did fall occasionally.[39]

The war years may not have led to a major increase in export volumes from Latin America, but they did drive export prices higher. Although the monopsony power of the United States limited the rise, it was nevertheless true that export prices increased at an annual rate of 9.8 percent for the region as a whole (see Table 8.3), with the highest rates of increase recorded by the Dominican Republic (whose sugar was still purchased by the British) and Ecuador and the lowest by Honduras (where banana prices continued to be "administered" by the fruit companies). For those republics that exported products which could be consumed locally (e.g., Argentina), the rise in export prices had a direct and immediate impact on the cost of living.

Inflation in the main trading partners (principally the United States), coupled with shipping shortages, drove up the dollar price of imports. For the region as a whole they rose less rapidly than export prices, but there were wide differences in the prices paid by individual countries. Countries that previously relied on the United States for imports and in which transport costs were modest (e.g., Mexico) faced the smallest increases; those republics far away and previously supplied from Europe (e.g., Argentina) suffered the biggest rise.

Under the abnormal wartime conditions the rise in the dollar price of imports was a poor guide to inflation in Latin America. This was due to the decline in import supply as a result of the war effort in the industrialized countries and to the shortage of international shipping, so import demand far exceeded available supply, providing innumerable opportunities

38 On these inflationary episodes, see pp. 111–13.
39 On price movements in the 1930s, see pp. 204–08.

Table 8.3. *Money, prices, and international reserves: annual average rates of growth, 1939–1945 (in percentages)*

Country	Export prices[a]	Import volume[b]	Money supply[c]	Prices Retail	Prices Wholesale	Foreign reserves[d]
Argentina	11.1	−16.0	17.7	5.0	12.3	22.8
Bolivia	9.3	+2.1	26.9	20.5		37.7
Brazil	15.9	+0.3	23.2	10.7	17.1[e]	
Chile	3.5	−3.7	20.9	14.9	19.3[f]	22.0
Colombia	6.8	−2.1	21.6	8.1		39.5
Costa Rica	7.0	−2.5	19.6	9.8	11.4	30.9
Cuba	n/a	n/a	28.8	12.8		49.0
Dominican Republic	16.7	−5.2	29.1	16.0	19.1	52.2
Ecuador	17.1	+2.7	27.0	17.7		50.5
El Salvador	10.6	+2.0	23.4	15.3		27.6
Guatemala	5.0	−3.1	21.3	10.0		33.3
Haiti	13.3	n/a	n/a	9.7		n/a
Honduras	1.3	0	20.9	20.4		51.8
Mexico	7.9	+13.8	25.5	13.4		30.6
Nicaragua	11.4	0	28.0[g]	27.3		34.6
Panama	14.5	+0.8	49.0	8.4		17.3
Paraguay	12.2	n/a	25.8	11.9		69.2
Peru	8.5	+0.6	24.2	10.5	12.9	24.2
Uruguay	9.6	−2.4	18.1	4.8		23.1
Venezuela	4.3	+2.4	16.4	4.7	6.3	26.0
Latin America	9.8	−0.7	19.6	12.6[h]	14.1[h]	29.6

[a] Based on unit value of exports.
[b] Based on quantum of imports.
[c] Currency and deposit money.
[d] Central Bank holdings of gold and foreign exchange (dollar equivalents).
[e] São Paulo only.
[f] Wages in manufacturing.
[g] Datum is for 1940–5.
[h] Unweighted.
Sources: CEPAL (1976); International Monetary Fund, *Yearbook of International Financial Statistics* (various issues between 1946 and 1951).

for windfall profits for those lucky enough to be allocated licenses. The quantum of imports delivered to Latin America fell by one-third between 1939 and 1942. Again, the republics traditionally supplied from Europe suffered the worst, with Argentina seeing a two-thirds drop in the volume of its imports between 1939 and 1943. Mexico, on the other hand, was able to take advantage of its geographical position and its improved relationship with the United States to increase the volume of its imports rapidly (see Table 8.3).

The sharp rise in dollar export and import prices was more than sufficient to provoke cost-of-living increases in Latin America. However, the main explanation for inflation in the war years was in fact a monetary one. The rise in the value of exports was not matched by the rise in the value of imports (despite the rise in their price), because the *volume* of imports fell (see Table 8.3). Latin America as a whole, as well as each of the twenty republics, ran a trade surplus that swamped the outflow of factor payments (e.g., profit remittances) and imports of services (e.g., shipping). The net inflow of gold and foreign exchange was swollen by capital receipts from the United States to finance direct investments, military expenditure, and social infrastructure.

The result was an abundance of foreign exchange that stood in marked contrast to the scarcity of the 1930s. International reserves, held in part in the United States, rose at a frenetic rate. Several republics managed to increase the dollar value of their reserves at an annual rate in excess of 50 percent between 1939 and 1945 (see Table 8.3). Every republic (except Panama) managed an annual growth rate in excess of 20 percent. Indeed, the increase in Argentina's foreign assets alone was greater than the total stock of Latin American reserves held at the end of 1939, although for those countries still trading with Great Britain (including Argentina) part of the increase consisted of blocked sterling balances in London.[40]

As exporters exchanged their foreign-currency earnings for local deposits through the banking system, the money supply started to rise. This increase in "money of external origin" drove up the money supply, and nominal demand rose far in excess of the available supply of goods (itself restricted by the decline in the quantum of imports). Thus wartime inflation was inevitable.[41] In a number of countries the problem was exacerbated by fiscal policy that added a domestic component to inflationary pressures and pushed prices to dangerously high levels.

The fiscal problem, which resulted in large deficits in a number of countries, arose for a number of reasons. On the revenue side, the fall in the volume of imports led to a decline in customs duties. Although the importance of customs revenue from imports had declined since the 1920s, in 1939 it still accounted for around 25 percent of government income in the larger republics and more than 50 percent in the smaller countries. Import tariffs were raised in many cases during the war, but the decline in the tax base (the quantum of imports) was often so steep (see Table 8.3) that by the end of the war customs duties had fallen to around 10 percent of total revenue in the three largest republics (Argentina, Brazil, Mexico), with large

40 Following the outbreak of war, the pound sterling became inconvertible. Thus countries such as Argentina, which had a trade surplus with Great Britain, were forced to accumulate sterling balances in London that could not easily be spent. See Fodor (1986), pp. 154–70.
41 There is a good discussion of wartime inflation problems in Harris (1944), Chapters 6–7.

reductions elsewhere. Governments were therefore forced to turn to other means of increasing revenue.

The most appropriate taxes to use under wartime conditions were direct. These had two advantages: they did not necessarily provoke price rises, and they reduced disposable income and purchasing power, thereby bringing nominal demand more into line with available supply. Direct taxes were still something of a novelty in Latin America, however, and even those republics which had introduced them before the war derived only modest yields from them because the tax base (the number of individuals and corporations liable to payment) was so small. Only Venezuela, with its tax on petroleum companies, obtained a high share of state income from direct taxes, although the widespread use of a profits tax in Colombia had pushed its yield to nearly 20 percent of all government revenue by the start of the war.[42]

Many countries made a major effort to raise revenue from direct taxes, and progress was not negligible. The Vargas administration in Brazil increased their yield from 8.5 percent of all revenue in 1939 to 26.5 percent in 1945.[43] Inevitably, however, the modest size of the base for direct taxes forced governments to turn to other forms of taxation to increase revenue. One popular, and almost invisible, source was the profit from the operation of multiple exchange-rate systems; by buying foreign exchange from exporters at the lowest (official) rate and selling to importers at the highest (free) rate, governments could turn a tidy profit. Such manipulations had inflationary consequences, however, because they raised the domestic currency cost of imports. The same was true of the higher rates for indirect taxes adopted universally by governments for consumer and other goods. Thus government revenue – at least in nominal terms – did rise during the war years despite the fall in imports, but the increase in indirect taxes, in particular those on consumer goods, gave a further twist to the inflationary spiral. Indeed, under wartime conditions it was fairly safe to assume that firms would pass any increase in indirect taxes on to consumers through higher prices.

The fiscal position would still have been manageable if government expenditures had been carefully controlled. Indeed, the more conservative republics (such as El Salvador and Guatemala) continued to keep a tight rein on public expenditures and avoided large budget deficits, and Venezuela

42 On fiscal problems during the war years, see Wallich (1944).
43 Brazil was among the first countries in Latin America to be forced to move away from reliance on import duties. In the early 1940s trade ratios declined sharply, and the share of consumer goods in total imports dropped below 20 percent. At the same time, the Vargas administration, by then committed to industrialization, had no desire to cripple manufacturing through high tariffs on intermediate and capital-goods imports. Thus, o estado novo – the name used by Vargas after 1937 to describe his authoritarian regime – had to make extensive use of fiscal reform. See Villela and Suzigan (1977), pp. 220–5.

began to reap a richer harvest from foreign companies as a result of its more aggressive oil policy. Generally, however, and for a variety of reasons, governments chose to expand their activities in the war years even if this implied a further increase in nominal demand and an addition to inflationary pressures.

One reason for increasing public expenditures, adopted explicitly in Colombia, was for countercyclical purposes. The first months of the war brought real hardship for some branches of the export sector, and unemployment was widespread. Public works, often targeted on rural areas, were seen as an appropriate policy response in keeping with the new Keynesian orthodoxy that was gaining favor throughout the world. As the export sector recovered and import supply fell, however; the additional purchasing power implied by an expansion of government expenditures was wholly inappropriate.

A more legitimate reason for increasing expenditures was the need for investments in social infrastructure in order to increase domestic supply. With the fall in imports the need for an increase in domestic supply was paramount; however, domestic producers were often unable to expand output because of deficiencies in transport, energy, and harbor facilities. Manufacturing, on the one hand, and intraregional trade, on the other, were particularly badly served by the social infrastructure inherited from the 1930s. Without public investment, even if it did imply government borrowing, it would have been very difficult to increase domestic supply.

Many republics chose the war years and the fight against the Axis powers to increase military spending. Although U.S. military aid was generous and covered part of the increase, it could not be expected to meet all needs. Some republics had more prosaic reasons for increasing military spending. Ecuador and Peru came to blows over a still-unresolved border dispute in the Amazon jungle.[44] And many of the Caribbean Basin dictators (for example, Anastasio Somoza in Nicaragua) used the war as a cover for strengthening their mechanisms of internal repression.[45] In Argentina Perón was not slow to reward the armed forces, whose military intervention had made it possible for him to rise to power after 1943.[46]

Government-expenditure patterns were also sensitive to the political changes of the war years. The alliance between the United States and the

---

44 War erupted in 1941 and proved to be a major embarrassment for the Pan-American movement. Under strong U.S. pressure a peace treaty involving substantial territorial gains for Peru was accepted in January 1942, but it was denounced in 1960 by Ecuador, and the matter was not finally resolved until the late 1990s. See Humphreys (1981), pp. 125–6.

45 William Krehm, writing in the 1940s, has provided an excellent account of how many Caribbean Basin dictators tried to use the war effort to enhance their own positions. See Krehm (1984).

46 Perón's rise to power was intimately associated with his domination of the organized labor movement. Nevertheless, the army was also a major beneficiary of the 1943 coup. See Potash (1980), Chapter 3.

Soviet Union had brought Communist parties and labor unions to prominence in many Latin American republics. The reward for "responsible"
behavior by these institutions often took the form of progressive labor legislation and increased social-security programs. Although not entirely new –
Uruguay had adopted its first public-sector pension scheme as early as
1896[47] – the wartime legislation marked a significant increase in social expenditures, the beneficiaries of which were generally a relatively privileged
minority in urban areas. A well-designed social-security program should at
first increase government revenue by more than expenditure (as happened
in Chile in the 1940s), but the abuse of such systems was often widespread
and a drain on government resources from the start.[48]

The consequence of government expenditures rising more rapidly than
revenue was wartime budget deficits. In a few exceptional cases these deficits
were not inflationary: Argentina, with its well-developed domestic capital
market, was able to fund much of the deficit through the issue of bonds
to the nonbank private sector, and Colombia achieved the same result after
1942 through legislation that forced companies to invest excess profits in
government securities.[49] Most of the republics, however, relied on borrowings from the banking system, which led to monetization of the deficit.
Central-bank credits to government grew by more than 20 percent a year
from 1939 to 1945 in Brazil, Ecuador, Mexico, Paraguay, and Peru. Those
governments that were lucky enough to secure foreign borrowing to cover
budget deficits still faced inflationary pressures, because the proceeds could
not be spent entirely on imports.

The combination of soaring international reserves and rising budget
deficits resulted in a monetary explosion (see Table 8.3). Even those republics with conservative fiscal policies (El Salvador, Guatemala, Venezuela)
suffered, because they tended to be the most open economies and therefore
the most likely to accumulate money of external origin. Although most of
the increase in the money supply came from external moneys (particularly
in the smaller Caribbean Basin republics), in a few republics (notably Brazil,
Chile, and Peru) the increase was mainly of domestic origin. This was also
true in Costa Rica, where the reformist Rafael Angel Calderón Guardia
administration ran huge budget deficits in support of its ambitious social
programs.[50]

The rapid rise in the money supply during the war years pushed up the
cost-of-living index in all republics. The increases in most republics were
far in excess of inflation rates in the United States and also exceeded the

47 This was a pension fund for teachers. The pension system was considerably extended under the
   presidency of José Batlle y Ordóñez (1903–7, 1911–15), although provision had also been made for
   accident insurance and unemployment benefits before the 1930s. See Mesa-Lago (1978), pp. 71–5.
48 The decade of the 1940s was one of the most active in the twentieth century for starting new
   social-security programs. See Mesa-Lago (1991), Tables 1–2.
49 See Triffin (1944), pp. 105–7.
50 See Rosenberg (1983), Chapter 3.

rise in import prices by a large margin. The cost-of-living index was not always the best guide to inflationary pressures, however. This was partly a reflection of its urban bias (in some cases it was confined to the capital city) and limited coverage (it did not cover all types of households). Even more important were the numerous attempts at price control by the authorities. These efforts, aided in many cases by technical assistance from the U.S. Office of Price Administration, could not eliminate inflation but did help to repress it. Thus the annual average increase in retail prices (see Table 8.3) was generally far below the increase in money supply – a difference that could not be explained by the increase in real output. A more accurate indicator of inflation was provided by wholesale prices, which were not subject to the same degree of price control. In those republics that published both sets of price changes, wholesale prices invariably outstripped the cost-of-living index (see Table 8.3).

Price controls were not the only measures adopted to reduce the rate of inflation, but they were the most effective. The Colombian measures to sterilize the inflow of foreign exchange and to finance the budget deficit in a noninflationary way, which we have already mentioned, were considered too radical elsewhere. A few countries, particularly those with multiple exchange rates, were prepared to see their currencies appreciate against the U.S. dollar (e.g., Uruguay[51]) in an effort to lower the domestic currency cost of imports, but currency appreciation was strongly resisted by exporters and disliked by industrialists. It was also unpopular with finance ministers, for whom it could mean a reduction in nominal tax receipts. Significantly, not a single republic was prepared to see its official exchange-rate revalued, despite the accumulation of foreign-exchange reserves. Similarly, no republics were prepared to raise the central-bank discount rate sharply in an effort to curtail monetary growth by the commercial banks. Monetary policy was not only passive, it was also extremely accommodating.

The excess purchasing power implied by rapid monetary growth affected assets as well as goods and services. Although stock-market indexes soared in those republics with an exchange, the narrow market and the wide spread between buying and selling rates made it unattractive to many investors.[52] Of much greater interest was the urban property market: In many cities land prices increased by a factor of ten or more during the war years.[53]

---

51 The free rate in Uruguay rose from 2.775 pesos per U.S. dollar in 1939 to 1.9 in 1945 – an appreciation of 31.5 percent. The official rate was unchanged at 1.899, however.

52 The range of financial assets offered was narrow. The index of industrial shares in Chile, Peru, and Venezuela, for example, was based on only ten or eleven stocks. See League of Nations (1945), Table 103.

53 Brazil, where urbanization was proceeding rapidly, was particularly affected by the rise in land values. The populations of Rio de Janeiro and São Paulo exceeded 2 million by the end of the 1940s, although the largest city in Latin America remained Buenos Aires. On the growth of Latin American cities in general, see Gilbert (1982).

Rapid urbanization had been under way in the major Latin American republics even before the war.[54] The acceleration in the rate of growth of population,[55] coupled with the problems of the agricultural sector, had begun to turn the rural labor shortage of the nineteenth century into the labor surplus of the late twentieth century. Inward-looking policies in the 1930s, which encouraged city-based activities, promoted rural–urban migration, and the growth of manufacturing, services, and public administration in the 1940s provided another major impetus. Owners of land and property in the center of cities and in the surrounding areas received a windfall gain from the explosion in real-estate prices: Many a postwar fortune could be traced to this phenomenon.

The other side of this inflationary coin was the growing inequality in the distribution of income. Although the owners of capital (including land) clearly benefited from the rapid appreciation in the price of assets, only a small number of wage and salary earners were able to protect their real earnings from the ravages of inflation. These privileged groups included the armed forces in a number of countries, where governments depended on their goodwill for survival, and even some workers in manufacturing, where competition from imports had ceased to be relevant in the firm's pricing decisions. Generally, however, most groups of workers saw their real wages and salaries undermined by the rise in the cost-of-living index, which provoked social unrest in the last months of the war.[56]

The postwar dilemma

The adaptation by the Western Hemisphere to wartime conditions and the priority given by the United States to the economic needs of its southern neighbors meant that for many Latin American republics the advent of peace was not an unmitigated blessing. As Asian supplies returned to the market the United States wound down its purchases of a number of primary products from Latin America, and the elaborate mechanisms for channeling goods, technical assistance, and capital from the United States – built up under the auspices of inter-American economic cooperation – withered

---

54 The precise extent of urbanization in Latin America as a whole before 1950 is subject to a considerable margin of error due to the different definitions used in each national census. Nevertheless, it has been estimated that the rural population fell from 67 percent of the total in 1940 to 63 percent in 1950. By then only Argentina, Chile, and Uruguay were classified as predominantly urban. See Wilkie (1990), Table 644, p. 137.

55 The annual average rate of growth of the region's population accelerated from 1.9 percent in the 1930s to 2.5 percent in the 1940s. A few countries (e.g., Costa Rica, Mexico, and Venezuela) even reached or surpassed 3 percent per year. See Sánchez-Albórnoz (1977), p. 203.

56 The social and political movements toward the end of the war are considered in Bethell and Roxborough (1988); see also Bethell and Roxborough (1992).

away. At the inter-American conference held in 1945 at Chapúltepec, Mexico, the United States reaffirmed its belief in free trade to a skeptical Latin American audience, and all wartime commodity agreements, such as that for coffee, came to an end.[57] The main priority for the United States became the reconstruction of Europe; following the outbreak of the Cold War in 1947 this goal became even more important. Official U.S. capital now flowed to Western Europe, and it was made clear to Latin America that financial support from the United States would have to come from private sources.[58]

Latin America therefore saw its share of the market for U.S. imports decline at the same time as the United States took a smaller share of Latin American exports (see Table 8.1). This decline, similar to what happened after the First World War, was predictable and unavoidable. The return to peacetime conditions also wiped out many of the gains that Latin American exporters had made in other Latin American countries, however. The share of Latin American exports going to other Latin American republics fell rapidly after the war (see Table 8.1), as manufactured imports from Europe and the United States drove out the Latin American products.

Some decline in intra-Latin American trade was inevitable, but it was made worse by exchange-rate policies. After the war years, during which Latin American inflation rates were far above inflation rates in Europe and North America, currencies were seriously overvalued. Local costs, including wages in the manufacturing sector, had risen rapidly, but nominal exchange rates remained virtually unchanged. This policy, defensible during the war when devaluation would have been ineffective, was continued after 1945, so by 1948 official exchange rates were still virtually unchanged. Under such circumstances, with Latin American inflation rates still far above the levels in the main trading partners, exporters of manufactured goods could not compete in price; and price competition was essential to compensate for inferior quality.

The decline in the proportion of exports going to the United States and Latin America was matched by a rise in the European share. But the economic reconstruction of Europe was at first fraught with problems, limiting the volume of goods that could be bought from Latin America. Germany remained devastated, France struggled to overcome wartime damage to its factories, and Great Britain had to hastily abandon the ill-conceived plan in 1947 to make sterling convertible.[59] Only when the Marshall Plan was

---

57 The Chapúltepec conference was a disappointment for many Latin American countries, which hoped that their wartime cooperation with the United States would be rewarded with a new economic order in inter-American affairs. See Thorp (1992).

58 See Rabe (1988), Chapter 2.

59 The convertibility of sterling was forced on Great Britain by the United States, which was anxious to restore more normal conditions in international finance, but it proved premature and had to be reversed. See Horsefield (1969), pp. 186–7.

Table 8.4. *External trade indicators, 1945–1948 (1945 = 100)*

Country	Export volume[a]	Export value[b]	Import volume[c]	Net barter terms of trade	Purchasing power of exports
Argentina	103	213	400	160	164
Bolivia	87	122	118	94	80
Brazil	121	179	165	96	116
Chile	100	160	139	119	118
Colombia	101	197	136	132	134
Costa Rica	167	397	110[d]	166	282
Cuba	n/a	177	n/a	n/a	n/a
Dominican Republic	104	188	145	118	120
Ecuador	98	196	162	159	157
El Salvador	118	214	158	88	107
Guatemala	100	170	191	109	108
Haiti	101	175	n/a	n/a	n/a
Honduras	146	196	176	84	127
Mexico	79	143	90	112	90
Nicaragua	217	380	148	129	267
Panama	175	254	95	99	176
Paraguay	48	126	n/a	n/a	n/a
Peru	82	153	121	111	94
Uruguay	70	147	130	115	88
Venezuela	155	313	314	157	235
Latin America	110	199	175	117	128

[a] Based on value of exports at constant (1963) prices.
[b] Based on dollar value of exports.
[c] Based on quantum of imports;
[d] Affected by the 1948 civil war.
Source: CEPAL (1976).

launched in 1948, leading to a massive transfer of financial resources from the United States, did the recovery of Europe become irreversible – and even then the Cold War limited reconstruction to Western Europe.[60]

Under these circumstances it is not surprising that the volume of exports from Latin America grew at only modest rates in the first few years after the war. From 1945 to 1948 (see Table 8.4), only Brazil and Venezuela among the larger republics managed growth in excess of 5 percent a year, and the mineral exporters (Bolivia, Chile, Mexico, and Peru) did particularly badly. Uruguay failed to take advantage of the reopening of the European market

60 The Soviet Union was originally intended to be a beneficiary of Marshall Plan aid, but the rapid deterioration in U.S.–U.S.S.R. relations after 1947 changed the situation completely. On the Marshall Plan, see Scammell (1980), pp. 30–4.

for its traditional products, and even Argentina – for whom the loss of the European market in the war had been particularly serious – failed to make much headway.

If the growth in export volumes was problematic, the rise in prices was another matter altogether. Commodity prices, which had been artificially restrained during the war, soared as trading conditions returned to normal. A number of republics (see Table 8.4) saw export prices double in the first three years after the war, and almost all republics enjoyed an increase of more than 50 percent. Import prices were also rising, but in general not as fast as export prices, so the majority of countries experienced an improvement in the net barter terms of trade (NBTT).

This improvement in the NBTT was clearly exceptional, resting as it did on the adjustment from war to peace. It would have been natural to expect a modest deterioration after the supply of primary products from other regions returned to normal. The outbreak of the Korean War produced a further period of abnormal conditions, however.[61] Export prices soared again as stocks were accumulated in the expectation of wartime shortages, and the NBTT for every Latin American country except Argentina hit a peak during the early 1950s. Mineral exporters, facing a rapid increase in demand for their products at the beginning of hostilities, benefited most in the first part of the war; and coffee exporters enjoyed a steady rise in prices and the NBTT, both of which peaked in 1954.

The rapid rise of export prices and the NBTT was partial compensation for the poor performance of export volumes. As a result the international reserve position – which had been so strong during the war years – remained temporarily buoyant. However briefly, every republic enjoyed a period of foreign-exchange abundance during which the balance of payments was not a binding constraint on growth. Furthermore, the accumulation of foreign exchange presented every republic after 1945 with an important decision: how to spend the accumulated balances before their real value was eroded by inflation. This was a crucial postwar dilemma.

One option was to use the foreign exchange to resolve the public external-debt problem. Those republics – the majority – that had defaulted on their foreign bonds in the 1930s had never repudiated the debt. Discussions continued with bondholder committees in the United States and Great Britain, although the foreign-exchange constraint in the 1930s ruled out any permanent solution. With the accumulation of foreign-exchange reserves it became possible to negotiate in earnest. At the same time the world inflation of the 1940s and the rise in commodity prices were rapidly reducing the real burden of the debt.

61 The Korean War (1950–4), and indirect confrontation between the United States and the Soviet Union through the two halves of Korea, raised the very real prospect of a Third World War. Stockpiling of strategic commodities by the developed countries was one immediate response.

The incentive to negotiate with the bondholders was not fear of government reprisals. On the contrary, foreign governments had not been particularly energetic on behalf of the bondholders in the 1930s, and during the Second World War the U.S. government had transferred official capital to Latin American republics irrespective of the status of the public external debt. However, after 1945 the prospect of a resumption of normal international capital flows acted as both a carrot and a stick for those governments that still had not settled with their foreign creditors. Chile, in particular, was quick to reach a settlement when it became clear that this was a precondition for a loan from the newly created International Bank for Reconstruction and Development (the World Bank).[62]

The decision to reach a settlement did not mean full payment. Unpaid interest was never capitalized in any of the agreements, and the principal was also reduced in a few special cases. In general the republics that had defaulted agreed to resume debt service on the principle, but at very low nominal rates of interest and with repayments stretched out over many years. The agreements did not impose a major burden on any of the republics, and in any case world inflation steadily reduced the real burden of debt-service payments.

Argentina, not for the first time, was the exception. At considerable sacrifice to itself, Argentina had serviced its external debt in full during the 1930s, although it had not been rewarded with any significant new capital inflows. The nationalist tide, which had led to the military coup in 1943 and had swept Perón to the first of his presidential election victories in 1946, persuaded Argentine policymakers to convert all external debt into internal securities, so the prewar foreign obligations of central, provincial, and municipal governments had been redeemed in full by 1949. This required Argentina to use a significant proportion of its accumulated foreign exchange, thus reducing its options in comparison with other republics.[63]

Argentina also spent a high proportion of its international reserves on nationalizing foreign-owned properties. The most spectacular purchase was that of the railway network, much of which had been in the hands of British and (to a lesser extent) French companies since its construction before the First World War. In 1948 Argentina spent the considerable sum of £150 million ($600 million) for the British railway companies, which is now widely thought to have been excessive. It should be remembered, however, that Argentina financed the purchase through its accumulated and

---

62 Chile had been refused a $40 million loan by the World Bank in September 1946. Following the announcement of an agreement with Chile's creditors, the World Bank made a $16 million loan in March 1948. See Jorgensen and Sachs (1989).

63 See Jorgenson and Sachs (1989).

still-inconvertible sterling balances in London. Thus at the time both sides thought they had secured a bargain.[64]

The nationalization of foreign-owned properties was not limited to Argentina. The larger republics, and even some of the smaller ones, brought into public ownership numerous public utilities, transport companies, and financial institutions, and some mining operations were also taken over. Mexico used its accumulated foreign exchange to reach an agreement with foreign companies over the terms of compensation for the expropriation of the oil industry in 1938. In many parts of Latin America the combination of buoyant international reserves and rising nationalism provided the ideal chemistry for a shift in the balance between the private sector and the public sector, and foreign capitalists were not the only ones affected.[65]

Debt settlement and nationalizations account for part of the disappearance of foreign-exchange reserves after 1945, but the main reason was the growth of imports. During the war all republics had been frustrated in their efforts to secure imports, and a great deal of pent-up demand existed. Households wanted access to consumer goods that had been unavailable or for which imperfect substitutes had been used. Firms wanted capital equipment to increase capacity and improve quality, and the shift from agriculture to industry was generating a strong demand for imported raw materials.

At first governments hoped that accumulated foreign-exchange reserves would be sufficient to meet the postponed demand for all classes of imports, but the immediate postwar growth proved to be excessive. In the three years after the end of hostilities, the volume of Latin America's imports grew by a massive 75 percent (see Table 8.4) and the value by an unsustainable 170 percent. Argentina, where imports had been particularly sharply reduced during the war, increased the volume of imports by 300 percent.[66] Among the major republics only Mexico, which had been the least affected by import shortages before 1945 and where severe balance-of-payments problems emerged as early as 1947, saw a drop in the volume of imports.

---

64 There is some speculation that Perón was convinced Great Britain would soon repudiate its sterling liabilities, thus leaving Argentina with a worthless asset. Nor could Argentina expect any favors from the United States, which was deeply hostile to the Perón administration in its first few years. See MacDonald (1990), pp. 137–43.

65 Nationalization could also involve domestic capitalists. Thus Perón created the Instituto Argentino para la Promoción y el Intercambio (IAPI), with a virtual monopoly on foreign trade, which displaced many local firms. IAPI permitted the Peronist government to drive a wedge between foreign and domestic prices for agricultural exports and to channel the profits into the industrialization program. See Torre (1991), pp. 80–1.

66 Argentina had suffered the consequences of U.S. displeasure for its wartime neutrality – a policy that led to a partial economic boycott in February 1942 and a particularly severe reduction in the supply of many imports. See Escudé (1990), pp. 63–8.

Much to the chagrin of policymakers the rate of growth of imports showed no signs of abating, and difficult choices had to be made. If import growth was to continue, foreign exchange would soon be exhausted unless the stock of reserves could be replenished through export expansion and foreign-capital inflows. If, on the other hand, this option was ruled out on the grounds that it was either not feasible or not desirable, the only alternative was to restrict the growth of imports. This basic choice provided every republic with a major postwar dilemma.

Import restriction was not new in Latin America. Indeed, since 1929 such a policy had been adopted by force of circumstance throughout the region and had contributed to widespread structural change and industrial growth. It had been implemented by governments that tended to view inward-looking development as a second-best option, however, and it lacked theoretical and intellectual support. The most important book in support of industrial protectionism, by the Romanian economist Mihail Manoilescu, had been translated into both Spanish and Portuguese, but the author's ideas and his fascist sympathies had been discredited by the end of the war.[67]

The immediate postwar years brought a major shift in the policy debate in much of Latin America, which encouraged a number of governments (but by no means all) to adopt inward-looking development and import restrictions as the best policy. The factors promoting this change were internal and external, intellectual and political, and their combined effect was to undermine the theoretical case for export-led growth based on primary products in many parts of the region.

One factor that had changed sharply since the 1920s was nationalism. The experience of the 1930s, the collapse of the international trade and payments system, and the willingness of the developed countries to exploit their greater economic, political, and even military power in their relations with Latin American states had all combined to produce a certain cynicism with regard to models of development that required an open door to foreign goods and capital. Hopes that wartime cooperation with the United States would lead to a new and fairer postwar division of labor were quickly dashed, and the tense wartime relationship between the United States and Argentina had unleashed a wave of nationalism that placed a premium on models of development which reduced dependence on foreign powers.[68]

A second factor was export pessimism. The problems faced by Europe in the aftermath of the war were interpreted in much of Latin America as evidence that it would be many years before the Old World again became a major consumer of imported primary products. At first the failure to increase European real incomes rapidly not only restricted the growth of demand

---

67 See Love (1994).

68 This helps to explain the attraction of industrialization in Argentina, which was seen by Perón as a way of rewarding his urban supporters and reducing dependence on foreign powers at the same time.

but also made it more difficult to dismantle the protectionist cocoon in which European agriculture was now draped. The Cold War brought the very real threat of a Third World War that would have brought a further major disruption to the fragile international trade and payments system.

Export pessimism was also reflected in the work of CEPAL,[69] created in 1948 with Raúl Prebisch in charge from 1950.[70] The first regional organization to be concerned with Latin American rather than Pan-American problems, CEPAL was associated from its very first documents with the idea that Latin America's NBTT were subject to secular decline, that the appropriate policy response was inward-looking development, and that this in turn necessitated an increase in the barriers to imports in order to promote industrialization. Although the theoretical and empirical basis of the *Cepalista* model turned out to be weak,[71] it nevertheless helped to shift the balance of the policy debate in a number of republics away from export-led growth and toward import restrictions.

The most compelling argument in favor of import restrictions was a shortage of foreign exchange, however. By the end of 1948 Argentina had exhausted most of its gold holdings and much of its foreign currency reserves. As early as 1947 Brazil was forced to adopt a system of import licenses in order to ration the use of foreign exchange.[72] In Mexico the balance-of-payments situation became so serious that the exchange-rate was devalued sharply in 1948 and again in 1949, losing almost half its value against the U.S. dollar in just over one year.[73]

A variety of factors therefore combined to make a model of development based on inward-looking development more attractive. Yet the response in Latin America was far from homogeneous. A few republics – Argentina, Brazil, Chile, and Uruguay – adopted the new model consistently and enthusiastically, but a number of others – including Colombia and Mexico – tried to combine the inward-looking model with policies that would also promote exports. The small republics, together with oil-rich Venezuela, were not affected by export pessimism and at first saw no reason to depart from traditional export-led growth based on primary products. Finally

69 At first the U.N. Economic Commission for Latin America (ECLA) was concerned exclusively with problems of the Latin American republics. Following decolonization in the Caribbean Basin, a number of former British colonies joined the organization, so in the 1970s ECLA became ECLAC – the Economic Commission for Latin America and the Caribbean. Since the Spanish acronym, CEPAL, did not change, it is usually used in preference to ECLA or ECLAC in this book.

70 The first director of CEPAL was the Mexican Gustavo Martínez Cabañas (1949–50), although Prebisch was the first to be offered the position. Prebisch did, however, move to Santiago in 1948 in order to write the introduction to CEPAL's first Economic Survey of Latin America. See ECLA (1949). Prebisch was the executive secretary from 1950 to 1963. See ECLAC (1988), p. 15.

71 The literature on this subject is huge. See, for example, Spraos (1983), Diakosavvas and Scandizzo (1991), and Powell (1991).

72 See Kahil (1973), pp. 250–8.

73 See Gold (1988), pp. 1128–30.

Bolivia, Paraguay, and Peru, having begun the immediate postwar years with ill-designed policies that discouraged exports without doing much for import-competing sectors, eventually switched to outward-looking policies based on export diversification. The latter was also adopted in Puerto Rico, where Operation Bootstrap provided massive incentives for U.S. firms to establish manufacturing subsidiaries, the output of which was then reimported tariff free into the U.S. mainland.[74]

The new inward-looking model implied restrictions on imports. This was achieved through import licenses, higher tariffs, and a complex system of exchange rates that reserved the lowest rate for essential imported inputs and the highest rate for luxury consumer goods. In the republics that followed inward-looking development the spread between the highest and lowest exchange-rate was high and became higher. In Argentina the 34 percent spread in 1945 had become 452 percent by 1951, at which point no fewer than seven exchange rates were in existence.[75] A similar pattern was found in Bolivia, Brazil, Chile, Paraguay, and Uruguay. By contrast, Colombia and Mexico – anxious to avoid damage to their export sectors – had both devalued and substantially unified their exchange rates by the early 1950s.[76]

The import restrictions adopted under the inward-looking model were extremely effective. Despite the improvement in the NBTT and the impact of the Korean War on commodity prices, the volume of imports had peaked as early as 1947 in Mexico, 1948 in Argentina, 1949 in Chile, and 1951 in Brazil and Uruguay. Furthermore, the restrictions had the desired effect of changing the structure of imports in favor of producer goods. The proportion of imports accounted for by consumer goods fell sharply in all inward-looking countries, dropping below 10 percent in Argentina and Brazil by the early 1960s.[77]

The outward-looking model survived, but it was now confined to the less important republics. Import restrictions were much less severe in this group of countries, multiple exchange rates were less common, and exchange-rate stability was widespread. At first the volume of imports increased steadily, in line with improvements in the NBTT and the purchasing power of exports (PPE). As the NBTT started to decline after the Korean War, however, opposition to an inward-looking model began to wane; by the mid-1960s every Latin American republic – even those that promoted exports – included in its arsenal a formidable battery of instruments to restrict imports and to encourage the import-competing sectors (see Chapter 9).

---

74 Operation Bootstrap transformed the productive structure of Puerto Rico, with industry replacing agriculture as the most important sector. See Dietz (1986), Chapter 4.
75 On Peronist economic policies, see Gerchunoff (1989).
76 On Mexican exchange-rate policy, see Solís (1983), pp. 118–22. For Colombia, see Ocampo (1987), pp. 252–62.
77 See Grunwald and Musgrove (1970), p. 20.

The new international economic order

From an early stage in the war the main Allied powers – in particular Great Britain and the United States – had begun to plan for the postwar period. All parties wanted to avoid the errors, mistakes, and beggar-my-neighbor policies of the interwar years. There was widespread recognition of the need for international supervision of balance-of-payments corrections, for mechanisms to promote exchange-rate stability, for new instruments to promote international capital flows, and for a global organization to oversee the elimination of barriers to international trade. There was also widespread recognition, at least during the war, of the need to promote orderly markets in primary commodities and to avoid damaging swings in commodity prices.

The first real progress toward the establishment of a new international economic order came at the Bretton Woods Conference in July 1944.[78] As the world's greatest creditor nation and with its economy enormously strengthened by wartime increases in production, the United States was in a unique position to dictate terms at the conference. Although almost half of the participating countries were Latin American, their ability to influence the final outcome was minimal. Even Great Britain, crippled by debt and war damage, was unable to win support for the radical ideas preferred by John Maynard Keynes.[79]

Bretton Woods therefore reflected U.S. preferences and priorities, including the creation of two new international organizations that would operate under United Nations auspices: the International Monetary Fund (IMF) and the International Bank for Reconstruction and Development (IBRD, or World Bank). Unlike League of Nations organizations, many of which had been housed in neutral Switzerland, these new organizations (later known as the "heavenly twins") were to be based in Washington, D.C. – a reflection of the new global balance of power. Trade issues, including commodity agreements and price control, were considered of secondary importance by the United States and were therefore postponed to a later conference.[80]

The postponement of trade issues did not unduly concern the Latin American participants at Bretton Woods, who were in general enthusiastic supporters of the new organizations. Indeed, all republics joined the "heavenly twins" virtually as founder members (except Haiti and Argentina,

78 See Van Dormael (1978), Chapter 16.
79 See Harrod (1951), Chapters 13–14. As the representative of a debtor nation with a weak balance-of-payments position, Keynes favored the creation of an international reserve currency, Bancor, which could be issued by fiat and which would have eased the liquidity problems of deficit countries.
80 Keynes was sensitive to the problems faced by primary-product exports, however, and at Bretton Woods he advocated a scheme for the stabilization of primary-product prices.

which joined in 1953 and 1956, respectively[81]). At first the IMF was widely supported in Latin America because borrowings from the fund were made automatic up to a certain level and because the conditions attached to additional borrowings were left undetermined at Bretton Woods. The right to borrow offered the possibility of avoiding painful adjustment programs every time an external shock to the balance of payments occurred, and it also avoided the need to maintain large foreign-currency reserves earning negative real rates of interest.[82]

Although some reservations were expressed by the region's economists at the IMF's commitment to fixed exchange rates, Latin American republics demonstrated unreserved enthusiasm for the World Bank. In a postwar environment in which bond finance had collapsed and direct foreign investment from Europe was ruled out by reconstruction of the Old World, the creation of a genuine multilateral organization committed to project loans appeared to provide Latin America with a counterweight to exclusive reliance on U.S. capital. Indeed, some of the World Bank's first loans in 1948–9 went to Latin American republics (Chile and Colombia), and the bank undertook a stream of high-level research in numerous republics that was aimed at identifying priority areas for public investment.[83]

Results fell short of expectations, however. Both the IMF and the World Bank, with voting power determined by share ownership,[84] gave a much higher priority to Europe than to Latin America, so the counterweight to dependence on U.S. capital was slight in practice. Furthermore, it was clear from the beginning of the Cold War that Latin America would not be a high priority for official U.S. capital flows and that the region would have to look to U.S. private capital to meet developmental and balance-of-payments requirements. Inevitably, therefore, Latin American attention began to turn to the international trade issues that had been postponed at Bretton Woods.

The first step toward the creation of an International Trading Organization (ITO), the third pillar in the planned new international economic order,

---

81 Because participation at Bretton Woods was restricted to independent countries that supported the Allied war effort, only forty-five delegations attended the crucial conference. Nineteen of them were from Latin America. Argentina did not participate, and membership had to be delayed until Perón was overthrown. Haiti's agreement to Bretton Woods was postponed for "technical" reasons. See Horsefield (1969), p. 117.

82 With dollar prices rising continuously after 1939 and a zero nominal return on international reserves, the real rate of interest was bound to be negative. Even when dollar inflation returned to modest levels at the end of the 1940s, the loss of real purchasing power on foreign-currency reserves was not negligible.

83 One of the best known is the report on Colombia compiled by Lauchlin Currie [see World Bank (1950)], which contributed to the long association of the author with numerous Colombian governments. See Sandilands (1990).

84 Votes were proportional to quotas, and the original quotas gave the nineteen Latin American republics (i.e., excluding Argentina) 7.9 percent of the total compared with 31.25 percent for the United States and 14.8 percent for the United Kingdom. See Horsefield (1969), p. 96.

took place in 1947 with the signing in Switzerland of a General Agreement on Tariffs and Trade (GATT) as a prelude to a wider conference to examine all issues related to trade policies. This crucial conference took place in Havana between November 1947 and March 1948, with Latin American republics much in evidence. Indeed, Chile and Brazil joined forces with Australia and India to press for special concessions on international trade and investment for developing countries – a group whose special interests were now being acknowledged for the first time.[85]

The Havana Charter, signed by fifty-three of the fifty-six countries present, went part of the way toward meeting Latin American concerns on international trade in general and primary commodities in particular.[86] However, the United States never ratified the charter, Great Britain postponed its decision until the United States made up its mind, and the whole idea of an ITO soon faded into obscurity. The world was left only with GATT, which initially commanded so little interest that only twenty-three countries – three of which (Brazil, Chile, and Cuba) were in Latin America – bothered to ratify the treaty. In the early 1950s a few other Latin American republics (Nicaragua, the Dominican Republic, Haiti, Peru, and Uruguay) joined GATT, but the majority of the republics, including some of those who had joined, considered the organization irrelevant and incapable of addressing the trade issues of primary concern to Latin America.

The perceived irrelevance of GATT stemmed from its inability to tackle the issues of trade in primary products. Agriculture was excluded from its terms of reference, so that it was in no position to tackle the numerous tariffs and nontariff barriers facing exporters of primary products. By contrast, trade in manufactures was addressed as a matter of urgency by GATT, with drastic cuts in trade barriers being applied by most member states.[87]

The failure of GATT to tackle the problems of international trade in primary commodities served to stiffen the resolve of those Latin American republics that were committed to inward-looking development. After more than a century of export-led growth, the most important republics had lost faith in the ability of the international marketplace to provide the necessary stimulus for growth and development. And yet, just as much of Latin America was turning inward, the world was about to embark on a remarkable twenty-five-year (1948–73) upswing that reestablished international

85 Concurrent with the notion of developing countries as a separate bloc was the recognition of development economics as a separate subdiscipline. See Arndt (1985), pp. 151–9, and the personal accounts of many of the pioneers of development economics in Meier (1984, 1987).

86 See Scammell (1980), p. 45.

87 The exclusion of agriculture from GATT provisions was due to a number of factors. The most important was the climate of insecurity that prevailed at the time, which made developed countries in particular reluctant to sacrifice access to food supplies on the altar of free trade. See Winters (1990), pp. 1288–1303.

trade as the engine of growth for most developed countries and many developing ones.

Several factors contributed to the dynamism of international trade in the postwar period. By the end of the 1940s Marshall Plan aid had eased the balance-of-payments problem in Europe, had helped to raise the rate of capital accumulation, and had accelerated the process of reconstruction. Currency reform in Germany and devaluation in France and Great Britain eliminated disequilibria in exchange-rate parities and paved the way for renewed exports from Europe to pay for the massive purchase of manufactured goods from the United States. In Asia commodity supply and purchasing power gradually returned to normal, and Japan, its defense spending now crippled by the constitution, pushed resources into productive investment at an unprecedented rate.[88]

GATT, prevented by its articles from tackling primary commodity trade and services, threw its energies into reducing the barriers to trade faced by manufactured goods. In a series of "rounds," tariff and nontariff barriers were progressively eliminated on those manufactured goods deemed of special importance to GATT members. With Latin America in self-imposed exile,[89] GATT negotiations reflected the interests of the developed countries that dominated the organization, and barriers to trade on manufactured goods of particular interest to developing countries either fell slowly (e.g., processed foods) or increased (e.g., textiles).

GATT stood for nondiscrimination, multilateralism, and most-favored-nation treatment. An exception was permitted in the case of free trade areas or customs union, however. The countries of Western Europe, determined to create conditions that would render another war impossible, exploited this opportunity to promote regional integration through the European Economic Community (EEC) and the European Free Trade Area.[90] The Soviet Union, though not a member of GATT, promoted its own version of regional integration through the Council for Mutual Economic Assistance, and trade between the countries of Eastern Europe rose rapidly as a result.

The reduction in the barriers to trade produced an unprecedented increase in world exports and imports. The value of international trade rose at an annual rate of 9.7 percent between 1948 and 1973, and the increase in volume was only slightly lower. Yet the trade was increasingly concentrated among the handful of developed countries that specialized in manufactured

---

88 On postwar reconstruction in the developed countries, see Scammell (1980), Chapter 5.

89 Many Latin American republics (e.g., Costa Rica, Mexico, and Venezuela) refused to join GATT until the 1980s or even later.

90 The European Economic Community (EEC), which became the European Community (EC) in the 1980s and the European Union (EU) in the 1990s, was established with six members [Belgium, France, (West) Germany, Italy, Luxembourg, and The Netherlands] by the Treaty of Rome in 1957. Great Britain, which at first found its imperial commitments inconsistent with EEC membership, formed the European Free Trade (EFTA), with Austria, Denmark, Norway, Sweden, and Switzerland, in 1960.

Table 8.5. *Latin America's shares of world and regional exports,*
1946–1975 (in percentages)

Year	Share of total world exports			Country shares of total Latin American exports				
	Total Latin America	Major countries[a]	All other republics	Argentina	Brazil	Cuba	Mexico	Venezuela
1946	13.5	8.9	4.6	25.5	21.2	11.6	6.9	11.1
1948	12.1	7.3	4.8	24.5	18.2	11.2	5.7	17.2
1950	10.7	6.7	4.0	18.4	21.2	10.4	8.3	14.5
1955	8.9	4.9	4.0	11.8	18.0	7.7	9.9	23.0
1960	7.0	3.5	3.5	12.8	15.0	7.2	9.0	27.2
1965	6.2	3.2	3.0	13.9	14.9	6.4	10.4	22.8
1970	5.1	2.8	2.3	12.0	18.5	7.1	9.5	17.7
1975	4.4	2.2	2.2	8.2	24.0	8.1	8.0	24.3

[a] Includes Argentina, Brazil, Chile, Colombia, Mexico, and Uruguay.
Sources: Derived from International Monetary Fund, *Yearbook of International Financial Statistics*; CEPAL (1976).

exports. Whereas as late as 1955 the trade in manufactured products between developed countries had accounted for a third of world trade, this had risen to nearly half by the end of the 1960s. Furthermore, the developed countries also surpassed the developing countries in the value of primary-product exports, so their total contribution to world trade had reached over 80 percent by 1969.[91]

The new international economic order therefore benefited primarily the developed countries. Only by participating in the spectacular growth of manufactured exports, as some Southeast Asian countries began to do from the late 1950s,[92] could the developing countries hope to extract major advantages from the expansion of world trade. Yet trade in primary products was not stagnant. Although very much the junior partner in the expansion of international trade, primary-product exports still managed to grow between 1950 and 1970 at 6 percent a year. This was impressive by historical standards and guaranteed those developing countries that maintained market share at least some benefits from the expansion of world trade.

A number of developing countries did indeed reap a modest harvest from the expansion of primary-product exports, but the major Latin American republics chose a different path. As a result Latin America's share of world exports fell steadily (see Table 8.5). Latin America, with 6.5 percent of the

91 See Scammell (1980), Table 8.5, p. 128.
92 The countries were Hong Kong, Singapore, South Korea, and Taiwan – collectively known as "the four dragons." By the 1990s the four had become eight, with the inclusion of Indonesia, Malaysia, the Philippines, and Thailand, or nine if the special case of the People's Republic of China is also taken into account.

world's population, accounted for 13.5 percent of the world's exports in 1946, but this share had fallen below 10 percent by 1955 and to 7 percent by 1960. Indeed, by 1965 the region's share of world exports had fallen below its share of population – perhaps for the first time since independence. With Latin America's share of world imports in a similar decline, the region was becoming increasingly divorced from the international trading system.

The decline in Latin America's share of world trade was not entirely due to inward-looking policies, and in any case not all republics eschewed export-led growth (see Chapter 9). Part of the problem was the concentration of Latin American exports in primary products at a time when primary-product trade was growing less rapidly than world trade. Following the Korean War, when the region's terms of trade had peaked, primary-product prices fell relative to the prices of manufactured goods. This decline in the NBTT lent support to those who accepted the hypothesis, vigorously espoused by CEPAL, of a long-run secular decline in the NBTT of primary-product exporters, and it was indeed a source of difficulties until the commodity price boom of the 1970s.[93]

An additional problem faced by Latin American primary-product exports was protection for agriculture in the developed countries and the discrimination of European powers in favor of former colonies. Neither was new, but the EEC's Common Agricultural Policy[94] was another blow to exporters of temperate products from Latin America, and the mantle of protection surrounding U.S. and Japanese farmers was an additional irritant.[95] European imperial preference was phased out, but in its place the EEC adopted a scheme giving tariff and other preferences to exports from a number of developing countries in competition with Latin America. The Lomé Convention,

---

93 The hypothesis of a long-run secular decline in the ratio of primary-product to manufactured-goods prices – still controversial – must be separated from the decline that almost all primary-product-exporting countries faced in the two decades after the early 1950s. This was hardly surprising in view of the high prices enjoyed by primary products as a result of the Korean War, but the subsequent decline in the NBTT inevitably imposed strains on the balance of payments. This was used by CEPAL in numerous publications as prima facie evidence of the validity of the long-run hypothesis. See, for example, ECLA (1970), pp. 3–31.

94 The Common Agricultural Policy (CAP) was established by the 1957 Treaty of Rome. At the time, the EEC was a net importer of foodstuffs, so the first impact of the CAP's high support prices for domestic farmers was ISA and trade diversion. The CAP was so effective, however, that the EEC was rapidly converted from a net food importer to a net food exporter, with major repercussions in the world markets for many commodities (e.g., sugar, beef, and wheat) of importance to Latin America, On the CAP, see Pinder (1991), Chapter 5.

95 U.S. farmers had received a large increase in protection under Roosevelt's New Deal, and the structure of deficiency payments survived into the postwar period. Japanese rice farmers were so highly protected that the local price has regularly exceeded the world price by a factor of four or five. See World Bank (1986), Chapter 6.

Table 8.6. *Commodity share and rank of total Latin American exports*
(in percentages)[a]

Commodity	1934–1938	Rank	1946–1951	Rank	1963–1964	Rank
Coffee	12.8	2	17.4	1	15.0	2
Oil	18.2	1	17.3	2	26.4	1
Sugar	6.1	4	10.2	3	8.6	3
Cotton	4.5	8	4.7	4	4.3	6
Copper	4.7	7	3.4	8	4.9	4
Wheat and wheat flour	5.1	6	4.2	6	1.7	
Beef and cattle	5.7	5	4.4	5	4.4	5
Wool	4.3	9	3.7	7	2.0	9
Maize	6.3	3	2.0		2.0	10
Fish and fishmeal	0		0.1		2.4	8
Hides	3.5	10	3.2	9	0.5	
Iron ore	0		0.1		2.8	7
Forest products	1.0		2.3	10	1.0	
Subtotal	72.2		73.0		76.0	
20 Products[b]	80.4		79.3		81.8	

[a] Only the top ten products in each period have been ranked.
[b] Listed products plus cacao, bananas, lead, zinc, tin, oil/oilseeds, and nitrates.
Source: Derived from Grunwald and Musgrove (1970), Table A.6, p. 21.

as it was eventually called, excluded all Latin American republics until Haiti and the Dominican Republic were allowed to join in 1989.[96]

Although the global obstacles surrounding trade in primary products were significant, they were not sufficient to explain the poor performance of Latin American exports. Not only did the rate of growth of the region's exports fall far below the rate of growth of world trade, it also fell short of the rate of growth of all developing countries and even fell below the rate of growth of all Western Hemisphere developing countries.[97] Although world trade in many primary products (e.g., cotton) was still relatively free, the region remained dependent on a handful of primary products in which it proved impossible to maintain – let alone increase – market share.

In the late 1930s (see Table 8.6) a mere twenty commodities accounted for 80 percent of Latin American exports – and this figure was virtually

96 The Lomé Convention was established shortly after Great Britain (along with Denmark and the Republic of Ireland) joined the EEC in 1973. It grew out of the Yaoundé Convention, which had allowed France to maintain the links to its colonies through the EEC in a network of preferential arrangements. With so many Caribbean countries linked to Europe through Lomé, the EEC eventually accepted the case for membership by the Dominican Republic and Haiti, leaving only Cuba and Puerto Rico without a formal tie. See Pinder (1991), pp. 177–81.

97 This was possible because a number of Caribbean countries (e.g., Trinidad and Tobago) were classified as part of the Western Hemisphere group of developing countries without being part of Latin America.

unchanged nearly thirty years later. Indeed, commodity concentration was even greater than these figures imply, because the top ten commodities accounted for nearly 70 percent of exports and the top five for nearly 50 percent. Thus in the absence of export diversification the growth of Latin American exports was determined by the performance of a handful of commodities.

Some of these commodities (e.g., sugar and maize) faced insuperable problems in world markets as a result of protection and discrimination, but others (e.g., oil and cotton) enjoyed favorable income elasticities and were relatively unaffected by trade barriers. If, however, we examine Latin America's world market share after the late 1930s for the ten leading products, we find only two (cotton and copper) that recorded an increase in the thirty years after 1934–8. Market share was lost in coffee, oil, sugar, wheat, beef, wool, maize, and hides.

In some cases the loss of market share was enormous. Thus despite the growth of Venezuela's oil income in the 1950s, Latin America's share of world oil exports fell from 53 percent to 29 percent in fewer than thirty years as cheaper Middle East production came on stream. Aggressive inward-looking policies, particularly in the Southern Cone, pushed down the region's market share in wheat, beef, and wool to levels that could not possibly be explained by trade discrimination alone. Indeed, under Perón Argentina felt obliged to pass laws forbidding the domestic consumption of meat on certain days in a desperate – if unsuccessful – attempt to discourage the switch of production from world to domestic markets.[98]

A few countries gained market share, but they were mainly small republics whose export performance had little impact on the regional totals. The same was true of export diversification, where the main success stories were found in Central America, the Dominican Republic, Ecuador, and Peru. In many cases one Latin American country's gain was simply another's loss. The gain in world market share for coffee by Central America, Ecuador, the Dominican Republic, and Mexico partially offset the huge loss by Brazil, although African exporters gained as well. The sugar gains in the 1960s were often a simple reflection of the real location of the U.S. import quota for Cuba after the rise of Fidel Castro.[99]

The secular boom in world trade could not last forever, and the volume rate of growth declined significantly after the first oil crisis in 1973. Yet in almost every year after 1945 world trade rose faster than world GDP,

98 This was coupled with tax and other incentives for exporters. See Gerchunoff (1989), pp. 71–8.
99 The reallocation of Cuba's sugar quota to the rest of Latin America in 1960 was one of the first retaliatory measures taken by the United States following the deterioration in relations between the two countries after the Cuban Revolution. Because so many Latin American countries benefited, the United States saw it as a useful device for securing the votes needed in the Organization of American States (OAS) to expel Cuba in 1962. See Domínguez (1989), pp. 23–6.

providing opportunities for those countries whose export structure had adapted to the new pattern of demand. The most dynamic branches of world trade were found in manufactured goods, and Latin American countries were slow to awaken to the new realities. Even those republics whose postwar export performance was satisfactory still specialized in primary products.

Puerto Rico, exploiting its unique relationship with the United States, had turned manufactured exports into a new engine of growth by the 1950s. However, duty-free access to the U.S. market and the almost unlimited supply of U.S. capital led most policymakers to dismiss the relevance of the Puerto Rican model. In the 1960s, when Mexico began to enjoy considerable success with manufactured exports to the United States from *maquiladoras* (assembly plants)[100] on the northern frontier, a number of policymakers in the rest of Latin America began to take export promotion more seriously. The success of the Southeast Asian economies in combining growth and equity on the back of manufactured exports was an additional invitation for policy reform.[101] Yet it took the debt crisis in the 1980s to finally convince all of the republics in the region that a major effort had to be made to break the dependence of exports on a handful of primary products (see Chapter 11).

Latin America therefore lost out on the opportunities created by the secular postwar boom in international trade. The limited success of a handful of smaller republics in promoting primary-product exports could not disguise the fact that the region as a whole had lost market share. Just as Latin America had promoted export specialization in the 1920s at a time when some shift of resources to the nonexport sector would have been more prudent, so did the region withdraw from the world market after 1945 at a time when export promotion offered enormous opportunities. On each occasion the "market" proved an elusive guide to resource allocation, with policymakers filling the vacuum and intervening to shift relative prices in the desired direction.[102] The case for inward-looking development had been credible in the uncertain environment of the late 1940s, but it looked much less plausible a decade later and was almost indefensible by the 1960s. The region paid a high price for the failure to adapt policy more quickly.

100 On the early growth of the industry, see Sklair (1989), Chapter 3.

101 The most common measure of income inequality, the Gini coefficient, was significantly lower in the four Asian dragons compared with Latin America in the 1950s, and the disparity widened in the subsequent years. See Fields (1980), Chapter 5.

102 By the late 1940s the complex structure of multiple exchange rates, tariffs, quotas, and licenses in many countries – not to mention the state marketing boards in Argentina – often made changes in domestic policy instruments more relevant for exporters than changes in world market prices. The impact of a small change in the world market price could easily be swamped, for example, by a decision to move the commodity to a different exchange-rate.

9

Inward-looking development in the postwar period

By the beginning of the 1950s, and even more so by the end of the Korean War, the Latin American republics were faced with a clear choice: to opt explicitly for an inward-looking model of development that would reduce their vulnerability to external shocks or to press ahead with export-led growth on the basis of some combination of export intensification and export diversification.[1]

This choice was not made in a vacuum. Each option favored different groups within society, giving a political twist to most of the economic arguments. At the same time, international and regional institutions pressed hard to influence the outcome. Although the International Monetary Fund (IMF) favored outward-looking policies as a solution to balance of payments problems, the Economic Commision for Latin America (CEPAL), under the dynamic leadership of Raúl Prebisch, defended inward-looking policies. With the deterioration in the net barter terms of trade (NBTT) after the Korean War (a key feature in CEPAL's case for inward-looking development), the intellectual pendulum began to swing toward import-substituting industrialization (ISI). Yet many governments were still reluctant to abandon export-led growth altogether, in recognition of the key role still played by the export sector in economic, social, and political terms.

For a number of republics that had built up a significant industrial base (Argentina, Brazil, Chile, Colombia, Mexico, and Uruguay) the solution was simple. The series of shocks – some favorable, but mainly hostile – to which their export sectors had been exposed since the late 1920s had generated a strong reaction against export-led growth and a broad measure of support for policies explicitly favoring industrialization. CEPAL had appeared to provide the theoretical justification for such policies, and ISI had already demonstrated its ability to generate rapid growth of output and employment in the manufacturing sector. Indeed, the "easy" stage of

---

1 "Export intensification" refers to an emphasis on traditional exports, raising their share of GDP and – in some cases – of total exports. "Export diversification" refers to the promotion of nontraditional exports.

ISI was already complete in these republics, for import suppression had reduced the share of consumer goods in total imports to modest levels.[2]

The other republics faced a greater dilemma. A few (Bolivia, Paraguay, Peru) had flirted with inward-looking policies in the first years after the Second World War, but the results had been disastrous – a collapse of foreign-exchange reserves, supply-side bottlenecks, and inflationary pressures. Peru adopted export-led growth with enthusiasm following a military coup in 1948, but the return to orthodoxy in Bolivia and Paraguay was to prove a long, drawn-out, and painful affair. Elsewhere the absence of a significant industrial base was seen as a critical obstacle to inward-looking policies, and the export-led model was at first retained – with varying degrees of conviction among the republics concerned. Both Venezuela (a winner in the commodity lottery) and Cuba (a loser) relied on export intensification (oil and sugar, respectively) to sustain the rate of growth of foreign-exchange earnings, while most of the other republics looked to export diversification.

The rate of growth of gross domestic product (GDP), and even GDP per head, was not unimpressive for many members of both groups, but dissatisfaction became widespread in the 1960s. The inward-looking group was racked by balance-of-payments crises, inflationary pressures, and labor strife. The outward-looking group also suffered from balance-of-payments problems and vulnerability to adverse external conditions. Both groups, therefore, saw regional integration as a partial solution to their problems. For the inward-looking group it provided an opportunity for export promotion without the full blast of international competition; for the outward-looking group it provided an opportunity for industrialization through regional ISI.

Each group shared one feature – an unequal distribution of income and wealth. Inherited from an earlier period, the distribution of income failed to improve significantly and in some cases deteriorated even further. New data sources, on both income and wealth concentration, revealed what many had always believed – that inequality was more marked in Latin America than in other parts of the world. The inability of the bottom deciles to provide an effective market for many goods and services was seen by some as an obstacle to further growth and development, but most attempts to improve the distribution of income and wealth were ineffective. Only Cuba, following the adoption of revolutionary socialist policies after 1958, experienced a major change in the share of income received by the poorest, although the price paid – stagnation of real consumption per head and confrontation with the United States – was a high one.

---

2 By 1948–9 the share of consumer goods in total imports was 13 percent in Argentina, 16 percent in Brazil, 12 percent in Chile, 20 percent in Colombia, and 17 percent in Mexico. See Grunwald and Musgrove (1970), p. 20.

The inward-looking model

The two decades after 1929 had forced Latin American governments to adopt a series of measures in defense of the balance of payments that had provided new opportunities for industrial growth. In most of those republics in which modern manufacturing had been established before the Great Depression, the opportunities were seized, and industrial growth advanced at a rapid rate. By the beginning of the 1950s industry in these republics, the LA6 (Argentina, Brazil, Chile, Colombia, Mexico, and Uruguay) had either become or was about to become the leading sector, with demand no longer overwhelmingly determined by the fortunes of the export sector. This relative autonomy appeared to have created the conditions for an explicit industrialization policy based on the home market.

The inward-looking model was adopted by nearly all the republics in which the first stages of industrialization had been completed. Peru, however, its industrial dynamism undermined by inappropriate policies throughout most of the first half of the twentieth century, opted for export-led growth after 1948 despite the existence of a modest industrial capacity. Venezuela had also seen the emergence of some modern manufacturing geared to the home market, with demand sustained by the growth of oil revenues, but industry was to remain the junior partner in the postwar model as successive governments exploited the apparently limitless opportunities created by a world economy based on cheap oil. Thus the full inward-looking model was at first confined to the LA6 – the focus of this section.

The inward-looking model rested on manufacturing. Other activities linked to the home market, such as construction, transport, and finance, were not neglected, but the base of the pyramid was seen to rest firmly on the shoulders of the industrial establishments that had grown up in a market sheltered from imports. However, the protection offered to industry had been ad hoc, often inconsistent, and geared to the defense of the balance of payments rather than the needs of industry. In addition to tariffs, it consisted of multiple exchange rates, import quotas and licenses, and occasional outright prohibition. Thus the first task of the policymakers was to introduce greater rationality into the protection offered industry.

The shift toward explicit protection for industry was not immune to external pressures. As members of the IMF (Argentina had finally joined in 1956), the inward-looking countries were under pressure to eliminate quotas and multiple exchange rates. Some resisted. Mexico persevered with its system of import quotas – introduced in 1947 – until the 1980s. Brazil not only maintained its multiple-exchange-rate system in the 1950s but even added a weekly foreign-exchange auction to determine the cost of

Table 9.1. *Nominal protection in Latin America, circa 1960 (in percentages)*

Country	Nondurable consumer goods	Durable consumer goods	Semimanufactured goods	Industrial raw materials	Capital goods	Overall average
Argentina	176	266	95	55	98	131
Brazil	260	328	80	106	84	168
Chile	328	90	98	111	45	138
Colombia	247	108	28	57	18	112
Mexico	114	147	28	38	14	61
Uruguay	23	24	23	14	27	21
EEC	17	19	7	1	13	13

Note: Nominal protection has been calculated as the simple arithmetic mean of approximate incidence (in ad valorem terms) of duties and charges. In the case of Uruguay, it has been calculated as the simple arithmetic mean of theoretical incidence (excluding surcharges and prior deposits) on the CIF value of imports.

Sources: Macario (1964), Table 5, p. 75; for Uruguay, Macario (1964), Table 3, p. 70.

many imports.[3] Generally, however, international pressure was successful, and protection came to rest heavily on more orthodox instruments.

The most important was the tariff. At a time when successive rounds of negotiations, under the auspices of the General Agreement on Tariffs and Trade (GATT), were rapidly lowering the tariffs applied by the developed countries, many Latin American republics – not just the inward-looking ones – were moving in the opposite direction. In addition, a number of republics made use of prior deposits for imports, which had a strong protectionist effect because they increased the local currency price at which imports would subsequently be resold.

Table 9.1 makes clear just how high these tariffs had become for the LA6 by the beginning of the 1960s. The height of these nominal tariff rates partly reflects the phasing out of multiple exchange rates and quotas. Mexico and Uruguay, for example, appeared to have lower tariffs than many other republics because most imports were still subject to quotas. Furthermore, the fact that exchange rates usually failed to move in line with the difference between world and domestic inflation rates led to tariffs being used to "compensate" industrialists for currency overvaluation. Nevertheless, by any standards the nominal rates of tariffs were extremely high – higher than Latin America had applied in earlier periods and far higher than any rates ever adopted in the developed countries. Indeed, as Table 9.1 shows,

3 See Bergsman (1970), pp. 30–2, in which Table 3.1 shows the enormous premium over the official exchange-rate that importers of consumer goods had to pay.

nominal protection in the European Economic Community (EEC) was far lower in every class of commodities.

The high nominal tariff rates drove a wedge between world and domestic prices and imposed a heavy burden on consumers. Yet for producers high nominal tariffs were only half the story. The crucial measure for the producer was the change in value added per unit of output created by the system of protection – taking account not only of the nominal tariff on competing imports but also the impact of tariffs and other forms of protection on the cost of inputs. This measure, known as the effective rate of protection (ERP),[4] was a more appropriate indicator of the incentives being offered to industry. Generally, the ERP was even higher than nominal protection for many classes of goods and was particularly high for consumer goods. Indeed, an ERP of 100 percent – by no means uncommon – implied that the value added per unit of output under the system of protection was double what it would have been under free trade.[5]

Faced with such high rates of protection (nominal and effective), it might have been assumed that the domestic private sector would respond with sufficient dynamism to make an appeal to foreign capital unnecessary. However, the domestic private sector, which had been responsible for most of the increase in manufacturing capacity before 1950, suffered from two severe limitations in the postwar period: It lacked access to the additional finance needed to support large-scale investments in new industries, and it lacked the technology required for mounting sophisticated industrial enterprises.

These two problems had not been crippling while industry was preoccupied with producing nondurable consumer goods under the stimulus of import substitution. This "easy" stage of ISI had not required huge capital investments in individual establishments, and the necessary technology was embodied in imported capital goods. However, the shift in the industrial structure toward consumer durables and toward intermediate and capital goods increased the minimum size of investment and demanded access to technology that could not always be purchased on the open market.

Thus the inward-looking republics – in some cases with reluctance – were obliged to revise their legislation on direct foreign investment and create the conditions deemed appropriate to attract multinational corporations (MNCs). Even Argentina had revised its views on foreign investment before Juan Perón's downfall in 1955, although the new legislative framework was

4 The ERP is defined as the proportionate change in value added (per unit of output) as a result of protection when compared with the free-trade situation. See Corden (1971), Chapter 3.

5 The ERP is difficult to measure accurately, because it must take into account the protection provided not only by tariffs but also by quotas, licenses, and multiple exchange rates. Thus estimates vary significantly, even for the same country. All estimates agree that the ERP for manufacturing in the 1950s and 1960s was very high, however. See Cardoso and Helwege (1992), pp. 94–6, in which Table 4.9 reports an average ERP for manufacturing in Uruguay, for example, of 384 percent.

not adopted until 1959.[6] Mexico, while reserving many sectors (e.g., oil, banking, insurance, and transport) for national capital, encouraged MNCs to invest in manufacturing – a task made difficult at first by the ill feeling inherited from oil nationalization in 1938. Brazil, where the program of industrialization was adopted with the greatest conviction, was so anxious to attract MNCs that it even passed legislation which actually favored foreign investors over domestic investors in some respects.[7]

The MNCs, at first dominated by U.S. companies, were invited to Latin America for their technology, marketing and management skills, and access to finance. What attracted the MNCs, however, was the captive market to which they had previously supplied exports. The high tariff wall may have kept out imports, but once inside the wall foreign investors were in turn protected from foreign competition. The richest pickings were often to be found in the production of consumer goods rather than in the intermediate and capital-goods industries that governments were hoping to see established. Foreign ownership was therefore not confined to the newer branches of industry, and much foreign investment simply involved the purchase of established domestic firms.[8] Thus some conflicts arose between the goals of governments and of MNCs. These conflicts, coupled with the use by MNCs of transfer prices to minimize tax burdens,[9] were producing a certain tension by the end of the 1960s. Furthermore, the relationship was not helped by government directives to foreign firms, particularly in the automobile industry, to increase the proportion of their inputs obtained from domestic sources.[10]

---

6 Foreign capital was given rights equal to national capital in December 1959. See Petrecolla (1989), p. 110. See also Katz and Kosacoff (2000), pp. 289–91.

7 Under the draconian exchange-control system in operation in Brazil, domestic firms often had difficulty securing the foreign exchange needed for imports of capital goods. In 1955, however, the monetary authority (SUMOC) issued Instruction 113, which allowed foreign firms to import equipment without any foreign-exchange transactions. It has been estimated that imports so favored would have cost 45 percent more in the absence of Instruction 113. See Bergsman (1970), pp. 73–5.

8 The foreign share of industrial production was significant even in long-established industries. By the end of the 1960s it varied from 15 percent to 42 percent in the food sectors of the major countries and from 14 percent to 62 percent in textiles. A particular favorite was the tobacco sector, in which the share was more than 90 percent in Argentina, Brazil, Chile, and Mexico. See Jenkins (1984), p. 34, Table 2.4.

9 Because subsidiaries of MNCs purchase from and sell to each other, they are often able to choose a nonmarket price for transactions that minimizes their global tax liability. In countries with high marginal tax rates, these "transfer prices" could then be used to raise the cost of imported inputs and lower the value of exports. See Vaitsos (1974). On intracompany transfers in general, see Grosse (1989), Chapter 10.

10 When the first automobiles were assembled in Brazil in the 1920s, the only domestic material input used was jute for stuffing the seats. See Downes (1992), p. 570. By 1970, following legislation in the 1950s to raise local content, imported inputs represented only 4 percent of the value of output. See Jenkins (1987), Chapter 4 and Table 5.2, p. 72.

In the absence of sufficient investment by the domestic private sector, a number of state-owned enterprises (SOEs) were set up to sustain the industrialization program. Although the main public investments were found in social infrastructure – energy, transport, and communications – some branches of industry were also considered appropriate for public investment on the grounds that the domestic private sector could not or would not provide the finance and that the products were too sensitive to be controlled by foreign companies. Brazil formed Petrobras in 1953 to control the oil industry and to complement existing public investments in manufacturing.[11] By the 1960s the profitability of the Brazilian automobile industry – dominated by MNCs – depended primarily on the price of inputs from SOEs (e.g., steel and electricity) and the oil policy of the Brazilian government. The steel industry was also a favorite target for SOEs throughout the inward-looking republics.

With so much emphasis in the LA6 on the manufacturing sector, it is hardly surprising that it expanded rapidly. As the leading sector, its rate of growth exceeded the rate of growth of GDP – pushing up the share of manufacturing in total net output. By the end of the 1960s the inward-looking countries had seen the share of manufacturing in GDP rise to a level similar to that in developed countries. Furthermore, the structure of industrial production had now shifted away from food processing and textiles toward metal-using industries and chemicals. The largest countries in Latin America – Argentina, Brazil, and Mexico – now warranted the label "semi-industrialized," and Chile and Colombia, with much smaller domestic markets, were not far behind. Only Uruguay, after a burst of industrial growth in the first decade after the war, found itself unable to sustain the dynamism of the manufacturing sector on the basis of its tiny domestic market.

The price paid for this industrial success was high. Shielded from international competition, much of the manufacturing sector was both high cost and inefficient in every sense. High unit costs arose not only from the need to pay more for tradable inputs than the world price but also because the domestic market was usually too small to support firms of optimum size.[12] Inefficiency stemmed from the distortions in factor prices, the lack of competition in the domestic market, and the tendency toward an oligopolistic structure with high entry barriers. The market leaders – including MNCs – could set prices above marginal cost, which the rest of the industry then

---

11 On the origins of Petrobras, see Philip (1982), Chapter 11.

12 Manufacturing products are in general subject to economies of scale, so unit costs of production fall as plant size rises. Carnoy (1972) demonstrated for a range of industrial commodities the excess costs associated with production runs limited to the national market.

followed. Inevitably, profit rates were often abnormally high in the protected industrial sectors.[13]

The high cost of industrial production made it difficult for manufactured goods to enter into international trade. The problem was compounded by the overvaluation of exchange rates and by the export pessimism surrounding policy throughout the 1950s. In addition, many subsidiaries of MNCs came to Latin America with contracts that ruled out exports to third countries (where they would have competed with production from the subsidiaries of the same MNCs). By the mid-1960s the proportion of manufacturing output exported and the contribution of manufacturing to total exports was still small. Only Mexico, where currency overvaluation had been eliminated through devaluations in 1948, 1949, and 1954, was able to make any significant progress in manufactured exports. But even in Mexico – despite the proximity of the U.S. market and the growth of border industries[14] – the contribution of industry to foreign-exchange receipts was still minor.

The inability of industry to penetrate world markets left export earnings dependent on primary products, although Mexico at least was able to supplement these with a growing trade in tourism.[15] However, primary-product exports by the inward-looking republics were negatively affected by a whole host of factors. In addition to deteriorating NBTT after the Korean War, the traditional export sector suffered from the antiexport bias implied by the new structure of protection for industry.[16] Forced by high tariffs to purchase inputs above world market prices, primary-product exporters still had to sell their output in world markets at international prices. In Perón's Argentina the state marketing board even paid farmers below world prices,[17] and everywhere in the LA6 currency overvaluation tended to

13 The rate of return (calculated as the ratio of net profits to capital and reserves) among ten leading MNCs in Brazil varied from 9.3 percent to 26.5 percent between 1967 and 1973. See Evans (1979), Table 4.4. This was high by international standards.

14 The measurement of the impact of the border industry in Mexico before the 1990s was complicated by the fact that balance-of-payments statistics excluded *maquiladoras* from the trade account, although their net exports were included in the current account. By 1970 these net exports were valued at $81 million, compared with $1,348 million for commodity exports.

15 The growth of the Mexican tourist industry, which mainly draws visitors from the United States, was impressive. By 1970 more than 2 million tourists were recorded – nearly half of the Latin American total. Although Mexicans themselves had a great propensity to travel abroad, the net contribution of tourism to the balance of payments was still important – $260 million in 1960 and $416 million in 1970. See ECLAC (1989), Table 258, p. 466.

16 Antiexport bias is defined as the proportionate difference between value added per unit of output in the protected domestic market and in the world market. It is therefore almost certain to be greater than the ERP for the same product. For an estimate of antiexport bias in Brazil in the 1960s, see Bergsman (1970), Table 3.9, p. 52.

17 On the state marketing board (IAPI), see Chapter 8, n. 65. See also Furtado (1976), pp. 186–7.

discourage the growth of primary-product exports.[18] Export diversification was limited, and export earnings continued to be dominated by a handful of traditional products. The bias against exports was so strong in Uruguay that the volume of exports fell sharply in the 1950s, and the value of exports in the early 1970s was still below what it had been twenty years earlier.[19]

The lack of dynamism of export earnings might not have mattered if the inward-looking model had succeeded in eliminating the need for imports – but it did not succeed. Although part of the new industrial output was indeed intended to replace imports, industry itself was import intensive. Intermediate and capital goods had to be imported, even if consumer goods could be eliminated. Foreign exchange was needed for payments of licenses, royalties, and the transfer of technology – not to mention remittances of profits. And many of the related nontraded goods and services, such as transport and telecommunications, were also import intensive. The need to suppress imports to protect the balance of payments produced major distortions with almost any scheme to replace imports – however inefficient – winning official support. Brazil operated an aggresive Law of Similars to encourage domestic production of import-competing goods with scant regard for efficiency issues.[20] Indeed, the net foreign exchange saved by some of these schemes was often close to zero because they themselves were so import intensive.[21]

The lack of dynamism of exports, coupled with the need for rising imports, produced an almost endless series of balance-of-payments problems in the inward-looking countries. Stabilization programs to eliminate balance-of-payments disequilibria tended to be costly, because imports could only be cut by reducing intermediate and capital-goods purchases, with negative effects on production and capacity. In addition, the tight balance-of-payments constraint meant that excess growth in the money supply could not spill over into consumer-goods imports, so monetary expansion – for example, through budget deficits – was associated with excess demand for domestic

18 The term "currency overvaluation" is used in two different ways. The first refers to an exchange-rate that is inconsistent with a balance-of-payments equilibrium, so the authorities are forced to use other import-restricting measures. The second refers to the change (appreciation) of the exchange-rate following the introduction of a system of protection designed to squeeze imports. Except for Mexico, where postwar devaluations eliminated the first kind of overvaluation for much of the 1950s, the LA6 all experienced currency overvaluation in both senses in the 1950s and 1960s.

19 As a consequence, Uruguay's share of world exports fell from 0.45 percent in 1946 to 0.08 percent in 1970 and 0.047 percent in 1975 – a tenfold decline in thirty years.

20 The Law of Similars allowed Brazilian manufacturers to request prohibition of any import they believed could be produced locally. Not until 1967 was the price of domestic production formally adopted as one of the criteria to inform the government's decision. See Bergsman (1970), pp. 34–5.

21 The gross savings of foreign exchange could be measured by the CIF value of the import replaced. However, the net savings needed to take into account imported components, imported machinery, licenses, royalties, profit remittances, and so forth. Even if the net savings were usually positive, they could still be small.

Table 9.2. *Exchange rates and inflation, 1950–1970*

Country	exchange-rate[a] (1960 = 100)			Annual average rate of inflation (in percentages)			
	1950	1960	1970	1950–1955	1955–1960	1960–1965	1965–1970
				LA6			
Argentina	17	100	482	17	38	27	20
Brazil	10	100	2,439	18	28	62	48
Chile	3	100	1,109	47	24	29	29
Colombia	28	100	269	4	10	14	11
Mexico	69	100	100	10	6	2	3
Uruguay	17	100	2,273	13	25	35	44
				LA14			
Bolivia	1	100	100	108[b]	6[c]	5	6
Costa Rica	100	100	118	2	2	1	2
Cuba	100	100	100	0	1[d]	n/a	n/a
Dominican Republic	100	100	100	0	0	3	2
Ecuador	100	100	166	2	0	0	5
El Salvador	100	100	100	4	0	0	1
Guatemala	100	100	100	3	−1	0	1
Haiti	100	100	100	1	1	4	3
Honduras	100	100	100	5	1	4	2
Nicaragua	100	100	100	11	−2	2	3
Panama	100	100	100	0	0	1	1
Paraguay	4	100	100	47	11	5	3
Peru	56	100	144	6	8	10	9
Venezuela	100	100	138	1	2	0	1

[a] Nominal exchange-rate (per U.S. dollar).
[b] Datum is for 1950–6.
[c] Datum is for 1957–60.
[d] Datum is for 1955–8.

Sources: Thorp (1971); Wilkie (1974 and 1990); World Bank (1983), vol. I; International Monetary Fund (1987). For inflation data in all decades since 1940, see Thorp (1998), Appendix V.

goods and high rates of inflation. Because monetary discipline tended to be weak in the LA6 and because domestic supply – particularly of agricultural goods – was relatively inelastic, most of the inward-looking countries suffered from acute exchange-rate instability and inflationary pressures (see Table 9.2).

The combination of balance-of-payments constraints, budget deficits, and supply-side bottlenecks produced a heated debate between structuralists and monetarists over the causes of inflation. The monetarist interpretation placed the emphasis on irresponsible fiscal policies, leading to large budget deficits, expansion of the money supply, and domestic inflation. In the monetarist model bottlenecks on the supply side were due to price controls (e.g., for agricultural goods) and price distortions (e.g., overvalued exchange rates) and were therefore a consequence of inflation rather than its cause. Structuralists did not deny that excess money creation was associated with inflation but instead argued that the money supply was largely passive, with the root cause of inflation lying in fiscal, agricultural, and balance-of-payments bottlenecks.[22]

The fiscal "bottleneck" was attributed by structuralists to the inelastic nature of tax revenue and the constant pressure to increase government expenditure in support of ISI programs. With the switch in policy from a tariff designed to raise revenue to a tariff designed to provide protection, the income from customs duties as a proportion of expenditure was steadily declining, and new sources of taxation had to be introduced. The "inelastic" nature of tax revenues was above all, however, a reflection of a tax system that was overreliant on indirect taxes which fell disproportionately heavily on the poor. The yield from direct taxes was disappointing, and high rates of inflation encouraged taxpayers to delay payment as long as possible. Even the notorious inflation tax, which reflected the erosion of money balances as a result of rising prices, was of declining utility as the public learned to economize on its money balances as a defense against inflation.[23]

The structuralists at first appeared to be on stronger ground in the case of the food-supply bottleneck, which they attributed to Latin America's antiquated land-tenure system, with its division between *minifundios* (small farms) and *latifundios* (large estates). Yet the poor performance of food supply in a country such as Argentina, which until the 1930s had enjoyed one of the most dynamic agricultural sectors in the world, could only be attributed to price controls and the deterioration of the internal and external terms of trade faced by farmers. Mexico recorded impressive rates of growth of agricultural output until the mid-1960s, which structuralists attributed to the land reform of the 1930s, but Mexican farmers never faced the price distortions found in Argentina, Chile, and Uruguay, and the competitive exchange-rate for much of the 1950s made agricultural exports profitable.[24]

---

22 The literature on the monetarist–structuralist debate is huge. See Thorp (1971); Wachter (1976); and Sheahan (1987), Chapter 5.

23 The inflation tax, if there is no real GDP growth, is the same as seigniorage. See Cardoso and Helwege (1992), pp. 150–4.

24 On the food-supply bottleneck, see Edel (1969). See also Cardoso (1981), who demonstrates theoretically how a food-supply bottleneck can propagate inflation. Parkin (1991), Chapter 5, has used the model as the basis for an empirical study of Brazilian inflation.

Balance-of-payments and inflation problems forced the inward-looking countries into standby agreements with the IMF. These programs were generally a failure that the IMF, committed to a monetarist approach, attributed to the unwillingness of governments to stick to unpopular policies and that many critics attributed to the IMF's monetarist approach.[25] In fact, the problem was rooted in the conflict between the IMF's outward-looking preferences and the inward-looking model of development adopted by the LA6. All IMF programs tended to emphasize policies that would overcome balance-of-payments disequilibrium through export expansion. The LA6 governments, however, remained committed to policies designed to eliminate the problem through import suppression. Not surprisingly, the commitment to IMF-inspired policies was only skin deep, and the short-run fall in real wages, output, and employment associated with the policies often overwhelmed any increase in exports associated with devaluation.[26]

The inward-looking model, particularly in the 1950s, is now seen as an aberration – condemned by Latin American leaders and international organizations alike. The distortions associated with the model have become legendary, and its achievements have been dismissed. Some of the distortions were inevitable: An inward-looking model designed to foster industrialization is bound to drive a wedge between domestic and international prices. Yet many of the distortions were far in excess of what was required. The damage to agriculture and to exports in Argentina and Uruguay could not be explained entirely by the industrialization program. Mexico, through offering huge incentives to industry, was still able to record satisfactory agricultural, export, and even price performances for much of this period through judicious use of public investments (e.g., in irrigation) and the avoidance (at least until the 1960s) of currency overvaluation.[27]

Yet although the excesses were often unnecessary the model – even in a less-distorted form – still cannot be defended. In semi-industrialized countries import suppression made no sense; exports had to expand to pay for the additional imports required to keep the productive apparatus efficient and technologically up to date. The semiclosed nature of the economies accentuated the inflationary pressures to which the inward-looking republics had been subject since the beginning of the Second World War. Furthermore, the model was adopted in an explicit form just when the world economy and international trade were embarking on their longest and fastest period of secular expansion. The timing of the model could not have been worse.

25 Fund stand-by programs in Latin America are analyzed in Remmer (1986), pp. 1–24.
26 A good example of a failed IMF program is Argentina after 1958. See Díaz-Alejandro (1965), pp. 145–53.
27 For a good survey of the case for and against ISI, drawing on recent developments in trade and growth theory, see FitzGerald (2000).

Outward-looking countries

Although they were not opposed to industrialization the remaining republics in Latin America (LA14) did not consider that a model based exclusively on inward-looking development was viable at the end of the 1940s. Structural change since the 1920s had been modest, and each of these fourteen republics still had the classic features of export-led growth economies, in which output, income, employment, and public revenue were highly correlated with the fortunes of a handful of primary-product exports.

The industrial sector in these republics was particularly weak. Unable to take much advantage of the opportunities provided by the restrictions on imports in two world wars and the 1930s, the manufacturing sector was too fragile at the end of the 1940s to provide a springboard for a new inward-looking model. Social infrastructure remained geared primarily to the needs of the export sector, and energy supply was inadequate for a major expansion of secondary activities. Although the acceleration in the rate of growth of population, coupled with rural–urban migration, had converted the earlier labor shortage into a labor surplus, the kind of skilled labor required by modern manufacturing was still scarce.

Furthermore, the economic elite in many of these republics was still politically powerful. Although they were willing to add investments in secondary and tertiary activities to their portfolios, they were not prepared to countenance policies overtly hostile to the primary-export sector, which remained their traditional base. The prime examples of this pragmatic approach to postwar opportunities were provided by the Trujillo family in the Dominican Republic and the Somoza dynasty in Nicaragua, who spread investments across a wide range of activities, with the export sector providing the core.[28]

This commitment to export-led growth was reinforced by the experience of three republics (Bolivia, Paraguay, and Peru), where the economic elite did lose political power after the war and where inward-looking policies were pursued briefly – with disastrous results. The politics and economics of Bolivia had been so intimately tied up with tin for more than half a century that the decline in influence of the *rosca* – the name given to the three enterprises that controlled the Bolivian tin industry – was bound to signal the advent of policies hostile to the export sector.[29] Yet Bolivia's experiment with inward-looking development after 1946 contributed substantially to the economic chaos that led to the revolution in 1952: The postrevolutionary decision to nationalize the tin industry and ignore economic considerations in its management crippled the country's

28 On the Somoza business interests in Nicaragua, see Booth (1982), Chapters 4–5. On Trujillo's interests in the Dominican Republic, see Moya-Pons (1990a).
29 See Whitehead (1991), pp. 535–9.

export earnings and economic growth for nearly a decade.[30] The sobering experience of hyperinflation in 1956 finally reconciled the new political elite to the need for greater rationality in economic decision making – including incentives for the export sector.[31]

The political turmoil in Paraguay in the decade before General Alfredo Stroessner seized power in 1954 was as acute as it was in Bolivia. Paraguay also suffered severely from the change of direction in Perón's Argentina – the republic to which Paraguay had informally attached itself throughout the first half of the twentieth century. Export earnings were hit, exchange-rate policy was undermined, and the incoherent set of inward-looking policies adopted pushed Paraguay close to hyperinflation.[32] Stroessner's rule laid the basis for a return to export-led growth, although Paraguay's traditional penchant for contraband trade – flagrantly promoted by the military clique close to Stroessner – makes it impossible to use official trade figures as a guide to performance.[33]

The failure of Peru's brief flirtation with inward-looking policies after the war is more surprising. Unlike Bolivia and Paraguay, Peru did at least have a diversified industrial sector and met many of the preconditions for the kind of industrialization program favored by CEPAL. Yet the efforts of the administration of President José Luis Bustamante after 1945 to switch resources from the export sector to the domestic market proved disastrous. The balance-of-payments current account deteriorated rapidly, foreign exchange reserves were drained, and annual inflation rates soared. The military coup in 1948, led by General Manuel Odría, paved the way for two decades of aggressive export-led growth. In 1968 another military intervention provided the catalyst for an equally dramatic shift in policy – this time in favor of inward-looking development.[34]

With Bolivia (slowly), Paraguay, and Peru returning to orthodoxy, the LA14 formed a bloc whose export performance stands in sharp contrast to the rest of Latin America. Whereas the six inward-looking countries – the LA6 – saw their share of world trade fall from 8.9 percent in 1946 to

30 The three giant mining companies that formed the *rosca* were nationalized after the revolution, and a state enterprise Corporación Minera de Bolivia (COMIBOL) was created as an umbrella organization. Political considerations were foremost in COMIBOL decisions for many years, and the company became almost legendary for its economic inefficiency. See Klein (1992), pp. 233–45.

31 The hyperinflationary episode in 1956 bore remarkable similarities to the catastrophic events in 1985, when inflation reached an annualized rate of 60,000 percent. The 1956 inflation was ended with a stabilization program designed with the help of a U.S. economist George Jackson Eder. See Eder (1968).

32 See Lewis (1991), p. 251, and Roett and Sacks (1991), p. 63.

33 The close involvement of the military under Stroessner in the contraband trade was an open secret. See Nickson (1989).

34 These twists and turns in the Peruvian economic model are well discussed in Thorp and Bertram (1978), Chapters 10–13.

3.5 percent in 1960, the LA14 experienced only a modest decline – a decline that could be explained almost entirely by their specialization in primary products at a time when primary-product trade was growing less rapidly than world trade. By 1960 the LA14 accounted for the same share of world trade as the LA6, and their share of the Latin American total had risen from one-third to one-half.[35] Five republics (Costa Rica, Ecuador, El Salvador, Nicaragua, and Venezuela) even managed to increase their share of world trade in the first fifteen years after the war.

In some cases export-led growth simply meant export intensification; that is, export earnings continued to depend almost entirely on long-established traditional primary products. Oil continued to account for virtually all of Venezuela's export earnings both before and after the consolidation of democracy at the end of the 1950s.[36] Although Middle Eastern oil production enjoyed lower unit costs, Venezuela's proximity to the United States and its generous treatment of the multinational oil companies (until nationalization in the mid-1970s) provided the basis for fast growth of exports in the 1950s.[37] Bolivia was unable to shake off its dependence on tin until the 1970s (when natural gas began to be exported in large quantities), so export recovery in the 1960s required a complete overhaul of the Corporación Minera de Bolivia (COMIBOL, the state-owned colossus responsible for all mineral exports from nationalized mines).[38] Cuba, both before and after the revolution that brought Castro to power in 1959, was almost wholly dependent on sugar for export earnings.[39] Because the contribution of exports to GDP remained high, Cuba continued to be an economy in which the volume and price of sugar exports provided the key to economic performance.[40]

In the majority of cases, however, outward-looking policies were accompanied by export diversification. Generally this meant the promotion of new primary products or the intense development of minor exports. Peru led the way, with the exploitation of lead, zinc, copper, and iron deposits by foreign firms and with the rapid growth of fish products. Fishmeal, used as an input by the poultry and hog industries in the developed countries,

---

35 See Table 8.5.

36 Venezuela's brief experiment with democracy after the Second World War had ended in military intervention. Democracy was finally established after elections in December 1958. See Ewell (1991).

37 See Randall (1987), Chapter 3.

38 COMIBOL received technical and financial assistance from U.S. and (West) German official sources after 1960. This went part of the way toward improving its efficiency, but losses remained common. See Dunkerley (1984), p. 105.

39 The World Bank devoted one of its first country studies to Cuba; the study emphasized the dependence of the island's economy on sugar. See Truslow (1951).

40 Despite the World Bank mission's recommendations that Cuba should become less dependent on sugar, on the eve of the revolution the crop still accounted for 30 percent of national income – the same ratio as in 1913. See Brundenius (1984), Table A2.2.

was particularly dynamic.[41] By 1970 nearly one-third of all export earnings in Peru came from fish products, compared with less than 1 percent in 1945. Ecuador benefited from the giant fruit companies' search for virgin lands suitable for growing bananas. By 1960 export earnings from bananas were dominating foreign-exchange receipts, and Ecuador had captured more than one-quarter of world exports.[42] Paraguay began to exploit its enormous agricultural potential by exporting cotton and growing soybeans and other such crops for conversion into exports of vegetable oils.[43]

In Central America export earnings and economic performance had been dependent on coffee and bananas for decades. With the control of malaria and the growth of social infrastructure, the fertile plains of the Pacific littoral were opened up after 1945 for the spread of cotton plantations to be followed in a few years by new cattle ranches and improvements in breeding stocks. The sugar industry, which had made steady progress in the 1950s, received a huge boost from the U.S. decision to reallocate the Cuban sugar quota to the rest of Latin America,[44] and by the mid-1960s the combined earnings from cotton, sugar, and beef were beginning to rival those from coffee and bananas.[45] At the end of the 1960s agroexporters in Guatemala began to experiment with cardamom, and within a decade it had captured 80 percent of world exports.[46]

Although export diversification mainly affected primary products, there were a handful of cases of diversification into secondary and even tertiary activities. Haiti, facing almost insuperable problems in expanding the supply of agricultural products, turned to light manufactures in the 1960s in a not very successful effort to sustain export earnings.[47] Panama, even before the Carter–Torrijos treaties in 1977, saw its income rise in line with canal operations.[48] The establishment of a free-trade zone in the port of Colón provided a major source of income from entrepôt activities; shipping

41 The rise of the fishmeal industry in Peru is the subject of an excellent monograph. See Roemer (1970).
42 The Ecuadorian banana boom is described in May and Plazo (1958), pp. 169–75. Plazo had been president of Ecuador from 1948 to 1952, when the boom began.
43 See Roett and Sacks (1991), Chapter 4.
44 Cuba's sugar quota was cut in July 1960. Ironically, it had been increased (to 3.12 million tons) as recently as December 1959. See Domínguez (1989), pp. 23–5.
45 See Bulmer-Thomas (1987), pp. 185–90.
46 Cardamom, a spice, is frequently added to coffee in Middle Eastern countries. On its growth in Guatemala, see Guerra Borges (1981), pp. 256–8.
47 The crisis in Haiti's primary exports, which can be traced in part to soil degradation, is analyzed in Lundahl (1992), Chapter 5. The only manufactured export with which Haiti had any real success was baseballs.
48 The Carter–Torrijos treaties restored Panamanian sovereignty over the Canal Zone and substantially increased the rental income from the canal's operations. However, direct value added from the canal had already risen from $44.1 million in 1950 to $152 million in 1970. See Weeks and Zimbalist (1991), p. 51.

registrations rose steadily; and earnings from banking, finance, and insurance turned Panama into one of the world's most important offshore financial centers and an increasingly attractive location for money-laundering by the continent's drug dealers (*narcotraficantes*). By 1970 only one-third of export earnings came from commodities, the remainder being accounted for by services.[49]

Export-led growth in the postwar period was not without its advantages and helped the smaller republics to avoid some of the excesses found in the inward-looking countries. The growth of exports, coupled with modest capital inflows, underpinned stable exchange rates. Nominal exchange-rate devaluation was rare among this group of republics, and in the 1960s ten of the LA14 maintained an unchanged exchange-rate to the U.S. dollar – in complete contrast to the exchange-rate performance of the LA6 (see Table 9.2). Because the outward-looking countries were relatively open,[50] exchange-rate stability brought price stability. Indeed, once the high-inflation episodes in Bolivia and Paraguay had been overcome in the 1950s, not one of the countries – with the possible exception of Peru – had a major problem with inflation (see Table 9.2). Thus, fixed exchange rates did not necessarily mean overvalued exchange rates, and most of these republics had little difficulty preserving a parity that made exports profitable.[51]

Price stability did not mean that monetary and fiscal policy was always orthodox. Some republics – for example, El Salvador and Guatemala – did conduct their domestic policies along extremely conservative lines, but many others indulged in the same loose fiscal and monetary policies that were causing so many problems in the inward-looking countries.[52] The public-revenue system was often antiquated, tax evasion was widespread, and domestic capital markets were undeveloped. Not surprisingly, budget deficits were quite common and were often financed by printing money. Yet the penalties for such largesse were quite different in the outward-looking

---

49 Paradoxically, this share drops after the implementation of the Carter–Torrijos treaties if – as happens in some estimates – exports from the Colón Free Trade Zone are treated as Panamanian commodity exports. On the transformation of the Panamanian balance of payments after 1979 (when the treaties were ratified by the United States), see International Monetary Fund (1986), pp. 507–8.

50 The (unweighted) ratio of exports plus imports to GDP for the LA6 was 25.3 percent in 1960. For the other republics (excluding Cuba) the unweighted average was 43 percent. See World Bank (1980), Table 3, p. 387.

51 In view of Latin America's reputation for currency depreciation, it is worth emphasizing the exceptional nature of currency stability in some republics. Panama has never altered its exchange-rate. The Haitian rate was fixed from before the First World War until 1991. The Dominican Republic, Honduras, and Guatemala had eighty, seventy, and sixty years, respectively, of currency stability before the debt crisis of the 1980s.

52 Costa Rica, where a welfare state had been created on social democratic lines since 1940, had frequent problems with budget deficits and was obliged to seek IMF support in 1961.

countries. The excess supply of money was reflected in balance-of-payments problems through the increase in imports – unmatched by exports – rather than through increases in domestic prices.[53]

Balance-of-payments problems were in fact quite common among this group, and stabilization programs, usually under the auspices of the IMF, were therefore inevitable.[54] Stabilization – designed primarily to resolve external disequilibrium – was much easier in the outward-looking countries, however. First, the relatively open nature of the economies meant that consumer goods still accounted for a significant proportion of total imports, and these could be cut without undue damage to the productive capacity of the economy.[55] Second, the IMF's orthodox measures for balance-of-payments improvement tended to fall on more fertile soil because all fourteen republics were already committed to some form of export-led growth. Thus almost all of the examples of "successful" IMF stabilization policies in the 1950s and 1960s tended to be found among the LA14.[56]

Numerous problems associated with export-led growth had produced a growing sense of dissatisfaction among many of the LA14 republics by the 1960s, however. One problem, emphasized by CEPAL and the cornerstone of its policies, was the deterioration in the NBTT. Although the high prices for commodities recorded during the Korean War could not possibly be expected to last, the subsequent fall in the NBTT caused balance-of-payments problems for many countries.[57] The number of commodities traded freely steadily declined as the developed countries introduced quotas on a range of products (e.g., beef) and as international commodity agreements (in sugar, cacao, coffee, and tin) were established to counteract the instability in world commodity prices.[58] Oil – even before the formation of the Organization of Petroleum Exporting Countries (OPEC) cartel[59] – was not exempt, for the

53 After Trujillo was assassinated in 1961 monetary policy was loosened in the Dominican Republic and the fiscal deficit increased. Yet prices rose only modestly, and the exchange-rate remained fixed, with monetary growth reflected primarily in higher imports.

54 For a careful analysis of many such programs, see Remmer (1986), pp. 1–24.

55 As later as 1970 the share of consumer goods in total imports was 20.2 percent for the LA14 (excluding Cuba), compared with 7.8 percent for the LA6. See ECLAC (1989), pp. 522 and 526.

56 The Bolivian stabilization program in 1956, the Costa Rican program in 1961, and the Dominican program in 1964 were examples of IMF-inspired programs that eliminated the main internal and external disequilibria. Even the Peruvian stabilization program in 1959, launched while the republic was still committed to a version of export-led growth, achieved external equilibrium, although it has not been without its critics. See Thorp (1967).

57 The NBTT for the region as a whole, which had peaked in 1954, declined by nearly 30 percent in the next eight years. See CEPAL (1976), p. 25.

58 These international commodity agreements are discussed in Rowe (1965), pp. 155–83. See also Macbean and Nguyen (1987).

59 OPEC was formed in 1961, with Venezuela playing a leading role. See Randall (1987), p. 35. Ecuador joined in the 1970s, before leaving in 1992, but no other Latin American oil producers have been members.

United States introduced quotas in 1959 to protect its domestic producers, a measure that affected Venezuela.[60] Lack of consideration for the environment in primary production began to impose supply constraints. Peru's fish stocks were clearly depleted by the 1970s,[61] and Haiti's inability to expand agricultural exports was linked to soil erosion.[62] In many countries the destruction of tropical forests to make way for cattle ranches disturbed climatic conditions, and even the water level in the Panama Canal locks (rain fed from rivers) began to be affected.[63]

In many republics export-led growth also witnessed a rise in foreign penetration, which was not always welcomed. Foreign companies dominated mineral exports everywhere except Bolivia and were firmly established in many dynamic branches of agroexports, such as bananas and sugar. Even where they did not control production (as in cotton), foreign interests often controlled processing, distribution, and marketing, and they held a privileged position in the supply of inputs at all stages in the transformation of raw materials.[64] Domestic interests tended to be dominant in those branches of activity in which rates of return were lower, thereby limiting the opportunities for capital accumulation both inside and outside the export sector.

Above all, dissatisfaction with export-led growth stemmed from the extreme difficulty of sustaining rapid growth of exports over the long run. Between 1960 and 1970 only Bolivia – its hostility to the export sector now reversed – was able to increase its share of world exports.[65] Between 1950 and 1970 only Nicaragua and Peru were able to do so. Even if a more modest target is set, the results are still disappointing: In the two decades after 1950 only Costa Rica, Nicaragua, and Peru were able to increase exports at least as fast as the growth of world trade in primary products.[66] Time and again the growth of exports ran into one or other of the enormous problems faced by almost all tropical producers. Cuban sugar exports in the 1950s were crippled by the terms and conditions of the International Sugar Agreement.[67] Ecuador's spectacular growth in bananas

60 See Grunwald and Musgrove (1970), p. 249.

61 See Roemer (1970), pp. 87–8.

62 Soil erosion and other explanations of Haiti's economic decline are explored in great detail in Lundahl (1979).

63 See Wadsworth (1982), pp. 167–71.

64 An excellent account of foreign penetration of the cotton and beef industries in Central America in this period can be found in Williams (1986).

65 This increase in the Bolivian share did not nearly compensate for the decline in share between 1946 and 1960, however.

66 World trade in primary products (in current dollars) increased at an annual rate of 6 percent between 1950 and 1970. See Scammell (1980), p. 127.

67 See Thomas (1971), p. 1142. In the six years after 1952 Cuba's share of world sugar production fell from 19.4 percent to 12.6 percent, with its quota in the "free" market virtually unchanged.

in the 1950s (reversed in the 1960s) simply displaced exports from Central America.[68] Peru's mineral investments ran into decreasing returns.[69] Venezuela began to suffer from the competition of low-cost Middle Eastern oil.[70] Bolivia remained the highest-cost tin producer among the major exporters, with COMIBOL able to avoid losses only when world prices were high.[71]

In only a few cases could a poor export performance be attributed to deliberate antiexport policies. After Trujillo was assassinated in 1961 the Dominican Republic experienced an interlude during which a shift away from dependence on sugar was attempted, but it was later reversed.[72] Revolutionary Cuba began by discouraging sugar exports in an effort to diversify the economy but was soon forced to return to dependence on sugar – with the Soviet Union replacing the United States as the main market.[73] The currency in Peru was almost certainly overvalued in the first half of the 1960s.[74] Generally, however, policy was favorable to exports – in marked contrast to the situation in inward-looking countries.

One by one, therefore, and with varying degrees of enthusiasm, the outward-looking countries began to reassess their policies toward the industrial sector. The experience of inward-looking policies in neighboring countries was studied carefully, and CEPAL, its influence at a peak in the late 1950s, was listened to with respect. Without abandoning the export sector, the LA14 explored how industrial promotion might be grafted onto export-led growth. The key instrument was usually an industrial promotion law that gave new manufacturing establishments special privileges to encourage industrial investment. Firms were allowed to import machinery and components at low or zero rates of duty, and tax holidays were granted on trading profits.[75] Development banks were set up to channel cheap credit to the manufacturing sector,[76] but care was taken to ensure

---

68 The Latin American share of world banana exports (nearly 70 percent) hardly changed in the 1950s and 1960s, although country shares changed sharply. See Grunwald and Musgrove (1970), Table 13.3, p. 372.

69 See Dore (1988), pp. 155–9.

70 See Grunwald and Musgrove (1970), Table 8.5, pp. 275–7.

71 See Latin America Bureau (1987).

72 The dependence on sugar was intimately linked to the size of the sugar quota provided by the United States. See Moya Pons (1990b), pp. 530–2.

73 The Soviet share of Cuban sugar exports (2 percent in 1959) had reached 49 percent in 1961 and 80 percent in 1978. See Brundenius (1984), Table 3.9, p. 76.

74 The 1959 stabilization program did not reduce inflation to international levels, and the real exchange-rate steadily appreciated until devaluation in 1967.

75 On the shift in economic policy in the five Central American republics, see Bulmer-Thomas (1987), Chapter 9.

76 Many of these development banks were established with the help of multilateral institutions, including the Inter-American Development Bank (created in 1961).

that the financial requirements of the export sector were still met in full.[77]

The result was a proliferation of high-cost, inefficient industries that were nonetheless highly profitable. Concentrated mainly in consumer goods, the new industries were protected from imports by tariffs that were usually lower than in inward-looking countries but were still high enough to generate major distortions. In those republics, such as Venezuela, where the returned value of exports was expanding domestic demand for manufactured goods while high tariffs discouraged consumer-goods imports, the rate of growth of industrial output was particularly rapid. Indeed, Venezuelan industrial output rose at an annual rate of 13 percent during the 1950s.

ISI, therefore, eventually came to be of importance in the smaller republics even if they resisted full-scale adoption of the inward-looking model. The new industry was even more import-intensive than in the larger republics, however, so the net savings of foreign exchange were modest. The small size of the market crippled the chances of exploiting economies of scale in many sectors and pushed unit costs far above world prices even without the additional distortions provided by tariffs.

Regional integration

By the end of the 1950s all of the Latin American republics had embarked on the first stage of industrialization, and some had even become semiindustrialized. Yet industry was generally high cost and inefficient, despite the abundance of cheap unskilled labor. Production runs were small, plant size was suboptimal, and unit costs in the new dynamic industries – even for the largest firms – were high by international standards. As a result manufactured goods did not enter the export list, and foreign-exchange earnings remained dependent on a handful of primary products. The intraregional trade that had developed in the war years – a trade that included manufactured goods – had largely collapsed, and industrial production was overwhelmingly confined to the domestic market. The narrowness of this market, exacerbated by the concentration of income in the top deciles (see pp. 298–312), allowed demand for many products to be satisfied by a small number of firms, so the structure of most industries approximated the conditions required for an oligopoly.[78]

---

77 In Central America agriculture (including livestock) received approximately the same share of total commercial bank lending in 1970 as in 1961 despite the rapid growth of industry. See Bulmer-Thomas (1987), Table 9.3, p. 186.

78 The combination of small production runs and oligopolistic structures gave Latin America the worst of both worlds. The former raised unit costs; the latter ruled out competitive markets. Because of market fragmentation, concentration ratios (i.e., the proportion of total sales accounted for by

The larger countries had expanded industrial production beyond non-durable consumer goods by establishing factories to produce consumer durables and intermediate (including basic) goods.[79] Even in the larger countries, however, industry was import intensive, so rapid economic growth was frequently associated with balance-of-payments problems. The capital-goods industries – hampered by market size – were slow to develop, so a growing proportion of the import bill consisted of machinery and equipment. Furthermore, because so much technology is embodied in capital goods, the region remained heavily dependent on technology that was imported from abroad and was designed for the markets of developed countries.

Similar problems were faced by industrialization programs in other developing countries. However, although a handful of countries in Southeast Asia – notably Hong Kong, Singapore, South Korea, and Taiwan – chose this moment (at the end of the 1950s) to reform policy in favor of promoting manufactured exports to the rest of the world, Latin America was still convinced that the obstacles in the path of its industrial exports remained overwhelming. As late as 1967 a CEPAL document stated that "The developing countries have neither the resources nor the technical ability to compete with others even in the developing area, and much less in the industrialized regions. And insofar as they might be able to do so, experience is showing that they would encounter very strong opposition."[80]

This export pessimism remained a feature of CEPAL's thinking for many years and, indeed, found an echo in other organizations around the world. Emphasis was placed on the need for asymmetry in international trade policy, with Raúl Prebisch leaving CEPAL in 1963 to lead the new U.N. Conference on Trade and Development (UNCTAD) in its long, and largely unsuccessful, search for privileged access to the markets of the developed countries for the manufactured exports of developing countries.[81]

For CEPAL, whose influence throughout Latin America was by now considerable, the solution was regional integration (RI). Inspired by the Treaty of Rome, which had led to the formation of the European Economic Community (EEC) in 1958, CEPAL saw the abolition of national tariff and nontariff barriers within Latin America as the means by which the domestic market could be enlarged, permitting the exploitation of economies of scale

the leading three or four firms) were usually lower in Latin American industry than in advanced countries. See, for example, Jenkins (1984), Table 4.2, p. 83, on the pharmaceutical industry.

79 "Basic goods" are those products used throughout the industrial sector as intermediate inputs (e.g., steel, chemicals, and processed fuels).

80 ECLA(1970), p. 140.

81 UNCTAD, created in 1964, did succeed in establishing the generalized system of preferences (GSP) in 1971, under which developing countries received unilateral tariff concessions on a broad range of manufactured and agroindustrial products. The concessions were so tightly fenced with qualifications and exceptions, however, that the net benefit from the GSP has been very modest. On the GSP, see Weston (1982).

and lowering unit costs while maintaining protection against imports from third countries. In CEPAL's vision RI would give a new impulse to industrialization throughout the region and provide an opportunity in the larger countries for building a sophisticated capital-goods industry with technological autonomy. The expansion of intraregional exports would permit intraregional imports to grow, thus alleviating the balance-of-payments constraint on development. It was also assumed that intraregional trade would be subject to much less instability than extraregional trade, so external shocks would become less important.[82]

CEPAL's vision would not have been sufficient in itself to push Latin America toward RI in the 1960s if it had not found support elsewhere. Indeed, ISI had created influential groups, some of whose members stood to lose from freer trade within Latin America, and nationalism was still a powerful political force that looked unfavorably on too close an association with neighboring countries. However, a limited version of RI – on a scale rather different from that envisaged by CEPAL – found support in a number of countries.

The first group was precisely those Southern Cone countries (Argentina, Chile, and Uruguay together with Brazil) that had suffered most from the drop in intraregional trade since the Second World War. As late as the first half of the 1950s this group of countries had kept a modest intraregional trade alive among themselves, in both primary and secondary products, through discriminatory use of all the trade instruments at their disposal. These mechanisms for trade promotion ran counter to the most-favored-nation (MFN) treatment preferred by international agencies (including GATT) under which a trade privilege extended to one trading partner should be extended to all. The elimination of these practices forced intraregional imports to compete on equal terms with extraregional imports, which had a severe impact on the value of the former. For this group of countries RI was therefore seen as a means of restoring intraregional trade to its previous levels.[83]

The second group of countries consisted of the Central American republics, in which modern manufacturing had scarcely begun. Although export-led growth had remained the dominant model throughout the 1950s, the deterioration in the NBTT after the Korean War and the widespread recognition that the national market was too small to support more than a handful of simple industries without major distortions persuaded the elite to experiment with a version of RI, provided it did not undermine traditional and nontraditional primary-product exports. Thus RI

---

82 CEPAL's key documents on intraregional trade are ECLA (1956) and (1959).
83 See Dell (1966), pp. 25–9.

was to remain the junior partner in a model that would give privileges to industry without withdrawing the advantages enjoyed by export agriculture.[84]

A commitment to RI, however visionary, could not conceal the enormous problems that integration faced in the Latin American context. No one took too seriously references to a Latin American common market, which implied free movement of labor and capital, but the choice between a customs union (with a common external tariff, or CET) and a free-trade area (which left each country free to impose national tariffs on third countries) could not be avoided. Furthermore, the preunion tariffs in Latin America, though high in all countries, varied considerably from country to country (see, for example, Table 9.1), so the abolition of tariffs on intraregional trade still implied different national adjustments. Even more worrisome, and scarcely recognized at the time, was the complete lack of harmonization in the area of exchange-rate, fiscal, and monetary policies.

The second problem was the scale of nontariff barriers to intraregional trade. Although quantitative restrictions on imports were being phased out (except in Mexico), the transport of goods between countries in Latin America was still fraught with problems. Freight rates to traditional markets in Europe and North America were much lower, and shipping routes were more widespread. Restrictions on national carriers could mean long delays for goods at the frontier as they were unloaded and reloaded, and intraregional trade could not escape the network of bureaucratic red tape designed to discourage imports in general.

The third problem was the welfare gains expected from RI. The traditional approach to this problem had assumed that welfare benefits could be identified with the excess of trade creation (TC) over trade diversion (TD), in which TC represented the replacement of high-cost domestic production by cheaper imports from a partner and TD represented the replacement of cheaper imports from a third country by more expensive imports from a partner.[85] Although the identification of net welfare benefits with the excess of TC over TD proved to be based on strong assumptions,[86] it was a source of concern that in the Latin American context TD was likely to exceed TC. The reason was not so much that national industrialists would resist the closure of high-cost factories (though that could be expected); it had more to do with RI being seen as a vehicle for the continuation of import substitution – in a regional context rather than a national one – with

---

84 See Bulmer-Thomas (1987), pp. 185–90.
85 See El-Agraa (1997), pp. 35–44.
86 One of the assumptions was full employment, so resources made idle by trade creation could then be switched into other activities. If the result of trade creation was an increase in unemployment, however, the welfare benefit was uncertain.

regional producers able to replace imports from the rest of the world as a result of the abolition of tariffs on intraregional trade.[87]

Even if it could be assumed that net welfare would improve despite TD in excess of TC, the distribution of net benefits among the member countries would be a further source of concern. The reason was simple. The gains from RI in this Latin American model tended to accrue to those countries that succeeded in replacing extraregional imports with national production and intraregional exports. Those countries that simply replaced cheap imports from the rest of the world with high-cost imports from a partner would be worse off. Thus welfare gains tended to be associated with capturing the new industries and running intraregional trade surpluses, whereas welfare losses were linked to intraregional trade deficits. A successful RI scheme therefore needed to find some way of compensating the losers or of allocating the new industries among all members, in defiance of market forces.[88]

A final problem, related to the distribution of benefits, concerned the system of intraregional payments. Although intraregional exports and imports must be equal, that was not true for any single country. Countries with deficits in intraregional trade would need to channel finance to surplus countries as a counterpart of the excess of imports over exports. If paid in hard currency, the settlement of intraregional balances would then exacerbate the balance-of-payments constraint for deficit countries – although the alleviation of this constraint was one of the reasons that had originally been given for promoting RI.

The technocrats at CEPAL and national policymakers were aware of many of these problems in the design of integration schemes in the 1960s, although the proposed solutions were far from adequate. The first scheme to be formally adopted was the Latin American Free Trade Association (LAFTA), which was established by the Treaty of Montevideo in February 1960 and eventually embraced the ten republics of South America, together with Mexico.[89] LAFTA set itself the target of abolishing all tariffs on intraregional trade by 1971 through periodic negotiations. These included annual negotiations on national schedules, under which individual countries undertook to cut tariffs facing member countries on a range of commodities to be agreed in bilateral discussions, and triannual negotiations on common

---

87 This was seen most clearly in Central America, where the virtual absence of prior industrialization meant that new manufacturing firms producing tradable goods were almost bound to replace imports from the rest of the world as a result of the new tariff system. See Bulmer-Thomas (1988), pp. 75–100.

88 Cline (1978), pp. 59–115, is an excellent treatment of this question.

89 Many accounts of LAFTA exist. See, for example, Bulmer-Thomas (1997). Vaitsos (1978) contains a comparative study of regional integration schemes, including LAFTA, in developing countries.

schedules that listed the commodities in which free trade would be progressively established.[90]

Progress under the national schedules was at first impressive, and in the first two years (1961–2) 7,593 tariff concessions were agreed. The ease of these negotiations was deceptive, however, because most of the tariff "concessions" were on commodities that did not enter into intraregional trade or were reductions in tariffs from redundant levels. In future years tariff negotiations under the national schedule would prove to be much more difficult, and by the end of the 1960s they had ground to a complete halt. Meanwhile, negotiations under the common schedule never passed beyond the first round in 1964, at which time free trade in a small number of primary products was agreed to "in principle," with the date of implementation progressively delayed.[91]

Thus LAFTA never achieved its aim of abolishing intraregional tariffs and its success in tackling the other problems faced by RI in the Latin American context was even more problematic. A payments system was constructed after 1965, with a multilateral clearing house that led to the automatic clearing of one-third of intraregional trade by 1970 and two-thirds by 1980[92] – not an insignificant achievement – but little was done to promote the interests of the less developed countries (Bolivia, Ecuador, and Paraguay[93]), and no regional development bank was created that could channel resources to the weakest members. Agreement was reached on a regime of industrial complementarity that allowed a subset of countries to push through tariff reductions in a particular industry, but this facility – used quite widely in the 1970s – mainly benefited MNCs with subsidiaries in different parts of Latin America.[94]

Frustrated by the lack of progress under LAFTA, the Andean countries formed the Andean Pact (AP) in 1969, the aims of which were more ambitious.[95] The target this time was a customs union with a CET and legislation to ensure that the benefits of RI accrued to domestic factors of

90 See Finch (1988), pp. 243–8.
91 The commodities were bananas, cacao, coffee, and cotton – all traditional primary-product exports from Latin America and the exact opposite of the kind of manufactured products the architects of LAFTA had hoped to promote.
92 See IDB (1984a), Table 1.1, p. 56.
93 The only significant concession was that the less-developed countries could move toward trade liberalization at a slower pace. This, however, did nothing to ensure them a "fair" share in the new industry to be created by regional integration. On the formal concessions offered, irrespective of their relevance, see IDB (1984a), p. 70.
94 The list of products affected by complementarity agreements is given in IDB (1984a), p. 156, n. 8. The list involves products in which MNCs were (and are) particularly active.
95 The original members of the Andean Pact were Bolivia, Chile, Colombia, Ecuador, and Peru. Venezuela joined in 1973, and Chile withdrew in 1976.

production rather than to MNCs.[96] An Andean development corporation was formed to channel external finance into regional infrastructure, special consideration was given to the needs of the least-developed members (Bolivia and Ecuador[97]), and RI was seen explicitly as a means of promoting an industrialization program.[98] Yet the AP fell at the first hurdle: A minimum CET was accepted in principle but was never implemented, and Chile withdrew in 1976 when its neoliberal policies on tariff reductions and foreign investment (see Chapter 10) proved inconsistent with membership of the AP.[99]

Like the AP, the Central American Common Market (CACM) – launched at the end of 1960 – set out to create a customs union with a CET.[100] Unlike LAFTA or the AP, however, the CACM did not have to confront established pressure groups in modern manufacturing that were hostile to intraregional tariff concessions. The low level of industrialization before 1960 made it relatively easy to free intraregional trade, and the CET was in place by 1965. A payments system was implemented that led to automatic clearing of more than 80 percent of intraregional trade by 1970, and a Central American Bank for Economic Integration (CABEI) channeled funds for regional infrastructure to all countries, with the weaker members (Honduras and Nicaragua) receiving a disproportionately large share of all loans. CABEI was the only effective mechanism for compensating the weaker members, however, because other such instruments were either abandoned or postponed.[101] The result was an RI scheme that undoubtedly generated net benefits but in which the distribution of benefits among members was

---

96 The most radical instrument of the new policy was Decision 24, which fixed a maximum rate for profit remittances and set a terminal year for majority ownership by foreign companies. Inevitably, Decision 24 provoked much friction, and its radical character was steadily eroded. See El-Agraa and Hojman (1988), pp. 262–3.

97 The list of concessions provided for Bolivia and Ecuador, including special treatment within the Andean Development Corporation, is given in IDB (1984a), pp. 74–5. Nevertheless, it is hard to quarrel with the IDB's assessment that "the Special Regime for the Andean LDCs [less-developed countries] has had very little effect and has not lived up to initial expectations."

98 This was to be achieved through the sectoral program of industrial development (SPID), the object of which "was to rationalise industrialisation by allocating plants in such a way that optimal utilisation in the context of even development is ensured." See El-Agraa and Hojman (1988), p. 264. In practice, the SPID did little to avoid the proliferation of suboptimal plants.

99 Chilean withdrawal is often erroneously attributed to the political differences between the right-wing dictatorship of General Augusto Pinochet Ugarte and the left-leaning governments in some other Andean republics. Without a doubt, these political differences did not help the smooth operation of the AP, but they were secondary to Chile's desire to implement a neoliberal economic program that was inconsistent with AP membership.

100 For an overview of regional integration in Central America from its origins to its relaunch in the 1990s, see Bulmer-Thomas (1998).

101 The most controversial instrument was the Integration Industries Scheme, which gave tariff-free privileges to a single firm in an industry in which economies of scale were deemed to be important. Only two firms were granted such privileges, amounting in effect to a regional monopoly, before

unequal. Honduras, in particular, ran increasingly large intraregional trade deficits, with trade diversion far outstripping trade creation and with the deficit having to be settled twice a year in hard currency out of extraregional exports.[102] Following the war between El Salvador and Honduras in 1969, which paralyzed trade between the two countries until 1980, Honduras withdrew from the CACM.[103]

With the partial exception of the CACM, Latin American efforts to create an institutional framework for promoting RI were not very successful. The growth of intraregional trade in LAFTA in particular, which could be attributed to official measures, was modest: Even by the end of the 1970s less than half of intraregional trade was in commodities covered by LAFTA concessions, and trade in the goods covered by LAFTA concessions had not grown as fast as had trade in nonconcessional products.[104] Intraregional trade as a proportion of total trade in the CACM peaked in 1970 and declined steadily thereafter.[105] After a decade of the AP, intraregional trade was still less than 5 percent of total trade.[106]

It would be wrong, however, wholly to dismiss the Latin American experiment in RI. Despite the institutional failures, intraregional trade not only expanded rapidly in absolute terms in the two decades after 1960, but for the region as a whole even grew in relative terms (i.e., as a proportion of total exports) until the late 1970s. As Table 9.3 makes clear, the share of intraregional exports in total exports had reached double digits by 1965 and came close to 18 percent a decade later. Furthermore, although intraregional trade had been dominated by primary products in the early 1960s, these declined in importance, and by 1975 trade in manufactured goods accounted for almost half of all intraregional exports (see Table 9.3) – in sharp contrast to extraregional exports, among which manufactured goods were relatively unimportant.[107]

it effectively collapsed as a result of private-sector (and U.S. government) opposition. See Ramsett (1969).

102 The Honduran problem, which was the major factor in its decision to leave the CACM, was illustrative of the difficulties faced by integration schemes in Latin America. As the weakest member of CACM, Honduras was in effect asked to replace imports from the rest of the world with higher-cost imports (before tariffs) from the region. Its exports to CACM, however, were primarily food products, which continued to be sold at world prices. Thus the terms of trade for Honduras deteriorated – precisely the opposite of what is supposed to happen in an integration scheme.

103 The war between the two countries arose out of the tensions generated by migration of Salvadorans to Honduras. See Bulmer-Thomas (1990a).

104 See IDB (1990), pp. 10–11.

105 At their peak intraregional exports represented 26 percent of total exports. The subsequent decline was only relative, however, and the absolute value of trade continued to grow until 1981.

106 See El-Agraa and Hojman (1988), Table 11.1(a), p. 261.

107 These were still only 16 percent of extraregional exports in 1975. See Thoumi (1989), Table 5, p. 13.

Table 9.3. *Intraregional exports by product group as percentages of total exports by product group, 1965, 1970, and 1975*

Exports	1965	1970	1975
Basic foodstuffs and raw materials			
1. Food and live	8.8	8.0	10.0
animals	(27.1)	(22.2)	(17.1)
2. Beverages and	7.6	12.2	8.5
tobacco	(0.3)	(0.5)	(0.4)
3. Crude materials,	9.4	9.9	8.2
inedible	(12.2)	(10.3)	(6.2)
4. Fuels and mineral	13.9	14.0	16.7
fuels	(31.5)	(22.9)	(29.3)
5. Animal and	13.3	14.6	16.6
vegetable oils and fats	(1.8)	(1.7)	(1.2)
Subtotal	(72.9)	(57.6)	(54.2)
Manufactured products			
Chemical elements	36.1	48.2	53.9
and compounds	(5.6)	(7.4)	(8.2)
Manufactured goods,	15.6	18.0	27.1
classified by material	(13.3)	(19.6)	(16.3)
Machinery and	70.2	51.0	52.6
transport equipment	(4.1)	(9.2)	(15.4)
Miscellaneous	70.0	55.2	38.5
manufactured articles	(3.7)	(5.5)	(5.3)
Subtotal	(26.7)	(41.7)	(45.2)
Other products	27.5	38.9	16.4
	(0.4)	(0.7)	(0.6)
Total	12.6	14.0	17.9
	(100)	(100)	(100)

Notes: Figures in parentheses refer to the composition of intraregional exports, in percentages. Based on trade data provided by members of the Inter-American Development Bank; statistics therefore exclude Cuba and include Barbados, Guyana, Jamaica, and Trinidad and Tobago.
Source: Thoumi (1989), Table 4, p. 10, and Table 5, p. 12.

Intraregional trade in manufactured exports was particularly rapid in machinery and equipment, supporting the argument of CEPAL that RI could be used as a basis for building a regional capital-goods industry, and increased its share of the total from 4 percent to 15 percent in the decade after 1965 (see Table 9.3). Indeed, exports of sophisticated manufactures depended heavily on the regional market in the 1960s, with 70 percent of all exports of both machinery and transport equipment and miscellaneous manufactured goods going to other Latin American republics. These ratios subsequently declined, as firms in the larger countries began to export equivalent goods to the rest of the world in the 1970s. Thus it could be claimed with some justification that the regional market had been the springboard for extraregional exports of high-technology goods.[108]

In view of the institutional paralysis apparent by the end of the 1960s, the growth of intraregional trade came to depend on the private sector rather than the public sector. Indeed, regional private-sector organizations – virtually nonexistent in 1960 – became more and more important, and in the 1970s the growth of trade was due almost entirely to their efforts. The window of opportunity provided by the regimes of industrial complementarity was exploited to the fullest, and trade in regional services – including consultancy, finance, insurance, and construction – also became important.[109] In a belated effort to match the contribution of the private sector, the region's governments created the Sistema Económico de América Latina (SELA), with membership expanded to include the English-speaking Caribbean, in 1975.[110] When the Treaty of Montevideo expired in 1980, LAFTA was replaced by the Latin American Integration Association (LAIA), which gave greater prominence to industrial complementarity and to private sector initiatives.[111]

The prominence of the private sector in intraregional exports was reflected in the geographical pattern of trade. The most important trade flows occurred between blocs of countries in close proximity. Thus in LAFTA Argentina, Bolivia, Brazil, Paraguay, and Uruguay formed a bloc that dominated intra-LAFTA trade and that was so important for the three smaller countries (Bolivia, Paraguay, and Uruguay) that it accounted for nearly 40 percent of their total exports by the end of the 1970s.[112] In the AP total trade was dominated by the flows between Colombia and Venezuela,[113] and trade between El Salvador and Guatemala accounted for more than half of all trade in the CACM.[114] Intraregional trade was highly concentrated, and

---

108 In 1965 exports of machinery and transport equipment to the regional market were twice as important as exports to the world market. The two markets were roughly equal in importance in the 1970s, but in the 1980s the world market became much more important. Most of these exports came from MNCs operating in Brazil and Mexico. See Blomström (1990).

109 This important area of trade has been almost totally neglected. For an honorable exception, see IDB (1984a), pp. 156–69.

110 SELA, based in Caracas, also embraced all those Latin American republics (Cuba, the Dominican Republic, Haiti, and Panama) that were not members of any integration scheme, as well as four members (Barbados, Guyana, Jamaica, and Trinidad and Tobago) of the Caribbean Free Trade Area (later the Caribbean Community, or CARICOM) and Suriname.

111 It is doubtful whether LAIA could have succeeded where LAFTA failed. However, LAIA – and intraregional trade – effectively collapsed as a result of the debt crisis that began in 1982.

112 In all three cases the intraregional exports went overwhelmingly to Argentina and Brazil. See Thoumi (1989), Table 14, p. 33.

113 This trade, however, consisted predominantly of Colombian exports to Venezuela by the end of the 1970s, so it was therefore vulnerable to import restrictions imposed by Venezuela.

114 By the end of the 1970s El Salvador was selling 60 percent of intraregional exports to Guatemala; the reverse figure was nearly 50 percent.

in many pairs of countries no trade took place at all.[115] The widening of the market anticipated by CEPAL was therefore rather modest, and the process was essentially driven by private-sector groups that exploited their knowledge of neighboring markets to establish additional outlets for production without significantly altering plant size and production runs.[116]

The unwillingness of the private sector to base investment decisions on a Latin American market was understandable. The failure of public-sector initiatives to establish an adequate framework for eliminating tariff and nontariff barriers to intraregional trade had been repeatedly demonstrated, and the geographical concentration of trade made it vulnerable to external shocks. Indeed, intraregional trade turned out to be even more unstable than extraregional trade. In almost all the republics subject to RI schemes, the coefficient of instability for intraregional exports was high – and higher than for extraregional exports.[117]

Intraregional trade was also procyclical. It tended to move in line with extraregional trade, with the movements exaggerated in both directions. Thus while the value of total trade was growing in the 1960s and 1970s, the value of intraregional trade grew even faster. On the other hand, when the value of total imports declined after 1981, intraregional trade suffered a collapse that would only be reversed as total imports started to increase again at the end of the decade. The procyclical nature of intraregional trade was a disappointment for those who had hoped that RI would increase the autonomy of the region in the face of external shocks. Yet it was hardly surprising. The composition of intraregional and extraregional exports was different, and it was not usually possible to switch exports from one market to the other in the short run.[118]

Growth, income distribution, and poverty

Before the Second World War statistical information on the Latin American republics was scarce. Some countries (e.g., Bolivia and Paraguay) could not even provide accurate information on the size of their populations, and

---

115 Mexico, for example, sold virtually nothing to Bolivia, Paraguay, or Uruguay, despite the fact that all four countries were members of LAFTA. Similarly, the trade links between CACM and LAFTA were modest.

116 The increase in business contacts produced an explosion in regional and subregional business associations. These increased from 3 in 1960, to 14 in 1971, and to 41 in 1983. See IDB (1984a), p. 159.

117 See Thoumi (1989), Table 25, p. 80. The only exception is Honduras, where the coefficient of instability between 1960 and 1982 was even higher for extraregional exports.

118 Even where it was possible, as in the case of machinery and transport equipment (see note 108), intraregional exports were vulnerable to the import restrictions that were usually imposed following an external shock.

national accounting data did not exist. By the 1950s, however, the situation had improved.[119] Although many deficiencies remained, all countries now provided a regular stream of statistics, and the participation of international agencies ensured a reasonable degree of cross-country comparability. CEPAL, in particular, was assiduous in collecting and preparing information, not only on the postwar period, but in some cases also on earlier decades. Thus it was possible to compare the growth and development of all of the republics in a consistent framework, in many cases with measures of income distribution and poverty becoming available for the first time.

The single most commonly used measure of growth is the GDP at constant prices. The region's rate of growth had increased in each of the three decades after 1940 – a satisfactory performance – and by the 1960s it averaged 5.4 percent per year (see Table 9.4). Only in Uruguay, Venezuela, and the Dominican Republic did the rate of growth fall in each decade, but in the latter two cases the rate was still high even in the 1960s. The Latin American rate of growth compared favorably with other developing countries – it was higher even than that of East Asia in the 1950s – and was faster than the rate of growth in the developed countries.

Population growth was accelerating for most of the period, however. In common with other developing countries, the republics of Latin America were in the midst of a demographic explosion as a result of a small increase in the birth rate and a large fall in the death rate.[120] Between 1900 and 1930 population grew by more than 2.5 percent a year only in Argentina, Honduras, and Cuba, but by the 1950s population was growing at this rate in thirteen republics. Furthermore, fast growth of population before 1930 implied a high rate of international immigration – bringing workers with skills and in some cases capital – whereas in the 1950s international emigration to Latin America had virtually ceased, so the additions to the population were young dependents.[121]

When the GDP figures are adjusted for population growth to give GDP per head (see Table 9.4), the position was still generally satisfactory. Only

---

119 The situation improved enormously when a concerted effort was made in the 1940s to achieve consistent regionwide coverage of key social and economic indicators under the auspices of inter-American cooperation. The *annus mirabilis* occurred in 1950, when almost all republics conducted a population census and many held an agricultural census. See Travis (1990).

120 In the early 1930s the crude death rate (CDR) had been above 20 per 1,000 in all republics except Argentina, Cuba, Panama, and Uruguay. See Wilkie (1990), Table 710. By the early 1960s it was below 20 in all republics except Bolivia and Haiti. By the 1960s the population of Latin America (276 million in 1970) was growing at 2.8 percent per year, compared with 1.9 percent in the 1930s and 2.5 percent in the 1940s.

121 Not only had mass migration to Latin America ceased, but emigration to the United States was accelerating. By the 1970s the Hispanic population of the United States, though dominated by emigrants of Mexican origin, was drawn from a wide range of countries.

Table 9.4. *Gross domestic product: growth rates and per head, 1950–1970*

Country	Growth rates (in percentages)		Per head (1970 prices in US$)			Rank
	1950–1960	1961–1970	1950	1960	1970	
Argentina	2.8	4.4	753	812	1,055	1
Bolivia	0.4	5.0	189	151	201	19
Brazil	6.9	5.4	187	268	364	12
Chile	4.0	4.3	561	631	829	3
Colombia	4.6	5.2	224	261	313	14
Costa Rica	7.1	6.0	318	394	515	8
Cuba	2.4^a	4.4^b	450^c	534^d	638^e	7
Dominican Republic	5.8	5.1	252	324	403	11
Ecuador	4.9	5.2	184	221	256	17
El Salvador	4.4	5.8	218	237	294	15
Guatemala	3.8	5.5	271	288	361	13
Haiti	1.9	0.8	95	99	84	20
Honduras	3.1	5.3	190	231	259	16
Mexico	5.6	7.1	362	467	656	6
Nicaragua	5.2	6.9	249	311	436	10
Panama	4.9	8.1	358	443	708	5
Paraguay	2.7	4.6	203	212	243	18
Peru	4.9	5.5	278	364	446	9
Uruguay	1.7	1.6	770	820	828	4
Venezuela	8.0	6.3	485	723	942	2
Latin America	**5.3**	**5.4**	**306**	**396**	**513**	

^{a} Datum is for 1950–8. See Brundenius (1984).
^{b} See Brundenius and Zimbalist (1989).
^{c} Derived from Maddison (1991) and Pérez-López (1991).
^{d} 1962. Derived from Brundenius and Zimbalist (1989), Table 5.8, p. 63, and spliced to estimate of GDP per head for 1970.
^{e} See Pérez-López (1991).
Sources: Wilkie (1974); World Bank (1980); IDB (1990). For GDP data at Purchasing Power Parity Exchange rates, see Thorp (1998), Appendix IX.

Haiti suffered a fall in living standards between 1950 and 1970; most republics saw GDP per head rise in each decade. For the region as a whole, performance compared reasonably well with other developing countries and was not far behind the developed countries, in which population growth was much more modest. The level of GDP per head in Latin America by the end of the 1960s put all Latin America except Haiti firmly in the group of countries described by the World Bank as "middle-income," with the first six countries in the ranking being described as "upper middle-income."[122]

122 See World Bank (1984), Table 1, which uses data for the early 1980s and also includes Brazil in this group.

The level of GDP per head is calculated in the prices of a given year. The distortions associated with ISI imparted an upward bias to the manufacturing component of GDP, because the value of net output far exceeded its value at world prices. However, the use of official exchange rates to convert national currencies to dollars imparted a downward bias to the figures, because purchasing-power parity exchange rates were generally lower.[123] These two biases did not necessarily cancel each other out, but there was no reason to dismiss the GDP and GDP per head figures as meaningless or – even worse – misleading. Furthermore, performance was satisfactory both among the group of countries that followed inward-looking development and the group that pursued a more outward-looking orientation, with the latter group experiencing the greater improvement over the two decades after 1950.[124]

The collection of information extended to social indicators – many of which also told an encouraging story. Life expectancy was rising, and infant and child mortality was falling. Primary- and secondary-school enrollments were increasing rapidly, both in absolute terms and as a proportion of the school-age population, and illiteracy was on the decline. Health indicators were all moving in the right direction. Latin America was becoming an increasingly urban society: By the end of the 1960s nearly 60 percent of the region's population was classified as urban (i.e., living in towns or cities with more than 1,000–3,000 people), compared with less than 40 percent in 1940. In the smaller republics the rural population was still in a majority, but everywhere it was in relative decline.[125]

The rapid urbanization of Latin America was a reflection of population growth, rural–urban migration, and the emphasis in many countries on urban-based activities. The principal cities grew at an astonishingly rapid rate, and urban sprawl, industrial pollution, and substandard housing became widespread. Mexico City, Buenos Aires, and São Paulo were now among the largest cities in the world.[126] Indeed, the attraction of the leading city in each republic was often so great that migration from other towns and cities was sometimes even more important than migration from rural areas.[127]

---

123 In 1970, for example, the official exchange-rate for Mexico was 12.5 pesos per U.S. dollar, whereas the purchasing-power parity rate (see CEPAL, 1978, p. 8) was 8.88. See also Thorp (1998), Appendix Table II.I, p. 317.

124 In the 1950s the (unweighted) average annual growth rate of real GDP for the two groups was the same (4.3 percent). In the 1960s the rate for the LA6 was 4.7 percent, whereas for the LA14 it was 5.1 percent.

125 See Wilkie (1990), Table 644, p. 137.

126 By 1970 four Latin American cities (Mexico City, São Paulo, Buenos Aires, and Rio de Janeiro) had more than 7 million inhabitants (roughly the same as New York or London). See Wilkie (1990), Table 634, p. 129.

127 Good case studies on migration in Latin America can be found in Peek and Standing (1982).

Under such circumstances it would not have been surprising to discover major problems in the workings of the labor market, particularly in urban areas. Rapid population growth in one decade always increases labor supply in following decades,[128] and rural–urban migration adds directly to the urban supply of labor. Moreover, in both rural and urban areas female participation rates – the proportion of the adult female population wishing to work – were on the increase.[129] The growth of real GDP, it is true, could be expected to increase the demand for labor, but the shift to urban-based activities, with higher productivity and higher capital–output ratios, would be expected to moderate labor absorption.[130]

Despite these problems evidence of growing unemployment or underemployment in Latin America during this period is weak. Indeed, in a series of historical studies the Programa Regional del Empleo para América Latina y el Caribe (PREALC), a division of the International Labour Organisation (ILO), discovered evidence of a decline in underemployment in the three decades after 1950 in the majority of countries examined (see Table 9.5).In all cases the proportion of the nonagricultural population classified as underemployed rose, but this was usually more than offset by the decline in underemployment among agricultural workers. Thus rural–urban migration was lowering the overall impact of underemployment and at the same time rendering it more visible, because it was becoming increasingly an urban problem rather than a rural one.

The growing presence of the underemployed in urban areas was a reminder that growth and development were not the same thing. Equally disturbing was the accumulation of evidence on the distribution of income and wealth. In the century before 1930 the majority of republics had seen export-led growth reinforce their colonial legacy of unequal distribution patterns. Partial evidence had suggested that the top quintile received a greater share of income than its counterpart abroad and that the opposite was true of the bottom quintile.

More complete studies after the Second World War confirmed this picture. Even more worrisome was the trend in the distribution of income.

128 Thus the rate of growth of the population economically active (PEA) accelerated from 2.1 percent in the 1950s, to 2.5 percent in the 1960s, and to 3.2 percent in the 1970s. This was even faster than the (lagged) rate of growth of population because of the increase in female participation in the PEA. See Deas (1991), Table 14.1, p. 219.

129 The growth of the female labor force, as a consequence, was extremely rapid and reached 4.7 percent per annum in the 1970s. See Deas (1991), Table 14.1, p. 219.

130 Agriculture typically has the lowest sectoral capital–output ratio. Thus a shift from agricultural activities to nonagricultural activities (equivalent to a shift from rural to urban sectors) implied a reduction in labor absorption for a given level of investment. The level of investment therefore needed to increase significantly to avoid a rise in unemployment.

Table 9.5. *Underemployment as percentage of population economically active, 1950, 1970, and 1980*

Country	1950	1970	1980
Argentina	22.8	22.3	28.2
	(7.6)	(6.7)	(6.8)
Bolivia	68.7	73.1	74.1
	(53.7)	(53.5)	(50.9)
Brazil	48.3	48.3	35.4
	(37.6)	(33.4)	(18.9)
Chile	31.0	26.0	29.1
	(8.9)	(9.3)	(7.4)
Colombia	48.3	40.0	41.0
	(33.0)	(22.3)	(18.7)
Costa Rica	32.7	31.5	25.1
	(20.4)	(18.6)	(9.8)
Ecuador	50.7	64.9	62.0
	(39.0)	(41.2)	(33.4)
El Salvador	48.7	44.6	49.0
	(35.0)	(28.0)	(30.1)
Guatemala	62.7	59.0	56.7
	(48.7)	(43.0)	(37.8)
Mexico	56.9	43.1	40.4
	(44.0)	(24.9)	(18.4)
Panama	58.8	47.5	36.8
	(47.0)	(31.7)	(22.0)
Peru	56.3	58.4	51.6
	(39.4)	(37.7)	(31.8)
Uruguay	19.3	23.7	27.0
	(4.8)	(6.9)	(8.0)
Venezuela	38.9	42.3	31.1
	(22.5)	(19.9)	(12.6)
Latin America	**46.1**	**43.8**	**38.3**
(14 countries)	(32.5)	(26.9)	(18.9)

Note: Figures in parentheses refer to underemployment in agriculture as percentage of agricultural labor force.
Source: Wells (1987), Table 2.1, pp. 96–7, based on estimates by PREALC.

Other regions of the world saw a modest improvement in the share of income received by the bottom quintile, but many Latin American republics witnessed a further decline (see Table 9.6). Thus by 1970 the average for Latin America was a mere 3.4 percent compared with 4.9 percent for all developing countries and 6.2 percent for developed countries. The Gini

Table 9.6. *Income distribution and poverty, circa 1960 and circa 1970*

Country	Income shares (in percentages) Poorest 20% circa 1960	Poorest 20% circa 1970	Richest 20% circa 1960	Richest 20% circa 1970	Gini index[a] circa 1970	Poverty index[b] circa 1970
Argentina	6.9	4.4	52.0	50.3	.425	8
Bolivia		4.0		59.0		
Brazil	3.8	3.2	58.6	66.6	.574	49
Chile		4.4		51.4	.503	17
Colombia	2.1	3.5	62.6	58.5	.520	45
Costa Rica	5.7	3.0	59.0	54.8	.466	24
Cuba	2.1	7.8	60.0	35.0	.25	
Dominican Republic					.493	
Ecuador		2.9		69.5	.625	
El Salvador	5.5		61.4		.539	
Guatemala		5.0		60.0		
Honduras		2.3		67.8	.612	65
Mexico	3.5	3.4	61.0	57.7	.567	34
Nicaragua		3.1		65.0		
Panama		2.5		60.6	.558	39
Paraguay		4.0				
Peru	2.5	1.9		61.0	.591	50
Uruguay		4.0			.449	
Venezuela	3.0	3.0	59.0	54.0	.531	25
Latin America	3.7	3.4				39

[a] See note 131 for an explanation of the Gini coefficient.
[b] Defined as the proportion of the population living below the poverty line.
Sources: World Bank (1980, 1983, 1990); Brundenius (1984); Sheahan (1987); Wilkie (1990); Cardoso and Helwege (1992).

coefficient (see Table 9.6), widely used to measure inequality in the distribution of income,[131] indicated that the degree of income concentration was extremely high in Latin America – far higher than in the developed countries at a comparable stage of their development – and that the concentration of income was becoming worse in precisely those countries (e.g.,

131 The Gini coefficient assumes a value of zero in the case of complete equality (i.e., when everyone receives the same income) and of unity in the case of complete inequality (i.e., when all income goes to one individual). The Gini coefficient in Western Europe had typically been in the range 0.3 to 0.4, and a similar range was reported in South Korea and Taiwan. On the measurement of income inequality, see Cowell (1977), pp. 121–9.

Brazil, Mexico) with the most dynamic performance.[132] Throughout Latin America the top quintile received around 60 percent of income (see Table 9.6) – a share that remained stubbornly high and that was much higher than in developed countries (around 45 percent).

The unequal distribution of income and the high Gini coefficients reflected the underlying distribution of assets – land, physical and financial capital, and human capital. The distribution of land was, if anything, even more unequal than the distribution of income, with Latin America's traditional division of agricultural holdings into *minifundios* and *latifundios* producing an extraordinary concentration of landholdings in very few hands.[133] Only Costa Rica, with its proud tradition of owner-occupation, enjoyed a predominance of family-sized farms, and even there the distribution of landholdings had become steadily more concentrated since independence.[134]

Urban wealth was also highly skewed. With shares only rarely traded in financial markets, ownership of the new activities was heavily concentrated in a relatively small number of extended families with interlocking directorates.[135] The main challenge to the hegemony of this group came not so much from a property-owning middle class as from MNCs, which had acquired a strong position in many of the most dynamic sectors by the end of the 1960s.[136] Yet this did little to reduce the concentration of income and wealth among domestic factors of production.

The profile of wages and salaries also suggested a spread of earnings between the highest and the lowest which was far higher than that found in developed countries.[137] In large part this spread reflected the unequal distribution of human capital – above all education – which left a large

---

132 The Gini coefficient in Brazil jumped from 0.5 to 0.6 between 1960 and 1970. See Cardoso and Helwege (1992), Table 9.10, p. 241.

133 The extent of land concentration became apparent in the 1950s with the publication of numerous agricultural censuses. In Ecuador, in 1954, farms in excess of 100 hectares (2.2 percent of all holdings) controlled 64.4 percent of the land, whereas the numerous subfamily farms (73.1 percent of the total) occupied only 7.2 percent of the farm area. See Zuvekas and Luzuriaga (1983), Table 4.1, p. 54.

134 Only 5 percent of farms in Costa Rica were rented as late as 1973. However, farms in excess of 500 hectares (1 percent of the total) occupied nearly 40 percent of the farm area. See Dirección General de Estadística y Censos (1974), Table 29.

135 The extent of family control is notoriously difficult to quantify in the absence of published balance sheets and company accounts, but a few studies have been conducted. See Strachan (1976) for the case of Nicaragua.

136 By the end of the 1960s MNC penetration into manufacturing was particularly marked, with foreign firms responsible for at least 30 percent of production almost everywhere and more than 40 percent in Brazil, Colombia, and Peru. See Jenkins (1984), Table 2.2, p. 32 and Table 2.4, p. 34.

137 On wage differentials in Latin America, across both occupations and industries, see Salazar-Carrillo (1982). See also Elías (1992), Chapter 6.

proportion of the labor force with little or no schooling. Thus, despite the growth of educational enrollments, in fourteen republics more than 40 percent of the labor force had fewer than three years of schooling by 1970.[138] Inevitably, the private rate of return to education was high under such circumstances, so those members of the labor force with secondary schooling or vocational training were able to command a high price for their services relative to the mass of unskilled – and uneducated – workers.[139]

One consequence of the unequal distribution of assets (including human capital) was a process of development in Latin America that concentrated the benefits of growth in the hands of the upper deciles. It was not so much that the poor were getting poorer – although occasionally that did happen – for even the bottom decile usually enjoyed some increase in real income.[140] The problem had much more to do with the unequal distribution of the benefits of growth. Furthermore, although there was a modest rise in living standards in the bottom deciles, the rapid growth of population increased the absolute numbers living in poverty as well as the numbers of those classified as extremely poor (destitute). Thus the relative decline in poverty was still consistent with the classification of a large proportion of the total population as poor (see Table 9.6).

At the end of the 1940s the low level of urbanization almost inevitably meant that the majority of the poor would be found in rural areas. Average rural incomes were below those in urban areas, and many agricultural workers were underemployed as a result of the seasonal nature of agricultural work. The extreme case was Cuba, where the sugar industry required cane cutters for only three months of the year and sought to deprive its workers of access to land in the remaining nine months in order to ensure their availability for the harvest.[141] Elsewhere the monopsony power of the local landlord often reduced the demand for labor below what it would have been in a competitive market, and the political power of the landowning class in many countries was sufficient to prevent the spread of minimum-wage legislation and trade unions to rural areas.[142]

---

138 See ECLAC (1989), Table 31, p. 57.

139 In Mexico, in the mid-1960s, senior executives were paid nearly ten times as much as were unskilled workers in industry, and middle-level executives were paid nearly four times as much. See Salazar-Carrillo (1982), p. 166.

140 The case of Brazil, where income inequality increased sharply in the 1960s, is illustrative. The bottom 40 percent still experienced a modest increase in income per head, although their share of total income fell sharply. See Cardoso and Helwege (1992), p. 240.

141 The problem of underemployment in the Cuban sugar industry was exacerbated in the years before the revolution by the decision of the sugar companies to reduce the length of the harvest in an attempt to reduce costs and remain internationally competitive. See Thomas (1971), Chapter 94.

142 The powerful landowning class in El Salvador resisted the introduction of minimum rural wages until 1965. Rural trade unions, however, continued to be banned. See White (1973), pp. 106, 120.

Rural–urban migration provided part of the rural labor force with an escape valve that also improved the situation for those who remained behind. Everywhere the proportion of the labor force in agriculture declined – sometimes rapidly – and in Argentina, Chile, and Uruguay the rural population even fell in absolute terms after 1960.[143] The problem of underemployment and poverty became an urban problem as well as a rural problem – so much so that by the end of the 1970s rapid urbanization meant that the poor were equally distributed between urban and rural areas, although a lower proportion of the urban population was classified as poor.[144]

Poverty and underemployment in urban areas were a reflection of a fast-growing labor force and relatively slow job creation in the modern, or formal, sector. The result was an explosion of the urban informal sector, in which productivity and wages of full-time employees were usually low and underemployment – visible and invisible – was widespread.[145] Some economists blamed the slow growth of job creation in the modern sector on distorted factor prices that artificially reduced the cost of capital and encouraged capital-intensive techniques in industry.[146] Others put the blame on red tape and the barriers to entry created by legislation.[147] There was some truth to both accusations, although the slow growth of modern-sector industrial jobs was partially offset by the expansion of state bureaucracies. Everywhere job creation was fastest in the service sectors, with the informal sector accounting for a growing proportion of urban employment.[148]

The growth of urban underemployment, coupled with the unequal distribution of the benefits of growth, offered a challenge for those governments that were sensitive to the needs of their electorates and a threat for those that ruled in the name of a small elite. At the same time, governments throughout the region were pressured to undertake social reform – for both economic and political reasons.

143 The urban population of Latin America increased by more than 50 million between 1960 and 1970, whereas the rural population increased by only 10 million. See IDB (1991), Table A.2, p. 262.

144 In 1970 the incidence of poverty (i.e., the proportion of the total population classified as poor) was 54 percent in rural areas and 29 percent in urban areas. A decade later the figures were 51 percent and 21 percent, respectively. See Deas (1991), Table 14.3, p. 224.

145 Thus although total underemployment was falling as a result of its decline in agriculture (see Table 9.5), underemployment in nonagricultural (mainly urban) activities rose from 13.6 percent of the PEA in 1950 to 16.9 percent in 1970 and 19.4 percent in 1980. See Wells (1987), p. 97.

146 The slogan of this school was "Get the factor prices right," and it was taken up with enthusiasm by the World Bank after 1970. See World Bank (1987), Part 2.

147 The most forceful statement of this position was provided by De Soto (1987), based on a wealth of Peruvian data.

148 Employment in the urban informal sector as a proportion of the employed labor force has been estimated to vary between 10.9 percent (Costa Rica) and 44 percent (Bolivia) at the start of the 1980s. This was before the debt crisis, which had the effect of substantially increasing the relative importance of the informal sector. See Thomas (1992), Table 4.2, p. 68.

The economic case for reform was put most forcibly by CEPAL, which argued that the unequal distribution of income reduced the effective market for industrial goods and narrowed the scope for ISI.[149] A redistribution of income, CEPAL argued, could provide a broader market for many goods that were either being imported or produced at high unit costs – which could inject new dynamism into the industrialization process. The success of the East Asian newly industrialized countries (NICs) began to be studied carefully in the 1960s, and it was considered no coincidence that both South Korea and Taiwan had begun their industrialization process after widespread land reform – albeit under Japanese occupation – had increased the proportion of households able to purchase consumer goods.[150]

Political pressure for reform came from reaction to the Cuban Revolution. The success of Fidel Castro's revolutionary movement, which swept to power on 1 January 1959, was widely attributed to the appalling social and economic conditions faced by many Cubans despite the fact that Cuba had had one of the more prosperous economies in Latin America.[151] The Alliance for Progress was launched in 1961 with a fanfare of reformist rhetoric by the leaders of the American republics,[152] and official capital inflows – helped by the creation of the Inter-American Development Bank (IDB) – were linked to the adoption of social and economic reform.[153]

For a variety of reasons reform was thus on the agenda by the early 1960s and in some cases much earlier. Both the ends and the means of reform were subject to a great deal of controversy, and numerous experiments were carried out with varying degrees of success. The most successful in the short term were often the least successful in the long run, as the Argentine experience had already shown – the dramatic increase in real urban wages in the first Perón administration had led to an intense struggle over distributive shares in the next decades, which generated macroeconomic instability and exacerbated inflationary problems.[154] The same was true of the sharp rise

149 See, for example, the article by Raúl Prebisch in ECLA (1970), pp. 257–78.
150 For a case study of income distribution in Taiwan, see Fei, Ranis, and Kuo (1979).
151 Cuba's real GDP per head in 1950 was the fifth highest in Latin America, as Table 9.4 makes clear.
152 The Alliance for Progress (ALPRO) was essentially a U.S. response to the hemispheric threat presented by the Cuban Revolution. Its massive targets for official and private capital transfers to Latin America were never met, although the transfers themselves increased substantially by comparison with the 1950s. The ALPRO had effectively collapsed by the end of the 1960s, for its emphasis on linking capital flows to reform was distasteful both to Latin American elites and to the Nixon administration in the United States.
153 The IDB made loans to all of the Latin American republics (except Cuba). Following decolonization in the Caribbean, membership was expanded to include a number of other countries. The IDB was an enthusiast for regional integration from the start and formed the Instituto para la Integración Económica de la América Latina (INTAL) to promote intraregional trade.
154 The wage share jumped from 36.8 percent of GNP in 1943–4 to 43.7 percent in 1950–2. The increase was even more marked when social-security contributions are taken into account. See Díaz-Alejandro (1970), Table 2.20, p. 122.

in real wages in the first two years (1970–3) of the socialist administration of Salvador Allende in Chile.[155]

A more indirect method of tackling the distribution of income was through fiscal policy. The tax system throughout the region relied heavily on indirect taxes, which are generally regressive, so a switch to direct taxes – in particular, progressive taxes on income – could be expected to improve the post-tax distribution of income.[156] At the same time the targeting of government expenditures on the lower income deciles could be expected to improve the social distribution of income (i.e., the distribution of income adjusted for the impact of government expenditures).

With the partial exceptions of Colombia and Costa Rica the results were disappointing on both counts.[157] New income taxes were introduced, but evasion was widespread, and only a small proportion of the adult population usually paid any income tax at all.[158] On the expenditure side, the bottom decile benefited from expenditures on primary schools and health clinics, but the middle and upper deciles were the principal beneficiaries of expenditures on secondary schools and universities. The bottom decile did not benefit from public-utility subsidies because they did not generally have access to the electricity and water provided by state-owned enterprises.[159] Even where fiscal policy played a positive role, it was usually not sufficient to outweigh the negative effect on distribution of regressive indirect taxes, which remained the most important source of government revenue.[160]

Expenditure on education was seen as an important means of improving income distribution in the long run, and all countries experienced a welcome rise in the proportion of the school-age population attending primary school. Nevertheless, the private rate of return on investment in secondary and tertiary education was usually higher than in primary schooling, and the largest percentage gains in enrollment were found in these sectors. Thus

155 In 1970 and 1971 real wages rose by 8.5 percent and 22.3 percent, respectively. In the next two years they fell by 11.3 percent and 38.6 percent as inflation accelerated ahead of nominal wage increases. See Larraín and Selowsky (1991), Table 7.11, p. 200.

156 A regressive tax is one in which the burden falls more heavily on the poor than on the rich. An example is a sales tax on food, because food constitutes a much higher proportion of the income of the poor than of the rich. By contrast, an income tax is likely to be progressive, provided the marginal rate is higher than the average rate, with the rich contributing proportionately more of their income than the poor. For a case study of how the Colombian fiscal system addressed these issues, see McLure et al. (1990).

157 The better performance of these two republics was almost certainly linked to their democratic systems, which made governments more sensitive to the needs of the electorate.

158 The most extreme case must surely be Nicaragua, where in the 1960s only 0.2 percent (1 in 500) of the population was paying income tax. See Watkins (1967), p. 405.

159 It has been demonstrated that in Colombia, where reform was generally taken seriously, the subsidy per head for education and health was highest in the top quintile, because this group benefited most from state support for universities. See Selowsky (1979), Table 1.6, p. 22.

160 See IDB (1984a), Table 29, p. 436.

the massive expansion of educational expenditures provided some assistance to the bottom deciles but contributed more to the welfare of the middle deciles. In Costa Rica, which had long prided itself on its commitment to education, the Gini coefficient fell during the 1960s, implying a shift toward greater equality, despite a fall in the share of income received by the bottom decile.[161]

A more radical answer to the question of distribution was provided by those who favored land reform (i.e., a redistribution of physical assets). Latin America was no stranger to land reform, the social function of land having been recognized as early as 1917 by the Mexican Constitution. Early attempts at land reform – Mexico in the 1930s,[162] Bolivia after the 1952 revolution,[163] and Guatemala during the last two years of the government of Jacobo Arbenz (1951–4)[164] – had been carried out mainly for political reasons, however. The new argument for land reform stemmed from the existence of an inverse relationship between the size of farms and their yield per hectare. Numerous studies demonstrated that small farms, which used more labor per unit of land, had higher yields than large farms, which used more capital per unit of land.[165] Thus it was claimed, on the basis of this "inverse yield law," that the redistribution of large farms into smaller plots would bring both more output and more employment.[166]

Land reform was widely attempted in the 1960s, but for most governments it was a cosmetic exercise designed to ensure compliance with the Alliance for Progress. Reluctance to attempt anything more radical was due not only to the political influence of the landowning class but also to the fear that redistribution would undermine export earnings, for agricultural exports came disproportionately from large estates.[167] Indeed, these fears proved to be justified in those republics (e.g., Chile and Peru) in which significant land reform was attempted from the 1960s onward.[168] Furthermore, Mexico was so concerned with avoiding any negative impact on agricultural exports from land reform that public expenditures (e.g., irrigation) and credit were concentrated on the largest farmers – whose share of

161 See Fields (1980), pp. 185–94.

162 On the changes in Mexican agriculture after the land reform, see Sanderson (1981).

163 The 1953 Agrarian Reform Law led eventually to the redistribution of about one-quarter of Bolivia's cultivable land. See Heath, Erasmus, and Buechler (1969).

164 The Guatemalan agrarian reform, enacted by President Arbenz during the most radical phase of the Guatemalan Revolution, was reversed as soon as the counterrevolution triumphed in 1954. On the agrarian reform itself, see Gleijeses (1991), Chapter 8.

165 See Barraclough (1973) for evidence demonstrating this inverse yield law.

166 The most sophisticated version of this argument can be found in Berry and Cline (1979).

167 This was considered so important in Honduras that numerous public initiatives were adopted to ensure a continuation of production for export even from the reformed sector. See Brockett (1988), Chapter 6.

168 See Thiesenhusen (1989), Chapters 5 and 7.

agricultural income rose accordingly.[169] Ironically, the fear of land reform was often sufficient to persuade large farmers to adopt superior techniques, including the new varieties of seeds associated with the Green Revolution, so the inverse yield law ceased to have the same force.[170] By the end of the 1970s the economic case for land reform had largely been undermined, although the political case remained strong in a number of smaller republics (e.g., Guatemala), in which the monopsony power of the landowning class was an obstacle to social and economic modernization.[171]

The expropriation, with or without compensation, of nonland assets provided an alternative, if even more radical, route to changing the distribution of income. Although nationalizations have not been uncommon in Latin America, they have mainly affected foreign companies. The most important exceptions were Chile under Allende (1970–3) and Cuba under Castro, although a number of private companies were nationalized by Perón and the revolutionary government in Bolivia expropriated the tin industry from its (mainly) Bolivian owners. By striking at the wealth from which the upper decile derived its income, nationalization in each of these cases had an immediate impact on the distribution of income. In Cuba, for example, the share of the top decile dropped from nearly 40 percent to 23 percent following wholesale nationalizations in the early 1960s.[172]

Nationalization may have been effective, but it was associated with widespread political upheaval and was far too radical for most Latin American governments. Although after 1959 Cuba was rapidly transformed into the Latin American country with the most equal distribution of income, it was not a model with much appeal. Statistics on income per head in Cuba have proved highly controversial, but there is agreement that performance in the 1960s was unimpressive.[173] Expenditures on health and education were transformed, but the absence of consumer goods meant that many basic needs could not be adequately met.[174] Cuba may have demonstrated that redistribution of income was feasible in the Latin American context, but the price paid was considered far too high by governments in the rest of the region.

169 See de Janvry (1990), pp. 123–31.
170 See Grindle (1986), Chapter 4.
171 With a majority of the labor force in rural areas and with one of the highest concentrations of landownership, Guatemalan society could not easily be changed without some sort of agrarian reform.
172 It dropped even further in the 1970s. See Brundenius (1984), Table 5.6 and Figure 5.1, p. 116.
173 Even the global social product (GSP), the measure used by the Cuban authorities themselves, showed little increase between 1962 and 1966. See Pérez-López (1991), Table 1, p. 11.
174 Brundenius constructed an estimate of basic-needs (food and beverages, clothing, housing, education, and health) expenditure per head in Cuba that showed almost no improvement over prerevolutionary levels by 1970. Only in the subsequent decade did the performance improve sharply. See Brundenius (1984), Table A2.28, p. 178.

The consequence was that, except for Cuba, the distribution of income remained unequal: Growth benefited the middle and upper deciles more than the bottom quintile despite a number of attempts at reform. The ineffectiveness of reform had a number of causes. Among them were the lack of democracy in many Latin American countries before the 1980s, governments that were unresponsive to the needs of the poorest groups, and the limited impact of the policy instruments available even to progressive administrations. With radical land reform and nationalization ruled out, short-run redistributive strategies rested heavily on fiscal and wage policy – neither of which was capable of making much of an impact.[175]

Inflation made the problem worse in the inward-looking republics. The modest gains made by the lower deciles during boom years were often wiped out by the stabilization programs that were periodically adopted to curb inflation. The success of a devaluation designed to restore external equilibrium was often assumed to depend on a fall in real wages, with particularly severe consequences for those low-paid workers who were unable to defend themselves through powerful trade unions.[176]

The ineffectiveness of reform also stemmed from the shift to urban-based activities. Although average rural incomes were invariably lower than average urban incomes, they were usually more equally distributed – at least at the bottom end of the scale.[177] Although the root cause of rural inequality was the unequal distribution of land, in the urban economy the problem stemmed from the rapid growth of a labor supply that was dominated by unskilled workers. Ultimately, the demographic transition – leading to a fall in the birth rate – and the spread of educational opportunities could be expected to improve the situation. Yet these effects would take many years to influence events, and in the meantime the shift of activity toward urban areas was setting in motion forces that reform programs were relatively powerless to reverse. Thus the rapid growth of the Latin American economies in the two decades after 1950 brought only modest gains for the bottom deciles in almost all of the republics.

---

175 Wage policy could be highly effective in the short term (see note 154), but it was less effective in the long run.

176 The impact of devaluation on real wages was made most explicit in a case study of Argentina by Díaz-Alejandro (1965).

177 This was clearest in the case of Brazil, where the bottom quintile in agriculture received a share of agricultural income twice as high as the bottom quintile in the nonagricultural sector, whereas the position of the top quintile was the exact reverse. See ECLA (1971), Table 9, p. 114.

10

New trade strategies and debt-led growth

At the beginning of the 1960s it was widely believed that regional integration would restore the dynamism of the inward-looking model of development in the larger republics and provide a platform for industrialization in the smaller countries. Yet by the end of the decade the mood had changed. Regional integration – at least in South America – had not brought the expected gains, and the inward-looking model seemed to be subject to diminishing returns. The prestige of CEPAL, which had nailed its colors to both inward-looking development and regional integration, declined despite the regional organization's best efforts to revise its approach to industrialization,[1] and the Latin American policymaking elite began to pay more attention to alternative ideas on trade and deveopment.[2]

The Achilles heel of inward-looking development remained the balance-of-payments constraint. After 1929 persistent balance-of-payments problems had persuaded more and more countries to abandon export-led growth based on primary products in favor of a new model that was expected to lower their vulnerability to external shocks. Yet balance-of-payments problems continued under inward-looking development as the policies adopted to favor industry undermined the export sector and shifted the composition of imports in the direction of complementary goods – the demand for which expanded rapidly in line with industrial growth.

Under the new model, therefore, vulnerability to external shocks remained acute, as events after 1970 clearly demonstrated. The collapse of the Bretton Woods system in 1971, following the inability of the U.S. administration to maintain the convertibility of dollars into gold at a fixed price, and the adoption by the major industrialized countries of floating currencies made it difficult for Latin American republics to sustain stable trade-weighted real exchange rates.[3] After the Arab–Israeli war in 1973 the

1 See, for example, ECLA (1963), where the need to promote extraregional as well as intraregional manufactured exports is recognized.
2 The emergence of alternative ideas about trade and development in the 1960s, emphasizing export promotion and market forces, is explored in Love (1994).
3 On the collapse of the Bretton Woods system, see Scammell (1980), Chapter 12.

Organization of Petroleum Exporting Countries (OPEC) was able to impose stringent export quotas on its members, and oil prices were quadrupled. For those republics in Latin America that were net importers of oil at the time – all except Bolivia, Colombia, Ecuador, and Venezuela[4] – the first oil shock was a harsh reminder of the limitations that could be placed on economic development by balance-of-payments constraints. The same lesson was driven home even more forcibly by the second oil shock after 1978.[5]

The inward-looking model of development had been rooted in export pessimism. As a result the incentives provided to the export sector – at least in the larger republics – had diminished, and almost all countries had seen their share of world trade decline. By the early 1970s, however, a number of changes had taken place in the world economy and international trade policy, which compelled Latin America to take a fresh look at the barriers to exports.

First, the persistent rise in real wages in the developed countries and the huge differential between wage rates in developed countries and those in developing countries encouraged a number of multinational corporations (MNCs) to establish a new international division of labor in which some of the simpler, more labor-intensive tasks could be performed outside the developed countries. This sourcing of inputs, in which only capital was mobile, contributed to the rapid rise in international trade in manufactured goods and provided opportunities for those developing countries that were able and willing to meet the requirements of MNCs.

Second, the success of some Southeast Asian countries (notably Hong Kong, Singapore, South Korea, and Taiwan), where export-led growth had been established on the basis of manufactured goods, was proving to be spectacular. Dismissed at first as a "special case" with little relevance for Latin America, the Asian experience eventually provided a major challenge for the export pessimists. Although numerous – and often contradictory – lessons were to be drawn from the experience of the newly industrializing countries (NICs) in Asia, their performance came under closer scrutiny in Latin America as their rates of growth of exports and gross domestic product (GDP) began to accelerate. Their resilience in the face of external shocks – such as the two oil crises – was also considered particularly impressive.[6]

Third, the work of the U.N. Conference on Trade and Development (UNCTAD) and other international organizations that lobbied for special trade privileges for the less-developed countries (LDCs) held out the

---

4 Mexico and Peru, though exporters of crude oil, were net importers until 1977 and 1978, respectively. See IDB (1982), Table 66-67.

5 The first oil shock, in 1973, raised the average price of a barrel from U.S. $3 to $12; the second, in 1979, from $12 to $30. Thus oil importers had to absorb a tenfold increase in price in less than a decade.

6 See Sachs (1985), pp. 523–73. The Asian NICs had seen their economies transformed through manufactured export growth, with GDP per head in the 1970s rising in excess of 5 percent per year. See Ranis and Orrock (1985), Table 4.3, p. 55.

prospect of privileged treatment for the LDC exports. The Generalized System of Preferences (GSP) was adopted by the majority of the developed countries at the start of the 1970s. Its promise of duty-free access to the markets of developed countries for nontraditional exports from LDCs proved to be much less generous than originally expected, but it did provide a modest window of opportunity that would be opened further in subsequent rounds of negotiations.[7] Meanwhile, the United States – which did not adopt the GSP until 1976 – had amended its tariff code in 1962 to permit the importation of goods from abroad with only value added subject to duty, provided the inputs were of U.S. origin.[8] Although clearly intended to benefit U.S. MNCs, the amendments provided opportunities for any Latin American republic that was able to attract investment into assembly-type operations.

Finally, export pessimism was further undermined by the commodity price boom in the 1970s. The collapse of the Bretton Woods system in 1971 brought to an end the system of fixed exchange rates that had underpinned monetary discipline in the main industrialized countries. Freed of the obligation to preserve exchange-rate parities, monetary policy in the developed countries became loose, and world liquidity – boosted by the huge U.S. budget deficits needed to finance the Vietnam War – soared. As a result primary commodities – not only oil – reached record prices, and the net barter terms of trade (NBTT) for many Latin American countries (including some oil importers) improved sharply during the 1970s.[9]

These changes in the international environment could not fail to be recognized in Latin America. They elicited three different responses – export promotion, export substitution, and primary-export development – each of which gave greater emphasis to the export sector and marked a shift from traditional import-substituting industrialization (ISI). Export promotion attempted to graft manufactured exports onto the inward-looking model; export substitution aimed at shifting resources out of protected sectors; and the primary-export development model sought to exploit the rise in world commodity prices. Yet none of the three models was notably successful: The decline in the share of world trade was not reversed,[10] and the region became increasingly dependent on foreign borrowing to fuel its economic growth.

---

7 One of the problems with the GSP was the limited use LDCs could make of tariff preferences because of the widespread use of quotas. In 1980, for example, total imports from LDCs covered by the GSP were $55.4 billion. Less than half of these imports were actually accorded GSP treatment, however, and they represented only 8.2 percent of total imports from LDCs. See Kelly et al. (1988), Table A25, p. 133.

8 See Sklair (1989), pp. 8–9. Item 807 was the crucial code, for it allowed goods to be exported to the United States with dutiable value calculated net of any U.S. inputs in the final product.

9 Taking 1970 as the base, the Latin American NBTT had increased by 50 percent within a decade. The increase for oil exporters was 176 percent. See ECLAC (1989), Table 276, pp. 506–7.

10 The Latin American share of world exports fell from 4.9 percent in 1970 to 4.6 percent in 1980. See Wilkie (1990), Table 2600, p. 674.

The combination of a small export sector and mounting debt-service obligations proved to be disastrous when the debt crisis finally erupted in 1982.

Export promotion

The export promotion (EP) strategy was based on the recognition that the domestic market was not large enough to support firms of optimal size in many branches of industry. At the same time the strategy remained committed to protecting manufacturing from international competition. Thus it attempted to graft onto ISI a new set of incentives that would make exports of manufactured goods possible. The EP strategy was therefore an industrialization strategy, in which firms were encouraged to exploit opportunities provided both by the protected domestic market and by the growth of world trade.

Six countries (Argentina, Brazil, Colombia, Mexico, Haiti, and the Dominican Republic) followed the EP strategy from the 1960s onward, although not consistently. Argentina abandoned the policy in the 1970s in favor of export substitution (see pp. 323–30). Haiti and the Dominican Republic tried to take advantage of the new international division of labor through incentives for foreign companies that assembled manufactured goods in export-processing zones (EPZs). Mexico encouraged assembly operations through its *maquiladora* industry on the northern border and – in view of its more sophisticated industrial base – also promoted other kinds of manufactured exports.

The Brazilian EP strategy began after the military coup in 1964. For the first three years, however, economic policy was dictated primarily by the needs of a stabilization program that laid the basis for future growth at the expense of a sharp reduction in real wages and a deterioration in the distribution of income.[11] This period of rapid growth, often known as the Brazilian miracle, began in 1967 and produced rates of change in all the macroeconomic aggregates (including exports) that far exceeded those in other Latin American countries and rivaled those in the Asian NICs.[12] Yet although export promotion was an important part of the Brazilian miracle, it was less crucial than certain other policies. In particular, the concentration of income in the upper deciles,[13] coupled with new credit facilities, provided

---

11 The stabilization program and its impact on distribution are disscussed in Fishlow (1973). See also Bacha (1977).

12 During the years of the Brazilian miracle (1967–73), real GDP rose at an annual rate of 10 percent. See Wells (1979), pp. 228–33.

13 The gain was most concentrated in the top 5 percent, for their share of income rose from 27.4 percent in 1960 to 36.3 percent in 1970. See Baer (1983), Table 27, p. 105. Because the population of Brazil was nearing 100 million in 1970, this elite group still represented a sizable market.

the necessary conditions for rapid growth of the consumer durable industries and made possible mass production of automobiles in Latin America for the first time.[14]

The ISI strategy through protection increased industrial value added per unit of output in the domestic market. At the same time, exporters of manufactured goods were penalized as a result of both overvalued exchange rates and tariffs on imported inputs. Thus for most manufactured goods the value added per unit of output in world markets was far lower than what could be secured in the domestic market.[15] This antiexport bias had to be eliminated, or at least reduced, if the EP strategy was to have any chance of success.

All of the instruments that could be used to reduce antiexport bias were controlled by the authorities. The exchange-rate was the most important, because a real, effective devaluation would increase the value added per unit of output for all exported commodities. Real devaluation would also raise the price of competing imports, however, thus providing additional incentives for firms selling in the domestic market. The EP strategy therefore needed to use fiscal and credit policy to provide additional incentives for exporters. The instruments available included selective tariff reductions and tax rebates, along with special credit facilities and other subsidies for exporters.[16]

The experience of EP countries with exchange-rate policy was mixed. Haiti and the Dominican Republic maintained exchange rates that were fixed in nominal terms to the U.S. dollar, which virtually ruled out the possibility of real devaluation. On the other hand, both countries avoided high rates of inflation for much of the 1970s, so at first the exchange-rate was not seriously overvalued. After the devaluation of 1954 Mexico also maintained a rate of exchange fixed to the U.S. dollar; however, the rate of inflation exceeded the rate of U.S. inflation (Mexico's main trading partner), so the currency steadily appreciated in real terms and undermined the EP strategy until a further maxidevaluation took place in 1976. Shortly thereafter Mexico discovered huge new deposits of oil, so the EP strategy was abandoned in favor of the promotion of oil exports.[17]

The other three counties all followed an exchange-rate strategy known as the "crawling peg," designed to preserve the real value of the currency through frequent minidevaluations following an initial realignment of the currency. This policy was adopted in Argentina in 1964, in Colombia in

14 Annual production of automobiles jumped from 57,300 in 1960 to 550,700 in 1975. This was comparable with production levels in many European countries.
15 Antiexport bias in Brazil (defined as [value added if sold domestically]/[value added if exported] − 1) exceeded 50 percent in eighteen of twenty-one manufacturing sectors in 1967. See Bergsman (1970), p. 51.
16 The range of instruments and their impact on antiexport bias is shown in Bulmer-Thomas (1988), pp. 105–15.
17 See Looney (1985), Chapters 5–6.

1967, and in Brazil in 1968. Although attractive to exporters, the crawling peg encouraged inflationary expectations, so Argentina abandoned it after 1967 in favor of a fixed nominal exchange-rate that rapidly became overvalued. So did Brazil, in the mid-1970s.[18] In Colombia the boom in coffee prices after 1975 pushed the exchange-rate to a level that undermined manufactured exports.[19] Exchange-rate policy was therefore far from consistent, although improvement in the performance of manufactured exports in all three countries was notable while the crawling peg was in operation.

Even where the official exchange-rate was overvalued authorities could still use a parallel rate to promote exports. Furthermore, a dual exchange-rate could be used to reward exporting firms differently from import-competing firms – thus lowering antiexport bias. One technique, used widely in the Dominican Republic, was to allow exporters to sell a certain proportion of their foreign exchange in the parallel market while surrendering the remainder at the official rate of exchange. By varying the proportions authorities could alter the incentives under the EP strategy.[20] To avoid exchange-rate losses by the central bank, a similar scheme had to operate for imports, with the lower exchange-rate reserved for essentials and a higher rate imposed on luxuries. Inevitably, this led to opposition from many importers, and the allocation of imports to each category often encouraged corruption.[21]

The EP strategy was intended not so much to lower the protection offered to firms selling in the protected market as to raise the incentives for firms exporting their products. Although tariff reform was adopted in each republic, the main purpose was to lower tariffs on imported inputs entering into production that was later exported. Some general tariff reductions did occur, particularly in Brazil in the second half of the 1960s, but trade liberalization never seriously threatened the profitability of the import-competing sectors, and in the 1970s a number of republics again raised tariffs following the first oil crisis.

Tariff rebates on imported inputs entering into exports (sometimes called drawback schemes) were widely used, and the scheme adopted in Colombia, under the Plan Vallejo, was particularly successful.[22] In Mexico, however, the widespread – and growing – use of import quotas and licenses in the 1960s undermined the effectiveness of drawback schemes, because the principal reason for high prices for inputs was the quota rather than the tariff.[23] Only in the extreme case of the *maquiladora* industry, where no tariff or

18 Brazil did not try to peg the nominal exchange-rate, but its rate of depreciation fell behind the difference between domestic and foreign rates of inflation. See Baer (1983), p. 166.

19 See Thorp (1991), pp. 167–71. See also Edwards (1984).

20 See Vedovato (1986), p. 163. Official devaluation against the U.S. dollar took place in 1985.

21 See Edwards (1989) for a general overview of exchange-rate problems in the Latin American context.

22 On the details of the Plan Vallejo, which laid the basis for export promotion in Colombia, see Díaz-Alejandro (1976). See also Thomas (1985), pp. 26–9.

23 On import quotas in Mexico and the increasing sophistication with which they were used, see ten Kate and Wallace (1980), pp. 43–54.

quota restrictions were placed on imported inputs, did the tariff policy unambiguously favor export promotion. The same was true of the EPZs in Haiti and the Dominican Republic, which offered extremely generous tax treatment to investors.[24]

The other main incentives offered to manufactured exports included tax rebates and subsidized credit. The typical instrument used to lower the tax burden on nontraditional exports was a certificate, equivalent to a fixed proportion of the FOB value of exports, that could be set against future tax liability. These *certificados de abonos tributarios* (CATs) were often generous and were also successful in promoting exports. Not surprisingly, they imposed a considerable fiscal burden on the governments concerned. The problem was further aggravated by the use of subsidized credit. In Brazil, the country that took this policy to its most extreme form, the total subsidy as a proportion of the FOB value of manufactured exports was approximately 25 percent by the beginning of the 1970s.[25]

The widespread use of subsidies in the EP strategy also ran counter to the rules of the General Agreement on Tariffs and Trade (GATT). Although Mexico, Haiti, and Colombia did not join GATT until the 1980s (Argentina joined in 1967), nonmembership did not provide protection against retaliatory measures because importing nations were still entitled to impose countervailing or antidumping duties against goods deemed to be unfairly subsidized.[26] In fact, nonmembership could make the risk of retaliation more likely because the offending country had no right of appeal to arbitration. However, the modest penetration of the world market by the EP countries meant that most of them – the main exception being Brazil – escaped retaliatory measures.

At a superficial level the EP strategy was successful. The proportion of manufactured goods in total exports rose sharply in each republic (see Table 10.1), the rise in the share corresponding closely to the period when the EP strategy was in force. Argentina was able to raise the contribution of manufactured goods in total exports to around 25 percent in the years when some version of the EP strategy was in force. Haiti had pushed the share above 50 percent by the late 1970s – the first republic in Latin America to do so – although the domestic value added associated with the new (mainly assembled) exports was still modest. In the Dominican Republic the increase in the 1970s corresponded closely to the early years of promotion of EPZs.[27]

---

24 On the spread of EPZs in developing countries, see Balasubramanyam (1988).

25 See Tyler (1983), pp. 97–107.

26 Under GATT rules a countervailing duty could be applied, in which the exporter was deemed to be receiving an illegitimate subsidy. An antidumping duty could be applied if the exporter was deemed to be selling the product at less than full cost. See Kelly et al. (1988).

27 Trade statistics for the Dominican Republic do not always include exports from the EPZs. If they are excluded, the share of manufactured goods in total exports is much smaller than shown in Table 10.1. See Mathieson (1988), pp. 41–63.

Table 10.1. *Export-promotion countries: manufactured exports, 1960–1980*

Country	Year	Manufactured exports Value (in millions of US$)	As percentage of total	Exports as percentage of GDP[a]
Argentina	1960	44.3	4.1	7.9
	1970	245.9	13.9	9.2
	1975[b]	717.9	24.4	7.2
Brazil	1960	28.4	2.2	6.7
	1970	420.5	15.4	6.5
	1980	7,491.9	37.2	5.6
Colombia	1960	6.9	1.5	17.5
	1970	78.5	10.7	14.2
	1980	775.3	19.7	15.8
Dominican	1970[c]	5.9	2.8	17.2
Republic	1980	166.1	23.6	18.4
Haiti	1960	3.6[d]	8.0[d]	15.8
	1970	18.2	37.8	12.3
	1980	199.7	58.6	17.6
Mexico	1960	122.3	16.0	8.4
	1970	391.3	32.5	7.7
	1975[e]	929.4	31.1	8.8

[a] 1980 prices.
[b] Assumed to follow export substitution after 1975 (see Table 10.2).
[c] Export promotion assumed to begin only after 1970.
[d] Data are for 1962.
[e] Assumed to follow primary export development after 1975.
Sources: IDB (1982), Table 3, p. 351, and Table 6, p. 353; ECLAC (1989), Table 281, p. 520, and Table 70, p. 105; World Bank (1989); Fass (1990), Table 1.8, p. 40.

The EP strategy, by shifting the composition of exports away from primary products, the prices of which were so volatile, reduced the instability of export proceeds. Because the markets for manufactured exports were not the same as the markets for primary-product exports, the geographical concentration of exports was also reduced. The shares of exports to the United States and the European Economic Community (EEC) fell in every case except Haiti, and a number of new nontraditional markets appeared. Brazil was particularly successful in winning markets in other developing countries: By the early 1980s the Middle East – its demand for imports swollen by the second huge round of increases in oil prices – and Africa accounted for more than 10 percent of all Brazilian exports and for a much higher proportion of its manufactured exports.[28]

28 See Wilkie (1990), Table 2614, p. 696.

The EP strategy was much less successful in opening the economies to foreign trade and in restoring the export sector as one of the engines of growth. The ratio of exports to GDP (see Table 10.1) hardly increased at all. Not one of the six republics managed permanently to reverse its decline in the share of world exports despite the fact that to a much higher degree foreign-exchange earnings now came from those commodities (manufactured exports) that were growing fastest in international trade. Thus export promotion failed to compensate fully for the poor performance of primary-product exports, which continued to be subject to antiexport bias. Only in exceptional periods, such as the coffee boom in Colombia and the oil bonanza in Mexico in the late 1970s, did the share in world trade increase, and in all such cases the improvement was due mainly to high prices for primary-product exports.

The economic development of the major countries that followed an EP strategy (Argentina, Brazil, Colombia, and Mexico) therefore continued to depend on the internal market, where the pattern of demand was heavily influenced by the distribution of income. The concentration of income in the upper deciles, which became even more concentrated in Brazil after 1964, did not lead to industrial stagnation – as CEPAL had argued it would – but it did encourage a structure of production that often gave preference to capital-intensive consumer durables for the rich over labor-intensive articles of basic consumption for the poor. Because the EP strategy promoted existing industry rather than encouraging the creation of new firms, it was by no means certain that the new exports would be labor intensive. Indeed, manufactured exports from both Brazil and Mexico were generally capital intensive, in defiance of received economic wisdom on international trade patterns,[29] and only Colombia was able to establish a pattern of manufactured exports that was labor intensive and contributed to an improvement in employment conditions and income distribution in the first half of the 1970s.[30]

The EP strategy was a brave attempt to rescue the inward-looking model of development without sacrificing the cocoon of protection that was still considered essential for industry. It was not without its successes: Industrial entrepreneurs had demonstrated that they were responsive to price and other incentives and that they could penetrate world markets, and export pessimism was seen to be unjustified – at least in the case of manufactured goods. Yet the strategy could not be regarded as an unqualified success in

29 The Hecksher–Ohlin theorem stated that countries would export those products which intensively used the factor of production in relative abundance. In the Latin American context the theorem therefore implied labor-intensive exports. Yet numerous studies had drawn attention to the capital-intensive nature of the new manufactured exports. See, for example, Tyler (1976).

30 See Urrutia (1985), pp. 117–122. An excellent case study of Colombian textiles, a labor-intensive export, is provided in Morawetz (1981).

any republic – not even Brazil – and Argentina had abandoned it by the mid-1970s.

There was no single reason for failure, but one explanation does stand out above all others: fluctuations in the real effective exchange-rate (REER). Although the importance of a competitive exchange-rate was recognized – the REER should be constant or falling (i.e., depreciating) – the EP strategy was blown off course by an appreciation on numerous occasions. We have already mentioned the impact of the Colombian coffee boom in the second half of the 1970s on the exchange-rate; Colombia also experienced an accelerating inflow of foreign exchange after the 1960s from the sale of drugs (marijuana and cocaine), which is widely considered to have undermined the REER.[31] In both the Dominican Republic and Mexico the determination to defend a fixed exchange-rate despite the differential between domestic and world rates of inflation eventually led to serious problems of currency overvaluation, which finally provoked major devaluations.

A second problem was the conflict between short- and long-run policies. The long-run exchange-rate policy demanded by the EP strategy was often in conflict with the short-run needs of stabilization programs in which a fixed exchange-rate was seen as a defense against inflationary pressures. Argentina was particularly susceptible to this conflict; and the crawling peg policy after 1964, which had been quite successful in promoting nontraditional exports, was replaced in 1967 by a maxidevaluation which it was hoped would permanently fix the nominal value of the currency.

The semipermanent character of stabilization programs in Argentina made it very difficult, if not impossible, to pursue a long-run exchange-rate policy consistent with the EP strategy,[32] but Argentina was not the only country to suffer. Following the first oil shock, which raised the share of oil in the import bill to 25 percent, Brazil allowed the REER to drift upward (i.e., to appreciate) in an effort to contain inflationary pressures. At the same time, the balance-of-payments constraint after 1973 persuaded Brazilian policymakers to give renewed emphasis to import-substitution programs designed to reduce the republic's dependence on imported energy.[33] Thus external shocks threatened the foundations of the EP strategy in Brazil, although increasing levels of subsidies still made it possible for manufactured exports to grow rapidly (see Table 10.1).

The barriers erected by developed countries against manufactured exports from developing countries, the importance of which CEPAL had stressed,

---

31 On exchange-rate appreciation, see Thomas (1985), Chapter 2. The economic impact of the drug industry on Colombia is examined in Arrieta et al. (1991), pp. 47–96.

32 See Guadagni (1989) and Maynard (1989) on the difficulties Argentina faced in trying to promote exports in the face of short-term stablization problems.

33 The most important of these was the alcohol program, which converted cane sugar into fuel and led to a reduction in the demand for imported oil. See Baer (1983), pp. 146–7.

proved to be less of a problem than many people had anticipated. The greatest difficulties were experienced by Brazil toward the end of the 1970s as voluntary export restraints (VERs) were imposed on a number of its manufactured exports.[34] This, however, was a measure of Brazil's success, for other – less successful – countries did not face the same barriers. Furthermore, the barriers were at least in part a response to Brazil's formidable array of subsidies. By contrast, Colombia was able to expand a range of labor-intensive manufactured exports (e.g., textiles) despite the fact that nontariff barriers were the rule rather than the exception,[35] and the republic also established a niche as the world's most important exporter of children's books. Mexican manufactured exports, particularly from the *maquiladoras*, were sensitive to the business cycle in the United States and were adversely affected by the U.S. recession in 1974, but this was no different from the situation facing all exporters of manufactured goods. Thus the deficiencies of the EP model could not easily be laid at the door of the developed countries despite the existence of protectionist tendencies in their commercial policies.

Export substitution

The EP strategy had at least demonstrated that Latin America could export manufactured exports. It had not, however, done much to eliminate the inefficiencies of domestic industry caused by the high levels of protection from international competition. It had provided new incentives for industrial exports while still encouraging import-competing production. Thus export promotion was coupled with continued import substitution in industry, and manufactured exports could only compete in the world market on the basis of numerous subsidies.

A more radical alternative to EP was the export substitution (ES) strategy. The underlying philosophy behind ES was that economic development in Latin America had been grossly distorted by ISI, state intervention, and corporatism. The solution was seen in a shift toward a more market-oriented and less-protected environment, which would lead to the elimination of antiexport bias. The economies would then become more open and more integrated into the world market, and domestic prices would move more closely into line with international prices. The reduction in protection

---

34 The developed countries made increasing use of VERs as a way of protecting their industry from import competition. Because the effect of a VER was an increase in the final price at which imports were sold, some exporters were able substantially to increase profits per unit of sales. On VERs in general, see Kelly et al. (1988).

35 International trade in textiles was regulated by the Multi-Fiber Arrangement, established in 1962, which laid down export and import quotas for all participating countries. See Farrands (1982).

and the elimination of antiexport bias would encourage exportables while discouraging importables. Thus the ES strategy was expected to lead to a large increase in the ratio of both exports and imports to GDP and could also lead to negative ISI; that is, the replacement of high-cost local industrial production by less expensive imports.

The ES strategy was pursued in the 1970s by the three Southern Cone countries (Argentina, Chile, and Uruguay), and a more modest experiment was carried out in Peru. Chile was the first to adopt the program following the overthrow of the socialist government of Salvador Allende in September 1973 and the imposition of the dictatorship of Augusto Pinochet. Uruguay was close on Chile's heels, following the collapse of democracy in 1973, and the program was endorsed in Argentina in 1976 after the military intervention against the Peronist regime. Thus the ES strategy was implemented in the Southern Cone by military dictatorships. The shift to free-market economies was coupled with political repression, making it difficult to disentangle the impact on performance of economic policies and authoritarian politics.[36] By contrast, the program was adopted in Peru after 1978 during the transition from military rule to civilian government.

The willingness of all four countries to embrace a strategy that was diametrically opposed to received wisdom in much of Latin America was a reflection of their deep frustration at the failure of alternative policies. The share of exports in GDP had shrunk to such modest levels that rapid growth – generating heavy demand for imports – was ruled out by balance-of-payments constraints. GDP per head had underperformed the rest of Latin America by a large margin, and throughout the Southern Cone the volume of exports per head had declined since 1950.[37] Chile and Uruguay had never strayed far from the path of ISI. Argentina's experiment with EP in the 1960s had been overwhelmed by a series of stabilization programs in the first half of the 1970s. Peru had preserved a traditional export-led model until the mid-1960s, but the military regimes after 1968 had promoted inward-looking development so aggressively that the republic's share of world trade had fallen by two-thirds in a single decade.

In all four countries balance-of-payments problems had contributed to inflationary pressures and inflation had undermined confidence in financial instruments, so financial repression was widespread.[38] Inflation was

---

36 For a brave attempt to do so, see Handelman and Baer (1989), Chapters 2–3. The economic programs in support of stabilization within the Southern Cone are analyzed in Díaz-Alejandro (1981).

37 Between 1950 and 1975 the volume of exports per head in Argentina, Chile, and Uruguay fell at an annual rate of 0.2 percent, 2.3 percent, and 1.2 percent, respectively. In the rest of Latin America it rose at an annual rate of 1.3 percent over the same period. See Ramos (1986), Table 1.1, p. 2.

38 Financial repression, sometimes also called shallow finance, is the term used to describe an economy with a low ratio of financial to real assets and a limited choice of financial instruments. It is usually associated with negative real rates of interest (i.e., inflation rates in excess of nominal interest rates). The classic works on financial repression are McKinnon (1973) and Shaw (1973).

further aggravated by class struggle, as different social groups fought to protect their real standard of living through increases in nominal incomes. When coupled with irresponsible fiscal policy, the result was an acceleration of inflation that contributed in no small part to the collapse of civilian government in the Southern Cone and to the fall of the military in Peru. Chile under Allende (1970–3) was the worst offender. Irresponsible fiscal and monetary policies, combined with a sharp decline in capital inflows, led to an acceleration in inflation from 33 percent in 1970 to 354 percent in 1973. Although foreign actors (particularly U.S. agencies) were heavily involved in destabilizing the Allende regime, the failure to curb inflationary pressures was perhaps the single most important factor in the fall of Allende.[39]

Thus the ES strategy (in effect an adjustment program) was implemented against a background of economic dislocation that demanded drastic stabilization measures. Although in theory it is possible to adopt stabilization and adjustment programs simultaneously, in practice it is very difficult – as many governments in Latin America have found to their detriment.[40] The instruments used to favor adjustment (e.g., competitive exchange rates and changes in relative prices) can undermine stabilization and vice versa. The conflict between the two kinds of programs was to prove severe in the countries that adopted the ES strategy and ultimately led to the failure of both.

The cornerstone of the ES strategy was trade liberalization. Initially a maxidevaluation was carried out to achieve a significant depreciation of the REER, and the currency was then periodically realigned to offset the difference between domestic and world inflation. The intention was to stabilize the REER after the initial devaluation. Political repression in the Southern Cone was so severe, however, that real wages fell further than implied by devaluation. This meant that the incentives offered to exporters were even greater than implied by the change in the REER.

Whereas real devaluation encouraged exports, tariff reductions and the phasing out of nontariff barriers were used to promote imports. This was a radical departure from the established practice in the rest of Latin America and was controversial even among the ES countries. Chile went farthest, reducing its nominal tariff to an average of 10 percent by 1979; indeed, Chile's commitment to lower tariffs was one of the reasons for its departure

39 The literature on the Allende period is huge. For the politics, see Kaufman (1988); for the economics, see de Vylder (1976).
40 The difference between stabilization programs and adjustment programs is essentially one of timing. Whereas stabilization is adopted to deal with disequilibria in the short term (e.g., a balance-of-payments crisis) without necessarily bringing about any change in the structure of the economy, adjustment is needed to shift factors of production over the longer term toward an allocation of resources that is more consistent with the country's dynamic comparative advantage. Thus adjustment programs can aggravate the problem of stabilization and vice versa. See Kahler (1990).

Table 10.2. *Export-substitution countries: structure of external trade,*
circa 1970–1980

Country	Year	A	B	C	D	E
Argentina	1975	7.2	16.4	24.4^a	3.1	1,287
	1980	11.2	26.2	23.1^a	14.2	4,774
Chile	1970	12.4	32.8	8.1^b	8.1^c	91
	1975	16.9	35.3	19.9	4.5	490
	1980	22.8	48.6	27.3	22.6^d	4,733^d
Peru	1978	15.8	25.2	3.9^a	8.7^e	192
	1980	14.0	27.4	14.1^a	16.0^d	1,728^d
Uruguay	1970	14.9	31.8	19.8^c	7.1^c	45
	1975	18.3	35.0	34.5	4.1	190
	1980	21.6	42.5	42.1	12.3^d	709

Key: A = Ratio of exports to GDP at 1980 prices;
B = Ratio of exports plus imports to GDP at 1980 prices;
C = Ratio of nontraditional exports to total exports;
D = Ratio of consumer-goods imports to total imports; and
E = Balance-of-payments current account deficit, in millions of U.S. dollars.
^{a} Nontraditional exports defined as manufactured goods.
^{b} Datum is for 1971.
^{c} Data are for 1973.
^{d} Data are for 1981.
^{e} Datum is for 1975.
Sources: IDB (1981), Table 3, p. 400, and Tables 8–9, p. 403, and (1982), Table 3, p. 351,
and Tables 6 and 7, p. 353; Ramos (1986), Tables 7.7–7.9 ECLAC (1989), Table 70,
p. 105, and Tables 281–3, pp. 520–7; World Bank (1991).

from the Andean Pact (AP), because unilateral tariff reduction was inconsistent with the AP's stated goal of a common external tariff (CET). Argentina and Peru had lowered tariffs to an average of 35 percent and 32 percent respectively, by the beginning of the 1980s. Uruguay concentrated on eliminating quotas and licenses for imports and made only modest progress on tariff reductions.[41]

Trade liberalization was successful at first: Exports rose rapidly and the openness of each economy increased (see Table 10.2). Imports also rose, but not so rapidly as to aggravate the balance-of-payments problem in the first stages of liberalization. Even more encouraging was the change in the composition of exports, with nontraditional exports (except in Argentina) rising sharply in importance (see Table 10.2). These new products, whether agricultural or industrial in origin, were able to compete in world markets in terms of price. Local firms, squeezed in the domestic market by rising imports and by the recessionary impact of falling real wages, were encouraged

41 See Ramos (1986), pp. 125–34.

to shift production into exports. Negative import substitution (i.e., the replacement of high-cost domestic production by imports) was therefore coupled with export growth – the essence of an export-substitution strategy.

The success of trade liberalization was much more limited in Peru than in the other countries – a reflection in part of the fact that it was adopted so late and abandoned so quickly. Much of the improvement in export earnings after 1978 was in fact due to an increase in the NBTT, so export performance continued to be overwhelmingly dominated by traditional products (mainly minerals). Imports responded to tariff reductions so strongly that the trade deficit became unacceptably large as the terms of trade deteriorated after 1980. The brief Peruvian experiment with trade liberalization and the ES strategy therefore went into reverse, as measures – including tariff increases – were adopted to protect the balance of payments even before the debt crisis erupted in 1982.[42]

The fight against inflation – a major preoccupation in all of the export-substitution countries, particularly the Southern Cone – was inspired by a monetarist perspective. The fiscal deficit was tackled primarily through cutting expenditure – helped by the fall in real wages – in an effort to reduce the rate of growth of the money supply. The domestic capital market was strengthened through a number of financial liberalization measures. Interest rates were freed, quantitative controls on credit were phased out, barriers to the entry of new financial institutions were reduced, and bank regulations were eased. The result was a sharp increase in financial intermediation, with the ratio of financial assets to GDP rising in all countries.

Thus the growth of the money supply was subject to two contradictory forces. The decline in the fiscal deficit reduced the need for the governments to rely on central-bank borrowing, but financial liberalization increased the time and savings deposits the public wished to hold. The second force proved stronger than the first, and the money supply grew so rapidly that the authorities became concerned about inflationary implications. Furthermore, many of the measures adopted in support of adjustment – exchange-rate devaluation, interest rate liberalization, abolition of price control, and so forth – were aggravating inflationary pressures and undermining the stabilization program.

Financial liberalization and the decline in fiscal deficits meant that the authorities in the Southern Cone had lost the ability to control the money supply through traditional means. Trade liberalization, however, had led to a significant opening of the economy in which – monetarists argued – any imbalance in the supply of and demand for money would be reflected in the balance of payments. This monetary approach to the balance of payments implied that the money supply was endogenous – not exogenous – and

42 See Beckerman (1989), pp. 122–6.

that it would adjust to whatever level the public wished to hold through changes in international reserves.[43]

The authorities therefore considered that inflation stabilization could best be achieved through further liberalization of the balance of payments – above all, the capital account – so international capital flows could provide the mechanism for equilibrating the supply of and demand for money. At the same time, trade liberalization was expected to eliminate the gap between local and world prices, so domestic inflation would fall into line with inflation in partner countries.

In all of these arguments the exchange-rate was seen to play a pivotal role – as the instrument for translating foreign prices into domestic prices, as the primary determinant of inflationary expectations, and as the equilibrating mechanism in the balance of payments. A shift therefore took place in the Southern Cone, from an exchange-rate policy designed to encourage exports to one designed to defeat inflation. Henceforth nominal devaluation was to be preannounced at a rate below the difference between domestic and foreign inflation in an effort to break inflationary expectations and to force firms to adopt international prices for their products.[44] The new policy began in Chile after 1976 and was followed two years later in Argentina and Uruguay. By 1979 Chilean policymakers were so confident of the correctness of the strategy that the nominal exchange-rate was pegged to the U.S. dollar – an almost unknown experience in Chilean economic history.

Both the exchange-rate policy and the experiment in financial liberalization in the Southern Cone proved to be disastrous. Inflation certainly fell, but neither far enough nor fast enough, so the REER appreciated steadily. Imports exploded, and exports were undermined by the overvalued exchange-rate. The current-account deficit in the balance of payments accelerated and was primarily financed by commercial borrowing from abroad. The unregulated nature of the borrowing produced a boom in consumer credit, so the composition of imports shifted away from producer goods to consumer goods (see Table 10.2). Despite the inflows of capital, domestic interest rates remained extremely high in real terms, and productive investment was crippled.[45] Financial institutions chose to conceal the non-performing nature of many of their loans by additional lending to firms in distress. As foreign lenders became aware of the unsustainable nature of the policies, capital inflows began to decline – thus forcing the authorities

43 On the monetary approach to the balance of payments in the Southern Cone, see Foxley (1983), pp. 114–25.

44 This exchange-rate policy was known as the *tablita*, because a table of exchange rates was regularly published giving the currency's value at future dates. On its role in Argentina, see Sjaastad (1989), pp. 259–64.

45 Real interest rates remained above 10 percent throughout the period of financial liberalization and often exceeded 20 percent. See Ramos (1986), Table 8.11, pp. 154–5.

to adopt emergency measures in support of the balance of payments and provoking a financial crisis.

The failure of the export-substitution strategy provoked a strong reaction in some circles against neoconservative economics in general. To some extent this was justified: The experiment with financial liberalization had proved costly, the assumptions on which it had been based were clearly inappropriate, and some markets had responded in an apparently perverse fashion.[46] Trade liberalization had been more successful, and the performance of nontraditional exports in particular had confirmed the lessons from the EP strategy of the importance of the REER. Nevertheless, the switch to an overvalued exchange-rate – coupled with lower tariffs – provoked such a strong demand for imports that the balance of payments remained a binding constraint that could be relaxed only through dangerously high levels of capital inflows.

The assumption that inflation could be controlled through the monetary approach to the balance of payments and an overvalued exchange-rate was particularly ill considered. The first stages of trade liberalization had increased the importance of exportables without leading to a massive reduction in importables, so the share of tradables in GDP had increased at first.[47] This encouraged the authorities to believe that all prices in the economy could be determined by reference to world prices, tariffs, and exchange rates. However, the overvalued exchange-rate not only discriminated against exports, but also led to widespread deindustrialization as imports replaced domestic production of manufactured goods. The result was a decline in the importance of tradables and an increase in the proportion of GDP accounted for by nontradables, prices of which were determined by domestic supply and demand rather than by world market conditions.

The Southern Cone economies therefore moved even further away from the assumptions on which the inflation-stabilization program had been based. Following the introduction in 1981–2 of drastic measures to protect the balance of payments (including exchange-rate devaluation), inflation rates again began to accelerate at the same time as output fell sharply. The drop in real GDP was exceptionally severe, pushing real income per head down to the level it had been at when the ES strategy began.[48]

The ES strategy failed to achieve any of its targets in either the Southern Cone or Peru. Inflation was not defeated, the balance of payments remained

---

46 The domestic saving rate (the ratio of gross national savings to GDP) remained low, or even fell, despite the incentives provided by high real interest rates. See Ramos (1986), pp. 141–58.

47 Tradables consist of exportables and importables. The former comprise those sectors in which net exports are positive and the latter those sectors in which net imports are positive. On the decline in the share of tradables in the Southern Cone, see Ramos (1986), Table 7.15, p. 133.

48 The drop was particularly steep in Chile, where the ES strategy had been pursued most vigorously. See Fortín and Anglade (1985), pp. 191–5.

a problem, and the growth rate of exports was not sustained. Furthermore, even the years of growth were accompanied by a deterioration in the distribution of income and a decline in real wages. Nevertheless, in its first phase the strategy had reinforced the lesson from the EP strategy: Nontraditional exports could indeed prosper under appropriate incentives.

Primary-export development

The remaining eleven Latin American republics – Bolivia, Ecuador, Paraguay, and Venezuela in South America, together with the five Central American countries, Panama, and Cuba – were not attracted by the ES strategy. At the same time, their fragile industrial base was considered too weak to support an EP strategy based on manufactured exports.

Throughout the postwar period – even in revolutionary Cuba – the basic model had remained export-led growth with ISI grafted on as a subsidiary activity. Many members of this group expected regional integration to put industrialization on a firmer basis by permitting ISI in a regional context rather than in a national context, but by the beginning of the 1970s disillusionment with the model was becoming widespread. Manufacturing was capital intensive, import intensive, and heavily dependent on foreign capital and technology. On the other hand, price stability, underpinned by fixed nominal exchange rates, was the rule rather than the exception, and there was therefore a natural reluctance to promote nontraditional exports in general and manufactured exports in particular through real exchange-rate depreciation.

Although the ES and EP strategies were therefore ruled out, an alternative model was made available by the commodity-price boom in the 1970s. The surge in prices for most primary products created exceptional opportunities for the members of the group – none of which had totally abandoned the traditional model of export-led growth based on mineral or agricultural exports. This strategy, which we may label primary-export development (PED), emphasized foreign-exchange earnings from primary products (together with services in Panama) and gave very little weight to manufactured exports.[49]

The PED strategy sought to take advantage of favorable conditions in international markets. Sometimes this took the form of an increase in the quantity exported (e.g., cotton in Central America);[50] other countries were content merely to reap the windfall associated with higher prices. This

---

49 In all eleven PED republics the share of manufactures in extraregional exports was low. The Central American countries had developed an important intraregional trade based on industrial products, however.

50 The cotton boom in Central America is well described in Williams (1986), Part I.

happened in the case of Venezuelan oil and Bolivian oil and tin, in which prices rather than volumes explained the sharp rise in export earnings.[51] The rise in world sugar prices after 1973 also forced the Soviet Union to raise the price paid to Cuba, so sugar still accounted for more than 80 percent of the island's total exports in 1980 despite the difficulties of increasing volumes.[52] The largest harvest, however, was reaped by countries that were able to increase volumes at a time of sharply rising prices. This happened in Central Ameria in the case of coffee, following the Brazilian frost in 1975 and the collapse of the export-quota system under the International Coffee Agreement (ICA).[53]

The PED strategy also involved the exploitation of new primary products. Bolivia became increasingly dependent on exports of natural gas from the Santa Cruz area after 1972, with a pipeline to Argentina. By the end of the 1970s more than half of all Bolivian exports were destined for the rest of Latin America and nearly 20 percent for its Southern Cone neighbor.[54] New oil production came on stream in Ecuador in 1972 and soon dominated the total value of exports.[55] Paraguay shifted out of meat and timber exports toward cotton and soybeans. Guatemala began to export crude oil in 1980.

Not all of the new exports were recorded. Exports of coca paste, mainly destined for processing plants in Colombia, rose rapidly in Bolivia and Ecuador and provided a stream of narcodollars – which helps to explain the combination of stable exchange rates and high domestic inflation in Bolivia.[56] Contraband flourished in Paraguay, where business circles (including the military) close to President Alfredo Stroessner exploited the country's geographical position and exchange-rate fixed to the U.S. dollar in order to buy from and sell to neighboring countries with fluctuating currencies.

51 Venezuela was restrained by export quotas agreed by OPEC. Bolivia, where unit costs of tin production were comparatively high and where oil reserves were nearly exhausted, was unable to increase output without major new investments; however, Bolivia's first tin smelter came on stream in the early 1970s, so the republic finally began to capture a higher share of the value added associated with tin production.

52 Since 1961 the Soviet Union had regularly paid Cuba above the world price for its sugar imports. The jump in world prices in 1974 forced the Soviet Union to follow suit, but the price paid was not subsequently lowered when the world price started to fall. Thus by the end of the 1970s Cuba was receiving from the Soviet Union a price that was about five times higher than what was available in the world market. See Brundenius (1984), Table 3.9, p. 76.

53 The ICA, established in 1963, was designed to keep prices within a certain range through the use of (variable) export quotas. The Brazilian frost lowered world production so much that export quotas had to be abandoned, however. Even so, the rest of the world was unable to compensate for the Brazilian decline, and prices rose rapidly – far exceeding the upper limit originally set by the ICA.

54 See ECLAC (1989), Table 289, pp. 564–5.

55 The oil boom in Ecuador and its impact on the rest of the economy are thoroughly analyzed in Bocco (1987).

56 For an empirical estimate of the impact of coca on the Bolivian economy, using a computable general equilibrium model, see De Franco and Godoy (1992).

Table 10.3. *Primary-export development countries: unit value and purchasing power of exports, 1970 and 1980*

Country	Unit value of exports in 1980 (1970 = 100)	Purchasing power of exports in 1980 (1970 = 100)	Exports / GDP (1980 prices, in percentages) 1970	1980
Bolivia	585	196	36.9	23.6
Costa Rica	299	150	38.2	33.9
Cuba	425	109[a]	15.5	8.1
Ecuador	278	350	15.6	25.0
El Salvador	292	157	28.8	34.8
Guatemala	275	185	21.1	22.2
Honduras	321	146	41.6	37.8
Nicaragua	282	165[b]	29.5	23.9
Panama	238	455	38.9	45.4
Paraguay	303	167	15.8	13.9
Venezuela	1,234	263	65.4	39.4

[a] Derived from Brundenius and Zimbalist (1989), Tables 9.2 and 9.3, assuming import prices rose at same rate as the Latin American average.
[b] Exports in 1980 were seriously disrupted by the 1979 revolution, so 1978 has been chosen as the reference year.
Sources: Brundenius (1984), Table 3.7, p. 75; Brundenius and Zimbalist (1989), Table 9.2, p. 146; ECLAC (1989), Table 275, p. 504, Table 279, p. 512, and Table 4.3, p. 70 .

The existence of these unrecorded activities must be borne in mind when we examine published statistics.[57] Yet even the official figures suggested a remarkable improvement in the fortunes of the export sector. The unit value of exports improved sharply in the decade after 1970, the value of exports jumped between 500 percent and 1,000 percent, and the purchasing power of exports (PPE) soared (see Table 10.3).[58] Although the steep rise in the price of oil after both 1973 and 1978 favored the main energy exporters (Bolivia, Ecuador, and Venezuela), the net oil importers in the group also recorded an impressive performance aided by high and rising prices for the main primary-product exports.

The abundance of foreign-exchange earnings underpinned exchange rates that had been pegged to the U.S. dollar even before the collapse of the Bretton Woods system. In the decade after 1970 the eleven republics

57 The impact of these illegal activities throughout Latin America has been the subject of wild speculation. For a sober and objective assessment of the impact of the drug trade on Colombia, see Arrieta et al. (1991).
58 The PPE measures the volume of imports that the value of exports can buy. It is calculated either by dividing the value of exports by the unit value of imports or by multiplying the volume of exports by the NBTT.

recorded only four devaluations against the U.S. dollar among them, and nine republics had no such devaluation at all.[59] International Monetary Fund (IMF) standby agreements were comparatively rare, and the degree of conditionality was generally mild.

Yet in general the PED strategy was not a success. Only Ecuador and Venezuela – both oil exporters – raised their share of world exports between 1970 and 1980, although in the Venezuelan case this was due entirely to price rather than to volume changes. Few of the republics expanded export earnings at a rate consistent with the accumulation of foreign debt. Their vulnerability to external shocks was as great as ever, and the weak domestic economy was still not sufficiently resilient to offer any real compensation. The existence of stable exchange rates proved to be an inadequate bulwark against inflationary pressures caused by monetary expansion and higher dollar prices for imports, so the distribution of income deteriorated further in many countries,[60] and the real exchange-rate became progressively overvalued.

The failure of the PED strategy was a particular disappointment for the three energy exporters (Bolivia, Ecuador, and Venezuela), which had most to gain from the massive redistribution of world oil income from consumers to producers after 1973. Venezuela, as a founding member of OPEC, had long believed that a policy of export quotas with high prices was preferable to a free market with low prices. Ecuador, following the establishment of military rule in 1972, shared the same view and joined OPEC in November 1973 – despite the strain this put on its relationship with the United States.

At first the development of energy exports in all three countries had depended heavily on foreign investment. Even Bolivia where Standard Oil had been nationalized in 1937, had offered exceptionally generous terms to Gulf Oil in the 1950s in the hope of promoting exports.[61] Governments in all three countries considered their primary duty to be the extraction of a rising proportion of the economic rent associated with nonrenewable natural products in order to channel resources toward the nonexport sector. This was achieved through reference prices,[62] taxation, and joint ventures, with government revenue increasingly dependent on the energy sector.

---

59 In the post–Bretton Woods era, characterized by floating exchange rates, a peg to the U.S. dollar did not rule out the possibility of depreciation against other currencies. For most of the PED countries, however, the United States was the main trading partner, so a fixed rate to the dollar approximated a stable effective (trade-weighted) exchange-rate.

60 Although a stable inflation rate in an indexed economy need not lead to an increase in income inequality, an acceleration in the inflation rate is almost bound to do so. This is because the lowest deciles typically can only respond with a lag to any increase in the inflation rate.

61 See Philip (1982), pp. 455–60.

62 The purpose of reference prices was to reduce the possibility of transfer pricing by the oil companies as part of their tax-minimization strategies. The reference price was the one adopted in calculating tax liability.

This "rent-seeking" approach had many advantages, but it still left foreign companies in charge of crucial strategic decisions about investment, production, and exports. The rising tide of nationalism proved irresistible, and in all three countries the energy sector finally came to be dominated by state-owned enterprises. Gulf Oil was expropriated in Bolivia in 1969,[63] leaving Yacimientos Petrolíferos Fiscales Bolivianos (YPFB) as the main operator in the energy field. Gulf Oil was also nationalized in Ecuador in 1976 – a rare occasion, on which a foreign company sought its own expropriation.[64] Anticipating the expiration of oil contracts in 1983, the Venezuelan government nationalized its oil industry – dominated by foreign companies since its beginnings in the 1920s – at the end of 1975.[65]

The energy sector proved to be the engine of growth only in Ecuador. Between 1970 and 1980 real GDP rose at an annual rate of 9.7 percent, while GDP per head recorded an impressive 6.5 percent rate of growth. Yet oil wealth led the country's military government to postpone the fiscal reforms that were long overdue, and the overvalued currency made possible by oil ruled out expansion of nontraditional exports. In Bolivia and Venezuela nationalization brought only modest gains: The mining sector's net output barely increased in both countries, and real GDP per head was virtually unchanged in Venezuela after 1970.[66] Both countries were rescued only by the spectacular improvement in the NBTT that pushed real gross domestic income up rapidly and gave the temporary illusion of prosperity.[67]

The windfall gain associated with the rise in energy prices was used by all three countries to try to promote new activities outside the energy sector. Venezuela led the way with nationalization of its iron-ore industry, joint ventures in its metal industry, and the promotion of automobile production. The radical military governments in Ecuador carried out a huge expansion of social investment in health, education, and housing. Bolivia even experimented with import substitution in agriculture (ISA) in an effort to reverse its dependence on imported foodstuffs. In all three countries ambition ran far ahead of what was justified by the (temporary) improvement in the terms of trade. Imports rose so rapidly that each country ran a deficit in the current account of the balance of payments during most of the years of high energy

---

63 See Philip (1982), Chapter 13.

64 See Brogan (1984), pp. 5–6.

65 See Lieuwen (1985), pp. 209–15.

66 GDP per head (in 1988 prices) in Venezuela increased from $4,941 in 1970 to only $5,225 in 1980. This was still the highest in Latin America, although it was below the level in oil-rich Trinidad and Tobago. See IDB (1989), Table B–I, p. 463.

67 Gross domestic income (GDI) is the GDP adjusted for the change in the terms of trade. It is therefore sensitive to the choice of base year. However, if 1970 is chosen as the base, the improvement in the NBTT for energy exporters leads to a rapid rise in GDI in the decade up to 1980.

prices,[68] leaving them dangerously vulnerable to the subsequent fall in the terms of trade.

The five Central American republics faced a different problem. As a net oil importer, the region stood to lose from the oil shocks of the 1970s. Prices of traditional exports (coffee, bananas, cotton, beef, and sugar) increased sharply at various points after 1970, however, so the terms of trade were by no means always unfavorable. Furthermore, the first oil crisis and the rise in price of imported inputs put a squeeze on industrial profits, which encouraged resources to shift away from manufacturing and the Central American Common Market (CACM) and back to primary-product exports.[69] Although the decline of CACM was only relative – total intraregional trade continued to grow[70] – the engine of growth was once again extraregional exports in general and traditional products in particular.[71]

In Central America PED produced a major increase in foreign-exchange earnings. Land rents rose, and the small-scale peasantry that produced food for the home market was squeezed. A similar squeeze on small-scale industry was taking place in urban areas as a result of the rise in costs of imported inputs. The result was a sharp increase in rural and urban proletarianization, with a growing proportion of the labor force dependent on wages.[72]

Although the Central American economies appeared to be booming in the 1970s, the proceeds were unequally distributed. Domestic inflation – virtually unknown in the 1950s and 1960s – began to accelerate, fueled by higher world prices and the explosion in money of external origin as a result of the increase in international reserves. In the absence of defense mechanisms and strong trade unions, the labor movement was unable to protect itself, and real wages fell in the first half of the 1970s.[73] The decline was later reversed in Costa Rica and Honduras, the two republics with the strongest trade unions, but the fall continued in El Salvador, Guatemala, and Nicaragua and contributed in no small measure to the growing social and political tension in those three countries.

The opposition to the Somoza dynasty in Nicaragua was not limited to labor groups and a broad-based movement – dominated by the Frente Sandinista de Liberación Nacional (FSLN) – finally succeeded in overthrowing

---

68 Bolivia and Ecuador were recording deficits in the current account of the balance of payments by 1975 (Venezuela by 1977). See World Bank (1991).

69 See Weeks (1985), pp. 147–50.

70 Intraregional imports suffered a modest decline over the previous year in 1971 and 1975, but in all other years they continued to grow until 1981.

71 The five traditional exports (coffee, bananas, cotton, sugar, and beef) accounted for 84 percent of extraregional exports in 1970. By 1979, after almost a decade of spectacular export growth, these five products represented almost exactly the same share of the total. See Bulmer-Thomas (1987), p. 204.

72 See Bulmer-Thomas (1987), pp. 218–24.

73 See Bulmer-Thomas (1987), Table 10.7, p. 219.

the dictatorship in July 1979.[74] The period of coalition rule was brief, and Nicaragua was soon embroiled in both a civil war and a confrontation with the United States that would destroy the economy in the space of a few years.[75] Civil wars in El Salvador[76] and Guatemala,[77] beginning at the end of the 1970s, added to Central America's grief, and the CACM was an early victim. By 1981 intraregional trade was falling in absolute terms, and the decline continued for several years.[78]

The three remaining republics – Cuba, Panama, and Paraguay – all offered contrasting styles of PED. Cuba, having reversed its hostility to monoculture and dependence on sugar in the mid-1960s, proceeded to build its socialist economy around the preferential prices and other forms of assistance provided by the Soviet Union and its East European allies. Relatively little sugar production reached the world market, so Cuba's shortage of foreign exchange remained acute. However, a Soviet decision to allow Cuba to sell in the free market any Soviet oil not required for domestic consumption stimulated energy-saving measures and rewarded Cuba – briefly – with a handsome dollar income.[79] Coupled with improvements in planning techniques and a switch from moral to material incentives, the Cuban economy enjoyed respectable rates of growth in the 1970s and first half of the 1980s.[80]

Panama's rulers had long recognized that its comparative advantage lay in its geographical position rather than in primary-product exports. Although exports of bananas, shrimp, sugar, and refined oil continued to grow, the real engine of growth in the 1970s was the export of services. Thus the PED strategy in the Panamanian context must be interpreted as meaning the promotion of tertiary exports.[81] The offshore banking center shot to prominence: More than 120 banks were participating by the beginning of the 1980s, and deposits totaled $43.5 billion at their peak in 1982.[82] The

---

74 See Booth (1982), Chapter 8.

75 See Bulmer-Thomas (1990b), pp. 353–65.

76 See Dunkerley (1982) on the origins of civil war in El Salvador.

77 A guerrilla war had been fought in Guatemala since 1960, but the security situation deteriorated markedly at the end of the 1970s. See McClintock (1985), Part III.

78 The decline was so severe that intraregional exports, which had constituted more than 25 percent of total exports at the end of the 1960s, fell below 10 percent by 1986.

79 This change in policy was not adopted until 1981, but it coincided with the peak of oil prices. By 1985 the dollar earnings from oil reexports were three times more valuable than convertible currency earnings from sugar exports to the world market. See Domínguez (1989), pp. 90, 207–8.

80 All commentators are agreed on the superior performance of the Cuban economy after 1970 compared with the previous decade. See Pérez-López (1991).

81 Tertiary exports are service exports (e.g., banking, insurance, and shipping). Thus Panama traditionally runs a huge deficit in the trade account and a large surplus in the service account of the balance of payments. In 1980, for example, the former was $959 million and the latter $649 million. See IDB (1983), Table 42, p. 369, and Table 43, p. 370.

82 On the rise (and subsequent decline) of the international banking center in Panama, see Weeks and Zimbalist (1991), pp. 68–83.

Colón Free Trade Zone became an important transshipment point for goods destined for all parts of Latin America,[83] and a transisthmian oil pipeline allowed Panama to recapture some of the income it lost because supertankers could not use the canal.[84] The number of ships flying the Panamanian flag steadily rose,[85] and the insurance industry was a successful by-product of both banking and shipping.[86]

Although the canal itself had provided the key to Panama's economic development from the first day of the republic's history, its control and ownership had been vested firmly in U.S. hands. The signing of the Carter–Torrijos treaties in 1977 and their ratification by the U.S. Congress in 1979 promised a new dawn: Sovereignty over the Canal Zone reverted to Panama, and Panamanian control was finally achieved in the year 2000.[87] Income from canal operations rose sharply, transactions with the Canal Zone ceased to be treated as if they were foreign trade, and exports from the Colón Free Trade Zone were finally credited to Panama.[88]

In Paraguay PED involved the search for new primary products (cotton and soybeans), which led to a decline in the importance of processed (industrial) exports.[89] However, the engine of growth in Paraguay was not limited to primary-product exports (or contraband) but included also construction. The decision to build two enormous hydroelectric dams (Itaipú and Yacyreta) in conjunction with Brazil and Argentina, respectively, boosted not only the construction sector but also all activities that supplied inputs to construction firms and to their vast labor force.[90] As a result, real GDP

83 At its peak, value added from the Free Trade Zone (i.e., reexports less imports) reached 10.3 percent of GDP. See Weeks and Zimbalist (1991), p. 67.

84 The inspiration for the oil pipeline was the need to find an efficient route by which Alaskan crude, discovered in the 1970s, could reach refineries on the east coast of the United States.

85 The Panamanian flag of convenience was used so widely that the country appeared to have one of the world's largest shipping fleets (37.1 million tons in 1980). However, nearly all of this fleet was owned by foreigners who found the Panamanian flag convenient for tax and employment purposes.

86 At first the service sectors in Panama formed a virtuous circle in which the expansion of one part promoted the growth of the others and encouraged new activities. (Money laundering, linked to the rise of the offshore banking center, also became an increasingly important part of the service economy.) The reverse was also true, however – as Panama found to its detriment in the second half of the 1980s.

87 The details of the treaties are provided in Major (1990) as part of an excellent account of the history of the Canal Zone.

88 In 1979 (the last year of the old system for IMF accounting purposes) Panama was estimated to have commodity exports of $356 million. In 1980 (under the new IMF accounting system) the figure jumped to $2,267 million as a result, above all, of the inclusion of reexports from the Free Trade Zone. Yet in both years the current-account deficit was almost identical. Users of the statistics should note, however, that not all international agencies use the same approach.

89 In large part this shift in the composition of exports was a reflection of low land prices in eastern Paraguay, which encouraged Brazilians – already heavily engaged in production of cotton and soybeans – to invest in the neighboring republic. See Baer and Birch (1984).

90 The boom produced an average annual increase in the net output of the construction sector of more than 30 percent in the last three years of the 1970s. Industry and commerce also grew by more than 10 percent a year in the same period. See Baer and Birch (1984), p. 790.

rose by 8.7 percent per year in the 1970s – a highly creditable performance by any standard.

The PED strategy had its successes, but in far too many countries the commodity-price boom had been treated as if it reflected a new long-run equilibrium. The volatile nature of commodity prices in the 1970s left both the private sector and the public sector unable to distinguish between temporary and permanent improvements in the external environment. Resource shifts into the primary-product export sector, which could not easily be reversed, were implemented on the basis of short-run price changes – an echo of the 1920s policy in many republics. When commodity prices started to fall and the terms of trade deteriorated, too many republics were left dangerously exposed.

Commodity-price increases were widely interpreted as reflections of increases in average or long-run real prices. PED countries responded to favorable external conditions with a huge rise in imports, so the current-account deficit often remained negative even in boom years for exports. The public sector was just as shortsighted as the private sector: Budgets swollen by exceptional levels of trade taxes were treated as normal, and expenditures rose rapidly to eliminate the surplus.[91]

The vulnerability of PED countries to external shock could have been offset by productive investment outside the primary-product export sector. As is shown, some efforts were made, and huge sums were borrowed on the international capital market. Yet most of the investments did not come on stream in time to increase resilience to external shock, much of the finance was wasted, and some republics suffered a serious loss of investment through capital flight.

Even the energy exporters among the PED countries – Bolivia, Ecuador, and Venezuela – suffered the same fate as their less fortunate fellow republics. Much the same was true of Mexico after new oil deposits were discovered in the second half of the 1970s. Although the improvement in terms of trade for energy-exporting countries proved to be longer lasting, it was not permanent. A strategy based on permanently high energy prices was not viable, and a risk-minimizing strategy required the adoption of adjustment programs to prepare for less favorable external conditions. The enormous economic rent associated with energy production could have offered a lubricant for relatively painless adjustment, but the resources were used instead for transfers and subsidies to households and the private sector. The investments required by adjustment were financed by foreign borrowing at a rate that could only be sustained if the improvement in the terms of trade proved to be permanent.

91 Venezuela, for example, ran a large central-government budget deficit even at the height of the oil boom in 1981.

The state, public enterprise, and capital accumulation

The driving force behind Latin America's economic development in the century before the 1930s had been the private sector. Although the domestic capitalist class may at times have played a secondary role to foreign investors, there was no doubting the hegemonic role of the private sector in all decisions to do with production, investment, and even distribution. The state occupied a distinctly secondary role, providing a regulatory framework that favored export-led growth, although members of the private sector still competed fiercely for a share of the rents made possible by state regulation.

The shift from traditional export-led growth to ISI complicated the task of public-policy management. In addition to dispensing privilege and providing a new regulatory framework involving a redistribution of national income, the state was also called on to make a large number of public investments in order to protect the profitability of the new model.

The complexity of the task and the rise of new social groups competing for state power generated frictions between the private sector and the public sector that on occasion undermined both political and economic stability. With rare exceptions, however, the state continued to see its general function as supporting private enterprise, although it was no longer possible to favor all factions of the private sector simultaneously. Thus the opposition of traditional agroexporters to Peronism in Argentina was consistent with state support for private investment in manufacturing, and the expropriation of private estates in Mexico in the 1930s did little to weaken the bond that was forming between the Mexican state and the emerging industrial bourgeoisie.

On those rare occasions when the state was deeply hostile to the private sector or wished sharply to restrict the range of activities left open to private enterprise, the inevitable counterrevolution usually proved triumphant. In Chile the brief socialist experiment after 1970 under President Allende,[92] when private investment collapsed as public enterprises were formed in all branches of the economy, ended in military dictatorship in September 1973 and in an excessive devotion to the virtues of the free market. Earlier flirtations with an enlarged role for the state in Guatemala under Jacobo Arbenz (1951–4),[93] in Peru under Juan Velasco Alvarado (1968–75),[94] or later in Nicaragua under the Sandinistas (1979–90)[95] proved to be only temporary: The private sector restored its economic hegemony after it reconquered state

---

92 The spread of state ownership under Allende is described in de Vylder (1976).

93 Although communist influence during the Arbenz presidency was considerable, the state's role in production remained essentially indirect rather than direct. Nevertheless, the private sector was quick to roll back the frontiers of state intervention after 1954.

94 FitzGerald (1976) provides a thorough analysis of the growth of state intervention under military rule in Peru. The retreat from state intervention is outlined in Thorp (1991), Chapter 5.

95 Nicaragua's state enterprises under the Sandinistas are examined in Colburn (1990).

power. Cuba, guided by the messianic Fidel Castro, was the only republic both to cripple the private sector and to defeat the counterrevolution, leaving the state as the sole source of virtually all investment and in control of production and distribution.[96]

Despite the complaints of some factions of the domestic capitalist class, the relationship between the public sector and the private sector was generally harmonious. The latter looked to the former for privileges, protection, and complementary investments, and the scope of state intervention became broader and more complex with every twist in the prevailing model of development. Yet the resources available to the state to carry out these functions were strictly limited. The ratio of revenue to GDP – a crude measure of tax effort – was low by international standards. The sole exception was Venezuela, where a high share of the oil rent was captured by the state even before nationalization.[97]

The modest tax effort in most of Latin America had a variety of explanations. Agrarian interests had successfully resisted a land tax in the nineteenth century, which pushed the fiscal burden onto regressive indirect taxes. The private sector had been unable to prevent the introduction of income taxes in the twentieth century, and the rate structure was usually progressive on paper, with marginal far above average rates, but exemptions were widespread and evasion (and avoidance), common. In the postwar period developed countries worried about "fiscal drag" (the process by which inflation increased real tax receipts as a result of high marginal tax rates), but Latin American republics worried about the Oliveira–Tanzi effect (the process by which inflation eroded the real value of tax receipts). Moreover, the growth of the urban informal sector – much of the activity of which is not detected by fiscal authorities – undermined the revenue from domestic sales taxes.

Revenue could be supplemented by borrowing, but the weakness of domestic capital markets and the limited access (before the 1970s) to foreign sources of credit put strict limits on the size of deficits that could be financed without major inflationary implications. The result was a ratio of central-government expenditure to GDP that was low by international standards. Indeed, as late as 1975 only four republics (Chile, Panama, Uruguay, and Venezuela)[98] exceeded the average ratio for all developing countries

96 The extent of state control in Cuba went far beyond what had been established even in Eastern Europe. For example, the Cuban revolutionary government, despite the fact that it inherited a distribution system in which small shopowners played a vital role, insisted on 100 percent state ownership in the commercial sector. See Mesa-Lago (1981), Table 1, p. 15.

97 In 1975, the year before the oil industry was nationalized, central-government revenue in Venezuela represented 34.6 percent of GDP. This was approximately three times higher than the percentage in Brazil or Mexico. See IDB (1983), Table 19, p. 356.

98 Five republics, if Cuba is included.

(22.4 percent), and only two (Chile and Panama) exceeded the average for industrial countries (28.6 percent).[99] Even defense expenditures, so often assumed to be the source of much profligacy, absorbed a low proportion of GDP in the mid-1970s (except in Chile and Cuba, where it exceeded 3 percent of GDP).[100]

A conflict thus arose between the extremely limited resources available to central government in most countries throughout the postwar period and the growing demands placed on the state by the private sector. Particular importance was attached to the rate of public investment, because capital accumulation by the state was seen as essential to sustaining a high rate of private investment. The "crowding out" of private investment by public expenditure was seen as much less of a threat than was the absence of profitable private-sector opportunities as a result of the lack of public investment. Furthermore, state intervention had acquired respectability during and after the 1940s, both through the influence of CEPAL and through the impact of project lending to the public sector by the World Bank and other international financial institutions.

The conflict was largely resolved through the expansion of state-owned enterprises (SOEs). Although indirect methods of state intervention, including the growth of provincial and even municipal governments, were not overlooked, the spread of SOEs was seen as the key to raising the rate of capital accumulation. Indeed, when expenditure by SOEs is included with other branches of government (central, provincial, and municipal), the public-expenditure share of GDP (with the exception of neoconservative Chile) is seen to have risen sharply after 1970 (see Table 10.4).

Although the first SOEs dated back to the colonial period, with profitable tobacco and alcohol monopolies providing a useful source of crown (later state) revenue, they had grown in importance after the First World War for a variety of reasons. First, public utilities owned by foreigners had been taken into state ownership throughout Latin America, and by the 1970s very few were still under foreign control. Early in the twentieth century the government of José Batlle y Ordóñez in Uruguay had been the pioneer in the field,[101] even creating public utilities to undermine the monopoly position enjoyed by foreign companies, and the power of foreign-owned public utilities had been finally broken by the wave of nationalizations at the end of the Second World War. This included foreign-owned railways, leaving

99 See IMF (1986), pp. 78–9.
100 In two Latin American republics (Costa Rica and Mexico) the rates of defense spending were among the lowest in the world. The former had abolished its army in 1948; the latter could never have justified the level of defense spending it would need if the United States were to invade, so it settled for a level of spending that was consistent with internal-security needs.
101 See Finch (1981), Chapter 7.

Table 10.4. *Public-sector spending in selected countries, 1970–1980*

Country	Consolidated nonfinancial public-sector expenditure as percentage of GDP			Current and investment expenditure by state-owned enterprises as percentage of GDP		
	1970	1975	1980	1970–1973	1974–1978	1979–1981
Argentina	38.6	46.4	49.1	12.5	17.0	19.5
Brazil	35.9	42.7	52.7	10.4	18.6	25.6
Chile	41.3	40.4	31.6	21.8	31.3	26.1
Colombia	25.9	27.6	29.4	6.4	6.0	8.4
Mexico	22.3	31.9	35.0	11.9	16.4	20.7
Peru	24.5	46.1	60.1	10.1	24.3	32.1
Venezuela	28.7	38.9	53.3	19.3	21.1	28.2

Sources: For all countries except Colombia, Larraín and Selowsky (1991), Table 1.1, p. 2, and Table 8.1, pp. 308–9; for Colombia, derived from IDB (1984b), Table 1, p. 148, and p. 171.

the state as the main investor in the railway network in most republics from the 1950s onward.

Second, the mining industry – for so long a major source of foreign investment – had proved irresistible to governments of a nationalist persuasion. The creation of a state-owned company in the 1940s to extract iron ore in Brazil[102] had been followed by nationalization of the tin industry in Bolivia in the 1950s[103] and by the spread of SOEs throughout the mining sector in Peru after 1968 under military rule.[104] The expropriation of foreign-owned copper companies under Allende in Chile was not reversed by the neoconservative Pinochet administration,[105] and the first administration of Carlos Andrés Pérez in Venezuela (1974–8) established state control over iron ore

102 This enterprise, Companhia Vale do Rio Doce, coupled with the Volta Redonda steel mill, gave the state substantial control over a basic input into the industrialization process.
103 The main target of the revolutionary government in Bolivia after 1952 was the political power of the mining oligarchy (the *rosca*). Because the *rosca* dominated the tin industry, nationalization was seen as the only solution. Other (smaller) mining companies were not affected. See Dunkerley (1984), pp. 56–60.
104 The new SOEs in the mining sector were Petroperú, Mineroperú, and Centromin. In addition, the state created enterprises for sugar exports, food marketing, fishing, energy supply, transport, housing, and finance. See FitzGerald (1976), pp. 47–48.
105 The decision to retain the state copper company, CODELCO, within the public sector was a reflection of the copper industry's vital contribution to the economy. Furthermore, part of the military budget was paid out of the revenue of CODELCO, making the armed forces resistant to any proposal to privatize the industry.

and bauxite production as part of its grand ambitions for diversification of the economy away from oil.[106]

Oil, both crude and refined, was also a favored target for SOEs. Indeed, Argentina had led the way in the 1920s with the formation of Yacimientos Petrolíferos Fiscales (YPF),[107] and Bolivia and Mexico had expropriated foreign-owned oil companies in the 1930s. By the end of the 1970s the state was an active investor in all oil-producing countries, and oil-refining was often in state hands even in oil-importing republics.[108] SOEs in oil, such as PEMEX in Mexico, Petrobras in Brazil, and PDVSA in Venezuela, were among the largest companies in Latin America and even appeared on *Fortune* magazine's list of the world's biggest firms.[109]

Long-term development finance had also proved a popular area for entry by SOEs. With financial repression almost everywhere and high rates of inflation in many countries, private financial institutions preferred short-term loans to favored clients over long-term lending to risky ventures. SOEs began to fill the gap from the 1930s onward with Nacional Financiera in Mexico[110] and CORFO in Chile[111] serving as models for many other countries. Although, on occasion, private commercial banks were taken over by the state, this was usually done to avert bankruptcy and closure. Indeed, before the 1980s only Costa Rica – and, of course, Cuba – had established a state monopoly on bank deposits.[112]

The consumer-goods industries set up under the ISI strategy were dominated by private enterprise, but the same was not true for all intermediate and capital-goods sectors. SOEs were set up in many countries in these branches of industry in order to fill the vacuum left by lack of private-sector interest. The steel industry was a favored candidate for SOEs: Public-sector capital played a leading role in the larger republics, where steel production

---

106 Bauxite is the raw material used in the production of aluminum. Because the conversion process is energy intensive, the abundance of cheap electricity in Venezuela appeared to make the industry suitable for the diversification program. See Rodríguez (1991), pp. 249–52.

107 See Lewis (1990), pp. 53–5.

108 Oil refining in Costa Rica, for example, was nationalized in 1968, although oil distribution remained within the private sector.

109 On the spread of SOEs in the oil industry in Latin America, see Vernon (1981), pp. 98–102.

110 Nacional Financiera, founded in 1934, rapidly expanded to fill the gap left by the unwillingness of the private sector to make long-term loans for development projects. See Brothers and Solís (1966), pp. 26–8.

111 CORFO, founded in 1939, had invested in forty-six companies, with a majority share in thirty-one, even before Allende came to power. See Larraín and Selowsky (1991), p. 93.

112 Nationalization of the banks was one of the first acts of the revolutionary junta that triumphed in the 1948 Costa Rican civil war. Control of credit was seen as crucial for long-term development plans, although it was not unrelated to the desire to strike at the economic heart of the oligarchy, which had been on the losing side in the war. See Cerdas Cruz (1990), pp. 386–7.

was seen as crucial for the dynamism of the industrialization program.[113] A similar argument was used for establishing SOEs in petrochemicals, and "national security" was often invoked to justify SOEs in ship building and arms production.[114]

The spread of SOEs was well illustrated by Brazil, where a dynamic private sector had welcomed the creation of public enterprises both before and after military intervention in 1964. The domestic private sector, MNCs, and the government formed a triple alliance, with public investments designed to improve private profitability and to encourage new private-sector initiatives. By the end of the 1970s Brazil had established 654 state enterprises, 198 of which were at the federal level[115]; the latter were spread across the economic spectrum, and embraced many of Brazil's largest companies. Indeed, 28 of the 30 largest companies in 1979 were SOEs – a huge increase from the 12 of 30 recorded in 1962.[116]

The Brazilian SOEs played a crucial role in determining the profitability of private-sector firms, both domestic and foreign. In the automobile industry, which was dominated by foreign companies, firms had to buy all of their electricity and most of their steel from SOEs, and the demand for automobiles was determined in part by the price of fuel (gasoline and alcohol) set by other public-sector firms and in part by state regulations governing consumer credit. As long as SOEs adopted price and investment policies that were consistent with private-sector profitability, their presence was welcomed by both the foreign and domestic elements of the capitalist class.

Sometimes, however, the formation of SOEs ran counter to private sector interests. State intervention in the production and distribution of foodstuffs, justified by governments in terms of the need to subsidize consumption by the poor, was usually frowned on by the private sector. National airlines, often run by the state for prestige reasons, were an area in which profitable private investment was possible. It was difficult to explain to a skeptical private sector the need for SOEs in tourism or even – as happened in a few countries – in nightclubs. Furthermore, Latin America, like Western Europe, could not escape the ratchet effect, under which a company would be kept in public ownership long after the original reason for its expropriation had ceased to apply.

113 Katz (1987) contains several good chapters (5–7) on steel enterprises in Latin America, including SOEs in Brazil and Mexico and a private-sector firm in Argentina.
114 National security was also invoked to justify the creation of state nuclear power plants in Argentina and Brazil. See Serrano (1992), pp. 51–65. Mexico also began to construct a nuclear power plant at the end of the 1970s, but this was more a reflection of the limitless ambitions unleashed by the oil boom.
115 Most of these enterprises, at all levels of government, were services, and many were research and development activities from which the private sector benefited. See Trebat (1983), Table 3.2.
116 See Evans (1979), Chapter 5.

Yet private-sector discontent with the extent of public ownership in Latin America was limited – until the 1980s. Even the ES countries, with their emphasis on market forces, private enterprise, and foreign investment, were not prepared to roll back the frontiers of the state to any significant degree. Chile carried out a privatization program in the 1970s, but most of this was the reprivatization of activities briefly taken into public ownership under Allende's socialist administration.[117] Indeed, under Pinochet Chile kept a number of industries (including copper) in the public sector, increasing their profitability, lowering their investments, and using the surpluses as an opportunity to lower tax rates on the private sector.[118]

Although the number of SOEs was often large, their contribution to real GDP was usually modest. Only in Venezuela, its economy dominated by oil, did SOEs account for more than 15 percent of net output in the late 1970s.[119] Furthermore, if Venezuela is excluded the average figure for Latin America was below the average both for developing countries and for developed ones. The bulk of value added was generated by the private sector – foreign and domestic – giving the capitalist class (in the absence of high effective rates of direct taxation) a strong influence over the distribution of national income.

The SOEs played a disproportionately important part in the process of capital accumulation, however. The presence of SOEs in capital-intensive branches of activity (e.g., mining and energy), coupled with private-sector preference for activities with low capital–output ratios and short gestation periods, was sufficient to explain most of this imbalance, although examples of wasteful or inefficient investment were by no means unknown. The contribution of SOEs to gross fixed investment tended to exceed its contribution to net output. Indeed, the share of SOEs in capital spending was far higher in Latin America than in LDCs as a whole and was even higher than in developed countries.[120]

Despite the presence of numerous socially profitable opportunities for investment and the lack of opposition from the private sector, public-sector capital accumulation was at first restrained by a shortage of finance. Modest surpluses in the current accounts of the public sector were far from sufficient to finance ambitious investment programs by the different branches of public administration. The profits of SOEs were often reduced by price

117 On the Chilean privatization program in the 1970s, see Edwards (1987), Chapter 4. See also Yotopoulos (1989).

118 This did not, however, rule out the growth of foreign investment in sectors with SOEs (including copper). Indeed, the foreign-investment climate was exceptionally favorable under Pinochet.

119 In Venezuela the share of SOEs in GDP at factor cost was a massive 27.5 percent. See Short (1984), p. 118.

120 The (weighted) average for the Latin American share of SOEs in gross domestic investment at the end of the 1970s was 29 percent, compared with 4 percent in the United States, 11 percent in Japan, and 17 percent in the United Kingdom. See Kuczynski (1988), Table 3.8, p. 54.

controls and sometimes by spiraling costs and even the reinvestment of profits could be blocked by the statutory requirement to make transfers to the central government.

This financial constraint was finally relaxed in the 1970s with the growth in international bank lending. Indeed, loans to the public sector – both general government and SOEs – were even more attractive for foreign banks than were loans to the private sector, because the former always carried a public guarantee of repayment. Large SOEs in the major Latin American countries were the most favored clients; in Mexico, PEMEX received a huge proportion of all new loans. SOE spending as a proportion of GDP rose steadily (see Table 10.4). As the financial constraint was relaxed, the contribution of the public sector to gross fixed capital formation soared. Only Chile, where the state had been responsible for virtually all new investment in the first half of the 1970s, experienced a decline in public-sector contribution to capital formation.[121]

The result was an impressive rate of gross fixed capital formation in Latin America in the 1970s. Although only Venezuela regularly achieved a rate of investment (as a proportion of GDP) of more than 20 percent in the 1950s, the average for Latin America never fell below 21 percent in the 1970s and exceeded 23 percent in every year between 1974 and 1981.[122] The investment rate, which had often compared unfavorably with other regions, at last began to reach the level required for long-run rapid growth of real GDP per head. The rate was not sustainable, however; the base, rooted in the shifting sands of international bank lending, was to prove extremely fragile and collapsed in the 1980s. Furthermore, the fall in bank lending not only reduced the scope for public investment but also undermined the whole model of capital accumulation on which Latin America's development had become based.

Debt-led growth

The defaults in the 1930s had effectively cut Latin America off from the private international bond market on which the region's foreign financing had heavily depended. Although both the scope and the sophistication of international capital markets had developed rapidly after the 1940s, the market for Latin American bonds remained of trivial importance. Some private-portfolio capital reached Latin America early in the postwar period, but it was mainly in the form of short-term trade credits at commercial rates of interest.

---

121 See Short (1984), pp. 115–22, for figures on individual countries.
122 See Wilkie (1990), Table 3437, p. 1057.

Direct foreign investment in Latin America had certainly increased after the 1940s and was at first widely welcomed by host governments that were anxious to increase access to foreign sources of capital. The financial contribution of MNCs to Latin America proved to be a disappointment, however. The capital was often raised locally, many investments represented the purchase of an existing firm, and there was no guarantee that the seller would reinvest the proceeds locally. Furthermore, the inflow of foreign direct investment in any year was often exceeded by the cumulative outflow of foreign exchange as a result of profits remitted abroad and payment of royalties.

As a capital-scarce region, Latin America expected to borrow from abroad to supplement the domestic savings needed to finance capital accumulation. A deficit in the current account of the balance of payments could legitimately be considered the "normal" state of affairs, provided it could be financed by autonomous (and voluntary) capital inflows. Yet the difficulty of increasing net inflows of private capital – portfolio or direct – left Latin America heavily dependent on official sources of foreign borrowing in the first two decades after the Second World War. As late as 1968 official sources of capital accounted for 60 percent of the region's public external debt.[123]

Official borrowings could be either bilateral or multilateral. The former referred to borrowings from a single country (e.g., the Export–Import Bank or the U.S. Agency for International Development) and the latter to loans from sources controlled by different countries. Multilateral sources had become important when the IMF and the World Bank were established at the Bretton Woods Conference, and the creation of the Inter-American Development Bank (IDB) in 1961 had added a third international financial institution (IFI) of great importance to Latin America.

In the 1960s ALPRO had given a boost to official capital flows to Latin America, and the IFIs in particular had increased their exposure. Bilateral flows (mainly from the United States) remained the most important, however, so the loss of interest in ALPRO by the administrations of Lyndon Johnson and Richard Nixon might have had serious implications for Latin America's foreign-financing needs.

That it did not do so was due to changes in the international financial system which made it attractive for foreign banks to lend to Latin America from the end of the 1960s onward. The origin of this policy change can be found in the formation of the eurodollar market,[124] which generated a huge pool of international liquidity under the control of international banks and for which new borrowers had to be found. Financed at first by U.S. trade

---

123 See IDB (1983), Table 58, p. 383.

124 The term "eurodollar" can be misleading, for it is often used to describe any currency holding outside the issuing country. Thus a Japanese yen deposit in the Panamanian international banking center can sometimes be included, as can U.S. dollar deposits in a London financial institution.

deficits and later swollen by the huge U.S. budget deficits associated with the Vietnam War, the stock of eurocurrency deposits jumped from $12 billion at the end of 1964 to $57 billion at the end of 1970.[125]

The growth of the eurocurrency market was only a first step in the transformation of bank lending to Latin America. The second was the spread of branch and representative offices of international banks in the Latin American market. Led at first by U.S. financial institutions (particularly Citicorp), the return of branch banking to Latin America after a long absence allowed foreign banks to service their corporate multinational clients in the region.[126] It also provided an invaluable conduit between Latin America and head offices for information about local conditions and profitable lending opportunities.

Because of the widespread defaults in the 1930s, however, inhibitions about the desirability of bank lending to Latin America remained. These inhibitions were finally overcome as a result of two changes in lending practices at the end of the 1960s. The first involved the use of syndicated loans, which allowed banks to spread the risk of lending to foreign countries over a large number (up to 500 in some cases) of lending institutions. The second involved the shift to flexible interest rates: Henceforth, debt contracts would require the borrower to pay a fixed premium over a reference rate of interest (e.g., the New York prime rate) that changed according to market conditions.

The combination of syndicated lending, flexible interest rates, and large premiums made lending to sovereign countries – previously dismissed as too risky – highly profitable. Citicorp's lending to Brazil alone accounted for 13 percent of its total profits by 1976.[127] Bank lending jumped from 10.5 percent of Latin America's public external debt in 1966 to 26.1 percent in 1972, with almost half the increase in the debt accounted for by loans from foreign banks.[128]

The first oil crisis further stimulated this profitable lending. The stock of eurocurrency deposits, swollen by petrodollars transferred from importers

---

125 See Griffith-Jones (1984), Table 5.3, p. 42.

126 See Stallings (1987), pp. 94–102.

127 See Sachs (1989), p. 8.

128 Debt figures are subject to a great deal of confusion, for a variety of reasons. First, it is necessary to distinguish between the public external debt and private external debt: The former refers to all debt (incurred by both the private sector and the public sector) that carries a state guarantee of repayment; the latter does not carry any public guarantee. Thus the total external debt contains an element of nonguaranteed private debt. Second, it is necessary to distinguish between commitments and disbursements, because there is often a considerable difference as a result of delays in releasing funds, suspension of payments, and so forth. Third, it is necessary to distinguish between short-term debt and long-term debt: Obligations that mature in less than 12 months are usually treated as short-term. It should be pointed out, however, that the share of bank lending in total debt – irrespective of its definition – grew rapidly in the 1970s.

to exporters of oil, jumped to $205 billion by the end of 1974. The second oil crisis provided another boost, and eurocurrency deposits stood at $661 billion by the end of 1981. Throughout the decade after 1973 the banks had to find new sources of profitable lending quickly. Latin America, where the initial growth of syndicated loans had proved so successful and where the international banks were now represented through a network of local offices, was an obvious market.

The willingness – indeed, eagerness – of the banks to supply Latin America with new loans could not be questioned. Yet Latin America was equally enthusiastic about receiving the loans. Thus the supply of and demand for loanable funds generally marched in tandem, although on occasion the banks' eagerness led to sales techniques that fell far short of normal professional and ethical standards.[129]

The demand for bank loans by Latin American borrowers stemmed from a variety of causes. By the end of the 1960s dissatisfaction with direct foreign investment had reached a peak, as reflected in Decision 24 of the Andean Pact; MNCs were needed, it was conceded, for their technological expertise in certain areas, but they could not be relied on to finance balance-of-payments deficits. New sources of capital were required. At the same time, official capital flows were in decline as a result of the demise of ALPRO.

Bank loans had an additional advantage over other sources of portfolio capital – they were virtually free of conditions. Whereas most Latin American governments had struggled to meet IMF conditionality at one time or another, new loans from the international banks came with very few strings attached. Indeed, the banks were unaware of the purposes for which most of their loans were used: Nearly 60 percent of all U.S. bank lending in the 1970s was devoted to "general purpose," "purpose unknown," or "refinancing."[130] Although SOEs were the major recipients of bank loans, central governments were also beneficiaries, with loans contracted for financing deficits in the budget, the balance of payments, or both.[131]

A final reason for the enthusiasm for bank loans was provided by the external shocks created by the two oil crises. For the oil importers (e.g., Brazil), access to bank lending without conditions offered a means of financing the balance-of-payments deficit implied by the higher price of oil without painful stabilization and adjustment programs and without sacrificing high rates of GDP growth. For the oil exporters, the high price of oil provided an opportunity either to expand oil production (e.g., Ecuador and Mexico) or to diversify the economy away from its dependence on oil

129 See Roddick (1988), pp. 24–34.
130 See Stallings (1987), Table 10, p. 131.
131 Nearly two-thirds of all U.S. portfolio investment in Latin America in the 1970s went to public and private corporations. Most of the remainder went to central governments. See Stallings (1987), Table 9, p. 128.

through massive investments in the non-oil economy (e.g., Venezuela). In both cases the scale of planned investment was far in excess of domestic resources and required access to foreign loans.

The banks were not the only source of new loans for Latin America – in the 1970s official capital flows also benefited from the growth of world liquidity – and by no means all bank lending went to the public sector. Thus all classes of debt grew rapidly. Wherever possible the banks looked for a public guarantee on loans, even if they were destined for the private sector. The Pinochet administration in Chile refused to give such a guarantee, however,[132] and Venezuela's abundant oil reserves were thought to make such guarantees unnecessary. Furthermore, banks were still prepared to lend to private-sector companies without public guarantees in the larger republics: One-quarter of all debt in both Argentina and Brazil at the end of 1982 was in the form of private, nonguaranteed, long-term loans.

The banks' enthusiasm for lending to Latin America did not extend equally to every republic. Their preference was overwhelmingly for lending to the large countries – Argentina, Brazil, Chile, Colombia, Mexico, and Venezuela. Their efforts to lend to Colombia were largely rebuffed until the administration of Julio César Turbay Ayala (1978–82), however, as a result of the republic's long conservative tradition in fiscal affairs.[133] As late as the end of 1982 Colombia still owed more than half its debt to the World Bank and other official creditors.

In fact, the banks' interest in the smaller republics was quite limited. With the exception of Costa Rica, Panama, and Uruguay, these countries continued to depend heavily on official sources of capital. El Salvador and Guatemala, for example, owed approximately 90 percent of their debt to official sources at the beginning of the 1980s and the proportion was above 50 percent in Bolivia, the Dominican Republic, Haiti, Honduras, Nicaragua, and Paraguay. The total debt of most of the smaller republics still grew rapidly, however, as a result of the increase in official capital flows and some bank lending.

The growth in Latin American debt from the late 1960s onward (see Table 10.5) was very fast. Nevertheless, at least until the second oil crisis, in 1978–9, it was sustainable because the nominal rate of interest on the debt was below the rate of growth of nominal exports. High levels of international liquidity, coupled with recession in the developed countries after the first oil shock, kept nominal rates of interest below the world rate

132 When it became clear that the financial system was on the verge of collapse because it could not make interest payments on the unguaranteed debt, the Pinochet regime intervened in 1983 to provide a guarantee as part of the refinancing package. See Ffrench-Davis (1988), pp. 122–32.

133 See Ocampo (1987) on the initial reluctance of the Colombian state to accept the new loans that banks were so eager to provide.

of inflation. Export earnings in Latin America soared as a result of higher prices for commodities. Thus Latin America could borrow internationally the resources it needed to pay the interest on the debt without running the risk of an unsustainable increase in the debt–export ratio. Only Peru, suffering from gross mismanagement of its fiscal and monetary affairs, ran into debt problems in the 1970s;[134] however, a rescue plan worked out with the IMF and the banks coincided with a boom in the NBTT at the end of the decade, so international creditors were able to delude themselves into thinking that the problem had been solved.

The second oil crisis proved to be a watershed in global economic management. The developed countries went into recession, bringing down the price of commodities and producing a sharp deterioration in the NBTT for Latin America's oil importers. This time, however, the developed countries tackled their structural imbalances through tight monetary policy, pushing world interest rates up to astronomical levels. By 1981 base rates in London and New York were more than 16 percent, which pushed the rate of interest payable on bank debt close to 20 percent.[135] With the growth of Latin America's export earnings slowing down sharply after 1980 and with receipts peaking in 1981 for both oil and non-oil exporters, debt-led growth was no longer sustainable.

Astonishingly, however, the banks and other creditors continued to lend even after the second oil crisis. Between the end of 1979 and 1982 (see Table 10.5), the stock of Latin American debt jumped from $184 billion to $314 billion. Inevitably, the debt–export ratio deteriorated sharply. As late as 1980 this ratio had been below 200 percent – a crude indicator of sustainability – in twelve republics. By 1982 only three republics (Guatemala, Haiti, and Paraguay) were so favored. Furthermore, the debt–service ratio – the proportion of export earnings required to pay interest and principal on the debt–jumped from a feasible 26.6 percent in 1975 to an impossible 59 percent in 1982 (see Table 10.5).

The continuation of lending to Latin America after the second oil crisis gave rise to an unprecedented import boom. Within the space of a few years imports had more than doubled, and the current-account deficit – despite the rise in the value of oil exports – had widened to $40 billion in 1981. Even more disturbing was the acceleration of capital flight – most of it illegal – as private agents in many Latin American republics lost confidence in public policies and anticipated currency devaluation. By the end of 1982 the foriegn assets of the private sector in Argentina, Mexico, and Venezuela

---

134 See Thorp and Whitehead (1979), pp. 136–8.
135 Even the U.S. real rate of interest was close to 10 percent. See Thorp and Whitehead (1987), Table 1.1, p. 3.

Table 10.5. *External debt indicators, 1960–1982*

Year	A	B	C	D
1960	7.2[a]	16.4	17.7[a]	3.6[a]
1970	20.8[a]	19.5	17.6[a]	5.6[a]
1975	75.4	42.9	26.6	13.0
1979	184.2	56.0	43.4	19.2
1980	229.1	56.6	38.3	21.2
1981	279.7	57.6	43.8	26.4
1982	314.4	57.6	59.0	34.3

Key: A = Total public, private, and short-term external debt, in billions of U.S. dollars;
B = Banks' share of public external debt (%);
C = Ratio of service payments (interest and amortization) to exports (%); and
D = Ratio of interest payments to exports (%).
[a] External public debt only.
Sources: CEPAL (1976), p. 25; IDB (1983), Tables 56, 58–60; (1984b), Table 1, p. 12, and Table 5, p. 21; (1989), Table E–6.

were estimated to be at least half the value of each country's public external debt.[136]

All warning signs were ignored by debtors and creditors until it was too late. Costa Rica and Nicaragua faced major debt problems in 1980, but both were dismissed as of limited relevance to the rest of Latin America.[137] The spectacle of oil-exporting countries – above all, Ecuador, Mexico, and Venezuela – facing current-account and budget deficits despite the enormous rise in oil prices was not considered grossly imprudent. The widespread deterioration of debt–service and debt–export ratios did not at first cause alarm. Only in 1982, as the value of exports from Latin America started to fall from its peak level of the previous year, did the pace of lending slacken. The terms of trade of non-oil exporters deteriorated sharply as the world recession drove down commodity prices. Ironically, however, it was an oil-exporting nation that precipitated disaster. When Mexico – no longer able to service its debt – threatened default in August, the debt crisis had finally arrived.

136 No definition of capital flight is completely satisfactory, but all estimates suggest that these three countries were the worst affected. See Sachs (1989), Table 1.5, p. 10.
137 See Bulmer-Thomas (1987), pp. 237–52.

11

Debt, adjustment, and the shift to a new paradigm

The Mexican government's August 1982 threat of default on its external public debt was the trigger that finally unleashed the debt crisis. The net flow of bank lending to Latin America ground to a halt, and the net transfer of resources suddenly turned negative. Even countries like Colombia, which had been prudent about accumulating foreign-debt obligations,[1] were affected as private financial institutions in the developed countries reversed their previously optimistic forecasts concerning Latin America.

The decline in bank lending set in motion a chain of events that was to lead by the end of the decade to a New Economic Model (NEM), based on exports, for the majority of republics.[2] The transition to a new trajectory was not painless and was far from complete even in those countries that were prepared to carry out the most far-reaching program of reforms. Yet countries had few alternatives, for the logic of the situation demanded a response from governments all along the political spectrum. The old growth model, based on a central role for the state in the process of capital accumulation, was attacked on one side by the decline in capital flows to state-owned enterprises (SOEs) and on the other by the emerging consensus in favor of neoliberal economics and a smaller state.

The NEM emerged in part as a pragmatic response to the series of adjustment and stabilization programs adopted in each republic in the 1980s. Forced by the negative transfer of resources to accumulate trade surpluses, Latin American republics finally gave higher priority to the question of export promotion, which had been on the agenda in most republics since the 1960s. Unable to borrow funds abroad, governments also began to address the problems of fiscal reform, inefficient state-owned enterprises, and indiscriminate subsidies.

---

1 Although subject to much the same pressure to accept new commercial bank lending as elsewhere in Latin America, Colombia was slow to accumulate debt until the administration of Julio César Turbay Ayala (1978–82). See Ocampo (1987), pp. 240–4.
2 On the NEM, and its principal components, see Edwards (1995), Bulmer-Thomas (1996), Thorp (1998), and Stallings (2000).

The NEM also reflected the unprecedented agreement among international financial institutions (IFIs), academics, and governments in the developed countries in favor of free markets, trade and financial liberalization, and privatization of public enterprises. This orthodoxy,[3] despite its fragile theoretical and empirical underpinnings, overwhelmed the remaining Latin American voices that supported inward-looking policies and an interventionist state. Governments that were ostensibly committed to shrinking the boundaries of the state came to power throughout the region, and the intellectual climate in Latin America turned sharply in favor of free-market economics. Research institutes and universities that were committed to the new orthodoxy flourished, while traditional centers that advocated even a reformed version of the old model were steadily eclipsed. Only in the area of hyperinflation, a phenomenon far removed from the experience of the developed countries, and in stabilization programs to fight it could an authentic Latin American voice still be heard.

The emergence of a new growth model transformed most areas of economic policy. Trade was liberalized, financial markets were deregulated, and public enterprises began to be offered for sale to the private sector. Those Latin American republics that had not yet joined the General Agreement on Tariffs and Trade (GATT) or its successor the World Trade Organization (WTO) applied for membership,[4] and several republics joined the Cairns Group in pursuit of free trade in agriculture.[5] The Latin American voice, previously almost inaudible, began to be heard in international trade negotiations, and the largest countries made clear their ambition to seek First World status.

Nowhere was the change in attitude more apparent than in relations with the United States. Although the U.S. invasion of Panama in December 1989 was condemned,[6] the points of friction between Latin America and the United States were steadily eroded. As the Cold War ended and the socialist experiment in Eastern Europe and the Soviet Union collapsed, Cuba became more isolated, and traditional U.S. security concerns, less pronounced. Drugs replaced communism in U.S. foreign-policy priorities, and drug-control programs necessitated a high degree of cooperation between the United States and many Latin American republics. The U.S. war

---

3 The new orthodoxy was first captured in an influential book by Bela Balassa, Gerardo Bueno, PedroPablo Kucynski, and Mario Henrique Simonsen, which was translated into Spanish and Portuguese and which circulated widely in Latin America. See Balassa (1986).

4 By 2000 all Latin American countries had become members of the WTO.

5 The Cairns Group was formed by those countries with agricultural exports that were particularly badly affected by nontariff barriers and those favoring a move toward free trade in agricultural products. Latin American members of the Group included Argentina, Brazil, and Uruguay.

6 The U.S. invasion was the culmination of a long campaign by both the Reagan and Bush administrations to remove Manuel Noriega from power in Panama. Unlike the invasion of Grenada in 1983, it was not covered in a multilateral cloak and was seen throughout Latin America as an unacceptable abuse of power in a post-Cold War environment. See Weeks and Zimbalist (1991), pp. 136–55.

on terrorism, following the tragic events of 11 September 2001, provided further opportunities for close cooperation between Latin America and the United States.

Trade liberalization also brought North America and South America closer together. Driven by the imperative of seeking markets for their non-traditional exports, many Latin American republics nonetheless feared the arbitrary nature of a world trading system in which protectionist voices remained powerful.[7] Access to the US market was seen as the key to successful export promotion, while the United States saw in hemispheric integration an opportunity to press its own trade agenda while locking Latin American governments into economic reforms that might otherwise have been reversed. The North American Free Trade Agreement (NAFTA), launched by Canada, Mexico, and the United States in 1994, was the first illustration of this new approach while the Free Trade Area of the Americas (FTAA), negotiations for which began in earnest in 1998, was the most ambitious goal.

By the beginning of the new millennium, the NEM had taken shape throughout Latin America. Economic reforms, many of them painful, had been adopted and the role of the state in economic activity had been much reduced. In contrast to the 1980s, there was some improvement in living standards in the 1990s. However, Latin America still suffered from many of the same problems. The region remained vulnerable to economic shocks and this vulnerability had been exacerbated by the impact of globalization – the process under which world product and factor markets had become increasingly integrated. Income distribution had not improved in most countries and the absolute numbers of those living in poverty continued to rise. The evidence to suggest that the shift to a new paradigm would bring about an improvement in growth and equity, both in comparison to Latin America's past and in comparison with emerging markets in Asia, was exceedingly thin.

From debt crisis to debt burden

At the time of the threatened Mexican default in August 1982, many of the major international banks had such high levels of exposure to Latin America that their financial viability was thought to be at risk. By the end of 1982 the ratio of Latin American loans to equity was in excess of 100 percent for sixteen of the eighteen leading international banks in Canada and the United States. Between them, these eighteen banks had extended

7 The Uruguay Round of GATT negotiations, launched in 1986 and finally completed in 1993, allowed the DCs to maintain a high level of protection against agricultural imports and delayed until 2005 the elimination of quotas on textiles and clothing.

nearly $70 billion in credits to the region, and one bank (Citicorp) had provided more than $10 billion.[8]

The high levels of exposure of the main international banks persuaded governments in the advanced countries to take a keen interest in the Latin American debt crisis. In the 1930s the appeal by private bondholders facing default had been met with public indifference, but in the 1980s the response of governments was swift and determined. The U.S. administration led the way, driven in part by the threat to the stability of the international financial system and in part by fear of the consequences of economic collapse in Mexico.[9]

Under the leadership of the Reagan administration a de facto creditors' cartel had soon been formed among the private and official (bilateral and multilateral) lenders to Latin America in an effort to establish a common set of rules that would nurse the debtors back to health while avoiding a major international banking crisis. Small banks, with little exposure to Latin America, were actively discouraged from reaching unilateral solutions with creditor countries, for they could have had serious implications for more exposed financial institutions. With as many as 500 banks involved in a single large loan, the task of representing the private creditors in all negotiations had to be delegated, and a small Bank Advisory Committee was set up for each country.

Creditor discipline was enforced not only by the existence of bank advisory committees but also by frequent formal and informal meetings between banks, governments, and IFIs. The role of the IFIs proved to be particularly important. As the institution responsible for its members' balance-of-payments problems, the International Monetary Fund (IMF) came to acquire a higher profile than it had ever enjoyed in its dealings with Latin America. As policy reform moved to the top of the agenda, the World Bank – now committed to structural and sectoral adjustment loans as well as to more traditional project lending – also acquired a key role in the design of strategies for handling the debt crisis.

The maintenance of creditor discipline did not, of course, guarantee the authority of the creditors' cartel. Latin America had a long history of default, which could not have provided much ground for optimism to any banker with a knowledge of the past. Yet the debtor countries at first accepted the rules of the game set down by the cartel and in most cases serviced their debts – despite the considerable economic and political costs – promptly and in full.[10] Even loans to the private sector, which had not received a

8 See Griffith-Jones, Marcel, and Palma (1987), Table 2.

9 Economic collapse in Mexico implied an increase in migration to the United States and massive political instability on the U.S. border. It is widely believed that if the debt crisis had begun further south (e.g., Argentina), the U.S. response would have been different. See Díaz-Alejandro (1984).

10 The exceptions (e.g., Nicaragua) were minor, and the sums involved did not represent any threat to the international financial system.

public guarantee (very important in Chile and Venezuela), were serviced, although in the Chilean case this was possible only after the government of Augusto Pinochet had intervened in the heavily indebted private banking sector in 1982–3 to avoid a probable financial collapse.[11]

That the debtor countries were willing to act in such an orthodox fashion can be attributed to the unwritten agreement both sides had appeared to reach by the end of 1982. The willingness of most debtor governments to meet their obligations stemmed from the belief – widely held by all parties to the negotiations – that the financial crisis was one of liquidity and not of solvency. The series of external shocks that had hit the region since the end of the 1970s (see pp. 346–52) and that had brought about the deterioration in the debt–service ratio was deemed to be temporary. Thus the continuation of new lending to Latin America would relieve the liquidity problem and grant the region a breathing space until external conditions became more "normal." Nominal interest rates (e.g., the U.S. prime rate) were expected to fall, the developed countries – that is, those belonging to the Organization for Economic Cooperation and Development (OECD) – were expected to resume growth, and primary-product prices were expected to recover. All of this, it was assumed, would create the conditions for an improvement in the debt–service ratio by lowering interest payments and increasing exports.

Provided private and official creditors were prepared to reschedule existing debts and to continue lending new money, Latin American governments were persuaded that a dignified exit from the debt crisis could be made. The creditors, however, made it clear that their cooperation would only be forthcoming in return for macroeconomic discipline and policy reform. Debt rescheduling, together with the prospect of new lending, was therefore made conditional on an agreement with the IMF – and often the World Bank as well – and the accumulation of arrears was only permitted in exceptional cases.

The conditionality of debt rescheduling and new lending thrust both the IMF and the World Bank into a key position. Cooperation between the two institutions and with creditor governments reached new heights. Little by little dissatisfaction with past Latin American economic policies began to crystallize into a coherent vision (the "Washington consensus") of what the creditors felt was appropriate for the region.[12] Stabilization and adjustment programs were adopted under the watchful eye of both the IMF and the World Bank in an effort to establish the macroeconomic and microeconomic conditions that would make debt servicing possible. Only a few countries were unaffected, either because rescheduling proved

11 State intervention in the banking system was in complete contrast to the privatization program favored by the Pinochet dictatorship throughout its existence. See Whitehead (1987), pp. 126–37.
12 The Washington Consensus was outlined in an influential book by Williamson (1990).

unnecessary (e.g., Colombia) or because political circumstances ruled out IMF support (e.g., Nicaragua).

At first the bargain struck between debtors and creditors appeared to succeed. World interest rates fell, growth was resumed in the developed countries, and the volume of Latin America's exports started to climb. The U.S. economy in particular experienced rapid growth after 1982, which created a massive boom in imports. In an ill-concealed attempt to reward its friends and punish its enemies, the Reagan administration created the Caribbean Basin Initiative (CBI), which gave duty-free access on a wide range of goods to numerous small countries in, or on the fringes of, the Caribbean Sea.[13] By mid-1985 the oil-importing countries in the region were benefiting from a significant weakening of petroleum prices.[14]

Yet the unwritten agreement suffered from two major problems. First, the increase in the volume of exports did not produce an increase in earnings as a result of the weakness of commodity prices – a reflection in part of the strength of the U.S. dollar.[15] The net barter terms of trade (NBTT) deteriorated in the first half of the 1980s for almost all republics, and the increase in export volumes was not sufficient to compensate for the fall in prices. The value of the region's exports in 1985 was no higher than in 1981, and a year later – after oil prices fell – it was nearly 20 percent lower. The debt–service ratio failed to improve,[16] and the liquidity crisis remained as grave as ever.

Second, the willingness of creditors to reschedule did not guarantee new lending. Official creditors – especially the international financial agencies – at first increased their lending to Latin America, but private sources began to dry up. Small banks proved particularly awkward, and new money packages for major debtors were held up for months as a result of the reluctance of a few creditors to increase their exposure. Furthermore, the new loans from official creditors had to be repaid, so that by 1987 even the three main IFIs were net recipients of capital from Latin America.[17]

13 The CBI, which began to function in 1984, at first excluded Guyana and Nicaragua, because of the tension between the governments of those countries and the Reagan administration. Membership was possible only after an improvement in diplomatic relations.

14 Latin America as a region is a net oil exporter and therefore benefits from high oil prices. However, the majority of countries are net oil importers, so more countries gain than lose when oil prices fall.

15 Because most commodity prices are denominated in dollars, world demand is negatively affected by an appreciation of the dollar, and commodity prices, ceteris paribus, tend to fall. This was only one of the factors behind the weakness of commodity prices in the first half of the 1980s, however. See Maizels (1992), pp. 7–20.

16 The debt–service ratio measures the proportion of exports devoted to payment of interest and principal on the debt. It is not an ideal measure of the debt repayment capacity, but it is the one most widely used. Between 1982 and 1988 the debt–service ratio exceeded 40 percent in every year and only fell below 30 percent after 1989. See IBD (1992), Table E-12.

17 The main IFIs for Latin America are the Inter-American Development Bank, the IMF, and the World Bank.

Numerous efforts were made to improve the efficiency and flexibility of debt renegotiations. A secondary market in bank debt began to appear, which allowed small banks to unload their unwanted exposure and reduced the number of creditors involved in reschedulings. Both creditors and debtors welcomed the adoption of "exit bonds," which allowed marginal creditors to depart in return for a paper loss on their loan. Debt–equity swaps, with the debt acquired in the secondary market, were used by some countries to convert external public debt into ownership of real assets, and debt conversions used the same mechanism to replace external debt with internal (domestic) debt serviceable in local currency. Debt-for-nature swaps – canceling debt in exchange for environmental improvements – became fashionable, and Harvard University even pioneered debt-for-scholarship schemes.

All of these innovations had merit, but they could not disguise the underlying problem. Without significant flows of new credits, Latin America was transferring to the rest of the world far more in interest and profit remittances than it was receiving in net capital inflows. This resource transfer, which had yielded an average positive inflow of $13 billion a year between 1979 and 1981, turned sharply negative in 1982 and remained so for the rest of the decade. By the mid-1980s the negative resource transfer had reached some $30 billion – equivalent to 4 percent of regional GDP and 30 percent of exports.

The negative resource transfer was aggravated by capital flight – much of which was not captured in official statistics. Even before the debt crisis broke, the private sector in many Latin American countries had begun to accumulate a significant stock of financial assets abroad (mainly in the United States) in response to interest-rate differentials, exchange-rate risk, and political uncertainty. Those countries with weak or nonexistent exchange controls were particularly affected, but even draconian rules on capital outflows (as in Brazil) could not prevent some financial hemorrhage.

The flight of capital continued after 1982 despite the tightening of exchange controls in all republics and was not limited exclusively to the very rich. Thousands of small savers in Argentina, Mexico, and Venezuela used foreign bank accounts to hedge against political and economic uncertainty. The decision by the Mexican government to convert dollar-denominated accounts in Mexico into pesos, following the nationalization of the banking system in 1982, was particularly badly received by a middle class that was facing high rates of inflation for the first time in many years. In 1983 alone, flight capital from Argentina, Brazil, Chile, Mexico, and Venezuela was estimated at $12.1 billion.[18] By the middle of the decade the stock of

---

18 The measurement of capital flight is fraught with problems, but all estimates agree that it was very significant in this period. For one estimate, see Felix and Caskey (1990), Table 1.7, p. 13.

foreign (mainly dollar) financial assets in the hands of the private sector in Argentina, Mexico, and Venezuela was almost as large as the debt owed to commercial banks by the public sector.

The negative net resource transfer, further aggravated by unrecorded capital flight, put a severe strain on the unwritten agreement between debtors and creditors. The need to transfer abroad such a high proportion of exports obliged all of the republics to adopt harsh and unpopular measures to curb imports. The expected renewal of voluntary bank lending never materialized, and the arm-twisting efforts of official creditors suffered from diminishing returns. By mid-1985 it was clear to all the main participants that the strategy was not working. As the leading creditor nation, the United States finally accepted the need for a new initiative.

The first public recognition that the position of the debtors was unsustainable came in 1985 with the announcement of the Baker Plan. Named after the U.S. Secretary of the Treasury at the time, the Baker Plan identified the crisis as one of liquidity rather than solvency, but the additional resources provided under the scheme were quite inadequate. By February 1987 Brazil had declared a moratorium and international banks rushed to declare their Latin American loans as value impaired. This forced them to make loan-loss provisions, but these were cushioned by permission from the fiscal authorities in their countries to write them off against tax.

The Baker Plan was followed by the Brady Plan in 1989, named after Nicholas Brady who succeeded James Baker as U.S. Treasury Secretary. This scheme was more radical as it offered private creditors a menu from which they could choose provided that they had met the conditions for adjustment stabilization agreed with the IMF. The most popular choice was to exchange the nominal value of bank debt for bonds with a lower face value with collateral provided by zero-coupon Treasury bills. These Brady bonds, as they were immediately dubbed, allowed banks to exit from their exposure to Latin America and therefore brought to an end the 1980s debt crisis.

It did not, of course, end the problem of indebtedness. The debt now took the form of bonds rather than bank loans, but the export sector in most countries was still very small in relation to both the size of the economy and the debt itself. Indeed, many commentators at the time argued that the Brady Plan, like the Baker Plan, was too little and too late.

We shall never know whether the critics were right or wrong as the Brady Plan was soon overtaken by events. For reasons discussed below, the main Latin American countries were suddenly the beneficiary of new capital inflows starting in 1990 that reversed the negative net transfer of resources for most of the decade. Instead of foreign currency scarcity, there was – at least until the Asian financial crisis in 1997 – foreign exchange

Table 11.1. *Total disbursed external debt[a] (US$mn):1990–2000*

	1990	1995	2000
Argentina	62,233	98,547	146,200
Bolivia	3,768	4,523	4,461
Brazil	123,439	159,256	236,157
Chile	18,576	22,026	36,849
Colombia	17,848	24,928	35,851
Costa Rica	3,924	3,889	4,050
Cuba	8,785[b]	10,504	11,100
Dominican Republic	4,499	3,999	3,676
Ecuador	12,222	13,934	13,564
El Salvador	2,076	2,168	2,795
Guatemala	2,487	2,936	3,929
Haiti	841	902	1,170
Honduras	3,588	4,242	4,685
Mexico	101,900	165,600	149,300
Nicaragua	10,616	10,248	6,660
Panama	3,795	3,938	5,604
Paraguay	1,670	1,439	2,491
Peru	19,996	33,515	28,353
Uruguay	4,472	4,426	5,492
Venezuela	36,615	38,484	31,545
Latin America	**434,565**	**609,504**	**733,932**

[a] Includes the public- and private-sector external debt. Also includes International Monetary Fund loans.

[b] 1993.

Source: ECLAC (2001), p. 761.

abundance. Some governments even issued new bonds in order to retire the Brady bonds.

The result was a surge in external indebtedness just after the Brady Plan was supposed to have ended the debt crisis (see Table 11.1). The main Latin American countries experienced a build-up of debt that was even greater than in the period before 1982. This time the creditors were largely anonymous, as they were bondholders rather than banks, making a coordinated creditor response almost impossible.

The capital inflows in the first half of the 1990s were mainly portfolio. Only one-third consisted of Direct Foreign Investment. A few countries, notably Chile, adopted restrictions on short-term capital inflows,[19] but most were only too happy to capture whatever foreign resources were available.

19 On Chile's approach to capital inflows at this time, see Labán and Larráin (1994)

The result was a dangerous increase in speculative capital and an excessive dependence on foreign capital for the financing of domestic investment.

The first evidence that the increase in debt was unsustainable came with the Mexican financial crisis in 1994. Dubbed the first such crisis of the twenty-first century by Michel Camdessus (the IMF's Director at the time), the Mexican crisis led to an unprecedented rescue package mounted by the IMF and coordinated by the United States. Mexico avoided default and the spreads on Latin American bonds returned to their previous levels, but it was an ominous warning of the difficulties that lay ahead.

This *tequila* crisis, as it was widely known, only temporarily reversed the net inflow of capital to Latin America, which continued almost unabated until the end of 1998. At this point the 1997 Asian financial crisis, coupled with the Russian default in August 1998, led to a reassessment by creditors of Latin American risk. Thus, the ability of governments and companies in Latin America to borrow their way out of difficulty came to an end as the century closed.

There have been three circumstances under which Latin American countries have been able to cope with the new debt reality. First, some countries (see below) have been able to increase the size of their export sectors in relation to GDP. Just as South Korea escaped the 1980s debt crisis because it was able to export its way out of trouble, so a handful of Latin American countries have been able to bring down the ratio of debt and debt servicing to exports through rapid growth of the export sector.

Second, some countries – for reasons explored below – have been able to finance a growing proportion of their current account deficits through DFI rather than debt. This "Asian" adjustment has been particularly helpful in Brazil where DFI after 1995 was sufficient to cover almost all financing needs. Indeed, Brazil became in the late 1990s the largest recipient of DFI in the developing world outside of China.

Third, many Latin American countries are too small to be attractive to foreign private creditors. Portfolio investors will not invest in equity markets with small turnover and little liquidity. Governments of such countries find it difficult to issue bonds. As a result, most smaller Latin American countries have been dependent on official sources of capital, which is subject to strict conditions as well as being rationed.

The generalized debt crisis of the 1980s did not, therefore, repeat itself in the 1990s, even if some countries had very serious debt problems. Brazil came close to a moratorium in 1998 before the devaluation of the *real* in January 1999 and faced further difficulties in mid-2002 in the run-up to the presidential elections. Ecuador defaulted on its Brady bonds in 2000 and Argentina defaulted on all its foreign debt at the end of 2001. The Argentine default caused a major financial crisis in the country and led many to argue that it heralded another generalized debt crisis in Latin America.

This did not happen, although contagion from Argentina proved to be very serious in Uruguay.[20]

External adjustment

The switch in 1982 from a net positive transfer of resources to a net negative one had enormous implications for Latin America. Despite the emphasis on inward-looking development since the 1930s, the region was still vulnerable to external shocks. Indeed, the combination of high financial exposure through external debt and relatively low trade dependence made the impact of the decline in capital flows severe. Although some countries in East Asia (e.g., South Korea) also suffered from debt problems, they had a much larger external trade sector with which to carry out the necessary adjustments. On the other hand, other countries with low trade dependence (e.g., India) did not suffer from the same degree of indebtedness. The Latin American combination – most marked in the larger republics – was particularly dangerous.[21]

In order to reverse the sign of the resource transfer, the external account had to be adjusted quickly. The balance of payments can be summarized as follows:

Credits	Debits
Exports of goods/services (E)	Imports of goods/services (M)
Net transfer receipts (T)	Net factor payments (F)
	Current-account deficit (B)
Net capital receipts (K)	Net fall in international reserves (R)

Interest payments on the external debt are included in net factor payments (F). Thus the balance-of-payments current-account deficit (B) can be written as follows:

$$B = (E + T) - (M + F) \qquad (11.1)$$

The equality between total incomings and outgoings means is expressed as follows:

$$E + T + K = M + F + R \qquad (11.2)$$

---

20 Brazil also faced a major debt problem in 2002, but this had less to do with contagion from Argentina and more to do with the increase in the risk premium associated with the presidential elections at the end of the year.

21 This contrast between Latin America and Asia is made by Fishlow (1991).

Table 11.2. *Net barter terms of trade, 1980–2000 (1995 = 100)*

	1980	1985	1990	1995	2000
Argentina	133.4	108.9	97.2	100.0	108.8
Bolivia	209.4	207.1	114.5	100.0	112.0
Brazil	67.2	56.4	60.3	100.0	91.5
Chile	177.9	137.4	84.1	100.0	73.6
Colombia	131.1	120.0	94.8	100.0	115.8
Costa Rica	78.2	80.3	71.7	100.0	95.8
Dominican Republic	178.3	147.3	97.4	100.0	102.0
Ecuador	264.9	210.3	141.1	100.0	123.8
El Salvador	77.5	53.6	69.3	100.0	82.7
Guatemala	112.6	79.2	97.9	100.0	84.7
Haiti	198.5	178.6	116.4	100.0	88.1
Honduras	116.5	99.5	80.9	100.0	103.8
Mexico	329.0	185.5	109.2	100.0	107.4
Nicaragua	126.2	96.1	119.1	100.0	77.3
Panama	115.8	102.7	69.1	100.0	99.8
Paraguay	57.0	52.1	86.6	100.0	84.2
Peru	200.0	137.6	92.5	100.0	80.9
Uruguay	85.3	85.9	100.2	100.0	86.2
Venezuela	240.7	227.1	141.6	100.0	157.4
Latin America	**161.6**	**125.5**	**94.4**	**100.0**	**103.6**

Source: ECLAC (2001), pp. 508–509.

Because external adjustment cannot be implemented in the long run by falls in reserves, R can be set to zero. After rearrangement we therefore find the following:

$$(F - K) = (E + T) - M \qquad\qquad (11.3)$$

The left-hand side $(F - K)$ is the (negative) net resource transfer, and the right-hand side approximates the trade balance.[22] Thus the switch from a positive inflow to a negative net resource transfer of $30 billion implied a trade surplus of approximately the same amount. Because the (positive) net transfer of resources (a trade deficit) in 1980 had been some 2 percent of gross domestic product (GDP), adjustment to the debt crisis required a massive shift in the external accounts equivalent to 6 percent of GDP for the region as a whole.

The adjustment problems associated with the creation of such a large trade surplus were made worse by the deterioration of the NBTT after 1980 (see Table 11.2). The recession in the developed countries at the beginning

22 The trade balance is $(E - M)$. Thus the right-hand side of equation (11.3) is the trade balance adjusted for net transfer receipts (T).

of the 1980s – the consequence of tight monetary policies and high real and nominal interest rates – took a heavy toll on the prices of Latin America's non-oil commodity exports. With most commodity prices denominated in dollars, the strength of the U.S. currency in the first half of the 1980s was a further blow to Latin America's export prices. Finally, oil and gas prices went into a sharp decline at the end of 1985, bringing serious problems for Latin America's main hydrocarbon exporters (Bolivia, Colombia, Ecuador, Mexico, Peru, and Venezuela).

The speed with which external adjustment had to be carried out, coupled with the deterioration in the NBTT, made it inevitable that the trade surplus would be secured primarily by import suppression. Export promotion, given the history of antiexport bias in many Latin American republics, could not generally be achieved quickly, and the world recession at the beginning of the 1980s was hardly a propitious climate for launching an export drive. Both the United States and the European Community (EC) – the two main markets – were subject to intense protectionist pressures that affected both traditional and nontraditional exports from Latin America. Sugar exporters were particularly badly hit by the additional support given by the U.S. government to domestic production, which led to a sharp decline over the 1980s in the U.S. sugar-import quota. Voluntary export restraints (VERs) proliferated in the EC, damaging the opportunities for nontraditional exports by the larger Latin American republics. International commodity agreements, which had helped to sustain prices above free-market levels, ran into further difficulties: The tin and coffee agreements collapsed, pushing world prices down to very low levels.[23]

Import suppression, despite its heavy social and economic costs, was familiar territory for all Latin American republics. A formidable arsenal of weapons had been forged over the years to control the demand for imports and to ration available foreign exchange. Quotas, licenses, high tariffs, and prior-import-deposit schemes were still widespread in most countries, and bureaucratic delays in processing requests for foreign exchange were legion.[24] Furthermore, the explosion in commercial lending to some Latin American republics had undoubtedly created an unsustainable boom in nonessential imports, which could be cut back quickly. In Mexico, for example, the value of imports had risen from $6.3 billion in 1975 to $24 billion in 1981.

All of the traditional weapons were used in an effort to suppress imports. Import tariffs were raised in many countries. Even countries such as Chile, which had reduced tariffs substantially in the period before the debt crisis,

---

23 The tin agreement collapsed in October 1985, with particularly severe implications for Bolivia. See Latin America Bureau (1987). The coffee agreement collapsed in 1990, with adverse effects on all coffee exporters.

24 A case study of Colombian import controls is provided by Ocampo (1990), pp. 369–87.

were forced to reverse trade-liberalization measures. Quotas and licenses were tightenened, and Brazil pressed ahead with the ambitious import-substitution programs it had launched after the first oil crisis to reduce dependence on imported energy.

The scale of the adjustment required meant that traditional weapons were not sufficient, however. No country could afford to neglect export promotion, despite all the difficulties, so measures needed to be taken that could suppress imports without harming exports. The exchange-rate, which so often had been overvalued, became a key instrument in external adjustment programs in many countries. Nominal devaluation was pushed to the point that real effective exchange-rate depreciation (RERD) was assured, providing a disincentive against imports and simultaneously a boost to exports. By the middle of the 1980s, the only republics that had suffered real exchange-rate appreciation were those still committed to a fixed nominal exchange-rate (El Salvador, Haiti, Honduras, and Panama) and those suffering from hyperinflation (Bolivia and Nicaragua).

The impact of these measures was considerable. The trade balance, which had been negative until 1982, became positive, with a surplus of $30 billion recorded in 1983 and nearly $40 billion in 1984. Although the measures taken to promote exports had some effect, with the volume of exports rising after 1982, the deterioration in the NBTT left the value of exports virtually unchanged. Thus the burden of adjustment to a large trade surplus was at first borne entirely by import suppression, and the value of imports fell from a peak of $100 billion in 1981 to $60 billion in 1983 – a level that was sustained for the next three years.

The cut in imports fell on both extraregional and intraregional imports. Many intraregional imports were vulnerable, in view of the fact that the goods usually competed with domestic production. Venezuelan imports from Colombia, which had traditionally provided the core of Andean Pact intraregional trade, collapsed after 1981. Intraregional imports in the Central American Common Market (CACM) fell by 60 percent in the six years after 1980 as nontariff barriers escalated and the political crisis deepened. Even where intraregional imports continued, payment could not always be guaranteed, and intraregional debts became a serious problem. Argentina regularly failed to meet payments on Bolivian natural-gas imports, and Nicaragua's consistent failure to pay for goods imported from the rest of Central America was a major contributor to CACM's crisis. Because one country's intraregional imports were another's exports, the fall in intraregional trade did nothing to ease the burden of regional external adjustment.[25]

The huge expansion in the export and reexport of drugs from many republics also played its part in easing the burden of external adjustment

25 Intraregional imports declined even more rapidly than extraregional imports, so their share of the total was reduced to 13.3 percent by 1990. See ECLAC (1992), Table 92, p. 151.

without being recorded in the official statistics. Although the estimates varied enormously, the flow of foreign currency into Colombia from the sale of cocaine was one of the factors behind the relatively modest fall in imports. By 1986 Bolivian imports had overtaken their level in 1980 for similar reasons. Money-laundering from drugs became an important feature of the Panamanian economy in the mid-1980s, and the reexport of narcotics played a significant role in Costa Rica, Guatemala, and Mexico.[26]

Import suppression was effective, but it was a short-term strategy with high costs. As inflation began to accelerate and real incomes continued to fall, it became clear that import suppression could not be used as a long-term response to a debt crisis that showed no signs of abating. By the mid-1980s an important policy change was taking place in a number of republics in favor of trade liberalization and export promotion in order to meet the demands of both debt servicing and renewed growth. As the decade came to a close, more and more republics opted for the new outward-looking strategy based on export-led growth. By the beginning of the 1990s a new trade orthodoxy had swept across Latin America, embracing all but a handful of republics.

Several factors contributed to the emergence of the new orthodoxy. It came to be recognized that the debt crisis was more than a short-run liquidity problem, that the commercial banks were not going to continue to lend to Latin America at the same rate as before, and that the region was going to have to compete for scarce funds in the international marketplace with other countries (including the United States, where the persistent balance-of-payments and budget deficits were a magnet for world savings). Even those Latin American countries that were successful in attracting foreign investment (direct and portfolio) did not expect to avoid an overall negative transfer of resources, and this was more likely to be combined with the renewal of growth in a strategy that emphasized export promotion rather than import suppression.

The emphasis on the need for export promotion was shared by the official creditors, including the IFIs. The World Bank and the IMF in particular, together with the U.S. Agency for International Development (USAID), used the leverage provided by conditionality to push the debtor countries in the direction of trade liberalization. An oversimplistic interpretation was given to export-led growth in East Asia and to inward-looking development in Latin America, from which the IFIs drew the conclusion that trade liberalization would quickly lead to renewed growth.[27] The pressure from

---

26 On the impact of the drug trade in Latin America, see Joyce and Malamud (1998). For case studies of Colombia and Bolivia, see Steiner (1999) and Gamarra (1999) respectively.

27 As a result of pressure from the Japanese government, the World Bank eventually produced a much more nuanced study of Asia. See World Bank (1993).

the IFIs was not sufficient on its own to persuade countries to move toward export-led growth, but it did contribute to the momentum in favor of trade liberalization in those countries in which an internal consensus in support of policy reform was emerging.

Microeconomic considerations were also important in explaining the policy shift. Few if any policymakers favored export-led growth on the basis of traditional exports. Priority was to be given to new nontraditional exports, including manufactured goods, in which Latin America was at a disadvantage because of the high cost of many commodity inputs caused by import suppression and other trade distortions. Trade liberalization was expected to bring the cost of material inputs closer into line with international costs, allowing local firms to exploit the long-run dynamic comparative advantage provided by the abundance of unskilled labor and natural resources.

The Southern Cone countries had experimented with export promotion policies in the 1970s, but these had been overwhelmed by the debt crisis and went into reverse. It was not until 1984 that Chile once again felt confident enough to return to the trade liberalization policies she had adopted so aggressively after 1975. Ecuador flirted briefly with tariff reductions in 1984, but Congress – not for the first time in recent Ecuadorian history – stymied the neoliberal instincts of the executive.

The most important shift away from ISI, however, came in Mexico in 1985 with the decision by the de la Madrid administration to join GATT. At a stroke, the quantitative restrictions that had underpinned Mexican industry for decades came under fire and a program of tariff reductions was also agreed. Those other Latin American countries that had not yet applied to GATT all did so in the following years so that by the end of the century every Latin American and Caribbean country except the Bahamas was a member of the the WTO.

The Mexican government's decision had less to do with globalization, a word that had only just been coined, and more to do with the need to expand the export sector. Paradoxical though it may seem, reducing tariffs and NTBs is often the first step toward promoting exports. The reason is the impact of import restrictions on the exchange-rate, which tends to become overvalued, and the increase in costs of export production from high tariffs on imported inputs.

Mexico's trade liberalization policies led to a deepening of the trade links with the United States and a rapid expansion of exports (see Table 11.3). The non-oil share of exports, most of which goes to the United States, went from 20 percent in the early 1980s to 80 percent in the early 1990s. At that point Mexico began to negotiate its entry into the free trade agreement launched by the United States and Canada in 1989. The result was NAFTA, which came into force on 1 January 1994. This has led to a further deepening of the trade ties between Mexico and the United States to the point where

Table 11.3. *Volume of exports of goods, 1985–2000 (1995 = 100)*

	1985	1990	1995	2000
Argentina	49.3	70.3	100.0	136.2
Bolivia	42.6	79.8	100.0	119.1
Brazil	71.3	79.6	100.0	137.4
Chile	36.7	63.3	100.0	159.6
Colombia	39.9	78.3	100.0	118.0
Costa Rica	36.6	54.7	100.0	190.1
Dominican Republic	18.5	21.3	100.0	160.4
Ecuador	42.3	55.9	100.0	99.3
El Salvador	78.0	66.2	100.0	195.0
Guatemala	71.3	73.9	100.0	178.4
Haiti	96.0	141.1	100.0	220.7
Honduras	60.5	90.5	100.0	146.8
Mexico	27.6	53.1	100.0	205.7
Nicaragua	75.1	62.9	100.0	166.3
Panama	47.6	79.9	100.0	92.3
Paraguay	19.6	39.2	100.0	58.8
Peru	64.9	69.7	100.0	165.7
Uruguay	51.4	82.2	100.0	135.0
Venezuela	52.1	76.2	100.0	122.8
Latin America	44.7	65.3	100.0	159.8

Source: ECLAC (2001), pp. 504–505.

Mexico now accounts for half of all trade between the United States and Latin America.[28]

This bilateral trade is not, however, typical of trade between the United States and Latin America. Mexico's trade with the United States consists mainly of manufactured goods and is largely intraindustry. Indeed, of the ten most important manufactured exports from Mexico to the United States, nine feature in the ten most important manufactured imports from the United States.[29] And Mexico has now become very dependent on exports to the United States, which account for 25 percent of GDP. Not surprisingly, Mexico went into recession in 2001 as a result of the economic slowdown in its northern neighbor.

Elsewhere in Latin America, trade liberalization has been much less successful in promoting exports (see Table 11.3). Tariffs have been reduced everywhere and some countries such as Bolivia and Chile have adopted a uniform tariff. However, export performance has been overwhelmingly affected by the value of the real exchange-rate. After the 1980s this often moved in the "wrong" direction. When trade barriers are reduced, the real

28 See Bulmer-Thomas and Page (1999)
29 See Bulmer-Thomas (2001a)

exchange-rate should depreciate, providing an additional incentive to exporters. However, in many cases this did not happen.

Why was the movement in the real exchange-rate so perverse? In many countries trade liberalization occurred just as capital returned to Latin America. The net inflows pushed up the value of the real exchange-rate and encouraged imports, but not exports. This was the problem in Mexico from 1990 to 1994, in Argentina after 1991 and Brazil from 1994 to 1998. As a result, export performance in many countries has been modest and Latin America's increasing share of world exports is mainly due to Mexico.

The disappointing performance of the export sector was one of the reasons for the reevaluation of regional integration. The schemes established in the 1960s had been discredited by the debt crisis, as they were so strongly associated with ISI – albeit at the regional level. However, a new attempt was made in the 1990s to launch integration schemes that would promote exports without encouraging protection against third countries. The Central American Common Market was relaunched in 1990, the Caribbean Community (CARICOM) in 1992 and the Andean Pact (renamed the Andean Community) in 1995. CEPAL denoted this revival of integration as "open" regionalism in contrast to the "closed" regionalism of the 1960s and 1970s.[30]

The most innovative new integration scheme was the Mercado Común del Sur (MERCOSUR), formally adopted in 1991. Linking Argentina, Brazil, Paraguay, and Uruguay (Bolivia and Chile became associate members in 1996), it had a clear political purpose as well as economic objectives. When the Clinton administration announced in 1994 U.S. support for a Free Trade Area of the Americas (FTAA), MERCOSUR was quick to negotiate as a bloc in order to prevent the United States from dominating the hemispheric agenda on regional integration. However, MERCOSUR's early promise was not fulfilled. The common external tariff was never adopted in full and the scheme suffered from the economic instability brought about both by external shocks and the absence of macroeconomic coordination.[31] Regional trade, as in the rest of Latin America and the Caribbean, failed to rise above 20 percent of total trade.

Trade liberalization is only one of the ways in which Latin America has adjusted externally. Just as important has been the liberalization of the capital account of the balance of payments and a new approach to foreign capital. The old hostility to DFI, so strong in the 1970s, has gone and country after country has introduced new legislation to promote DFI with very few sectors or activities reserved for foreign capital.

As part of this new approach to DFI, all Latin American governments have divested themselves of state-owned enterprises (SOEs). A few of these

30 See Devlin and Estevadeordal (2001)
31 See Bouzas and Soltz (2001)

behemoths still exist, particularly in the oil industry, but they are now the exception rather than the rule. Even Cuba has participated in this process of privatization with the added twist that the purchase of the assets is restricted to foreigners. Elsewhere domestic private groups have been active in the purchase of SOEs, but so have foreigners. As a result, the stock of DFI has surged in public utilities, airlines, railways, and steel companies and other sectors where SOEs were previously common.[32]

It is perhaps in the mining sector that the transformation has been most marked. Latin America has a long history of discrimination against DFI in mining, going back to the formation of YPF (an oil monopoly) by the Argentine state in 1922 if not before. The rationale for this was complex and included resentment at foreign company practices, rent-seeking by cash-strapped governments and nationalism. Yet, nearly two centuries after the end of colonialism in most of Latin America, it is still the mineral resources that most attract foreign companies. Thus, Latin America had little choice but to liberalize access of foreign capital into the mining sector if it wanted to receive DFI.

The liberalization of the capital account has not been limited to DFI. On the contrary, for most of the 1990s the foreign investment coming to Latin America was private portfolio capital. This was not in the form of bank lending, the dominant form of foreign capital in the 1970s, but bonds and to a lesser extent equity. Trade credits from banks and other short-term loans continued, but in general the international banks were only too quick to seize the opportunity for exit offered by the Brady bonds.

The growth of the international bond market was dramatic and the main Latin American governments and companies tapped into it with relative ease. They were given a head start by the issuance of Brady bonds that transformed what had become almost an exotic form of Latin American debt into one with broad appeal. Furthermore, this foreign currency market was open to nationals (both companies and individuals), providing a welcome hedge against devaluation and an opportunity for portfolio diversification.

The international bond markets offered Latin America an opportunity to issue debt at lower real interest rates than in the shallow domestic financial markets. This was so even after making allowance for expected exchange-rate movements provided that the country risk premium could be held to a moderate level. Governments therefore put a huge effort into reducing the risk premium through sophisticated "road shows" in New York and London as well as greater transparency on the fiscal accounts and rules on company disclosures.

These efforts did not go unrewarded by the ratings agencies. By the beginning of the new millennium Chile had been given an A- on its long-term foreign currency debt, Colombia – despite the high levels of domestic

---

32 On the new approach to foreign investment in Latin America, see the articles in Baer (1998).

violence – received a B+ as did El Salvador, which had been embroiled in civil war as late as the early 1990s. The ratings agencies were more circumspect about the big three (Argentina, Brazil, and Mexico), although Mexico was rewarded with investment grade status during 2000 as the era of the one-party state finally came to an end.

The ratings, modest country risk premiums, and low international interest rates all encouraged Latin American governments, as well as larger companies, to switch out of domestic currency debt into foreign bonds. The result was an unhealthy expansion of external indebtedness in many countries, particularly Argentina and Brazil, that were vulnerable to a widening of the risk premium and any unwillingness of the bond markets to refinance. When Argentine difficulties finally surfaced in 2000, the country was found to account for 25 percent of all emerging market fixed interest debt.

If Latin America's attempts to tap into the international bond market were too successful, the opposite was true of its efforts to attract equity capital. All attempts to broaden the appeal of the local stock markets failed. Only a small number of stocks were listed, most domestic companies preferring to remain 100 percent controlled by their family shareholders. Most of the listed stocks were not actively traded so that liquidity was a serious problem. The larger firms sought a listing as American Depositary Receipts (ADRs) on the New York exchange and mergers and acquisitions by foreign companies led some of the most important companies to delist. By 2000 only two markets – São Paulo and Mexico City – had any appeal for foreign investors and stocks in these markets accounted for 80 percent to 90 percent of the typical Latin American fund.

Latin America's liberalization of the capital account was therefore very problematic. Many of the smaller countries remained unattractive to foreign capital regardless of what they did, while DFI flowed primarily to mineral extraction and former SOEs. Assembly plants set up by foreign companies flourished in parts of the Caribbean Basin, but this was a reflection of temporary tax breaks in the United States more than anything else. The larger countries, on the other hand, became too dependent on the foreign currency bond market. Mexico was the first to suffer (in 1994), but was rescued by its international creditors and was able to use currency depreciation to build up a massive export capacity. Argentina and Brazil were not so fortunate.

Internal adjustment, stabilization, and the exchange-rate problem

By reducing the flow of new capital to Latin America the debt crisis forced each republic to cut imports and, if possible, increase exports quickly. This external adjustment was mirrored by a process of internal adjustment that was designed to lower aggregate demand to a level consistent with the reduced level of imports and to provide the price and other incentives for a shift of supply from the home market to the world market.

The trade surplus provided the foreign exchange for the net transfer of resources to the creditors in the developed countries. The trade surplus in most countries accrued to the private sector, however, whereas most of the external debt was in the hands of the public sector. Thus an internal transfer problem arose, in which the public sector had to secure access to the foreign exchange earned by the private sector. Only in those republics, such as Chile, Mexico, and Venezuela, with a high share of export earnings accruing to SOEs was the internal transfer of resources relatively straightforward.[33]

Internal adjustment was therefore a complicated process involving a reduction in aggregate demand, a shift in supply, and an internal transfer from the private sector to the public sector. Each element of adjustment ran the risk of aggravating inflationary pressures. If aggregate demand fell too slowly, excess demand would emerge even in a recession, because the cut in imports after 1981 had reduced aggregate supply quickly. The shift in supply from the home market to the world market implied a change in relative prices that was likely to cause an increase in absolute (nominal) prices.[34] Finally, the internal transfer of foreign exchange to the public sector would be highly inflationary if the government printed money to secure control of the resources rather than using tax revenue to generate a sufficient level of public savings.

The problem of internal adjustment was therefore inseparable from both external adjustment and inflation stabilization. At the same time, most Latin American republics entered the debt crisis with serious problems of internal instability, including high levels of inflation. In 1981, the last year before the eruption of the debt crisis, only five republics (Chile, the Dominican Republic, Guatemala, Honduras, and Panama) enjoyed annual inflation rates of less than 10 percent, and in each case the exchange-rate was pegged in nominal terms to the U.S. dollar. Of the remaining republics,[35] five had annual inflation rates between 20 percent and 50 percent, three between 50 percent and 100 percent, and one (Argentina) above 100 percent.

Central-government budget deficits had also begun to increase before the debt crisis, and in 1981 almost half the countries had a deficit in excess of 5 percent of GDP, with only Chile and Venezuela running a budget

33 This is no doubt one reason why governments committed to privatization were reluctant to transfer ownership of mineral companies generating huge foreign-exchange receipts. Even in Pinochet's Chile, the state-owned copper company remained in public hands.

34 Because nominal prices for domestic goods and services are rigid downward, a change in relative prices implies a change in absolute prices.

35 International comparisons of inflation rates almost always exclude Cuba, partly because data are lacking and partly because most markets in Cuba are not cleared through price adjustments.

surplus. Public-sector deficits, which included the losses of SOEs and the deficits of municipal and state administrations, were usually even larger than those of the central government.[36] With domestic capital markets in many republics unwilling or unable to absorb large issues of government paper, the inflationary consequences of even modest budget deficits could be considerable.

External adjustment led to a sharp cut in imports and domestic recession, with severe implications for government revenue. Smaller republics, still dependent on import duties for a high share of government revenue, suffered particularly from the decline in imports. Although at first tariff rates were increased in several republics, this could not offset the impact of the sharp decline in the value and volume of imports. The recession drove many firms and workers from the formal sector to the informal sector, making it more difficult for the state to extract direct and indirect taxation from the production and distribution of goods.[37] At the same time, incentives to encourage a shift of supply from the home market to the world market often implied a tax reduction for exporters. Not surprisingly, central-government revenue as a proportion of GDP fell in most republics in the first years of the crisis.

Although cuts were made in public expenditures as a result of numerous stabilization programs, the difficulty of increasing revenue after the debt crisis meant that few if any republics were able to generate a primary surplus large enough to finance out of income the purchase of foreign exchange from the private sector for debt servicing.[38] Furthermore, many countries operated a multiple exchange-rate system in which the public sector was able to "buy" foreign exchange at a special rate, which implied huge exchange-rate losses for the central bank.[39] These losses typically did not enter into the definition of the budget deficit, so the latter often gave a misleading impression of fiscal and monetary orthodoxy.

Many countries simply printed money in order to purchase the foreign exchange needed for debt servicing. However, the largest republics (Argentina, Brazil, and Mexico) were able to issue bonds or other financial instruments to the private sector as a means of carrying out the internal transfer. Although in theory this was noninflationary, in practice it had serious inflationary consequences. First, the nominal and real domestic rate of interest had to rise sharply to persuade the private domestic sector to absorb government debt. Second, the debt itself was highly liquid (particularly in

36 See Larraín and Selowsky (1991), Table 8.1.

37 See Cardoso and Helwege (1992), pp. 231–6.

38 The primary budget balance is calculated before deduction of interest payments. Thus a primary surplus is needed if an overall budget deficit is to be avoided.

39 A good example is provided by Costa Rica, where the official exchange-rate (used for debt payments by the government) remained at 20 colones per U.S. dollar after 1982 but the interbank rate and free market rates steadily depreciated. See Consejo Monetario Centroamericano (1991), p. 38.

Brazil), so it was virtually quasi-money. Third, the internal debt rose so rapidly that nominal interest payments began to absorb a growing proportion of government revenue and undermined the public sector's financial balance. Both Argentina and Brazil eventually declared a partial default on their internal debt, temporarily destroying private-sector confidence in the domestic capital market and raising the cost of future borrowing for the government.[40]

By the mid-1980s inflation was substantially higher in almost all republics than it had been before the debt crisis. As inflation accelerated, it became clear that the budget deficit and the rate of inflation were interdependent. Although the orthodox claim that large budget deficits would lead to inflation could not be denied, it was also true that the acceleration of inflation caused a widening of the budget deficit – at least when expressed in nominal terms.

There were several explanations for the causal relationship between accelerating inflation and the size of the nominal budget deficit. First, nominal expenditure tended to rise more rapidly than nominal revenue. Many governments found it extremely difficult to cut public expenditure when so much of it consisted of wages and salaries on the one hand (including the armed forces) and interest payments on the external and internal debt on the other. Second, real tax revenue was eroded by the ability of the public to delay payment in a context of rising inflation (the Oliveira–Tanzi effect).[41] Third, real domestic interest rates needed to rise to persuade the public to hold government debt in an increasingly risky environment. With inflation accelerating, this implied an even more rapid rise in nominal interest rates, so the rate of growth of internal debt-service payments outstripped the increase in nominal revenues.

Some governments went further and argued that the fiscal stance could only be measured by the real deficit, that is, the nominal financial deficit adjusted for inflation. This included adjustments not only for real interest payments on the real value of the internal and external debt but also for the inflation tax – the depreciation in the real value of money holdings as a result of inflation.[42] Because the inflation tax often yielded substantial resources, governments could claim that fiscal policy was strict at a time when other indicators suggested it was loose. Mexico, for example, ran a real financial surplus in 1982 as a result, above all, of the impact of the inflation tax on the measurement of the real deficit at a time when both the primary balance and the financial nominal balance were in deficit.[43]

---

40 These partial defaults in Argentina and Brazil are discussed in Welch (1993).
41 The Oliveira–Tanzi effect is outlined in more detail in Cukierman (1988), pp. 49–53.
42 The inflation tax is outlined in Cardoso and Helwege (1992), pp. 150–4. Alternative concepts of the real budget deficit are explored in Buiter (1983).
43 See Ros (1987), Table 4.6, p. 83.

Although the measurement of the fiscal position under accelerating inflation was fraught with problems, few economists were persuaded of the wisdom of abandoning conventional indicators. Furthermore, the yield from the inflation tax proved to be a dwindling advantage to governments as the tax base (the real value of money holdings) declined. During the 1980s, following the debt crisis, the ratio of the money supply (M1) to GDP fell in almost all the high-inflation countries as the private sector learned to economize on its money balances and found alternative sources of liquidity (often the U.S. dollar). In Brazil, for example, the ratio collapsed to 3.9 percent in 1985 compared with 21 percent in low-inflation Venezuela.[44]

In a few republics the failure to adopt appropriate stabilization and adjustment programs in response to the debt crisis led to hyperinflation – usually defined as a monthly rate of inflation in excess of 50 percent. By the end of 1984 Bolivia was covering only 2 percent of government expenditure with tax revenue, and the rate of inflation in 1985 exceeded 8,000 percent.[45] Even this extraordinary figure was surpassed by Nicaragua in 1988, when defense expenditure was given overriding priority and the process of printing money pushed inflation above 33,000 percent – one of the highest rates ever recorded in Latin America. The last months of the García administration in Peru (1985–90) were marred by a similar story, with a flight from domestic currency and huge fiscal deficits pushing inflation above 7,000 percent in 1990. Both Argentina and Brazil, the true size of their fiscal deficits concealed by creative accounting at all levels of government, slid into hyperinflation at various points, with administrations in both republics in the early 1980s unwilling to make the fight against inflation their highest priority.[46]

Internal adjustment required the adoption of stabilization programs throughout Latin America. Because the rescheduling of debt was generally possible only if a country had signed an agreement with the IMF, the fund found itself playing a key role in the design and implementation of the first wave of stabilization programs in the 1980s. Only five countries were able to avoid submitting to IMF conditionality during this first wave – Cuba (not a member of the IMF), Nicaragua (denied IMF support through U.S. pressure), Colombia (which never rescheduled), and Paraguay and Venezuela (where IMF balance-of-payments support was not needed).

The close involvement of the IMF in the design of stabilization programs meant that policy was orthodox at first. Although the IMF remained committed to currency devaluation, financial liberalization, and domestic credit

44 With the acceleration in the rate of inflation in Venezuela at the end of the 1980s, the monetary ratio fell sharply.

45 Morales (1988) contains a good account of the hyperinflationary episode and the subsequent stabilization program.

46 See the chapters on Argentina and Brazil in Bruno, Fischer, Helpman, and Liviatan (1991).

control, the IMF-inspired programs emphasized the need to reduce the fiscal deficit through increases in revenue and cuts in expenditure. The call for fiscal discipline was reinforced in several republics by agreements with the World Bank on structural adjustment and with USAID on reductions in public-sector activity.

The need to reduce public expenditure was frustrated by the rising proportion of public revenue absorbed by interest payments on the debt (internal and external) and the reluctance of governments to cut the public-sector wage bill too drastically. Thus the burden of adjustment fell disproportionately on capital rather than on current expenditure, with the share of investment in total public expenditure falling in the 1980s in almost all republics. Public works, health, and education all suffered grievously from the reductions.

Public-expenditure cuts were not sufficient to restore fiscal discipline. Indeed, the growth of interest payments on the debt (internal and external) meant that total public expenditure continued to rise in many countries as a proportion of GDP despite the curbs on government spending. In Brazil total central-government expenditure jumped from 27 percent of GDP in 1981 to 51 percent in 1985.[47] Even Mexico, where fiscal austerity was applied with greater conviction, saw an increase from 21 percent in 1981 to 31 percent in 1987. In both cases the explanation was provided by the disproportionately rapid rise in interest payments, which were taking more than 50 percent of total Mexican central-government expenditure by 1987 compared with less than 10 percent in 1980.[48]

Orthodox stabilization programs therefore had to address the revenue side of the equation. Yet the circumstances could hardly have been less favorable. Recession after 1981 and the flight into the informal sector made tax collection harder, and external adjustment required numerous tax concessions to stimulate exports. Thus a policy of increasing tax rates (direct and indirect) was unlikely to meet with much success, and the first wave of stabilization programs – with substantial prodding from the IMF – tended to emphasize the need to raise tariffs on all services provided by the public sector in order to reduce losses by SOEs.

As the present or expected profitability of SOEs increased following these price rises, the possibility of selling public-sector assets to the private sector (privatization) became more realistic. Yet despite IMF pressure only Chile – continuing the policies adopted after 1973 – made much use of privatization as a solution to the fiscal problem in the first half of the 1980s. Governments in other republics at first remained unconvinced, either because they feared that public-sector assets could only be sold to the private sector at prices

47 See IDB (1991), Table C-2, p. 284.
48 See IDB (1991), Table C-17, p. 292.

that did not reflect their present discounted value or because they feared the damage to long-run growth from public-sector disinvestment. As the fiscal crisis continued, however, and as it became clear that foreign lending to SOEs would remain restricted, other governments joined the bandwagon in favor of privatization, so by the 1990s the sale of public-sector assets was contributing to fiscal revenue in all republics.

The first wave of stabilization programs after the debt crisis were not very successful. Despite the high profile adopted by the IMF and the widespread use of fund conditionality, inflation accelerated in most republics after 1981. Failure to meet agreed targets led the IMF to suspend many of its standby agreements and extended fund facilities. Brazil signed seven letters of intent with the IMF in the space of a few years, and targets were often broken before the first funds were released.[49]

The IMF blamed governments for lack of fiscal and monetary discipline, but it was clear that the problem was far more deep rooted. Of the fourteen countries that suffered from internal disequilibrium and inflation before the debt crisis, only one (Costa Rica) had made real progress on stabilization by the mid-1980s.[50] The shock to internal stability delivered by the debt crisis was generally too severe to be handled within the framework of an orthodox IMF-inspired stabilization program because the inherited problem of instability was already so acute. Even some of those countries that had avoided severe internal disequilibrium before 1982 (e.g., the Dominican Republic, Guatemala, and Honduras) were unsuccessful in carrying out the necessary internal adjustments after the debt crisis.

As the limitations of an orthodox response became clear, interest in heterodox stabilization programs increased. A new theory of inflation began to gain acceptance, one that emphasized its inertial character and addressed the question of a coordinated reduction in prices in order to lower inflationary expectations.[51] The orthodox approach was criticized for its reliance on market forces to break expectations in a context in which inflationary expectations were sustained by exchange-rate devaluation, nominal interest-rate increases, and the rise in public-sector tariffs. Without any nominal anchors the rate of inflation in the orthodox approach could easily drift upward despite the recession and tight fiscal and monetary policies.

Heterodox stabilization programs were adopted in a number of Latin American republics in the second half of the 1980s. A central element in the programs was a sharp change in relative prices at the beginning to remove distortions, followed by a freeze on certain prices (including nominal wage rates) to break inflationary expectations. The widespread use of indexation in high-inflation countries was ended with only a few exceptions. As inflation came down, it was assumed that the Oliveira–Tanzi effect would begin

49 See Dias Carneiro (1987), pp. 48–58.
50 See Bulmer-Thomas (1987), pp. 244–52.
51 On inertial inflation, see Amadeo et al. (1990).

to operate in reverse – increasing real tax revenue and encouraging an increase in real-money balances (and private-sector savings). Architects of the programs recognized that the price freeze could not be expected to last forever. A frozen exchange-rate would lead to currency overvaluation, fixed nominal wages to a fall in real wages, and price control to the emergence of new distortions, but it was assumed that by the time the freeze was lifted inflationary expectations would have been permanently lowered.[52]

Heterodox stabilization programs were not without their successes. The hyperinflation in Bolivia was stopped dead in 1985, following the adoption of a program that froze money wages, reformed the fiscal system completely, and liberalized the market for foreign exchange.[53] The Mexican program, launched in December 1987 with a tripartite agreement among business, unions, and government, also brought inflation down rapidly, with the controlled exchange-rate playing a crucial role in breaking inflationary expectations. As inflation came down, nominal interest rates also fell, and the fiscal burden implied by high levels of debt servicing became more tolerable.[54] Nicaraguan hyperinflation was stopped in 1991 after adoption of a fixed exchange-rate, a tight monetary policy, and access to foreign assistance to support additional imports.[55]

The heterodox programs in Bolivia, Mexico, and Nicaragua did not ignore the need for fiscal discipline. Thus heterodox measures were combined with orthodox policies in a judicious mix. By contrast, the heterodox programs launched in Argentina in 1985 (the Austral Plan[56]) and Brazil in 1986 (the Cruzado Plan[57]) were notable for the absence of a tight fiscal policy. At first the rate of inflation fell sharply, in response to the freeze on prices and the fixing of the exchange-rate, but nominal aggregate demand continued to outstrip available supply, and inflationary pressures soon reemerged. As the distortions in relative prices reappeared, price controls had to be lifted before fiscal discipline had been restored. The result was an explosion in the rate of inflation that soon surpassed the rate before the adoption of the heterodox programs.[58]

The failure of heterodox programs in Argentina and Brazil did not at first lead to a restoration of orthodoxy. On the contrary, governments in both countries were even willing to freeze domestic financial assets in a desperate attempt to bring both inflation and the budget deficit under control. Yet by the beginning of the 1990s, after a decade of failed stabilization programs,

---

52 A good analytical treatment of heterodox stabilization programs can be found in Alberro (1987).

53 See Pastor (1991). There is some dispute as to whether the Bolivian program was really heterodox, however.

54 A number of good accounts of the Mexican stabilization program exist. See, for example, Ortiz (1991).

55 See IDB (1992), pp. 140–1.

56 On the Austral Plan, see Machinea and Fanelli (1988), pp. 111–52.

57 On the Cruzado Plan, see Modiano (1988), pp. 215–58.

58 See Cardoso (1991), pp. 143–77.

the need to combine orthodox fiscal measures (including privatization) with heterodox policies was finally recognized.

The first country to reap the results of the new approach was Argentina. The *Ley de Convertibilidad* in 1991 introduced a virtual currency board under which the local currency was pegged to the U.S. dollar and the monetary base was backed by foreign exchange reserves. Inflation had fallen to insignificant levels within a few years and by the end of the decade was negative (i.e., prices were falling).[59] Brazil adopted the *Real* plan in mid-1994, which enabled annual inflation to fall to 2.5 percent in 1998. When the currency was devalued sharply at the beginning of 1999, it was widely assumed that inflation would return. However, this did not happen and inflation has remained under control.[60]

Monetary policy, which has been transformed in Latin America since the early 1980s, must take much of the credit for the lowering of inflation. Central banks have become much more autonomous (e.g., Brazil) and some have been given complete independence (e.g., Mexico). Regulation of the banking systems have been improved and the entry of foreign banks has increased efficiency even if competition is still limited. The ability of the public sector to monetize fiscal deficits has been severely curtailed. The outcome, as is shown in the next section, has been a big fall in inflation in Latin America to rates that have not been seen for decades. Indeed, such has been the improvement in the quality and credibility of monetary policy that nominal exchange-rate devaluation is no longer necessarily a guide to the rate of inflation.[61]

The most serious weakness in monetary policy has been the failure to lower the real cost of borrowing. This is partly due to the shallowness of the financial markets, but is also due to the huge spread between borrowing and lending rates. Indeed, it is not unknown for the real lending rate to be close to zero while the real borrowing rate is above 10 percent. Lack of competition in the financial markets is primarily to blame and this has not yet been overcome through liberalization of the capital account of the balance of payments. In practice, only the largest Latin American companies have access to the international capital market so that small and medium-sized enterprises (SMEs) are restricted to borrowing in the domestic market and are crippled by high rates.

This unsatisfactory state of affairs arises in part because financial institutions have become major creditors to the public sector and are not so dependent on private sector business. Foreign-currency bonds are often held

59 Inflation, however, returned in 2002 as a result of the collapse of the currency following debt default at the end of 2001.

60 See Ferreira and Tullio (2002)

61 This is illustrated by Brazil, where annual inflation was kept below 10 percent despite the massive nominal devaluation after January 1999.

by domestic agents and these are principally the banks. Thus, the banks benefit from the country risk premium and the banks are also the most likely to hold the domestic currency debt issued by governments.

High interest rates on public debt made it impossible for governments to eliminate fiscal deficits. This gave the impression that fiscal policy did not improve after the debt crisis. In fact, it did, but it is necessary to distinguish between the primary balance (net of interest payments) and the nominal balance. The primary balance moved into surplus in most countries, as taxes increased, defence spending was cut, and subsidies to SOEs were eliminated. Equity considerations have been largely sacrificed in the search for increased revenues with an emphasis on broad-based sales taxes, particularly value-added taxes. And federal countries such as Brazil made serious efforts to control spending by provincial governments. However, interest payments on the public debt – both domestic and foreign – remained a drain on state finances leading to nominal deficits that were sometimes large even when the primary balance was in surplus.

The tightness of fiscal policy, in terms of macroeconomic stability, is more closely approximated by the primary than the nominal balance. Thus, fiscal policy was restrictive in many countries at the cost of lower investment and also at the expense of social spending. Targeting of social spending on lower income groups, promoted by the World Bank in particular, became more popular and enjoyed some success – notably in Chile. However, the impact of social spending did not in general improve the distribution of income.[62]

The reasons for this have been complex, but two stand out. First, educational spending on universities – a large part of the total – favored the middle and upper deciles of the income distribution. Second, state spending on pensions went overwhelmingly to the middle classes in Latin America rather than the poor. Although many governments have privatized – in whole or in part – their pension systems, there is a long lag before state liabilities cease since older workers remain in the state system and continue to benefit until they die.[63]

While something approaching a consensus developed in relation to fiscal and monetary policy in Latin America since the debt crisis, the same could not be said about exchange-rate policy. All Latin American countries, except dollarized Panama, devalued in the 1980s and early 1990s in an effort to adjust the external sector both to create resources to service the debt and to promote exports. However, the similarity ended there. One group, led by Argentina, marched resolutely toward fixed currencies and *de facto* dollarization. Another group, led by Chile, adopted a crawling peg with a real exchange-rate target. While the third group, led by Mexico after 1994 and joined by Brazil in 1999, opted for exchange-rate flexibility.

---

62 See the various case studies in Lustig (1995).
63 For a case study of Chile, see Scott (1996).

The first group initially enjoyed great success. Inflation came down to international levels and was accompanied by financial deepening. However, the risk premium did not disappear and a spread remained between domestic and foreign interest rates. Thus, the logic of this group has been to move toward *de jure* dollarization with Ecuador and El Salvador joining Panama.

Argentina appeared to be moving in this direction with nearly 70 percent of bank deposits denominated in dollars by the fourth quarter of 2001. However, default on the external debt at the end of 2001 triggered a devaluation of the currency and a difficult period of *pesoification* in 2002 as the authorities struggled to reverse the dollarization of the 1990s.

The second group also enjoyed initial success in achieving the target. However, the difficulty of attracting foreign capital after the Asian financial crisis led to a dismantling of restrictions on foreign capital inflows and a move toward full currency flexibility. Only the smaller countries, such as Costa Rica, were able to persevere with real exchange-rate targeting. Other countries, including Chile and Colombia, effectively joined the third group at the end of the 1990s.

Thus, Latin America found itself divided into two camps on exchange-rate policy. In the fixed exchange-rate group, dollarization appeared to be the logical step or at least a monetary union based on a regional currency. In the other group, formal dollarization looked increasingly unlikely, although the dollar was often used in pricing assets.

Growth, equity, and inflation since the debt crisis

It is not easy at this distance to judge Latin America's economic performance since the debt crisis. There is, for example, a sharp contrast between the adjustment of the 1980s, the recovery of the 1990s and the stagnation at the start of the new millennium. Nevertheless, certain patterns emerge with clarity.

The rate of growth of GDP per head since 1981 – the last year before the debt crisis – is shown in Table 11.4. The result is not impressive. In the first decade, GDP per head for the region as a whole fell by 0.9 percent at an annual rate and only four countries – three if the special case of Cuba is excluded – managed a positive growth rate.[64] It can be argued that the long-run performance should not be judged by the 1980s, as this was a period of adjustment to the excesses of ISI and the debt crisis. However, even if the analysis is confined to the period since 1990, the results are still disappointing with a low annual rate of growth of GDP per head (1.2 percent) for the region as a whole.

---

64 Cuba was still benefiting from Soviet bloc subsidies in the 1980s, which insulated it from the impact of the debt crisis. See Mesa-Lago (2000), Part III.

Table 11.4. *Growth of GDP per head (US$ at 1995 prices), 1981–2001*

	1981–90	1991–2001
Argentina	−2.1	2.1
Bolivia	−1.9	1.0
Brazil	−0.4	1.1
Chile	1.4	4.2
Colombia	1.6	0.6
Costa Rica	−0.7	1.8
Cuba	2.8	−1.6
Dominican Republic	0.2	3.8
Ecuador	−0.9	−0.1
El Salvador	−1.5	2.0
Guatemala	−1.6	1.2
Haiti	−2.9	−2.8
Honduras	−0.8	0.3
Mexico	−0.2	1.5
Nicaragua	−4.1	0.5
Panama	−0.7	2.4
Paraguay	0	−0.9
Peru	−3.3	1.8
Uruguay	−0.6	1.8
Venezuela	−3.2	0.3
Latin America	−0.9	1.2

Source: ECLAC (2001), pp. 740–741.

Since the debt crisis only one country (Chile) has been able unambiguously to exceed its performance during the inward-looking phase of development from 1950 to 1980, although the Dominican Republic (see Table 11.4) has since 1990 achieved a very credible performance in GDP per head (3.8% annual increase). Argentina improved its long-run rate of growth of real GDP per head in the 1990s, but this was undermined by a deep recession after 1998 that lasted four years. The other cases of superior growth are all rather unusual. El Salvador, for example, grew rapidly for part of the 1990s, but this was after a long civil war and the rate of growth was heavily influenced by the remittances sent by all those who had left the country for the United States.[65]

Mexico's performance has been an illustration of the costs and benefits of globalization. One of the first to adjust, Mexico was also quick to liberalize its current and capital accounts and to integrate its economy into the North American economic space.[66] Although performance could be damaged by

65 On the performance of the Salvadorean economy after the civil war, see Segovia (2002).
66 On Mexico's integration into the U.S. economic sphere, see FitzGerald (2001).

domestic mistakes, as in the excessive buildup of debt in the early 1990s, the long-run trend toward a greater dependence on the U.S. market has become clear.

When the U.S. economy performed well, Mexico benefited handsomely. Growth was export led and export expansion generated a boom in other parts of the economy despite the weak backward linkages from the *maquila* industry on the northern border. The economy became less dependent on oil and manufactured exports became less dependent on the assembly industry. However, Mexico went into recession as soon as the U.S. economy slowed down. With 25% of its GDP in exports and 85% of its exports going to the United States, this was perhaps inevitable.

Argentina's performance has been a case study in the dangers of inconsistent policies. On many criteria, Argentina in the 1990s was the most neoliberal economy in Latin America with widespread privatization, complete capital account liberalization, and a large measure of trade liberalization. Yet the exchange-rate policy, under which the local currency was pegged to the U.S. dollar under a virtual currency board regime, imposed fiscal obligations on the government that were never fully respected. The result was a lack of fiscal discipline leading to a massive increase in external debt. As long as the economy grew rapidly, the debt problem could be contained. It became unsustainable, however, when growth stopped after 1998 and the authorities had no instruments at their disposal with which to stimulate the economy.[67]

The other big disappointment has been Brazil. The largest economy in the region, Brazil has consistently failed to achieve its potential. Adjustment and liberalization were delayed until the 1990s so that this harsh judgement may prove premature. However, greater fiscal and monetary responsibility, low inflation, trade and financial liberalization, and the promotion of DFI have not yet enabled Brazil to shift to a higher long-run sustainable growth rate.

The obstacles to faster growth in Brazil are numerous. The rate of investment is held back by low domestic savings, as in so many parts of Latin America and unlike in Asia; foreign capital cannot be relied on to close the gap. High real interest rates discourage borrowing by the private sector for productive purposes. Exports have not responded to devaluation and remain less than 10 percent of GDP (compared with over 20 percent in China at the end of the 1990s). Brazil's income inequality, one of the worst in the world, also acts as a break on its economic performance, although this is more controversial. At the very least Brazil does not enjoy the benefits such as high savings rates that are supposed to accompany an unequal distribution of income.

67 See Mussa (2002).

The transition from ISI would have required greater attention to foreign trade with or without globalization. The reason is that Latin America saw its share of world trade decline steadily after 1950 to the point where it had reached a mere 3.5 percent in 1980 (much lower than its share of world population). Although some of this decline could be attributed to a specialization in primary products at a time when primary products trade was growing less fast than total trade, it was also due to the relentless anti-export bias associated with the inward-looking model of development.

The strategy to reverse the decline in world market share has had two components. First has been the greater attention to the export sector through policies designed to favor traded over nontraded goods and within tradeables to favor exportables over importables. Second has been the desire to diversify exports away from primary products toward manufactured goods and even services.

The results for Latin America as a whole at first appear impressive, but they are too heavily influenced by Mexico. Thus, the share of world exports has indeed increased since the mid-1980s, but this is mainly due to Mexico's export boom. By 2000 Mexico accounted for half of all Latin America's exports. Excluding Mexico, the Latin American performance has been much less satisfactory, although some smaller countries – notably Chile, but also Costa Rica – did increase world market share.[68]

Aggregate figures for Latin America are always heavily influenced by Brazil and trade is no exception. Thus, the poor performance of Latin America (excluding Mexico) reflects the Brazilian export sector's lack of dynamism. This has been all the more puzzling in view of the increase in export competitiveness after the devaluation in January 1999. The Brazilian authorities tended to blame agricultural protectionism in rich countries for this sad state of affairs, but in truth it has been much more complex.

The diversification of Latin America's exports away from primary products has been more encouraging. Once again, the results have been heavily influenced by Mexico, but this time they are reinforced by Brazil. Diversification has had several causes. In smaller countries it has been helped by the growth of the maquila industry. Haiti, for example, has one of the lowest ratios of primary product to total exports and this is entirely due to the assembly plants exporting light manufactures to the United States. In Costa Rica the establishment by INTEL of a computer chip factory at the end of the 1990s doubled the gross value of exports within two years. In larger countries it also reflects investments by MNCs as part of the production chain linking subsidiaries across the world.

Regional integration has also been an important cause of diversification. The new phase of integration has encouraged the export of manufactured

68 See Steinfatt and Contreras (2001).

goods to neighboring countries. Indeed, despite the absence of formal discrimination against agricultural products, almost all intraregional trade in Latin America is in manufactures and a growing proportion of this is intraindustry trade as well. However, the impact of regional integration would appear to be quite limited as each scheme – with the notable exception of NAFTA – has found it difficult to increase the share of total trade that is intraregional trade. This peaked at 20 percent in MERCOSUR, 15 percent in the CACM, and 10 percent in the Andean Community and CARICOM.

Equity in Latin America is usually measured by reference to both poverty and income distribution.[69] Much was expected from the new paradigm in this respect. Export-led growth, it was argued, would lead to a concentration on labor-intensive exports creating employment that would reduce poverty and pushing up the wages of unskilled workers to improve income distribution. The reduction of inflation would eliminate the inflation tax, which falls so heavily on the poor, and lead to an improvement in equity. Finally, the targeting of social spending was expected to have the same effect.[70]

Sadly, the expected benefits have not in general materialized. As Table 11.5 shows, the proportion of households living in poverty rose in the 1980s. It fell in the 1990s, but by the beginning of the new millennium it was only back to where it had been in 1980. Since population growth has continued throughout this period, many more Latin Americans are living in poverty than at the start of the debt crisis.

The assumption that the NEM would improve equity was not entirely flawed. The elimination of the inflation tax did have a positive impact, as the reduction in poverty in Brazil after 1994 showed. The targeting of social spending could also be very beneficial, as the case of Chile demonstrated in the 1990s. However, exports were not generally intensive in unskilled labor. Primary products continued to be intensive in natural resources and manufactured goods were usually intensive in skilled labor. The result was an increase in real wages for skilled workers rather than for the unskilled.

This is one reason why income distribution has failed to improve in Latin America. The region went into the debt crisis with some of the highest indicators of inequality in the world, but the NEM did little or nothing to change this. Chile, the most successful new paradigm country, enjoyed a reduction in the Gini coefficient[71] in rural areas in the 1990s, but suffered an increase in urban areas. The reverse was true of Mexico. Brazil, the country

---

69 There is a growing literature on this topic. See, for example, Morley (1995), Bulmer-Thomas (1996), Berry (1998), Ganuza (2000), and Stallings (2000).

70 See Morley (2000).

71 The Gini coefficient is the best known measure of income distribution varying from zero (compete equality) to one (complete inequality).

Table 11.5. *Percentage of households below poverty line: 1980, 1990, and 2000*

	Circa 1980	Circa 1990	Circa 2000
Argentina[a]	N/A	12	16
Bolivia[a]	N/A	49	42
Brazil	39	41	30
Chile	N/A	33	18
Colombia	39	50	49
Costa Rica	22	24	18
Dominican Republic	N/A	N/A	32[b]
Ecuador[a]	N/A	56	58
El Salvador	N/A	48[c]	44
Honduras	N/A	75	74
Mexico	32	39	38
Nicaragua	N/A	68	65
Panama	36	36	24
Paraguay[a]		42[d]	41
Uruguay[a]	9	12	6
Venezuela	22	34	44
Latin America	35	41	35

[a] Urban area.
[b] 1997.
[c] 1995.
[d] 1994.
Source: 1980 date from ECLAC (2001), pp. 64–5; 1990 and circa 2000 from CEPAL (2001), pp. 221–222.

with the most unequal distribution of income in Latin America, saw its Gini coefficient rise in both urban and rural areas in the 1990s.[72]

The most impressive Latin American performance has been in terms of inflation stabilization. This has been a success story with only minor qualifications, as Table 11.6 makes clear. Given the long history of chronic inflation in many countries before 1980, this is all the more remarkable. Furthermore, as was shown earlier, the impact of adjustment programs in the 1980s at first exacerbated inflationary pressures through the impact of currency depreciation, increases in sales taxes and the ending of subsidies on the price level.

The fall in inflation rates at the beginning of the 1990s was mainly at-tributable to real exchange-rate appreciation.[73] The inflows of capital led to currency overvaluation that reduced inflation, but undermined external

[72] Figures on the Gini coefficient in rural and urban areas in Latin America can be found in CEPAL (2001), Tables 23 and 24, pp. 237–9.
[73] See Devlin, Ffrench-Davis, and Griffith-Jones (1995).

Table 11.6. *Variations in consumer price index (%)*

	1993	1994	1995	1996	1997	1998	1999	2000
Argentina	7.4	3.9	1.6	0.1	0.3	0.7	−1.8	−0.7
Bolivia	9.3	8.5	12.6	7.9	6.7	4.4	3.1	3.4
Brazil	2489.1	929.3	22.0	9.1	4.3	2.5	8.4	5.3
Chile	12.2	8.9	8.2	6.6	6.0	4.7	2.3	4.5
Colombia	22.6	22.6	19.5	21.6	17.7	16.7	9.2	8.8
Costa Rica	9.0	19.9	22.6	13.9	11.2	12.4	10.1	11.0
Dominican Republic	2.8	14.3	9.2	4.0	8.4	7.8	5.1	9.0
Ecuador	31.0	25.4	22.8	25.6	30.6	43.4	60.7	91.0
El Salvador	12.1	8.9	11.4	7.4	1.9	4.2	−1.0	4.3
Guatemala	11.6	11.6	8.6	10.9	7.1	7.5	4.9	5.8
Haiti	44.4	32.2	24.8	14.7	15.6	7.5	9.7	19.0
Honduras	13.0	28.9	26.8	25.3	12.7	15.6	10.9	10.1
Mexico	8.0	7.1	52.1	27.7	15.7	18.6	12.3	9.0
Nicaragua	19.5	14.4	11.1	12.1	7.3	18.5	7.2	9.9
Panama	0.9	1.3	0.8	2.3	−0.5	1.4	1.5	0.7
Paraguay	20.4	18.3	10.5	8.2	6.2	14.6	5.4	8.6
Peru	39.5	15.4	10.2	11.8	6.5	6.0	3.7	3.7
Uruguay	52.9	44.1	35.4	24.3	15.2	8.6	4.2	5.1
Venezuela	45.9	70.8	56.6	103.2	37.6	29.9	20.0	13.4
Latin America	**876.6**	**333.1**	**25.8**	**18.2**	**10.4**	**10.3**	**9.5**	**8.7**

Source: ECLAC (2001), p. 743.

competitiveness at the same time. The classic example is provided by Argentina, where the rate of inflation fell from over 50 percent a month at the beginning of 1991 to an annual rate of 0.1 percent by 1996 (see Table 11.6). However, the cost for Argentina in terms of lost competitiveness was high. The real exchange-rate appreciated by anything from 30 percent to 50 percent depending on which domestic price deflator is used.

A fall in inflation due to currency overvaluation is not sustainable. However, inflation rates remained low even when real exchange rates depreciated. The reasons were both economic and psychological. Tight fiscal and monetary policies allowed the authorities to compensate for the impact of currency falls, while trade liberalization lowered tariffs and increased competition in the tradeable goods sector at the same time. Inflation reduction also had a psychological component. Inflationary expectations were broken in the first half of the 1990s, allowing governments to phase out indexation and making it less likely inflation would return.

This section has concentrated on the traditional measures of macroeconomic performance: growth, equity, and inflation. However, the two decades after 1980 witnessed an important change in Latin America that consolidated a trend beginning even earlier. This was the demographic transition, under which the fall in death rates beginning in the 1920s was finally matched by a fall in death rates. Thus, the main Latin American countries faced a more manageable annual increase in population, although a number of the smaller countries such as Honduras and Nicaragua remained stuck in the first phase of the demographic transition (high birth rates and low death rates).

Latin America and globalization

Latin America began the process of adjustment to globalization in the mid-1980s. The objectives were not only to counter the negative impact of the debt crisis, but also to reverse the disengagement of the region from the world's product and factor markets. This reversal had been a consequence of several decades of inward-looking development coupled with a growing hostility to foreign direct investment.[74]

The goal of countering the negative impact of the debt crisis has been only partially successful. Latin America did succeed in extricating itself from the debt overhang represented by commercial bank loans, but at the expense of a huge increase in bond indebtedness. In part this was due to the exchange of bank loans for bonds under the Brady Plan, but it was also due to the ease of tapping the international bond market in the 1990s.

The bond markets proved just as fickle as commercial creditors. Capital flowed to Latin America in abundance when global liquidity was strong,[75] but the inflow proved vulnerable to events over which Latin America had no control. The Mexican financial crisis in 1994 affected all of Latin America although the circumstances in other countries were very different. The Asian financial crisis in 1997 and the Russian default the following year proved to be the catalyst for a rise in the country risk premiums in Latin America despite the lack of synchronization in the real economies of emerging markets. Last, but not least, the terrorist attack on the United States in September 2001 led to an increase in risk aversion and a flight to quality from which Latin America inevitably suffered.

Adjustment to globalization has therefore not ended Latin America's debt problems, although they now take new forms. Debt in the 1990s increased faster than nominal GDP, leading to a rise in the debt/GDP ratio. Similarly, the increase in the dollar value of exports was in many cases insufficient to reduce the debt–service ratio (interest plus amortization as a share of exports). The rate of domestic saving rose, but capital formation needed to rise as well as a result of the neglect of investment in the 1980s.

---

74 The literature on globalization is vast. For a critique, see Stiglitz (2002).
75 See Devlin, Ffrench-Davis and Griffith-Jones (1995).

Thus, the gap between domestic savings and investment remained leading to a need for foreign resources.[76]

The second objective – integration into global product and factor markets – was also only partially successful. The share of trade (exports plus imports) in GDP rose, but this only meant that trade was growing faster than GDP. Given the bias against exports and imports under ISI, this rising trade ratio was hardly surprising. More relevant is Latin America's share of world exports.

This share increased after 1990, but the rise is entirely explained by Mexico. Indeed, when Mexico is excluded from the Latin American figure, the ratio fell after 1990. Just as disturbing is the failure of all the Latin American integration schemes, excluding NAFTA, to increase world market share of exports in the 1990s. Latin America's export performance may have been superior to what had gone before, but it still did not measure up against the competition from outside – particularly East Asia.

Mexico's outstanding export performance has many explanations. On the supply side, competitiveness was increased through tax reform (including tariff reductions) and the adoption (after 1994) of a flexible exchange-rate. Yet these measures were common to almost all countries in the region. What was different in Mexico's case was the demand side. Even before NAFTA was launched, Mexico had become increasingly integrated into the North American economic space with many firms taking investment decisions on a regional rather than national basis. Direct foreign investment linked Mexico to its northern neighbor and Mexican firms began to acquire a presence in the United States.

Mexico's trading links with the United States proved so strong that they dominated all Latin America's trade links. In the decade from 1988 to 1998, Latin America's exports to the United States grew at 14 percent a year compared with U.S. imports from all sources of 7.8 percent. By contrast, Latin America's exports to the European Union, Japan and other industrial countries grew more slowly than their imports from all sources. Thus, Latin America's share of U.S. imports increased – mainly due to Mexico – while its share of other markets declined. These other markets were of little importance to Mexico, but of much greater significance for the rest of Latin America.

Latin America's integration into world product markets was therefore disappointing. However, there was one notable exception – the drugs trade. Despite all efforts at interdiction, including crop spraying, financial support for substitutes, and draconian measures against money laundering, the export of narcotics from Latin America continued unabated. A decline in production in one country simply led to an increase in another; a clampdown

76 On the weakness of domestic saving in Latin America, see Reinhart (1999).

on distribution through one channel always led to the emergence of other conduits. A few voices were heard calling for legalization of the drugs trade, but the importing countries were not yet ready for such drastic steps.

Latin America's integration into global factor markets was more successful than its integration into product markets. By the end of the 1990s the region's share of global direct foreign investment had risen to about 10 percent — more than double what it had been a decade before — and DFI was spread around the region, attracted not just to Mexico but to other countries as well. The region was also well represented — perhaps too well — in the global bond market where Argentina alone accounted for 25 percent of all emerging market debt by 2000.

The other global factor market (labor) remained subject to major restrictions, although this had not prevented widescale migration from Latin America to other parts of the world — notably the United States. Migratory movements were also important within Latin America; Bolivians and Paraguayans, for example, formed a large part of the Argentine labor force by the end of the century and Nicaraguans represented at least 10 percent of the Costa Rican population. These labor movements led to a massive flow of remittances to relatives in Latin America as well as to a modest transfer of technology.

Where Latin America still lags far behind is in the knowledge economy. Its educational deficit remains severe despite high-level recognition in the 1990s of the need for accelerated investment. The use of the Internet is at very low levels compared with developed countries. By the beginning of the new millennium, there were only 34 personal computers per 1,000 people compared with 229 in the Eurozone and 311 in the United States. Signs of a productivity revolution inspired by the New Economy, as in the North America, were conspicuous by their absence.

Thus, the long march toward globalization has not brought the benefits many expected. Growth rates have been disappointing and remain below those before 1980 in most countries. The region has opened up to foreign trade, but the basis for Latin America's renewed integration into the world economy remains unclear. Labor is abundant, but it is not cheap compared with many countries in Asia. Capital is scarce domestically and can only be obtained from abroad at high cost. The region is still rich in natural resources, but the pattern of world demand and residual protectionism does not favor agricultural exports. That leaves mining exports and it is a sad comment on 500 years of economic history that Latin America's comparative advantage is still seen by many to lie with precious metals and other minerals.

12

Conclusions

The economic development of Latin America since independence is a story of unfulfilled promise. Despite the abundance of natural resources and a favorable ratio of land to labor, and after nearly two centuries of freedom from colonial rule, not one republic has achieved the status of a developed country. Furthermore, the gap between living standards in Latin America and those in the developed countries has steadily widened since the early nineteenth century, when – by some accounts – the subcontinent was the most prosperous of the developing-country regions.[1]

Even though the collapse of Iberian rule ended restrictions on commerce, Latin America continued to operate in a world in which rules were made by others. Unable to break into the charmed circle of advanced capitalist countries, Latin America has remained a peripheral region in which external influence has been preeminent. Trade cycles, investment and consumption patterns, the accumulation of debt, and the transfer of technology have all been driven by forces over which Latin America has exercised little control. Even during the period of inward-looking development, the ability of external events to shape internal dynamics was powerful.

Peripheral status has often been used to explain Latin American backwardness.[2] Other countries faced the same constraints, however, and still managed to transform their position while abiding by the rules of the game. The United States, a peripheral country at the beginning of the nineteenth century, had overtaken Great Britain in terms of living standards by the beginning of the twentieth century through a productivity revolution based on technology and investment.[3] The Scandinavian countries had seen their economies transformed through export-led growth based on primary

---

1 Estimates of GDP per head at the beginning of the nineteenth century, admittedly crude, suggest that Latin America was the richest of the now Third World regions. See Maddison (2001), Tables A1-c, A2-c, A3-c, and A4-c.

2 See, for example, Frank (1969), Cardoso and Faletto (1979), and, with a more nuanced perspective, Furtado (1976). A critical evaluation of such views can be found in Kay (1989).

3 By 1913, GDP per head in the United States was nearly 10 percent higher than in the United Kingdom. See Maddison (2001), p. 185.

products by the beginning of the twentieth century.[4] Public support made it possible for the Industrial Revolution to spread to a number of central European countries in the late nineteenth century.[5] The British dominions achieved record levels of exports per head to raise living standards throughout their economies.[6] Japan exchanged its military prowess for an industrial machine that conquered the world after 1945.[7] Newly industrialized countries (NICs) in East Asia exploited the opportunities for labor-intensive manufactured exports made possible by the rapid growth of world trade after 1950.[8] A handful of smaller countries (e.g., the Bahamas) have recently raised living standards to developed-country levels on the back of service exports.[9]

In isolation each of these examples could be dismissed as a special case. Taken together, however, they demonstrate that escape from the periphery has always been possible. External constraints may have been formidable, but never overwhelming. Thus Latin America can find little consolation in the lessons to be derived from world economic history. Indeed, free of formal colonial rule, most Latin American countries have enjoyed a degree of independence denied to many nations that did indeed escape peripheral status. Thus the main reasons for the relative backwardness of Latin America are to be found within the region itself.[10]

Latin America's economic development since independence falls relatively easily into two distinct, but partially overlapping phases, followed by a third, which has only recently begun. The first corresponds to traditional export-led growth based on primary products. Slow to begin, it reached its apex in the first decade of the twentieth century and faded away in the wake of the Great Depression. The second corresponds to inward-looking development. Based on import substitution, which had begun in the larger republics late in the nineteenth century, it peaked in the quarter-century after the Second World War. A third phase, shaped by globalization, became dominant after the debt crisis of the 1980s.

Timing has not been kind to Latin America. The region's experiment with traditional export-led growth gathered momentum in almost inverse proportion to the relative advantage enjoyed by primary products over

4 See Blomström and Meller (1991), Chapters 2, 4, 6, and 8.

5 See Berend (1982), Chapter 5.

6 Lewis (1989), pp. 1574–81, is an illuminating comparison between Argentina and two dominions (Australia and Canada). See also Cortés Conde (1997).

7 See Ohkawa and Rosovsky (1973), Chapter 2.

8 See Lin (1988), where East Asian and Latin American performances are contrasted.

9 On long-run economic performance in the Caribbean, see Bulmer-Thomas (2001b) and Nicholls (2001).

10 This is not to deny that negative external shocks have been important at times, but over the long run it is difficult to sustain the thesis that the influence of external factors has been persistently negative.

manufactured goods in international trade. Changes in the industrial structure and consumption patterns of the developed countries, together with technical progress in reducing primary commodity inputs per unit of output, had shifted international trade in favor of manufactured goods by the end of the nineteenth century.[11] The climax in inward-looking development was reached as the world economy embarked on a period of sustained and rapid growth in international trade.

Timing is not simply a matter of chance, however. The slow progress in the nineteenth century reflected the delays so many countries encountered in removing the obstacles on the supply side of export expansion. Inward-looking development was prolonged far beyond what had at first been justified by turmoil in international markets. The scope for the promotion of nontraditional exports had been apparent long before it became fashionable in the region. Firms and individuals may have been responsive to price signals, but the signals themselves did not always reflect the changes in the world economy. The absence of some markets, the segmentation of others, and inconsistent public policies meant that relative prices were slow to move into line with the opportunities provided by the world economy.

The first phase of Latin America's postindependence development was based on primary-product exports. Rapid growth was expected to transform the entire economy, increasing productivity in the nonexport sector and leading to a rise in income per head. Judged by this standard, export-led growth was generally a failure. By the late 1920s, after a century of experimentation with different export products, most Latin American countries were recording negligible growth rates. Indeed, in a few cases there may even have been a decline in living standards.

The modest growth record can be seen in Table 12.1. By the end of the 1920s gross domestic product (GDP) per head varied from $121 to $592 (at 1970 prices), with the majority of countries squeezed into the bottom of the range. Income per head at the time of independence (at 1970 prices) must have fallen in a range from $100 (the subsistence level) to $300.[12] However, modern scholarship suggests that most of Latin America, favored by generous land–man ratios and hospitable climates, was above the subsistence level at the time of independence, so the range can be narrowed to the upper section of the band ($150 to $300).[13] This gives a matrix of

---

11 For much of the nineteenth century the growth of trade in primary products and in manufactured goods had been comparable. By 1913, however, trade in manufactured goods was growing much faster. See Lewis (1978).

12 The current lowest level of income per head in the world (at 1970 prices), $100, can be considered the subsistence level. The (price-adjusted) estimates in Bairoch and Lévy Leboyer (1981), Table 1.7, suggest a maximum of $300 per head in Latin America at the time of independence.

13 Exports per head in Latin America in 1829–31 are estimated to have been twice as high as exports per head for all Third World countries and some twenty times greater than for Africa and Asia. See

Table 12.1. *Annual rate of growth of GDP per head, circa 1820 to 1928 (in percentages)*

Country	GDP per head 1928 (in 1970 prices)	1820s GDP per head (in 1970 prices)[a]			
		150	200	250	300
Argentina	571	1.3	1.1	0.8	0.6
Brazil	160	0.1	−0.2	−0.4	−0.6
Chile	501	1.2	0.9	0.7	0.5
Colombia	158	0.1	−0.2	−0.4	−0.6
Costa Rica	219	0.4	0.1	−0.1	−0.3
Cuba	298	0.7	0.4	0.2	0
Ecuador	152	0	−0.3	−0.5	−0.7
El Salvador	121	−0.2	−0.5	−0.7	−0.9
Guatemala	195	0.3	0	−0.2	−0.4
Honduras	223	0.4	0.1	−0.1	−0.3
Mexico	252	0.5	0.2	0	−0.2
Nicaragua	189	0.3	−0.1	−0.3	−0.5
Peru	163	0.1	−0.2	−0.4	−0.6
Puerto Rico	468	1.1	0.9	0.6	0.4
Uruguay	592	1.4	1.1	0.9	0.7
Venezuela	197	0.3	0	−0.2	−0.4
Latin America	262	0.6	0.3	0.1	−0.1

Note: The growth rates have been calculated using different assumptions about the level of GDP per capita in the 1820s, ranging from $150 to $300.
[a] Data are assumed to refer to 1828, so annual rate of growth is calculated over 100 years.
Source: For GDP per head, 1928, see Table A.3.2.

possible annual growth rates from which only a handful of countries emerge with any credit. The vast majority saw only the most modest rise in living standards, so the gap between living standards in Latin America and the developed countries increased steadily.[14]

At the root of the failure of export-led growth was the slow growth of exports. As the engine of growth within the export-led model, the export sector needed to grow rapidly to raise average living standards throughout the economy. Yet, with rare exceptions, export growth was either modest or cyclical until the sustained boom at the beginning of the twentieth century. Indeed, the first half-century of independence was marred by repeated failures in many republics to seize the opportunities that foreign trade presented. Sometimes the commodity lottery was to blame, pushing resources into exports that subsequently declined in importance; often the problem

Bairoch and Etemard (1985), Table 1.5, p. 27. Thus it is improbable that Latin American income per head was close to subsistence level at the time of independence.
14 See Albala Bertrand (1993), Tables 2.1 and 2.4.

was associated with a scarcity of factor inputs that could not easily be resolved through relative price changes; and nearly always the growth of the export sector was impeded by infrastructure problems.

Export-led growth was not the same as rapid growth of exports, however. Nothing was automatic about the growth of the nonexport sector in response to an export expansion, so the mechanics of the export-led growth model could not be taken for granted. The commodity lottery could favor the transfer of productivity gains from one sector to another, but it could also undermine it. Furthermore, the nonexport sector faced many of the same problems encountered by the export sector: lack of infrastructure, scarcity of factors of production, and a shortage of complementary inputs. The biggest problem of all, however, was the growth of the internal market. Translating expansion of the export sector into effective demand for the products of the nonexport sector was not a simple matter when internal transport links were so dismal and when labor markets were artificially distorted to prevent real wages from rising. Foreign penetration of the export sector – particularly minerals – further reduced the stimulus to the nonexport economy associated with any given rise in exports.[15]

The difficulties encountered in transforming the nonexport sector were well illustrated by the manufacturing sector. By the First World War the export engine had begun to fire in all republics, but modern industry could be found in only a handful. Whereas the Scandinavian countries had seen the emergence of firms providing the capital goods and other inputs needed by their export sectors, Latin American republics were heavily dependent on imports to meet the same demand. The rapid rise of the export sector in the British dominions had contributed to the emergence of factories providing finished goods for the local market, but in most of Latin America these purchases were satisfied by a combination of cottage industry and imports. In relation to its size and income per head, Latin America was underindustrialized before the First World War.[16]

Many obstacles had to be overcome before modern manufacturing could take root. The supply of energy was inadequate, transport costs for inputs and outputs were usually high, and the machinery had to be imported. Yet this was no different from the problem facing those peripheral countries (such as Romania and Switzerland) in which modern manufacturing was becoming established. What was different was official neglect. The ideology of Ricardian comparative advantage was taken seriously, the exchange of primary-product exports for manufactured imports was considered optimal, and state intervention favored the export sector. Occasional efforts to provide a measure of industry protection through tariff increases were countered by

---

15 A good analytical treatment of these issues can be found in Lewis (1989).
16 This was particularly true of Argentina. See Chapter 5, n. 78.

fluctuating real exchange rates, which could lower the cost of imports faster than customs duties were raising them, and an almost complete absence of credit facilities.

Where modern industry had been established, it was always high cost and usually inefficient.[17] Manufactured exports were possible only under the artificial circumstances provided by war and other disruptions to normal trade channels. Primary export substitution,[18] based on the export of labor-intensive manufactured products, was almost completely unknown in Latin America, whereas it contributed handsomely to the escape from the periphery of a number of other primary-product-exporting countries. Despite access to cotton at world prices and real wages at a fraction of British costs, the textile industry in Latin America had difficulty replacing imports from developed countries, yet alone generating a surplus for export.

One route to higher living standards under traditional export-led growth, favored particularly in Scandinavia, was an increase in domestic value added from processing primary products. Yet, despite the modest nature of cascading tariffs[19] and other trade-distorting devices in the nineteenth century, few examples of vertical integration within Latin American countries exist. Many of the primary exports returned transformed within imported finished products. Sometimes, as in the case of steel products based on iron ore, this was understandable. Often, as in the case of garments made from wool, it was less easy to justify. Only in Argentina, where the trade in live cattle and wheat gave way to chilled meat and flour, was there a serious attempt to capture the value added associated with each stage of the product chain.

The Argentine example showed that export-led growth could work well in the Latin American context. Argentina had been relatively slow to start its impressive export expansion, and there were numerous defects in the way the export-led model functioned, but the mechanics of export-led growth did not work flawlessly anywhere. Most countries that were peripheral at the beginning of the twentieth century regarded Argentina as a legitimate model, envying its wealth of commodity exports and diversified markets. Despite the relatively low level of industrialization, by the beginning of the twentieth century Argentina had achieved a level of income per head that attracted immigration from all over the world. Furthermore, the standard

---

17 "Inefficiency" is used in many different senses by economists. Here it refers both to the absence of allocative efficiency – a result of distorted factor prices – and to technical inefficiency; that is, the failure to maximize output for given inputs.

18 The phrase "primary-export substitution," first coined by Ranis (1981), refers to the policy switch in some East Asian countries in the late 1950s in favor of exporting simple manufactured goods that until then had been subject to import-substituting industrialization (ISI).

19 The tariff is said to be "cascading" when it rises in proportion to the degree of processing of the imported product. Such a tariff encourages exporting countries to ship their products in an unprocessed form and (even more important) provides a disincentive for exporting manufactured goods based on local natural resources.

of living was much more securely based in Argentina than in neighboring Uruguay, where rapid urbanization and a welfare state rested uneasily on an unchanged level of exports per head.

If Argentina was the undisputed success story during the first phase of postindependence development, the opposite was true in the second (inward-looking) phase. Yet there was nothing inevitable about this, and, indeed, the relative decline of the Argentine economy was not widely apparent until the 1950s. Poised on the threshold of developed-country status in the 1920s, Argentina will now have to continue to wait to join the club to which it has so long aspired. Although agricultural protectionism in the developed countries hurt Argentina badly, it was the accumulation of (avoidable) policy errors during the inward-looking phase that finally led to the republic's fall from grace.

The inward-looking phase in Latin America has acquired an almost mythical status as a result of the strong desire of contemporary social scientists to contrast it (unfavorably) with the modern version of export-led growth. Although much of this criticism is justified, it should not be exaggerated.[20] Inward-looking development was a legitimate response to the turmoil in international markets after 1913. The problem was that the phase began too slowly in Latin America and went on for too long. In the 1930s and even the 1940s the export-led growth model was still seen as providing the only coherent long-run option in many republics. Thus inward-looking development did not become the paradigm for the region until world trade had started to expand rapidly after the Second World War. The opportunity cost of the inward-looking model then became increasingly high, as the advantages to be reaped from international specialization were abandoned in favor of growing protection.

Although the costs of the inward-looking model eventually proved excessive, the benefits at first appeared substantial. The annual rate of growth of real GDP per head (see Table 12.2) increased for virtually all republics under inward-looking development compared with the rates estimated for the export-led growth phase (see Table 12.1). Many republics attained the 1.5 percent annual increase in real income per head in the half-century before 1980 that could have been regarded as a legitimate target in the nineteenth century. The goalposts had been moved, however. In mature capitalist countries (such as the United States) the long-run rate was now close to 2 percent, and the newly industrialized countries of Europe secured increases that were closer to 3 percent.[21]

---

20 One of the few objective assessments of the ISI model (throughout the developing countries) can be found in Bruton (1989).

21 Some of these countries (e.g., Finland, Greece, Hungary, and Spain) tripled the value of real GDP per head between 1950 and 1970. See Bairoch and Lévy-Leboyer (1981), Table 1.4.

Table 12.2. *Annual rate of growth of GDP
per head, circa 1928 to 1980 (in percentages)*

Country	GDP growth rate
Argentina	1.2
Brazil	2.9
Chile	1.3
Colombia	2.0
Costa Rica	2.2
Cuba	2.2
Ecuador	2.4
El Salvador	1.6
Guatemala	1.5
Honduras	0.6
Mexico	2.6
Nicaragua	0.8
Peru	2.7
Puerto Rico	3.2
Uruguay	1.0
Venezuela	3.6
Latin America[a]	2.1

[a] Based on the listed countries, with the exception
of Puerto Rico.
Source: Table A.3.2.

Judged by this more exacting standard, only a handful of Latin American
countries (Brazil, Mexico, Peru, Puerto Rico, and Venezuela) recorded an
adequate performance, and almost all of them had performed badly during
the period of traditional export-led growth. Furthermore, none of the countries that had done best under export-led growth could be included among
the success stories of inward-looking development. Indeed, if Argentina,
Chile, Cuba, and Uruguay had sustained a long-run rate of growth of 3 percent a year (as happened in a few countries) throughout the inward-looking
phase, they would have reached developed-country status before the advent
of the debt crisis.[22]

It is tempting to look for some causal explanation in the inverse relationship between country performance in the two phases. Republics (Brazil?)
that had done least well under export-led growth were perhaps more willing to sacrifice export interests on the altar of inward-looking development;
countries with successful export sectors (Cuba?) may have been more reluctant to abandon a tried-and-true formula. Well-entrenched export groups
could be relied on to provide a spirited defense of their commercial interests,

---

22 In the 1980s Argentina and Uruguay, for example, would have had a level of real GDP per head
close to $3,000 (at 1970 prices) – comparable to the level in a number of European countries.

and the emerging industrial sector would find more room to maneuver in a country with fragmented export interests. In order to overcome the resistance of a previously successful export sector (Argentina?), extreme measures may have been required that destabilized the economy or offered such huge incentives for inward-looking development (Uruguay?) that major price distortions were introduced. This line of analysis should not be pursued too far, however. Counterexamples exist, and many countries performed poorly during both phases.

The inward-looking phase favored the larger economies with their big domestic markets. The new activities promoted by import substitution were generally subject to economies of scale, so unit costs varied inversely with the length of production runs. Yet the optimal plant size tended to rise over time, and the delay in adopting inward-looking policies could be costly. Small factories were set up in the 1950s and 1960s throughout Latin America with suboptimal production levels and high unit costs; the same establishments might have been able to compete internationally if they had been founded a generation earlier.

The inward-looking phase saw the emergence of modern industry in all republics. The ratio of manufacturing net output to GDP rose rapidly, even in the smaller republics, but this was little consolation. Protected by a tariff wall that became progressively higher, the new factories often required additional nontariff barriers to satisfy the domestic market. As competition from imports vanished, pressure to improve quality and design dissipated. Competition among domestic producers might have relieved the situation, but oligopoly was much more common, with barriers to entry provided by high initial capital costs.

Oligopoly was associated with a high rate of return on capital in many branches of industry, an incentive for both foreign and domestic capital, but it did not lead to the research and development associated with high economic rents in developed countries. Subsidiaries of multinational companies, unlike their counterparts in developed countries, faced no internal or external threat to their dominant market position; domestic firms were usually content to follow the example set by the industry leaders. As a result, most of the change in output could be explained by increases in factor inputs with little increase in total factor productivity.[23] Sources-of-growth analysis for the larger countries has shown that the productivity of capital during the inward-looking phase hardly changed at all.[24]

This was an inadequate basis for shifting industrial production toward the world market once the trade in manufactured products began to accelerate

23 Total factor productivity measures the output per unit of all factor inputs. This means it is necessary to take a (weighted) average of the factor inputs.

24 See Elías (1992) for a rare application of sources-of-growth analysis to the major Latin American republics. On factor productivity growth in the twentieth century, see Hofman (2000).

after the Second World War. Export pessimism endured longer in Latin America than could possibly have been justified by the remaining pockets of protection in the advanced capitalist countries, and the lessons from the East Asian NICs were at first dismissed as irrelevant. Latin America played virtually no part in reshaping the rules of international trade after the war, despite having been on the winning side, and the General Agreement on Tariffs and Trade (GATT) was seen as a club for rich countries.

The regional-integration experiments of the 1960s were an attempt to overcome the limitations of the inward-looking model. Inspired in part by the success of the European Economic Community, the Latin American versions lacked the political commitment and vision that emerged in Europe from the ashes of two world wars and the loss of millions of lives. The erosion of national sovereignty and the implicit tax on consumers of agricultural products were regarded by European decision makers as an acceptable price to pay for internal security and external industrial competitiveness. Latin America aspired to the benefits, but it was not prepared to meet the costs. By the 1970s regional integration had degenerated into artificial schemes for promoting multinational investments, although intraregional trade – much of which enjoyed no privileges – continued to rise.

If the Great Depression and the Second World War finally crippled the export-led growth model, the debt crisis of the 1980s ended the inward-looking phase. No amount of import compression could release the resources needed to service debts and expand production. The tentative measures already adopted in support of nontraditional exports were strengthened, and new schemes were adopted throughout the region to shift resources back to the export sector. Trade was liberalized, and firms were at last forced to compete against imports. The ratio of exports to GDP finally began to rise again.

It is difficult to evaluate the new model and its impact on Latin America, since it has not been in operation very long, but some of the problems can already be identified. Some of the more successful countries during the inward-looking phase (Brazil?) have found it relatively harder to adopt the discipline associated with the new model. Many of the "nontraditional" exports under the new model have become "traditional" and are facing the same problems their more venerable predecessors encountered. The commodity lottery may be less important now than it was in the past, but natural resources (in an unprocessed form) are still subject to low income elasticities and price competition from synthetic products. There is still great reluctance to complete the processing of primary products in the country of origin, and high-technology manufactured exports are still confined to a few larger countries.

The secular boom in world trade after 1950 was quite exceptional – a golden age in response to the accumulation of trade restrictions over the previous two decades. Even if the trade pessimists are wrong, world exports should not be expected to rise again at their golden-age rate. The conclusion of GATT's Uruguay Round at the end of 1993 and the launch of the Doha Round in 2001 were considerable achievements, but they did not herald the end of trade frictions. Thus the new export-led growth model will need to harness the stimulus from trade more efficiently if the nonexport sector is to be transformed. The commodity lottery may have declined in importance, as manufactured goods slowly replace primary products in the export list, but the mechanics of export-led growth are as important as ever.

Harnessing the engine of growth, whether it has been the export sector or import-substituting industry, to ensure the development of the rest of the economy has always been difficult in Latin America. In the presence of formidable barriers – physical, economic, and financial – the initial stimulus has often withered away before reaching low-productivity activities in distant regions. Public policy has rightly been seen as crucial in the destruction of these barriers.

The policy environment has also been important in nurturing the engine of growth itself. The swashbuckling entrepreneur who cut a swath through the tropical jungle in pursuit of profit may have captured the imagination of the outside world,[25] but no foreign capitalists and very few domestic ones have ever invested a cent before the ground rules have been agreed on with the government. If the public sector was at first unable to provide adequate infrastructure, credit, or basic inputs, it could still offer land, labor legislation, and tariff concessions. The emergence of an engine of growth was usually intimately linked to these changes in public policy, and very few powerful export sectors or even import-competing complexes arose spontaneously in Latin America.

These sectoral policies have a long, and often successful, history in Latin America. Meat in Argentina, coffee in Guatemala, and oil in Venezuela are all commodities for which the policy framework was a vital ingredient in the emergence of a dynamic export sector in the first phase of postindependence development. Basic industry in Brazil, textiles in Colombia, and *maquiladoras* in Mexico are examples from the second phase. Export-processing zones (EPZs) in the Caribbean Basin are examples from the third phase. Although failures (e.g., coffee in nineteenth-century Honduras) did occur, successes were numerous. The state had sufficient control over resources to influence their allocation and often simply responded to pressure from the private sector in favor of particular activities.

The exchange-rate has played a leading part in the evolution of sectoral policies. Fluctuating real effective exchange rates have been a powerful and

---

25 See, for example, the biography of Minor Cooper Keith, founder of the United Fruit Company, by Stewart (1964).

transparent instrument for shifting resources into or out of chosen sectors. Currency movements have sometimes backfired, driving resources out of privileged areas as a result of unintended appreciation. Yet this has only reinforced public and private awareness of the effectiveness of exchange-rate policy. Since independence it has been the single most important instrument controlled by the authorities. This has remained true even during periods of fixed nominal exchange rates, under the gold, silver, or dollar standard, because real exchange rates can change rapidly.

The sectoral dimension of public policy has always been the easiest part. The policy framework has contributed to the (often substantial) economic rents in the favored sector. As signs of exhaustion emerged in the engine of growth, the need to invest these rents in other areas with higher social rates of return became paramount. Taxation could have played a leading role in easing the transfer. Yet fiscal policy has been quite inadequate in Latin America throughout its postindependent history. The result has been a tendency toward inertia in the allocation of resources, with favored activities retaining their privileged position long after it was socially justified. Perhaps the best example is coffee, which remains one of the leading exports from Latin America after nearly a century in which world supply has shown an irresistible tendency to outstrip demand.

Inadequate fiscal resources and antiquated tax structures have usually prevented Latin American governments from making the modest expenditures needed to increase the flexibility of the economic system. Potentially productive regions remained trapped by the almost complete absence of communications, unable to develop an agricultural surplus and provide a market for industrial goods. Illiteracy has remained a scourge for much of the postindependence period, hindering technological progress and discouraging innovation. Labor productivity growth has been restrained by inadequate expenditure on disease control and a health system geared to the needs of the upper deciles.[26]

Sometimes the pressure to increase public expenditure has overcome the inhibitions resulting from insufficient revenue. Where capital markets were undeveloped and foreign borrowing was restricted, the results invariably were monetary expansion and inflation. Such episodes were usually short lived in the first phase of development, even though Argentina, Brazil, and Chile had already acquired an inflationary reputation by the end of the nineteenth century. Hyperinflation was also not unknown, although this phenomenon was always associated with war or civil war before the 1940s. Generally, however, Latin American governments accepted the constraints on public spending implied by modest tax revenues in the first phase of

26 The health subsidy per household in Colombia, for example, was 26 percent higher for the top quintile than for the bottom quintile, according to one definition. See Selowsky (1979), pp. 94–7.

development. Indeed, the suspension of debt-service payments was a more common response than monetary expansion to the gap between revenue and expenditure.

The second phase of development was associated with the spread of inflation. The new model generated shifts in demand that could not easily be accommodated within the relatively inflexible systems inherited from the first phase. The structuralists were correct in drawing attention to these bottlenecks that contributed to inflationary pressures. The relative decline in the importance of foreign supply and the absolute decline in imported consumer goods meant, however, that monetary lack of discipline was more likely to be punished by domestic price increases. The monetarist case for orthodox monetary policy and flexible prices could not easily be dismissed.

Even during the second phase of development many Latin American republics sustained low inflation rates and exchange-rate stability. Not until the 1980s did inflation become endemic in the region, with virtually all countries suffering from double-digit annual rates and with episodes of hyperinflation more common. Inflation, however, played havoc with Latin America's attempts to integrate into global product and factor markets, while undermining the economic reforms. Inflation stabilization programs in the 1990s were helped by the impact of capital inflows on the real exchange-rate, bringing a permanent adjustment to moderate rates of inflation in most countries.

The losers from inflation acceleration in the 1980s were the poor: Income inequality increased in many countries, and the absolute numbers of people living in poverty rose. Poverty (both absolute and relative) and inequality have been constant features of the Latin American landscape in the postindependence period, however; Latin America has been scarred by gaps in living standards between the poorest and richest that have given it a reputation (almost certainly deserved) as the region with the most unequal distribution of income in the world.

Throughout its independent history Latin America has been marked by extremes of inequality – in the distribution of income and wealth and even between regions within the same country. Inequality has brought a concentration of power, with the state reflecting the interests of the dominant group. Under such circumstances change has often been achieved only through violence, and economic development has suffered accordingly. High rates of investment, favored in theory by inequality, have been comparatively rare, and the rich have consumed a higher proportion of their income than have their counterparts abroad. The gap between private investment and the rate of capital formation required to increase living standards rapidly was filled by the public sector after the Second World War, but this stretched the resources of the state beyond the limits of prudence. The process collapsed in the 1980s.

The problem of inequality was inherited from the colonial period, in which the distribution of assets (principally land) favored a concentration of income. Fiscal policy, as in all countries at that time, did not aim at redistribution, and the transfers to the poor through Church wealth were too modest to make much of an impact on income inequality. Only in Costa Rica, where the abundance of land and absence of labor made family farming the only option, were income and wealth more equally distributed.[27]

The first phase of economic development after independence provided an opportunity to correct the inherited problem of inequality. An export-led growth model based on labor-intensive primary products at a time of labor scarcity was a potentially powerful formula for altering the relative returns to factors of production and for shifting the distribution of income in favor of the lower deciles. Capital was also scarce, however, and the owners of land (joined later by foreign investors) became the owners of the new capital, controlling the dynamics of export-led growth. The labor market was subject to coercion, and access to land was artificially restricted to produce a labor force for the expanding sectors at a fixed or even lower real wage. Currency depreciation became an additional device for lowering real costs in the export sector without the need to engage in coercion.

Market forces were therefore manipulated to undermine the shift in the distribution of income that should have occurred in the first phase of development, and state intervention exacerbated the problem. The inherited problem of wealth inequality was made worse by land grants from the public domain and concessions to the owners of capital – domestic and foreign – which again concentrated income in the upper deciles. The privatization of Church wealth – an additional opportunity to redistribute income and improve equality – was yet another occasion on which the rich and powerful were able to add to their holdings of land, even thwarting the redistributive intentions of certain governments.[28]

The second, inward-looking, phase may have led at first to an improvement in the distribution of income in some countries (not enough statistics are available for anyone to be certain). The shift of resources from low-productivity agriculture and cottage industry to sectors protected from international competition by high tariffs, coupled with the spread of urban trade unions and mass political parties, was a potent cocktail while labor scarcity remained widespread. However, the emergence of a labor surplus throughout Latin America after the Second World War undermined what little progress had been made. By the end of the second phase income and

---

27 Costa Rica's egalitarianism, however, did not survive the disappearance of the land frontier. By the late twentieth century the distribution of income was only marginally more equal in Costa Rica than in the rest of Latin America.

28 This was clearly the case during the reform period in Mexico under Benito Juárez.

wealth were demonstrably concentrated in the upper deciles, and Gini coefficients were sliding into higher and higher bands.

The third phase of development, once again based on exports, began with an opportunity to improve the distribution of income and wealth through privatization of state assets. Like Church wealth in the nineteenth century, however, state assets in the late twentieth century have been transferred overwhelmingly to the upper deciles. Defense mechanisms to prevent a concentration of ownership have broken down, much state property has been sold at prices that do not reflect its market value, and few attempts have been made to ensure that the proceeds of sale are used by government agencies to improve the position of the lower deciles. Privatization may still be desirable on efficiency grounds, but the opportunity for decreasing inequality has been lost. Meanwhile, the new model of export-led growth has not led to a transfer of income shares from rich to poor, although in many countries it has reduced the proportion of household living in poverty.

For most of the postindependence period, therefore, the dynamics of the dominant model of economic development have either preserved the existing level of inequality or have exacerbated it. Countervailing forces have usually depended on state intervention, and public policy in Latin America in the twentieth century has often had a redistributive dimension. Its impact, however, has been much more limited. The orthodox instruments at the disposal of the state have been blunt and ineffective; the unorthodox instruments have tended to produce political chaos and counterrevolution. It has been an unpleasant dilemma.

The biggest disappointment has been fiscal policy. Used to great effect by developed countries, fiscal policy in Latin America has had only the most modest impact on the distribution of income. Marginal rates of direct taxation may have exceeded average rates, but dependence on indirect taxes has given the fiscal system a regressive character. The small number of income-tax payers has made it difficult to alter post-tax income on the revenue side. Any hope that social expenditure could be targeted on the poor has been frustrated by the ability of the middle and even upper classes to reap most of the benefits from spending on health, education, and social security. The lowest deciles have remained outside the system, lacking voice and political influence,[29] with their major gain to be found in the spread of primary education.

One of the problems with fiscal policy has been the constant need to consider its other functions in the design of redistributive policy. Taxation plays many roles, in addition to redistributing income, and expenditure must be financed by domestic or foreign resources, with numerous implications for resource allocation. Only oil-rich Venezuela has been able to use the fiscal

---

29 On the concept of "voice," see Hirschman (1981).

system primarily as a tool for redistributing income without much consideration of efficiency and private-sector incentives. Budget deficits caused by expenditures targeted on the poor have led to fiscal imbalance, so the targeted group has been often punished with accelerating inflation.

Unorthodox policies in favor of redistribution have been subject to no such restrictions.[30] Designed to "soak the rich," they have usually been effective in the short run but counterproductive in the long run. The massive redistribution of income under Juan Domingo Perón contributed to the crisis in Argentine society in the subsequent forty years. The Chilean experiment under Salvador Allende ended in military dictatorship. The Peruvian one under Alan García led to hyperinflation. In the end the poor in Nicaragua suffered more under the Sandinistas than they had under the Somoza dynasty. Although the Cuban experiment under Castro has endured, it is by no means certain that gains have outweighed losses.

The prospects for improvement in income distribution remain poor until the demographic transition has eliminated Latin America's labor surplus. That will take time. The crude birth rate will not fall into line with the death rate until the middle of the twenty-first century, although the gap has been narrowing. Unorthodox remedies remain problematic, so any improvement in the medium term will require a strengthening of orthodox policies. This serves to underline the case for fiscal reform and a change in the pattern of public expenditure – both areas that need priority research.[31]

If the state has been relatively passive (and ineffective) in distribution, it has been more active in the sphere of production. Not all of the monopolies inherited from the colonial authorities were sold off, the embryonic banking sector had to be nurtured by the state, and even nineteenth-century railways often had a public-sector component. The twentieth century saw an expansion into public utilities, mining, basic industries (including oil refining), and communications, and even agriculture and construction have experienced state involvement. Direct state participation in production has been complemented by an array of indirect measures to promote output and to affect the allocation of resources among the different branches of the economy.

Such an active role for the state, during a period in which the state has usually been relatively weak and little more than an expression of the class interests of the dominant groups, would have been unthinkable without acceptance by the private sector. Indeed, most state intervention – certainly before the 1970s – can be attributed to the market failures that tend to arise in poor countries with limited infrastructure and few producers. The state may have been prepared to compete with foreign private interests

---

30 See Ascher (1984) for accounts of several unorthodox redistributive programs in Latin America.
31 Both the World Bank and the Inter-American Development Bank began to give much higher priority to fiscal reform and poverty reduction at the beginning of the 1990s.

(as with nineteenth-century railways) or even expropriate them (as with twentieth-century oil), but the private domestic sector was generally assured of sufficient economic space to develop its own interests without direct competition from the public sector.

Although market failures have been widespread in Latin America, for most of its history the state has lacked the resources with which to respond. Thus state intervention before 1940 was in fact much more modest than activist ideology might have suggested.[32] As soon as the resources at the disposal of the state have increased, governments have tended to expand the range of their activities. The inconvertible sterling balances controlled by Perón were an open invitation to purchase British properties after the Second World War. Oil rents extracted by the Venezuelan state since 1940 have provided the lubricant for penetrating virgin territory. Access to seemingly unlimited foreign resources in the 1970s was an irresistible temptation for virtually every government.

State intervention has now gone into reverse as the public sector withdraws from areas it invaded after 1940.[33] A more traditional relationship has been restored, with the state subject to fiscal restraint and scarce resources. Only a few "sacred cows" remain, protected above all by their ability to create and transfer rents to the public sector.

The profitability of the private sector remains highly sensitive to state intervention in the broadest sense, however. In the first phase of development the profitability of the export sector often hinged on the matrix of instruments controlled by the state. Indeed, with volatile world markets, state intervention was seen as essential to protect the private sector from the inevitable fluctuations implied by peripheral status. Coffee valorization in Brazil was a public response to a private-sector crisis: Export (and import) duties were varied in line with the needs of the export sector. Public infrastructure was geared to the needs of primary products. In the second (inward-looking) phase, private profitability was perhaps even more sensitive to the level at which public instruments were set. The exchange-rate, tariffs, quotas, and licenses were usually a more important guide to success or failure in the import-competing sector than were intrafirm decisions on the allocation of resources and investment.

The state, therefore, has neither wished nor been able to withdraw from the production arena, as favored by the classical liberals. On those occasions when the state has been forced by its weakness to remain essentially passive, the result has been not so much an explosion of private sector initiative as an absence of new activity. Indeed, the delay in promoting export growth (let alone export-led growth) in so many nineteenth-century Latin American

32 See Whitehead (1994).
33 The state has even withdrawn from some areas (e.g., public utilities) invaded before 1940.

countries can be attributed in part to the failure of the state to address even the most minimal requirements of the export sector.

Although state intervention has generally complemented and encouraged private investment, it has not produced competition. On the contrary, the formal sector in Latin America has been subject to imperfect competition, oligopolistic structures, and (on occasion) outright monopoly. Where there has been a mass of sellers, as in some branches of agricultural production, they have usually faced a limited number of buyers. Indeed, each link in the processing chain has tended to be associated with an increase in concentration. Only in the urban informal sector, a relatively recent phenomenon, have competition and a large number of buyers and sellers been a normal state of affairs.

Oligopoly and market concentration are not necessarily the enemy of economic progress. The long-run keys to development and a higher standard of living are capital accumulation, technical progress, and an increase in total factor productivity – all associated in many countries with firms that enjoy market power. Although allocative efficiency is undermined by imperfect competition, oligopoly has been associated in many countries with economic rents that have made possible a faster long-run rate of growth. However "perfect" competition may be in the urban informal sector, it is difficult to believe that this is the route to a rapid increase in living standards through total factor-productivity growth.

Latin America's oligopolistic structures may have yielded above-normal profits and substantial economic rents, but they have not traditionally been associated with technical progress, investment booms, or total factor-productivity growth.[34] Rents in the primary-product export sector were diluted through consumption expenditures in the capitals of Europe, with long-run profitability assured by land abundance and a pliant state; supranormal profits during the inward-looking phase were often transferred abroad, with profitability guaranteed by the absence of international competitors. The stimulus to use the rents productively, so manifest in the United States in the nineteenth century or in Japan since the Second World War, has been absent.

The transfer of assets to the domestic private sector, whether through alienation of church wealth, expropriation of foreign property, or privatization of state assets, has never been used to enhance the competitive environment. Instead, new (often family-based) conglomerates have emerged to challenge the hegemony of established groups and join the charmed circle with influence and power over state decisions. The rent-seeking tactics of the inward-looking phase, based on the transfer of state privileges from

---

34 The slow rate of technical progress and the low level of research and development is the main theme of a major study of Latin American economic backwardness in Fajnzylber (1990), Chapter 2.

one group to another, are now being replaced by rent-creating strategies based on access to international markets and cost reductions. Yet the new phase of development will be no more successful than its predecessors unless a way can be found to transform rents into technical progress and total factor-productivity growth.

It is unrealistic to expect all Latin American republics to perform equally well in the new phase. The losers easily outnumbered the winners from the first phase of development; if the second phase produced a greater number of successes, failures – some quite spectacular – were still numerous. No single formula can ever guarantee a favorable outcome for all members of this particular club. Yet it would be surprising indeed if the third phase were not associated with a rapid rise in living standards in some Latin American republics, bringing their GDP per head up to the level of the poorer developed countries by the middle of the twenty-first century. That is the ray of hope to which those who still live in crushing poverty must turn their gaze. Yet, even if the goal is clear, the route forward is uncertain. Those countries that stumble through the incompetence, corruption, or greed of their elites can expect to be severely punished. That is the warning the privileged must heed.

APPENDIX 1

Data sources for population and exports before 1914

Population

The quality of population census data in nineteenth-century Latin America leaves much to be desired. Enumeration was often incomplete, the Indian population was occasionally ignored, and the margin of error was substantial. All estimates of total population must therefore be regarded with caution. However, twentieth-century scholarship has done much to remedy the deficiencies of nineteenth-century statistics. As a result figures exist for Latin American countries from the mid-nineteenth century onward, which can be combined to give estimates for all of Latin America at various intervals. For present purposes I chose the years 1850, 1870, 1890, and 1912[1].

For most of the period before the First World War, Puerto Rico was part of the Latin American community, and Panama did not exist as an independent country. In the interests of consistency, I therefore included figures for Puerto Rico after 1898 (following its annexation by the United States), and I continued to include Panama in the Colombian figures after 1903 (following its declaration of independence from Colombia).

Table A.1.1 gives the population figures for the relevant years. The 1850 data are from Sánchez-Albórnoz (1986), p. 122, with the exception of the five Central American republics, for which the data were taken from Woodward (1985), p. 478, and reflect more recent scholarship on Central American population figures. For later years the main source is Mitchell (1993), with intercensal years interpolated using the implied geometric annual rate of growth. The exceptions are the Dominican Republic, Haiti, and Uruguay, where interpolation has been made on the basis of the figures in Sánchez-Albórnoz (1986), p. 122. For the other countries (Australia, Canada, New Zealand, and the United States) I used Mitchell (1993). The interested reader should also consult Maddison (2001), Table A2-f, p. 198, which provides estimates of population growth rates for a sample of countries from 1820–70 and for all countries from 1870 onward.

Exports

The figures on exports for nineteenth-century Latin America are varied. Some countries (e.g., Brazil and Chile) have complete and consistent series; others (e.g., Haiti and Honduras) have

---

1 For 1900 and 1910, there is a complete set of population statistics in Thorp (1998), Appendix Table 1.1, p. 313.

Table A.1.1. *The population of Latin America, circa 1850 to circa 1912*
(in thousands)

Country	Circa 1850	Circa 1870	Circa 1890	Circa 1912
Argentina	1,100	1,793	3,366	7,333
Bolivia	1,374	1,495	1,626	1,866
Brazil	7,230	9,808	14,334	24,386
Chile	1,443	1,943	2,600	3,414
Colombia[a]	2,200	2,819	3,610	5,363
Costa Rica	101	137	228	355
Cuba	1,186	1,459	1,617	2,364
Dominican Republic	146	242	400	729
Ecuador	816	1,013	1,257	1,708
El Salvador	366	493	785	1,107
Guatemala	847	1,080	1,331	1,772
Haiti	938	1,150	1,409	1,860
Honduras	230	265	355	570
Mexico	7,662	9,100	11,282	14,262
Nicaragua	274	337	379	558
Paraguay	350	221	350	565
Peru	2,001	2,568	2,972	4,561
Puerto Rico	495	667	835	1,152
Uruguay	132	286	621	1,144
Venezuela	1,490	1,752	2,305	2,387
Latin America	30,381	38,628	51,662	77,456
Australia	786	1,609	3,067	4,545
Canada[b]	2,546	3,790	4,975	7,591
New Zealand	27	246	617	1,076
United States	23,192	39,818	62,948	94,569

[a] Includes Panama.
[b] Includes Newfoundland.
Sources: The 1850 data are from Sánchez-Albórnoz (1986), p. 122 (excluding Central America) and Woodward (1985), p. 478 (for Central America). For later years and for non–Latin American countries, the main source is Mitchell (1993), with intercensal years interpolated using the implied geometric annual rate of growth. The exceptions are the Dominican Republic, Haiti, and Uruguay, for which interpolation has been done on the basis of the figures in Sánchez-Albórnoz (1986), p. 122.

only the most partial data. In addition, data are presented in a variety of currencies, which must be converted into a common unit of account (I chose the U.S. dollar). This requires knowledge of the relevant exchange rates which – for the nineteenth century – is not always simple to acquire.

In order to calculate figures on exports per head (as used in Chapter 3), it was necessary to construct estimates of exports for the same years as for population: 1850, 1870, 1890, and 1912. In view of the fluctuations in exports from year to year, I used three-year averages wherever possible. In four cases (Puerto Rico in 1850; Cuba, Honduras, and Paraguay in

Table A.1.2. *Latin American exports, circa 1850 to circa 1912 (three-year averages, in thousands of US$)*

Country	Circa 1850	Circa 1870	Circa 1890	Circa 1912
Argentina	11,310	29,667	109,000	454,420
Bolivia	7,500	12,916	20,200	34,625
Brazil	35,850	83,880	136,977	346,828
Chile	11,308	27,625	52,750	152,750
Colombia[a]	4,133	18,600	20,533	32,800
Costa Rica	1,150	2,900	8,633	9,612
Cuba	26,333	67,000[b]	90,000	153,000
Dominican Republic	500	1,200	3,233	11,300
Ecuador	1,594	4,133	5,833	13,496
El Salvador	1,185	3,586	5,301	9,229
Guatemala	1,404	2,655	10,030	12,871
Haiti	4,499	7,425	14,166	11,300
Honduras	1,125	951[c]	2,874	2,668
Mexico	24,313	21,276	50,000	152,883
Nicaragua	1,010	1,178	3,833	6,051
Paraguay	451	1,582[d]	2,990	4,833
Peru	7,500	25,834	9,910	43,000
Puerto Rico	6,204[e]	6,421	9,167	46,242
Uruguay	7,250	13,333	27,667	57,600
Venezuela	4,865	11,961	19,050	25,026
Latin America	**159,484**	**344,123**	**602,147**	**1,580,534**
Australia	13,000	101,833	161,833	395,333
Canada[f]	16,325	77,132	107,825	393,833
New Zealand	578	23,882	47,700	106,333
United States	162,000	400,000	859,667	2,307,000

[a] Includes Panama.
[b] Datum is for 1877.
[c] Datum is for 1882.
[d] Datum is for 1879.
[e] Datum is for 1844.
[f] Includes Newfoundland.

1870) it was not possible to form an estimate of exports. In these four cases I estimated exports for the nearest available year and calculated exports per head by adjusting the population figures (again using interpolation). Annual growth rates for exports or exports per head used in Chapter 3 reflect this difference in the choice of base or terminal year.

The figures for exports (in U.S. dollars) are given in Table A.1.2. The sources used are so numerous that they are listed separately below.[2] Information is given not only on the source for each year but also on the original currency (a) and on the exchange rate used to

2 The interested reader should also consult Maddison (2001), Table F-1, p. 360 and, for post-1900 data, Thorp (1998), Appendix VI.

convert primary data (where appropriate) into U.S. dollars (b). Note that exchange rates are expressed as units of domestic currency per U.S. dollar, except for the pound sterling/U.S. dollar rate, which is given as the number of U.S. dollars per pound (assumed to equal five throughout the 1850–1912 period). The data on exports per head (see Table 3.5) were then obtained from Table A.1.1 and A.1.2.

Argentina

1850. Mulhall and Mulhall (1885). (a) Gold pesos. (b) 1.
1870. Mitchell (1993). (a) Gold pesos. (b) 1.
1890. Mitchell (1993). (a) Gold pesos. (b) 1.
Cortés Conde (1985), Table 14, p. 365, contains a lower (unofficial) estimate for exports in 1880–90.
1912. Mitchell (1993). (a) Paper pesos. (b) 2.27. See Mills (n.d.), pp. 200–1.

Bolivia

1850. Klein (1992), Table 2, p. 320, for average silver production in 1840–9 and 1850–9 (I used the average of the two periods). Peñaloza Cordero (1983) for silver price in 1850 in U.S. dollars. I then assumed that silver constituted two-thirds of all exports in 1850.
1870. Based on growth of silver production, using Klein (1992), Table 2, p. 32. I assumed that the 1870 figure was equal to the average of 1860–69.
1890. Bureau of the American Republics (1892a) contains an unofficial U.S. dollar estimate, which is more reliable than the official estimate.
1912. Mitchell (1993). (a) Bolivianos. (b) 2.57. See Mills (n.d.), pp. 200–1.

Brazil

For all years, Leff (1982). (a) Pounds sterling. (b) 5.

Chile

1850. Palma (1979), Appendix 11. (a) Constant (1900) pounds sterling. I have adjusted the figure to current pounds using the UK wholesale price index in Appendix 3 of the same source. (b) 5.
All other years. Mitchell (1993). (a) Gold pesos. (b) 2.666. See Mills (n.d.), pp. 200–1.

Colombia

1850, 1870, and 1890. Urrutia and Arrubla (1970), using McGreevey's unofficial U.S. dollar series (including gold).

1912. Mitchell (1993) excludes gold, so it could not be used. Instead, I used Levine (1914), Eder (1912), and League of Nations (1926). (a) Gold pesos. (b) 1. For 1912 I added in the figure for Panama. See Mitchell (1993).

Costa Rica

1850. Molina (1851). (a) Pesos. (b) 1.
1870. Mitchell (1993). (a) Pesos. (b) 1.
1890. Mitchell (1993). (a) Pesos. (b) 1.50. See Bureau of the American Republics (1892b).
1912. Mitchell (1993). (a) Pesos. (b) 2.15. See Young (1925).

Cuba

1850. Mitchell (1993). (a) Pesos. (b) 1.
1870. Mitchell (1993). (a) Pesos. (b) 1. The datum is for 1877.
1890. Mitchell (1993). (a) Pesos. (b) 1. The datum is for 1892 (assumed to be the same as in 1890).
1912. Mitchell (1993). (a) Pesos. (b) 1.

Dominican Republic

1850. No official estimate exists. Exports per head are assumed to be 70 percent of Haitian figure.
1870. Mitchell (1993). (a) Pesos. (b) 1. The datum is for 1872 (assumed to be the same as in 1870).
1890 and 1912. Mitchell (1993). (a) Pesos. (b) 1.

Ecuador

1850. Rodríguez (1985), p. 191. The datum is the average of 1847 and 1853. (a) Sucres. (b) 1.
1870. Rodríguez (1985), p. 197. (a) Sucres. (b) 1.
1890. Mitchell (1993). (a) Sucres. (b) 1.428. See Bureau of the American Republics (1892c).
1912. Mitchell (1993). (a) Sucres. (b) 2.05. See Mills (n.d.), pp. 200–1.

El Salvador

1850. Lindo-Fuentes (1990). (a) Pesos. (b) 1.
1870. Lindo-Fuentes (1990). (a) Pesos. (b) 1.
1890. Lindo-Fuentes (1990). (a) Pesos. (b) 1.267. See Young (1925).
1912. Mitchell (1993). (a) Colones. (b) 2.42. See Young (1925).

Guatemala

1850. Mitchell (1993). (a) Pesos. (b) 1. The datum is for 1851 (assumed to be the same as in 1850).

1870. Mitchell (1993). (a) Pesos. (b) 1.

1890. Mitchell (1993). (a) Pesos. (b) 1.39. See Young (1925).

1912. Mitchell (1993). (a) Gold pesos. (b) 1.

Haiti

1850. Benoit (1954). I used quantity of coffee exports multiplied by the Brazilian export unit value in dollars – see IBGE (1987) – and assumed that coffee represented 88 percent of total exports – see St. John (1888), pp. 328–32.

1870. Benoit (1954). The same as for 1850, but assuming that coffee is 80 percent of total exports.

1890. Bureau of the American Republics (1892d). (a) U.S. dollars.

1912. Pan-American Union (1952). (a) U.S. dollars.

Honduras

1850. Squier (1856). (a) U.S. dollars.

1870. Molina Chocano (1982). (a) Pesos. (b) 1. The datum is for 1882.

1890. Molina Chocano (1982). (a) Pesos. (b) 1.428. See Young (1925). The datum is for 1889 (assumed to be the same as in 1890).

1912. Mitchell (1993). (a) Gold pesos. (b) 1. Smuggled exports are thought to have been important. See Bureau of the American Republics (1904).

Mexico

1850. Herrera Canales (1977), p. 161. (a) Pesos fuertes. The figure for 1828 is 14,488,793 pesos fuertes; for 1856, 28,000,000 pesos fuertes. The implied annual rate of growth is 2.38 percent, and I used this to derive the 1850 figure. (b) 1.

1870. Average of 1870–2. Herrera Canales (1977), p. 161. (a) Pesos fuertes. (b) 1.

1890. Mitchell (1993). (a) Pesos. (b) 1.333. See Rosenzweig Hernández (1989), p. 174.

1912. Mitchell (1993). (a) Pesos. (b) 2 (fixed under the gold standard).

Nicaragua

1850. Woodward (1985). (a) U.S. dollars. The datum is for 1851 (assumed to be the same as in 1850).

1870. Woodward (1985). (a) U.S. dollars. The datum is the average of 1870 and 1871.

1890. Bureau of the American Republics (1892e) (a) U.S. dollars.

1912. Young (1925). (a) U.S. dollars. Mitchell (1993) could not be used because it excludes gold.

Paraguay

1850. Bourgade (1892). (a) Pesos. (b) 1. The datum is the average of 1851, 1852, and 1853 (assumed to be the same as in 1850).

1870. Mitchell (1993). (a) Pesos. (b) 1. The datum is for 1879.

1890. Mitchell (1993). (a) Gold pesos. (b) 1.

1912. Mitchell (1993). (a) Gold pesos. (b) 1.

Peru

1850. Mitchell (1993). (a) Pesos. (b) 1. See Gootenberg (1989), p. 164. The datum is for 1851 (assumed to be the same as in 1850).

1870. Mitchell (1993). (a) Soles. (b) 0.8. See Gootenberg (1989), p. 164.

1890. Thorp and Bertram (1978), p. 334. (a) Pounds sterling. (b) 5.

1912. Mitchell (1993). (a) Soles. (b) 2. See Mills (n.d.), pp. 200–1.

Puerto Rico

1850. Dietz (1986), p. 18. (a) Pesos. (b) 1. The datum is for 1844.

1870. Dietz (1986), p. 18. (a) Pesos. (b) 1. The datum is the average of 1865 and 1874.

1890. Bergad (1983), p. 146. (a) Pesos. (b) 1. The datum is the sum of coffee and sugar.

1912. Clark (1975), p. 607. (a) U.S. dollars.

Uruguay

1850. Mulhall and Mulhall (1885), p. 580. The datum is the average for 1841–60. See also Acevedo (1902), vol. 2, p. 146. (a) U.S. dollars.

1870. Mitchell (1993). (a) Pesos fuertes. (b) 1.

1890. Mitchell (1993). (a) Pesos fuertes. (b) 1.

1912. Finch (1981), p. 124. This is an unofficial estimate (the average of 1911 and 1913), which is considered more accurate than the official values in Mitchell (1993).

Venezuela

1850. Bureau of the American Republics (1892h). (a) U.S. dollars. Imports and exports are reversed by mistake in the source.

1870. Bureau of the American Republics (1892h). (a) U.S. dollars. The datum is for 1872–3 (assumed to be the same as in 1870).

1890. Bureau of the American Republics (1892h). (a) U.S. dollars. The datum is the average of 1889 and 1890.

1912. Mitchell (1993). (a) Bolívares. (b). 5.18. See Mills (n.d.), pp. 200–1.

All other countries are from Mitchell (1993).

APPENDIX 2

The ratio of exports to gross domestic product, the purchasing power of exports, and the volume of exports, circa 1850 to circa 1912

The criteria used in Chapter 3 for measuring the success or failure of export-led growth require information on the ratio of exports to GDP and the purchasing power of exports before 1914. This appendix explains the methods I used to calculate the statistics.

The ratio of exports to GDP

Calculation of the required rate of growth of exports in equation (3.1) involves estimation of the ratio of exports to GDP (w). Because w can be assumed to change over time, it is necessary to estimate it at the beginning (circa 1850) and at the end (circa 1912) of the period.

The ratio of exports to GDP is the same as the ratio of exports per head to GDP per head. Table 3.5 provides data on exports per head in current dollars for all countries at different time intervals, and Figure 5.1 provides data on GDP per head circa 1912 for fourteen countries at constant (1970) dollars (see Appendix 3). Estimates for w in 1912 can therefore be obtained by converting the GDP data to current dollars using a deflator obtained from U.S. price indexes. See Mitchell (1993). Assuming that 1970 equals 100, the 1912 price index can be calculated as 35. Thus the GDP data were converted to current dollars by multiplying by 0.35. This allows calculation of w in 1912 for the fourteen countries that provided GDP data. In the case of the other six countries (Bolivia, Dominican Republic, Ecuador, Haiti, Paraguay, and Venezuela) it could safely be assumed that all had a level of GDP per head in 1912 between the regional average and the lowest recorded rates (found in Brazil, El Salvador, and Peru). This gave a range of between $40 and $80 in current prices, and my final choice was made on the basis of a variety of indicators.

The estimates of exports per head, GDP per head, and w for 1912 are shown in Table A.2.1. Because Latin America had been following export-led growth before 1912, it is safe to assume that in almost all cases the estimate of w was higher at the end of the period than at the beginning. The exception is Uruguay, where the stagnation of exports per head, coupled with evidence of a rise in living standards, suggests that by 1912 w had fallen from its previous level.

In Chapter 3 the criterion for the success or failure of export-led growth is whether or not the rate of growth of exports exceeds the minimum required rate as indicated by Figures 3.1 and 3.2. The minimum rate is given, ceteris paribus, by the highest value for w. Thus the estimates of export shares for 1912 are the most important, because (with the exception

419

Table A.2.1. *The ratio of exports to GDP, w, 1850 and 1912 (based on current prices, in US$)*

Country	w in 1850	Exports per head in 1912	GDP per head in 1912	w in 1912	Range of w
Argentina	0.2	62.0	188	0.33	0.2–0.3
Bolivia	0.1	18.6	(60)	0.31	0.1–0.3
Brazil	0.1	14.2	44	0.32	0.1–0.3
Chile	0.1	44.7	140	0.32	0.1–0.3
Colombia	0.1	6.4	45	0.14	0.1–0.2
Costa Rica	0.2	27.1	76	0.36[a]	0.2–0.4
Cuba	0.3	64.7	148[b]	0.44	0.3–0.4
Dominican Republic	0.1	15.5	(65)	0.24	0.1–0.2
Ecuador	0.1	7.9	(40)	0.20	0.1–0.2
El Salvador	0.1	8.3	39	0.21[a]	0.1–0.2
Guatemala	0.1	7.2	65	0.11[a]	0.1–0.2
Haiti	0.1	6.1	(40)	0.15	0.1–0.2
Honduras	0.1	4.7	67	0.07[a]	0.1–0.2
Mexico	0.1	10.7	78	0.14	0.1–0.2
Nicaragua	0.1	10.8	54	0.2[a]	0.1–0.2
Paraguay	0.1	8.6	(40)	0.22	0.1–0.2
Peru	0.1	9.4	37	0.25	0.1–0.3
Puerto Rico	0.2	40.1	118	0.34	0.2–0.3
Uruguay	0.4	50.3	195	0.26	0.3–0.4
Venezuela	0.1	10.5	(50)	0.21	0.1–0.2
Latin America	0.1	20.4	81	0.25	0.1–0.25

Note: Data in parentheses are estimated values.

[a] The export figure is for 1912, but the GDP figure is for 1920. This biases the estimate of w downward. The bias has been taken into account in calculating the w range for Guatemala and Honduras, the countries that are most affected.

[b] Because the estimate of GDP in Alienes (1950), as reported in Brundenius (1984), p. 140, is in current prices, this measure was used in preference to deflating the constant price estimate in Table A.3.2.

of Uruguay) they determine the maximum values for w. In setting the upper limit for the w range, the numbers in Table A.2.1 were rounded up or down to correspond to the values chosen for w in Figures 3.1 and 3.2.

The data required to estimate w in 1850 with accuracy are not available.[1] However, the figures on exports per head and the assumption that w was generally rising over time mean that plausible assumptions can be made. The estimates in Table A.2.1 for 1850 refer to the bottom end of the range for w (with the exception of Uruguay, which is assumed to have had a higher ratio of exports to GDP in 1850 than in 1912).

1 There are crude estimates for a few countries. See Maddison (1995), p. 202 for Brazil and Mexico and Díaz, Lüders, and Wagner (1998), AE 16, for Chile.

Table A.2.2. *Price indices for imports, circa 1850 to circa 1912*
(base year = 100)

Years	United Kingdom export prices	Brazilian import prices	Chilean import prices	U.S. export prices	Average	Annual rate of change (in percentages)
1850–1870	119	115	118	n/a	117	+0.8
1870–1890	73	75	75	n/a	74	−1.5
1890–1912	108	136	161	113	130	+1.3
1850–1912	94	117	143	n/a	118	+0.3

Sources: For U.K. data, Mitchell (1988); for Brazilian data, IBGE (1987); for Chilean data, Palma (1979); for U.S. data, Wilkie (1990).

The "guesstimates" of w for 1850, coupled with the data on exports per head in 1850, can be used to obtain the implied levels of GDP per head in 1850 at current prices. For Latin America as a whole this yields a level of GDP per head of around $50. Adjusted for the (small) rise in U.S. dollar prices between 1850 and 1912, this implies a rate of growth of real GDP per head in Latin America of 0.5 percent per year between 1850 and 1912. Without any pretensions to accuracy, this figure seems plausible.

The purchasing power of exports

Chapter 3 uses estimates of the purchasing power of exports (PPE) at various points between 1850 and 1912. Because the PPE for any country is obtained by dividing the change in the value of exports by the change in import prices, it can only be calculated if information is available on each country's import unit values. It is not unreasonable to assume that the change in import prices (in dollar or sterling terms) was the same for all countries, however, because they were purchasing similar goods from similar sources.

In Table A.2.2 a number of price indexes are presented for different time periods before 1912, each of which is an approximation to Latin America's import unit values. The unweighted average of the four indexes is then assumed to measure the change in Latin America's import prices, and the final column of the table shows the implied annual average rate of change in each period. These are the adjustment factors that were applied to the rate of growth of the value of exports in Table 3.4 to obtain the rate of growth of the PPE.

The volume of exports

A small number of countries provide sufficient information to calculate the rate of growth of the volume of exports at different intervals before 1912. The results are shown in Table A.2.3 for Argentina, Brazil, Chile, Cuba, Ecuador, Mexico, and Peru.[2]

2 See also Maddison (2001), p. 361, and Thorp (1998), p. 337.

Table A.2.3. *Rates of growth of the volume of exports, circa 1850*
to circa 1912 (in percentages)

Country	1850–1870	1870–1890	1890–1912	1850–1912
Argentina[a]	n/a	5.2	5.2	5.2
Brazil	3.4	1.8	3.7	3.0
Chile	4.1	5.0	2.5	3.8
Cuba[b]	5.6	0.3	4.7	3.5
Ecuador[c]	2.7	2.5	3.7	3.0
Mexico	n/a	n/a	6.5	n/a
Peru	4.4	−4.5	7.2	2.5

[a] The dates are 1875–9 to 1890–4, 1890–4 to 1910–4, and 1875–9 to 1910–4.
[b] Based on sugar only.
[c] Based on cacao only.
Sources: For data on Argentina, Díaz-Alejandro (1970); for data on Brazil, IBGE (1987); for data on Chile, Palma (1979); for data on Cuba, Mitchell (1993); for data on Ecuador, Rodríguez (1985); for data on Mexico, Rosenzweig Hernández (1989); for data on Peru, Hunt (1973).

Comparison between the figures in Table A.2.3 and the rate of growth of the value of exports reveals whether export prices were rising or falling. Only Cuba shows a marked downward trend in prices, which is consistent with the evolution of sugar prices after 1850. Elsewhere, the value of exports grew more rapidly than the volume of exports between 1850 and 1912, implying an increase in export prices. In the 1870–90 subperiod, however, export prices appear to have fallen in Chile, Ecuador, and Peru.

APPENDIX 3

Gross domestic product per head,
1913, 1928, 1980, and 2000

The level of gross domestic product (GDP) per head is widely used to measure economic performance, growth rates, and differences in the standard of living between countries. Although all Latin American countries have produced estimates of GDP per head since 1950, the information for earlier years is much less systematic. This appendix brings together all of the available information as consistently as possible to provide statistics for 1913, 1928, 1980, and 2000.

The basic source is CEPAL (1978), which gives time-series data for all Latin American countries (except Cuba and Puerto Rico) on GDP at factor cost using 1970 prices. The GDP figures therefore differ from GDP at market prices because they exclude net indirect taxes. The data on individual countries are in local currency (at 1970 prices) and can be converted to U.S. dollars by using the appropriate exchange-rate. I have used annual average exchange rates in 1970, as reported in World Bank (1983). These are shown in the first column of Table A.3.1

These exchange rates are official and therefore differ from the purchasing-power parity (PPP) exchange rates used in many international comparisons. PPP exchange rates are important in comparisons between developing and developed countries. They are less relevant in comparisons between a group of relatively similar developing countries. Even so, PPP rates, as reported by CEPAL (1978), are also given in Table A.3.1 They are uniformly lower than official exchange rates, and the proportionate difference is shown in the third column. This can be thought of as the adjustment factor that is needed to convert GDP per head at official rates to GDP per head at PPP rates.[1]

Data on GDP per head are given in this appendix for 1913 (on the eve of the First World War), for 1928 (on the eve of the Great Depression), for 1980 (on the eve of the debt crisis), and for 2000. These benchmark data are then used for various purposes throughout this book. CEPAL (1978) contains an estimate of GDP at factor cost in 1913 only for Argentina and in 1928 only for Argentina, Brazil, Colombia, and Mexico. However, numerous other official and unofficial calculations of GDP can be spliced onto the CEPAL time-series data to give estimates for other countries in 1913 and 1928. Finally, it is possible to put together crude estimates of GDP per head for Cuba and Puerto Rico, neither of which is included in

---

1 Thorp (1998), Appendix II, estimates the growth of GDP per head using data derived from PPP exchange-rate. Maddison (2001), p. 195, does the same, although the number of countries before 1950 is smaller and prices are in 1990 U.S. dollars rather than 1970 U.S. dollars.

Table A.3.1. *Official and purchasing-power exchange rates,* 1970 *(per US$)*

Country	Official exchange-rate	Purchasing-power parity exchange-rate	Official exchange rate/purchasing-power parity exchange-rate	Currency
Argentina	3.78	2.95	1.28	Peso
Bolivia	11.88	9.03	1.32	Peso
Brazil	4.59	4.14	1.11	New cruzeiro
Chile	0.0122	0.01	1.22	Peso
Colombia	18.44	10.68	1.73	Peso
Costa Rica	6.62	5.09	1.30	Colón
Dominican Republic	1.0	0.87	1.15	Peso
Ecuador	25.0	14.0	1.79	Sucre
El Salvador	2.5	1.70	1.47	Colón
Guatemala	1.0	0.81	1.23	Quetzal
Haiti	5.0	3.99	1.25	Gourde
Honduras	2.0	1.75	1.14	Lempira
Mexico	12.5	8.88	1.41	Peso
Nicaragua	7.0	6.41	1.09	Córdoba
Panama	1.0	0.76	1.32	Balboa
Paraguay	126.0	85.41	1.48	Guaraní
Peru	38.7	30.72	1.26	Sol
Uruguay	0.25	0.20	1.25	Peso
Venezuela	4.5	3.96	1.14	Bolívar

Sources: Official exchange rates from World Bank (1983); purchasing-power parity exchange rates from CEPAL (1978).

CEPAL (1978), so data exist for sixteen countries in 1913 and 1928.[2] For 1980 and 2000 it is possible to estimate GDP per head for all twenty Latin American republics as well as Puerto Rico.

The data for 1913 and 1928 for the sixteen countries are weighted by population to give an estimate of GDP per head for Latin America. The estimates for Latin America in 1980 and 2000, however, are based only on the twenty Latin American republics. Puerto Rico, which by 1980 had a GDP per head almost twice as high as the next-richest country (see Table A.3.2), was excluded from the weighted average figure in order to avoid biasing the estimate upward. Its inclusion would raise Latin American GDP per head by nearly 3 percent.

The data for 1980 are derived from World Bank (1983) except where indicated below. The data for 2000 are derived from World Bank (2002a), using growth rates of GDP per head at constant prices (1995 U.S. dollars). In the case of Cuba, the growth rate from 1980

---

2 Thorp (1998), Appendix II and Appendix IX, provides an estimate for Ecuador for 1913 and 1928 and for Venezuela for 1913. I have included these estimates is this Appendix, although they were not used in the statistical analysis in Chapters 5 and 7.

Table A.3.2. *GDP per head at factor cost, 1913, 1928, 1980 and 2000 (1970 prices in US\$ at official exchange rates)*

Country	1913	1928	1980	2000
Argentina	537	571	1,044	1107
Bolivia			288	272
Brazil	125	160	691	747
Chile	399	501[a]	979	1739
Colombia	128	158	442	553
Costa Rica	218[b]	219	679	783
Cuba	390	298	948	859
Dominican Republic			530	811
Ecuador	67	152	513	453
El Salvador	112[b]	121	278	299
Guatemala	185[b]	195	417	408
Haiti			137	77
Honduras	191[b]	223	307	293
Mexico	223[c]	252	972	1128
Nicaragua	155[b]	189	288	201
Panama			910	1113
Paraguay			620	564
Peru	106	163	649	579
Puerto Rico	338	468[d]	2,222[e]	3255[e,f]
Uruguay	557	592[d]	979	1154
Venezuela	114	197	1,237	910
Latin America	**223**	**262**	**758**	**804**

[a] Datum is for 1929.
[b] Data are for 1920.
[c] Datum is for 1910.
[d] Data are for 1930.
[e] Not included in the Latin American average.
[f] Datum is for 1997.

to 1990 was obtained from Thorp (1998), Appendix IX and for 1990 to 2000 from World Bank (2002a).

The data for the four reference years are presented in Table A.3.2 The statistics can differ from those found in other sources for a variety of reasons. First, wherever possible the statistics refer to GDP at factor cost. This is lower than GDP at market prices because net indirect taxes were excluded. It is also different from gross national product, national disposable income, and other proxies for living standards. Second, the data in Table A.3.2 are sensitive to the choice of base year. Venezuela's GDP for example, would look much more impressive if 1980 rather than 1970 were the base year, because it would reflect the huge rise in oil prices in the 1970s. Third, the results are affected by the choice of the exchange-rate for conversion of domestic currencies into U.S. dollars. Finally, not all sources use the same statistics on population, and this can cause the data to vary, particularly in earlier years.

The sources and methods used for each country are listed below. In order to avoid repetition, certain general features can first be mentioned. Wherever possible, the figures are the three-year average of GDP at factor cost in domestic currency divided by the three-year average of population divided by the exchange-rate. Thus, for example, 1928 is the average of 1927 to 1929. The population data before 1980 were obtained from Wilkie (1974) unless otherwise stated; the population data for 1980, from World Bank (1983), except for Cuba and Puerto Rico. The population data for 2000 are from World Bank (2002a). The data on the five Central American republics upto 1980 are taken from Bulmer-Thomas (1987), Table A.3.2, adjusted to official exchange rates using the conversion factors derived from Table A.3.1 For 2000, they are derived from World Bank (2002a).

Argentina

1913. CEPAL (1978).
1928. CEPAL (1978).
1980. World Bank (1983).
2000. World Bank (2002a).

Bolivia

1980. World Bank (1983).
2000. World Bank (2002a).

Brazil

1913. CEPAL (1978) for 1920, adjusted to 1913 by Haddad (1974).
1928. CEPAL (1978).
1980. World Bank (1983).
2000. World Bank (2002a).

Chile

1913. CEPAL (1978) for 1940, adjusted to 1929 by Palma (1984) and to 1913 by Palma (1979).
1928. CEPAL (1978) for 1940, adjusted to 1929 by Palma (1984).
1980. World Bank (1983). The source gives GDP at market prices in 1977 prices; that datum was converted to U.S. dollars at the 1977 exchange-rate (21.529) and then to 1970 prices, using the U.S. GDP deflator from 1970 to 1977 (0.65).
2000. World Bank (2002a).

Colombia

1913. CEPAL (1978) for 1929, adjusted to 1913 by L. Zimmerman in *Arme in Rijke Landen* (1964), as cited in Maddison (1991), Table 1.7, p. 6.

1928. CEPAL (1978).

1980. World Bank (1983).

2000. World Bank (2002a).

Cuba

1913. The datum is real national income per head and was obtained from Alienes (1950), as reported in Brundenius (1984), Table A.2.1, p. 140, adjusted from current 1913 prices to 1970 prices by a weighted average of sugar and nonsugar prices. The change in the sugar price (+7.79 percent) was obtained from League of Nations sources for 1913 and from Inter-American Development Bank sources for 1970. The change in the nonsugar price (+206 percent) was assumed to be the same as the change in U.S. wholesale prices. The weights given to sugar and nonsugar prices were obtained from the shares of sugar (0.28) and nonsugar (0.72) net output in GDP in 1913. See Brundenius (1984), Table A.2.1, p. 140. That gave a weighted average rise in prices of 150 percent between 1913 and 1970; the increase was then applied to the estimate in current prices in Alienes (1950), to give 1913 real national income per head at 1970 prices.

1928. The ratio of 1928 real national income per head (1926 prices) to 1913 real national income per head (1926 prices) in Alienes (1950) was applied to the 1913 figure (see above) to give 1928 real national income per head at 1970 prices.

1980. The datum was obtained by adjusting the 1970 figure for GDP per head in current dollars – see Pérez-López (1991) – by the growth of real GDP between 1970 and 1980, as reported in Brundenius and Zimbalist (1989), Table 5.8, p. 63.

2000. World Bank (2002a).

Dominican Republic

1980. World Bank (1983). The data refer to GDP at market prices.

2000. World Bank (2002a).

Ecuador

1980. World Bank (1983). The data refer to GDP at market prices. The source gives GDP at 1975 prices; that datum was converted to U.S. dollars at the 1975 exchange-rate (25.0) and then to 1970 dollars, using the U.S. GDP deflator between 1970 and 1975 (0.727).

2000. World Bank (2002a).

Haiti

1980. World Bank (1983). The data refer to GDP at market prices. The source gives GDP at 1976 prices; that datum was converted to U.S. dollars at the 1976 exchange-rate (5.0) and then to 1970 dollars, using the U.S. GDP deflator between 1970 and 1976 (0.69).
2000. World Bank (2002a).

Mexico

1913 and 1928. Solís (1983), Table III-1, pp. 79–80, adjusted from 1960 prices to 1970 prices by the GDP deflator obtained by comparing Solís (1983) and CEPAL (1978) for 1970. The 1913 datum is for 1910.
1980. World Bank (1983).
2000. World Bank (2002a).

Panama

1980. World Bank (1983). The data refer to GDP at market prices.
2000. World Bank (2002a).

Paraguay

1980. World Bank (1983). The data refer to GDP at market prices. The source gives GDP at 1977 prices; that datum was converted to U.S. dollars at the 1977 exchange-rate (126) and then to 1970 dollars, using the U.S. GDP deflator between 1970 and 1977 (0.65).
2000. World Bank (2002a).

Peru

1913 and 1928. CEPAL (1978) for 1950, adjusted to 1913 and 1928 by Boloña (1981) as reported in Maddison (1991), Table 1.7, p. 6. The 1928 datum refers to 1929.
1980. World Bank (1983). The data refer to GDP at market prices. The source gives GDP at 1973 prices; that datum was converted to U.S. dollars at the 1973 exchange-rate (38.7) and then to 1970 dollars, using the U.S. GDP deflator between 1970 and 1973 (0.86).
2000. World Bank (2002a).

Puerto Rico

1913. Assumes that GDP per head grew at 1.5 percent per year between 1913 and 1930.
1928. The figure is for 1930. Dietz (1986), p. 244, provides a table that was used to obtain an estimate of 1950 GDP at 1970 market prices; that datum was then adjusted to 1940,

using an index formed from net income at constant prices between 1940 and 1950. See Dietz (1986), p. 205. That in turn was converted to 1930, using an index formed from net dollar income in current prices between 1930 and 1940, assuming no change in prices between 1930 and 1940. See Perloff (1950), Table 49, p. 160.

1980. Derived from Dietz (1986), Table 5.1, p. 244.

2000. World Bank (2002a).

Uruguay

1913. Assumes the same ratio to Argentina as in 1928.

1928. The datum is for 1930. CEPAL (1978) for 1935, adjusted by the change in real GDP between 1930 and 1935. See Millot, Silva, and Silva (1973), Table 23.

1980. World Bank (1983). The source gives GDP at 1978 prices; that datum was converted to U.S. dollars at the 1978 exchange-rate (6.125) and then to 1970 dollars, using the U.S. GDP deflator between 1970 and 1978 (0.60).

2000. World Bank (2002a).

Venezuela

1928. CEPAL (1978) for 1936, adjusted by the change in real GDP between 1928 and 1936. See Rangel (1970), as reported in McBeth (1983), Table 17, p. 114.

1980. World Bank (1983). The data refer to GDP at market prices. The source gives GDP at 1968 prices; that datum was converted to U.S. dollars at the 1968 exchange-rate (4.5) and then to 1970 prices, using the U.S. GDP deflator between 1968 and 1970 (1.076).

2000. World Bank (2002a).

Bibliography

Abente, D. (1989). "Foreign Capital, Economic Elites and the State in Paraguay during the Liberal Republic (1870–1936)," *Journal of Latin American Studies* 21 (1): 61–88.

Abreu, M. de P. (2000). "Argentina and Brazil during the 1930s: the impact of British and US international economic policies." In Thorp, R. (ed.), *Latin America in the 1930s: The Role of the Periphery in World Crisis*. Basingstoke: Palgrave.

Abreu, M. de P., and Bevilaqua, A. (2000). "Brazil as an export economy, 1880–1930." In Cardenas, E., Ocampo, J., and Thorp, R. (eds.), *An Economic History of Twentieth Century Latin America, Vol. I: The Export Age. The Latin American Economies in the Late Nineteenth and Early Twentieth Centuries*. Basingstoke: Palgrave.

Acevedo, E. (1902). *Historia económica de la República de Uruguay*. 2 vols. Montevideo: El Siglo Ilustrado.

Adams, F. (1914). *Conquest of the Tropics*. New York: Doubleday.

Albala Bertrand, J. M. (1993). "Evolution of Aggregate Welfare and Development Indicators in Latin America and the OECD, 1950–85." In Abel, C., and Lewis, C. M. (eds.), *Welfare, Poverty and Development in Latin America*. Basingstoke, Eng.: Macmillan/St. Antony's College.

Albert, B. (1988). *South America and the First World War: The Impact of the War on Brazil, Argentina, Peru and Chile*. Cambridge University Press.

Alhadeff, P. (1986). "The Economic Formulae of the 1930s; a Reassessment." In Di Tella, G., and Platt, D. C. M. (eds.), *The Political Economy of Argentina, 1880–1946*. Basingstoke, Eng.: Macmillan/St. Antony's College.

Alienes, J. (1950). *Características fundamentales de la economía cubana*. Havana: Banco Nacional de Cuba.

Amadeo, E., et al. (1990). *Inflación y establización en América Latina: nuevos modelos estructuralistas* Bogotá: Tercer Mundo Editores.

Anna, T. (1985). "The Independence of Mexico and Central America." In Bethell, L. (ed.), *The Cambridge History of Latin America, Vol. III: From Independence to c. 1870*. Cambridge University Press.

Arndt, H. W. (1985). "The Origins of Structuralism," *World Development* 13 (2): 151–9.

Arriaga, E. (1968). *New Life Tables for Latin American Populations in the Nineteenth and Twentieth Centuries*. Berkeley: University of California.

Ascher, W. (1984). *Scheming for the Poor: The Politics of Redistribution in Latin America*. Cambridge, Mass.: Harvard University Press.

Bacha, E. (1977). "Issues and Evidence in Recent Brazilian Economic Growth," *World Development* 5 (1–2): 47–67.

Baer, W. (1969). *The Development of the Brazilian Steel Industry*. Nashville, Tenn.: Vanderbilt University Press.

Baer, W. (1983). *The Brazilian Economy: Growth and Development*. New York: Praeger.

Baer, W. (ed.) (1998). *The Changing Role of International Capital in Latin America. Quantitative Review of Economics and Finance*, 38 (3).

Baer, W., and Birch, M. H. (1984). "Expansion of the Economic Frontier: Paraguayan Growth in the 1970s," *World Development* 12 (8): 783–98.

Bairoch, P., and Etemard, B. (1985). *Commodity Structure of Third World Exports*. Geneva: Libraire Droz.

Bairoch, P., and Lévy-Leboyer, M. (eds.) (1981). *Disparities in Economic Development since the Industrial Revolution*. Basingstoke, Eng.: Macmillan.

Bairoch, P., and Toutain, J. (1991). *World Energy Production*. Geneva: Libraire Droz.

Bakewell, P. (1984). "Mining in Colonial Spanish America." In Bethell, L. (ed.), *The Cambridge History of Latin America: Vol. II: Colonial Latin America*. Cambridge University Press.

Balassa, B., et al. (1986). *Towards Renewed Economic Growth in Latin America: Summary, Overview and Recommendations*. Washington, D.C.: Institute for International Economics.

Balasubramanyam, V. (1988). "Export Processing Zones in Developing Countries: Theory and Empirical Evidence." In Greenaway, D. (ed.), *Economic Development and International Trade*. Basingstoke, Eng.: Macmillan.

Ballesteros, M., and Davis, T. E. (1963). "The Growth of Output and Employment in Basic Sectors of the Chilean Economy, 1908–1957," *Economic Development and Cultural Change* 11: 152–76.

Banco de Guatemala (1989). *Banca Central*, No. 1. Guatemala City: Banco de Guatemala.

Banco de la República (1990). *El Banco de la República: Antecedentes, evolución y estructura*. Bogotá: Banco de la República.

Baptista, A. (1997). *Bases cuantitativas de la economía venezolana, 1830–1995*. Caracas: Ediciones Fundación Polar.

Barbier, E. B. (1989). *Economics, Natural-Resource Scarcity and Development*. London: Earthscan Publications Ltd.

Barraclough, S. (ed.) (1973). *Agrarian Structure in Latin America*. Lexington, Mass.: Heath.

Batou, J. (1990). *One Hundred Years of Resistance to Underdevelopment*. Geneva: Libraire Droz.

Batou, J. (1991). *Between Development and Underdevelopment*. Geneva: Libraire Droz.

Bauer, A. (1986). "Rural Spanish America, 1870–1930." In Bethell, L. (ed.), *The Cambridge History of Latin America, Vol. IV: c. 1870–1930*. Cambridge University Press.

Bauer Paíz, A. (1956). *Cómo opera el capital yanqui en Centroamérica (el caso de Guatemala)*. Mexico, D.F.: Editorial Ibero-Mexicana.

Bazant, J. (1985). "Mexico from Independence to 1867." In Bethell, L. (ed.), *The Cambridge History of Latin America, Vol. III: From Independence to c. 1870*. Cambridge University Press.

Beatty, E. (2000). "The impact of foreign trade on the Mexican economy: terms of trade and the rise of industry, 1880–1923." *Journal of Latin American. Studies*, 32 (2): 399–434.

Beckerman, P. (1989). "Austerity, External Debt, and Capital Formation in Peru." In Handelman, H., and Baer, W. (eds.), *Paying the Costs of Austerity in Latin America*. Boulder, Colo.: Westview.

Benoit, P. (1954). *1804–1954: cent cinquante ans de commerce exterieur d'Haiti*. Port-au-Prince: Institut Haitien de Statistique.

Berend, I. T. (1982). *The European Periphery & Industrialization: 1780–1914*. Cambridge University Press.

Bergad, L. (1983). *Coffee and the Growth of Agrarian Capitalism in Nineteenth Century Puerto Rico*. Princeton, N.J.: Princeton University Press.

Bergquist, C. (1978). *Coffee and Conflict in Colombia, 1886–1910*. Durham, N.C.: Duke University Press.

Bergsman, J. (1970). Brazil: *Industrialization and Trade Policies*. London: Oxford University Press.

Berry, A. (1983). "A Descriptive History of Colombian Industrial Development in the Twentieth Century." In Berry, A. (ed.), *Essays on Industrialization in Colombia*. Tempe: Center for Latin American Studies, Arizona State University.

Berry, A. (1987). "The Limited Role of Rural Small-Scale Manufacturing for Late-Comers: Some Hypotheses on the Colombian Experience," *Journal of Latin American Studies* 19 (2): 279–94.

Berry, A. (ed.) (1998). *Poverty, Economic Reform and Income Distribution in Latin America*. Boulder, Colo.: Lynne Rienner.

Berry, A., and Cline, W. (1979). *Agrarian Structure and Productivity in Developing Countries*. Baltimore: Johns Hopkins University Press.

Bethell, L. (1970). *The Abolition of the Brazilian Slave Trade*. Cambridge University Press.

Bethell, L. (1985). "The Independence of Brazil." In Bethell, L. (ed.), *The Cambridge History of Latin America, Vol. III: From Independence to c. 1870*. Cambridge University Press.

Bethell, L. (ed.) (1991). *The Cambridge History of Latin America, Vol. VIII: Latin America since 1930: Spanish South America*. Cambridge University Press.

Bethell, L., and Roxborough, I. (1988). "Latin America between the Second World War and the Cold War: Some Reflections on the 1945–8 Conjuncture," *Journal of Latin American Studies* 20 (1): 167–89.

Bethell, L., and Roxborough, I. (1992). *Latin America between the Second World War and the Cold War, 1944–1948*. Cambridge University Press.

Blakemore, H. (1974). *British Nitrates and Chilean Politics, 1886–1896: North v Balmaceda*. London: Athlone Press.

Blakemore, H. (1986). "Chile from the War of the Pacific to the World Depression, 1880–1930." In Bethell, L. (ed.), *The Cambridge History of Latin America, Vol. V: c. 1870 to 1930*. Cambridge University Press.

Blaug, H. (1976). *Economic Theory in Retrospect*, 3d ed. Cambridge University Press.

Blomström, M. (1990). *Transnational Corporations and Manufacturing Exports from Developing Countries*. New York: United Nations.

Blomström, M., and Meller, P. (eds.) (1991). *Diverging Paths: Comparing a Century of Scandinavian and Latin American Economic Development*. Washington, D.C.: Inter-American Development Bank.

Bocco, A. M. (1987). *Auge petrolero, modernización y subdesarrollo: El Ecuador de los años setenta*. Quito: Corporación Editora Nacional.

Bogart, E. L. (1908). *The Economic History of the United States*. London: Longmans.

Boloña, C. (1981). "Tariff Policies in Peru, 1880–1980." D.Phil. dissertation, Oxford University.

Bonilla, H. (1985). "Peru and Bolivia from Independence to the War of the Pacific." In Bethell, L. (ed.), *The Cambridge History of Latin America, Vol. III: From Independence to c. 1870*. Cambridge University Press.

Booth, J. A. (1982). *The End and the Beginning – The Nicaraguan Revolution*. Boulder, Colo.: Westview.

Bourgade, E. de (1892). *Paraguay: The Land and the People, National Wealth and Commercial Capabilities*. London: George Philip.

Bouzas, R. and Soltz, H. (2001). "Institutions and regional integration: the case of MERCOSUR." In Bulmer-Thomas, V. (ed.), *Regional Integration in Latin America and the Caribbean: The Political Economy of Open Regionalism*. London: Institute of Latin American Studies.

Brading, D. (1978). *Haciendas and Ranchos in the Mexican Bajío: León, 1700–1860*. Cambridge University Press.

Bratter, H. (1939). "Foreign exchange control in Latin America." *Foreign Policy Report*, 14, (23): 274–88.

Broadberry, S. N. (1986). *The British Economy between the Wars: A Macroeconomic Survey*. Oxford: Basil Blackwell.

Brockett, C. D. (1988). *Land, Power and Poverty: Agrarian Transformation and Political Conflict in Central America*. Boston: Unwin Hyman.

Brogan, C. (1984). *The Retreat from Oil Nationalism in Ecuador, 1976–1983*. London: Institute of Latin American Studies.

Brothers, D. S., and Solís M. L. (1966). *Mexican Financial Development*. Austin: University of Texas Press.

Brown, J. (1979). *A Socio-Economic History of Argentina, 1776–1860*. Cambridge University Press.

Browning, D. (1971). *El Salvador: Landscape and Society*. Oxford: Oxford University Press.

Brundenius, C. (1984). *Revolutionary Cuba: The Challenge of Economic Growth with Equity*. Boulder, Colo.: Westview.

Brundenius, C., and Zimbalist, A. (1989). *The Cuban Economy: Measurement and Analysis of Socialist Performance*. Baltimore: Johns Hopkins University Press.

Bruno, M., Fischer, S., Helpman, E., and Liviatan, N. (eds.). (1991). *Lessons of Economic Stabilization and Its Aftermath*. Cambridge, Mass.: MIT Press.

Bruton, H. (1989). "Import Substitution." In Chenery, H., and Srinivasan, T. N. (eds.), *Handbook of Development Economics*, Vol. 2. Amsterdam: North-Holland.

Bryce, J. (1912). *South America: Observations and Impressions*. London: Macmillan.

Buiter, W. (1983). "Measurement of the Public Sector Deficit and the Implications for Policy Evaluation and Design," *IMF Staff Papers* 30 (2). Washington, D.C.

Bulmer-Thomas, I. (1965). *The Growth of the British Party System*. 2 vols. London: Baker.

Bulmer-Thomas, V. (1987). *The Political Economy of Central America since 1920*. Cambridge University Press.

Bulmer-Thomas, V. (1988). *Studies in the Economics of Central America*. Basingstoke, Eng.: Macmillan/New York: St. Martin's.

Bulmer-Thomas, V. (1990a). "Honduras since 1930." In Bethell, L. (ed.), *The Cambridge History of Latin America, Vol. VII: Latin America since 1930: Mexico, Central America and the Caribbean*. Cambridge University Press.

Bulmer-Thomas, V. (1990b). "Nicaragua since 1930." In Bethell, L. (ed.), *The Cambridge History of Latin America, Vol VII: Latin America since 1930: Mexico, Central America and the Caribbean*. Cambridge University Press.

Bulmer-Thomas, V. (ed.) (1996). *The New Economic Model in Latin America and its Impact on Income Distribution and Poverty*. London: ILAS and Macmillan/New York: St. Martin's Press.

Bulmer-Thomas, V. (1997). "Regional integration in Latin America before the debt crisis: LAFTA, CACM and the Andean Pact." In El-Agraa, A. (1997), *Economic Integration Worldwide*. Basingstoke: Macmillan.

Bulmer-Thomas, V. (1998). *Reflexiones sobre la Integración Centroamericana*. Tegucigalpa: Banco Centroamericana de Integración Económica.

Bulmer-Thomas, V., and Page, S. (1999). "Trade relations in the Americas: MERCOSUR, the Free Trade Area of the Americas and the European Union." In Bulmer-Thomas, V., and Dunkerley, J. (eds.), *The United States and Latin America; the New Agenda*. Cambridge, Mass.: The David Rockefeller Center for Latin American Studies, Harvard University/ London: Institute of Latin American Studies.

Bulmer-Thomas, V. (2001a). "Regional integration and intra-industry trade." In Bulmer-Thomas, V. (ed.), *Regional Integration in Latin America and the Caribbean: The Political Economy of Open Regionalism*. London: Institute of Latin American Studies.

Bulmer-Thomas, V. (2001b). "The wider Caribbean in the 20th century: A long-run development perspective." *Integration and Trade*, 15 (5): 5–56.

Bureau de Publicidad de la América Latina (1916–1917). *El 'Libro Azul' de Panamá*. Panama City: Bureau de Publicidad de la América Latina.

Bureau of the American Republics (1892a). *Handbook of Bolivia*. Washington, D.C.: Government Printing Office.

Bureau of the American Republics (1892b). *Handbook of Costa Rica*. Washington, D.C.: Government Printing Office.

Bureau of the American Republics (1892c). *Handbook of Ecuador*. Washington, D.C.: Government Printing Office.

Bureau of the American Republics (1892d). *Handbook of Haiti*. Washington, D.C.: Government Printing Office.

Bureau of the American Republics (1892e). *Handbook of Nicaragua*. Washington, D.C.: Government Printing Office.

Bureau of the American Republics (1892f). *Handbook of Paraguay*. Washington, D.C.: Government Printing Office.

Bureau of the American Republics (1892g). *Handbook of the Argentine Republic*. Washington, D.C.: Government Printing Office.

Bureau of the American Republics (1892h). *Handbook of Venezuela*. Washington, D.C.: Government Printing Office.

Bureau of the American Republics (1904). *Honduras: Geographical Sketch, Natural Resources, Laws, Economic Conditions, Actual Development, Prospects of Future Growth*. Washington, D.C.: Government Printing Office.

Burns, E. B. (1980). *The Poverty of Progress: Latin America in the Nineteenth Century*. Berkeley: University of California Press.

Burns, E. B. (1991). *Patriarch and Folk: The Emergence of Nicaragua 1798–1858*. Cambridge, Mass.: Harvard University Press.

Bushnell, D. (1970). *The Santander Regime in Gran Colombia*. Westport, Conn.: Greenwood.

Bushnell, D., and Macaulay, N. (1988). *The Emergence of Latin America in the Nineteenth Century*. New York: Oxford University Press.

Cantarero, L. A. (1949). "The Economic Development of Nicaragua, 1920–1947." Ph.D. dissertation, University of Iowa.

Cárdenas, E. (2000). "The Great Depression and Industrialization: The Case of Mexico." In Thorp, R. (ed.), *Latin America in the 1930s: The Role of the Periphery in World Crisis*. Oxford: Palgrave/St. Antony's College.

Cárdenas, E., and Manns, C. (1989). "Inflación y estabilización monetaria en México durante la revolución," *El Trimestre Económico* 56 (221): 57–79.

Cárdenas, E., Ocampo, J., and Thorp, R. (eds.) (2000). *An Economic History of Twentieth Century Latin America, Vol. I: The Export Age. The Latin American Economies in the Late Nineteenth and Early Twentieth Centuries*. Basingstoke: Palgrave.

Cardoso, E. (1981). "Food Supply and Inflation," *Journal of Development Economics* 8 (3): 269–84.

Cardoso, E. (1991). "From Inertia to Megainflation: Brazil in the 1980s." In Bruno, M., Fischer, S., Helpman, E., and Liviatan, N. (eds.), *Lessons of Economic Stabilization and Its Aftermath*. Cambridge, Mass.: MIT Press.

Cardoso, E., and Helwege, A. (1992). *Latin America's Economy: Diversity, Trends and Conflicts*. Cambridge, Mass.: MIT Press.

Cardoso, F. H., and Brignoli, H. (1979a). *Historia económica de América Latina. Vol. I: Sistemas agrarios e historia colonial*. Barcelona: Editorial Crítica.

Cardoso, F. H., and Brignoli, H. (1979b). *Historia económica de América Latina. Vol. 2: Economías de exportación y desarrollo capitalista*. Barcelona: Editorial Crítica.

Cardoso, F. H., and Faletto, E. (1979). *Dependency and Development in Latin America*. Berkeley: University of California Press.

Carnoy, M. (1972). *Industrialization in a Latin American Common Market*. Washington, D.C.: Brookings Institution.

Carr, R. (1984). *Puerto Rico: A Colonial Experiment*. New York: New York University Press.

Carroll, H. (1975). *Report on the Island of Porto Rico*. New York: Arno Press.

Catão, L. (1991). "The International Transmission of Long Cycles between 'Core' and 'Periphery' Economies: A Case Study of Brazil and Mexico, c. 1870–1940." D.Phil. dissertation, Cambridge University.

CEPAL (1959). *El desarrollo económico de la Argentina*, 3 vols. Santiago, Chile: United Nations.

CEPAL (1976). *América Latina: Relación de precios del intercambio*. Cuadernos Estadísticos de la Cepal. Santiago, Chile: United Nations.

CEPAL (1978). *Series históricas del crecimiento de América Latina*. Cuadernos Estadísticos de la Cepal. Santiago, Chile: United Nations.

CEPAL (2001). *Panorama Social de América Latina, 2000–1*. Santiago, Chile: United Nations.

Cerdas Cruz, R. (1990). "Costa Rica since 1930." In Bethell, L. (ed.), *The Cambridge History of Latin America, Vol. VII: Latin America since 1930: Mexico, Central America and the Caribbean*. Cambridge University Press.

Chalmers, H. (1944). "Inter-American Trade Policy." In Harris, S. E. (ed.), *Economic Problems of Latin America*. New York: McGraw-Hill.

Chalmin, P. G. (1984). "The Important Trends in Sugar Diplomacy before 1914." In Albert, B., and Graves, A. (eds.), *Crisis and Change in the International Sugar Economy, 1860–1914*. Norwich, Eng.: ISC Press.

Chenery, H. (1960). "Patterns of Industrial Growth," *American Economic Review* 50 (3): 624–54.

Chowning, M. (1990). "The Management of Church Wealth in Michoacán, Mexico, 1810–1856: Economic Motivations and Political Implications," *Journal of Latin American Studies* 22 (3): 459–96.

Clarence-Smith, W. (2000). *Cocoa and Chocolate, 1765–1914*. London and New York: Routledge.

Clark, V., et al. (1975). *Porto Rico and Its Problems*. New York: Arno Press.

Clark, W. (1911). *Cotton Goods in Latin America, Part II*. U.S. Dept of Commerce and Labor, Washington, D.C.: Government Printing Office.

Cline, W. R. (1978). "Benefits and Costs of Economic Integration in Central America." In Cline, W. R., and Delgado, E. (eds.), *Economic Integration in Central America*. Washington, D.C.: Brookings Institution.

Coatsworth, J. (1978). "Obstacles to Economic Growth in Nineteenth Century Mexico," *American Historical Review* 83 (1): 80–100.

Coatsworth, J. (1981). *Growth against Development – The Economic Impact of Railroads in Porfirian Mexico*. Dekalb: Northern Illionois University Press.

Coatsworth, J. (1993). "Notes on the comparative economic history of Latin America and the United States." In Bernecker, W., and Tobler, H. (eds.), *Development and Underdevelopment in America*. Berlin and New York: Walter de Gruyter.

Coatsworth, J. (1998). "Economic and institutional trajectories in nineteenth century Latin America." In Coatsworth, J., and Taylor, A. (eds.), *Latin America and the World Economy since 1800*. Cambridge, Mass.: The David Rockefeller Center for Latin American Studies, Harvard University.

Colburn, F. D. (1990). *Managing the Commanding Heights: Nicaragua's State Enterprises*. Berkeley: University of California Press.

Collier, S. (1986). *The Life, Music and Times of Carlos Gardel*. Pittsburgh, Pa.: University of Pittsburgh Press.

Connell-Smith, G. (1966). *The Inter-American System*. London: Oxford University Press.

Conniff, M. L. (1985). *Black Labor on a White Canal: Panama, 1904–1981*. Pittsburgh, Pa.: University of Pittsburgh Press.

Consejo Monetario Centroamericano (1991). *Boletín Estadístico 1991*. San José, Costa Rica: Consejo Monetario Centroamericano.

Contreras, M. (2000). "Bolivia, 1900–39: mining, railways and education." In Cardenas, E., Ocampo, J. and Thorp, R. (eds.), *An Economic History of Twentieth Century Latin America, Vol. I: The Export Age. The Latin American Economies in the Late Nineteenth and Early Twentieth Centuries*. Basingstoke: Palgrave.

Corden, W. M. (1971). *The Theory of Protection*. Oxford: Clarendon Press.

Cortés Conde, R. (1985). "The Export Economy of Argentina, 1880–1920." In Cortés Conde, R., and Hunt, S. J. (eds.), *The Latin American Economies: Growth and the Export Sector, 1880–1930*. New York: Holmes & Meier.

Cortés Conde, R. (1986). "The Growth of the Argentine Economy c. 1870–1914." In Bethell, L. (ed.), *The Cambridge History of Latin America, Vol. V: c. 1870–1930*. Cambridge University Press.

Cortés Conde, R. (1997). *La Economía Argentina en el Largo Plazo*. Buenos Aires: Editorial Sudamericana.

Cortés Conde, R. (2000). "The vicissitudes of an exporting economy: Argentina, 1875–1930." In Cardenas, E., Ocampo, J., and Thorp, R. (eds.), *An Economic History of Twentieth Century Latin America, Vol. I: The Export Age. The Latin American Economies in the Late Nineteenth and Early Twentieth Centuries*. Basingstoke: Palgrave.

Council of Foreign Bondholders. (1931). *Annual Report*. London: Council of Foreign Bondholders.

Cowell, F. A. (1977). *Measuring Inequality*. Oxford: Philip Allan.

Cramer, G. (1998). "Argentine riddle: The Pinedo Plan of 1940 and the political economy of the early war years." *Journal of Latin American Studies*, 30 (3): 519–50.

Cuddington, J. T., and Urzúa, C. M. (1989). "Trends and Cycles in the Net Barter Terms of Trade: A New Approach," *Economic Journal* 99 (396): 426–42.

Cukierman, A. (1988). "The End of High Israeli Inflation: An Experiment in Heterodox Stabilization." In Bruno, M., et al. (eds.), *Inflation Stabilization: The Experience of Israel, Argentina, Brazil, Bolivia and Mexico*. Cambridge, Mass.: MIT Press.

Cumberland, W. W. (1928). *Nicaragua: An Economic and Financial Survey*. Washington, D.C.: Government Printing Office.

Dalton, L. (1916). *Venezuela*. London: T. Fisher Unwin.

Dawson, F. G. (1990). *The First Latin American Debt Crisis: The City of London and the 1822–25 Loan Bubble*. New Haven, Conn.: Yale University Press.

Dean, W. (1969). *The Industrialization of São Paulo, 1880–1945*. Austin: University of Texas Press.

Dean, W. (1987). *Brazil and the Struggle for Rubber: A Study of Environmental History*. Cambridge University Press.

Deas, M. (1982). "The Fiscal Problems of Nineteenth-Century Colombia," *Journal of Latin American Studies* 14 (2): 287–328.

Deas, M. (1985). "Venezuela, Colombia and Ecuador: The First Half-Century of Independence." In Bethell, L. (ed.), *The Cambridge History of Latin America, Vol. III: From Independence to c. 1870*. Cambridge University Press.

Deas, M. (1986). "Colombia, Ecuador and Venezuela, c. 1880–1930." In Bethell, L. (ed.), *The Cambridge History of Latin America, Vol. V: c. 1870–1930*. Cambridge University Press.

Deas, M. (ed.) (1991). *Latin America in Perspective*. Boston: Houghton Mifflin.

De Franco, M., and Godoy, R. (1992). "The Economic Consequences of Cocaine Production in Bolivia: Historical, Local and Macroeconomic Perspectives," *Journal of Latin American Studies* 24 (2): 375–406.

de Janvry, A. (1990). *The Agrarian Question and Reformism in Latin America*. Baltimore: Johns Hopkins University Press.

Dell, S. (1966). *A Latin American Common Market?* London: Oxford University Press.

Denny, H. (1929). *Dollars for Bullets: The Story of American Rule in Nicaragua*. New York: Dial Press.

De Soto, H. (1987). *El otro sendero: La revolución informal*. Buenos Aires: Editorial Sudamericana.

Devlin, R., Ffrench-Davis, R., and Griffith-Jones, S. (1995). "Surges in capital flows and development: an overview of policy issues." In Ffrench-Davis, R. and Griffith-Jones, S. (eds.), *Coping with Capital Surges: The Return of Finance to Latin America*. Boulder, Colo.: Lynne Rienner.

Devlin, R., and Estevadeordal, A. (2001). "What's new in the new regionalism in Latin America?" In Bulmer-Thomas, V. (ed.), *Regional Integration in Latin America and the Caribbean: The Political Economy of Open Regionalism*. London: Institute of Latin American Studies.

de Vries, M. G. (1986). *The IMF in a Changing World*. Washington, D.C.: International Monetary Fund.

de Vylder, S. (1976). *Allende's Chile*. Cambridge University Press.

Diakosavvos, D., and Scandizzo, P. (1991). "Trends in the Terms of Trade of Primary Commodities, 1900–1982: The Controversy and Its Origins," *Economic Development and Cultural Change* 39 (2): 231–64.

Dias Carneiro, D. (1987). "Long-Run Adjustment, the Debt Crisis and the Changing Role of Stabilisation Policies in the Recent Brazilian Experience." In Thorp, R., and Whitehead, L. (eds.), *Latin American Debt and the Adjustment Crisis*. Basingstoke, Eng.: Macmillan/St. Antony's College.

Díaz, J., Lüders, R., and Wagner, G. (1998). "Economía chilena 1810–1995: Evolución cuantitativa del producto total y sectorial." Pontificia Universidad Católica, Instituto de Economía, Documento de Trabajo, No. 186.

Díaz-Alejandro, C. F. (1965). *Exchange Rate Devaluation in a Semi-Industrialized Country: The Experience of Argentina, 1955–1961*. Cambridge, Mass.: MIT Press.

Díaz-Alejandro, C. F. (1970). *Essays on the Economic History of the Argentine Republic*. New Haven, Conn.: Yale University Press.

Díaz-Alejandro, C. F. (1976). *Colombia (Foreign Trade Regimes and Economic Development)*. New York: National Bureau of Economic Research.

Díaz-Alejandro, C. F. (1981). "Southern Cone Stabilization Plans." In Cline, W. R., and Weintraub, S. (eds.), *Economic Stabilization in Developing Countries*. Washington, D.C.: Brookings Institution.

Díaz-Alejandro, C. F. (1984). "Latin American Debt: I Don't Think We Are in Kansas Anymore," *Brookings Papers on Economic Activity*, 2.

Díaz-Alejandro, C. F. (2000). "Latin America in the 1930s." In Thorp, R. (ed.), *Latin America in the 1930s: The Role of the Periphery in World Crisis*. Basingstoke, Eng.: Palgrave/St. Antony's College.

Diederich, B. (1982). *Somoza and the Legacy of US Involvement in Central America*. London: Junction Books.

Dietz, J. L. (1986). *Economic History of Puerto Rico: Institutional Change and Capitalist Development*. Princeton, N.J.: Princeton University Press.

Dirección General de Estadística (México) (1933). *Censo industrial*. México, D.F.: Direction General de Estadística.

Dirección General de Estadística y Censos (Costa Rica) (1930). *Anuario estadístico 1929*. San José: Dirección General de Estadística y Censos.

Dirección General de Estadística y Censos (Costa Rica) (1974). *Censo agropecuario*. San José: Dirección General de Estadística y Censos.

Domínguez, J. (1989). *To Make a World Safe for Revolution: Cuba's Foreign Policy*. Cambridge, Mass.: Harvard University Press.

Dore, E. (1988). *The Peruvian Mining Industry: Growth, Stagnation and Crisis*. Boulder, Colo.: Westview.

Downes, R. (1992). "Autos over Rails: How US Business Supplanted the British in Brazil, 1910–28," *Journal of Latin American Studies* 24 (3): 551–83.

Drake, P. W. (1989). *The Money Doctor in the Andes: The Kemmerer Missions, 1923–1933*. Durham, N.C.: Duke University Press.

Duncan, K., et al. (1977). *Land and Labour in Latin America: Essays on the Development of Agrarian Capitalism in the Nineteenth and Twentieth Centuries*. Cambridge University Press.

Dunkerley, J. (1982). *The Long War: Dictatorship and Revolution in El Salvador*. London: Junction Books.

Dunkerley, J. (1984). *Rebellion in the Veins: Political Struggle in Bolivia, 1952–1982*. London: Verso.

Eakin, M. (1989). *British Enterprise in Brazil: The St. John d'el Rey Mining Company and the Morro Velho Gold Mine, 1830–1960*. Durham, N.C.: Duke University Press.

Echeverri Gent, E. (1992). "Forgotten Workers: British West Indians and the Early Days of the Banana Industry in Costa Rica and Honduras," *Journal of Latin American Studies* 24 (2): 275–308.

ECLA (1949). *Economic Survey of Latin America, 1948*. New York: United Nations.

ECLA (1951). *Economic Survey of Latin America, 1949*. New York: United Nations.

ECLA (1956). *Study of Inter-American Trade*. New York: United Nations.

ECLA (1959). *Inter-American Trade: Current Problems*. New York: United Nations.

ECLA (1963). *Towards a Dynamic Development Policy for Latin America*. New York: United Nations.

ECLA (1965). *External Financing in Latin America*. New York: United Nations.

ECLA (1970). *Development Problems in Latin America*. Austin: University of Texas Press.

ECLA (1971). *Income Distribution in Latin America*. New York: United Nations.

ECLAC (1988). *ECLAC 40 Years (1948–1988)*. Santiago, Chile: United Nations.

ECLAC (1989). *Statistical Yearbook for Latin America and the Caribbean, 1988*. Santiago, Chile: United Nations.

ECLAC (2001). *Statistical Yearbook for Latin America and the Caribbean, 2000*. Santiago, Chile: United Nations.

Edel, M. (1969). *Food Supply and Inflation in Latin America*. New York: Praeger.

Eder, G. J. (1968). *Inflation and Development in Latin America: A Case History of Inflation and Stabilization in Bolivia*. Ann Arbor: University of Michigan.

Eder, P. (1912). *Colombia*. London: T. Fisher Unwin.

Edwards, S. (1984). "Coffee, Money and Inflation in Colombia," *World Development* 12 (11/12): 1107–17.

Edwards, S. (1989). "Exchange Controls, Devaluations and Real Exchange Rates: The Latin American Experience," *Economic Development and Cultural Change* 37 (3): 457–94.

Edwards, S. (1995). *Crisis and Reform in Latin America: From Despair to Hope*. Oxford: Oxford University Press.

Edwards, S., and Cox Edwards, A. (1987). *Monetarism and Liberalization: The Chilean Experiment*. Chicago: University of Chicago Press.

Eichengreen, B., and Portes, R. (1988). *Settling Defaults in the Era of Bond Finance*. Birkbeck College, Discussion Paper in Economics, 1988/8.

El-Agraa, A. (1997). "The theory of economic integration." In El-Agraa, A. (ed.), *Economic Integration Worldwide*. Basingstoke: Macmillan.

El-Agraa, A. M., and Hojman, D. (1988). "The Andean Pact." In El-Agraa, A. M. (ed.), *International Economic Integration*. Basingstoke, Eng.: Macmillan.

Elías, V. (1992). *Sources of Growth: A Study of Seven Latin American Economies*. San Francisco: International Center for Economic Growth.

Engerman, S., and Sokoloff, K. (2000). "Technology and industrialization, 1790–1914." In Engerman, S., and Gallman, R. (eds.), *The Cambridge Economic History of the United States, Vol. II, The Long Nineteenth Century*. Cambridge: Cambridge University Press.

Enock, R. (1919). *Mexico*. London: T. Fisher Unwin.

Escudé, C. (1990). "US Political Destabilisation and Economic Boycott of Argentina during the 1940s." In Di Tella, G., and Watt, C. (eds.), *Argentina between the Great Powers, 1939–46*. Pittsburgh, Pa.: University of Pittsburgh Press.

Evans, P. (1979). *Dependent Development: The Alliance of Multinational, State and Local Capital in Brazil*. Princeton, N.J.: Princeton University Press.

Ewell, J. (1991). "Venezuela since 1930." In Bethell, L. (ed.), *The Cambridge History of Latin America, Vol. VIII: 1930 to the Present*. Cambridge University Press.

Fajnzylber, F. (1990). *Unavoidable Industrial Restructuring in Latin America*. Durham, N.C.: Duke University Press.

Farrands, C. (1982). "The Political Economy of the Multifibre Arrangement." In Stevens, C. (ed.), *EEC and the Third World: A Survey. Vol. II: Hunger in the World*. London: Hodder and Stoughton/ODI/Institute of Development Studies.

Fass, S. M. (1990). *Political Economy in Haiti: The Drama of Survival*. New Brunswick, N.J.: Transaction Publishers.

Fei, J., Ranis, G., and Kuo, S. (1979). *Growth with Equity: The Taiwan Case*. New York: Oxford University Press.

Felix, D., and Caskey, J. P. (1990). "The Road to Default: An Assessment of Debt Crisis Management in Latin America." In Felix, D. (ed.), *Debt and Transfiguration? Prospects for Latin America's Economic Revival*. Armonk, N.Y.: M. E. Sharpe, Inc.

Ferns, H. S. (1960). *Britain and Argentina in the Nineteenth Century*. Oxford: Clarendon Press.

Ferns, H. (1992). "The Baring Crisis Revisited," *Journal of Latin American Studies* 24 (2): 241–73.

Ferreira, A., and Tullio, G. (2002). "The Brazilian exchange rate crisis of January 1999." *Journal of Latin American Studies*, 34 (1): 143–64.

Fetter, F. (1931). *Monetary Inflation in Chile*. Princeton, N.J.: Princeton University Press.

Ffrench-Davis, R. (1988). "The Foreign Debt Crisis and Adjustment in Chile: 1976–86." In Griffith-Jones, S. (ed.), *Managing World Debt*. New York: Harvester Wheatsheaf.

Ffrench-Davis, R., Muñoz, O., and Palma, J. G. (1994). "The Latin American Economies, 1950–1990." In Bethell, L. (ed.), *The Cambridge History of Latin America, Vol. VI: Latin America since 1930: Economy, Society and Politics*, Part 1. Cambridge University Press.

Fields, G. S. (1980). *Poverty, Inequality and Development*. Cambridge University Press.

Finch, M. H. J. (1981). *A Political Economy of Uruguay since 1870*. Basingstoke, Eng.: Macmillan.

Finch, M. H. J. (1988). "The Latin American Free Trade Association." In El-Agraa, A. M. (ed.), *International Economic Integration*. Basingstoke, Eng.: Macmillan.

Fischel, A. (1991). "Politics and Education in Costa Rica." Ph.D. dissertation, University of Southampton.

Fisher, J. (1985). *Commercial Relations between Spain and Spanish America in the Era of Free Trade, 1778–1796*. Liverpool: Centre for Latin American Studies, University of Liverpool.

Fishlow, A. (1972). "Origins and Consequences of Import Substitution in Brazil." In Di Marco, L. (ed.), *International Economics and Development*. New York: Academic Press.

Fishlow, A. (1973). "Some Reflections on Post–1964 Brazilian Economic Policy." In Stepan, A. (ed.), *Authoritarian Brazil: Origins, Policies, and Future*. New Haven, Conn.: Yale University Press.

FitzGerald, E. V. K. (1976). *The State and Economic Development: Peru Since 1968*. Cambridge University Press.

FitzGerald, H. (1992). *ECLA and the Formation of Latin American Economic Doctrine in the 1940s*. Working Paper Series, No. 106. The Hague: Institute of Social Studies.

FitzGerald, E. V. K. (2000). "ECLA and the theory of import-substituting industrialisation in Latin America." In Cardenas, E., Ocampo, J., and Thorp, R. (eds.), *An Economic History of Twentieth Century Latin America. Volume 3: Industrialization and the State in Latin America*. Basingstoke: Palgrave.

FitzGerald, E. V. K. (2001). "The winner's curse: premature monetary integration in the NAFTA." In Bulmer-Thomas, V. (ed.), *Regional Integration in Latin America and the Caribbean: The Political Economy of Open Regionalism*. London: Institute of Latin American Studies.

Floyd, R. H., Gray, C., and Short, R. (1984). *Public Enterprise in Mixed Economies: Some Macroeconomic Aspects*. Washington, D.C.: International Monetary Fund.

Fodor, J. (1986). "The Origin of Argentina's Sterling Balances, 1939–43." In Di Tella, G., and Platt, D. C. M. (eds.), *The Political Economy of Argentina, 1880–1946*. Basingstoke, Eng.: Macmillan/St. Antony's College.

Fodor, J., and O'Connell, A. (1973). "La Argentina y la economía atlántica en la primera mitad del siglo XX," *Desarrollo Económico* 13 (49): 1–67.

Foner, P. S. (1963). *A History of Cuba and Its Relations with the United States, Vol. II: 1845–1895*. New York: International Publishers.

Ford, A. G. (1962). *The Gold Standard, 1880–1914: Britain v Argentina*. Oxford: Oxford University Press.

Fortín, C., and Anglade, C. (1985). *The State and Capital Accumulation in Latin America, Vol. I: Brazil, Chile, Mexico*. Pittsburgh, Pa.: University of Pittsburgh Press.

Foxley, A. (1983). *Latin American Experiments in Neo-Conservative Economics*. Berkeley: University of California Press.

Frank, A. G. (1969). *Capitalism and Underdevelopment in Latin America*. New York: Monthly Review Press.

Fritsch, W. (1988). *External Constraints on Economic Policy in Brazil, 1889–1930*. Basingstoke, Eng.: Macmillan.

Furtado, C. (1963). *The Economic Growth of Brazil*. Berkeley: University of California Press.

Furtado, C. (1976). *Economic Development of Latin America: A Survey from Colonial Times to the Cuban Revolution*, 2d ed. Cambridge University Press.

Gallman, R. (2000). "Economic growth and structural change in the long nineteenth century." In Engerman, S., and Gallman, R. (eds.), *The Cambridge Economic History of the United States, Vol. II, The Long Nineteenth Century*. Cambridge: Cambridge University Press.

Gallo, E. (1986). "Argentina: Society and Politics, 1880–1916." In Bethell, L. (ed.), *The Cambridge History of Latin America, Vol. V: c. 1870 to 1930*. Cambridge University Press.

Gamarra, E. (1999). "The United States and Bolivia: Fighting the drug war." In Bulmer-Thomas, V., and Dunkerley, J. (eds.), *The United States and Latin America: The New Agenda*. Cambridge, Mass.: The David Rockefeller Center for Latin American Studies, Harvard University/London: Institute of Latin American Studies.

Ganuza, E., Taylor, L., and Morley, S. (eds.) (2000). *Política Macroeconómica y Pobreza en América Latina y el Caribe*. New York: United Nations Development Programme, Inter-American Development Bank and ECLAC.

García, R. (1989). *Incipient Industrialization in an "Underdeveloped Country." The Case of Chile, 1845–1879*. Stockholm: Institute of Latin American Studies.

Gerchunoff, P. (1989). "Peronist Economic Policies, 1946–55." In Di Tella, G., and Dornbusch, R. (eds.), *The Political Economy of Argentina, 1946–83*. Basingstoke, Eng.: Macmillan.

Gilbert, A. J. (ed.) (1982). *Urbanization in Contemporary Latin America*. Chichester, Eng.: John Wiley.

Giles, J., and Williams, C. (2000a). "Export-led growth: A survey of the empirical literature and some non-causality results. Part 1." *Journal of International Trade and Economic Development*, 9 (3): 261–337.

Giles, J., and Williams, C. (2000b). "Export-led growth: A survey of the empirical literature and some non-causality results. Part' 2." *Journal of International Trade and Economic Development*, 9 (4): 445–70.

Gleijeses, P. (1991). *Shattered Hope: The Guatemalan Revolution and the United States, 1944–1954*. Princeton, N.J.: Princeton University Press.

Gleijeses, P. (1992). "The Limits of Sympathy: The United States and the Independence of Spanish America," *Journal of Latin American Studies* 24 (3): 481–505.

Gold, J. (1988). "Mexico and the Development of the Practice of the International Monetary Fund," *World Development* 16 (10): 1127–42.

Gómez-Galvarriato, A. (1998). "The evolution of prices and real wages in Mexico from the Porfiriato to the Revolution." In Coatsworth, J., and Taylor, A. (eds.), *Latin America and the World Economy since 1800*. Cambridge, Mass.: The David Rockefeller Center for Latin American Studies, Harvard University.

Gonzales, M. J. (1989). "Chinese Plantation Workers and Social Conflict in Peru in the Late Nineteenth Century," *Journal of Latin American Studies* 21 (3): 385–424.

Gootenberg, P. (1989). *Between Silver and Guano: Commercial Policy and the State in Post-Independence Peru*. Princeton, N.J.: Princeton University Press.

Gootenberg, P. (1991). "North–South: Trade Policy, Regionalism and *Caudillismo* in Post-Independence Peru," *Journal of Latin American Studies* 23 (2): 273–308.

Gravil, R. (1970). "State Intervention in Argentina's Export Trade between the Wars," *Journal of Latin American Studies* 2 (2): 147–66.

Greenhill, R. (1977a). "The Brazilian Coffee Trade." In Platt, D. C. M. (ed.), *Business Imperialism, 1840–1930: An Inquiry Based on British Experience in Latin America*. Oxford: Clarendon Press.

Grieb, K. J. (1979). *Guatemalan Caudillo: The Regime of Jorge Ubico, Guatemala – 1931 to 1944*. Athens: Ohio University Press.

Griffin, K. (1969). *Under-Development in Spanish America*. London: George Allen and Unwin Ltd.

Griffith-Jones, S. (1984). *International Finance and Latin America*. London: Croom Helm.

Griffith-Jones, S., Marcel, M., and Palma, G. (1987). *Third World Debt and British Banks: A Policy for Labour*. London: Fabian Society.

Grindle, M. (1986). *State and Countryside: Development Policy and Agrarian Politics in Latin America*. Baltimore: Johns Hopkins University Press.

Grosse, R. (1989). *Multinationals in Latin America*. London: Routledge.

Ground, R. L. (1988). "The Genesis of Import Substitution in Latin America," *CEPAL Review*, No. 36: 179–203.

Grunwald, J., and Musgrove, P. (1970). *Natural Resources in Latin American Development*. Baltimore: Johns Hopkins University Press.

Guadagni, A. A. (1989). "Economic Policy during Illia's Period in Office." In Di Tella, G., and Dornbusch, R. (eds.), *The Political Economy of Argentina, 1946–83*. Basingstoke, Eng.: Macmillan.

Gudmundson, L. (1986). *Costa Rica before Coffee: Society and Economy on the Eve of the Export Boom*. Baton Rouge: Louisiana State University Press.

Gwynne, R., and Kay, C. (2000). "Views from the periphery: Futures of neoliberalism in Latin America." *Third World Quarterly*, 21 (1):141–56.

Guerra Borges, A. (1981). *Compendio de geografía económica y humana de Guatemala*. Guatemala City: Universidad de San Carlos.

Gupta, B. (1989). "Import Substitution of Capital Goods: The Case of Brazil 1929–1979." D.Phil. dissertation, University of Oxford.

Gylfason, T. (1999). "Exports, inflation and growth." *World Development*, 27 (6): 1031– 57.

Haber, S. (1989). *Industry and Underdevelopment: The Industrialisation of Mexico, 1890–1940*. Stanford, Calif.: Stanford University Press.

Haber, S. (1992). "Assessing the Obstacles to Industrialization: The Mexican Economy, 1830–1940," *Journal of Latin American Studies* 24 (1): 1–32.

Haber, S. (1997). "Financial markets and industrial development: a comparative study of governmental regulation, financial innovation and industrial structure in Brazil and Mexico, 1840–1930." In Haber, S. (ed.), *How Latin America Fell Behind*, Stanford: Stanford University Press.

Haddad, C. (1974). "Growth of Brazilian Real Output, 1900–47." Ph.D. dissertation, University of Chicago.

Hale, C. A. (1986). "Political and Social Ideas in Latin America, 1870–1930." In Bethell, L. (ed.), *The Cambridge History of Latin America, Vol. IV: c. 1870 to 1930*. Cambridge University Press.

Handelman, H., and Baer, W. (eds.) (1989). *Paying the Costs of Austerity in Latin America*. Boulder, Colo.: Westview.

Hanley, A. (1998). "Business finance and the São Paulo Bolsa, 1886–1917." In Coatsworth, J., and Taylor, A. (eds.), *Latin America and the World Economy since 1800*. Cambridge, Mass.: The David Rockefeller Center for Latin American Studies, Harvard University.

Hanson, S. (1938). *Argentine Meat and the British Market*. Stanford, Calif.: Stanford University Press.

Harpelle, R. N. (1993). "The Social and Political Integration of West Indians in Costa Rica: 1930–50," *Journal of Latin American Studies* 25 (1): 103–20.

Harris, S. (1944). "Price Stabilization Programs in Latin America." In Harris, S. (ed.), *Economic Problems of Latin America*. New York: McGraw-Hill.

Harrod, R. S. (1951). *The Life of John Maynard Keynes*. London: Macmillan.

Haslip, J. (1971). *The Crown of Mexico: Maximilian and His Empress Carlota*. New York: Holt, Rinehart & Winston.

Herrera Canales, I. (1977). *El comercio exterior de México, 1821–1875*. Mexico, D.F.: Colegio de México.

Hewitt de Alcantara, C. (1976). *Modernizing Mexican Agriculture*. Geneva: UNRISD.

Hillman, J. (1988). "Bolivia and the International Tin Cartel, 1931–1941," *Journal of Latin American Studies* 20 (1): 83–110.

Hillman, J. (1990). "Bolivia and British Tin Policy, 1939–1945," *Journal of Latin American Studies* 22 (2): 289–315.

Hirschman, A. O. (1963). *Journeys towards Progress: Studies of Economic Policy Making in Latin America*. New York: Twentieth Century Fund.

Hirschman, A. O. (1981). *Essays in Trespassing*. Cambridge University Press.

Hoetink, H. (1986). "The Dominican Republic, c. 1870–1930." In Bethell, L. (ed.), *The Cambridge History of Latin America, Vol. V: c. 1870 to 1930*. Cambridge University Press.

Hofman, A. (2000). *The Economic Development of Latin America in the 20th Century*. Cheltenham: Edward Elgar.

Holloway, T. (1980). *Immigrants on the Land: Coffee and Society in São Paulo, 1886–1934*. Chapel Hill: University of North Carolina Press.

Hood, M. (1975). *Gunboat Diplomacy, 1895–1905: Great Power Pressure in Venezuela*. London: George Allen & Unwin.

Hopkins, A. G. (1994). "Informal Empire in Argentina: An Alternative View," *Journal of Latin American Studies*, 26 (2).

Horn, P. V., and Bice, H. E. (1949). *Latin American Trade and Economics*. New York: Prentice-Hall.

Horsefield, J. K. (1969). *The International Monetary Fund, 1945–1965. Vol. I: Chronicle*. Washington, D.C.: International Monetary Fund.

Hughlett, L. J. (ed.) (1946). *Industrialization of Latin America*. New York: McGraw-Hill.

Humphreys, R. A. (1946). *The Evolution of Modern Latin America*. Oxford: Clarendon Press.

Humphreys, R. A. (1961). *The Diplomatic History of British Honduras*. Oxford: Oxford University Press.

Humphreys, R. A. (1981). *Latin America and the Second World War, 1939–1942*. London: Athlone Press.

Humphreys, R. A. (1982). *Latin America and the Second World War, 1942–1945*. London: Athlone Press.

Hunt, S. (1973). *Prices and Quantum Estimates of Peruvian Exports, 1830–1962*. Woodrow Wilson School Research Program in Economic Development, Discussion Paper No. 31. Princeton, N.J.: Princeton University.

Hunt, S. (1985). "Growth and Guano in 19th Century Peru." In Cortés Conde, R., and Hunt, S. (eds.), *The Latin American Economies: Growth and the Export Sector, 1880–1930*. New York: Holmes and Meier.

Imlah, A. (1958). *Economic Elements of the Pax Britannica*. Cambridge University Press.

Instituto Brasileiro de Geografia e Estatística (IBGE) (1987). *Estatísticas históricas do Brasil*. Rio de Janeiro: IBGE.

Inter-American Development Bank (IDB) (1982). *Economic and Social Progress in Latin America: The External Sector, 1982 Report*. Washington, D.C.: IDB.

Inter-American Development Bank (IDB) (1983). *Economic and Social Progress in Latin America: Natural Resources, 1983 Report*. Washington, D.C.: IDB.

Inter-American Development Bank (IDB) (1984a). *Economic and Social Progress in Latin America: Economic Integration, 1984 Report*. Washington, D.C.: IDB.

Inter-American Development Bank (IDB) (1984b). *External Debt and Economic Development in Latin America: Background and Prospects*. Washington, D.C.: IDB.

Inter-American Development Bank (IDB) (1989). *Economic and Social Progress in Latin America 1989 Report*. Washington, D.C.: IDB.

Inter-American Development Bank (IDB) (1991). *Economic and Social Progress in Latin America 1991 Report*. Washington, D.C.: IDB.

International Monetary Fund (1986b). *Yearbook of Balance of Payments Statistics 1986*. Washington, D.C.: International Monetary Fund.

International Monetary Fund (1987). *Yearbook of International Financial Statistics 1987*. Washington, D.C.: International Monetary Fund.

Irigoin, M. (2000). "Inconvertible paper money, inflation and economic performance in early 19th century Argentina." *Journal of Latin American Studies*, 32 (2): 333–59.

James, E. W. (1945). "A Quarter Century of Road-Building in the Americas," *Bulletin of the Pan American Union* 79 (1): 609–18.

Jenkins, R. (1984). *Transnational Corporations and Industrial Transformation in Latin America*. Basingstoke, Eng.: Macmillan.

Jenkins, R. (1987). *Transnational Corporations and the Latin American Automobile Industry*. Basingstoke, Eng.: Macmillan.

Jenkins, R. (ed.) (2000). *Industry and Environment in Latin America*, London and New York: Routledge.

Jones, C. (1977a). "Commercial Banks and Mortgage Companies." In Platt, D. C. M. (ed.), *Business Imperialism, 1840–1930: An Inquiry Based on British Experience in Latin America.* Oxford: Clarendon Press.

Jones, C. (1977b). "Insurance Companies." In Platt, D. C. M. (ed.), *Business Imperialism 1840–1930: An Inquiry Based on British Experience in Latin America.* Oxford: Clarendon Press.

Jones, C. L. (1940). *Guatemala Past and Present.* Minneapolis: University of Minnesota Press.

Jorgensen, E., and Sachs, J. (1989). "Default and Renegotiation of Latin American Foreign Bonds in the Interwar Period." In Eichengreen, B., and Lindert, P. (eds.), *The International Debt Crisis in Historical Perspective.* Cambridge, Mass.: MIT Press.

Joseph, E. (1982). *Revolution from Without: Yucatán, Mexico and the United States, 1880–1924.* Cambridge University Press.

Joslin, D. (1963). *A Century of Banking in Latin America.* London: Oxford University Press.

Joyce, E., and Malamud, C. (eds.) (1998). *Latin America and the Multinational Drug Trade,* London: ILAS/Macmillan.

Kahil, R. (1973). *Inflation and Economic Development in Brazil, 1946–1963.* Oxford: Clarendon Press.

Kahler, M. (1990). "Orthodoxy and Its Alternatives: Explaining Approaches to Stabilization and Adjustment." In Nelson, J. M. (ed.), *Economic Crisis and Policy Choice: The Politics of Adjustment in the Third World.* Princeton, N.J.: Princeton University Press.

Karlsson, W. (1975). *Manufacturing in Venezuela: Studies on Development and Location.* Stockholm: Latinamerika-institutet i Stockholm.

Karnes, T. L. (1978). *Tropical Enterprise: Standard Fruit and Steamship Company in Latin America.* Baton Rouge: Louisiana State University Press.

Katz, F. (1981). *The Secret War in Mexico: Europe, the United States and the Mexican Revolution.* Chicago: University of Chicago Press.

Katz, J. M. (1987). *Technology Generation in Latin American Manufacturing Industries.* Basingstoke, Eng.: Macmillan.

Katz, J., and Kosacoff, B. (2000). "Import-substituting industrialization in Argentina, 1940–80: Its achievements and shortcomings." In Cardenas, E., Ocampo, J., and Thorp, R. (eds.), *An Economic History of Twentieth Century Latin America. Volume 3: Industrialization and the State in Latin America.* Basingstoke: Palgrave.

Kay, C. (1989). *Latin American Theories of Development and Underdevelopment.* London: Routledge.

Kelly, M., et al. (1988). *Issues and Developments in International Trade Policy.* Washington, D.C.: International Monetary Fund.

Kepner, C. (1936). *Social Aspects of the Banana Industry.* New York: Columbia University Press.

Kepner, C., and Soothill, J. (1935). *The Banana Empire: A Case Study in Economic Imperialism.* New York: Vanguard Press.

Kindleberger, C. (1987). *The World in Depression.* London: Penguin.

Kirsch, H. W. (1977). *Industrial Development in a Traditional Society: The Conflict of Entrepreneurship and Modernization in Chile.* Gainesville: University Presses of Florida.

Klarén, P. F. (1986). "The Origins of Modern Peru, 1880–1930." In Bethell, L. (ed.), *The Cambridge History of Latin America, Vol. V: c. 1870 to 1930.* Cambridge University Press.

Klein, H. S. (1982). *Bolivia: The Evolution of a Multi-Ethnic Society.* New York: Oxford University Press.

Klein, H. S. (1992). *Bolivia: The Evolution of a Multi-Ethnic Society.* 2d ed. New York: Oxford University Press.

Knape, J. (1987). "British Foreign Policy in the Caribbean Basin, 1938–1945: Oil, Nationalism and Relations with the United States," *Journal of Latin American Studies* 19 (2): 279–94.

Knight, A. (1986a). *The Mexican Revolution: Vol. I: Porfirians, Liberals and Peasants.* Lincoln: University of Nebraska Press.

Knight, A. (1986b). *The Mexican Revolution: Vol. II: Counter-revolution and Reconstruction.* Lincoln: University of Nebraska Press.

Knight, A. (1990). "Mexico, c. 1930–46." In Bethell, L. (ed.), *The Cambridge History of Latin America, Vol. VII: Latin America since 1930: Mexico, Central America and the Caribbean.* Cambridge University Press.

Knight, F. (1990). *The Caribbean: The Genesis of a Fragmented Nationalism.* 2d ed. Oxford: Oxford University Press.

Kock-Petersen, S. A. (1946). "The Cement Industry." In Hughlett, L. J. (ed.), *Industrialization of Latin America.* New York: McGraw-Hill.

Koebel, W. H. (n.d.). *Central America.* New York: Scribners.

Koebel, W. H. (1911). *Uruguay.* London: T. Fisher Unwin.

Koebel, W. H. (1919). *Paraguay.* London: T. Fisher Unwin.

Korol, J. C., and Sábato, H. (1990). "Incomplete Industrialization: An Argentine Obsession," *Latin American Research Review* 25 (1): 7–30.

Krehm, W. (1984). *Democracies and Tyrannies of the Caribbean.* Westport, Conn.: Lawrence Hill.

Kuczynski, P. (1988). *Latin American Debt.* Baltimore: Johns Hopkins University Press.

Labán, R., and Larraín, F. (1994). "The Chilean experience with capital mobility." In Bosworth, B., Dornbusch, R., and Labán, R. (eds.), *The Chilean Economy: Policy Lessons and Challenges.* Washington, D.C.: Brookings Institution Press.

Lafeber, W. (1978). *The Panama Canal: The Crisis in Historical Perspective.* New York: Oxford University Press.

Langley, L. (1968). *The Cuban Policy of the United States: A Brief History.* New York: Wiley.

Langley, L. D. (1983). *The Banana Wars: An Inner History of American Empire 1900–1934.* Lexington: University Press of Kentucky.

Larraín, F., and Selowsky, H. (1991). *The Public Sector and the Latin American Crisis.* San Francisco: ICS Press.

Latin America Bureau (LAB) (1987). *The Great Tin Crash, Bolivia and the World Tin Market.* London: LAB.

League of Nations (1925). *Statistical Yearbook.* Geneva: League of Nations.

League of Nations (1926). *Statistical Yearbook.* Geneva: League of Nations.

League of Nations (1927). *Statistical Yearbook.* Geneva: League of Nations.

League of Nations (1928). *Statistical Yearbook.* Geneva: League of Nations.

League of Nations (1930). *International Yearbook of Agricultural Statistics, 1929/30.* Geneva: League of Nations.

League of Nations (1931). *Statistical Yearbook.* Geneva: League of Nations.

League of Nations (1933). *International Yearbook of Agricultural Statistics, 1932/3.* Geneva: League of Nations.

League of Nations (1938). *Public Finance.* Geneva: League of Nations.

League of Nations (1945). *Statistical Yearbook, 1942/4.* Geneva: League of Nations.

Leff, N. H. (1968). *The Brazilian Capital Goods Industry, 1929–1964.* Cambridge, Mass.: Harvard University Press.

Leff, N. H. (1982). *Underdevelopment and Development in Brazil. Vol. I: Economic Structure and Change, 1822–1947.* London: George Allen & Unwin.

León Gómez, A. (1978). *El escándalo del ferrocarril: Ensayo histórico.* Tegucigalpa: Imprenta Soto.

Levi, D. (1987). *The Prados of São Paulo: An Elite Family and Social Change, 1840–1930.* Athens: University of Georgia Press.

Levin, J. (1960). *The Export Economies: Their Pattern of Development in Historical Perspective.* Cambridge, Mass.: Harvard University Press.

Levine, V. (1914). *South American Handbooks: Colombia*. London: Pitman.

Lewis, A. (1978). *Growth and Fluctuations, 1870–1913*. London: Allen & Unwin.

Lewis, C. (1986). "Industry in Latin America before 1930." In Bethell, L. (ed.), *The Cambridge History of Latin America, Vol. IV: c. 1870 to 1930*. Cambridge University Press.

Lewis, C. (1983). *British Railways in Argentina, 1857–1914*. London: Institute of Latin American Studies.

Lewis, P. H. (1990). *The Crisis of Argentine Capitalism*. Chapel Hill: University of North Carolina Press.

Lewis, P. H. (1991). "Paraguay since 1930." In Bethell, L. (ed.), *The Cambridge History of Latin America, Vol. VIII: Latin America since 1930: Spanish South America*. Cambridge University Press.

Lewis, W. A. (1989). "The Roots of Development Theory." In Chenery, H., and Srinivasan, T. N. (eds.), *Handbook of Development Economics*. Amsterdam: North-Holland.

Libby, D. C. (1991). "Proto-Industrialization in a Slave Society: The Case of Minas Gerais," *Journal of Latin American Studies* 23 (1): 1–35.

Lieuwen, E. (1965). *Venezuela*. London: Oxford University Press.

Lieuwen, E. (1985). "The Politics of Energy in Venezuela." In Wirth, J. D. (ed.), *Latin American Oil Companies and the Politics of Energy*. Lincoln: University of Nebraska Press.

Lin, C. (1988). "East Asia and Latin America as Contrasting Models," *Economic Development and Cultural Change* 36 (3): S153–S197.

Lindo-Fuentes, H. (1990). *Weak Foundations: The Economy of El Salvador in the Nineteenth Century, 1821–1898*. Berkeley: University of California Press.

Linke, L. (1962). *Ecuador: Country of Contrasts*. London: Oxford University Press.

Lipsey, R. (2000). "U.S. foreign trade and the balance of payments, 1800–1913." In Engerman, S., and Gallman, R. (eds.), *The Cambridge Economic History of the United States. Vol. II: The Long Nineteenth Century*. Cambridge: Cambridge University Press.

Lockhart, J., and Schwartz, S. B. (1983). *Early Latin America: A History of Colonial Spanish America and Brazil*. Cambridge University Press.

Lomnitz, L., and Pérez-Lizaur, M. (1987). *A Mexican Elite Family, 1820–1980*. Princeton, N.J.: Princeton University Press.

Looney, R. E. (1985). *Economic Policymaking in Mexico: Factors Underlying the 1982 Crisis*. Durham, N.C.: Duke University Press.

Love, J. (1994). "Economic Ideas and Ideologies in Latin America since 1930." In Bethell, L. (ed.), *The Cambridge History of Latin America, Vol. VI: Latin America since 1930: Economy, Society and Politics*, Part 1. Cambridge University Press.

Lundahl, M. (1979). *Peasants and Poverty: A Study of Haiti*. London: Croom Helm.

Lundahl, M. (1992). *Politics or Markets? Essays on Haitian Underdevelopment*. London: Routledge.

Lustig, N. (ed.) (1995). *Coping with Austerity: Poverty and Inequality in Latin America*. Washington, D.C.: Brookings Institution Press.

Lynch, J. (1985a). "The Origins of Spanish American Independence." In Bethell, L. (ed.), *The Cambridge History of Latin America, Vol. III: From Independence to c. 1870*. Cambridge University Press.

Lynch, J. (1985b). "The River Plate Republics from Independence to the Paraguayan War." In Bethell, L. (ed.), *The Cambridge History of Latin America, Vol. III: From Independence to c. 1870*. Cambridge University Press.

Macario, S. (1964). "Protectionism and Industrialization in Latin America," *Economic Bulletin for Latin America* 9 (1): 62–101.

Macbean, A., and Nguyen, T. (1987). "International Commodity Agreements: Shadow and Substance," *World Development* 15 (5): 575–90.

McBeth, J. S. (1983). *Juan Vicente Gómez and the Oil Companies in Venezuela, 1908–1935*. Cambridge University Press.

McClintock, M. (1985). *The American Connection, Vol. II, State Terror and Popular Resistance in Guatemala*. London: Zed Books.

McCloskey, D., and Zecker, J. (1981). "How the Gold Standard Worked, 1880–1913." In McCloskey, D. (ed.), *Enterprise and Trade in Victorian Britain*. London: Allen & Unwin.

McCreery, D. (1983). *Development and the State in Reforma Guatemala, 1871–1885*. Athens: Center for International Studies, Ohio University.

MacDonald, C. A. (1990). "The Braden Campaign and Anglo-American Relations in Argentina, 1945–6." In Di Tella, G., and Watt, C. (eds.), *Argentina between the Great Powers, 1939–46*. Pittsburgh, Pa.: University of Pittsburgh Press.

McDowall, D. (1988). *The Light: Brazilian Traction, Light and Power Company, 1899–1945*. Toronto: University of Toronto Press.

McGreevey, W. P. (1971). *An Economic History of Colombia, 1845–1930*. Cambridge University Press.

McGreevey, W. P. (1985). "The Transition to Economic Growth in Colombia." In Cortés Conde, R., and Hunt, S. (eds.), *The Latin American Economies: Growth and the Export Sector, 1880–1930*. New York: Holmes and Meier.

Machinea, J. L., and Fanelli, J. M. (1988). "Stopping Hyperinflation: The Case of the Austral Plan in Argentina, 1985–87." In Bruno, M., et al. (eds.), *Inflation Stabilization: The Experiences of Israel, Argentina, Brazil, Bolivia and Mexico*. Cambridge, Mass: MIT Press.

McKinnon, R. I. (1973). *Money and Capital in Economic Development*. Washington, D.C.: Brookings Institution.

McLure, C., et al. (1990). *The Taxation of Income from Business and Capital in Colombia*. Durham, N.C.: Duke University Press.

Maddison, A. (1985). *Two Crises: Latin America and Asia, 1929–38 and 1973–83*. Paris: Organization for Economic Cooperation and Development.

Maddison, A. (1991). "Economic and Social Conditions in Latin America, 1913–1950." In Urrutia, M. (ed.), *Long Term Trends in Latin American Economic Development*. Washington, D.C.: Inter-American Development Bank.

Maddison, A. (1995). *Monitoring the World Economy, 1820–1992*. Paris: OECD, Development Centre Studies.

Maddison, A. (2001). *The World Economy: A Millennial Perspective*. Paris: OECD, Development Centre Studies.

Maizels, A. (1963). *Industrial Growth and World Trade*. Cambridge University Press.

Maizels, A. (1970). *Growth and Trade: An Abridged Version of Industrial. Growth and World Trade*. Cambridge University Press.

Maizels, A. (1992). *Commodities in Crisis*. Oxford: Clarendon Press.

Major, J. (1990). "The Panama Canal Zone, 1904–79." In Bethell, L. (ed.), *The Cambridge History of Latin America, Vol. VII: Latin America since 1930: Mexico, Central America and the Caribbean*. Cambridge University Press.

Manchester, A. (1933). *British Preeminence in Brazil, Its Rise and Decline: A Study in European Expansion*. Chapel Hill: University of North Carolina Press.

Marichal, C. (1989). *A Century of Debt Crises in Latin America: From Independence to the Great Depression*. Princeton, N.J.: Princeton University Press.

Marichal, C. (1997). "Obstacles to the development of capital markets in nineteenth-century Mexico." In Haber, S. (ed.), *How Latin America Fell Behind*. Stanford: Stanford University Press.

Marquez, G. (1998). "Tariff protection in Mexico, 1892–1909: Ad valorem tariff rates and sources of variation." In Coatsworth, J., and Taylor, A. (eds.), *Latin America and the World Economy since 1800*. Cambridge, Mass.: The David Rockefeller Center for Latin American Studies, Harvard University.

Marshall, O. (1991). *European Immigration and Ethnicity in Latin America: A Bibliography*. London: Institute of Latin American Studies.

Mathieson, J. A. (1988). "Problems and Prospects of Export Diversification: Case Studies – Dominican Republic." In Paus, E. (ed.), *Struggle against Dependence: Nontraditional Export Growth in Central America and the Caribbean*. Boulder, Colo.: Westview.

May, S., and Plaza, G. (1958). *The United Fruit Company in Latin America*. Washington, D.C.: National Planning Association.

Maynard, G. (1989). "Argentina: Macroeconomic Policy, 1966–73." In Di Tella, G., and Dornbusch, R. (eds.), *The Political Economy of Argentina, 1946–83*. Basingstoke, Eng.: Macmillan/St. Antony's College.

Mecham, J. L. (1961). *The United States and Inter-American Security, 1889–1960*. Austin: University of Texas Press.

Meier, G. M. (1984). *Pioneers in Development*. New York: Oxford University Press/World Bank.

Meier, G. M. (1987). *Pioneers in Development (Second Series)*. New York: Oxford University Press/World Bank.

Mendels, F. (1972). "Proto-industrialization: The First Phase of the Industrialization Process," *Journal of Economic History* 32 (2): 241–61.

Menjívar, R. (1980). *Acumulación originaria y desarrollo del capitalismo en El Salvador*. San José, Costa Rica: EDUCA.

Mesa-Lago, C. (1978). *Social Security in Latin America: Pressure Groups, Stratification and Inequality*. Pittsburgh, Pa.: University of Pittsburgh Press.

Mesa-Lago, C. (1981). *The Economy of Socialist Cuba: A Two-Decade Appraisal*. Albuquerque: University of New Mexico Press.

Mesa-Lago, C. (2000). *Market, Socialist and Mixed Economies: Comparative Policy and Performance, Chile, Cuba and Costa Rica*. Baltimore: Johns Hopkins University Press.

Meyer, M. C., and Sherman, W. L. (1979). *The Course of Mexican History*. New York: Oxford University Press.

Miller, R. (1993). *Britain and Latin America in the 19th and 20th Centuries*. London and New York: Longman.

Miller, S. (1990). "Mexican Junkers and Capitalist Haciendas, 1810–1910: The Arable Estate and the Transition to Capitalism between the Insurgency and the Revolution," *Journal of Latin American Studies* 22 (2): 229–63.

Millot, J., Silva, C., and Silva, L. (1973). *El desarrollo industrial del Uruguay de la crisis de 1929 a la postguerra*. Montevideo: Instituto de Economía, Universidad de la República.

Mills, G. J. (n.d.), *South American Handbooks: Argentina*. London: Pitman.

Mitchell, B. (1980). *European Historical Statistics*. London: Macmillan.

Mitchell, B. (1983). *International Historical Statistics: Australasia and Americas*. London: Macmillan.

Mitchell, B. (1988). *British Historical Statistics*. 2d ed. London: Macmillan.

Mitchell, B. (1993). *International Historical Statistics. The Americas, 1750–1988*. Basingstoke, Eng.: Macmillan.

Modiano, E. M. (1988). "The Cruzado First Attempt: The Brazilian Stabilization Program of February 1986." In Bruno, M., et al. (eds.), *Inflation Stabilization: The Experiences of Israel, Argentina, Brazil, Bolivia and Mexico*. Cambridge, Mass.: MIT Press.

Molina, F. (1851). *Bosquejo de la República de Costa Rica*. New York: S. W. Benedict.

Molina Chocano, G. (1982). *Estado liberal y desarrollo capitalista en Honduras*. Tegucigalpa: Universidad Nacional de Honduras.

Morales, J. A. (1988). "Inflation Stabilization in Bolivia." In Bruno, M., et al. (eds.), *Inflation Stabilization: The Experiences of Israel, Argentina, Brazil, Bolivia and Mexico*. Cambridge, Mass.: MIT Press.

Morawetz, D. (1981). *Why the Emperor's New Clothes Are Not Made in Colombia: A Case Study in Latin American and East Asian Manufactured Exports*. New York: Oxford University Press.

Moreno Fraginals, M. (1986). "Plantation Economies and Societies in the Spanish Caribbean, 1860–1930." In Bethell, L. (ed.), *The Cambridge History of Latin America, Vol. IV: c. 1870–1930*. Cambridge University Press.

Morley, S. (1995). *Poverty and Inequality in Latin America: The Impact of Adjustment and Recovery in the 1990s*. Baltimore: Johns Hopkins University Press.

Morley, S. (2000). *La Distribución de Ingreso en América Latina y el Caribe*. Santiago: CEPAL y Fondo de Cultura Económica.

Moya Pons, F. (1985). "Haiti and Santo Domingo: 1790–c. 1870." In Bethell, L. (ed.), *The Cambridge History of Latin America, Vol. III: From Independence to c. 1870*. Cambridge University Press.

Moya Pons, F. (1990a). "The Dominican Republic since 1930." In Bethell, L. (ed.), *The Cambridge History of Latin America, Vol. VII: Latin America since 1930: Central America and the Caribbean*. Cambridge University Press.

Moya Pons, F. (1990b). "Import-Substitution Industrialization Policies in the Dominican Republic, 1925–61," *Hispanic American Historical Review* 70 (4): 539–77.

Mulhall, M. G., and Mulhall, E. T. (1885). *Handbooks of the River Plate*. London: Trubner & Co.

Munro, D. (1964). *Intervention and Dollar Diplomacy in the Caribbean, 1900–1921*. Princeton, N.J.: Princeton University Press.

Mussa, M. (2002). *Argentina and the Fund: From Triumph to Tragedy*. Washington, D.C.: Institute for International Economics.

Nicholls, S. (2001). "Panel data modelling of long-run per capita growth rates in the Caribbean: An empirical note." *Integration and Trade*, 15 (5): 57–82.

Nickson, A. (1989). "The Overthrow of the Stroessner Regime: Re-establishing the Status Quo," *Bulletin of Latin American Research* 8 (2): 185–209.

O'Brien, T. (1996). *The Revolutionary Mission: American Enterprise in Latin America, 1900–1945*. Cambridge: Cambridge University Press.

Ocampo, J. A. (1984). *Colombia y la economía mundial, 1830–1910*. Bogotá: FEDESAROLLO.

Ocampo, J. A. (1987). "Crisis and Economic Policy in Colombia, 1980–5." In Thorp, R., and Whitehead, L. (eds.), *Latin American Debt and the Adjustment Crisis*. Basingstoke, Eng.: Macmillan/St. Antony's College.

Ocampo, J. A. (1990). "Import Controls, Prices and Economic Activity in Colombia," *Journal of Development Economics*, 32 (2): 369–87.

Ocampo, J. A. (1991). "The Transition from Primary Exports to Industrial Development in Colombia," In Blömstrom, M., and Meller, P. (eds.), *Diverging Paths: Comparing a Century of Scandinavian and Latin American Economic Development*. Washington, D.C.: Inter-American Development Bank.

Ocampo, J. (2000). "The Colombian economy in the 1930s." In Thorp, R. (ed.), *Latin America in the 1930s: The Role of the Periphery in World Crisis*. Basingstoke: Palgrave.

Ocampo, J., and Botero, M. (2000). "Coffee and the origins of modern economic development in Colombia." In Cardenas, E., Ocampo, J., and Thorp, R. (eds.), *An Economic History of Twentieth Century Latin America. Vol. I: the Export Age. The Latin American Economies in the Late Nineteenth and Early Twentieth Centuries*. Basingstoke: Palgrave.

Ocampo, J. A., and Montenegro, S. (1984). *Crisis mundial, protección e industrialización: Ensayos de historia económica colombiana*. Bogotá: Fondo Editorial CEREC.

O'Connell, A. (2000). "Argentina into the Depression: Problems of an Open Economy." In Thorp, R. (ed.), *Latin America in the 1930s: The Role of the Periphery in World Crisis*. Basingstoke, Eng.: Palgrave/St. Antony's College.

Oddone, J. A. (1986). "The Formation of Modern Uruguay, c. 1870–1930." In Bethell, L. (ed.), *The Cambridge History of Latin America, Vol. V: c. 1870–1930*. Cambridge University Press.

Ohkawa, K., and Rosovsky, R. (1973). *Japanese Economic Growth: Trend Acceleration in the Twentieth Century*. Stanford, Calif.: Stanford University Press.

Oribe Stemmer, J. E. (1989). "Freight Rates in the Trade between Europe and South America, 1840–1914," *Journal of Latin American Studies* 21 (1): 23–59.

Ortega, L. (1990). "El proceso de industrialización en Chile, 1850–1970." Paper presented at the 10th World Congress of Economic History. Leuven.

Ortiz, G. (1991). "Mexico beyond the Debt Crisis: Toward Sustainable Growth with Price Stability." In Bruno, M., Fischer, S., Helpman, E., and Liviatan, N. (eds.), *Lessons of Economic Stabilization and Its Aftermath*. Cambridge, Mass.: MIT Press.

Palma, G. (1979). "Growth and Structure of Chilean Manufacturing Industry from 1830 to 1935." Ph.D. dissertation, Cambridge University.

Palma, G. (2000a). "From an Export-Led to an Import-Substituting Economy: Chile, 1914–39." In Thorp, R. (ed.), *Latin America in the 1930s: The Role of the Periphery in World Crisis*. Basingstoke, Eng.: Palgrave/St. Antony's College.

Palma, G. (2000b). "Trying to 'tax and spend' oneself out of the 'Dutch Disease': The Chilean economy from the War of the Pacific to the Great Depression." In Cárdenas, E., Ocampo, J., and Thorp, R. (eds.), *An Economic History of Twentieth Century Latin America. Vol. I: The Export Age. The Latin American Economies in the Late Nineteenth and Early Twentieth Centuries*. Basingstoke: Palgrave.

Pan-American Union (1952). *The Foreign Trade of Latin America Since 1913*. Washington, D.C.: Pan-American Union.

Parkin, V. (1991). *Chronic Inflation in an Industrialising Economy: The Brazilian Experience*. Cambridge University Press.

Pastor, M. (1991). "Bolivia: Hyperinflation, Stabilisation and Beyond," *Journal of Development Studies* 27 (2): 211–37.

Pastore, M. (1994). "Trade contraction and economic decline: The Paraguayan economy under Francia, 1810–40." *Journal of Latin American Studies*, 26 (3): 539–593.

Pederson, L. (1966). *The Mining Industry of the Norte Chico, Chile*. Evanston, Ill.: Northwestern University.

Peek, P., and Standing, G. (1982). *State Policies and Migration: Studies in Latin America and the Caribbean*. London: Croom Helm.

Peláez, C. (1972). *Historia de industrialização brasileira*. Rio de Janeiro: APEC.

Peñaloza Cordero, L. (1983). *Nueva historia económica de Bolivia de la independencia a los albores de la guerra del Pacífico*. La Paz: Editorial Los Amigos del Libro.

Pérez-López, J. (1974). "An Index of Cuban Industrial Output, 1950–58." Ph.D. dissertation, State University of New York at Albany.

Pérez-López, J. (1977). "An index of Cuban industrial output: 1930–58." In Wilkie, J., and Ruddle, K. (eds.), *Quantitative Latin American Studies: Methods and Findings, Statistical Abstract for Latin America Supplement Series 6*. Los Angeles: UCLA.

Pérez-López, J. F. (1991). "Bringing the Cuban Economy into Focus: Conceptual and Empirical Challenges," *Latin American Research Review* 26 (3): 7–53.

Perloff, H. S. (1950). *Puerto Rico's Economic Future: A Study in Planned Development*. Chicago: University of Chicago Press.

Petrecolla, A. (1989). "Unbalanced Development, 1958–62." In Di Tella, G., and Dornbusch, R. (eds.), *The Political Economy of Argentina, 1946–83*. Basingstoke, Eng.: Macmillan/St. Antony's College.

Phelps, D. M. (1936). *Migration of Industry to South America*. New York: McGraw-Hill.

Philip, G. (1982). *Oil and Politics in Latin America: Nationalist Movements and State Companies*. Cambridge University Press.

Pinder, J. (1991). *European Community: The Building of a Union*. Oxford: Oxford University Press.

Platt, D. C. M. (1971). "Problems in the Interpretation of Foreign Trade Statistics before 1914," *Journal of Latin American Studies* 3 (2): 119–30.

Platt, D. C. M. (1972). *Latin America and British Trade, 1806–1914*. London: Adam & Charles Black.

Platt, D. C. M. (ed.) (1977). *Business Imperialism, 1840–1930: An Inquiry Based on British Experience in Latin America*. Oxford: Clarendon Press.

Potash, R. (1969). *The Army and Politics in Argentina, 1928–45: Yrigoyen to Perón*. Stanford, Calif.: Stanford University Press.

Potash, R. (1980). *The Army and Politics in Argentina, 1945–62: Perón to Frondizi*. Stanford, Calif.: Stanford University Press.

Potash, R. A. (1983). *The Mexican Government and Industrial Development in the Early Republic: The Banco de Avío*. Amherst, Mass.: Stanford.

Powell, A. (1991). "Commodity and Developing Country Terms of Trade: What Does the Long Run Show?" *Economic Journal* 101 (409): 1485–96.

Prado, L. (1991). "Commercial Capital, Domestic Market and Manufacturing in Imperial Brazil: The Failure of Brazilian Economic Development in the XIXth Century." Ph.D. dissertation, University of London.

Prados de la Escosura, L., and Amaral, S. (eds.) (1993). *La Independencia Americana: consecuencias económicas*, Madrid: Alianza Editorial.

Rabe, S. (1988). *Eisenhower and Latin America: The Foreign Policy of Anticommunism*. Chapel Hill: University of North Carolina Press.

Ramos, J. (1986). *Neoconservative Economics in the Southern Cone of Latin America, 1973–1983*. Baltimore: Johns Hopkins University Press.

Ramos Mattei, A. (1984). "The Growth of the Puerto Rican Sugar Industry under North American Domination: 1899–1910." In Albert, B., and Graves, A. (eds.), *Crisis and Change in the International Sugar Economy, 1860–1914*. Norwich, Eng.: ISC Press.

Ramsett, D. (1969). *Regional Industrial Development in Central America: A Case Study of the Integration Industries Scheme*. New York: Praeger.

Randall, L. (1977). *A Comparative Economic History of Latin America, 1500–1914. Vol. I: Mexico*. New York: Institute of Latin American Studies, Columbia University.

Randall, L. (1987). *The Political Economy of Venezuelan Oil*. New York: Praeger.

Rangel, D. (1970). *Capital y desarrollo: El rey petróleo*. 2 vols. Caracas: Universidad Central de Venezuela.

Ranis, G. (1981). "Challenges and Opportunities Posed by Asia's Superexporters: Implications for Manufactured Exports from Latin America." In Baer, W., and Gillis, M. (eds.), *Export Diversification and the New Protectionism: The Experiences of Latin America*. Champaign: Bureau of Economic and Business Research, University of Illinois.

Ranis, G., and Orrock, L. (1985). "Latin American and East Asian NICs: Development Strategies Compared." In Durán, E. (ed.), *Latin America and the World Recession*. Cambridge University Press/Royal Institute of International Affairs.

Razo, A., and Haber, S. (1998). "The rate of growth of productivity in Mexico, 1850–1933." *Journal of Latin American Studies*, 30 (3): 481–517.

Reed, N. (1964). *The Caste War of Yucatán*. Stanford, Calif.: Stanford University Press.

Regalsky, A. M. (1989). "Foreign Capital, Local Interests and Railway Development in Argentina: French Investments in Railways, 1900–1914," *Journal of Latin American Studies* 21 (3): 425–52.

Reinhart, C. (1999). *Accounting for Saving: Financial Liberalization, Capital Flows and Growth in Latin America and Europe*. Washington, D.C.: Inter-American Development Bank.

Remmer, K. (1986). "The Politics of Economic Stabilisation: IMF Standby Programs in Latin America, 1954–84," *Comparative Politics* 19 (6): 1–24.

Reynolds, C. W. (1965). "Development Problems of an Export Economy: The Case of Chile and Copper." In Mamalakis, M., and Reynolds, C. W., *Essays on the Chilean Economy*. Homewood, Ill.: Irwin.

Rippy, J. F. (1945). *Historical Evolution of Hispanic America*. New York: Appleton-Century-Crofts, Inc.

Rippy, J. F. (1959). *British Investments in Latin America, 1822–1949: A Case Study in the Operations of Private Enterprise in Retarded Regions*. Minneapolis: University of Minnesota Press.

Rock, D. (1986). "Argentina in 1914: The Pampas, the Interior, Buenos Aires." In Bethell, L. (ed.), *The Cambridge History of Latin America, Vol. V. c. 1870 to 1930*. Cambridge University Press.

Rock, D. (1987). *Argentina, 1516–1987: From Spanish Colonization to Alfonsín*. Berkeley: University of California Press.

Rock, D. (1991). "Argentina, 1930–46." In Bethell, L. (ed.), *The Cambridge History of Latin America, Vol. VIII: Latin America since 1930: Spanish South America*. Cambridge University Press.

Rockland, H. A. (1970). *Sarmiento's Travels in the United States in 1847*. Princeton, N.J.: Princeton University Press.

Roddick, J. (1988). *The Dance of the Millions: Latin America and the Debt Crisis*. London: Latin America Bureau.

Rodríguez, L. (1985). *The Search for Public Policy: Regional Politics and Public Finance in Ecuador, 1830–1940*. Berkeley: University of California Press.

Rodríguez, M. (1991). "Public Sector Behavior in Venezuela." In Larraín, F., and Selowsky, M. (eds.), *The Public Sector and the Latin American Crisis*. San Francisco: ICS Press.

Roemer, M. (1970). *Fishing for Growth: Export-Led Development in Peru, 1950–1967*. Cambridge, Mass.: Harvard University Press.

Roett, R., and Sacks, R. S. (1991). *Paraguay: The Personalist Legacy*. Boulder, Colo.: Westview.

Ros, J. (1987). "Mexico from the Oil Boom to the Debt Crisis: An Analysis of Policy Responses to External Shocks, 1978–85." In Thorp, R., and Whitehead, L. (eds.), *Latin American Debt and the Adjustment Crisis*. Basingstoke, Eng.: Macmillan/St. Antony's College.

Rosenberg, M. (1983). *Las luchas por el seguro social en Costa Rica*. San José: Editorial Costa Rica.

Rosenzweig Hernández, F. (1989). *El desarrollo económico de México, 1800–1910*. Toluca, Mex.: El Colegio Mexiquense / Instituto Tecnológico Autónomo de México.

Rowe, J. (1965). *Primary Commodities in International Trade*. Cambridge University Press.

Sachs, J. (1985). "External Debt and Macroeconomic Performance in Latin American and East Asian NICs," *Brookings Papers* 2.

Sachs, J. D (1989). *Development Country Debt and the World Economy*. Chicago: University of Chicago Press.

St. John, S. (1888). *Hayti or the Black Republic*. London: Smith Elder.

Salazar-Carrillo, J. (1982). *The Structure of Wages in Latin American Manufacturing Industries*. Miami: Florida International University.

Salvucci, R. J. (1987). *Textiles and Capitalism in Mexico: An Economic History of the Obrajes, 1539–1840*. Princeton, N.J.: Princeton University Press.

Salvucci, R. (1997). "Mexican national income in the era of independence, 1800–1840." In Haber, S. (ed.), *How Latin America Fell Behind*. Stanford: Stanford University Press.

Samper, M. (1990). *Generations of Settlers: Rural Households and Markets on the Costa Rican Frontier, 1850–1935*. Boulder, Colo.: Westview.

Sánchez-Albórnoz, N. (1977). *La población de América Latina desde los tiempos precolombianos al año 2000.* Madrid: Alianza Universidad.

Sánchez-Albórnoz, N. (1986). "The Population of Latin America, 1850–1930." In Bethell, L. (ed.), *The Cambridge History of Latin America, Vol. IV: c. 1870–1930.* Cambridge University Press.

Sanderson, S. (1981). *The Transformation of Mexican Agriculture: International Structure and the Politics of Rural Change.* Princeton, N.J.: Princeton University Press.

Sandilands, R. (1990). *The Life and Political Economy of Lauchlin Currie: New Dealer, Presidential Adviser and Development Economist.* Durham, N.C.: Duke University Press.

Scammell, W. M. (1980). *The International Economy since 1945.* Basingstoke, Eng.: Macmillan.

Schneider, J. (1981). "Terms of Trade Between France and Latin America, 1826–1856: Causes of Increasing Economic Disparities?" In Bairoch, P., and Lévy-Leboyer, M. (eds.), *Disparities in Economic Development since the Industrial Revolution.* Basingstoke, Eng.: Macmillan.

Schneider, R. M. (1991). *Order and Progress: A Political History of Brazil.* Boulder, Colo.: Westview.

Schoonover, T. D. (1991). *The United States in Central America, 1860–1911: Episodes of Social Imperialism and Imperial Rivalry in the World System.* Durham, N.C.: Duke University Press.

Schoonover, T. (1998). *Germany in Central America: Competitive Imperialism, 1821–1929.* Tuscaloosa: University of Alabama Press.

Scott, C. (1996). "The distributive impact of the New Economic Model in Chile." In Bulmer-Thomas, V. (ed.) (1996), *The New Economic Model in Latin America and its Impact on Income Distribution and Poverty.* London: ILAS and Macmillan/New York: St. Martin's Press.

Segovia, A. (2002). *Transformación Estructural y Reforma Económica en El Salvador.* Guatemala: F & G Editores.

Selowsky, M. (1979). *Who Benefits from Government Expenditure? A Case Study of Colombia.* New York: Oxford University Press/World Bank.

Serrano, M. (1992). *Common Security in Latin America: The 1967 Treaty of Tlatelolco.* London: Institute of Latin American Studies.

Shaw, E. S. (1973). *Financial Deepening in Economic Development.* New York: Oxford University Press.

Sheahan, J. (1987). *Patterns of Development in Latin America: Poverty, Repression, and Economic Strategy.* Princeton. N.J.: Princeton University Press.

Short, R. P. (1984). "The Role of Public Enterprise; An International Statistical Comparison." In Floyd, R. H., Gray, C., and Short, R. (eds.), *Public Enterprise in Mixed Economies: Some Macroeconomic Aspects.* Washington, D.C.: International Monetary Fund.

Singer, M. (1969). *Growth, Equality and the Mexican Experience.* Austin: University of Texas Press.

Sjaastad, L. A. (1989). "Argentine Economic Policy, 1976–81." In Di Tella, G., and Dornbusch, R. (eds.), *The Political Economy of Argentina, 1946–83.* Basingstoke, Eng.: Macmillan/St. Antony's College.

Sklair, L. (1989). *Assembling for Development: The Maquila Industry in Mexico and the United States.* Boston: Unwin Hyman.

Smith, P. (1969). *Politics and Beef in Argentina's Patterns of Conflict and Change.* New York: Columbia University Press.

Smith, R. (1972). *The United States and Revolutionary Nationalism in Mexico, 1916–32.* Chicago: University of Chicago Press.

Smith, R. F. (1986). "Latin America, the United States and the European Powers, 1830–1930." In Bethell, L. (ed.), *The Cambridge History of Latin America, Vol. IV: c. 1870 to 1930.* Cambridge University Press.

Solís, L. (1983). *La realidad económica mexicana: Retrovisión y perspectivas*. Mexico, D.F.: Siglo Veintiuno.

Solomou, S. (1990). *Phases of Economic Growth, 1850–1973: Kondratieff Waves and Kuznets Swings*. Cambridge University Press.

Solomou, S. *The South American Handbook, 1924*. London: South American Publications.

Spender, J. (1930). *Weetman Pearson, First Viscount Cowdray*. London: Cassell.

Spraos, J. (1983). *Inequalising Trade?* Oxford: Clarendon Press.

Squier, E. G. (1856). *Notes on Central America*. London: Samper Low.

Staley, E. (1944). *World Economic Development*. Montreal: International Labour Office.

Stallings, B. (1987). *Banker to the Third World: US Portfolio Investment in Latin America, 1900–1986*. Berkeley: University of California Press.

Stallings, B., and Peres, W. (2000). *Growth, Employment and Equity: The Impact of the Economic Reforms in Latin America and the Caribbean*. Washington, D.C.: Brookings Institution Press.

Stein, S. (1957). *The Brazilian Cotton Manufacture*. Cambridge, Mass.: Harvard University Press.

Steiner, R. (1998). "Colombia's income from the drug trade." *World Development*, 26 (6): 1013–31.

Steiner, R. (1999). "Hooked on drugs: Colombia-US relations." In Bulmer-Thomas, V., and Dunkerley, J. (eds.), *The United States and Latin America: The New Agenda*. Cambridge, Mass.: The David Rockefeller Center for Latin American Studies, Harvard University/ London: Institute of Latin American Studies.

Steinfatt, K., and Contreras, P. (2001). "Trade and investment flows in the Americas." In Salazar-Xirinachs, J., and Robert, M. (eds.), *Towards Free Trade in the Americas*. Washington, D.C.: Brookings Institution Press.

Stewart, W. (1964). *Keith and Costa Rica: The Biography of Minor Cooper Keith, American Entrepreneur*. Albuquerque: University of New Mexico Press.

Stiglitz, J. (2002). *Globalization and Its Discontents*. London: Allen Lane.

Stokes, S. (2001). *Mandates and Democracy: Neoliberalism by Surprise in Latin America*. Cambridge: Cambridge University Press.

Strachan, H. W. (1976). *Family and Other Business Groups in Economic Development: The Case of Nicaragua*. New York: Praeger.

Stubbs, J. (1985). *Tobacco on the Periphery: A Case Study in Cuban Labour History, 1860–1958*. Cambridge University Press.

Summerhill, W. (1998). "Railroads in Imperial Brazil, 1854–89." In Coatsworth, J., and Taylor, A. (eds.), *Latin America and the World Economy since 1800*. Cambridge, Mass.: The David Rockefeller Center for Latin American Studies, Harvard University.

Sunkel, O. (1982). *Un siglo de historia económica de Chile, 1830–1930: Dos ensayos y una bibliografía*. Madrid: Ediciones Cultura Hispánica.

Sunkel, O., and Cariola, C. (1985). "The Growth of the Nitrates Industry and Socio-economic Change in Chile, 1880–1930." In Cortés Conde, R., and Hunt, S. (eds.), *The Latin American Economies: Growth and the Export Sector, 1880–1930*. New York: Holmes and Meier.

Swerling, B. (1949). *International Control of Sugar, 1918–1941*. Stanford, Calif.: Stanford University Press.

Syrquin, M. (1988). "Patterns of Structural Change." In Chenery, H., and Srinivasan, T. (eds.), *Handbook of Development Economics*, vol. 1. Amsterdam: North-Holland.

Taylor, C. C. (1948). *Rural Life in Argentina*. Baton Rouge: Louisiana State University Press.

Temin, P. (2000). "The Great Depression." In Engerman, S., and Gallman, R. (eds.), *The Cambridge Economic History of the United States. Vol. III. The Twentieth Century*. Cambridge: Cambridge University Press.

ten Kate, A., and Wallace, R. B. (1980). *Protection and Economic Development in Mexico.* Westmead, Eng.: Gower.

Thiesenhusen, W. C. (1989). *Searching for Agrarian Reform in Latin America.* Boston: Unwin Hyman.

Thomas, H. (1971). *Cuba or the Pursuit of Freedom.* London: Eyre & Spottiswoode.

Thomas, J. (1992). *Informal Economic Activity.* New York and London: Harvester Wheatsheaf.

Thomas, V. (1985). *Linking Macroeconomic and Agricultural Policies for Adjustment with Growth: The Colombian Experience.* Baltimore: Johns Hopkins University Press.

Thomas, J. (1995). *Surviving in the City: The Urban Informal Sector in Latin America.* London: Pluto Press.

Thompson, A. (1992). "Informal Empire? An Exploration in the History of Anglo-Argentine Relations, 1810–1914," *Journal of Latin American Studies* 24 (2): 419–36.

Thomson, G. (1985). "Protectionism and Industrialization in Mexico, 1821–1854." In Abel, C., and Lewis, C. *Latin America: Economic Imperialism and the State.* London: Athlone Press.

Thomson, G. (1989). *Puebla de los Angeles: Industry and Society in a Mexican City, 1700–1850.* Boulder, Colo.: Westview.

Thorp, R. (1967). "Inflation and Orthodox Economic Policy in Peru," *Bulletin of the Oxford University Institute of Economics and Statistics* 29 (3): 185–210.

Thorp, R. (1971). "Inflation and the Financing of Economic Development." In Griffin, K. (ed.), *Financing Development in Latin America.* Basingstoke, Eng.: Macmillan.

Thorp, R. (1986). "Latin America and the International Economy from the First World War to the World Depression." In Bethell, L. (ed.), *The Cambridge History of Latin America, Vol. IV: c. 1870 to 1930.* Cambridge University Press.

Thorp, R. (1991). *Economic Management and Economic Development in Peru and Colombia.* London: Macmillan.

Thorp, R. (1992). "A Reappraisal of the Origins of Import Substituting, Industrialisation, 1930–50," *Journal of Latin American Studies* 24 (Quincentenery Suppl.): 181–98.

Thorp, R. (1994). "The Latin American Economies, 1939–c. 1950." In Bethell, L. (ed.), *The Cambridge History of Latin America, Vol. VI: Latin America since 1930: Economy, Society and Politics,* Part 1. Cambridge University Press.

Thorp, R. (1998). *Progress, Poverty and Exclusion: An Economic History of Latin America in the 20th Century.* Washington, D.C.: Inter-American Development Bank.

Thorp, R. (ed.) (2000). *Latin America in the 1930s: The Role of the Periphery in World Crisis.* Basingstoke, Eng.: Palgrave/St. Antony's College.

Thorp. R., and Bertram, G. (1978). *Peru, 1890–1977: Growth and Policy in an Open Economy.* Basingstoke, Eng.: Macmillan.

Thorp, R., and Whitehead, L. (eds.) (1979). *Inflation and Stabilisation in Latin America.* Basingstoke, Eng.: Macmillan/St. Antony's College.

Thorp, R., and Whitehead, L. (eds.) (1987). *Latin American Debt and the Adjustment Crisis.* Basingstoke, Eng.: Macmillan/St. Antony's College.

Thoumi, F. E. (1989). *Las exportaciones intrarregionales y la integración latinoamericana y del Caribe en perspectiva.* Washington, D.C.: Banco Interamericano de Desarrollo.

Torre, J. C., and de Riz, L. (1991). "Argentina since 1946." In Bethell, L. (ed.), *The Cambridge History of Latin America, Vol. VIII: Latin America since 1930: Spanish South America.* Cambridge University Press.

Travis, C. (1990). *A Guide to Latin American and Caribbean Census Material: A Bibliography and Union List.* London: British Library/Standing Conference of National and University Libraries/Institute of Latin American Studies.

Trebat, T. (1983). *Brazil's State-Owned Enterprises, A Case Study of the State as Entrepreneur.* Cambridge University Press.

Tregarthen, G. (1897). *The Story of the Nations: Australia*. London: T. Fisher Unwin.

Triffin, R. (1944). "Central Banking and Monetary Management in Latin America." In Harris, J. (ed.), *Economic Problems of Latin America*. New York: McGraw-Hill.

Truslow, F. A. (1951). *Report on Cuba*. Baltimore: Johns Hopkins University Press.

Tulchin, J. (1971). *The Aftermath of War: World War I and US Policy toward Latin America*. New York: New York University Press.

Twomey, M. (2000). "Patterns of foreign investment in Latin America in the twentieth century." In Cardenas, E., Ocampo, J., and Thorp, R. (eds.), *An Economic History of Twentieth Century Latin America. Vol. I: The Export Age. The Latin American Economies in the Late Nineteenth and Early Twentieth Centuries*. Basingstoke: Palgrave.

Tyler, W. (1976). *Manufactured Export Expansion and Industrialization in Brazil*. Tubingen: Mohr.

Tyler, W. (1983). "The Anti-Export Bias in Commercial Policies and Export Performance: Some Evidence from Recent Brazilian Experience," *Weltwirtschaftliches Archiv* 119 (1): 97–107.

Urrutia, M. (1985). *Winners and Losers in Colombia's Economic Growth of the 1970s*. New York: Oxford University Press/World Bank.

Urrutia, M., and Arrubla, M. (eds.) (1970). *Compendio de estadísticas históricas de Colombia*. Bogotá: University Nacional de Colombia.

Vaitsos, C. (1974). *Intercountry Income Distribution and Transnational Enterprises*. Oxford: Oxford University Press.

Vaitsos, C. (1978). "Crisis in Regional Economic Cooperation (Integration) among Developing Countries: A Survey," *World Development* 6 (6): 719–70.

Van Dormael, A. (1978). *Bretton Woods: Birth of a Monetary System*. London: Macmillan.

Vedovato, C. (1986). *Politics, Foreign Trade and Economic Development: A Study of the Dominican Republic*. London: Croom Helm.

Véliz, C. (1961). *Historia de la marina mercante de Chile*. Santiago: Ediciones de la Universidad de Chile.

Vernon, R. (1981). "State-owned Enterprises in Latin American Exports." In Baer, W., and Gillis, M. (eds.), *Export Diversification and the New Protectionism*. Cambridge, Mass.: National Bureau of Economic Research.

Versiani, F. (1979). *Industrial Investment in an 'Export' Economy: The Brazilian Experience before 1914*. London: Institute of Latin American Studies.

Versiani, F. (2000). "Before the Depression: Brazilian Industry in the 1920s." In Thorp, R. (ed.), *Latin America in the 1930s: The Role of the Periphery in World Crisis*. Basingstoke, Eng.: Palgrave/St. Antony's College.

Villela, A., and Suzigan, W. (1977). *Política do governo e crescimento da economia brasileira*. Rio de Janeiro: IPEA/INPES.

Viotti da Costa, E. (1986). "Brazil: The Age of Reform, 1870–1889." In Bethell, L. (ed.), *The Cambridge History of Latin America, Vol. V: c. 1870 to 1930*. Cambridge University Press.

Vivian, E. (1914). *South American Handbooks: Peru*. London: Pitman.

Wachter, S. (1976). *Latin American Inflation: The Structuralist–Monetarist Debate*. Lexington, Mass.: Lexington Books.

Wadsworth, F. (1982). "La deforestación, muerte del Canal de Panamá." In Heckadon Moreno, S., and McKay, A. (eds.), *Colonización y destrucción de bosques en Panamá*. Panama City: Asociación Panameña de Antropología.

Walle, P. (1914). *Bolivia. Its People and Its Resources. Its Railways, Mines and Rubber-Forests*. London: T. Fisher Unwin Ltd.

Wallich, H. (1944). "Fiscal Policy and the Budget." In Harris, S. (ed.), *Economic Problems of Latin America*. New York: McGraw-Hill.

Wallich, H. (1950). *Monetary Problems of an Export Economy*. Cambridge, Mass.: Harvard University Press.

Watkins, V. (1967). *Taxes and Tax Harmonization in Central America*. Cambridge, Mass.: Harvard University Press.

Webster, C. K. (ed.) (1938). *Britain and the Independence of Latin America, 1812–1830*. 2 vols. Oxford: Oxford University Press.

Weeks, J. (1985). *The Economies of Central America*. New York: Holmes and Meier.

Weeks, J., and Zimbalist, A. (1991). *Panama at the Crossroads: Economic Development and Political Change in the Twentieth Century*. Berkeley: University of California Press.

Wells, J. (1979). "Brazil and the Post-1973 Crisis in the International Economy." In Thorp, R., and Whitehead, L. (eds.), *Inflation and Stabilisation in Latin America*. Basingstoke, Eng.: Macmillan.

Wells, J. (1987). *Empleo en América Latina: Una búsqueda de opciones*. Santiago, Chile: PREALC.

Weston, A. (1982). "Who Is More Preferred? An Analysis of the New Generalised System of Preferences." In Stevens, C. (ed.), *EEC and the Third World: A Survey*, vol. 2. London: Overseas Development Institute.

White, A. (1973). *El Salvador*. London: Ernest Benn Ltd.

Whitehead, L. (1987). "The Adjustment Process in Chile: A Comparative Perspective." In Thorp, R., and Whitehead, L. (eds.), *Latin American Debt and the Adjustment Crisis*. Basingstoke, Eng.: Macmillan/St. Antony's College.

Whitehead, L. (1991). "Bolivia since 1958." In Bethell, L. (ed.), *The Cambridge History of Latin America, Vol. VIII: Latin America since 1930: Spanish South America*. Cambridge University Press.

Whitehead, L. (1994). "State Organization in Latin America since 1930." In Bethell, L. (ed.), *The Cambridge History of Latin America, Vol. VI: Latin America since 1930: Economy, Society and Politics*, Part 2. Cambridge University Press.

Wickizer, C. (1943). *The World Coffee Economy with Special Reference to Control Schemes*. Stanford, Calif.: Stanford University Press.

Wilcox, M., and Rines, G. (1917). *Encyclopaedia of Latin America*. New York: Encyclopaedia Amazona Corporation.

Wilkie, J. W. (1974). *Statistics and National Policy*, supplement 3. Los Angeles: University of California.

Wilkie, J. W. (1990). *Statistical Abstract of Latin America*, 28. Los Angeles: University of California.

Williams, G. (1991). *The Welsh in Patagonia: The State and the Ethnic Community*. Cardiff: University of Wales Press.

Williams, J. (1920). *Argentine International Trade under Inconvertible Paper Money, 1880–1900*. Cambridge, Mass.: Harvard University Press.

Williams. R. E. (1986). *Export Agriculture and the Crisis in Central America*. Chapel Hill: University of North Carolina Press.

Williams, R. W. (1916). *Anglo-American Isthmian Diplomacy, 1815–1915*. London: Oxford University Press.

Williamson, J. W. (1990). *Latin American Adjustment: How Much Has Happened?* Washington, D.C.: Institute for International Economics.

Williamson, J. (1998). "Real wages and relative factor prices in the Third World, 1820–1940: Latin America." Cambridge, Mass.: HIER Discussion Paper 1853, Department of Economics, Harvard University.

Williamson, J. (1999). "Real wages, inequality and globalization in Latin America before 1940." *Revista de Historia Económica*, No. Especial.

Winters, L. A. (1990). "The Road to Uruguay," *Economic Journal* 100 (403): 1288–1303.

Woodward. R. L. (1985). "Central America from Independence to c. 1870." In Bethell, L. (ed.), *The Cambridge History of Latin America, Vol. III: From Independence to c. 1870.* Cambridge University Press.

World Bank (1950). *The Basis of a Development Program for Colombia.* Baltimore: Johns Hopkins University Press.

World Bank (1980). *World Tables.* 2d ed. Washington, D.C.: International Bank for Reconstruction and Development/World Bank/Oxford University Press.

World Bank (1983). *World Tables.* 3d ed. Washington, D.C.: International Bank for Reconstruction and Development/World Bank/Oxford University Press.

World Bank (1984). *World Development Report 1984.* Washington, D.C.: International Bank for Reconstruction and Development/World Bank/Oxford University Press.

World Bank (1986). *World Development Report 1986.* Washington, D.C.: International Bank for Reconstruction and Development/World Bank/Oxford University Press.

World Bank (1987). *World Development Report 1987.* Washington, D.C.: International Bank for Reconstruction and Development/World Bank/Oxford University Press.

World Bank (1989). *World Development Report 1989.* Washington, D.C.: International Bank for Reconstruction and Development/World Bank/Oxford University Press.

World Bank (1990). *World Development Report 1990.* Washington, D.C.: International Bank for Reconstruction and Development/World Bank/Oxford University Press.

World Bank (1991). *World Tables. 1991.* Washington, D.C.: International Bank for Reconstruction and Development/World Bank/Oxford University Press.

World Bank (1993). *The East Asian Miracle: Economic Growth and Public Policy.* Washington, D.C.: International Bank for Reconstruction and Development.

World Bank (2002). *World Development Report 2002.* Washington D.C.: International Bank for Reconstruction and Development/World Bank/Oxford University Press.

World Bank (2002a). World Development Indicators (CD-ROM). Washington, D.C.: International Bank for Reconstruction and Development.

Wythe, G. (1945). *Industry in Latin America.* New York: Columbia University Press.

Yotopoulos, P. A. (1989). "The (Rip)Tide of Privatization: Lessons from Chile," *World Development* 17 (5): 683–702.

Young, D. (1966). *Member for Mexico: A Biography of Weetman Pearson, First Viscount Cowdray.* London: Cassell.

Young, J. P. (1925). *Central American Currency and Finance.* Princeton, N.J.: Princeton University Press.

Zuvekas, C., and Luzuriaga, C. (1983). *Income Distribution and Poverty in Rural Ecuador, 1950–1979.* Tempe: Center for Latin American Studies, Arizona State University.

Index